The Perils of Anarchy:
Contemporary Realism and International Security

International Security Readers

Strategy and Nuclear Deterrence (1984)

Military Strategy and the Origins of the First World War (1985)

Conventional Forces and American Defense Policy (1986)

The Star Wars Controversy (1986)

Naval Strategy and National Security (1988)

Military Strategy and the Origins of the First World War,
revised and expanded edition (1991)

—published by Princeton University Press

Soviet Military Policy (1989)

Conventional Forces and American Defense Policy, revised edition (1989)

Nuclear Diplomacy and Crisis Management (1990)

The Cold War and After: Prospects for Peace (1991)

America's Strategy in a Changing World (1992)

The Cold War and After: Prospects for Peace, expanded edition (1993)

Global Dangers: Changing Dimensions of International Security (1995)

The Perils of Anarchy: Contemporary Realism and International Security (1995)

—published by The MIT Press

The Perils of Anarchy

Contemporary Realism and International Security

AN *International Security* READER

EDITED BY

Michael E. Brown
Sean M. Lynn-Jones
and Steven E. Miller

THE MIT PRESS
CAMBRIDGE, MASSACHUSETTS
LONDON, ENGLAND

The contents of this book were first published in *International Security* (ISSN 0162-2889), a publication of The MIT Press under the sponsorship of the Center for Science and International Affairs at Harvard University. Except as otherwise noted, copyright in each article is owned jointly by the President and Fellows of Harvard College and of the Massachusetts Institute of Technology.

William C. Wohlforth, "Realism and the End of the Cold War," 19:3 (Winter 1994/95); Kenneth N. Waltz, "The Emerging Structure of International Politics," 18:2 (Fall 1993); John J. Mearsheimer,"Back to the Future: Instability in Europe after the Cold War," 15:1 (Summer 1990); Christopher Layne, "The Unipolar Illusion: Why New Great Powers Will Rise," 17:4 (Spring 1993); Peter Liberman, "The Spoils of Conquest," 18:2 (Fall 1993); Stephen M. Walt, "Alliance Formation and the Balance of World Power," 9:4 (Spring 1985); Randall Schweller, "Bandwagoning for Profit: Bringing the Revisionist State Back In," 19:1 (Summer 1994); Christopher Layne, "Kant or Cant: The Myth of the Democratic Peace," 19:2 (Fall 1994); John J. Mearsheimer, "The False Promise of International Institutions," 19:3 (Winter 1994/95); Charles L. Glaser, "Realists as Optimists: Cooperation as Self-Help," 19:3 (Winter 1994/95); Paul Schroeder, "Historical Reality vs. Neo-realist Theory," 19:1 (Summer 1994); Fareed Zakaria, "Realism and Domestic Politics: A Review Essay," 17:1 (Summer 1992); Lisa L. Martin, "Institutions and Cooperation: Sanctions During the Falkland Islands Conflict," 16:4 (Spring 1992).

Selection and preface, copyright © 1995 by the President and Fellows of Harvard College and of the Massachusetts Institute of Technology.

Library of Congress Cataloging-in-Publication Data
Brown, Michael E. (Michael Edward), 1954–
    The perils of anarchy : contemporary realism and international
security / edited by Michael E. Brown, Sean M. Lynn-Jones and Steven
E. Miller.
        p. cm. — (International security readers)
    Includes bibliographical references (p.).
    ISBN 0-262-52202-0
    1. International relations   2. Security, International.
3. Realism. 4. Anarchism. 5. Anarchism. I. Lynn-Jones, Sean M.
II. Miller, Steven E. III. Title. IV. Series.
JX1391.B688 1995
327.1'.01—dc20   94-24041
                                                           CIP

Contents

The Contributors

MICHAEL E. BROWN is Co-Editor of *International Security* and Senior Research Fellow at the Center for Science and International Affairs, Harvard University.

SEAN M. LYNN-JONES is Co-Editor of *International Security* and a Research Fellow at the Center for Science and International Affairs, Harvard University.

STEVEN E. MILLER is Editor-in-Chief of *International Security* and Director of the International Security Program at the Center for Science and International Affairs, Harvard University.

WILLIAM C. WOHLFORTH is Assistant Professor of Political Science at Princeton University.

KENNETH N. WALTZ is Professor of Political Science at the University of California (Berkeley).

JOHN J. MEARSHEIMER is Professor of Political Science at the University of Chicago.

CHRISTOPHER LAYNE is a foreign and defense policy consultant in Los Angeles.

PETER LIBERMAN is Assistant Professor of Political Science at Tulane University in New Orleans.

STEPHEN M. WALT is Associate Professor of Political Science at the University of Chicago.

RANDALL SCHWELLER is Assistant Professor of Political Science at Ohio State University.

CHARLES L. GLASER is Acting Dean of the Irving B. Harris Graduate School of Public Policy Studies at the University of Chicago.

PAUL W. SCHROEDER is Professor of History and Political Science at the University of Illinois (Urbana-Champaign).

FAREED ZAKARIA is Managing Editor of *Foreign Affairs*.

LISA L. MARTIN is Associate Professor of Government at Harvard University.

Acknowledgments

The editors gratefully acknowledge the assistance that has made this book possible. A deep debt is owed to all those at the Center for Science and International Affairs, Harvard University, who have played an editorial role at *International Security*. Special thanks go to Mera Kachgal at CSIA and to Sally Gregg at MIT Press for their invaluable help in preparing this volume for publication.

Preface | Sean M. Lynn-Jones and Steven E. Miller

$\mathbf{R}$ealism is at the center of many contemporary debates about the theory and practice of international politics. Realists continue to engage in a spirited debate with their critics, and different schools within realism argue over the merits of contending realist theories. These debates have contributed to much intellectual ferment and spurred scholars to refine contemporary realism. This volume contains several important contributions to the continuing debates over realist theory.[1]

There is a long and rich tradition of realist thinking about international politics. Thucydides, Machiavelli, and Hobbes all have contributed to the evolution of realist thought. They and other writers have emphasized the enduring importance of power, conflict, and military force in international politics. The contemporary realists represented in this volume focus on similar issues.

Realism is a general approach to international politics, not a single theory. There are many different realist theories of international politics, but most realists share the following core beliefs about the nature of international politics.[2] First, realists believe that states are the most important actors in international politics. They therefore focus on explaining the behavior of states and tend to pay less attention to individuals and transnational actors like corporations and multinational organizations. Second, realists regard anarchy—the absence of any common sovereign—as the distinguishing feature of international life. Without a central authority to enforce agreements or to guarantee security, states must rely on their own means to protect their interests. Third, realists assume that states seek to maximize either their power or their security. Some realists focus on power as an end in itself, whereas others regard it as a means to security. Fourth, realists usually assume that states generally adopt rational policies that aim to achieve power and/or security. Fifth, realists normally agree that states will tend to rely on the threat or use

---

1. An earlier volume, Sean M. Lynn-Jones and Steven E. Miller, eds., *The Cold War and After: Prospects for Peace*, expanded edition (Cambridge, Mass.: The MIT Press, 1993) covered related themes, but concentrated on explanations of the long postwar peace and whether it will continue after the Cold War. Two essays from that volume are reprinted here because they present important realist theories before applying them to the post–Cold War world.

2. For other discussions of the elements and assumptions of realism, see Robert O. Keohane, "Realism, Neorealism and the Study of World Politics," in Keohane, ed., *Neorealism and its Critics* (New York: Columbia University Press, 1986), pp. 7–16; Robert Gilpin, "The Richness of the Tradition of Political Realism," in Keohane, *Neorealism and its Critics*, pp. 304–305; and Stephen M. Walt, "Alliances, Threats, and U.S. Grand Strategy: A Reply to Kaufman and Labs," *Security Studies*, Vol. 1, No. 3 (Spring 1992), pp. 473–474. In addition, most realists spell out their assumptions when they explicate their own theories.

of military force to secure their objectives in international politics. Sixth, most realists believe that aspects of the international system—especially the distribution of power among states—are the most important causes of the basic patterns of international politics and foreign policy. Although realists may recognize that state-level factors matter, they emphasize the importance of international factors.

Realism is not monolithic. There are several schools of thought within the realist approach. Most observers draw a distinction between classical realists and structural realists, who are also known as neorealists.[3] Classical realists generally argue that power is the most significant factor in international politics. States attempt to maximize their power, at least partly because the desire for increased power is rooted in human nature. Rational states define their national interests in terms of power. States often seek to create a balance of power, an equilibrium among states that sometimes preserves peace and at least helps to preserve the independence of the great powers.[4]

Structural realists share the classical realist emphasis on power, but they attempt to build a deductive, social-scientific theory of international politics. Instead of assuming that human nature contains an innate drive for power, structural realists posit that states seek to preserve their security. They argue that the anarchic structure of international politics shapes most international outcomes. In an anarchic international system, states must rely on self-help to guarantee their survival. States will build up their own military arsenals and form alliances to balance against more powerful—and therefore more threatening—states. War and conflict are likely in such a world, but they become less likely in a bipolar world that has only two great powers.[5]

---

3. The terms "structural realism" and "neorealism" are generally used interchangeably. Note that Barry Buzan, Charles Jones, and Richard Little, *The Logic of Anarchy: Neorealism to Structural Realism* (New York: Columbia University Press, 1993) uses neorealism to refer to Kenneth Waltz's theory and refers to more general systemic theories as structural realism.

4. The seminal work in the classical realist tradition is Hans J. Morgenthau, *Politics Among Nations: The Struggle for Power and Peace* (New York: Knopf, 1948 and later editions). Other important works include E.H. Carr, *The Twenty Years' Crisis: An Introduction to the Study of International Relations* (London: Macmillan, 1939); Henry Kissinger, *A World Restored: Castlereagh, Metternich, and the Problem of Peace, 1812–1822* (Boston: Houghton Mifflin, 1957); Morgenthau, *Scientific Man vs. Power Politics* (Chicago: University of Chicago Press, 1946); Martin Wight, *Power Politics*, edited by Hedley Bull and Carsten Holbraad (Harmondsworth, Great Britain: Penguin, 1978); and Arnold Wolfers, *Discord and Collaboration: Essays on International Politics* (Baltimore, Md.: The Johns Hopkins University Press, 1962).

5. The seminal exposition of structural realism is Kenneth N. Waltz, *Theory of International Politics* (Reading, Mass.: Addison-Wesley, 1979). See also Waltz, *Man, the State, and War: A Theoretical Analysis* (New York: Columbia University Press, 1959); Waltz, "The Origins of War in Neorealist Theory," in Robert I. Rotberg and Theodore K. Rabb, eds., *The Origin and Prevention of Major Wars* (Cambridge: Cambridge University Press, 1989); and Waltz, "Reflections on *Theory of International*

The division between classical realism and structural realism no longer fully captures the complexity of the contemporary debate among realists. Some of the most important debates are between different variants of structural realism. In addition, a new generation of classical realists has challenged important elements of structural realism. Finally, some scholars have argued for realist theories of hegemonic rivalry and war, which cannot easily be classified as classical or structural.

There are two important debates among structural realists. First, several writers have distinguished between the "aggressive" and "defensive" variants of structural realism.[6] The aggressive version of the theory holds that the international system fosters conflict and aggression. Security is scarce, making international competition intense and war likely. Rational states often are compelled to adopt offensive strategies in their search for security. In this volume, John Mearsheimer's "Back to the Future" is the preeminent example of this variant of realism. Defensive realists, on the other hand, argue that the international system does not necessarily generate intense conflict and war. States that understand the international system will realize that security is plentiful and that defensive strategies are the best route to security. In this volume, the essays by Stephen Walt and Charles Glaser represent defensive realism.[7]

Second, structural realists are divided on whether the most important determinant of international outcomes and foreign policies is the distribution of power or the level and sources of threats. In this volume, Kenneth Waltz, John Mearsheimer, and Christopher Layne represent the first position. They emphasize the importance of the polarity of a system—the number of great powers it has—as well as the role of changes in the relative power of states. Stephen Walt and Charles Glaser, on the other hand, argue that the overall distribution of power is less important than the level and direction of threats. Walt's "balance-of-threat" theory claims that states react to threats. The level of threat

Politics: A Response to My Critics," in Keohane, ed., *Neorealism and Its Critics*, pp. 322–345. For critical discussions of the differences between classical and structural realism see Keohane, "Realism, Neorealism and the Study of World Politics," and Richard Ashley, "The Poverty of Neorealism," in Keohane, ed., *Neorealism and Its Critics*, pp. 255–300.

6. Jack Snyder uses these terms in *Myths of Empire: Domestic Politics and International Ambition* (Ithaca, N.Y.: Cornell University Press, 1991), pp. 11–12, and Fareed Zakaria adopts "defensive realism" in his contribution to this volume. Whether these terms will be accepted widely remains to be seen.

7. For other important statements of similar arguments, see Stephen Van Evera, "Primed for Peace: Europe After the Cold War," *International Security*, Vol. 15, No. 3 (Winter 1990/91), pp. 7–57 at 11–17; and Barry R. Posen, *The Sources of Military Doctrine: France, Britain, and Germany Between the World Wars* (Ithaca, N.Y.: Cornell University Press, 1984), especially pp. 68–69. Robert Jervis articulated the theoretical underpinnings of defensive realism in "Cooperation Under the Security Dilemma," *World Politics*, Vol. 30, No. 2 (January 1978), pp. 167–214.

posed by a given state depends not only on its overall power, but also on its geographic proximity, offensive power, and offensive intentions.[8] Glaser adopts a similar approach, arguing that the severity of the security dilemma determines whether power can easily be translated into threat when offense has the advantage, increases in power translate easily into threats, and cooperation becomes more difficult.[9]

Structural realism also has been challenged by a new generation of classical realists. These new classical realists share Waltz's belief that the distribution of power is an important determinant of international politics and foreign policy, but they disagree with most structural realists on the goals of states and the role of domestic factors in shaping those goals. In particular, they question whether it is theoretically useful to assume that security is the prime goal of states, arguing that security is a malleable concept that states can pursue in many different ways. Unlike earlier classical realists, however, they do not posit that state behavior can be explained by individuals' lust for power. Instead, they argue that states seek to maximize their influence or that state goals vary. Fareed Zakaria and Randall Schweller make these arguments in their contributions to this volume. William Wohlforth adopts a broadly similar position. Some new classical realists also reject the claim that the internal politics of a state and its goals and values are relatively unimportant.[10] Like some earlier classical realists,[11] they place more weight on state-level differences, especially the distinction between revisionist and status-quo powers. Randall Schweller's essay emphasizes this point.

Finally, structural realism has been challenged by realist theories of hegemonic rivalry and war. Unlike structural realism, which tends to see international politics as a series of attempts to balance against potential hegemons, theories of hegemonic rivalry argue that international politics has been shaped by the rise and fall of successive hegemonic states that have dominated their respective international orders. War is particularly likely dur-

---

8. For a more complete explication of balance-of-threat theory, see Walt, *The Origins of Alliances* (Ithaca, N.Y.: Cornell University Press, 1987), especially pp. 263–266.

9. For a similar argument with historical evidence, see Ted Hopf, "Polarity, the Offense-Defense Balance, and War," *American Political Science Review*, Vol. 85, No. 2 (June 1991), pp. 476–493.

10. Although most structural realists do not deny that internal factors sometimes are important—especially in determining a given state's foreign policy—they construct theories that rely on systemic factors to explain outcomes in international politics. See, in particular, Waltz, *Theory of International Politics*, chaps. 2–4.

11. For important examples, see Arnold Wolfers, "The Balance of Power in Theory and Practice," in Wolfers, *Discord and Collaboration*, pp. 125–126; and Kissinger, *A World Restored*.

ing periods of hegemonic transition.[12] Such theories cannot easily be classified as classical or structural, because they share the former's assumption that states are not content with security but seek to maximize their power or influence, while often attempting to build a deductive theory that is as social-scientific as structural realism. In this volume, William Wohlforth's essay draws on realist theories of hegemonic rivalry to criticize structural realism and to explain the end of the Cold War.

In addition to the debates among realists, contemporary debates over realist theory have featured vigorous exchanges between realists and their critics, often called "anti-realists." Anti-realists have offered many different criticisms of realism. Liberal institutionalists argue that international institutions can make cooperation possible even in an anarchic international system. Critical theorists (sometimes known as post-structuralists or post-modernists) have attacked the epistemological foundations of realism. Proponents of the "democratic peace" hypothesis have argued that the absence of wars between democracies challenges the realist claim that domestic factors are less important than international ones, and that international politics is necessarily a realm of conflict. Other theorists have contended that domestic factors such as strategic culture, levels of modernization, and norms and values are more important than international factors in shaping grand strategy and foreign policy. Numerous commentators have faulted realism for failing to predict the end of the Cold War. Others have charged that realism is excessively preoccupied with states and ignores other important actors, such as ethnic groups and social movements. Several examples of these anti-realist arguments are included in the final section of this volume. Many of the realist essays collected in this volume respond to at least some of these criticisms.

The first section of this book explores how realist theories can shed light on changing international orders of the past, present, and future. Realism suggests that changes in the distribution of power in an international system have important implications for levels of conflict, war, and peace, and for the foreign policies of individual states. The four essays here use the insights of realist

---

12. Important works that present realist theories of hegemonic rivalry and power transitions include Robert Gilpin, *War and Change in World Politics* (Cambridge: Cambridge University Press, 1981); and A.F.K. Organski, *World Politics* (New York: Knopf, 1968). A variant of these theories has been employed in the realm of international political economy to argue that international economic cooperation and stability are most likely when a hegemonic power exists to make and enforce rules. See Charles P. Kindleberger, *The World in Depression, 1929–1939* (Berkeley: University of California Press, 1973); and Stephen D. Krasner, "State Power and the Structure of International Trade," *World Politics*, Vol. 28, No. 3 (April 1976), pp. 317–343.

theories to explain why the Cold War ended, and to predict how the international system will be changed by the end of hostility between superpowers.

In "Realism and the End of the Cold War," William Wohlforth argues that realist theories of hegemonic rivalry and power transitions can shed light on the transformation of the international system wrought by the peaceful decline and dissolution of the Soviet Union. In contrast to other scholars who claim that realist theories have been invalidated by the end of the Cold War, Wohlforth finds that realism explains much about the end of U.S.-Soviet antagonism. Realist theories focus on the consequences of changes in the international distribution of power. In Wohlforth's view, a shift in the distribution of power—the relative decline of Soviet power—caused Moscow to retrench strategically and to seek a peaceful rapprochement with the United States. Wohlforth argues that Soviet perceptions of the distribution of power must be examined in any full account of the Cold War's end. When Soviet leaders perceived that their country was falling further behind the United States and its Western allies, they adopted "new thinking" and a more moderate foreign policy. Because the Soviet Union was a declining challenger, not a declining hegemon, it more readily accepted its loss of power without launching a preventive war. Wohlforth concedes that realist theories are "terribly weak" because they cannot always offer clear predictions and explanations, but concludes that they remain stronger than the alternatives, which are even more indeterminate. In his view, realist scholars need to focus on how states actually perceive relative power, instead of relying on quantitative indicators of power such as gross national product, population, military force levels, and defense spending. Scholars should test realist theories by tracing how leaders' assessments of power shape their choices about foreign policy.

Kenneth Waltz's "The Emerging Structure of International Politics" uses neorealist theory to assess how the international order is evolving in the aftermath of the Cold War. He focuses on how the structure of the international system is changing, and on what effects those changes will have. In Waltz's view, the post-1945 emergence of bipolarity gave rise to the Cold War, in which the United States and the Soviet Union adopted similarly competitive policies toward one another. The changing structure of international politics in the 1980s made the end of the Cold War possible. Waltz argues that the world remains bipolar for now, because Russia can still take care of itself militarily, and because no other great power has emerged; however, he claims that bipolarity is altered, because the United States is no longer balanced by any other country. In such circumstances, balance-of-power theory predicts that other states will strive to hold the United States in check. The existence of preponderant U.S. power will motivate other states to distance themselves from the United States. In the absence of a Soviet threat, Waltz argues that "NATO's days are not numbered, but its years are." In the longer run, other countries will rise to great-power status so that they can protect their interests. Waltz writes that "the door to the great-power club will swing open if the EC, Germany, China, or Japan knock on it," and that "for a country to choose not to become a great power is a structural anomaly." Thus Waltz argues that we can expect the emerging world eventually to hold four or five great powers. Traditional patterns of great-power competition have been modified, however, by the advent of nuclear deterrence, which enables any state with survivable nuclear force to protect itself without relying on allies or on matching its competitors militarily and economically.

Like Waltz, John Mearsheimer draws upon structural realism to analyze the implications of the changing international distribution of power. Mearsheimer's well-known article, "Back to the Future: Instability in Europe after the Cold War," employs neorealist theory to present a pessimistic vision of Europe's future. Mearsheimer contends that Europe has enjoyed peace for the past 45 years for two key reasons: bipolar systems tend to be peaceful, and the presence of nuclear weapons has induced general caution. If the Soviet Union and the United States withdraw from Europe, he argues, Europe will devolve to multipolarity, and a renewed era of wars and major crises may erupt on that continent. Although others believe that European peace and stability will be preserved because economic interdependence causes peace, because democracies do not fight one another, or because war is becoming obsolescent among industrialized countries, Mearsheimer suggests that these theories are inapplicable or wrong. He also warns that more European countries, including a united Germany, will seek nuclear arsenals if the superpowers withdraw. If not carefully managed, this trend toward nuclear proliferation may create new risks of major crises and wars.[13]

---

13. For alternative visions of Europe's future, see Jack Snyder, "Averting Anarchy in the New Europe," *International Security*, Vol. 14, No. 4 (Spring 1990), pp. 5–41; and Stephen Van Evera, "Primed for Peace: Europe After the Cold War," Vol. 15, No. 3 (Winter 1990/91), pp. 7–57. For a more general theoretical rejoinder, see Robert Jervis, "The Future of World Politics: Will it Resemble the Past?" *International Security*, Vol. 16, No. 3 (Winter 1992/92), pp. 39–73. Letters from Stanley Hoffmann, Robert Keohane, Bruce Russett, and Thomas Risse-Kappen replying to Mearsheimer's arguments, as well as Mearsheimer's responses, can be found in "Correspondence: Back to the Future, Part II: International Relations Theory and Post-Cold War Europe," *International Security*, Vol. 15, No. 2 (Fall 1990), pp. 191–199, and "Correspondence: Back to the Future, Part III: Realism and the Realities of European Security," *International Security*, Vol. 15, No. 3 (Winter 1990/91), pp. 216–222.

In "The Unipolar Illusion: Why New Great Powers Will Rise," Christopher Layne analyzes the implications of the apparent emergence of a unipolar world in which the United States is the sole superpower. Applying neorealist theory to the future of international politics, he argues that the unipolar world is a passing condition, because new great powers will inevitably rise. Neorealism predicts that states will balance against potential hegemons by building up their own power and by forming alliances. Layne finds support for these predictions in two historical "unipolar moments," French predominance in the late seventeenth century and British hegemony during the "Pax Britannica" of the mid-nineteenth century. He concludes that a U.S. strategy of attempting to retain international primacy is not likely to succeed, and he outlines an alternative grand strategy aimed at protecting U.S. interests in the inevitable transition to a multipolar world.

The next three essays in this collection turn from how realism explains broad changes in international orders to the more specific causes of aggression and alignment. Most scholars recognize that countries often have gone to war because they expect that aggression will bring rewards. Peter Liberman's "The Spoils of Conquest" asks whether conquest still pays in the modern world. He notes that this question lies at the root of important debates over the way the world works, and over what foreign policies states should follow. Realists claim that conquest pays, so states have economic and security incentives to expand. Only defensive alliances stand in the way of imperial adventures. Liberals, on the other hand, argue that occupying a conquered state drains more wealth than it delivers up to the conqueror, and that therefore conquest does not pay; the world is a safer place than the realists imagine. Liberman takes account of several cases of twentieth-century conquest, including the Nazi occupation of Europe, the Japanese Empire, and the Soviet sphere of influence in Eastern and Central Europe. He finds that conquest does pay in the modern era. Modernization itself has made conquest more profitable by increasing the economic wealth of societies, thereby making them more appealing targets for aggressors. Modernization also has made it easier for conquerors to control populations, because the citizens of modern states have more to lose and can be coerced more easily than the populations of nonmodernized societies. Liberman concludes that the potential spoils of conquest will continue to tempt states to start aggressive wars, and that civilian-based resistance movements are unlikely to thwart conquerors.

In "Alliance Formation and the Balance of World Power," Stephen Walt considers the causes of alliances. He identifies several prominent explanations of international alignments: states ally against external threats (balancing); states ally with external threats (bandwagoning); states ally with other states that share a common ideology; states ally with states that offer them foreign aid; and states ally with states that successfully penetrate and manipulate their domestic politics. Walt assesses the merits of each hypothesis, and reaches two conclusions. First, external threats are the most powerful causes of alliances. Second, states usually balance against an external threat instead of band-wagoning with it. Ideology, economic aid, and political penetration turn out to be very weak sources of alignment. Unlike balance-of-power theorists, Walt contends that states balance against threats, not against power. He argues that how threatening a state is depends on its aggregate power, offensive power, proximity, and offensive intentions.

The debate over balancing and bandwagoning has critical implications for the formulation of grand strategy and the definition of vital interests. States that believe that balancing predominates over bandwagoning are less likely to attempt to expand, and will worry less about the solidarity of their defensive alliances. When bandwagoning is seen to predominate, aggression becomes more tempting, states worry about maintaining their credibility, and defensive alliances are fragile. Randall Schweller's "Bandwagoning for Profit: Bringing the Revisionist State Back In" recognizes these implications, but challenges Walt's conclusion that balancing is more common than bandwagoning. He offers a different perspective on whether states ally more often with the weaker or with the stronger side in a conflict. Schweller notes that while scholars like Walt and Waltz have argued that states balance against threatening increases in others' power, foreign-policy practitioners through the ages have believed that states bandwagon with power. Seeking to explain this discrepancy, Schwel-ler argues that it is a mistake to view balancing and bandwagoning as opposite behaviors motivated by the same goal of achieving security. Schweller suggests that Walt's definition of bandwagoning limits the term to cases in which states actually capitulated and then aligned with a threatening country. He points out that states frequently bandwagon opportunistically, as well as when threat-ened, and that bandwagoning may thus indeed be far more common than balancing. More generally, Schweller argues that neorealist theory cannot ac-count for much of international politics, including a particular state's decision to balance or bandwagon, because it does not recognize that states have different goals. He divides states into status-quo and revisionist powers. Status-quo powers are generally content with what they have, so they tend to balance against threats and to seek security. Revisionist powers, on the other hand, want to add to their wealth, power, or prestige, so they tend to initiate wars of conquest or to jump on the bandwagon of more powerful aggressor states.

The following three essays present realist approaches to the causes of peace in international politics. The first two offer realist rebuttals of important non-realist explanations of peace. The third argues that realism itself can explain many instances of peace and international cooperation.

The observation that democracies have not made war on one another has fired the imaginations of theorists and practitioners alike during the 1980s and 1990s.[14] Some scholars think that it is "as close as anything we have to an empirical law in international relations,"[15] and seek to explain how it works, while others dispute its very existence. Christopher Layne, in "Kant or Cant: The Myth of the Democratic Peace" scrutinizes the claim that democracies rarely, if ever, go to war with one another. Taking issue with what has become the conventional wisdom, Layne claims that the "democratic peace" is a myth. Layne argues that the deductive logic of the two main explanations proffered for its workings—institutional or structural constraints, and democratic norms and cultures—are not as persuasive as realist explanations that emphasize the distribution of military capabilities. Reviewing four historical cases of "near misses"—where democracies came close to making war with one another, but refrained from doing so—he looks in vain for the empirical indicators that the democratic-peace explanations are valid. He finds no evidence that democratic leaders tried harder to avoid wars with other states, that they justified their actions on the grounds that democracies should not fight one another, or that public opinion in democracies opposed war with other democracies. Layne warns that the democratic-peace theory is dangerous; founded on "wishful thinking," it suggests an interventionist U.S. foreign policy that would lead not to peace, but to more wars fought to spread democracy throughout the world.[16]

John Mearsheimer's "The False Promise of International Institutions" rebuts arguments that international institutions can reduce the risk of war sig-

---

14. For important examples of this argument, see Michael Doyle, "Kant, Liberal Legacies, and Foreign Affairs," parts 1 and 2, *Philosophy and Public Affairs*, Vol. 12, Nos. 3 and 4 (Summer and Fall 1983), pp. 205–235 and 323–353; and Bruce Russett, *Grasping the Democratic Peace: Principles for a Post–Cold War World* (Princeton, N.J.: Princeton University Press, 1993).

15. Jack S. Levy, "Domestic Politics and War," in Rotberg and Rabb, eds., *The Origin and Prevention of Major Wars*, p. 88.

16. For an affirmation of the "democratic peace" hypothesis that analyzes several of the historical cases considered by Layne, see John M. Owen, "How Liberalism Produces Democratic Peace," *International Security*, Vol. 19, No. 2 (Fall 1994), pp. 87–125. See also the exchange of correspondence in the Spring 1995 issue of *International Security*.

nificantly. He explicates three "anti-realist" arguments for how institutions can promote peace: (1) the liberal-institutionalist claim that international institutions promote cooperation by preventing cheating and providing information; (2) the critical theorists' argument that the adoption of new norms and ideas can eliminate war, even in an anarchic international system; and (3) arguments for collective security, which usually contend that wars would become unlikely if all states pledged to defend any victim of aggression. Mearsheimer does not deny that institutions sometimes matter, but he finds little empirical evidence or logical support for claims that institutions can increase the chances of peace. Instead, he concludes that realist theory correctly suggests that wars will be a recurrent feature of international politics, and that realism more successfully identifies the conditions for peace than any of the contending anti-realist theories.

In "Realists as Optimists: Cooperation as Self-Help," Charles Glaser argues that realist theory can explain international peace and cooperation. Realists and their critics have exaggerated the extent to which the nature of the international system makes war likely or inevitable. Both camps have been too pessimistic in their interpretation of realism. In Glaser's view, the logic of realism can lead to predictions of peace and cooperation. These benign outcomes are most likely when the offense-defense balance of military technology favors the defense. This condition creates a mild security dilemma, which enables security-seeking states to pursue security for themselves without undermining it for others. Whether the security dilemma is often mild is an empirical question, not a theoretical one; war is not a necessary consequence of international anarchy and other realist assumptions. Realists who are pessimistic about the prospects for peace and cooperation need to show that offense usually has the advantage, and that the security dilemma is frequently severe. Glaser recognizes that states may not behave peacefully even if international conditions encourage peace, but contends that these outcomes may reflect domestic conditions or state-level pathologies, not the structure of international politics.

The essays in the final section of this volume present several prominent criticisms of contemporary realist theory. These criticisms by no means exhaust the range of challenges to realism, but the arguments offered in these essays directly confront the arguments presented elsewhere in this volume.

In "Historical Reality vs. Neo-realist Theory," Paul Schroeder takes all realists to task for misreading history. He reviews the Westphalian era from 1648 to 1945 to see whether history actually supports, as realists argue, the propositions that states tend to balance against power or threat; that they are not threat; that they are not functionally differentiated in international politics; that potential hegemons are countered by the balancing efforts of other states; and that unipolar periods motivate other states to rise to great power status. Schroeder argues that the more one examines these historical generalizations about the conduct of international politics, the more doubtful, "indeed strange," these generalizations appear. He suggests that Waltz's neorealist theory does not help to explain most of European diplomatic history, and cites Layne's essay, "The Unipolar Moment," as an example of how neorealism produces or rests upon problematic interpretations of history.

In "Realism and Domestic Politics," a review essay on Jack Snyder's *Myths of Empire: Domestic Politics and International Ambition,* Fareed Zakaria assesses Snyder's attempt to improve upon realist theories by incorporating domestic politics into his model of international relations. Zakaria's arguments may be directed at Snyder's domestic-political explanation of over-expansion, but he makes it clear that they also apply to many of the variants of realism presented in this volume, including the essays by Waltz, Walt, and Glaser. Zakaria argues that "defensive realism"—the attempt to explain foreign policy as a response to external threats—is a weak theory, because states respond to shifts in relative power, not threats. He contends that attempts to build a realist theory on the assumption that states seek security are conceptually flawed. Such theories, in his view, fail to explain much of international politics and ultimately must "smuggle in" domestic factors to explain international politics and foreign policy. Zakaria suggests that realist theory should instead assume that states seek to maximize their influence in international politics.

Lisa Martin's "Institutions and Cooperation: Sanctions During the Falkland Islands Conflict" presents important elements of the institutionalist challenge to realism. She argues that realism is wrong to posit that states always pursue their narrowly-defined self-interests. Membership in international institutions can change how states define their interests and produce different policies. Martin examines European Economic Community (EEC) cooperation on multilateral sanctions against Argentina during the 1982 Falklands crisis. She finds that states acted against their interests in ways that they would not have in the absence of the institution of the EEC. Only Britain had a strong interest in imposing sanctions on Argentina; however, other EEC members supported sanctions because Britain was able to link sanctions to other important EEC issues, and forge a coalition by striking bargains across issues. Martin concludes that realists have underestimated the importance of international institutions in promoting international cooperation.

The essays included in this volume are not intended to provide a comprehensive overview of the state of contemporary realism. They do not cover all the issues raised in the debates between realists and their critics and among realists themselves. For example, they devote relatively little attention to the controversy over whether states seek absolute or relative gains.[17] The essays do, however, demonstrate that realism continues to be a source of vibrant debates and theoretical innovations. The editors hope that this collection stimulates additional debate, research, and better theories.

---

17. Several important articles on that issue are included in David A. Baldwin, ed., *Neorealism and Neoliberalism: The Contemporary Debate* (New York: Columbia University Press, 1993). See also Robert Powell, "Anarchy in International Relations: The Neorealist-Neoliberal Debate," *International Organization*, Vol. 48, No. 2 (Spring 1994), pp. 313–344.

Part I:
Realism and International Order,
Old and New

Realism and the End of the Cold War

William C. Wohlforth

$\mathbf{M}$odern realism began as a reaction to the breakdown of the post–World War I international order in the 1930s. The collapse of great-power cooperation after World War II helped establish it as the dominant approach to the theory and practice of international politics in the United States. During the Cold War, efforts to displace realism from its dominant position were repeatedly thwarted by the continued salience of the U.S.-Soviet antagonism: although indirect, the connection between events and theory was undeniable.

Now, the U.S.-Soviet antagonism is history. Suddenly, unexpectedly, and with hardly a shot fired in anger, Russian power has been withdrawn from the Elbe to the Eurasian steppe. A central question faces students and practitioners of international politics. Do the rapid decline and comparatively peaceful collapse of the Soviet state, and with it the entire postwar international order, discredit the realist approach?

Scholars have answered this question in two ways. Most argue that the events of the late 1980s and early 1990s utterly confound realism's expectations, and call into question its relevance for understanding the post–Cold War world.[1] Others—realist and non-realist alike—disagree, maintaining that the

---

William C. Wohlforth is Assistant Professor at the Department of Politics, Princeton University. He is the editor of Witnesses to the End of the Cold War *(Baltimore, Md.: The Johns Hopkins University Press, forthcoming 1995).*

I am grateful to Chip Blacker, David Dessler, Lynn Eden, David Holloway, Oliver Meier, Michael McFaul, Sarah Mendelson, Jon Mercer, and Pascal Venneson for their most helpful comments on earlier drafts. I wrote this article while a Social Science Fellow at Stanford University's Center for International Security and Arms Control. My thanks to the Center and the Carnegie Corporation of New York for supporting my fellowship.

---

1. See Charles W. Kegley, Jr., "The Neoidealist Moment in International Studies? Realist Myths and the New International Realities," *International Studies Quarterly*, Vol. 37, No. 2 (June 1993), pp. 131–147, and the sources cited therein; Richard Ned Lebow, "The Long Peace, the End of the Cold War, and the Failure of Realism," and Rey Koslowski and Friedrich Kratochwil, "Understanding Change in International Relations: The Soviet Empire's Demise and the International System," both in *International Organization*, Vol. 48, No. 2 (Spring 1994); Friedrich Kratochwil, "The Embarrassment of Changes: Neo-Realism as the Science of *Realpolitik* without Politics," *Review of International Studies*, Vol. 19, No. 1 (January 1993), pp. 63–80; John Lewis Gaddis, "International Relations Theory and the End of the Cold War," *International Security*, Vol. 17, No. 3 (Winter 1992/93), pp. 5–58; Thomas Risse-Kappen and Richard Ned Lebow, "International Relations Theory and the Transformation of the International System," draft introduction (September 1993) for Risse-Kappen and

---

International Security, Winter 1994/95 (Vol. 19, No. 3)

post-1989 transformation of international politics is not an appropriate test for theory. The end of the Cold War, they argue, was "merely a single data point." Even if it is inconsistent with realism it is insufficient to falsify it, because international relations theories are capable only of predicting patterns of behavior; they cannot make point predictions. And many scholars are pessimistic about the capacity of social science theory to explain unique and complex historical events involving revolutionary change. Therefore, our evaluation of theory should look to future patterns rather than past events.[2]

Both answers are wrong. Realist theories are not invalidated by the post-1989 transformation of world politics. Indeed, they explain much of the story. Realism is rich and varied, and cannot be limited just to structural realism, which deals poorly with change.[3] Many criticisms of realism based on the post-1989 system transformation contrast the most parsimonious form of realism, Kenneth Waltz's structural realism, with the richest and most context-specific alternative explanations derived from liberalism, the new institutionalism, or constructivism. This is not a fair or convincing approach to the evaluation of theories.

Instead, a thoroughly realist explanation of the Cold War's end and the relatively peaceful nature of the Soviet Union's decline that relies entirely on the propositions of pre-1989 theory is in many ways superior to rich explanations based on other theoretical traditions. But to carry on as if there are no lessons in this series of events for international relations theory in general and realist theories in particular is as indefensible intellectually as the claim that

---

Lebow, eds., *International Relations Theory and the End of The Cold War*, forthcoming; Richard Rosecrance and Arthur A. Stein, "Beyond Realism: The Study of Grand Strategy," in Rosecrance and Stein, eds., *The Domestic Bases of Grand Strategy* (Ithaca, N.Y.: Cornell University Press, 1993). Other important works in the post–Cold War debate are discussed below.

2. On theory and revolutionary change, see Peter J. Katzenstein, "International Relations Theory and the Analysis of Change," in Ernst-Otto Czempiel and James N. Rosenau eds., *Global Changes and Theoretical Challenges: Approaches to World Politics for the 1990s* (Lexington, Mass.: D.C. Heath, 1989). Lebow attributes the "data point" quotation to a "prominent participant" in a 1991 conference on international relations theory in Lebow, "The Long Peace, the End of the Cold War, and the Failure of Realism," pp. 251–252. The two most important collections on international theory published after the Cold War look almost entirely to the future (especially of the European Union and NATO) to evaluate competing theories: Sean M. Lynn-Jones and Steven E. Miller, eds., *The Cold War and After: Prospects for Peace—An* International Security *Reader* (Cambridge: MIT Press, 1993); and David A. Baldwin, ed., *Neorealism and Neoliberalism: The Contemporary Debate* (New York: Columbia University Press, 1993).

3. Kenneth N. Waltz, *Theory of International Politics* (New York: McGraw-Hill, 1979). For analyses, see Robert Keohane, ed., *Neorealism and its Critics* (New York: Columbia University Press, 1986); and Barry Buzan, Charles Jones, and Richard Little, *The Logic of Anarchy: Neorealism to Structural Realism* (New York: Columbia University Press, 1993).

the post-1989 transformation single-handedly invalidates any and all realist theories. As critics of realism rightly note, the events of the last half-decade highlight the indeterminacy of realist predictions about state behavior. Realist theories can be made more determinate, but only in *ex post* explanation rather than *ex ante* prediction. Realist theories are terribly weak. They are too easy to confirm and too hard to falsify. They do not come close to the ideal of scientific theory. Their strength is only evident when they are compared to the alternatives, which suffer from similar or worse indeterminacy but do not possess comparable explanatory power. The proper attitude toward the realist approach, even on the part of its defenders, ought to be reluctant acceptance conditioned on a determination to improve it, or to dispose of it if something better comes along.

I perform four basic tasks in this article. First, I discuss briefly the intellectual challenge presented by the post-1989 changes in world politics. What exactly should we expect this series of events to tell us about international relations theories? How much should we expect such theories to tell us about these events? This issue surely ought to lie at the center of any assessment of the Soviet collapse, but thus far it has not. Second, I outline the realist explanation of recent change in world politics that I elaborate upon further throughout the article. Third, I examine the many critiques of realism based on the end of the Cold War and the Soviet collapse: (a) predictive failure; (b) lack of correlation between independent and dependent variables; and (c) important patterns of state behavior defying realist expectations and explanations. Finally, I suggest some preliminary lessons that ought to be drawn from the post-1989 experience, and outline their implications for further research.

The Cold War's End and Social Science Theory

Like the French Revolution or the decline and fall of Rome, the Cold War's end is an event whose importance commands attention but whose complexity frustrates explanation. Few who took up the study of international politics during the Cold War will be content with the notion that the waning of that conflict is simply a single observation no more important than hundreds of others.

And like other complex events in history, the end of the Cold War is unique. The precise set of antecedent conditions and the precise nature of the outcome never occurred before and are exceedingly unlikely ever to recur. So the case cannot be explained in the ideal-scientific manner, as an instance of a general law. That is, the Cold War's end cannot easily be characterized as a type of outcome generally associated with a particular set of antecedent conditions: "Given such-and-such conditions, international systems tend to be transformed; since those conditions obtained in 1987, the Cold War ended as a result."[4] There are simply too many important novel elements in the Cold War story and too few other events even roughly comparable for an explanation of this type to work.

However, if we concentrate on the event itself, we face the familiar problem of too many variables and too few independent observations. International relations theories are almost never monocausal. The claim is rarely "A, not B, caused E," but rather "both A and B caused E but A was more important."[5] Establishing whether nuclear weapons, the balance of power, domestic politics, liberal values, the personalities of leaders, or other factors were truly "most important" in bringing the Cold War to an end is a predictably inconclusive business. In the language of statistics, the researcher faces negative degrees of freedom. If we accept the statistician's view of causality, causal inference cannot be made on the basis of negative degrees of freedom, so the causes of a single outcome cannot be established, and a single outcome will be compatible with numerous theories.[6]

The problem is clear: weak theories that at best can make probabilistic predictions confront a single, complex, but fatefully important event. The solution is twofold. First, it is necessary to disaggregate the event.[7] Elements of the larger event may be susceptible to general explanation. Different theories may explain different regularities that came together to produce the end of the Cold War. At the very least, disaggregation simplifies analysis and clarifies the

---

4. The impossibility of applying the "covering-law" model to the explanation of complex or "aggregative" historical events is discussed in Ernest Nagel, *The Structure of Science: Problems in the Logic of Scientific Explanation* (New York: Harcourt, Brace and World, 1961), pp. 568–575; and Carl G. Hempel, *Aspects of Scientific Explanation* (New York: Free Press, 1965), chap 12. David Dessler's paper, "Scientific Realism is Just Positivism Reconstructed," prepared for delivery at the annual meeting of the International Studies Association, Washington, D.C., March 28–April 1, 1994, alerted me to these sources.

5. See Nagel, *Structure of Science*, pp. 584–588, for the many ways one cause can be said to be "more important" than others.

6. Degrees of freedom are the number of observations minus the number of independent variables minus one. We are all familiar with this logic. Was it worn spark plugs or a dirty air filter that caused our poor gas mileage? We'll never know if we do both repairs simultaneously and only measure gas mileage in one period. We need at least three observations (one with no change; one with new plugs and old filter; and one with old plugs and new filter). But our confidence in any finding would be increased by further observations, to control for different driving conditions, weather, number of passengers, or types of gasoline used.

7. This solution is proposed by Nagel, *Structure of Science;* and Hempel, *Aspects of Scientific Explanation.*

dependent variable. Second, having selected a piece of the puzzle whose explanation may fall under the purview of a given theory, it is still necessary to go "beyond correlations," in David Dessler's phrase, and toward "a direct examination of a theory's postulated generative processes."[8] The only way to evaluate theory in each instance is to trace the process through which the posited cause produced (or influenced) the outcome. Having posited a cause, and shown a correlation, it will still be necessary to show empirically the mechanism that connects cause to effect.[9]

For the purposes of international theory, it is reasonable to separate the great-power element of the whole case: dramatic change in Soviet security policy; the emergence of a deep détente between the superpowers after 1987; Moscow's peaceful acquiescence in regime changes in East-Central Europe, and the subsequent collapse of its alliance and the reunification of Germany in 1989 and 1990. These events do not constitute the entire story, but they are an important part of it that is particularly relevant to international relations theory. Realist theories of all stripes highlight a single independent variable: the balance of power. They describe recent international change primarily as the result of declining relative Soviet power conditioned by the global distribution of power. For the purpose of evaluating realism, then, much post-1987 international change can be defined as a single series of events, linked by a single generative cause. A causal analysis of that link implies close examination of the influence of power on great-power decision-making during the Cold War endgame.

Strictly speaking, no particular finding about the Cold War's end will suffice to "falsify" an entire research program, such as realism. For a single series of events to constitute a critical test of a theory, it must not only be inconsistent with the theory but be unambiguously ruled out by it.[10] However it may

---

8. David Dessler, "Beyond Correlations: Toward a Causal Theory of War," *International Studies Quarterly*, Vol. 35, No. 3, (September 1991), pp. 337–355.
9. The "scientific" status of analyzing causal mechanisms is disputed among philosophers and methodologists of social science. Cf. Dessler, ibid.; Alexander L. George and Timothy J. McKeown, "Case Studies and Theories of Organizational Decision Making," in *Advances in Information Processing in Organizations*, Vol. 2 (Greenwich, Conn.: JAI Press, 1985); and Alexander L. George, "Case Studies and Theory Development: The Method of Structured, Focused Comparison," in Paul Gordon Lauren, ed., *Diplomacy: New Approaches in History, Theory and Policy* (New York: The Free Press, 1979), with Gary King, Robert O. Keohane and Sidney Verba, *Designing Social Inquiry: Scientific Inference in Qualitative Research* (Princeton, N.J.: Princeton University Press, 1994), who maintain that causality can only be understood statistically, and therefore that "process tracing" is merely another method of increasing the sample.
10. See Karl R. Popper, *Conjectures and Refutations: The Growth of Scientific Knowledge* (New York: Harper & Row, 1963), p. 117. I am indebted to David Dessler for helping me navigate Popper's arguments.

appear to critics of realism, realist theories do not rule out an event-series involving the emergence of deep superpower détente and the relatively peaceful contraction of Soviet power. But the importance of the exercise goes beyond formal arguments about theory-testing. If realism can be shown to have nothing to say about the Cold War's end, its relevance to the postwar world can be called into doubt. And a rigorous search for the causal mechanisms at work in important cases adds to our historical understanding. The clash of theories over the explanation of important events leads to a better understanding of those events.

An Outline of a Realist Explanation

Recent changes in world politics can be explained by realist hypotheses, derived from classical realism and from theories of hegemonic rivalry and power-transition, which have been obscured in recent years by the more influential structural variant.[11] The account I offer is simply an extension of the general realist system of explanation to a specific case with inevitably unique features that could not be anticipated and probably will not recur. Its power derives from the fact that it captures central causal relationships and is connected to a set of theories that have proven their utility in a great many different instances.

The Cold War was caused by the rise of Soviet power and the fear this caused in the West. The end of the Cold War was caused by the relative decline in Soviet power and the reassurance this gave the West. Stalin, Khrushchev, and Brezhnev may have had many reasons for competing with the United States, ranging from genuine fear to ideological conviction, but a necessary condition for competition was their perception that they had the *capability* to do so. Gorbachev may have had numerous reasons for seeking to withdraw from the rivalry with the United States, but a necessary precondition was the perception of *reduced capability* to continue competing.

Realists of all kinds view change in state behavior as adaptation to external constraints conditioned by changes in relative power. The best way to make

---

11. This kind of analysis is applied to the entire Cold War in Wohlforth, *The Elusive Balance: Power and Perceptions During the Cold War* (Ithaca, N.Y.: Cornell University Press, 1993). The only other effort to apply realist ideas systematically to an analysis of the Cold War's end that I have located is Kenneth Oye's "Explaining the End of the Cold War: Morphological and Behavioral Adaptations to the Nuclear Peace," draft chapter (December 1992) for Risse-Kappen and Lebow, eds., *International Relations Theory and the End of The Cold War.* I share Oye's emphasis on relative Soviet decline, but focus less on nuclear weapons, while introducing new arguments for the absence of war.

sense of the recent international change and to think about the future of world politics is to view the Cold War as a credible but ultimately failed Soviet challenge to U.S. hegemony.[12] What made the Cold War era seem so different from earlier eras in world history was the reduced uncertainty about alliance choices and the consequent stability of central power relations over four decades. The great popularity of structural realism was very largely due to the fact that it seemed to explain this state of affairs. An alternative explanation, truer to classical balance-of-power theory, is that the Cold War was explained by the Soviet Union's near-domination of Eurasia.[13] Of course, the real degree of Russia's power and threat was arguable, but it was clearer in the Cold War than during any other time of peace. Moscow's position resembled France's in 1813 or Germany's in 1917 and 1941, thus accounting for the stability of the opposing coalition. This was a novel situation, and it came to an end in novel ways.

There are three keys to understanding the peculiarities of the Cold War's end and the Soviet Union's sudden but peaceful collapse that have not been addressed heretofore. First, *decision-makers' assessments of power are what matters.* For any balance-of-power theory to explain state behavior, it must specify the mechanism through which capabilities are translated into actions. That mechanism can only be the assessments of the people who act on behalf of states. One reason balance-of-power theories cannot make deterministic predictions about state behavior is that so many factors can influence assessments of capabilities. As Hans Morgenthau argued almost a half century ago, power is composed of a complex combination of material and non-material factors. Even if, unlike Morgenthau, we distinguish carefully between power as *influence* and power as *capabilities*, the basic insight holds.[14] Capability contains vitally im-

---

12. Distinguishing features of works on hegemonic rise and decline include a focus on hierarchy as an ordering principle, hegemonic rivalry and power transitions. See Robert Gilpin, *War and Change in World Politics* (Cambridge: Cambridge University Press, 1980); A.F.K. Organski, *World Politics* (New York: Knopf, 1968); Karl Deutsch, *The Analysis of International Relations* (Englewood Cliffs, N.J.: Prentice-Hall, 1968); Organski and Jacek Kugler, *The War Ledger* (Chicago: University of Chicago Press, 1980); and Michael Howard, *The Causes of Wars* (Cambridge: Harvard University Press, 1984), chap. 1. For an effort to formalize and test power-transition theory, see Woosang Kim and James D. Morrow, "When do Power Shifts Lead to War?" *American Journal of Political Science,* Vol. 36, No. 4 (November 1992), pp. 896–922.

13. For theoretical analyses of balance-of-power theory that powerfully explicate this view, see R. Harrison Wagner, "What was Bipolarity?" *International Organization,* Vol. 47, No. 1 (Winter 1993), pp. 77–106; and Wagner, "Peace, War, and the Balance of Power," *American Political Science Review,* Vol. 88, No. 3 (September 1994), pp. 593–607.

14. Hans Morgenthau, *Politics Among Nations: The Struggle for Power and Peace* (New York: Knopf, 1948), Part 3. I define power as resources throughout this article. For empirical and conceptual

portant non-material elements that make it very difficult or even impossible to measure. Rational decision-makers may revise assessments of capabilities dramatically and suddenly when confronted with new information about non-material elements of capability, even when material measures change only slightly. Crude quantitative indicators of capabilities cannot accurately represent decision-makers' assessments.

The corollary of a perceptual approach to power is the realization that expectations inform policy. All policies are future-oriented. All decisions are bets on the future. A decision to reform, retrench, or go to war reflects expectations about future trends and assessments of the likely effect of today's policies on tomorrow's distribution of relative power. Theories of hegemonic rivalry suggest that during power transitions, sets of expectations that make decisions for war seem attractive are likely to occur. As in the case of assessments of power, it is difficult to make deterministic predictions about decision-makers' expectations in any case. How any state reacts to perceived decline will be determined by decision-makers' expectations. Obviously, if they conclude that decline is reversible, they will be less likely to opt for risky, forceful solutions to decline and more likely to choose retrenchment and reform. Robert Gilpin argued in 1981 that the two superpowers' basic ideological faith in the future was one of the factors that stabilized the Cold War.[15] What is striking about the Cold War's end is how very late in the game the Soviet leaders clung to this faith.

Second, *declining challengers are more likely than declining hegemons to try to retrench and reform rather than opt for preventive war.* It is vital to note that in the 1980s, the Soviet Union was not a declining hegemon, but a declining challenger. From 1917 onward, the Soviet Union stood formally for revision of the international status quo. Its real commitment to revisionism varied, and as its relative power grew its revisionist impulse assumed increasingly typical great-power forms. But the country's post-1945 hegemonic status and consequent conservatism in the Central European region should not be confused with global hegemony. Worldwide, successive Soviet leaderships chafed against an American-dominated system. They never doubted who the real hegemon was.

---

analysis of how decision-makers assess power, see Aaron L. Friedberg, *The Weary Titan: Britain and the Experience of Relative Decline, 1895–1905* (Princeton, N.J.: Princeton University Press, 1988); Wohlforth, *Elusive Balance;* and Wohlforth, "The Perception of Power: Russia in the Pre-1914 Balance," *World Politics,* Vol. 39, No. 3 (April 1987), pp. 353–381.

15. Gilpin, *War and Change,* p. 240. For more on the relationship between risk attitudes and the likelihood of war in power transitions, see Kim and Morrow, "When do Power Shifts lead to War?"

Theories of hegemonic rivalry do not make deterministic predictions about individual states' reactions to decline. But they do suggest that hegemons are more likely to react violently to decline than either a challenger that never became powerful enough to contemplate taking over leadership, or a state not directly contending for leadership. For all such theories, the danger point, when war is most likely (though not inevitable), is a *transition* in relative position, not the rapid decline of a challenger. Soviet power rose and fell without reaching such a transition point. Theorists of hegemonic war, perhaps under Thucydides' spell, tended to concentrate on dynamic challengers and moribund hegemons. They always thought of the problem of peaceful change as one of accommodating the demands of a rising challenger. In the 1950s and 1960s, the Soviet Union seemed to fit the bill. But roles were mixed in the Cold War endgame. Rigid, Spartan Soviet Russia was the moribund challenger, and dynamic, Athenian America the rising defender.

The third key is that *sudden decline or civil strife on the losing side of a struggle is less destabilizing globally than such decline or strife on the winning side.*[16] Internal strife on the losing side ratifies the previously-existing power relationship; it merely confirms what political actors knew to be the case just prior to the advent of the strife. Thus, it provides no incentive to renew the struggle. Civil strife on the winning side, of course, gives the losing party an incentive to carry on with the struggle. This helps to account not only for the relatively peaceful nature of Soviet decline and collapse, but also for the widespread obsession (both in the West and in Moscow) with U.S. decline during the Cold War. If we accept that the Soviet Union was behind the United States in power terms, then Soviet rise and U.S. decline were much more dangerous in terms of power-transition theory than vice-versa. Unlike structural realism, which insists on seeing the two superpowers as identical "sensible duopolists,"[17] this explanation sees the Soviet Union as occupying a quite different international position than United States and expects different consequences from changes in its relative power.

It follows that the basic hierarchy of the international system—with the United States at the top—has not only not been challenged by the Soviet collapse, but has been decisively reinforced by it.[18] This leads to a portrayal of

---

16. This is merely an extension of the logic in Geoffrey Blainey, *The Causes of War*, (New York: The Free Press, 1973), p. 82.
17. Waltz, *Theory of International Politics*, p. 203.
18. This conclusion resembles the views of Marxist world-system theorists. See Richard Herrmann, "International Relations Theory and the End of the Cold War," draft chapter (July 1993) for Lebow and Risse-Kappen, *International Relations Theory*. It is important to stress, however, that the realist

the near future of world politics as strikingly different from that suggested by structural realism. While structural realists focus on the war-proneness of the emerging multipolarity, theories of hegemonic rivalry highlight the relative stability and order that the existence of a clear hierarchy of prestige and power will impart to great-power relations. In short, there are (non-structural) realist reasons for regarding the near future of great-power relations relatively optimistically, even ignoring such important factors as the existence of nuclear weapons and the unprecedented popularity of liberal and democratic values.

Realists and Their Critics

Together, these non–structural realist arguments help explain change in Soviet security policy, the consequent emergence of deep superpower détente, the Soviet Union's adoption of reform and retrenchment rather than violent opposition to decline, and the ability of the international system to accommodate unprecedented power and territorial changes without great-power war. Objections to such an explanation can be anticipated by examining the post–Cold War debate on international theory. Below, I examine three lines of criticism: (1) egregious predictive failure; (2) lack of correlation between independent and dependent variables; (3) state behavior inconsistent with realist predictions, including the Soviet withdrawal from East-Central Europe, the high levels of great-power cooperation, and a potentially "critical" absence of great-power war. Many of these criticisms point to areas where realist theories must either improve or make more modest claims. Yet most of them are most damaging to the structural version of realism, whose inability to deal adequately with international change is acknowledged even by its most ardent defenders.

FAILURE TO PREDICT
Rational actors learn from predictive failures. One can reject the premise that prediction is a necessary condition of explanation yet still conclude that widespread failure to anticipate vitally important events even in general terms should cause us to wonder about the theories on which expectations were based.[19]

---

explanation proposed here regards military power, prestige, and security, and thus the U.S.-Soviet rivalry, as central, while world-system theorists see the Soviet challenge as peripheral. See, for example, Immanuel Wallerstein, *Geopolitics and Geoculture: Essays on the Changing World-System* (Cambridge: Cambridge University Press, Edition de la Maison des Sciences de L'Homme, 1992), chap. 1, who continues to see post-1989 systems changes as results of U.S. decline.

19. For a general critique of international relations theories, based on their failure to anticipate the Cold War's end, see Gaddis, "International Relations Theory"; on realism in particular, see Kra-

Most scrutiny has been directed at structural realism. The main charge against this theory is that it not only failed to anticipate change, but led those who believed in it to expect the opposite: stability. To the extent that structural realism sought to explain the Cold War by reference to bipolarity, this criticism appears justified. Ambiguity surrounds the definition of bipolarity, but its most common meaning is the concentration of capabilities in two powers, in this case the United States and the Soviet Union.[20] In 1988, Waltz argued that the Cold War was "firmly rooted in the structure of postwar international politics, and will last as long as that structure endures."[21] It is difficult to avoid the conclusion that any reasonably intelligent consumer of Waltz's theory in 1988 would have expected the Cold War to last as long as the bipolar structure itself. The Cold War ended over the course of the next two years; however, according to Waltz in 1993, "bipolarity endures, but in an altered state." In short, the Cold War's end caused an important amendment to be added to the theory: while bipolarity leads to Cold War, "altered bipolarity" leads to détente.[22]

However accurate, such criticisms miss Waltz's main contention: that a theory of international politics cannot predict state behavior or explain international change.[23] Waltz and his followers often employed the theory to discuss Cold War statecraft, but its core predictions are only two: balances will form;

---

tochwil, "The Embarrassment of Changes"; and Lebow, "The Long Peace, the End of the Cold War, and the Failure of Realism." For a helpful discussion of the relative importance of prediction in assessing theory, see David Dessler, "Explanation, Prediction, Critique: The Aims of Rationalistic International Relations Theory," College of William and Mary, unpublished ms., May 1994.

20. That was how it was seen by the postwar realists in opposition to whom Waltz first articulated his arguments about bipolarity. See Hans Morgenthau, *Politics Among Nations*, chap. 19; Morgenthau discusses the new postwar structure of power in the 1948 edition of his classic text, although he does not use the term "bipolarity"; John H. Herz, *International Politics in the Atomic Age* (New York: Columbia University Press, 1959), chap. 7; and Kenneth Waltz, "The Stability of a Bipolar World," *Daedalus* (Summer 1964), pp. 881–909. On the vexing ambiguities surrounding the concept, see Wagner, "What was Bipolarity?" Ned Lebow also develops a penetrating critique in "The Long Peace, the End of the Cold War, and the Failure of Realism."

21. Waltz, "The Origins of War in Neorealist Theory," in Robert I. Rotberg and Theodore K. Rabb, eds., *The Origin and Prevention of Major Wars* (Cambridge: Cambridge University Press, 1989), p. 52. That structure would likely endure for some time because Waltz, like most international relations theorists, believed that "national rankings change slowly. War aside, the economic and other bases of power change little more rapidly." In addition, "the barriers to entering the super-power club have never been higher or more numerous." Waltz, *Theory of International Politics*, p. 177.

22. Waltz, "The Emerging Structure of International Politics," *International Security*, Vol. 18, No. 2 (Fall 1993), pp. 48–52.

23. "The behavior of states and statesmen," Waltz states, "is indeterminate." *Theory of International Politics*, p. 68; "Changes in, and transformation of, systems originate not in the structure of a system but in its parts. Systems change, or are transformed, depending on the resources and aims of their units and on the fates that befall them." Waltz, "Reflections on *Theory of International Politics*: A Response to my Critics," in Keohane, *Neorealism and its Critics*, p. 343.

and bipolar systems are less war-prone than multipolar ones, due to reduced uncertainty about alliance choices. The latter prediction seems borne out by the history of the Cold War and even its end. The bipolar structure, it could be argued, was so primed for peace that even German reunification and Soviet dissolution did not upset the great powers' repose. The continued tendency of all the great powers to bandwagon with the United States after the Soviet collapse does contradict the theory's prediction of balancing. But Waltz always allowed that unit causes could delay system incentives for prolonged periods. The epistemological modesty of the theory renders it hard to criticize (and to falsify).

Theories of hegemonic rivalry clearly benefit in this instance from their focus on change. They urge the reader to think of any international system as temporary, and to look for the underlying causes of change, which accumulate slowly but are realized in rare, concentrated bursts. They encourage scholars and policy-makers to be on the lookout for gaps between the capabilities of states and the demands placed upon them by their international roles. It is thus no surprise that the predictions that look best in hindsight came from people who thought in these terms. An example is the sociologist Randall Collins, who identified early the Soviet geopolitical overstretch as the basic harbinger of international change. Relying on a theory whose central variables were relative capability and geopolitical position, he began predicting the collapse of the Soviet Union in the late 1970s, noting that the loss would result not mainly from ethnic revolt or a single major war but from the geopolitical exhaustion of the imperial center and "a loss of political confidence" among the Russians.[24]

The main criticism of theories of hegemonic rivalry is that none generated the kind of explanation I suggested above—even speculatively—before the fact.[25] In general, realists of all types tended to associate large-scale interna-

---

24. Randall Collins, *Weberian Sociological Theory* (New York: Cambridge University Press, 1986), chaps. 7, 8. See also Randall Collins, "Some Principles of Long Term Social Change: The Territorial Power of States," in Louis Kriesberg, ed., *Research in Social Movements, Conflicts and Change*, Vol. 1 (Greenwich, Conn.: JAI Press, 1978), pp. 1–34; Randall Collins and David Waller, "What Theories Predicted the State Breakdowns and Revolutions of the Soviet Bloc?" in Louis Kriesberg and David R. Segal, eds., *Research in Social Movements, Conflicts and Change*, Vol. 14 (Greenwich, Conn.: JAI Press, 1992); and Ted Hopf's letter, "Getting the End of the Cold War Wrong," *International Security*, Vol. 18, No. 2 (Fall 1993), pp. 202–208, which alerted me to Collins's work. Another, much better known prediction is Andrei Amalrik, *Will the Soviet Union Survive until 1984?* (New York: Harper and Row, 1970), whose scenario of collapse centers on the Soviet leadership's resort to a diversionary war with China.

25. I first put together the argument sketched out above in the spring of 1990, after the collapse of Moscow's outer empire, but before the collapse of its inner one. William C. Wohlforth, "Gorbachev's Foreign Policy: From New Thinking to Decline," in Wolfgang Danspeckgruber, ed., *Emerging Dimensions of European Security Policy* (Boulder, Colo.: Westview, 1991), pp. 47–62.

tional change with war. In particular, those who did contemplate Soviet decline in the context of the Cold War tended to assume that Moscow would not face decline gracefully.[26] The reasons for these assumptions are not intrinsic to the theory. There is no barrier in the theory that prevents one from pulling together various strands and constructing a scenario for the relatively peaceful ending of the Cold War rivalry. Many theorists of power transition and hegemonic rivalry themselves thought that retreat to more defensible positions and domestic reform were quite often the best strategies for a declining state. Indeed, those who thought that the United States was overextended urged precisely such a course on the U.S. government.

One explanation, as Ted Hopf argues, is that curiously little effort was devoted to thinking about how the Cold War might end.[27] At least one reason for that neglect is the difficulty of assessing power. The debate focused like a laser beam on U.S. decline, even as the Soviet Union was entering the initial stages of its final crisis. While many did identify a gap between Soviet capabilities and commitments, very few shared Collins's dire assessment. Most international relations theorists in the 1980s relied on the dominant assessment then prevalent among Sovietologists: the Soviet Union was in deep trouble, but a very long way from collapse. That Sovietological assessment mirrored the prevalent mood in Moscow's policy-making circles. The possibility of precipitous Soviet decline seemed so remote and so speculative up until 1989 that little analytical energy was devoted to working through scenarios involving a declining challenger in the context of a prolonged great-power rivalry.[28]

---

26. On the association of war and change see, for a small sampling of quotations, Gilpin, *War and Change*, p. 15; A.F.K. Organski, *World Politics* (New York: Knopf, 1985), p. 333; Robert Jervis, *The Meaning of the Nuclear Revolution* (Ithaca, N.Y.: Cornell University Press), p. 34; J.W. Burton, *International Relations: A General Theory* (Cambridge, Mass.: Cambridge University Press, 1967), pp. 76–77. In *Theory of International Politics,* Waltz discusses various roads to structural transformation without explicitly connecting them to war; however, he insisted that the only structural transformation in history, from multi- to bipolarity, was caused by World War II. For mid-1980s thinking on Soviet decline, see Kurt M. Campbell, "Prospects and Consequences of Soviet Decline," in Joseph S. Nye, Graham T. Allison, and Albert Carnesale, eds., *Fateful Visions: Avoiding Nuclear Catastrophe* (Cambridge, Mass.: Ballinger, 1988); and Paul M. Kennedy, *The Rise and Fall of the Great Powers* (New York: Random House, 1987), esp. pp. 488–514.
27. Hopf, "Getting the End of the Cold War Wrong."
28. As Raymond Aron remarked to Hedley Bull at a 1982 conference, Soviet decline was "the most important and indeed most neglected question in contemporary international relations scholarship." Cited by Campbell, "Prospects and Consequences of Soviet Decline," p. 153. On the stability assumption in Sovietology, see Thomas Remington, "Sovietology and System Stability," in *Post-Soviet Affairs,* Vol. 8, No. 3 (July–September 1992), pp. 239–269. Other good post-mortems on Sovietology include the articles by Robert Tucker and George Breslauer in the same issue; Alexander Dallin, "Causes of the Collapse of the USSR," *Post-Soviet Affairs,* Vol. 8, No. 4 (December 1992), pp. 279–302; Peter Rutland, "Sovietology: Notes for a Post-Mortem," *The National Interest,* Vol. 31 (Spring 1993), pp. 109–123.

It is not surprising, then, that when people did contemplate Soviet decline or large-scale international change they took the easiest intellectual route: induction. That is, episodes of rapid international change appeared to be associated historically with war, and empires rarely accepted their decline with graceful resignation.[29] Major international change and precipitous Soviet decline seemed remote enough that writers felt it sufficient to note in passing that analogous events in the past had usually been accompanied by large-scale violence. They did not ponder at length whether the set of perceptions and expectations that had accompanied such violence in the past was really as likely to appear in this instance.

This inductive association of war and major change is an important reason so many scholars failed to prepare intellectually for the transformation of world politics that occurred after 1989. Most analysts assumed, implicitly or explicitly, that the relevant political actors themselves would be constrained by the association of war and change, and precisely for that reason believed that change was most likely to be marginal in the near term. Fearing that radical change would raise the specter of war, the key political actors would endeavor to moderate their behavior in a rational cost-benefit calculation. So all the indications of new Soviet perceptions of power and interest, and of impending revolution in Eastern Europe, that stand out so clearly in hindsight were balanced at the time by the feeling that the magnitude of change would be managed by decision-makers apprehensive about potential instability and war. The notable feature of those analysts now regarded to have "got it most right" about the Soviet Union's fate is their dispassionate consideration of violence as the road to Soviet dissolution.

If scholars had thought more about the problem of how the Cold War system might end, they would not have met insuperable theoretical barriers blocking rough anticipation of the likely nature of international change. Indeed, they might have overcome the danger that always accompanies historical induction: *selection bias*, whereby scholars highlighted only those cases of international

---

29. See Jack Levy, "Declining Power and the Preventive Motivation for War," *World Politics*, Vol. 40, No. 1 (April 1988), p. 97. The association between war and change is hard to measure, but Paul F. Diehl and Gary Goertz, "Territorial Change and Militarized Conflict," *Journal of Conflict Resolution*, Vol. 32, No. 1 (March 1988), pp. 103–122, do find that if territorial change is "important" and "among the major powers" it tends to be associated with war. Also relevant here is: Jack Levy, *War in the Modern Great Power System, 1495–1975* (Lexington: University Press of Kentucky, 1983). Note that it usually takes a war to convince contemporaries and scholars in retrospect that a state has either become or ceased to be a "great power." See Levy, *War in the Modern Great Power System*, p. 24.

change and national decline that were associated with violence, and down-played or ignored other cases.[30] Because they were accustomed to thinking about the Cold War in terms of rising Soviet power and precarious U.S. hegemony (or, in the 1980s, in terms of two "sensible duopolist" superpowers adjusting to a bipolar structure) they were not inclined to sift the historical record for evidence about declining challengers.

However, if more analytical energy had been devoted to thinking through scenarios of systemic change, exponents of both structural realism and theories of hegemonic rivalry might have focused upon the unique features of the post–World War II international system in terms of both types of theory. For structural realists, bipolarity was a world-historical first. For hegemony theorists, never before had a challenger come so close to dominating Eurasia in peacetime, and never had such a challenger begun to decline well before the main status-quo states. Both theories thus should have led to the suspicion that change might be different this time around, even apart from such important new features as nuclear weapons.

The predictive failure of realist theories, including those that self-consciously addressed the problem of change in world politics, was linked to the difficulty of assessing power. The gap between a state's capabilities and its international role is easy to identify in hindsight, after capabilities have been put to some test. Before the fact, however, the existence or significance of such a gap will always be a matter of speculation. Any capabilities-based theory which recognizes that capabilities contain significant non-material elements must recognize the impossibility of making precise power assessments.

THE CORRELATION BETWEEN "POWER" AND "CHANGE"
Realists see change as the result of the rise and decline of states' relative power conditioned by the nature of the overall distribution of capabilities. A structural realist account of the Cold War's end would feature bipolarity, whose simplicity and ease of management might explain the comparatively peaceful nature of the change. Theories of hegemonic rivalry would highlight the U.S.-dominated hierarchy of world politics in explaining the same outcome. For either version, relative decline explains the change in Soviet behavior and interests that was the necessary condition for the emergence of deep superpower

---

30. Note Bruce Bueno de Mesquita's different argument about case selection bias in this theory in, "Pride of Place: The Origins of German Hegemony," *World Politics*, Vol. 43, No. 1 (October 1990), pp. 28–52.

détente, the revolutions in East-Central Europe, and the reunification of Germany. In this section, I aim to develop a richer understanding of the connection between decline and international change that defuses many criticisms of realism.

THE RELATIONSHIP BETWEEN DECLINE AND POLICY CHANGE. Perhaps the central theme of recent challenges to realism is the proposition that the realist emphasis on declining relative power is inconsistent with the "Gorbachev revolution." While acknowledging that change in Soviet security policy was the key permissive cause of the Cold War's end, many recent analyses question whether declining power caused that change. Rather, they feature other explanatory variables, such as the emergence of industrial society in the West,[31] emergence of civil society in East-Central Europe and a legitimization crisis of the communist parties,[32] Soviet modernization,[33] the Soviet domestic political competition between hard-liners and soft-liners,[34] domestic politics in both the Soviet Union and Western Europe,[35] Soviet elite or leadership learning,[36] the existence of nuclear weapons and superpower learning about them,[37] or some combination of these factors.[38]

---

31. Daniel Deudney and G. John Ikenberry, "The International Sources of Soviet Domestic Change," *International Security*, Vol. 13, No. 3 (Winter 1991/92), pp. 74–118.
32. Kratochwil, "The Embarassment of Changes"; and Koslowski and Kratochwil, "Understanding Change."
33. Jack Snyder, "The Gorbachev Revolution: A Waning of Soviet Expansionism?" *International Security*, Vol. 12, No. 4 (Winter 1987/88), pp. 93–131; and *Myths of Empire: Domestic Politics and International Ambition* (Ithaca, N.Y.: Cornell University Press, 1991), chap. 6.
34. Matthew Evangelista, "Internal and External Constraints on Soviet Grand Strategy," in Rosecrance and Stein, *Domestic Bases of Grand Strategy*; Richard Anderson, "Why Competitive Politics Inhibits Learning in Soviet Foreign Policy," in Robert Jervis and Jack Snyder, eds., *Dominoes and Bandwagons: Strategic Beliefs and Great Power Competition in the Eurasian Rimland* (New York: Oxford University Press, 1991).
35. Thomas Risse-Kappen, "Did 'Peace Through Strength' End the Cold War? Lessons from INF," *International Security*, Vol. 16, No. 1 (Summer 1991), pp. 162–188.
36. George Breslauer, "What Have We Learned about Learning?" in Breslauer and Phillip Tetlock, eds., *Learning in U.S. and Soviet Foreign Policy* (Boulder, Colo.: Westview, 1991); and Andrew Bennett, "Patterns of Soviet Military Interventionism, 1975–1990: Alternative Explanations and their Implications," in William Zimmerman, ed., *Beyond the Soviet Threat: Rethinking American Security Policy in a New Era* (Ann Arbor: University of Michigan Press, 1992). Janice Gross Stein, "Political Learning by Doing: Gorbachev as Uncommitted Thinker and Motivated Learner," in *International Organization*, Vol. 48, No. 2 (Spring 1994), pp. 155–183, stresses individual learning by Gorbachev.
37. Steve Weber, "Security after the Revolutions of 1989 and 1991: The Future with Nuclear Weapons," in Patrick J. Garrity and Steven A. Maaranen, eds., *Nuclear Weapons in the Changing World: Perspectives from Europe, Asia and North America* (New York: Plenum Press, 1992).
38. For accounts that combine the learning and the leadership competition/domestic politics approaches, see Sarah E. Mendelson, "Internal Battles and External Wars: Politics, Learning and the Soviet Withdrawal from Afghanistan," *World Politics*, Vol. 45, No. 3 (April 1993), pp. 327–360;

This literature faces a basic problem, however: the centrality of economic reform to the rise and demise of the Gorbachev revolution.[39] The problem for anti-realists (and realists) is that the declining-relative-capabilities explanation is difficult to differentiate from the domestic explanation focusing on the need to revitalize the economy.[40] This is the basic dilemma of much international relations theory: the difficulty of assigning relative weight to internal versus international factors when they continually influence one another. For surely no critic of realism thinks that the Soviet leaders would have initiated reforms if their economy had been bounding along at six percent a year while the West was mired in a depression. As Alexander Zinoviev put it in 1989, "if there were no West . . . the state of the communist economy would be extolled as the height of perfection, the communist system of power—as the height of democracy, the population's living conditions—as an earthly paradise."[41] And surely no realist thinks that the end of the Cold War can be explained adequately without reference to the peculiar mix of centralized authority, weakness and brittleness that we now know was characteristic of the Soviet domestic order.

Any realist discussion of international change must combine the domestic and international levels of analysis. A realist explanation cannot offer a comprehensive account of precisely why a given state's domestic political, social, and economic institutions decline in comparison to those of competing powers. Instead, it makes only two claims, both of which distinguish it from an account focusing solely on domestic politics. First, definitions of interests are related to perceived relative power. A given state's leadership seeks greater influence on the world stage when it thinks it can, and resolves to retrench internationally

---

and George Breslauer, "Explaining Soviet Policy Changes: The Interaction of Politics and Learning," in Breslauer, ed., *Soviet Policy in Africa: From the Old to the New Thinking* (Berkeley, Calif.: Berkeley-Stanford Program in Soviet Studies, 1992). For an argument in favor of combining many of the theories listed above, see Daniel Deudney and G. John Ikenberry, "Soviet Reforms and the End of the Cold War: Explaining Large-Scale Historical Change," *Review of International Studies*, Vol. 17, No. 3 (Summer 1991), pp. 225–250. A convincing effort to combine international influences and domestic institutional and ideational factors is Jeff Checkel, "Ideas, Institutions, and the Gorbachev Foreign Policy Revolution," *World Politics*, Vol. 45, No. 2 (January 1993), pp. 271–300.
39. Coit D. Blacker, *Hostage to Revolution: Gorbachev and Soviet Security Policy, 1985–1991* (New York: Council on Foreign Relations, 1993), makes a compelling case for the primacy of economic reform in the whole story, connecting it to changes in security policy. As Deudney and Ikenberry note in "The International Sources of Soviet Domestic Change," p. 80: "About the character of the crisis there is wide agreement. Virtually every commentator of these events points to economic stagnation as the decisive impetus for change."
40. Most analyses critical of realism acknowledge the importance of economic decline to the whole story, but some authors, discussed below, question its significance compared to other variables.
41. Alexander Zinoviev, "The Missing World War III, the Crisis of Communism, and the Offense of Democracy," *Détente*, No. 15 (1989), p. 5.

when it feels it must. The impetus to address economic deficiencies must be understood in terms of the relative economic efficiency of rival states and the strategic implications of the economy. Second, relative decline is connected to the costs of international competition or security. In the case of the Soviet Union and the Cold War's end, perceived relative decline was a necessary condition for the adoption of perestroika and "new thinking," and decline was connected to the burdens imposed by the Soviet Union's international position.

Many recent criticisms of realism maintain that changes in the Soviet political elite's preferences had little or nothing to do with changes in relative Soviet capabilities. They argue that the Soviet Union was not in decline—or at least that Soviet decline was not noticeably worse than earlier periods—until after Gorbachev began his reforms.[42] They argue that Gorbachev's reforms were a cause rather than a consequence of decline. Since they argue that Soviet decline was not particularly acute, many critics of realism see Gorbachev-era change in Soviet security policy as a willful intellectual revolution, not a reaction to the grim realities of the shifting scales of power.[43] In general, these anti-realists stress Gorbachev's intentionality: he wanted to do what he did because his preferences had changed in ways realists would never expect; he wished to give up "socialism" and join the West.

These arguments do not stand up to scrutiny. Critics of realism contrast a simplistic view of the relationship between decline and policy change against a nuanced and complex view of the relationship between their favored ex-

---

42. See, e.g., Lebow, "Stability and Change in International Relations: A Critique of Realism," esp. p. 266; Friedrich Kratochwil, "The Embarrassment of Changes"; and Stein, "Political Learning by Doing." The strongest case against the declining-capabilities view of Gorbachev is Evangelista, "Internal and External Constraints on Soviet Grand Strategy," in Rosecrance and Stein, *Domestic Bases of Grand Strategy*. See also John Meuller, "The Impact of Ideas on Grand Strategy," in ibid., p. 53.

43. This is an old debate. See Stephen Sestanovich, "Gorbachev's Foreign Policy: A Diplomacy of Decline," *Problems of Communism*, (January–February 1988), pp. 1–15; and the important sources cited in Richard K. Herrmann, "Soviet Behavior in Regional Conflicts: Old Questions, New Strategies, and Important Lessons," *World Politics*, Vol. 44, No. 3 (April 1992), pp. 432–465. The debate is surely not over. On the importance of external causes for Soviet retrenchment, see Celeste A. Wallander, "Opportunity, Incrementalism, and Learning in the Extension and Retraction of Soviet Global Commitments," and Richard Weitz, "The Soviet Retreat from Third World Conflicts: The Importance of Systemic Factors," both in *Security Studies*, Vol. 1, No. 3 (Spring 1992), pp. 514–579, and Celeste A. Wallander and Jane E. Prokop, "Soviet Security Strategies Toward Europe—After the Wall, With Their Backs Up Against It," in Robert O. Keohane, Joseph S. Nye and Stanley Hoffmann, eds., *After the Cold War: International Institutions and State Strategies in Europe*, (Cambridge: Harvard University Press, 1993). Finally, for a strong argument in favor of a cognitive learning explanation for Soviet retrenchment, see Andrew Bennett, "Patterns of Soviet Military Interventionism, 1975–1990: Alternative Explanations and their Implications."

planatory variable and policy change. They also compare incompatible measures. Their nuanced explanations filled with rich case detail are evaluated against quantitative indicators of "power." They ignore perceptions of power. However, if one wants to know whether change in ideas is caused by changes in power relations, one must investigate changing ideas about power.

A causal evaluation of a power-centric theory would have to trace the influence of power as assessed by the individuals and organizations concerned. Critics of realism, who do not do this, often ignore relative decline. The ABC of realism is that relative gains and losses are what matters. Data on absolute Soviet economic performance or defense expenditures are uninteresting to realists; even Soviet-U.S. comparisons are insufficient. The issue is the Soviet Union's capabilities relative to those powers aligned against it on the world stage.

TRACING THE INFLUENCE OF POWER. Tracing the influence of power assessments on the evolution of policy is a complex task requiring all the historian's skill and care in evaluating evidence, and maximum access to archival materials. [44] The documentary record of Soviet decision-making in the Gorbachev era is sparse, yet a surprising amount of evidence has come to light. This evidence suggests the importance of many factors: the sense of security provided by nuclear weapons; the force of Gorbachev's convictions; the exigencies of domestic politics; luck, chance and caprice. But the available evidence also suggests that the story cannot be told now and will not be able to be told in the future without according an important causal role to the problem of relative decline. The keys to keep in mind in any causal evaluation are that power is always relative; that perceptions and expectations link power to policy; and that rational assessments can change quickly when new evidence becomes available.

What perceptions of power surrounded the initial decisions to opt for reform, and how did feedback from the new policies feed into subsequent decisions? Most Sovietologists were long aware that reform sentiments had existed within and around the Soviet Communist Party elite since Khrushchev's Twentieth Party Congress. But through the 1960s and 1970s the Soviet leadership had a robust view of the Soviet Union's relative capabilities; this view was buttressed

---

44. As difficult as it is, it can and has been done, especially for the periods preceding the two world wars. Examples include Friedberg, *The Weary Titan*; Wohlforth, "The Perception of Power"; Risto Ropponen, *Die Kraft Russlands* (Helsinki: Historiallisia tutkimiksia, 1968); and Ernest R. May, ed., *Knowing One's Enemies: Intelligence Assessments before the Two World Wars*, (Princeton, N.J.: Princeton University Press, 1986).

by foreign governments, led by the United States, which viewed it as a rising power that had to be accommodated politically. That set of perceptions contrasted starkly with the views in the early 1980s, when reform ideas began to get through to members of the top leadership.[45]

Two factors helped bring reform notions to the fore in the early 1980s: the system-wide decline in socialism's economic performance—dramatically highlighted by the Solidarity movement in Poland—against a backdrop of economic recovery in the West; and the Soviet Union's awful geopolitical position, with every other major power in the entire world, in every region, allied or aligned against Moscow. Each general secretary from Brezhnev on acknowledged these problems openly in speeches and policy pronouncements, and official concern was detectable even in the pages of the censored press and scholarly journals. Reformist analysts at research institutes penned pessimistic classified assessments arguing for new policies to address both problems.[46] The situation seemed doubly grim because many Soviet analysts were changing the way they measured power. They began to replace the old brute indicators of steel production and energy consumption with new measures that highlighted efficiency and high technology.

The ideas for foreign and domestic policy change that began to get through to the top leadership in this period were not new, but the combination of external and internal problems was. Gorbachev and members of his inner circle date the immediate origins of the reforms precisely to the 1982–83 period. The key issue around which the reformers mobilized was the need to hold a party plenum to consider the issue of the scientific-technical revolution which, they argued, was passing socialism by and would continue to do so in the absence of reforms. The program Gorbachev announced to the April 1985 party plenum one month after his selection as general secretary had been developed in 1983 and 1984.[47]

---

45. Wohlforth, *Elusive Balance*, chaps. 7, 8.

46. On open acknowledgment of problems, see Wohlforth, *Elusive Balance*, pp. 224–229, and sources cited therein. For classified institute assessments of the international situation, see Robert English, "Russia Views the West: Intellectuals, Ideology and Foreign Policy, " Ph.D. dissertation, Princeton University, forthcoming in 1994, chap. 7.

47. Transcript of Michael McFaul's summer 1992 interview with N.I. Ryzhkov for the Hoover Institution's oral history project, pp. 127, 136–138. Gorbachev dated the immediate origins of his reforms to 1982: see John Gooding, "Perestroika as a Revolution from Within," *Russian Review*, Vol. 51, No. 1 (January 1992), p. 46, fn. 29. Other accounts concur: Yegor Ligachev, *Inside Gorbachev's Kremlin*, trans. Catherine A. Fitzpatrick, Michele A. Berdy, and Dorbochna Dyrcz-Freeman (New York: Pantheon, 1993), chap. 1; N.I. Ryzhkov, *Perestroika: Istoriia Predatel'stv* (Moscow: Novosti,

Thus, the impetus for innovation and even the contours of the new policies are inexplicable without reference to the interconnected problems of perceived relative decline and overextension. The policy that emerged from these circumstances sought to bring capabilities and commitments into line while reducing the cohesion and hostility of the opposing coalition of states through careful appeasement. This would reduce the threat, potentially facilitate valuable cooperation with more advanced rival states, and allow a reallocation of domestic resources to assist in the long-term revitalization of Soviet socialism. "New thinking" ideas and policy concepts—many of them western in origin—provided the policy's intellectual undergirding. Two central ideas suggested how Moscow might reduce its massive commitment to military power at minimal cost to itself: recognition of the security dilemma, and belief in the prevalence of balancing behavior in world politics. Together they suggested a simple recipe for successful retrenchment: reduce other states' sense of threat, and they will reduce their commitment to defense and the tightness of their anti-Soviet alignment.[48]

The drive behind the policy contained two elements: the perceived costs that drove intellectual change and the expected benefits to be derived from such change. The more advanced the perception of decline, the higher the perceived costs of the status quo, and the greater the incentive for intellectual change and the willingness to take risks for expected gain. Both elements were important. Perceptions of decline and high costs drove tough intellectual change and the acceptance of uncomfortable trade-offs. The expected benefits made each trade-off easier to stomach. Criticisms of realism ignore or downplay the cost side of the ledger. Tracing the influence of perceptions of capabilities on Soviet decision-making shows that increased awareness of decline and of the high costs of existing policies was associated with change from hallowed precepts.

Though the supporting ideas were well-developed among key Gorbachev aides, the initial foreign policy was an admixture of old and new. What ensued from 1985 was a trial-and-error learning process, with the radicalization of

---

1993), chap. 2; Georgy Arbatov, *The System: An Insider's Life in Soviet Politics* (New York: Random House, 1993), chap. 9; and the interviews in Stephen F. Cohen and Katrina vanden Heuvel, *Voices of Glasnost: Interviews with Gorbachev's Reformers* (New York: Norton, 1989). Jeff Checkel, "Ideas, Institutions, and the Gorbachev Foreign Policy Revolution," analyzes how the early-1980s international situation provided opportunities for policy entrepreneurs at research institutes to get their novel ideas to the leadership.

48. For a concise analysis, see Oye, "Explaining the End of the Cold War: Morphological and Behavioral Adaptations to the Nuclear Peace"; for more detail, Blacker, *Hostage to Revolution,* and Wohlforth, *Elusive Balance,* chap. 9.

policy proceeding in step with mounting feedback about the depth of social-ism's competitive disadvantage. What gave new thinking clear meaning and imposed clarity on Gorbachev's preferences were concrete and costly unilateral Soviet concessions. What made these concessions happen was dire perceived necessity. The relative strength of one's country and its international position become more evident when one tries to change these things for the better. The failure of the more conservative versions of perestroika constituted new evidence about Soviet capabilities. As these failures accumulated domestically, Gorbachev became more forthcoming internationally.[49] Feedback about the resilience and reformability of socialism was obviously part of any assessment of Soviet capabilities, and this feedback did not accumulate linearly, but in fits and starts. The concentrated, non-linear nature of change does not mean that it is unconnected to perceived capabilities.

The more conservative the person (in Soviet terms), the greater the need for negative feedback before he or she could retreat from old convictions. Thus, regardless of where Gorbachev "really" stood, it took considerable negative feedback about Soviet power and prospects before large conservative sectors of the ruling elite could stomach retreats. The concessions to the West that led to renewed U.S.-Soviet détente were driven by two factors: the expected benefit in decreased international tensions and increased cooperation; and the high costs of existing security policy. For many moderates and conservatives in the Soviet leadership, such concessions were hard to take. But moderates and even conservatives shared Gorbachev's desire to rescue socialism, which in the immediate situation was largely a resource allocation problem. They all wanted to get their hands on the human and material resources of the defense sector. As Gorbachev lectured the Politburo in a February 1988 session: "Yes, we achieved military-strategic parity with the United States. And no one reckoned how much it cost us. But a reckoning was necessary. Now it is clear that without significant reductions in military expenditures we cannot resolve the problems of perestroika." The general secretary was preaching to the converted, for by 1987 he had assembled a strong Politburo majority on this issue.[50]

---

49. Blacker, *Hostage to Revolution*, captures this process brilliantly.
50. From the diary of Gorbachev's principal foreign-policy adviser, Anatoly S. Chernyaev, in his memoir of these years, *Shest' let s Gorbachevym: Po dnevnikovym zapisiam* (Moscow: Progess, 1993), p. 253. He notes that Gorbachev "examined each one of his major actions (and initiatives) from both angles—internal and external." Former Foreign Minister Aleksandr Bessmertnykh recalls, "When Gorbachev came into power in Moscow, the economic statistics already indicated that the economy was doing not so good. So when you were talking about SDI and arms control, the economic element was sometimes, in my view, Gorbachev's number one preoccupation." Fred I. Greenstein and William C. Wohlforth, eds., "Retrospective on the End of the Cold War," *Princeton*

By looking at how the more traditionally-minded members of the Soviet leadership moved toward support for foreign-policy retrenchment, we get a rough measure of the influence of the cost side of the ledger. The budgetary connection turns out to be important in all issues, from regional conflicts to arms control to the reduction of the Soviet presence in East-Central Europe. Policies were changed when they were seen to be too costly. Gorbachev wanted to get out of Afghanistan from the outset of his tenure, but "with honor." So the question was: on what terms? Washington insisted on its right to continue arming the mujaheddin rebels. While the political costs of the intervention vastly outweighed the material costs, budget constraints did provide an argument for accepting potential loss of prestige. In internal debates, Foreign Minister Eduard Shevardnadze argued for massive subsidies to prop up Moscow's Afghan clients in the face of troop withdrawals and continued U.S. involvement. It was the pragmatic prime minister, Nikolai Ryzhkov, who countered that "the country cannot give up such a quantity of finances. . . . We understand that we must help, but we must reckon with the real situation."[51]

Similar considerations surrounded Gorbachev's dramatic arms control concessions. Ryzhkov later reconstructed his view of the perceptions that informed Soviet arms control policy in the 1986–88 period:

The main reason the negotiations broke through and agreement was achieved on intermediate-range missiles was our excessively high expenditures on defense. We understood perfectly well that we had to put an end to this confrontation. The Americans were twice as rich as we were, so we correspondingly felt our expenditures twice as much as they did. If five percent of gross national product was enough for them, we had to devote ten percent. We clearly understood that the country could not bear the share of state expenditures that existed at that time.[52]

University Center of International Studies Monograph Series No. 6, 1994, p. 17. Many scholars who focus on the domestic sources for reform note that arguments about international competitiveness were crucial in getting more conservative members of the Soviet elite to support radical reform. See, e.g., Ed Hewett, *Reforming the Soviet Economy* (Washington, D.C.: Brookings Institution, 1988), esp. pp. 365–367; and Jerry Hough, *Opening up the Soviet Economy* (Washington, D.C.: Brookings Institution, 1988), esp. pp. 17–26. Concern over relative decline was also critical in obtaining military support for reform. See, e.g., Russell Bova, "The Soviet Military and Economic Reform," *Soviet Studies*, Vol. 40, No. 3 (July 1988), esp. p. 394; and Dale Herspring, *The Soviet High Command, 1967–1989: Personalities and Politics* (Princeton, N.J.: Princeton University Press, 1990), chaps. 5 and 6.

51. Ryzhkov interview transcript, p. 176; The "with honor" quote is from Gorbachev aide Anatoly S. Chernyaev's discussion of Gorbachev's views as of 1985 in *Shest' let s Gorbachevym*, pp. 57–58. Chernyaev also supports Ryzhkov's view of Shevardnadze's position, recounting the foreign minister's support for deploying special forces to Afghanistan to aid the beleaguered regime in January 1989, pp. 270–273.

52. Ryzhkov interview transcript, p. 179.

The Soviet decision revealed to the world in Gorbachev's December 1988 speech to the UN General Assembly, unilaterally to reduce conventional deployments in Central Europe by 500,000 troops, was not an easy one. After all, it implied a substantially reduced Soviet presence on the socialist allies' territory. Why contemplate such a reduction? Gorbachev explained the reasoning to the Politburo in November, 1988:

If we publicize how matters really stand: we spend two and a half times more than the U.S. on military needs, and not a single country in the world, not to mention the 'less developed' ones we shower with weapons without receiving anything in return, spends more per capita for those purposes than we do. If we bring glasnost to this fact, then our entire new thinking and our whole new foreign policy will go to the devil. . . .*But that's not even the most important aspect.* We cannot resolve the tasks of perestroika if we allow the army to remain as it is. All our best scientific-technical resources go there.[53]

Gorbachev concluded that "the problem of our [military] presence" had to be discussed with the allies as soon as possible, to which Ryzhkov added, "if we do not do this, we can forget about any increase in the standard of living. Appoint any government you want, and it will not resolve that task." According to Chief of Staff Marshal Sergei Akhromeev, even the top brass agreed. He reports in his posthumously published memoirs that "at the beginning of 1988, the leadership of the general staff had practically arrived at a difficult conclusion: a unilateral reduction of our military forces was possible, given the current military-political situation, and necessary, given the country's economic condition."[54]

Not long after the November Politburo meeting, Ryzhkov pushed through a decision to start demanding hard currency for energy shipments to the socialist allies. Once again, the decision to inflict such pain on the allies was tough. And once again, the reason given was the acute state of the domestic economy, which had to assume primary importance. Even Gorbachev's liberal advisers, such as Anatoly Chernyaev and Georgy Shakhnazarov, saw Ryzhkov's decision as brutal and unfair to countries whose energy dependence on the Soviet Union had been imposed by Stalinist hegemony, but they too saw the equally brutal Soviet economic woes as overriding such concerns.[55] These were not decisions they wanted to make, but ones they felt forced to accept.

---

53. From Chernyaev's diary, *Shest' let s Gorbachevym*, pp. 255–256; emphasis added.
54. Sergei F. Akhromeev and Georgy M. Kornienko, *Glazami Marshalla i Diplomata* (Moscow: Mezhdunarodnye otnosheniia, 1992), p. 211.
55. Author's interview with Anatoly S. Chernyaev, Moscow, December 1993.

In short, Gorbachev and his colleagues in the leadership did not want to retreat from the world stage, give up socialism, make endless concessions to the West, or become liberal democrats. The evidence we have shows Gorbachev and others in the leadership reluctantly giving up their vision of socialism, the power of the Soviet Union, and the importance of its place in the world only under pressure. Cognitive change was compelled by mounting negative feedback. It is difficult to account for the series of wrenching Soviet decisions that set in motion the forces that ended the Cold War and precipitated the end of the post–World War II international system in the absence of hard perceived necessity. One cannot imagine Gorbachev—much less Ryzhkov or Ligachev— acquiescing in risky moves and retreating from hallowed precepts in the absence of dire need. Preferences clearly changed. The relative value of "socialism's international positions" or "the Motherland's international standing" declined in favor of "revitalizing the economy." But preferences changed under the impact of negative feedback about socialism's capability to do what was asked of it.

ANOMALIES OF THE END OF THE COLD WAR

Many accounts argue that three aspects of great-power behavior in the Cold War's endgame are anomalous in terms of both history and realism: the Soviet Union's decision to withdraw from East-Central Europe; the highly cooperative behavior of the other great powers; and the absence of great-power war. However, although it appeared to require an intellectual revolution in Moscow, a policy of careful appeasement and retrenchment is a historically common response to relative decline. The Roman, Byzantine, and Venetian empires attempted such strategies when they confronted the dilemma of decline. The modern cases of Edwardian Britain, Anwar Sadat's Egypt, and even Yasser Arafat's Palestine Liberation Organization come to mind.

WITHDRAWING FROM THE OUTER EMPIRE. Many observers would endorse Richard Ned Lebow's contention that "the Soviet retreat from Eastern Europe went far beyond any conception of retrenchment." The validity of this contention depends on how advanced Soviet perceptions of decline were when the decision was made to abandon the Central European allies. The less acute the perceptions of decline that surrounded the decision to give up the region, the more anomalous it appears to be. Lebow describes the decision as a conscious one taken by the leader of a country whose international position was no worse than that of Brezhnev's Soviet Union. "Gorbachev may have been surprised by the pace of change, but not by its results. He and his advisors had been discussing the possibility of cutting loose Eastern Europe as far back as 1987."[56] The implication is that Gorbachev would not have been surprised in those 1987 discussions by a proposal to exchange the Soviet Union's European alliance—with a reunified Germany joining a still-robust NATO—for a few billion Deutschmarks and a few trainloads of free German foodstuffs. However, the overwhelming bulk of evidence on Soviet decision-making about East-Central Europe contradicts this view.

People undoubtedly discussed cutting the allies loose in 1987, just as Lavrenty Beria discussed abandoning East Germany in 1953. The early discussions about East-Central Europe about which we have evidence have two common features: no concrete decisions flowed from them, and the payoffs of Soviet withdrawal were imagined to be much richer than what Moscow got in 1990. The existing secondary accounts, memoirs, interview-based reconstructions, and such internal documents as are available do not support the notion of a planned withdrawal from East-Central Europe. A more accurate characterization would be that the Soviet leadership tried fitfully to reduce the costs of the alliance while delicately urging reforms on its hard-line member governments. Less than a year after its adoption, the new approach produced unexpected results that forced Moscow to acquiesce in a series of painful retreats, often presented as *faits accomplis* whose reversal by force would have been very costly. The Soviets never resolved to get out until events pushed them out.[57]

The pattern of Gorbachev's policy toward the Warsaw Pact allies is similar to that in other areas. Like the new thinking as a whole, it contained substantial ambiguity, reflecting in part Gorbachev's own ambivalence about facing tough trade-offs. In 1988, the Soviet leadership decided to bring home some troops and reduce the costs of the alliance through a reduction in subsidies. Publicly, the policy proclaimed "non-intervention" and "freedom of choice."[58] What did

---

56. Lebow, "The Long Peace, the End of the Cold War, and the Failure of Realism," p. 262.
57. For more evidence concerning Soviet decision-making on East-Central Europe, see Blacker, *Hostage to Revolution;* Jeffrey Gedmin, *The Hidden Hand: Gorbachev and the Collapse of East Germany,* (Washington, D.C.: AEI Press, 1992); Ronald D. Asmus, J.F. Brown, and Keith Crane, *Soviet Foreign Policy and the Revolutions of 1989 in Eastern Europe,* R-3903-USDP (Santa Monica, Calif.: Rand, 1991); and Timothy Garten Ash, *In Europe's Name: Germany and the Divided Continent* (New York: Random House), chaps. 3, 6 and 7. Note also the contemporary interviews with Soviet officials reported in Don Oberdorfer, *The Turn: From the Cold War to a New Era* (New York: Poseidon, 1991); Michael Beschloss and Strobe Talbott, *At The Highest Levels: The Inside Story of the End of the Cold War* (Boston: Little, Brown, 1993); Stephen Kull, *Burying Lenin: The Revolution in Soviet Ideology and Foreign Policy* (Boulder, Colo.: Westview, 1992); and finally consult the recollections of Soviet officials in Greenstein and Wohlforth, "Retrospective on the End of the Cold War."
58. The public articulation of the policy is expertly documented in Asmus, Brown, and Crane, *Soviet Foreign Policy and the Revolutions of 1989.*

this mean? Gorbachev maintained that the allies had exercised freedom of choice when they chose socialism. In the immediate circumstances, the policy translated into a convenient "hands off" attitude: Moscow would not intervene to save hard-line regimes in trouble, but neither would it intervene against them or on behalf of reformers. What would Moscow do if a Warsaw Pact member chose capitalism and NATO membership? If the West intervened in the region, would Moscow? How would intervention be defined? The answers were unknown at the time, in the capitals of both NATO and Warsaw Pact member states, and even in Moscow itself. The ambiguity was removed when trade-offs were clearly faced, which in this instance did not occur until late in 1989.

· The German issue is illustrative. By 1988, Soviet aides were indeed making suggestions for new thinking on the German question. The more radical among them suggested long-term plans for a confederative solution in return for German neutrality and the consequent de-fanging of NATO. These suggestions were rebuffed by cautious and conservative officials in the Central Committee and the Foreign Ministry and an indifferent or distracted top leadership. As late as the summer of 1989, top decision-makers simply did not think the situation dire enough to warrant risky diplomatic initiatives. East German accounts confirm a hands-off attitude from Moscow throughout.[59] There is simply no evidence for the existence of a long-range plan to "cut loose" East-Central Europe, or even of any planning for such a contingency. When the situation did begin to unravel, the indications are that Soviet policy plunged

---

59. On Soviet assessments in 1988 and 1989, see Igor Maximychev (formerly minister-councilor of the Soviet Embassy in the Federal Republic of Germany), "What 'German Policy' We Need," *International Affairs*, No. 9 (September 1991), pp. 53–64, in which he says, "If there is anything to reproach our former 'German policy' with it is immobility and hidebound conservatism rather than a pursuit of any major change in the center of Europe," p. 54; and Maximychev, "Possible 'Impossibilities'," *International Affairs*, No. 6 (June 1993), pp. 108–117. See also the testimony of new-thinking Soviet German expert Viacheslav Dashichev, whose innovative proposals on the German question were repeatedy ignored by higher-ups in 1988 and 1989, "Dann erhebt sich das Volk," *Der Spiegel*, January 21, 1991, especially pp. 137, 140. Also valuable are the memoirs of Yuly A. Kvitsinskiy, the Soviet ambassador to the Federal Republic of Germany, who was continually frustrated in 1989 by the failure of his superiors to share his dire assessment: "In the summer of 1989 no one in the Moscow leadership could imagine that such an economically developed and prosperous member of the Warsaw Pact as the GDR would disappear from the map of Europe one year later." Kwizinskij, *Vor dem Sturm: Errinerungen eines Diplomaten* (Berlin: Siedler, 1993), pp. 13–14; see esp. chaps. 1 and 10. Finally, Chernyaev, *Shest' let s Gorbachevym*, recounts Gorbachev's ambivalence about the "fraternal allies" and his sense that the problem would be best tackled later. See e.g., pp. 81–82; 268–269. For recollections from within the German Democratic Republic confirming the "hands off" attitude, see especially Egon Krenz, *Wenn Mauern Fallen: Die friedliche Revolution: Vorgeschichte, Ablauf, Auswirkungen* (Vienna: Paul Neff Verlag, 1991); and also Günter Schabowski, *Das Politbüro: Ende eines Mythos* (Hamburg: Rohwolt, 1990).

into rudderless confusion. Gorbachev's top military adviser, Marshal Akhromeev, reported in his memoirs that the Soviets still lacked any planning for German unification as of the December 1989 Malta summit.[60] As late as March 1990, the West Germans perceived a lack of policy definition on the Soviet side.[61]

If there is no evidence of an early Soviet intention to free East-Central Europe, it is clear that Gorbachev made positive decisions not to intervene to prop up collapsing allied regimes during the fall and winter of 1989. But those decisions were made by a leader with new and extremely alarming information about his country's capabilities and prospects. In East-Central Europe, as elsewhere, Gorbachev's strategy was a reaction to the perceived relative decline of the Soviet Union, but it was based on the idea of reforming socialism. Until the fall of 1989, the feedback generated by Gorbachev's policy was mixed but generally favorable. The foreign policy was achieving cooperation, beginning to disassemble the opposing alignment of great powers, and seemed on the verge of facilitating major transfers of resources away from the defense sector. But just as this positive feedback was logged in, the revolutions in East-Central Europe generated the most compelling and disturbing evidence yet about the lack of viability of Soviet-type institutions.

None of this sank in immediately. It is vital not to forget the slowness with which the Soviet leadership came to an appreciation of the meaning of these events. The evidence suggests that both the Soviet leaders and their western counterparts began to absorb the lessons only late in the fall of 1989. Until very late in the game, all sides thought that the Warsaw Pact could be maintained despite regime changes in the region. On September 28, the Politburo approved an analytical paper on the situation in Poland signed by Shevardnadze, Aleksandr Yakovlev, Defense Minister Dmitry Yazov, and KGB chief Vladimir Kryuchkov. The document listed pressures for and against continued Polish membership in the alliance and concluded that the Poles would not raise the question of leaving the alliance "in the near future."[62] Even a month later, as East Germany was reeling under the impact of huge demonstrations and a

---

60. Akhromeev and Kornienko, *Glazami Marshalla i Diplomata*, p. 253.
61. They consciously exploited this, according to top Kohl adviser Horst Teltchik in *329 Tage: Innenansichten der Einigung* (Berlin: Siedler, 1991), p. 187.
62. It did acknowledge that Poland's membership might assume a "formal character." "Ob obstankovke v Pol'she, vozmozhnykh viariantakh ee razvitiia, perspektivakh sovetsko-pol'skikh otnoshenii"; and attached note of 29/09/89. Photocopies of Protokol No. P166/23 of the Politburo session of 28/09/89, CPSU Central Committee. In author's possession. Courtesy of David Holloway.

mass exodus, policymakers in Moscow (and the West) believed that a reform communist government would save the country and with it the Warsaw Pact, at least for a time.[63]

When the issue was finally presented as "spill blood or lose socialism," the amount of blood that would have had to be spilled was already great and the weaknesses of socialism had already been revealed in new and disturbing ways. By the time it became evident that losing socialism meant losing the Warsaw Pact, the constraints on Soviet actions were even greater. It is likely that private assessments of Soviet power were much more pessimistic than public ones.[64] These assessments must already have been quite gloomy by the time of the Central European revolutions of 1989, making the likely costs of any intervention or intimidation very high indeed. Ryzhkov found the aid to Afghanistan hard to bear in 1987, and subsidies to the allies painful in 1988. By then, the whole Politburo thought that the military presence in Central Europe was too costly. It is no wonder that they balked from an intervention that would have been frighteningly expensive in its own right, certainly in money and probably in blood; would have cut off Western credits and markets; and would have saddled them with their allies' massive hard currency debts.

Assessments of power can change quickly. The Soviet Union's reversal of external fortunes in 1989 was dramatically sudden. In that year alone, the issue of precipitous decline *vis-à-vis* the United States was transformed from looming threat to pressing reality.[65] What is "core" and what is "periphery" changes with changed power assessments. By August 1989, Shevardnadze, sitting with aides on the Black Sea coast of his native Georgia and contemplating the meaning of events in Poland, concluded that the long-term implications for the integrity of the Soviet Union itself were dire. For them, the Baltics and Georgia had suddenly become the core and the Warsaw Pact the periphery.[66]

---

63. See Krenz, *Wenn Mauern Fallen*, Part III and pp. 223–227; See also Gorbachev's December 1989 summit disucssion with Bulgaria's Petar Mladenov in *Gipfelgespräche*, pp. 143–160, and the sources in fns. 57 and 59 for more evidence on the "perestroika illusion" transferred to East-Central Europe.
64. See, in particular, Akhromeev and Kornienko, *Glazami Marsalla i Diplomata;* and Chernyaev, *Shest' let s Gorbachevym.*
65. Akhromeev and Kornienko, ibid., p. 254.
66. As related by Shevardnadze's aide Sergei Tarasenko in Greenstein and Wohlforth, "Retrospective on the End of the Cold War," p. 29. Here, Tarasenko mentions only the connection between East-Central Europe and Moscow's inner empire. In a later follow-up interview, he recalled that the beach party was thinking about a much more prolonged process of imperial dissolution than turned out to be the case. In addition, Tarasenko stressed that Shevardnadze's Georgian nationality led him to be more sensitive to this issue than others in the leadership. Chernyaev reports in detail on Gorbachev's "illusions" about the survivability of the Soviet Union in *Shest' let s Gorbchevym,* esp. chaps. 7–8.

GREAT-POWER COOPERATION. To many critics, the high levels of great-power cooperation during the Cold War endgame confound realist expectations.[67] Why did the western powers act so cooperatively rather than exploit Soviet weakness?

The West's cooperative behavior in the late 1980s does not present a puzzle for a realism that differentiates between revisionist and status-quo powers. Status-quo powers only go on the offensive in world politics to nip rising challengers in the bud or to buy the allegiance of allies that have their own revisionist projects. For the United States, sitting atop a global hierarchy that had recently seemed challenged by rising Soviet power, Moscow's decline provided relief without temptation. The only formally revisionist power in the West was the Federal Republic of Germany, but even it restrained itself until all had concluded that the German Democratic Republic was beyond rescue. Until quite late in 1989, the NATO allies wished mainly to keep what they had. If Gorbachev delivered those goods, they were all for him. Such cooperation is no anomaly for realists. They are not surprised when capitulation brings cooperation; it is always available at that price.[68]

Moreover, describing western behavior toward the Gorbachev-era Soviet Union as "cooperative" obscures as much as it tells. Cooperation was on offer on the very same terms that had been available for decades: Soviet acceptance of the status quo as seen in NATO capitals. The issue went beyond the territorial status quo in Europe, which had been settled *de facto* since the early 1960s and *de jure* since the early 1970s. The issue was whether Moscow would accept the West's definition of the security problem. What was so remarkable about

---

67. Deudney and Ikenberry, "The International Sources of Soviet Domestic Change"; Snyder, "Myths, Modernization, and the Post-Gorbachev World," in Lebow and Risse-Kappen, *International Relations Theory and the End of The Cold War*; Weber, "Security after the Revolutions of 1989 and 1991: The Future with Nuclear Weapons," in Garrity and Maaranen, *Nuclear Weapons in the Changing World*; and Meuller, "The Impact of Ideas on Grand Strategy," in Rosecrance and Stein, *Domestic Bases of Grand Strategy*.

68. Structural realism, which does not regard a state's attitude toward the status quo as a necessary part of the theory, also suggests strong reasons for western reluctance to hasten the decline and fall of Soviet power. One of the theory's basic policy messages is how peaceful and easily managed bipolarity is, compared to multipolarity. Conservative western powers thus would not only lack an interest in hastening Soviet decline, but would face an incentive to preserve Soviet power. As Robert Jervis notes, the balance-of-power logic often leads to restraint *vis-à-vis* the loser; "From Balance to Concert: A Study of International Security Cooperation," in Kenneth A. Oye, ed., *Cooperation under Anarchy* (Princeton, N.J.: Princeton University Press, 1986), p. 65; for evidence on the tradition of restraint as practiced in the Hellenic city-states system, see Adam Watson, *The Evolution of International Society: A Comparative Historical Analysis,* (London: Routledge, 1992), chap. 5.

Gorbachev's diplomacy in the years after 1987 was less its brilliance or strategic acumen than its slowly growing acceptance of the official Western view of the security problem.

Western officials believed that the Soviets were accepting their view of the situation for two reasons: first, because they had been right and the Soviets wrong all along; and second, because the distribution of power was now shifting in the West's favor. Key U.S. officials seemed to believe that not only were broader trends in the correlation of forces moving in their favor, but particularly that President Reagan's arms buildup was pushing Gorbachev toward concessions. An influential section of the administration thought that the Soviet Union was on its last legs, and that the United States should do nothing to slow the process.[69] Even officials inclined to be more forthcoming to Moscow believed that the balance of power was on the U.S. side of the negotiating table. The leader of that group, former Secretary of State George Shultz, wrote:

The Soviets were picking up our ideas and playing them back to us as though they had just invented them. That was fine with me. The more Gorbachev wanted to play the role of "creative world statesman for peace" by *coming toward our agenda*, the more we should stand back and applaud him in that performance.[70]

In 1987, Gorbachev, exasperated by U.S. refusal to make any concessions in negotiations on the Anti–Ballistic Missile treaty, complained that "U.S. policy is one of extorting more and more concessions. Two great powers should not treat each other that way." "I'm weeping for you," Shultz responded with a smile.[71] This is hardly a story of the emergence of cooperation between equals. It is rather a tale of cooperation emerging on the terms set by the stronger party, and that is how U.S. officials saw things, both at the time and in retrospect.[72]

---

69. See Kurt M. Campbell, "Prospects and Consequences of Soviet Decline," pp. 154–157.
70. George Shultz, *Turmoil and Triumph: My Years as Secretary of State* (New York: Charles Scribner's Sons, 1993), p. 894; emphasis in original.
71. Ibid., p. 723.
72. Two excellent sources of contemporary U.S. perceptions are Don Oberdorfer, *The Turn;* and Beschloss and Talbott, *At The Highest Levels.* See also: Shultz, *Turmoil and Triumph;* Thomas Banchoff "Official Threat Perceptions in the 1980s: The United States," and Michael Jochum, "The United States in the 1980s: Internal Estimates," both in Carl-Christoph Schweitzer, ed., *The Changing Western Analysis of the Soviet Threat* (New York: St. Martin Press, 1990); Caspar W. Weinberger, *Fighting for Peace: Seven Critical Years in the Pentagon* (New York: Warner, 1990), pp. 30, 34; Lou Cannon, *President Reagan: The Role of a Lifetime* (New York: Simon and Schuster, 1991), pp. 296–298. Some U.S. officials held to this robust view of U.S. power well before the Gorbachev years. See, e.g., Alexander Haig, *Caveat: Realism, Reagan and Foreign Policy* (New York: Macmillan, 1984), pp. 96, 107.

It is a view shared by moderate conservatives in the Gorbachev leadership, such as Marshal Akhromeev and First Deputy Foreign Minister Georgy Kornienko.[73] Akhromeev and many other officials on the Soviet side strongly felt the weakness of their position at the December 1989 Malta summit.[74] The U.S. National Security Council's Soviet expert, Robert Blackwill, after perusing the classified minutes of all previous superpower summits, concluded that Malta was the first at which the drive for cooperation outweighed competitive impulses.[75] Realists would say this was not mere coincidence.

Soviet diplomacy changed dramatically in the last quarter of 1989, in rational reaction to new evidence about relative Soviet power. Up to that point, Gorbachev had been seeking, by a series of increasingly bold strokes, a favorable change in the status quo. He expounded a vision of a demilitarized, denuclearized Europe in which a reforming Soviet Union and wealthy Europeans could cooperate on all matters from the economy to the environment. Such a situation would be vastly superior to the status quo in which a powerful nuclear NATO held a long list of trade restrictions against the Warsaw Pact, and a European Community was on the verge of a new wave of exclusionary economic integration. When the revolutions in East-Central Europe began to call socialism's viability into question, Gorbachev's line changed to an emphatic endorsement of the status quo. From December 1989 onward, his policy became increasingly focused on enlisting Western support for stabilizing the Soviet Union's eroding international position. Only at this point did the Western powers, led by the United States, move "beyond containment" to deep cooperation with Moscow.[76]

It is important to note, however, that western governments were uniformly unwilling to take any significant political or security risks to help Moscow, although critics constantly urged such a course on them. The West's behavior was conservative, even when this would be very damaging to Gorbachev. It is true that for a brief period in the fall of 1989, NATO powers endeavored to

---

73. Akhromeev and Kornienko, *Glazami Marshalla i Diplomata,* chaps. 6 and 7.
74. Ibid., p. 254.
75. Oberdorfer, *The Turn,* p. 379. Sergei Tarasenko later recalled that at Malta, both his boss, Shevardnadze, and Gorbachev "felt that the Soviet Union was in free fall, that our superpower status would go up in smoke unless it was reaffirmed by the Americans." Quoted in Beschloss and Talbott, *At the Highest Levels,* p. 153.
76. Soviet European policy in general is covered by Blacker, *Hostage to Revolution,* chap. 3; Gorbachev's brief shift to a status quo policy is detailed in Wohlforth, *Elusive Balance,* chap. 9; Beschloss and Talbott, *At the Highest Levels,* chaps. 6 and 7, document the Bush administration's move "beyond containment."

help Gorbachev keep the Warsaw Pact together out of a visceral fear of "instability." The more evidence accumulated about the weakness of the Soviet Union in general and Mikhail Gorbachev in particular, the more weight conservative "stability" arguments should have assumed in Western calculations. However, they did not elicit increased Western willingness to sacrifice other goals on Moscow's behalf. Much subsequent Western support was symbolic, while actual Western positions were devastating for Soviet prospects. The most dramatic example is West Germany's policy on reunification, which continually used the prospect of substantial future German aid and cooperation to Russia as bait for Soviet acceptance of tough concessions now. At Malta, Bush told Gorbachev that he was for perestroika's success and he promised not to "dance on the remains of the Berlin Wall." But he bluntly told the General Secretary that the United States would support German reunification and that its position on the Baltic states was unchangeable.[77]

THE MISSING WORLD WAR III. Realism's association of war and change was undeniable, and widely shared. Indeed, most thoughtful criticisms of realism accepted its fundamental argument that managing change peacefully was the basic problem of international politics. The problem was not the accuracy of realism's central analysis, but its pessimism about solutions.[78] In the present case, two questions emerge. Why was the international system able to accommodate massive changes in power and territory peacefully? Why did the Soviet Union refrain from resisting its decline violently?

As I argued above, theories of hegemonic rivalry identify power transitions as likely points for war. Leading states express conflicting claims about the governance of the international system, and when states perceive a gap between others' claims and their capabilities, they may unleash war. A rising challenger may conclude that the defending dominant state no longer possesses the capabilities to sustain its claim to leadership. A defender may conclude that its capability to sustain its status will decline relative to challengers in the future, and so unleash war now. Since military capability can only be measured by fighting, both states may rationally prefer war to negotiation.

---

77. See Teltschik, *329 Tage*, for reporting on contemporary West German views of Soviet stability and Gorbachev's vulnerability. He describes the process by which small Western grants and large symbolic promises served as a crucial "catalyst" for German reunification within NATO on pp. 230–286. For the Bush-Gorbachev discussions at Malta, see Gorbachev, *Gipfelgespräche: Geheime Protokolle aus meiner Amtszeit*, pp. 94–129, esp. p. 120.

78. Keohane, for example, argued that we needed a theory of peaceful change not despite but because of realism's pessimism in this regard. "Structural Realism and Beyond," in Keohane, *Neorealism and its Critics.*

Such a potential for transition never occurred in the Cold War. The Soviet Union was arguably closest to military dominance of Eurasia in 1945, just when it was most exhausted from the war. It regained the initiative in subsequent decades, but even in the darkest Cold War days, the most pessimistic U.S. assessments placed the point of danger years in the future. All U.S. fears over various "gaps" in favor of Moscow concerned reversible trends, not existing relationships. Once Soviet power began to decline relative to the United States and its allies, it should have been evident that, absent a reversal of fortunes, no hegemonic war was in the offing. Soviet decline reaffirmed rather than reversed the existing hierarchy of world politics. Only the re-emergence of Russian power or the rise of new powers would once again set up the kind of contradiction that had governed world politics since 1945. With Russian decline, the system was at least temporarily primed for peace.

Moscow's reluctance to resist decline violently is connected to the Soviet leadership's prudent decision to deal with decline by reform and retrenchment. Belief in the necessity and the possibility of reform via resource reallocation smoothed domestic resistance to external appeasement and increased the perceived value of Western cooperation. Declining empires are often very reluctant to use force to arrest decline, aware as they are of their internal fragility. The Byzantine, Ottoman, Manchu Chinese, and Tsarist Russian imperial elites all acutely perceived the risks associated with foreign wars against more efficient rivals.[79] But declining empires also often take the violent path, as Austria-Hungary did in 1914. What explains such different reactions to the same problem?

Realism is on weak ground here, for the choice of how to react to external conditions is made by state authorities who will be influenced by domestic considerations. The argument that international conditions determine domestic choice is impossible to sustain, which is why realists never make it. Nevertheless, existing theories seem needlessly underspecified. International factors about which we may form generalizations surely must play a role. In the present case, the Soviet Union's position as a challenging power is an extremely important contextual factor in explaining its reaction to decline. The point is obvious but needs to be made: challengers, by definition, do not like the status quo. It is always hard for Americans, whose country sits prosperously atop the global hierarchy, to see the extent to which other states' elites might resent the existing international order. The popular structural-realist view of the two

---

79. Stephen Peter Rosen, "The Decline of Multinational Empires: Introduction and Overview," Harvard University, unpublished ms., n.d.

superpowers as structurally identical "duopolists" may also have fed the widespread American perception that Soviets shared the U.S. political elite's attachment to the status quo.

It is true that some Soviet experts and diplomatic professionals came to view NATO, extended deterrence, and the rest of the Cold War panoply as good things. But this is not true of the Soviet elite as a whole, and it certainly does not reflect what we know of the views of Gorbachev and his closest associates. During the Cold War, Soviets saw themselves as endeavoring to increase their influence at the expense of the United States. But they saw the main contours of their policy as a series of reactions to strategic moves by the dominant global power. The great costs of their alliance system and defense complex were seen as imposed in part by the United States. If a hegemonic state believes it benefits from the status quo, its decline leads to the desire to cling to that status quo. A challenger, on the other hand, sees the status quo as unfavorable and is likely to be disinclined to make sacrifices on its behalf.

Critics rightly point to the existence of different domestic factions with different answers to international dilemmas as evidence of the indeterminacy of system-level explanations. In the Soviet case, a harder-line alternative to Gorbachev waited in the wings. But it is necessary to evaluate the influence of international conditions on the domestic struggle. Among the many factors that account for the failure of Soviet reactionaries to seize the political agenda, international ones must be given their due.[80] The Soviet Union's position as frustrated challenger accounts in part for the frustration of Soviet reactionaries, for the international status quo was widely viewed as part of the Soviet Union's problem. Its preservation was not an attractive solution. Gorbachev's new thinking did appear to many as an effective response to the country's external dilemmas until at least late in 1989. Indeed, to the extent that Gorbachev's radical diplomacy upset staid NATO foreign ministries and defense bureaucracies, Soviet conservatives could find something in it to applaud.

Conclusion

The post-1989 system transformation does not constitute a critical case for realism. Realist theories emerge from the end of the Cold War no weaker (though certainly no stronger) than they entered it. The end of the Cold War

---

80. I consider other factors that weakened the Soviet reactionaries in Wohlforth, "From the Gulf to the Abyss: The Soviet Union's Last Foreign Policy," in Wolfgang Danspeckgruber and Charles Tripp, eds., *The Gulf War and the New World Order* (Boulder, Colo.: Westview, forthcoming 1994).

international system was occasioned by the decline and collapse (or temporary contraction) of a great multinational state. Whatever the cause, this global transformation was realized when a great power abandoned valuable territory. This is a source of change which is quite consistent with realism. Post–Cold War post-mortems on realism have concentrated their fire on the wrong target—structural realism—whose long-acknowledged inadequacy for understanding change was on prominent display after 1989. The difficulty of conceptually and empirically separating structure from units is especially evident when power relations are in a state of flux. The temptation to measure structure after the fact is strong. It is hard to discern what the structure is at present, or exactly how we will know when it has changed.

The explanation I offer is an amalgam of classical realism and the hegemonic variant of neorealism coupled with a pragmatic empirical focus on decision-makers' capabilities assessments. The weaknesses of such an explanation are numerous. Despite its attention to historical contingency and complexity, it misses important elements of the story. A truly satisfactory account would include the personal strengths and weaknesses of Gorbachev and other central decision-makers, the precise causes of socialism's poor performance, the rise of national sentiments throughout the Soviet world, and many other factors. But to discuss the implications of these events for our general understanding of international politics we need theory, as weak and indeterminate as it may be. My explanation is derived from a set of theories that have demonstrated their utility for understanding a very wide range of diplomatic and military interactions among states and other social groups over very long spans of international history. It therefore provides a useful framework for comparing this episode of change with past and potential future cases. It zeroes in on a single independent variable while examining its impact in a way that accounts for complexity. It provides leverage for understanding the essential process of change in this case. It helps to establish a baseline from which to measure how much and in what ways the essentials of world politics have changed from earlier eras. It passes the twin tests of helping to understand and explain this event-series, and generating lines for further historical and comparative research to answer more basic questions about international politics. In particular, it suggests two lessons for theory, with implications for further research.

The first lesson is that a causal analysis of power is necessary, to enrich (some might say to weaken) realism in order to save it. One can construct rationalist and realist accounts that examine actors' beliefs and ideas, and this is the only way that realism can sensibly account for change in terms of power. There is no need to jettison all rationalist and realist assumptions the moment ideas are taken into account. Many realist theories escape damage from the post-1989 transformation by ducking out of the line of fire. But if they wish to account for specific episodes of change, they must take a perceptual approach to power. "Power" explains "change" only if it is viewed phenomenologically.

Critics of realism are right that capabilities, as they are usually measured by political scientists, have little to do with what happened in world politics after 1987. There is little reason to suppose that gross capabilities indicators are any better at approximating decision-makers' assessments or expectations at other times. Indeed, such indicators are highly misleading because they lull their users into a false sense that the power curves of nations move gracefully, incrementally, perhaps even predictably. That assumption, more than any other problem intrinsic to international relations theory, is the primary reason for the failure at least to anticipate in general terms the way the Cold War would end.

Most scholars, including most realists, are reluctant to undertake empirical examination of the influence of power on policy. Their reluctance is understandable: studying power assessments is a clear step away from parsimony; it is laborious; and many may doubt whether operative assessments can ever be reliably reconstructed. Further, it reduces the scholar to the level of the decision-maker: rather than issuing all-knowing pronouncements on the invisible structures to which hapless decision-makers must react, the scholar shuffles humbly after the statesman, sharing his flawed views of power, perhaps repeating his mistakes. Many realists will not accept these limitations. On the other hand, those who do favor in-depth historical case studies also appear disinclined to analyze power assessments. We face a familiar contradiction: competing theories seem never to meet on the same methodological ground. This contradiction is costly, for the debate will never be resolved as long as realists and their critics refuse to examine how capabilities actually get assessed by real actors.

The second lesson follows from the first: episodes of revolutionary change must be studied in a theoretically-informed way. Classical realism identified two keys for understanding international politics: the capabilities and the interests of states. The problem is that these variables are hard to measure reliably. Capabilities can only be measured when they are put to some test. Interests can only be reliably gauged when decision-makers accept unambiguous trade-offs. Scholars have therefore assumed that major wars constitute the only opportunity to test the capabilities and intentions of states. Wars generated the most evidence of the highest quality about power and interests, and since power and interests explain state behavior, major international change was concentrated in periods of war.

However, even in the absence of war, central causal variables can change radically in a short time. Revolutions or civil strife, as well as wars, may exert profound influence not only on scholars but also on the decision-makers they theorize about. Whatever independent variable one wishes to propose as an explanation of these events, it must have somehow varied a lot in a short time in order to account for the change, or else decision-makers must have received information about it unevenly, in concentrated bursts, rather than incrementally. If we accept the proposition that assessments of power and interest may rationally change quickly in certain periods, then such periods possess unique importance for theory. If that is so, it may not be necessary to invoke "intervening" variables, such as norms, regimes, or institutions, to account for the non-linear, concentrated nature of international change.[81] And it may be misleading to exclude periods of revolutionary change from the theoretical enterprise.

One area for further research is how decision-makers updated their assessments of power (and interests) in key historical cases. The temptation is to look immediately at periods of war. But it would be very helpful to sift the historical record with the suspicion that we have been biased toward associating war and change, missing other events that may have equal diagnostic utility for measuring power and interest. Another potentially significant bias may be the assumption that all declining states face the same incentives to use force: we may find that many of our inductive generalizations do not hold water, or we may discover superior generalizations. Perhaps we should weaken the hold exercised by Thucydides' portrayal of the hegemonic struggle between Athens and Sparta; perhaps we have studied the Napoleon Bonapartes too much and the Napoleon IIIs too little.

Looking to the future of world politics, two contradictory conclusions emerge. The first is that there are sound realist reasons to be at ease about the near future of great-power relations. The fact that the challenger rather than the defender exhausted itself in the struggle augurs well for international stability among the major powers. Presumably, the law of uneven growth would have to operate for many years to the United States' disadvantage before new challengers arise. Second, however, if my argument about percep-

---

81. Stephen Krasner persuasively presents the opposing view in "Sovereignty: An Institutional Perspective," *Comparative Political Studies*, Vol. 21, No. 1 (April 1988), pp. 66–94.

tions of power has any plausibility, then there are grounds for caution about confident projections of power relations based on the crude indicators so beloved of political scientists. Such indicators can account neither for the Cold War nor for its sudden end. Either power does not matter, or popular indices of power are not even roughly accurate indicators.

This leads to the frankly inductive warning for the West: keep a weather eye on Russia. Russia has often experienced rapid shifts in relative power with dire international consequences. In this century alone, Russia's sudden decline after the 1905 war with Japan and its equally sudden rise in the years before 1914 were important preconditions for World War I; its apparent weakness conditioned the disastrous diplomacy of the 1930s; its sudden rise in apparent power as a result of World War II set the Cold War in motion; its perceived forward surge in the late 1950s and early 1960s set the stage for the dangerous crises of that era; and its apparent sudden decline in the late 1980s was the catalyst for the greatest upheaval in international relationships in half a century. Russia may be down now, but prudent policymakers should not count it out.

The Emerging Structure of International Politics

Kenneth N. Waltz

$\mathbf{F}$or more than three hundred years, the drama of modern history has turned on the rise and fall of great powers. In the multipolar era, twelve great powers appeared on the scene at one time or another. At the beginning of World War II, seven remained; at its conclusion, two. Always before, as some states sank, others rose to take their places. World War II broke the pattern; for the first time in a world of sovereign states, bipolarity prevailed.

In a 1964 essay, I predicted that bipolarity would last through the century.[1] On the brow of the next millennium, we must prepare to bid bipolarity adieu and begin to live without its stark simplicities and comforting symmetry. Already in the fall of 1989, Undersecretary of State Lawrence Eagleburger expressed nostalgia for the "remarkably stable and predictable atmosphere of the Cold War," and in the summer of 1990, John Mearsheimer gave strong reasons for expecting worse days to come.[2]

For almost half a century it seemed that World War II was truly "the war to end wars" among the great and major powers of the world. The longest peace yet known rested on two pillars: bipolarity and nuclear weapons. During the war, Nicholas Spykman foresaw a postwar international order no different "from the old," with international society continuing "to operate within the same fundamental power patterns."[3] Realists generally shared his

Kenneth N. Waltz is Ford Professor of Political Science at the University of California, Berkeley. He has written Man, The State, and War: A Theoretical Analysis *(1959),* Foreign Policy and Democratic Politics: The American and British Experience *(1967, reissued 1992),* Theory of International Politics *(1979), and numerous essays. His "Nuclear Myths and Political Realities" won the Heinz Eulau award for best article in the* American Political Science Review *in 1990.*

For their thoughtful comments, I should like to thank Karen Adams, David Arase, Jamais Cascio, James Fearon, Robert Gilpin, Robert Keohane, Sean Lynn-Jones, Robert Powell, and Steve Weber.

1. Kenneth N. Waltz, "The Stability of a Bipolar World," *Daedalus*, Vol. 93, No. 3 (Summer 1964).
2. Lawrence Eagleburger, quoted in Thomas Friedman, "U.S. Voicing Fears That Gorbachev Will Divide West," *New York Times*, September 16, 1989, pp. 1, 6; John J. Mearsheimer, "Back to the Future: Instability in Europe After the Cold War," *International Security*, Vol. 15, No. 1 (Summer 1990), pp. 5–56.
3. Nicholas J. Spykman, *America's Strategy in World Politics: The United States and the Balance of Power* (New York: Harcourt, Brace and Company, 1942), p. 461.

International Security, Vol. 18, No. 2 (Fall 1993), pp. 44–79
© 1993 by the President and Fellows of Harvard College and the Massachusetts Institute of Technology.

expectation. The behaviors of states, the patterns of their interactions, and the outcomes their interactions produced had been repeated again and again through the centuries despite profound changes in the internal composition of states. Spykman's expectations were historically well grounded and in part borne out. States have continued to compete in economic, military, and other ways. The use of force has been threatened, and numerous wars have been fought on the peripheries. Yet, despite deep ideological and other differences, peace prevailed at the center of international politics. Changes in structure, and in the weaponry available to some of the states, have combined to perpetuate a troubled peace.[4] As the bipolar era draws to a close, we must ask two questions: What structural changes are in prospect? What effects may they have?

The End of Bipolarity—and of the Cold War

The conflation of peace and stability is all too common. The occurrence of major wars is often identified with a system's instability.[5] Yet systems that survive major wars thereby demonstrate their stability. The multipolar world was highly stable, but all too war-prone. The bipolar world has been highly peaceful, but unfortunately less stable than its predecessor.

Almost as soon as their wartime alliance ended, the United States and the Soviet Union found themselves locked in a cold war. In a world of two great powers, each is bound to focus its fears on the other, to distrust its intentions, and to impute offensive intentions even to defensive measures. The competition of states becomes keener when their number reduces to two. Neorealist, or structural, theory leads one to believe that the placement of states in the international system accounts for a good deal of their behavior.[6] Through most of the years of the Cold War the United States and the Soviet Union were similarly placed by their power. Their external behaviors therefore should have shown striking similarities. Did they? Yes, more than has usually been realized. The behavior of states can be compared on many

---

4. On the causes of multipolar-conventional war and of bipolar-nuclear peace, see esp. Waltz, "Stability," *The Spread of Nuclear Weapons: More May Be Better*, Adelphi Paper No. 171 (London: International Institute for Strategic Studies [IISS], 1981); and Waltz, *Theory of International Politics* (New York: McGraw-Hill, 1979). John Lewis Gaddis and Mearsheimer have offered similar explanations. See Gaddis, "The Long Peace," *International Security*, Vol. 10, No. 4 (Spring 1986), pp. 99–142. Since the reasoning is now familiar, I refrain from summarizing it here.
5. I made this mistake in "The Stability of a Bipolar World," but have since corrected the error.
6. Neorealist, or structural, theory is developed in Waltz, *Theory of International Politics*.

counts. Their armament policies and their interventions abroad are two of the most revealing. On the former count, the United States in the early 1960s undertook the largest strategic and conventional peacetime military buildup the world had yet seen. We did so while Khrushchev tried at once to carry through a major reduction in conventional forces and to follow a strategy of minimum deterrence, even though the balance of strategic weapons greatly favored the United States. As one should have expected, the Soviet Union soon followed in America's footsteps, thus restoring the symmetry of great-power behavior. And so it was through most of the years of the Cold War. Advances made by one were quickly followed by the other, with the United States almost always leading the way. Allowing for geographic differences, the overall similarity of their forces was apparent. The ground forces of the Soviet Union were stronger than those of the United States, but in naval forces the balance of advantage was reversed. The Soviet Union's largely coastal navy gradually became more of a blue-water fleet, but one of limited reach. Its navy never had more than half the tonnage of ours. Year after year, NATO countries spent more on defense than the Warsaw Treaty Organization (WTO) countries did, but their troops remained roughly equal in numbers.

The military forces of the United States and the Soviet Union remained in rough balance, and their military doctrines tended to converge. We accused them of favoring war-fighting over deterrent doctrines, while we developed a war-fighting doctrine in the name of deterrence. From the 1960s onward, critics of military policy urged the United States to "reconstitute its usable war-fighting capability." Before he became secretary of defense, Melvin R. Laird wrote that "American strategy must aim at fighting, winning, and recovering," a strategy that requires the ability to wage nuclear war and the willingness to strike first.[7] One can find many military and civilian statements to similar effect over the decades. Especially in the 1970s and 1980s, the United States accused the Soviet Union of striving for military superiority. In turn, the Republican platform of 1980 pledged that a Republican administration would reestablish American strategic superiority. Ronald Reagan as president softened the aspiration, without eliminating it, by making it his goal to establish a "margin of safety" for the United States militarily. Military

---

7. Melvin R. Laird, *A House Divided: America's Strategy Gap* (Chicago: Henry Regnery, 1962), pp. 53, 78–79.

competition between the two countries produced its expected result: the similarity of forces and doctrines.

Comparison on the second count, interventionist behavior, requires some discussion because our conviction that the United States was the status quo and the Soviet Union the interventionist power distorted our view of reality. The United States as well as the Soviet Union intervened widely in others' affairs and spent a fair amount of time fighting peripheral wars. Most Americans saw little need to explain our actions, assumed to be in pursuit of legitimate national interests and of international justice, and had little difficulty in explaining the Soviet Union's, assumed to be aimed at spreading Communism across the globe by any means available. Americans usually interpreted the Soviet Union's behavior in terms of its presumed intentions. Intentions aside, our and their actions were similar. The United States intervened militarily to defend client states in China, Korea, and Vietnam, and even supported their ambitions to expand. The Soviet Union acted in Afghanistan as the United States did in Vietnam, and intervened directly or indirectly in Angola, Mozambique, and Ethiopia.

David Holloway quotes a Soviet work, *War and the Army*, published in 1977, as follows: "Before the Socialist state and its army stands the task of defending, together with other Socialist states and their armies, the whole Socialist system and not only its own country." Beyond that broad purpose, Soviet forces were to help liberated countries thwart counterrevolution.[8] America assumed similar missions. Defending against or deterring attacks on the United States required only a fraction of the forces we maintained. We mounted such large forces because we extended defensive as well as deterrent forces to cover Western Europe, the Persian Gulf area, Northeast Asia, and other parts of the world from Central America to the Philippine Islands. We identified our security with the security of other democratic states and with the security of many undemocratic states as long as they were not Communist, and indeed even with some Communist ones. The interests we identified with our own were even more widely embracing than those of the Soviet Union. At the conclusion of the Second World War, the Soviet Union began edging outward. In response, one finds Clark Clifford advising President Harry S. Truman as early as 1946 that America's mission was to be not merely the tiresome one of containing the Soviet Union but

---

8. David Holloway, *The Soviet Union and the Arms Race*, second ed. (New Haven: Yale University Press, 1984), p. 81.

also the ennobling one of creating and maintaining "world order."[9] We zestfully accepted the task.

Before World War II, both the United States and the Soviet Union had developed ideologies that could easily propel them to unilateral action in the name of international duty: interventionist liberalism in the one country, international Communism in the other. Neither, however, widely exported its ideology earlier. The postwar foreign policies of neither country can be understood apart from the changed structure of international politics, exercising its pressures and providing its opportunities. More than the Soviet Union, the United States acted all over the globe in the name of its own security and the world's well-being. Thus Barry Blechman and Stephen Kaplan found that in the roughly thirty years following 1946, the United States used military means in one way or another to intervene in the affairs of other countries about twice as often as did the Soviet Union.[10]

The Soviet Union's aim was to export its ideology by planting and fostering Communist governments in more and more countries, and America's was to plant and foster democratic ones. President Reagan thought that we should worry about the Soviet Union's establishing a "military beachhead" in Nicaragua "inside our defense perimeters," thus threatening the safe passage of our ships through the Caribbean.[11] Throwing the cloak of national security over our interventions in Central America hardly concealed our rage to rule or to dictate to others how to govern their countries. Vice President George Bush, in February of 1985, set forth what we expected of Nicaragua and the signs of progress we looked for. He mentioned these: "That the Sandinistas bring the Democratic leaders back into the political process; that they hold honest, free and fair elections; that they stop beating up on the church, the unions and the business community and stop censoring the press; that they sever control of the army from the Sandinista party; and that they remove that most insidious form of totalitarian control, the neighborhood spy system called the 'SDC (Sandinista Defense Committee)'."[12] According to a senior official, the Reagan administration "debated whether we had the right to

---

9. Arthur Krock, *Memoirs* (New York: Funk and Wagnalls, 1968), appendix A, p. 480.

10. Barry Blechman and Stephen S. Kaplan, *Force Without War: U.S. Armed Forces as a Political Instrument* (Washington, D.C.: Brookings, 1978).

11. "Excerpts from Reagan's Speech on Aid for Nicaragua Rebels," *New York Times,* June 25, 1986, p. A12.

12. "Excerpts from Remarks by Vice President George Bush," Press Release, Austin, Texas, February 28, 1985.

dictate the form of another country's government. The bottom line was yes, that some rights are more fundamental than the right of nations to nonintervention, like the rights of individual people. . . . We don't have the right to subvert a democratic government but we do have the right against an undemocratic one."[13] The difference between the United States and the Soviet Union has been less in their behaviors than in their ideologies. Each sought to make other countries over in its own image. Stalin said of World War II: "This war is not as in the past. Whoever occupies a territory also imposes on it his own social system. Everyone imposes his own system as far as his army can reach. It cannot be otherwise."[14] The effort to impose one's own social system continued into the Cold War, with the aim to be accomplished by peaceful means if possible.

Rooted in the postwar structure of international politics, the Cold War for more than four decades stubbornly refused to evolve into a warm peace. The Cold War could not end until the structure that sustained it began to erode. Bipolarity worked against détente in the 1970s. The changing structure of international politics worked for détente in the 1980s.

Structural change begins in a system's unit, and then unit-level and structural causes interact. We know from structural theory that states strive to maintain their positions in the system. Thus, in their twilight years great powers try to arrest or reverse their decline. We need to look only at the twentieth century for examples. In 1914, Austria-Hungary preferred to fight an unpromising war rather than risk the internal disintegration that a greater Serbia would threaten. Britain and France continued to act as though they were great powers, and struggled to bear the expense of doing so, well into the 1950s.[15] At the end of that decade, when many Americans thought that we were losing ground to the Soviet Union, John F. Kennedy appealed to the nation with the slogan, "Let's get the country moving again." And Defense Secretary Dick Cheney resisted a 50 percent cut in defense spending spread throughout the 1990s with the argument that this "would give us the

---

13. Quoted in Robert W. Tucker, *Intervention and the Reagan Doctrine* (New York: Council on Religion and International Affairs, 1985), p. 5.
14. Quoted in Josef Joffe, "After Bipolarity: Eastern and Western Europe: Between Two Ages," in *The Strategic Implications of Change in the Soviet Union*, Adelphi Paper No. 247 (London: IISS, Winter 1989/90), p. 71.
15. *The Economist* apparently believes that Britain and France were great powers well into the 1950s, claiming that the Suez Crisis of 1956 "helped destroy Britain and France as great powers"; June 16, 1990, p. 101.

defense budget for a second-class power, the budget of an America in decline."[16]

The political and economic reconstruction attempted by the Soviet Union followed in part from external causes. Gorbachev's expressed wish to see the Soviet Union "enter the new millennium as a great and flourishing state" suggests this.[17] Brezhnev's successors, notably Andropov and Gorbachev, realized that the Soviet Union could no longer support a first-rate military establishment on the basis of a third-rate economy. Economic reorganization, and the reduction of imperial burdens, became an externally imposed necessity, which in turn required internal reforms. For a combination of internal and external reasons, Soviet leaders tried to reverse their country's precipitous fall in international standing but did not succeed.

The Rise and Fall of Great Powers

In the fairly near future, say ten to twenty years, three political units may rise to great-power rank: Germany or a West European state, Japan, and China. In a shorter time, the Soviet Union fell from the ranks, making the structure of international politics hard to define in the present and difficult to discern in the future. This section asks how the structure of international politics is likely to change.

The Soviet Union had, and Russia continues to have, impressive military capabilities. But great powers do not gain and retain their rank by excelling in one way or another. Their rank depends on how they score on a combination of the following items: size of population and territory, resource endowment, economic capability, military strength, political stability and competence. The Soviet Union, like Tsarist Russia before it, was a lopsided great power, compensating for economic weakness with political discipline, military strength, and a rich territorial endowment. Nevertheless, great-power status cannot be maintained without a certain economic capability. In a conventional world, one would simply say that the years during which Russia with its many weaknesses will count as a great power are numbered, and that the numbers are pretty small ones. Although Russia has more than

---

16. Michael R. Gordon, "Cheney Calls 50% Military Cut a Risk to Superpower Status," *New York Times*, March 17, 1990, p. 4.
17. "Succession in Moscow: First Hours in Power, Gorbachev in His Own Words," *New York Times*, March 12, 1985, p. A16.

enough military capability, technology advances rapidly, and Russia cannot keep pace. In a nuclear world, however, the connection between a country's economic and technological capability, on the one hand, and its military capability, on the other, is loosened.

With conventional weapons, rapid technological change intensifies competition and makes estimating the military strengths of different countries difficult. In 1906, for example, the British *Dreadnought*, with the greater range and firepower of its guns, made older battleships obsolete. With nuclear weapons, however, short of a breakthrough that would give the United States either a first-strike capability or an effective defense, Russia need not keep pace militarily with American technology. As Bernard Brodie put it: "Weapons that do not have to fight their like do not become useless because of the advent of newer and superior types."[18] Since America's nuclear weapons are not able to fight Russia's, the strategies of the two countries are decoupled. Each country can safely follow a deterrent strategy no matter what the other may do.[19] In contrast, the development of either a first-strike capability or an effective strategic defense would carry the world back to conventional times: weapons would once again be pitted against weapons. All of the parties to the strategic competition would again become concerned over, or obsessed with, the balance of advantage between offensive and defensive forces. Worry about the possibly uneven development of weapons would drive competition to high intensity. A country with a decisive but possibly fleeting offensive advantage would be tempted to strike before another country could find ways of safeguarding its forces. A country with an effective defense, fearing that an adversary might find ways to overcome it, would be tempted to launch a preventive blow. Fortunately, as far ahead as the imagination can reach, no offensive or defensive breakthrough that would negate deterrent forces is in sight.

So long as a country can retaliate after being struck, or appears to be able to do so, its nuclear forces cannot be made obsolete by an adversary's technological advances. With deterrence dominant, a second-strike force need only be a small one, and it is easy to say how large the small force needs to be: large enough to sustain a first strike without losing the ability

---

18. Bernard Brodie, *War and Politics* (New York: Macmillan, 1973), p. 321.
19. Some Soviet commentators understand this. See, especially, Andrei Kokoshin, "The Future of NATO and the Warsaw Pact Strategy: Paper II," in *The Strategic Implications of Change in the Soviet Union*, Adelphi Paper No. 247 (London: IISS, Winter 1989/90), pp. 60–65.

to retaliate with some tens of warheads. Both the United States and the Soviet Union have long had warheads and delivery systems that far exceed the requirement of deterrence. Moreover, deterrent strategies make large conventional forces irrelevant. They need only be big enough to require an adversary to attack on a scale that reveals the extent of its aggressive intentions. A trip-wire force is the only conventional component that a deterrent nuclear strategy requires.[20]

Nuclear weaponry favors status-quo countries by enabling them to concentrate attention on their economies rather than on their military forces. This is good news for a country in straitened circumstances. By relying on deterrence, Russia can concentrate on turning resources in the military sector of her economy—a favored and presumably rather efficient one—to civilian uses.

Nuclear weaponry widens the range within which national economic capabilities may vary before the boundary between the great and the major powers is reached. Nuclear weapons alone do not make states into great powers. Britain and France did not become great powers when they became nuclear ones. Russia will not remain a great power unless it is able to use its resources effectively in the long run. While it is trying to do so, its large population, vast resources, and geographic presence in Europe and Asia compensate for its many weaknesses. Russia's vulnerabilities are low, as is its need for Third-World intervention forces. The ability of Russia to play a military role beyond its borders is low, yet nuclear weapons ensure that no state can challenge it. Short of disintegration, Russia will remain a great power—indeed a great defensive power, as the Russian and Soviet states were through most of their history.

How does the weakened condition of Russia affect the structure of international politics? The answer is that bipolarity endures, but in an altered state. Bipolarity continues because militarily Russia can take care of itself and because no other great powers have yet emerged. Some of the implications of bipolarity, however, have changed. Throughout the Cold War, the United States and the Soviet Union held each other in check. With the waning of Soviet power, the United States is no longer held in check by any other country or combination of countries. According to Herbert Butterfield, Francois Fénélon, a French theologian and political counselor who died in

---

20. For fuller treatment of this and other strategic questions, see Waltz, "Nuclear Myths and Political Realities," *American Political Science Review,* Vol. 84, No. 3 (September 1990).

1715, was the first person to understand balance of power as a recurring phenomenon rather than as a particular and ephemeral condition. He believed that a country wielding overwhelming power could not for long be expected to behave with moderation.[21] Balance-of-power theory leads one to predict that other countries, alone or in concert, will try to bring American power into balance. What are the possibilities?

Because nuclear weapons alter the relation between economic capability and military power, a country with well less than half of the economic capability of the leading producer can easily compete militarily if it adopts a status-quo policy and a deterrent strategy. Conversely, the leading country cannot use its economic superiority to establish military dominance, or to gain strategic advantage, over its great-power rivals.

Can one then say that military force has lost its usefulness or simply become irrelevant? Hardly. Nuclear weapons do, however, narrow the purposes for which strategic power can be used. No longer is it useful for taking others' territory or for defending one's own. Nuclear weapons bend strategic forces to one end: deterring attacks on a country's vital interests. Partly because strategic weapons serve that end and no other, peace has held at the center of international politics through five postwar decades, while wars have often raged at the periphery. Nuclear weapons have at once secured the vital interests of states possessing them and upheld the international order.

Nuclear countries can neither gain nor lose much in military conflicts with one another. Winning big, because it risks nuclear retaliation, becomes too dangerous to contemplate. George Ball has labelled the retaliatory threat a "cosmic bluff,"[22] but who will call it? Nothing that might be gained by force is worth risking the destruction of one's cities even if the attacker somehow knew that the attacked would be unlikely to retaliate. Nuclear weaponry solves the credibility problem; put differently, nuclear weapons create their own credibility. The mere possibility of nuclear use causes extreme caution all around. Logic says that once the deterrent threat has failed, carrying it

---

21. Herbert Butterfield, "The Balance of Power," in Butterfield and Martin Wight, eds., *Diplomatic Investigations* (London: George Allen and Unwin, 1966), p. 140. Fénélon may have been first, but the idea was in the air. See Daniel Defoe, *A True Collection of the Writings of the Author of the True Born Englishman, Corrected by himself* (London, printed and to be sold by most booksellers in London, Westminster, 1703), p. 356.
22. Quoted by David Garnham, "Extending Deterrence with German Nuclear Weapons," *International Security*, Vol. 10, No. 1 (Summer 1985), p. 97.

out at the risk of one's own destruction is irrational. But logic proves unpersuasive because a would-be attacker cannot be sure that logic will hold.

Nuclear weapons produced an underlying stillness at the center of international politics that made the sometimes frenzied military preparations of the United States and the Soviet Union pointless, and efforts to devise scenarios for the use of their nuclear weapons bizarre. Representative Helen Delich Bentley remarked in the fall of 1989 that, "after having spent more than $1 trillion for defense in the last 10 years, we find ourselves not stronger but greatly weakened."[23] She was right. Our most recent military buildup, beginning with the Carter administration and running through most of Reagan's, was worse than irrelevant because it burned up resources that could have safely been put to constructive use.

If the leaders of a country understand the implications of nuclear weapons, they will see that with them they can enjoy a secure peace at reasonable cost. Because nuclear weapons widen the range of economic capabilities within which great powers and would-be great powers can effectively compete, the door to the great-power club will swing open if the European Community (EC), Germany, China, or Japan knock on it.[24] Whether or not they do so is partly a matter of decision: the decision by Japan and Germany to equip themselves as great powers or, in the case of Western Europe, the collective decision to become a single state. But in political as in other realms, choices are seldom entirely free. Late in the nineteenth century, the United States faced such a decision. Economically it qualified as a great power; militarily it chose not to become one. Some observers thought that the Spanish-American War marked America's coming of age as a great power. But no state lacking the military ability to compete with other great powers has ever been ranked among them. America's ability to do so remained latent. We entered World War I belatedly, and then we depended heavily on the matériel of our allies. In his memoirs, Lloyd George remarked that in the great battles of April to June 1918, American aviators flew French planes. He added that the "light and medium artillery used up to the end of the War by the American Army was supplied by the French. The heaviest artillery was supplied by the British. No field guns of American pattern or manufac-

---

23. Helen Delich Bentley, letter to the *New York Times*, November 20, 1989, p. A18.
24. Earlier I said the opposite, arguing that for would-be great powers the military barriers to entry were high. As nuclear technology became widely available, and warheads smaller and thus easier to deliver, second-strike forces came within the reach of many states. See Waltz, "The Stability of a Bipolar World," pp. 895–896.

ture fired a shot in the War. The same thing applies to tanks."[25] At the end of World War II, the United States dismantled its military machine with impressive—or alarming—rapidity, which seemed to portend a retreat from international affairs. Quickly, however, the world's woes pressed upon us, and our leaders saw that without our constructive efforts the world would not become one in which we could safely and comfortably live.

Some countries may strive to become great powers; others may wish to avoid doing so. The choice, however, is a constrained one. Because of the extent of their interests, larger units existing in a contentious arena tend to take on system-wide tasks. As the largest powers in the system, the United States and the Soviet Union found that they had global tasks to perform and global interests to mind.

In discussing the likely emergence of new great powers, I concentrate on Japan as being by population and product the next in line. When Japan surrendered on August 15, 1945, Homer Bigart of the *New York Herald Tribune* wrote that, "Japan, paying for her desperate throw of the dice at Pearl Harbor, passed from the ranks of the major powers at 9:05 a.m. today."[26] In 1957, when Carter, Herz, and Ranney published the third edition of their *Major Foreign Powers*,[27] Japan was not among them. In 1964, projecting national economic growth rates to see what countries might become great powers by the end of the century, I failed even to consider Japan. Yet now Japan is ready to receive the mantle if only it will reach for it.

Much in Japan's institutions and behavior supports the proposition that it will once again take its place among the great powers. In most of the century since winning its Chinese War of 1894–95, Japan has pressed for preeminence in Asia, if not beyond. From the 1970s onward, Japan's productivity and technology have extended its influence worldwide. Mercantilist policies enhance the role of the state, and Japan's policies have certainly been mercantilist. Miyohei Shinohara, former head of the economics section of the Japanese Economic Planning Agency, has succinctly explained Japan's policy:

The problem of classical thinking undeniably lies in the fact that it is essentially "static" and does not take into account the possibility of a dynamic change in the comparative advantage or disadvantage of industries over a

---

25. David Lloyd George, *War Memoirs, 1917–1918* (Boston: Little, Brown, 1936), pp. 452–453.
26. Quoted by Richard Severa, "Homer Bigart, Acclaimed Reporter, Dies," in *New York Times*, April 17, 1991, p. C23.
27. Gwendolyn M. Carter, John H. Herz, John C. Ranney, *Major Foreign Powers* (New York: Harcourt, Brace, 1957).

coming 10- or 20-year period. To take the place of such a traditional theory, a new policy concept needs to be developed to deal with the possibility of intertemporal dynamic development.[28]

The concept fits Japan's policy, but is not a new one. Friedrich List argued in the middle of the nineteenth century that a state's trade policy should vary with its stage of economic development. He drew sharp distinctions between exchange value and productive power, between individual and national interests, and between cosmopolitan and national principles. Free trade serves world interests by maximizing exchange value, but whether free trade serves a nation's interest depends on its situation.[29] States with primitive economies should trade their primary products freely and use foreign earnings to begin to industrialize. At that stage, protective tariffs work against the development of manufactures. A state at an intermediate level of development should protect only those infant industries that have a fair chance of achieving a comparative advantage. Such a state should aim not to maximize "value" but to develop its "productive power." Exposed to competition from states that are more advanced economically, a state's industries may die in infancy. Where potential productive power exists, a state should use tariffs to promote its development. List likens nations who slavishly follow "the School's" free-trade theory to "the patient who followed a printed prescription and died of a misprint."[30] To clinch the point that cheap imports work against the development of a nation's industries, he observed that "the worst of all things" would be for American farmers to be given their manufactured goods by England.[31] Exchange value would be maximized at the

---

28. Miyohei Shinohara, *Industrial Growth, Trade, and Dynamic Patterns in the Japanese Economy* (Tokyo: University of Tokyo Press), 1982, p. 24. Shinohara says that List was the first to develop "the theory of infant industry protection," but thinks that he would be surprised by Japan's thorough application of it. List, however, did not invent the theory. Instead, he applied it to developing countries and used it to attack economists' belief that free trade serves the interests of all nations. The belief that Japan invented what is sometimes called "strategic trade theory" is widespread. See Bruce R. Scott, "National Strategies: Key to International Competition," in Scott and George C. Lodge, eds., *U.S. Competitiveness in the World Economy* (Boston: Harvard Business School Press, 1985), pp. 95, 138. To give another example, Paul R. Krugman describes as a "new trade theory" what in fact was anticipated by List in every particular. "Introduction: New Thinking about Trade Policy," in Krugman, ed., *Strategic Trade Policy and the New International Economics* (Cambridge, Mass.: MIT Press, 1986).
29. Frederick List, *National System of Political Economy*, trans. G.A. Matile (Philadelphia: Lippincott, 1856), pp. 74, 79, 244, 253.
30. Margaret Hirst, *Life of Friedrich List And Selections from his Writings, 1909* (New York: Augustus M. Kelley, 1965), p. 289. "The School" refers to Adam Smith, David Ricardo, and their followers.
31. Ibid., p. 51n.

expense of America's future productive power.[32] At the final stage of development, attained in List's day only by England, free trade is again the sensible policy. "For such a country," he wrote, "the cosmopolitan and the national principle are one and the same thing."[33] With rapid technological change, one must wonder whether the final stage ever arrives. List, however, appeared to believe, as Smith did earlier and Keynes did later, that in a distant day nations would have accumulated all of the riches to which their resources entitled them.[34]

The United States acquiesced in Japan's protectionist policies when Japan was in List's intermediate stage of development, but objected more and more strenuously as its economy became more fully developed. Some Japanese and American voices have joined in urging Japan to loosen its economic policies, although most of the Japanese voices have been muted. A policy report of The Japan Forum on International Relations suggested that the government modify its policies to overcome its mercantilist reputation, to divorce its overseas development assistance from commercial interests that appear self-serving, and to drop "infant industry policies."[35] But will Japan do so? Major changes of policy would be required. Japan's imports of products that it manufactures have, according to Clyde Prestowitz, been "nearly nil." According to Lester Thurow, rather than allowing foreign companies to establish a Japanese market for products of superior technology, the Japanese have welcomed such products "only when they have lost the technological edge."[36]

Japan might take effective steps toward opening her economy, but I doubt it. Shinohara accepts that as "a new major economic power" Japan has an obligation to work "for stable growth of the world economy." But doing so,

---

32. Cf. Shinohara: "The 'comparative technical progress criterion' pays more attention to the possibility of placing a particular industry in a more advantageous position in the future. . . . The term could be called the 'dynamized comparative cost doctrine'." Shinohara, *Industrial Growth*, p. 25. Cf. also Scott, who wrote that an interdependent world calls for "emphasis on baking relative to distributing the pie"; Scott, "National Strategies," p. 137.
33. List, *National System*, p. 79.
34. On Smith and Keynes, see Robert Heilbroner, "Reflections, Economic Predictions," *New Yorker*, July 8, 1991, pp. 70–77.
35. *Japan Forum on International Relations*, "Japan, the United States and Global Responsibilities," April, 1990, pp. 18–24.
36. Clyde V. Prestowitz, Jr., *Trading Places: How We Allowed Japan to Take the Lead* (New York: Basic Books, 1988), p. 76; Lester C. Thurow, "Global Trade: The Secret of Success" (review of Michael E. Porter's *The Competitive Advantage of Nations*), *New York Times*, Book Review Section, May 27, 1990, p. 7.

he adds, does not require Japan to drop policies designed "to nourish infant industries over a span of 5–10 years." A "degree of protection may be justified." In a dynamic world, "competition tends to become brutal," and theories "framed in a surrealistic and hypothetical world when Adam Smith and David Ricardo were predominant are no longer applicable."[37] Whether culturally ingrained or rooted in the structure of government, Japan's economic policy is not likely to take a new direction. Why should more than marginal concessions be made, when the policies Japan has followed have been so successful? If a country has followed one road to success, why should it turn onto another one? The United States may accuse Japan of unfair trade practices, or the United States may instead, as Bruce Scott suggests, recognize that Japan has a strategy of "creating advantages rather than accepting the status quo." Simply put, its "approach may be more competitive than ours."[38]

The likelier course for Japan to follow is to extend its economic policies regionally. Thus the policy announced by Ministry of International Trade and Industry (MITI) Minister Tamura in Bangkok in January of 1987 called for integrating other Asian nations, especially the Association of Southeast Asian Nations (ASEAN), more closely with Japan's economy. The five-year economic plan, released by the Economic Planning Agency in May of 1988, calls, in the words of David Arase, "for the construction of an international division of labor through more imports, more FDI, and more ODA (Foreign Direct Investment and Official Development Assistance)." Japan now uses ODA, not simply to develop new sources of supply and to open new markets, but more broadly "to integrate the Asian-Pacific region under Japanese leadership." The "flying geese" pattern of development and the notion of an "Asian Brain" that manipulates "capital, technology, and trade to construct a regional division of labor tightly coordinated from Tokyo," are made explicit in a major Economic Planning Agency policy study.[39]

Japan's successful management of its economy is being followed by the building of a regional economic bastion. Quite a few Japanese talk and write as though this represents their future. Other leading states have taken notice. The United States made a defensive gesture of despair by putting the "Super-301" retaliation trade-sanction clause in the 1988 Omnibus Trade and Com-

---

37. Shinohara, *Industrial Growth*, pp. 113, 118–119.
38. Scott, "National Strategies," p. 100; cf. p. 131.
39. David Arase, "U.S. and ASEAN Perceptions of Japan's Role in the Asian-Pacific Region," in Harry H. Kendall and Clara Joewono, eds., *ASEAN, Japan, and the United States* (Berkeley: Institute of East Asian Studies, 1990), pp. 270–275.

petitive Act to be used as a lever for the opening of Japan's economy more widely to America's—and of course to others'—exports, and the EC strove to achieve economic unity in 1992 partly out of fear that a disunited Europe could not stand up to Japanese and American competition. Economic competition is often as keen as military competition, and since nuclear weapons limit the use of force among great powers at the strategic level, we may expect economic and technological competition among them to become more intense. Thus, as Gorbachev reminded the Central Committee in May of 1986, the Soviet Union is "surrounded not by invincible armies but by superior economies."[40]

One may wonder, however, why less concern for military security should be followed by more concern for the ability of one's country to compete economically. Should one not expect reduced concern for security to go hand-in-hand with reduced concern for one's competitive position? Among many negative answers that can be given to this question, I emphasize four strong ones.

1. Despite changes that constantly take place in the relations of nations, the basic structure of international politics continues to be anarchic. Each state fends for itself with or without the cooperation of others. The leaders of states and their followers are concerned with their standings, that is, with their positions *vis-à-vis* one another. Michael Mastanduno has related the results of Robert Reich's asking various groups whether they would prefer that over the next decade Japan's economy grow by 75 percent and America's by 25 percent, or that Japan's economy grow by 10.3 percent and America's by 10 percent. Of six different audiences, only the one made up of economists preferred the former, and they did so unanimously.[41] (Clearly, Friedrich List and Bruce Scott were not present.)

2. One may wonder why, with worries over military security reduced, and with the disappearance of the Soviet Union, concern for relative gains should take precedence over concern for absolute ones. With a 75 percent and 25 percent increase in production respectively, Japan and the United States would both be markedly better off at the end of a decade. With a 10.3 percent and 10 percent gain, both countries would be just about stagnant. On the

40. Quoted by Dusko Doder and Louise Branson, *Gorbachev: Heretic in the Kremlin* (New York: Viking, 1990), p. 207.
41. Michael Mastanduno, "Do Relative Gains Matter? America's Response to Japanese Industrial Policy," *International Security*, Vol. 16, No. 1 (Summer 1991), pp. 73–74.

face of it, the preference of five out of six groups for the latter condition appears to be irrational. But the "face" is merely a mask disguising international-political reality. Friedrich Engels's understanding that economic competition is ultimately more important than military competition is reflected in his remark that industrial espionage was in his day a more serious business, and a business more fiercely conducted, than military espionage. Technical and economic advances accumulate. One technological breakthrough may lead to others. Economic growth rates compound. By projecting adjusted national growth rates of gross domestic product (GDP) from the period 1950 to 1980 into the year 2010 using 1975 international dollars, William Baumol and his associates arrived at an expected GDP per capita of $19,000 for the United States and of $31,000 for Japan. That disparity will result if the United States grows at 1.90 percent yearly and Japan at 4.09 percent. Yet if the United States should raise its average annual rate from 1.90 to 3.05 percent, the two countries would be tied for first place among the sixteen countries for which calculations are shown.[42]

3. Prosperity and military power, although connected, cannot be equated. Yet with the use of military force for consequential advantage negated at least among nuclear powers, the more productive and the more technologically advanced countries have more ways of influencing international outcomes than do the laggards. America's use of economic means to promote its security and other interests throughout the past five decades is sufficient illustration. The reduction of military worries will focus the minds of national leaders on their technological and economic successes and failures.

4. Uncertainty is a synonym for life, and nowhere is uncertainty greater than in international politics. Anarchy places a premium on foresight. If one cannot know what is coming, developing a greater resource base for future use takes precedence over present prosperity. Reflecting Reich's informal finding, a *Newsweek*/Gallup poll of September 1989 showed that 52 percent of Americans thought the economic power of Japan was a greater threat to the United States than the military power of the Soviet Union.[43] Whatever the limitations on the national use of force, the international political realm continues to be an intensely competitive one. Concern over relative gains continues to be the natural preoccupation of states.[44] If Japan's methods

---

42. William J. Baumol, Sue Anne Batey Blackman, and Edward N. Wolff, *Productivity and American Leadership: The Long View* (Cambridge, Mass.: MIT Press, 1989), Table 12.3, p. 259.
43. "The Perceived Threat: A Newsweek Poll," *Newsweek*, October 9, 1989, p. 64.
44. For incisive analysis of the relative-gains problem, see Joseph M. Grieco, "Understanding

continue to prove successful, other countries will emulate or counter them. Many have argued that, as Richard Barnet has put it, with the "globalization" of the economy, states have "lost the power to manage stable economies within their frontiers."[45] Japan certainly has not and is not likely to do so. To manage "globalization," leading states are likely to strengthen their economic influence over states on which they depend or to which they are closely connected. Since incentives to compete are strong, the likely outcome is a set of great powers forming their own regional bases in Asia, Europe, and America, with Russia as a military power on the economic fringe.[46] Japan will lead the east Asian bloc, now forming; questions about China's and northeast Asia's roles are as yet unresolved. Western Europe, including the EC, trades increasingly among the countries that the EC comprises, while its global imports and exports are gradually declining.[47] And if the North American Free Trade Agreement (NAFTA) succeeds, the United States will be at the center of the world's largest economic bloc with presently about six trillion dollars in annual trade. Countries and regions that lag in the race will become more and more dependent on others.

National Preferences and International Pressures

Economically, Japan's power has grown and spread remarkably. But does that indicate a desire to play the role of a great power? Japan's concerted regional activity, its seeking and gaining prominence in such bodies as the IMF and the World Bank, and its obvious pride in economic and technological achievements all indicate that it does. Confidence in economic ability and technical skill leads a country to aspire to a larger political role. "Both Britain

---

the Problem of International Cooperation: The Limits of International or Neoliberal Institutionalism and the Future of Realist Theory," in David Baldwin, ed., *Neorealism and Neoliberalism: The Contemporary Debate* (New York: Columbia University Press, 1993); and Robert Powell, "Absolute and Relative Gains in International Relations Theory," *American Political Science Review*, Vol. 85, No. 4 (December 1991) pp. 1303–1320.

45. Richard J. Barnet, "Reflections, Defining the Moment," *New Yorker*, July 16, 1990, p. 56.

46. Krugman among others has argued that the postwar free-trade system is giving way to regional trading blocs. This outcome, he believes, "is as good as we are going to get" and has the advantage that regional pacts "can exclude Japan." Louis Uchitelle, "Blocs Seen as Imperiling Free Trade," *New York Times*, August 26, 1991, p. D1. Cf. Steve Weber and John Zysman, "The Risk That Mercantilism Will Define the New Security System," in Wayne Sandholtz, et al., *The Highest Stakes* (New York: Oxford University Press, 1992), pp. 167–196.

47. Wayne Sandholtz and John Zysman, "1992: Recasting the European Bargain," *World Politics*, Vol. 42, No. 1 (October 1989), pp. 122–123.

and the United States," Yojiro Eguchi of the Nomura Research Institute remarked in 1974, "created and ran international systems with themselves at the top when they were leading creditors." Noting that in ten years Japan's external assets would far exceed America's at their peak, he concluded that "now it is Japan's turn to come up with an international system suited to itself."[48] No country has a better claim than Japan to being a larger partner in managing the world's economy.

Like Japan, Germany has recently shown an inclination to play a more prominent role in the world. President Bush described the Houston meeting of heads of government held in July of 1990 as the first economic summit conference of the "post-postwar era." Chancellor Kohl emerged at the summit as a dominant leader, and Prime Minister Thatcher noted that, "there are three regional groups at this summit, one based on the dollar, one on the yen, one on the Deutschmark."[49] The terms of German unification, which were to have been worked out by the four victors of World War II together with the two Germanies, were instead negotiated by Kohl and Gorbachev at a meeting in the Caucasus. West Germany is the leading state in Europe in both economic and conventional military power. East Germany added a gross domestic product only one sixth as large as West Germany's, but this is far short of its potential. For some years the eastern part of Germany will be a drain on its economy. For Germany's place in the world, how much does that matter? We often underestimate the economic disparities among great powers now, as we did in prenuclear days. To cite a striking example, Japan and the United States in 1940 had GNPs of $9 billion and $100 billion, respectively, and per capita incomes of $126 and $754.[50] In the prenuclear era, a poor country aspiring to a place among the great ones had to discipline its people and harness its resources to its military aims. In the nuclear era, countries with smaller economic bases can more easily achieve great-power status. Although a united Germany's GDP is smaller than Japan's, in one

48. Quoted by Richard Rosecrance and Jennifer Taw, "Japan and the Theory of International Leadership," *World Politics*, Vol. 42, No. 2 (January 1990), p. 207.
49. R.W. Apple, Jr., "A New Balance of Power," *New York Times*, July 12, 1990, p. A1.
50. Figures expressed in current prices. U.S. data from *Historical Statistics of the United States: Colonial Times to 1970*, Part 1 (Washington, D.C.: U.S. Department of Commerce, Bureau of the Census, 1975), p. 224. Japanese data derived from B.R. Mitchell, *International Historical Statistics: Africa and Asia* (New York: New York University Press, 1982), p. 732; *National Income and Statistics of Various Countries 1938–1947* (Lake Success, N.Y.: Statistical Office of the United Nations, 1948), Appendix III, pp. 246–247; Thelma Liesner, *Economic Statistics 1900–1983: United Kingdom, United States of America, France, Germany, Italy, Japan* (New York: Facts on File, 1985), p. 117.

sense Germany is already more of an economic presence globally than Japan, and even rivals the United States. In four of the seven years from 1986 through 1992, Germany's exports were larger than America's, and they were always larger than Japan's. (See Table 1.) Moreover, Germany is in the best position to play a leading role in eastern Europe, Ukraine, and Russia. *Newsweek* quoted a top adviser to Chancellor Kohl as saying, "We *want* to lead. Perhaps in time the United States will take care of places like Central America, and we will handle eastern Europe."[51] Ironically, Japan in Asia and Germany in eastern Europe are likely in the next century to replay roles in some ways similar to those they played earlier.

The effect of national economic capability varies over the centuries. Earlier, enough national productivity to sustain a large military force, however much the people had to stint themselves, could make a state a great power. Now, without a considerable economic capability no state can hope to sustain a world role, as the fate of the Soviet Union has shown. In the mercantilist era, international economics was national politics. During the nineteenth century, the link was weakened, but no longer. Oligopolistic firms care about relative gains and market shares. Similarly, states in today's international politics are not merely trying to maximize value in the present but also to secure their future positions. As I have said before, the distinction between high and low politics, once popular among international political economists, is misplaced. In self-help systems, how one has to help oneself varies as circumstances change.

Table 1. Exports In Billions of U.S. Dollars.

	1986	1987	1988	1989	1990	1991	1992
U.S.	227.16	254.12	322.43	363.81	393.59	421.73	447.47
Germany	243.33	294.37	323.32	341.23	410.10	402.84	422.27
Japan	210.76	231.29	264.86	273.93	287.58	314.79	340.00

SOURCE: These data are based on 1975 (Japan), 1980 (Germany), and 1987 (U.S.) prices as indexed by the IMF, *International Financial Statistics*, Vol. XLV, No. 1 (Washington, D.C.: International Monetary Fund, January 1992), p. 72; and Vol. XLVI, No. 4 (April 1993), p. 58.

51. "The New Superpower," *Newsweek*, February 26, 1970, p. 17.

The increased international activity of Japan and Germany reflects the changing structure of international politics. The increase of a country's economic capabilities to the great-power level places it at the center of regional and global affairs. It widens the range of a state's interests and increases their importance. The high volume of a country's external business thrusts it ever more deeply into world affairs. In a self-help system, the possession of most but not all of the capabilities of a great power leaves a state dependent on others and vulnerable to those who have the instruments that the lesser state lacks. Even though one may believe that fears of nuclear blackmail are misplaced, will Japan and Germany be immune to them? In March of 1988, Prime Minister Takeshita called for a defensive capability matching Japan's economic power.[52] Whether or not he intended to, he was saying that Japan should present itself in great-power panoply before the nations of the world. A great power's panoply includes nuclear weapons.

Countries have always competed for wealth and security, and the competition has often led to conflict. Why should the future be different from the past? Given the expectation of conflict, and the necessity of taking care of one's interests, one may wonder how a state with the economic capability of a great power can refrain from arming itself with the weapons that have served so well as the great deterrent.

Since the 1950s, West European countries have feared that the American deterrent would not cover their territories. Since the 1970s, Japan has at times expressed similar worries. The increase of Soviet Far Eastern Forces in the late 1970s led Japan to reexamine its view of the Soviet threat. It is made uneasy now by the near-doubling of China's military budget between 1988 and 1993. Its three-million strong army, undergoing modernization, and the growth of its sea and air power-projection capabilities produce apprehension in all of China's neighbors and add to the sense of instability in a region where issues of sovereignty and territorial disputes abound. The Korean peninsula has more military forces per square kilometer than any other portion of the globe. Taiwan is an unending source of tension. Disputes exist between Japan and Russia over the Kurile Islands, and between Japan and China over the Senkaku Islands. China and Britain have had trouble agreeing on the future of Hong Kong. Cambodia is a troublesome problem for both Vietnam and China. Half a dozen countries lay claim to all or some of the

---

52. Arase, "U.S. and ASEAN Perceptions of Japan's Role in the Asian-Pacific Region."

Spratly Islands, strategically located and supposedly rich in oil. The presence of China's ample nuclear forces and the presumed development of North Korea's, combined with the drawdown of American military forces, can hardly be ignored by Japan, the less so since economic conflicts with the United States cast doubt on the reliability of American military guarantees. Reminders of Japan's dependence and vulnerability multiply in large and small ways. In February of 1992, Prime Minister Miyazawa derided America's labor force for its alleged lack of a "work ethic," even though productivity per man-hour is higher in America than it is in Japan. This aroused Senator Ernest F. Hollings, who responded by fliply referring to the atomic bomb as, "Made in America by lazy and illiterate Americans, and tested in Japan."[53] His remark made more Japanese wonder whether they indeed may require a nuclear military capability of their own. Instances in which Japan feels dependent and vulnerable will increase in number. For example, as rumors about North Korea's developing nuclear capabilities gained credence, Japan became acutely aware of its lack of observation satellites. Uncomfortable dependencies and perceived vulnerabilities will lead Japan to acquire greater military capabilities, even though many Japanese may prefer not to.

In recent years, the desire of Japan's leaders to play a militarily more assertive role has become apparent, a natural response to Japan's enhanced economic standing. Again the comparison with America at the turn of the previous century is striking, when presidents wanted to develop America's military forces (and also to annex more countries). Congress served as a brake;[54] in Japan, public opinion now serves the same purpose. Yet the key question is not whether the Japanese people wish their country to become a great power. The key question is whether its people and its leaders will begin to feel that Japan needs the range of capabilities possessed by other countries in its region, and in the world, in order, as Andrew Hanami has put it, to cope defensively and preventively with present and possible future problems and threats.[55] The many American voices that have urged Japan to carry a larger share of her security burden, and the increasing tilt of American public

---

53. David E. Sanger, "Japan Premier Joins Critics of American's Work Habits," *New York Times*, February 4, 1992, p. A1; "Senator Jokes of Hiroshima Attack," *New York Times*, March 4, 1992, p. A12.
54. Fareed Zakaria, "The Rise of a Great Power: National Strength, State Structure, and American Foreign Policy, 1865–1908" (Harvard University, PhD dissertation, forthcoming November 1993), ch. 3.
55. Andrew Hanami, "Japan's Strategy in Europe," unpublished conference paper, October 1992, p. 2.

opinion against Japan, have led her leaders to wonder how far they can count on the United States for protection. In the emerging multipolar world, can Japan expect to continue to rent American military forces by paying about 60 percent of their cost, while relying on the American strategic deterrent? The great powers of the world must expect to take care of themselves.

Yoichi Funabashi has praised Japan for fulfilling its international responsibilities in non-military ways. In his view, Japan is a "global civilian power," taking its place in a world in which humane internationalism is replacing the heavily military politics of the Cold War.[56] One wonders. The United States put its security interests above its concern for economic competitiveness throughout the years of the Cold War. It no longer does so. As military worries fall, economic worries rise. Competition continues, and conflict turns increasingly on technological and economic issues. Conflict grows all the more easily out of economic competition because economic comparisons are easier to make than military ones. Militarily, one may wonder who is the stronger but, in a conventional world, will not find out until a war is fought. Economically, however, the consequences of price and quality differentials quickly become apparent. Decreased concern over security translates directly into increased concern over economic competitiveness because the United States is no longer so willing to subordinate the second concern to the first one.

For a country to choose not to become a great power is a structural anomaly. For that reason, the choice is a difficult one to sustain. Sooner or later, usually sooner, the international status of countries has risen in step with their material resources. Countries with great-power economies have become great powers, whether or not reluctantly. Japanese and German reasons for hesitating to take the final step into the great-power arena are obvious and need not be rehearsed. Yet when a country receives less attention and respect and gets its way less often than it feels it should, internal inhibitions about becoming a great power are likely to turn into public criticisms of the government for not taking its proper place in the world. Pride knows no nationality. How long can Japan and Germany live alongside other nuclear states while denying themselves similar capabilities? Conflicts and crises are certain to make them aware of the disadvantages of being without the military instruments that other powers command. Japanese and German nuclear

---

56. "Japan's Better Example," Editorial, *New York Times,* April 20, 1992, p. A16.

inhibitions arising from World War II will not last indefinitely; one might expect them to expire as generational memories fade. The probability of both countries' becoming nuclear powers in due course is all the higher because they can so easily do so. There is only one nuclear technology, and those who have harnessed the atom for peaceful purposes can quickly move into the nuclear military business. Allocating costs between nuclear and conventional armaments is difficult, the more so since some weapons systems have both conventional and nuclear uses. Everyone agrees, however, that nuclear weaponry accounts for the lesser part of a country's defense budget.

For Germany and Japan the problems of becoming a nuclear power are not economic or technological; they are political. In time, internal inhibitions can be overcome, but other countries will be made uneasy if Germany or Japan become nuclear powers. We have been through this before. Americans treated the prospect of China's becoming a nuclear power as almost unthinkable. Yet China and other countries have become nuclear powers without making the world a more dangerous one. Why should nuclear weapons in German and Japanese hands be especially worrisome? Nuclear weapons have encouraged cautious behavior by their possessors and deterred any of them from threatening others' vital interests. What reasons can there be for expecting Germany and Japan to behave differently? Some countries will fear the effects that may follow if Germany or Japan go nuclear, but who will try to stop them? A preventive strike, launched before any warheads can possibly have been made, would be required. Israel's destruction of Iraq's nuclear facility in June of 1981 set the precedent. Would anyone want to follow it by striking at Germany or Japan? The question answers itself.

Moreover, the internal and external problems of becoming a nuclear power are not as great as they once were. Israel for years denied the existence of its nuclear forces, but no longer bothers to lie about them. One may wonder whether Japan, now stockpiling plutonium, is already a nuclear power or is content to remain some months or moments from becoming one. Consistently since the mid-1950s, the Japanese government has defined all of the weapons of the Self-Defense Forces as conforming to constitutional requirements. Nuclear weapons purely for defense would be deemed constitutional.[57]

---

57. Norman D. Levin, "Japan's Defense Policy: The Internal Debate," in Kendall and Joewono, *ASEAN, Japan, and the United States.*

Japan has to worry about China, and China has to worry about Japan, while both are enmeshed in the many problems of their region. Yet one often hears this question asked: Why should Japan want nuclear weapons? To argue that it does not misses the point. Any country in Japan's position is bound to become increasingly worried about its security, the more so because China is rapidly becoming a great power in every dimension: internal economy, external trade, and military capability.

From 1965 to 1980, China's annual economic growth rate averaged 6.8 percent and from 1980 to 1990, 9.5 percent. Western economists estimate that China can sustain growth rates between 6 and 9 percent without serious inflationary problems. An economy that grows at 8 percent yearly doubles in size every nine years. The World Bank estimated that China's GDP in 1990 was $364,900 million.[58] Data on China are suspect, but to any periodic visitor the rapidity of its material progress is obvious. If it manages to maintain an effective government and a measure of economic freedom for its industrious people, within a decade it will be in the great-power ranks. Modernizing its three-million-strong army, buying ships and airplanes abroad and building its own as well, China will rapidly gain in power-projection capability. America, with the reduction of its forces, a Cold War–weary people, and numerous neglected problems at home, cannot hope to balance the growing economic and military might of a country of some 1.2 billion people while attending to other security interests. Unless Japan responds to the growing power of China, China will dominate its region and become increasingly influential beyond it.

Although most Japanese now shy away from the thought that their country will once again be a world power, most Chinese do not. Balance-of-power politics in one way or another characterize all self-help systems. Nations have to make choices. They can always choose not to develop counterweights to the dominant power, presently the United States, or not to balance against a rapidly growing one, such as China. India, Pakistan, perhaps North Korea, and China all wield nuclear military force capable of deterring others from

---

58. World Bank, *World Development Report, 1992: Development and the Environment* (Oxford: Oxford University Press, 1992), pp. 220, 222. Recalculating GDP according to the purchasing power of its currency at home, the IMF concluded that China's GDP in 1992 was $1.66 trillion. The World Bank, applying purchasing-power parity differently, arrived at a figure of $2.6 trillion, a bit higher than Japan's. But one must remember that China's GDP is shared by a huge population. Using the new method, the IMF estimates America's per-capita income at $22,200, Japan's at $19,100, Germany's at $19,500, and China's at $1,450. Steven Greenhouse, "New Tally of World's Economies Catapults China Into Third Place," *New York Times*, May 20, 1993, A1.

threatening their vital interests. Increasingly Japan will be pressed to follow suit and also to increase its conventional abilities to protect its interests abroad.

Two points about nuclear weapons remain. First, some commentators have asserted that Japan and Germany cannot become nuclear powers because they have too little land and too great a concentration of targets on it. Roger Hilsman has claimed that "no nation with territory that is less than continental size can now play the nuclear game." He argues that Japan, Germany, and England have "come to understand this."[59] But direct access to the oceans solves the problem of force vulnerability for all three of the countries mentioned, and target concentration does not matter since it is easy to make enough warheads to cover the targets one cares to, no matter how dispersed they may be. Territorially small countries are no worse off than big ones. Invulnerability of delivery systems, not dispersal of targets, is the crucial consideration.

Second, an argument of a different sort holds that by monopolizing certain technologies, Japan can manipulate the military balance to its advantage. It can substitute economic for military means. Diet member Shintaro Ishihara is one of the authors of *The Japan That Can Say No*, a work that became famous in the United States before it was published in Japan. He advanced the notion that if "Japan sold chips to the Soviet Union and stopped selling them to the United States, this would upset the entire military balance." But because nuclear weapons resist obsolescence, the act he imagines would not have the effects he foresees. Ishihara, nevertheless, asserts more broadly that "economic warfare is the basis for existence in the free world," and believes that in that kind of struggle there "is no hope for the U.S."[60] Countries naturally play their strong suits up and play their weak ones down. Both Stalin and Mao belittled nuclear weaponry when only the United States had it. Neither superiority in the chip business nor a broader technological lead will enable Japan to secure the sources of its oil. Nor will conventional forces, along with economic superiority, substitute for nuclear deterrence.

The case of Western Europe remains. Economically and militarily the possibilities are easily drawn. The achievement of unity would produce an instant great power, complete with second-strike nuclear forces. But politically the European case is complicated. Many believe that the EC has moved

---

59. Roger Hilsman, "How Dead Is It?" *New York Newsday*, March 18, 1990, p. 5.
60. Quoted in Flora Lewis, "Japan's Looking Glass," *New York Times*, November 8, 1989, p. A21.

so far toward unity that it cannot pull back, at least not very far back. That is probably true, but it is also probably true that it has moved so far toward unity that it can go no farther. The easier steps toward unity come earlier, the harder ones later, and the hardest of all at the end. Economic unity is not easily achieved, but the final decision to form a single, effective political entity that controls foreign and military policies as well as economic ones is the most difficult, made more so because the number of states the EC comprises has now grown to twelve, and an additional four have candidate status. Especially in Britain and France, many believe that their states will never finally surrender their sovereignty. Indeed, the Maastricht Treaty on European Union had trouble securing the assent of Denmark and France, and its economic and social provisions remain controversial in Britain. Common foreign and defense policies are to be concluded only by heavily qualified majorities, and the defense policies "of certain member states" are to be respected.[61] The Community's external policy thereby becomes nearly a cipher. Germans may ultimately find that reunification and the renewed life of a great power are more invigorating than the struggles, complications, and compromises that come during, and would come after, the uniting of Western Europe.

Despite severe difficulties, three factors may enable Western Europe to achieve political unity. The first is Germany, the second is Japan, and the third is the United States. Uneasiness over the political and economic clout of Germany, intensified by the possibility of its becoming a nuclear power, may produce the final push to unification. And West Europeans, including many Germans, doubt their abilities to compete on even terms with Japan and America unless they are able to act as a political as well as an economic unit. Indeed, without political unification, economic unity will always be as impaired as it is now.

If the EC fails to become a single political entity, the emerging world will nevertheless be one of four or five great powers, whether the European one is called Germany or the United States of Europe. The next section asks what differences this will make in the behavior and interaction of states.

---

61. Council of the European Communities, Commission of the European Communities, *Treaty on European Union*, as signed in Maastricht on February 7, 1992 (Luxembourg: Office for Official Publications of the European Communities, 1992), Title V, Articles J.8, No. 2; J.3, No. 3; and J.4, Nos. 3 and 4.

Balance of Power Politics: Old Style, New Style

The many who write of America's decline seem to believe that its fall is imminent. What promised to be the American century will be halved by Japan's remarkable economic resurgence, or so they say. Yet the economic and technological superiority of Japan over the United States is not foreordained. Technologically, Japan and the United States are about on a par; but in economic growth and technological progress the trend favors Japan. We should notice, however, that, with a low birth rate, essentially no immigration, and an aging population, productivity is the only road to growth unless more women can be effectively used in the workforce. And to increase production becomes more difficult as Japan approaches the limit of what present technology offers. Under these circumstances, high growth rates threaten to bring inflation. And since aging populations consume more and save less, Japan and the United States are likelier to converge in their growth rates than to diverge, with Japan moving rapidly to a position of economic superiority. One may expect the economic gap between America and Japan to narrow further, but more slowly, given America's impressive resource base and the tendency of countries to respond energetically to intimations of decline. One must be careful: American voices of doom in the 1950s had little effect on our policies until Sputnik was lofted in 1957. In the 1970s, the Soviet Union did not move to check its declining fortunes but tried, only to fail, in the 1980s. The United States in the 1980s concentrated on competing militarily—and pointlessly—with a moribund Soviet Union. In the 1990s, it will surely heed the economic and technological challenges of Japan.

The structure of international politics is changing not because the United States suffered a serious decline, but because the Soviet Union did so, while Japan, China, and Western Europe continued to progress impressively. For some years to come and for better or worse, the United States will be the leading country economically as well as militarily.

What about Germany? If Germany should become a great power, it would be at the bottom of the list. Japan, with about 60 percent of America's gross domestic product, can easily compete militarily. But can Germany, with about half of Japan's, do so? I believe that it can for two reasons, easily adduced from the second part of this essay. First, offensive and defensive advantage has been transformed by nuclear weapons into deterrent strength easily achieved. Second, an adequate economic base together with the ability to develop an area of operations beyond one's borders is enough to enable a country to vault into the great-power category. Germany is better placed than a British-French combination would be to achieve the second. Many possibilities are open. Germany's beginning to act as a great power may, instead of goading Western Europe to unite, cause Britain and France to do so. But the second possibility is even less likely than the unlikely first one.

Changes spawn uncertainties and create difficulties, especially when the changes are structural ones. Germany, Japan, and Russia will have to relearn their old great-power roles, and the United States will have to learn a role it has never played before: namely, to coexist and interact with other great powers. The United States, once reflexively isolationist, after 1945 became reflexively interventionist, which we like to call "internationalism." Whether isolationist or internationalist, however, our policies have been unilaterally made. The country's involvement became global, but most of the decisions to act abroad were made without much prior consultation with other countries. This was entirely natural: Who pays the piper calls the tune. Decisions are made collectively only among near-equals.

Events have rent the veil of internationalism that cloaked America's post-war policies. Watching the Germans directing Western policy toward the Soviet Union in the summer of 1990, Representative Lee Hamilton remarked that "this is an example of the new multi-polar world that's going to make us learn a new meaning for the word 'consult.' These days it doesn't mean us going to Europe and telling them what to do."[62] In the spring of the same year, the United States tried to shape the charter of a new Bank for Eastern Europe because we would not enjoy there the veto over policies that we had in such organizations as the World Bank and the International Monetary Fund. This prompted a *New York Times* correspondent to remark that for "the first time in the postwar period, Washington is participating in the establishment of a multilateral lending institution that it will not control—reflecting the decline of this country's relative global weight."[63] The old and the new great powers will have to relearn old roles, or learn new ones, and figure out how to enact them on a shifting stage. New roles are hard to learn, and actors may trip when playing on unfamiliar sets. Under the circumstances,

---

62. R.W. Apple, Jr., "As Bush Hails Decision Many See Bonn Gaining," *New York Times*, July 17, 1990, p. A9.
63. Clyde H. Farnsworth, "U.S. Threatens Not to Join Bank for East Europe If Soviets Benefit," *New York Times*, March 15, 1990, p. A1.

predictions about the fates of states and their systems become harder to make.

Units in a self-help system engage in balancing behavior. With two great powers, balancing is done mainly by internal means. Allies have been useful and have therefore been wanted, but they were not essential in the security relations of the big two. Because one of the foundations of the postwar peace—nuclear weapons—will remain, and one—bipolarity—will disappear, we have to compare the problems of balancing in conventional and nuclear worlds. In a bipolar-conventional world, a state has to estimate its strength only in relation to one other. In a multipolar-conventional world, difficulties multiply because a state has to compare its strength with a number of others and also has to estimate the strength of actual and potential coalitions. Moreover, in a conventional world, no one category of weapons dominates. States have to weigh the effectiveness of present weapons, while wondering about the effects that technological change may bring, and they have to prepare to cope with different strategies. "To be sure," Georg Simmel remarked, "the most effective presupposition for preventing struggle, the exact knowledge of the comparative strength of the two parties, is very often only to be obtained by the actual fighting out of the conflict."[64] In a conventional world, miscalculation is hard to avoid.

In a nuclear world one category of weapons is dominant. Comparing the strategic strength of nations is automatically accomplished once all of them have second-strike forces. Even should some states have larger and more varied strategic forces than others, all would effectively be at parity. The only way to move beyond second-strike forces is to create a first-strike capability or to put up an effective strategic defense. Since no one will fail to notice another state's performing either of those near-miracles, war through miscalculation is practically ruled out. Since no one has been able to figure out how to use strategic nuclear weapons other than for deterrence, nuclear weapons eliminate the thorny problems of estimating the present and future strengths of competing states and of trying to anticipate their strategies. And since nuclear states easily generate second-strike forces, they do not need one another's help at the strategic level. Strategically, nuclear weapons make alliances obsolete, just as General de Gaulle used to claim.[65]

---

64. Georg Simmel, "The Sociology of Conflict," *American Journal of Sociology*, Vol. 9 (January 1904), p. 501.
65. Waltz, "Nuclear Myths and Political Realities."

Nuclear weapons eliminate neither the use of force nor the importance of balancing behavior. They do limit force at the strategic level to a deterrent role, make estimating the strategic strength of nations a simple task, and make balancing easy to do. Multipolarity abolishes the stark symmetry and pleasing simplicity of bipolarity, but nuclear weapons restore both of those qualities to a considerable extent. Nuclear weapons have yet another beneficial effect on the relations of the nations that have them. Conventional states shy away from cooperating for the achievement of even large absolute gains if their uneven division would enable some to turn their disproportionate gain into a military advantage. Because states with second-strike forces cannot convert economic gain into strategic advantage, an important part of the relative–absolute gains problem is negated. And since nuclear countries cannot make important gains through military conquest without inviting retaliation, the importance of conventional forces is reduced. The elimination of one and the reduction of another military concern means that the relative–absolute gains problem will be rooted much more in worries about how the distribution of gains from joint ventures may affect the economic and technological progress of competing states. Economic competition will provide plentiful sources of conflict, but we should prefer them to military ones.

Balance-of-power theory leads one to expect that states, if they are free to do so, will flock to the weaker side. The stronger, not the weaker side, threatens them, if only by pressing its preferred policies on other states. John Dryden gave the thought poetic expression:

But when the chosen people grew more strong,
The rightful cause at length became the wrong.[66]

Though this was written three centuries ago as a comment on Great Britain, according to Anthony Lewis, the Israeli government found that the couplet fit its case closely enough to merit proscription for Arab readers. Even if the powerful state's intentions are wholly benign, less powerful states will, from their different historical experiences, geographic locations, and economic interests, interpret events differently and often prefer different policies. Thus within NATO, Western European countries differed with American interpretations of the Soviet Union's behavior, the nature of the threats it entailed, and the best means of dealing with them.

---

66. From John Dryden, "Absalom and Acitophel."

In a multipolar world, the United States as the strongest power will often find other states edging away from it: Germany moving toward Eastern Europe and Russia, and Russia moving toward Germany and Japan.[67] Yet despite the collapse of the Soviet Union and the dissolution of the WTO, American policy continues to bank on NATO's continued cohesion and influence. In the words of Secretary of State James Baker, NATO "provides one of the indispensable foundations for a stable European security environment."[68] But we must wonder how long NATO will last as an effective organization. As is often said, organizations are created by their enemies. Alliances are organized against a perceived threat. We know from balance-of-power theory as well as from history that war-winning coalitions collapse on the morrow of victory, the more surely if it is a decisive one. Internal and external examples abound. In Britain, large parliamentary majorities make party discipline difficult to maintain. In Poland, Solidarity struggled to prevail; once it did so, it split into various factions. Coalitions formed to counter Napoleon defeated him twice and collapsed both times. Victory in World War II turned wartime allies into peacetime adversaries.

As the Soviet Union began to unravel, Josef Joffe, an astute observer of American and European affairs, saw that the United States would soon be "set to go home." He asked, "who will play the role of protector and pacifier once America is gone?"[69] Europe and Russia may for a time look on NATO, and on America's presence in Western Europe, as a stabilizing force in a time of rapid change. In an interim period, the continuation of NATO makes sense. In the long run, it does not. The presence of American forces at higher than token levels will become an irritant to European states, whose security is not threatened, and a burden to America acting in a world that is becoming more competitive politically and economically as it becomes less so militarily.

How can an alliance endure in the absence of a worthy opponent? Ironically, the decline of the Soviet Union in Eastern Europe entailed the decline

---

67. Karl-Heinz Hornhues, deputy majority leader of the Bundestag, reported that Russian leaders suggested that Germany and Russia form a counterweight to the United States. Marc Fisher, "Germany Says Russia Seeks a Policy Ally," *International Herald Tribune*, February 3, 1993, p. 6.
68. James Baker, "Euro-Atlantic Architecture: From West to East," Address to the Aspen Institute, Berlin, Germany, June 18, 1991, *U.S. Department of State Dispatch*, June 24, 1991, p. 439. For an incisive analysis of the roles and relations of the United States, Western Europe, and the Soviet Union, see Christopher Layne, "Toward German Unification?" *Journal of Contemporary Studies*, Vol. 7, No. 4 (Fall 1984), pp. 7–37.
69. Joffe, "After Bipolarity," pp. 75–76.

of the United States in the West. Without the shared perception of a severe Soviet threat, NATO would never have been born. The Soviet Union created NATO, and the demise of the Soviet threat "freed" Europe, West as well as East. But freedom entails self-reliance. In this sense, both parts of Europe are now setting forth on the exhilarating but treacherous paths of freedom. In the not-very-long run, they will have to learn to take care of themselves or suffer the consequences. American withdrawal from Europe will be slower than the Soviet Union's. America, with its vast and varied capabilities, can still be useful to other NATO countries, and NATO is made up of willing members. NATO's days are not numbered, but its years are. Some hope that NATO will serve as an instrument for constraining a new Germany. But once the new Germany finds its feet, it will no more want to be constrained by the United States acting through NATO than by any other state.

Conclusion

A number of scholars have written suggestively about the relation between the standing of states and their propensity to fight. A.F.K. Organski and Robert Gilpin argue that peace prevails once one state establishes primacy. The hegemonic state lacks the need to fight, and other states lack the ability.[70] Some states, however, may concert to challenge the superior one, and when leading states decline, other states rise to challenge them. Unrest at home may accompany the decline of states, tempting them to seek foreign wars in order to distract their people. Or they may take one last military fling hoping to recoup their fortunes. Japan, China, and Germany are now the rising states, and Russia the declining one. But even if they wished to, none could use military means for major political or economic purposes. In the presence of nuclear weapons, any challenge to a leading state, and any attempt to reverse a state's decline, has to rely on political and economic means.

John Mueller believes that war among developed states became obsolescent after World War II for reasons that have little to do with nuclear weapons. War has lost its appeal, and "substantial agreement has risen around the twin propositions that prosperity and economic growth should be central national goals and that war is a particularly counterproductive device for

---

70. A.F.K. Organski, *World Politics* (New York: Knopf, 1958); Robert Gilpin, *War and Change in World Politics* (Cambridge: Cambridge University Press, 1981).

achieving these goals."[71] Norman Angell was not wrong, but merely pre-
mature, when he concluded that wars would no longer be fought because
they do not pay.[72] John Mearsheimer, however, makes the telling point that,
"if any war could have convinced Europeans to forswear conventional war,
it should have been World War I, with its vast casualties." But then if
Mearsheimer is right in believing that an "equality of power . . . among the
major powers" minimizes the likelihood of war, World War I should never
have been fought.[73] The opposing alliances were roughly equal in military
strength, and their principal members understood this. Yet, as we well know,
war is always possible among states armed only with conventional weapons.
Some rulers will sooner or later convince themselves that subtle diplomacy
will prevent opponents from uniting and that clever strategy will enable
them to win a swift victory at an affordable price.

Peace is sometimes linked to the presence of a hegemonic power, sometimes to a balance among powers. To ask which view is right misses the
point. It does so for this reason: the response of other countries to one among
them seeking or gaining preponderant power is to try to balance against it.
Hegemony leads to balance, which is easy to see historically and to understand theoretically. That is now happening, but haltingly so because the
United States still has benefits to offer and many other countries have become
accustomed to their easy lives with the United States bearing many of their
burdens.

The preceding paragraph reflects international-political reality through all
of the centuries we can contemplate. But what about the now-widespread
notion that because there may be more major democratic states in the future,
and fewer authoritarian ones, the Wilsonian vision of a peaceful, stable, and
just international order has become the appropriate one? Democratic states,
like others, have interests and experience conflicts. The late Pierre Bérégovoy,
when he was prime minister of France, said in 1992 that a European power
was needed "because it's unhealthy to have a single superpower in the
world."[74] He believed this not because the one superpower is undemocratic,
but simply because it is super. The stronger get their way—not always, but

---

71. John Mueller, *Retreat from Doomsday: The Obsolescence of Major War* (New York: Basic Books, 1989), pp. 219, 222.
72. Norman Angell, *The Great Illusion* (London: Heinemann, 1914).
73. Mearsheimer, "Back to the Future," p. 18.
74. Quoted in Flora Lewis, "Europe's Last-Minute Jitters," *New York Times*, April 24, 1992, p. A35.

more often than the weaker. Democratic countries, like others, are concerned with losing or gaining more in the competition among nations, a point richly illustrated by intra-EC politics.

If democracies do not fight democracies, then one can say that conflict among them is at least benign. Unfortunately there are many problems with this view. Few cases in point have existed. When one notes that democracies have indeed sometimes fought other democracies, the proposition dissolves. The American-British War of 1812 was fought by the only two democratic states that existed, and conflict and bitterness between them persisted through the century and beyond. In the 1860s, the northern American democracy fought the southern one. Both parties to the Civil War set themselves up as distinct and democratic countries and the South's belligerence was recognized by other countries. An important part of the explanation for World War I is that Germany was a pluralistic democracy, unable to harness its warring internal interests to a coherent policy that would serve the national interest.[75] One might even venture to say that if a Japanese-American war had occurred in recent years, it would have been said that Japan was not a democracy but rather a one-party state. From Kant onward, it has been implied that democracies do not fight democracies, but only if they are democracies of the right sort. Propositions of this type are constants in the thinking of those who believe that what states are like determines how they behave.

And there is the rub. A relative harmony can, and sometimes does, prevail among nations, but always precariously so. The thawing of the Cold War led to an expectation that the springtime buds of peace will blossom. Instead it has permitted latent conflicts to bloom in the Balkans and elsewhere in eastern Europe, in parts of what was greater Russia and later the Soviet Union, and in the Middle East. Unity in Western Europe has become more difficult to achieve partly because there is no real threat to unite against.

Yet in placid times, and even in times that are not so placid, the belief that power politics is ending tends to break out. Brent Scowcroft has written recently that balancing "interests off each other" is a "peculiar conception that was appropriate for certain historical circumstances." He foresees instead a world in which all pursue "the same general goals."[76] John Steinbruner

---

75. See Waltz, "America as a Model for the World? A Foreign Policy Perspective," *PS*, Vol. XXIV, No. 4 (December 1991), pp. 667–670.
76. Brent Scowcroft, in "Geopolitical Vertigo and the U.S. Role," *New Perspectives Quarterly*, Vol. 9, No. 3 (Summer 1992), pp. 6–9.

envisions a world in which people accept a "configuration of cooperative forces" because militarily "they cannot manage anything else." He adds that an "arrangement that does this" must be open to all who wish to belong.[77] These ideas are among the many versions of the domino theory, so long popular in America. Once the bandwagon starts to roll, it collects the bystanders. Stephen Van Evera believes that if we get through the present difficult patch, meaning mainly that if democracies emerge in Eastern Europe and the former Soviet Union, then "for the first time in history, the world's major countries would all share common political and economic systems and enjoy the absence of ideological conflict." The major causes of war would be "tamed," and "possibilities for wider great power cooperation to prevent war worldwide would be opened."[78] In contrast, this article has used structural theory to peer into the future, to ask what seem to be the strong likelihoods among the unknowns that abound. One of them is that, over time, unbalanced power will be checked by the responses of the weaker who will, rightly or not, feel put upon. This statement, however, implies another possibility. The forbearance of the strong would reduce the worries of the weak and permit them to relax. Fareed Zakaria has pointed out that two countries, when overwhelmingly strong, did not by their high-handed actions cause other powers to unite against them—Great Britain and the United States in their heydays.[79] Both exceptions to the expected balancing behavior of states can easily be explained. Britain could not threaten the major continental powers; its imperial burdens and demographic limitations did not permit it to do so. The United States was held in check by its only great-power rival.

What is new in the proclaimed new world order is that the old limitations and restraints now apply weakly to the United States. Yet since foreign-policy behavior can be explained only by a conjunction of external and internal conditions, one may hope that America's internal preoccupations will produce not an isolationist policy, which has become impossible, but a forbearance that will give other countries at long last the chance to deal with their own problems and to make their own mistakes. But I would not bet on it.

---

77. John Steinbruner, "Defense Budget Priorities," Institute of International Studies, *Currents*, Vol. 1, No. 4 (Supplement), March 30, 1992, p. 3.
78. Stephen Van Evera, "Preserving Peace in the New Era," *Boston Review*, Vol. 17, No. 6 (November/December 1992), p. 4.
79. Fareed Zakaria, "Is Realism Finished?" *The National Interest*, No. 30 (Winter 1992/93), p. 24.

Back to the Future | *John J. Mearsheimer*

Instability in Europe
After the Cold War

The profound changes now underway in Europe have been widely viewed as harbingers of a new age of peace. With the Cold War over, it is said, the threat of war that has hung over Europe for more than four decades is lifting. Swords can now be beaten into ploughshares; harmony can reign among the states and peoples of Europe. Central Europe, which long groaned under the massive forces of the two military blocs, can convert its military bases into industrial parks, playgrounds, and condominiums. Scholars of security affairs can stop their dreary quarrels over military doctrine and balance assessments, and turn their attention to finding ways to prevent global warming and preserve the ozone layer. European leaders can contemplate how to spend peace dividends. So goes the common view.

This article assesses this optimistic view by exploring in detail the consequences for Europe of an end to the Cold War. Specifically, I examine the effects of a scenario under which the Cold War comes to a complete end. The Soviet Union withdraws all of its forces from Eastern Europe, leaving the states in that region fully independent. Voices are thereupon raised in the United States, Britain, and Germany, arguing that American and British military forces in Germany have lost their principal *raison d'être*, and these forces are withdrawn from the Continent. NATO and the Warsaw Pact then dissolve; they may persist on paper, but each ceases to function as an alliance.[1] As a result, the bipolar structure that has characterized Europe since

This article emerged from a paper written for a February 1990 conference at Ditchley Park, England, on the future of Europe, organized by James Callaghan, Gerald Ford, Valéry Giscard d'Estaing, and Helmut Schmidt. An abridged version of this article appears in the *Atlantic*, August 1990. I am grateful to Robert Art, Stacy Bergstrom, Richard Betts, Anne-Marie Burley, Dale Copeland, Michael Desch, Markus Fischer, Henk Goemans, Joseph Grieco, Ted Hopf, Craig Koerner, Andrew Kydd, Alicia Levine, James Nolt, Roger Petersen, Barry Posen, Denny Roy, Jack Snyder, Ashley Tellis, Marc Trachtenberg, Stephen Van Evera, Andrew Wallace, and Stephen Walt for their most helpful comments.

John Mearsheimer is Professor and Chair of the Department of Political Science, University of Chicago.

1. There is considerable support within NATO's higher circles, including the Bush administration, for maintaining NATO beyond the Cold War. NATO leaders have not clearly articulated the concrete goals that NATO would serve in a post–Cold War Europe, but they appear to conceive the future NATO as a means for ensuring German security, thereby removing possible German motives for aggressive policies; and as a means to protect other NATO states against

International Security, Summer 1990 (Vol. 15, No. 1)
© 1990 by the President and Fellows of Harvard College and of the Massachusetts Institute of Technology.

the end of World War II is replaced by a multipolar structure. In essence, the Cold War we have known for almost half a century is over, and the postwar order in Europe is ended.[2]

How would such a fundamental change affect the prospects for peace in Europe?[3] Would it raise or lower the risk of war?

I argue that the prospects for major crises and war in Europe are likely to increase markedly if the Cold War ends and this scenario unfolds. The next decades in a Europe without the superpowers would probably not be as violent as the first 45 years of this century, but would probably be substantially more prone to violence than the past 45 years.

This pessimistic conclusion rests on the argument that the distribution and character of military power are the root causes of war and peace. Specifically, the absence of war in Europe since 1945 has been a consequence of three factors: the bipolar distribution of military power on the Continent; the rough military equality between the two states comprising the two poles in Europe,

---

German aggression. However, the Germans, who now provide the largest portion of the Alliance's standing forces, are likely to resist such a role for NATO. A security structure of this sort assumes that Germany cannot be trusted and that NATO must be maintained to keep it in line. A united Germany is not likely to accept for very long a structure that rests on this premise. Germans accepted NATO throughout the Cold War because it secured Germany against the Soviet threat that developed in the wake of World War II. Without that specific threat, which now appears to be diminishing rapidly, Germany is likely to reject the continued maintenance of NATO as we know it.

2. I am not arguing that a complete end to the Cold War is inevitable; also quite likely is an intermediate outcome, under which the status quo is substantially modified, but the main outlines of the current order remain in place. Specifically, the Soviet Union may withdraw much of its force from Eastern Europe, but leave significant forces behind. If so, NATO force levels would probably shrink markedly, but NATO may continue to maintain significant forces in Germany. Britain and the United States would withdraw some but not all of their troops from the Continent. If this outcome develops, the basic bipolar military competition that has defined the map of Europe throughout the Cold War will continue. I leave this scenario unexamined, and instead explore what follows from a complete end to the Cold War in Europe because this latter scenario is the less examined of the two, and because the consequences, and therefore the desirability, of completely ending the Cold War would still remain an issue if the intermediate outcome occurred.

3. The impact of such a change on human rights in Eastern Europe will not be considered directly in this article. Eastern Europeans have suffered great hardship as a result of the Soviet occupation. The Soviets have imposed oppressive political regimes on the region, denying Eastern Europeans basic freedoms. Soviet withdrawal from Eastern Europe will probably change that situation for the better, although the change is likely to be more of a mixed blessing than most realize. First, it is not clear that communism will be promptly replaced in all Eastern European countries with political systems that place a high premium on protecting minority rights and civil liberties. Second, the longstanding blood feuds among the nationalities in Eastern Europe are likely to re-emerge in a multipolar Europe, regardless of the existing political order. If wars break out in Eastern Europe, human rights are sure to suffer.

the United States and the Soviet Union; and the fact that each superpower was armed with a large nuclear arsenal.[4] Domestic factors also affect the likelihood of war, and have helped cause the postwar peace. Most importantly, hyper-nationalism helped cause the two world wars, and the decline of nationalism in Europe since 1945 has contributed to the peacefulness of the postwar world. However, factors of military power have been most important in shaping past events, and will remain central in the future.

The departure of the superpowers from Central Europe would transform Europe from a bipolar to a multipolar system.[5] Germany, France, Britain, and perhaps Italy would assume major power status; the Soviet Union would decline from superpower status but would remain a major European power, giving rise to a system of five major powers and a number of lesser powers. The resulting system would suffer the problems common to multipolar systems, and would therefore be more prone to instability.[6] Power inequities could also appear; if so, stability would be undermined further.

The departure of the superpowers would also remove the large nuclear arsenals they now maintain in Central Europe. This would remove the pacifying effect that these weapons have had on European politics. Four principal scenarios are possible. Under the first scenario, Europe would become nuclear-free, thus eliminating a central pillar of order in the Cold War era. Under the second scenario, the European states do not expand their arsenals to compensate for the departure of the superpowers' weapons. In a third scenario, nuclear proliferation takes place, but is mismanaged; no steps are

---

4. It is commonplace to characterize the polarity—bipolar or multipolar—of the international system at large, not a specific region. The focus in this article, however, is not on the global distribution of power, but on the distribution of power in Europe. Polarity arguments can be used to assess the prospects for stability in a particular region, provided the global and regional balances are distinguished from one another and the analysis is focused on the structure of power in the relevant region.
5. To qualify as a pole in a global or regional system, a state must have a reasonable prospect of defending itself against the leading state in the system by its own efforts. The United States and the Soviet Union have enjoyed clear military superiority over other European states, and all non-European states, throughout the Cold War; hence they have formed the two poles of both the global and European systems. What is happening to change this is that both the Soviet Union and the United States are moving forces out of Central Europe, which makes it more difficult for them to project power on the Continent and thus weakens their influence there; and reducing the size of those forces, leaving them less military power to project. Because of its proximity to Europe, the Soviet Union will remain a pole in the European system as long as it retains substantial military forces on its own territory. The United States can remain a pole in Europe only if it retains the capacity to project significant military power into Central Europe.
6. Stability is simply defined as the absence of wars and major crises.

taken to dampen the many dangers inherent in the proliferation process. All three of these scenarios would raise serious risks of war.

In the fourth and least dangerous scenario, nuclear weapons proliferate in Europe, but the process is well-managed by the current nuclear powers. They take steps to deter preventive strikes on emerging nuclear powers, to set boundaries on the proliferation process by extending security umbrellas over the neighbors of emerging nuclear powers, to help emerging nuclear powers build secure deterrent forces, and to discourage them from deploying counterforce systems that threaten their neighbors' deterrents. This outcome probably provides the best hope for maintaining peace in Europe. However, it would still be more dangerous than the world of 1945–90. Moreover, it is not likely that proliferation would be well-managed.

Three counter-arguments might be advanced against this pessimistic set of predictions of Europe's future. The first argument holds that the peace will be preserved by the effects of the liberal international economic order that has evolved since World War II. The second rests on the observation that liberal democracies very seldom fight wars against each other, and holds that the past spread of democracy in Europe has bolstered peace, and that the ongoing democratization of Eastern Europe makes war still less likely. The third argument maintains that Europeans have learned from their disastrous experiences in this century that war, whether conventional or nuclear, is so costly that it is no longer a sensible option for states.

But the theories behind these arguments are flawed, as I explain; hence their prediction of peace in a multipolar Europe is flawed as well.

Three principal policy prescriptions follow from this analysis. First, the United States should encourage a process of limited nuclear proliferation in Europe. Specifically, Europe will be more stable if Germany acquires a secure nuclear deterrent, but proliferation does not go beyond that point. Second, the United States should not withdraw fully from Europe, even if the Soviet Union pulls its forces out of Eastern Europe. Third, the United States should take steps to forestall the re-emergence of hyper-nationalism in Europe.

METHODOLOGY: HOW SHOULD WE THINK ABOUT EUROPE'S FUTURE?
Predictions on the future risk of war and prescriptions about how best to maintain peace should rest on general theories about the causes of war and peace. This point is true for both academics and policymakers. The latter are seldom self-conscious in their uses of theory. Nevertheless, policymakers'

views on the future of Europe are shaped by their implicit preference for one theory of international relations over another. Our task, then, is to decide which theories best explain the past, and will most directly apply to the future; and then to employ these theories to explore the consequences of probable scenarios.

Specifically, we should first survey the inventory of international relations theories that bear on the problem. What theories best explain the period of violence before the Cold War? What theories best explain the peace of the past 45 years? Are there other theories that explain little about pre–Cold War Europe, or Cold War Europe, but are well-suited for explaining what is likely to occur in a Europe without a Soviet and American military presence?

Next, we should ask what these theories predict about the nature of international politics in a post–Cold War multipolar Europe. Will the causes of the postwar peace persist, will the causes of the two world wars return, or will other causes arise?

We can then assess whether we should expect the next decades to be more peaceful, or at least as peaceful, as the past 45 years, or whether the future is more likely to resemble the first 45 years of the century. We can also ask what policy prescriptions these theories suggest.

The study of international relations, like the other social sciences, does not yet resemble the hard sciences. Our stock of theories is spotty and often poorly tested. The conditions required for the operation of established theories are often poorly understood. Moreover, political phenomena are highly complex; hence precise political predictions are impossible without very powerful theoretical tools, superior to those we now possess. As a result, all political forecasting is bound to include some error. Those who venture to predict, as I do here, should therefore proceed with humility, take care not to claim unwarranted confidence, and admit that later hindsight will undoubtedly reveal surprises and mistakes.

Nevertheless, social science *should* offer predictions on the occurrence of momentous and fluid events like those now unfolding in Europe. Predictions can inform policy discourse. They help even those who disagree to frame their ideas, by clarifying points of disagreement. Moreover, predictions of events soon to unfold provide the best tests of social science theories, by making clear what it was that given theories have predicted about those events. In short, the world can be used as a laboratory to decide which theories best explain international politics. In this article I employ the body of theories that I find most persuasive to peer into the future. Time will reveal whether these theories in fact have much power to explain international politics.

The next section offers an explanation for the peacefulness of the post–World War II order. The section that follows argues that the end of the Cold War is likely to lead to a less stable Europe. Next comes an examination of the theories underlying claims that a multipolar Europe is likely to be as peaceful, if not more peaceful, than Cold War Europe. The concluding section suggests policy implications that follow from my analysis.

Explaining the "Long Peace"

The past 45 years represent the longest period of peace in European history.[7] During these years Europe saw no major war, and only two minor conflicts (the 1956 Soviet intervention in Hungary and the 1974 Greco-Turkish war in Cyprus). Neither conflict threatened to widen to other countries. The early years of the Cold War (1945–63) were marked by a handful of major crises, although none brought Europe to the brink of war. Since 1963, however, there have been no East-West crises in Europe. It has been difficult—if not impossible—for the last two decades to find serious national security analysts who have seen a real chance that the Soviet Union would attack Western Europe.

The Cold War peace contrasts sharply with European politics during the first 45 years of this century, which saw two world wars, a handful of minor wars, and a number of crises that almost resulted in war. Some 50 million Europeans were killed in the two world wars; in contrast, probably no more than 15,000 died in the two post-1945 European conflicts.[8] Cold War Europe is far more peaceful than early twentieth-century Europe.

Both Europeans and Americans increasingly assume that peace and calm are the natural order of things in Europe and that the first 45 years of this century, not the most recent, were the aberration. This is understandable,

---

7. The term "long peace" was coined by John Lewis Gaddis, "The Long Peace: Elements of Stability in the Postwar International System," *International Security*, Vol. 10, No. 4 (Spring 1986), pp. 99–142.
8. There were approximately 10,000 battle deaths in the Russo-Hungarian War of October–November 1956, and some 1500–5000 battle deaths in the July–August 1974 war in Cyprus. See Ruth Leger Sivard, *World Military and Social Expenditures 1989* (Washington, D.C.: World Priorities, 1989), p. 22; and Melvin Small and J. David Singer, *Resort to Arms: International and Civil Wars, 1816–1980* (Beverly Hills, Calif.: Sage, 1982), pp. 93–94.

since Europe has been free of war for so long that an ever-growing proportion of the Western public, born after World War II, has no direct experience with great-power war. However, this optimistic view is incorrect.

The European state system has been plagued with war since its inception. During much of the seventeenth and eighteenth centuries war was underway somewhere on the European Continent.[9] The nineteenth century held longer periods of peace, but also several major wars and crises. The first half of that century witnessed the protracted and bloody Napoleonic Wars; later came the Crimean War, and the Italian and German wars of unification.[10] The wars of 1914–45 continued this long historical pattern. They represented a break from the events of previous centuries only in the enormous increase in their scale of destruction.

This era of warfare came to an abrupt end with the conclusion of World War II. A wholly new and remarkably peaceful order then developed on the Continent.

THE CAUSES OF THE LONG PEACE: MILITARY POWER AND STABILITY

What caused the era of violence before 1945? Why has the postwar era been so much more peaceful? The wars before 1945 each had their particular and unique causes, but the distribution of power in Europe—its multipolarity and the imbalances of power that often occurred among the major states in that multipolar system—was the crucial permissive condition that allowed these particular causes to operate. The peacefulness of the postwar era arose for three principal reasons: the bipolarity of the distribution of power on the Continent, the rough equality in military power between those two polar states, and the appearance of nuclear weapons, which vastly expanded the violence of war, making deterrence far more robust.[11]

---

9. For inventories of past wars, see Jack S. Levy, *War In the Modern Great Power System, 1495–1975* (Lexington: University Press of Kentucky, 1983); and Small and Singer, *Resort to Arms*.

10. Europe saw no major war from 1815–1853 and from 1871–1914, two periods almost as long as the 45 years of the Cold War. There is a crucial distinction, however, between the Cold War and these earlier periods. Relations among the great powers deteriorated markedly in the closing years of the two earlier periods, leading in each case to a major war. On the other hand, the Cold War order has become increasingly stable with the passage of time and there is now no serious threat of war between NATO and the Warsaw Pact. Europe would surely remain at peace for the foreseeable future if the Cold War were to continue, a point that highlights the exceptional stability of the present European order.

11. The relative importance of these three factors cannot be stated precisely, but all three had substantial importance.

These factors are aspects of the European state system—of the character of military power and its distribution among states—and not of the states themselves. Thus the keys to war and peace lie more in the structure of the international system than in the nature of the individual states. Domestic factors—most notably hyper-nationalism—also helped cause the wars of the pre-1945 era, and the domestic structures of post-1945 European states have been more conducive to peace, but these domestic factors were less important than the character and distribution of military power between states. Moreover, hyper-nationalism was caused in large part by security competition among the European states, which compelled European elites to mobilize publics to support national defense efforts; hence even this important domestic factor was a more remote consequence of the international system.

Conflict is common among states because the international system creates powerful incentives for aggression.[12] The root cause of the problem is the anarchic nature of the international system. In anarchy there is no higher body or sovereign that protects states from one another. Hence each state living under anarchy faces the ever-present possibility that another state will use force to harm or conquer it. Offensive military action is always a threat to all states in the system.

Anarchy has two principal consequences. First, there is little room for trust among states because a state may be unable to recover if its trust is betrayed. Second, each state must guarantee its own survival since no other actor will provide its security. All other states are potential threats, and no international institution is capable of enforcing order or punishing powerful aggressors.

States seek to survive under anarchy by maximizing their power relative to other states, in order to maintain the means for self-defense. Relative power, not absolute levels of power, matters most to states. Thus, states seek opportunities to weaken potential adversaries and improve their relative power position. They sometimes see aggression as the best way to accumulate more power at the expense of rivals.

This competitive world is peaceful when it is obvious that the costs and risks of going to war are high, and the benefits of going to war are low. Two aspects of military power are at the heart of this incentive structure: the distribution of power between states, and the nature of the military power

---

12. The two classic works on this subject are Hans J. Morgenthau, *Politics Among Nations: The Struggle for Power and Peace*, 5th ed. (New York: Knopf, 1973); and Kenneth N. Waltz, *Theory of International Politics* (Reading, Mass.: Addison-Wesley, 1979).

available to them. The distribution of power between states tells us how well-positioned states are to commit aggression, and whether other states are able to check their aggression. This distribution is a function of the number of poles in the system, and their relative power. The nature of military power directly affects the costs, risks, and benefits of going to war. If the military weaponry available guarantees that warfare will be very destructive, states are more likely to be deterred by the cost of war.[13] If available weaponry favors the defense over the offense, aggressors are more likely to be deterred by the futility of aggression, and all states feel less need to commit aggression, since they enjoy greater security to begin with, and therefore feel less need to enhance their security by expansion.[14] If available weaponry tends to equalize the relative power of states, aggressors are discouraged from going to war. If military weaponry makes it easier to estimate the relative power of states, unwarranted optimism is discouraged and wars of miscalculation are less likely.

One can establish that peace in Europe during the Cold War has resulted from bipolarity, the approximate military balance between the superpowers, and the presence of large numbers of nuclear weapons on both sides in three ways: first, by showing that the general theories on which it rests are valid; second, by demonstrating that these theories can explain the conflicts of the pre-1945 era and the peace of the post-1945 era; and third, by showing that competing theories cannot account for the postwar peace.

THE VIRTUES OF BIPOLARITY OVER MULTIPOLARITY. The two principal arrangements of power possible among states are bipolarity and multipolarity.[15]

---

13. The prospects for deterrence can also be affected by crisis stability calculations. See John J. Mearsheimer, "A Strategic Misstep: The Maritime Strategy and Deterrence in Europe," *International Security*, Vol. 11, No. 2 (Fall 1986), pp. 6–8.

14. See Robert Jervis, "Cooperation Under the Security Dilemma," *World Politics*, Vol. 30, No. 2 (January 1978), pp. 167–214; and Stephen Van Evera, "Causes of War" (unpub. PhD dissertation, University of California at Berkeley, 1984), chap. 3. As noted below, I believe that the distinction between offensive and defensive weapons and, more generally, the concept of an offense-defense balance, is relevant at the nuclear level. However, I do not believe those ideas are relevant at the conventional level. See John J. Mearsheimer, *Conventional Deterrence* (Ithaca: Cornell University Press, 1983), pp. 25–27.

15. Hegemony represents a third possible distribution. Under a hegemony there is only one major power in the system. The rest are minor powers that cannot challenge the major power, but must act in accordance with the dictates of the major power. Every state would like to gain hegemony, because hegemony confers abundant security: no challenger poses a serious threat. Hegemony is rarely achieved, however, because power tends to be somewhat evenly distributed among states, because threatened states have strong incentives to join together to thwart an aspiring hegemon, and because the costs of expansion usually outrun the benefits before domination is achieved, causing extension to become overextension. Hegemony has never

A bipolar system is more peaceful for three main reasons. First, the number of conflict dyads is fewer, leaving fewer possibilities for war. Second, deterrence is easier, because imbalances of power are fewer and more easily averted. Third, the prospects for deterrence are greater because miscalculations of relative power and of opponents' resolve are fewer and less likely.[16]

In a bipolar system two major powers dominate. The minor powers find it difficult to remain unattached to one of the major powers, because the major powers generally demand allegiance from lesser states. (This is especially true in core geographical areas, less so in peripheral areas.) Furthermore, lesser states have little opportunity to play the major powers off against each other, because when great powers are fewer in number, the system is more rigid. As a result, lesser states are hard-pressed to preserve their autonomy.

In a multipolar system, by contrast, three or more major powers dominate. Minor powers in such a system have considerable flexibility regarding alliance partners and can opt to be free floaters. The exact form of a multipolar system can vary markedly, depending on the number of major and minor powers in the system, and their geographical arrangement.

A bipolar system has only one dyad across which war might break out: only two major powers contend with one another, and the minor powers are not likely to be in a position to attack each other. A multipolar system has many potential conflict situations. Major power dyads are more numerous, each posing the potential for conflict. Conflict could also erupt across dyads involving major and minor powers. Dyads between minor powers could also lead to war. Therefore, *ceteris paribus*, war is more likely in a multipolar system than a bipolar one.

Wars in a multipolar world involving just minor powers or only one major power are not likely to be as devastating as a conflict between two major

---

characterized the European state system at any point since it arose in the seventeenth century, and there is no prospect for hegemony in the foreseeable future; hence hegemony is not relevant to assessing the prospects for peace in Europe.

16. The key works on bipolarity and multipolarity include Thomas J. Christensen and Jack Snyder, "Chain Gangs and Passed Bucks: Predicting Alliance Patterns in Multipolarity," *International Organization*, Vol. 44, No. 2 (Spring 1990), pp. 137–168; Karl W. Deutsch and J. David Singer, "Multipolar Power Systems and International Stability," *World Politics*, Vol. 16, No. 3 (April 1964), pp. 390–406; Richard N. Rosecrance, "Bipolarity, Multipolarity, and the Future," *Journal of Conflict Resolution*, Vol. 10, No. 3 (September 1966), pp. 314–327; Kenneth N. Waltz, "The Stability of a Bipolar World," *Daedalus*, Vol. 93, No. 3 (Summer 1964), pp. 881–909; and Waltz, *Theory of International Politics*, chap. 8. My conclusions about bipolarity are similar to Waltz's, although there are important differences in our explanations, as will be seen below.

powers. However, local wars tend to widen and escalate. Hence there is always a chance that a small war will trigger a general conflict.

Deterrence is more difficult in a multipolar world because power imbalances are commonplace, and when power is unbalanced, the strong become hard to deter.[17] Power imbalances can lead to conflict in two ways. First, two states can gang up to attack a third state. Second, a major power might simply bully a weaker power in a one-on-one encounter, using its superior strength to coerce or defeat the minor state.[18]

Balance of power dynamics can counter such power imbalances, but only if they operate efficiently.[19] No state can dominate another, either by ganging up or by bullying, if the others coalesce firmly against it, but problems of geography or coordination often hinder the formation of such coalitions.[20] These hindrances may disappear in wartime, but are prevalent in peacetime, and can cause deterrence failure, even where an efficient coalition will eventually form to defeat the aggressor on the battlefield.

First, geography sometimes prevents balancing states from putting meaningful pressure on a potential aggressor. For example, a major power may not be able to put effective military pressure on a state threatening to cause trouble, because buffer states lie in between.

In addition, balancing in a multipolar world must also surmount difficult coordination problems. Four phenomena make coordination difficult. First, alliances provide collective goods, hence allies face the formidable dilemmas of collective action. Specifically, each state may try to shift alliance burdens onto the shoulders of its putative allies. Such "buck-passing" is a common feature of alliance politics.[21] It is most common when the number of states

---

17. Although a balance of power is more likely to produce deterrence than an imbalance of power, a balance of power between states does not guarantee that deterrence will obtain. States sometimes find innovative military strategies that allow them to win on the battlefield, even without marked advantage in the balance of raw military capabilities. Furthermore, the broader political forces that move a state towards war sometimes force leaders to pursue very risky military strategies, impelling states to challenge opponents of equal or even superior strength. See Mearsheimer, *Conventional Deterrence*, especially chap. 2.
18. This discussion of polarity assumes that the military strength of the major powers is roughly equal. The consequences of power asymmetries among great powers is discussed below.
19. See Stephen M. Walt, *The Origins of Alliances* (Ithaca: Cornell University Press, 1987); and Waltz, *Theory of International Politics*, pp. 123–128.
20. One exception bears mention: ganging up is still possible under multipolarity in the restricted case where there are only three powers in the system, and thus no allies available for the victim state.
21. See Mancur Olson and Richard Zeckhauser, "An Economic Theory of Alliances," *Review of Economics and Statistics*, Vol. 48, No. 3 (August 1966), pp. 266–279; and Barry R. Posen, *The*

required to form an effective blocking coalition is large. Second, a state faced with two potential adversaries might conclude that a protracted war between those adversaries would weaken both, even if one side triumphed; hence it may stay on the sidelines, hoping thereby to improve its power position relative to each of the combatants. (This strategy can fail, however, if one of the warring states quickly conquers the other and ends up more powerful, not less powerful, than before the war.) Third, some states may opt out of the balancing process because they believe that they will not be targeted by the aggressor, failing to recognize that they face danger until after the aggressor has won some initial victories. Fourth, diplomacy is an uncertain process, and thus it can take time to build a defensive coalition. A potential aggressor may conclude that it can succeed at aggression before the coalition is completed, and further may be prompted to exploit the window of opportunity that this situation presents before it closes.[22]

If these problems of geography and coordination are severe, states can lose faith in the balancing process. If so, they become more likely to bandwagon with the aggressor, since solitary resistance is futile.[23] Thus factors that weaken the balancing process can generate snowball effects that weaken the process still further.

The third major problem with multipolarity lies in its tendency to foster miscalculation of the resolve of opposing individual states, and of the strength of opposing coalitions.

War is more likely when a state underestimates the willingness of an opposing state to stand firm on issues of difference. It then may push the other state too far, expecting the other to concede, when in fact the opponent will choose to fight. Such miscalculation is more likely under multipolarity because the shape of the international order tends to remain fluid, due to the tendency of coalitions to shift. As a result, the international "rules of the road"—norms of state behavior, and agreed divisions of territorial rights and other privileges—tend to change constantly. No sooner are the rules of a given adversarial relationship worked out, than that relationship may become a friendship, a new adversarial relationship may emerge with a previous

---

Sources of Military Doctrine: France, Britain, and Germany between the World Wars (Ithaca: Cornell University Press, 1984).
22. Domestic political considerations can also sometimes impede balancing behavior. For example, Britain and France were reluctant to ally with the Soviet Union in the 1930s because of their deep-seated antipathy to communism.
23. See Walt, *Origins of Alliances*, pp. 28–32, 173–178.

friend or neutral, and new rules must be established. Under these circumstances, one state may unwittingly push another too far, because ambiguities as to national rights and obligations leave a wider range of issues on which a state may miscalculate another's resolve. Norms of state behavior can come to be broadly understood and accepted by all states, even in multipolarity, just as basic norms of diplomatic conduct became generally accepted by the European powers during the eighteenth century. Nevertheless, a well-defined division of rights is generally more difficult when the number of states is large, and relations among them are in flux, as is the case with multipolarity.

War is also more likely when states underestimate the relative power of an opposing coalition, either because they underestimate the number of states who will oppose them, or because they exaggerate the number of allies who will fight on their own side.[24] Such errors are more likely in a system of many states, since states then must accurately predict the behavior of many states, not just one, in order to calculate the balance of power between coalitions.

A bipolar system is superior to a multipolar system on all of these dimensions. Bullying and ganging up are unknown, since only two actors compete. Hence the power asymmetries produced by bullying and ganging up are also unknown. When balancing is required, it is achieved efficiently. States can balance by either internal means—military buildup—or external means—diplomacy and alliances. Under multipolarity states tend to balance by external means; under bipolarity they are compelled to use internal means. Internal means are more fully under state control, hence are more efficient, and are more certain to produce real balance.[25] The problems that attend efforts to balance by diplomatic methods—geographic complications and coordination difficulties—are bypassed. Finally, miscalculation is less likely than in a multipolar world. States are less likely to miscalculate others' resolve, because the rules of the road with the main opponent become settled over time, leading both parties to recognize the limits beyond which they cannot push the other. States also cannot miscalculate the membership of the opposing coalition, since each side faces only one main enemy. Simplicity breeds certainty; certainty bolsters peace.

24. This point is the central theme of Waltz, "The Stability of a Bipolar World." Also see Geoffrey Blainey, *The Causes of War* (New York: Free Press, 1973), chap. 3.
25. Noting the greater efficiency of internal over external balancing is Waltz, *Theory of International Politics*, pp. 163, 168.

There are no empirical studies that provide conclusive evidence of the effects of bipolarity and multipolarity on the likelihood of war. This undoubtedly reflects the difficulty of the task: from its beginning until 1945, the European state system was multipolar, leaving this history barren of comparisons that would reveal the differing effects of multipolarity and bipolarity. Earlier history does afford some apparent examples of bipolar systems, including some that were warlike—Athens and Sparta, Rome and Carthage—but this history is inconclusive, because it is sketchy and incomplete and therefore does not offer enough detail to validate the comparisons. Lacking a comprehensive survey of history, we cannot progress beyond offering examples pro and con, without knowing which set of examples best represents the universe of cases. As a result the case made here stops short of empirical demonstration, and rests chiefly on deduction. However, I believe that this deductive case provides a sound basis for accepting the argument that bipolarity is more peaceful than multipolarity; the deductive logic seems compelling, and there is no obvious historical evidence that cuts against it. I show below that the ideas developed here apply to events in twentieth century Europe, both before and after 1945.

THE VIRTUES OF EQUALITY OF POWER OVER INEQUALITY. Power can be more or less equally distributed among the major powers of both bipolar and multipolar systems. Both systems are more peaceful when equality is greatest among the poles. Power inequalities invite war by increasing the potential for successful aggression; hence war is minimized when inequalities are least.[26]

How should the degree of equality in the distribution of power in a system be assessed? Under bipolarity, the overall equality of the system is simply a function of the balance of power between the two poles—an equal balance creates an equal system, a skewed balance produces an unequal system. Under multipolarity the focus is on the power balance between the two leading states in the system, but the power ratios across other potential conflict dyads also matter. The net system equality is an aggregate of the degree of equality among all of the poles. However, most general wars under multipolarity have arisen from wars of hegemony that have pitted the leading state—an aspiring hegemon—against the other major powers in the system. Such wars are most probable when a leading state emerges, and can hope

---

26. This discussion does not encompass the situation where power asymmetries are so great that one state emerges as a hegemon. See note 15.

to defeat each of the others if it can isolate them. This pattern characterized the wars that grew from the attempts at hegemony by Charles V, Philip II, Louis XIV, Revolutionary and Napoleonic France, Wilhelmine Germany, and Nazi Germany.[27] Hence the ratio between the leader and its nearest competitor—in bipolarity or multipolarity—has more effect on the stability of the system than do other ratios, and is therefore the key ratio that describes the equality of the system. Close equality in this ratio lowers the risk of war.

The polarity of an international system and the degree of power equality of the system are related: bipolar systems tend more toward equality, because, as noted above, states are then compelled to balance by internal methods, and internal balancing is more efficient than external balancing. Specifically, the number-two state in a bipolar system can only hope to balance against the leader by mobilizing its own resources to reduce the gap between the two, since it has no potential major alliance partners. On the other hand, the second-strongest state in a multipolar system can seek security through alliances with others, and may be tempted to pass the buck to them, instead of building up its own strength. External balancing of this sort is especially attractive because it is cheap and fast. However, such behavior leaves intact the power gap between the two leading states, and thus leaves in place the dangers that such a power gap creates. Hence another source of stability under bipolarity lies in the greater tendency for its poles to be equal.

THE VIRTUES OF NUCLEAR DETERRENCE. Deterrence is most likely to hold when the costs and risks of going to war are obviously great. The more horrible the prospect of war, the less likely it is to occur. Deterrence is also most robust when conquest is most difficult. Aggressors then are more likely to be deterred by the futility of expansion, and all states feel less compelled to expand to increase their security, making them easier to deter because they are less compelled to commit aggression.

---

27. This point is the central theme of Ludwig Dehio, *The Precarious Balance: Four Centuries of the European Power Struggle*, trans. Charles Fullman (New York: Knopf, 1962). Also see Randolph M. Siverson and Michael R. Tennefoss, "Power, Alliance, and the Escalation of International Conflict, 1815–1965," *American Political Science Review*, Vol. 78, No. 4 (December 1984), pp. 1057–1069. The two lengthy periods of peace in the nineteenth century (see note 10 above) were mainly caused by the equal distribution of power among the major European states. Specifically, there was no aspiring hegemon in Europe for most of these two periods. France, the most powerful state in Europe at the beginning of the nineteenth century, soon declined to a position of rough equality with its chief competitors, while Germany only emerged as a potential hegemon in the early twentieth century.

Nuclear weapons favor peace on both counts. They are weapons of mass destruction, and would produce horrendous devastation if used in any numbers. Moreover, if both sides' nuclear arsenals are secure from attack, creating a mutually assured retaliation capability (mutual assured destruction or MAD), nuclear weapons make conquest more difficult; international conflicts revert from tests of capability and will to purer tests of will, won by the side willing to run greater risks and pay greater costs. This gives defenders the advantage, because defenders usually value their freedom more than aggressors value new conquests. Thus nuclear weapons are a superb deterrent: they guarantee high costs, and are more useful for self-defense than for aggression.[28]

In addition, nuclear weapons affect the degree of equality in the system. Specifically, the situation created by MAD bolsters peace by moving power relations among states toward equality. States that possess nuclear deterrents can stand up to one another, even if their nuclear arsenals vary greatly in size, as long as both sides' nuclear arsenals are secure from attack. This situation of closer equality has the stabilizing effects noted above.

Finally, MAD also bolsters peace by clarifying the relative power of states and coalitions.[29] States can still miscalculate each other's will, but miscalculations of relative capability are less likely, since nuclear capabilities are not elastic to the specific size and characteristics of forces; once an assured destruction capability is achieved, further increments of nuclear power have little strategic importance. Hence errors in assessing these specific characteristics have little effect. Errors in predicting membership in war coalitions also have less effect, since unforeseen additions or subtractions from such coalitions will not influence war outcomes unless they produce a huge change in the nuclear balance—enough to give one side meaningful nuclear superiority.

THE DANGERS OF HYPER-NATIONALISM. Nationalism is best defined as a set of political beliefs which holds that a nation—a body of individuals with characteristics that purportedly distinguish them from other individuals—

---

28. Works developing the argument that nuclear weapons are essentially defensive in nature are Shai Feldman, *Israeli Nuclear Deterrence: A Strategy for the 1980s* (New York: Columbia University Press, 1982), pp. 45–49; Stephen Van Evera, "Why Europe Matters, Why the Third World Doesn't: American Grand Strategy after the Cold War," *Journal of Strategic Studies*, Vol. 13, No. 2 (June 1990, forthcoming); and Van Evera, "Causes of War," chap. 13.

29. See Feldman, *Israeli Nuclear Deterrence*, pp. 50–52; and Van Evera, "Causes of War," pp. 697–699.

should have its own state.[30] Although nationalists often believe that their nation is unique or special, this conclusion does not necessarily mean that they think they are superior to other peoples, merely that they take pride in their own nation.

However, this benevolent nationalism frequently turns into ugly hyper-nationalism—the belief that other nations or nation-states are both inferior and threatening and must therefore be dealt with harshly. In the past, hyper-nationalism among European states has arisen largely because most European states are nation-states—states comprised of one principal nation—and these nation-states exist in an anarchic world, under constant threat from other states. In such a situation people who love their own nation and state can develop an attitude of contempt and loathing toward the nations who inhabit opposing states. The problem is exacerbated by the fact that political elites often feel compelled to portray adversary nations in the most negative way so as to mobilize public support for national security policies.

Malevolent nationalism is most likely to develop under military systems that require reliance on mass armies; the state may exploit nationalist appeals to mobilize its citizenry for the sacrifices required to sustain large standing armies. On the other hand, hyper-nationalism is least likely when states can rely on small professional armies, or on complex high-technology military organizations that do not require vast manpower. For this reason nuclear weapons work to dampen nationalism, since they shift the basis of military power away from pure reliance on mass armies, and toward greater reliance on smaller high-technology organizations.

In sum, hyper-nationalism is the most important domestic cause of war, although it is still a second-order force in world politics. Furthermore, its causes lie largely in the international system.

THE CAUSES OF THE LONG PEACE: EVIDENCE

The historical record shows a perfect correlation between bipolarity, equality of military power, and nuclear weapons, on the one hand, and the long peace, on the other hand. When an equal bipolarity arose and nuclear weapons appeared, peace broke out. This correlation suggests that the bipolarity

---

30. This definition is drawn from Ernest Gellner, *Nations and Nationalism* (Ithaca: Cornell University Press, 1983), which is an excellent study of the origins of nationalism. Nevertheless, Gellner pays little attention to how nationalism turns into a malevolent force that contributes to instability in the international system.

theory, the equality theory, and the nuclear theory of the long peace are all valid. However, correlation alone does not prove causation. Other factors still may account for the long peace. One way to rule out this possibility is to enumerate what the three theories predict about both the pre-war and postwar eras, and then to ask if these predictions came true in detail during those different periods.

BEFORE THE COLD WAR. The dangers of multipolarity are highlighted by events before both world wars. The existence of many dyads of potential conflict provided many possible ways to light the fuse to war in Europe. Diplomacy before World War I involved intense interactions among five major powers (Britain, France, Russia, Austria-Hungary, and Germany), and two minor powers (Serbia, and Belgium). At least six significant adversarial relationships emerged: Germany versus Britain, France, Russia, and Belgium; and Austria-Hungary versus Serbia and Russia. Before World War II five major powers (Britain, France, the Soviet Union, Germany, and Italy) and seven minor powers (Belgium, Poland, Czechoslovakia, Austria, Hungary, Romania, and Finland) interacted. These relations produced some thirteen important conflicts: Germany versus Britain, France, the Soviet Union, Czechoslovakia, Poland, and Austria; Italy versus Britain and France; the Soviet Union versus Finland and Poland; Czechoslovakia versus Poland and Hungary; and Romania versus Hungary. This multiplicity of conflicts made the outbreak of war inherently more likely. Moreover, many of the state interests at issue in each of these conflicts were interconnected, raising the risk that any single conflict that turned violent would trigger a general war, as happened in both 1914 and 1939.

Before World War II Germany was able to gang up with others against some minor states, and to bully others into joining with it. In 1939 Germany bolstered its power by ganging up with Poland and Hungary to partition Czechoslovakia, and then ganged up with the Soviet Union against Poland. In 1938 Germany bullied the Czechs into surrendering the Sudetenland, and also bullied the Austrians into complete surrender.[31] By these successes Germany expanded its power, leaving it far stronger than its immediate neighbors, and thereby making deterrence much harder.

German power could have been countered before both world wars had the other European powers balanced efficiently against Germany. If so, Ger-

---

31. Austria is not a pure case of bullying; there was also considerable pro-German support in Austria during the late 1930s.

many might have been deterred, and war prevented on both occasions. However, the other powers twice failed to do so. Before 1914 the scope of this failure was less pronounced; France and Russia balanced forcefully against Germany, while only Britain failed to commit firmly against Germany before war began.[32]

Before 1939, failure to balance was far more widespread.[33] The Soviet Union failed to aid Czechoslovakia against Germany in 1938, partly for geographic reasons: they shared no common border, leaving the Soviets with no direct access to Czech territory. France failed to give effective aid to the Czechs and Poles, partly because French military doctrine was defensively oriented, but also because France had no direct access to Czech or Polish territory, and therefore could not easily deploy forces to bolster Czech and Polish defenses.

Britain and France each passed the buck by transferring the cost of deterring Germany onto the other, thereby weakening their combined effort. The Soviet Union, with the Molotov-Ribbentrop Pact, sought to turn the German armies westward, hoping that they would become bogged down in a war of attrition similar to World War I on the Western Front. Some of the minor European powers, including Belgium, the Netherlands, Denmark, and the Scandinavian states, passed the buck to the major powers by standing on the sidelines during the crises of 1938 and 1939.

Britain and the United States failed to recognize that they were threatened by Germany until late in the game—1939 for Britain, 1940 for the United States—and they therefore failed to take an early stand. When they finally recognized the danger posed by Germany and resolved to respond, they lacked appropriate military forces. Britain could not pose a significant military threat to Germany until after it built up its own military forces and coordinated its plans and doctrine with its French and Polish allies. In the meantime

---

32. Britain's failure to commit itself explicitly to a Continental war before the July Crisis was probably a mistake of great proportions. There is evidence that the German chancellor, Bethmann-Hollweg, tried to stop the slide towards war once it became apparent that Britain would fight with France and Russia against Germany, turning a Continental war into a world war. See Imanuel Geiss, ed., *July 1914: The Outbreak of the First World War* (New York: Norton, 1967), chap. 7. Had the Germans clearly understood British intentions before the crisis, they might have displayed much greater caution in the early stages of the crisis, when it was still possible to avoid war.

33. See Williamson Murray, *The Change in the European Balance of Power, 1938–1939: The Path to Ruin* (Princeton: Princeton University Press, 1984); Posen, *Sources of Military Doctrine;* and Arnold Wolfers, *Britain and France between Two Wars: Conflicting Strategies of Peace from Versailles to World War II* (New York: Norton, 1968); and Barry R. Posen, "Competing Images of the Soviet Union," *World Politics*, Vol. 39, No. 4 (July 1987), pp. 579–597.

deterrence failed. The United States did not launch a significant military buildup until after the war broke out.

Multipolarity also created conditions that permitted serious miscalculation before both world wars, which encouraged German aggression on both occasions. Before 1914, Germany was not certain of British opposition if it reached for continental hegemony, and Germany completely failed to foresee that the United States would eventually move to contain it. In 1939, Germany hoped that France and Britain would stand aside as it conquered Poland, and again failed to foresee eventual American entry into the war. As a result Germany exaggerated its prospects for success. This undermined deterrence by encouraging German adventurism.

In sum, the events leading up to the world wars amply illustrate the risks that arise in a multipolar world. Deterrence was undermined in both cases by phenomena that are more common under a multipolar rather than a bipolar distribution of power.[34]

Deterrence was also difficult before both wars because power was distributed asymmetrically among the major European powers. Specifically, Germany was markedly stronger than any of its immediate neighbors. In 1914 Germany clearly held military superiority over all of its European rivals; only together were they able to defeat it, and then only with American help. 1939 is a more ambiguous case. The results of the war reveal that the Soviet Union had the capacity to stand up to Germany, but this was not apparent at the beginning of the war. Hitler was confident that Germany would defeat the Soviet Union, and this confidence was key to his decision to attack in 1941.

Finally, the events leading up to both world wars also illustrate the risks that arise in a world of pure conventional deterrence in which weapons of mass destruction are absent. World War I broke out partly because all of the important states believed that the costs of war would be small, and that successful offense was feasible.[35] Before World War II these beliefs were less widespread, but had the same effect.[36] The lesser powers thought war would

---

34. The problems associated with multipolarity were also common in Europe before 1900. Consider, for example, that inefficient balancing resulted in the collapse of the first four coalitions arrayed against Napoleonic France. See Steven T. Ross, *European Diplomatic History, 1789–1815: France Against Europe* (Garden City, N.Y.: Doubleday, 1969).

35. Stephen Van Evera, "The Cult of the Offensive and the Origins of the First World War," *International Security*, Vol. 9, No. 1 (Summer 1984), pp. 58–107. Also see Jack Snyder, *The Ideology of the Offensive: Military Decision-Making and the Disasters of 1914* (Ithaca: Cornell University Press, 1984).

36. Mearsheimer, *Conventional Deterrence*, chaps. 3–4.

be costly and conquest difficult, but the leaders of the strongest state—Germany—saw the prospect of cheap victory, and this belief was enough to destroy deterrence and produce war. Had nuclear weapons existed, these beliefs would have been undercut, removing a key condition that permitted both wars.

What was the role of internal German politics in causing the world wars? So far I have focused on aspects of the international system surrounding Germany. This focus reflects my view that systemic factors were more important. But German domestic political and social developments also played a significant role, contributing to the aggressive character of German foreign policy. Specifically, German society was infected with a virulent nationalism between 1870 and 1945 that laid the basis for expansionist foreign policies.[37]

However, two points should be borne in mind. First, German hyper-nationalism was in part fueled by Germany's pronounced sense of insecurity, which reflected Germany's vulnerable location at the center of Europe, with relatively open borders on both sides. These geographic facts made German security problems especially acute; this situation gave German elites a uniquely strong motive to mobilize their public for war, which they did largely by fanning nationalism. Thus even German hyper-nationalism can be ascribed in part to the nature of the pre-1945 international system.

Second, the horror of Germany's murderous conduct during World War II should be distinguished from the scope of the aggressiveness of German foreign policy.[38] Germany was indeed aggressive, but not unprecedentedly so. Other states have aspired to hegemony in Europe, and sparked wars by their efforts; Germany was merely the latest to attempt to convert dominant into hegemonic power. What was unique about Germany's conduct was its policy of mass murder toward many of the peoples of Europe. The causes of this murderous policy should not be conflated with the causes of the two

37. See Ludwig Dehio, *Germany and World Politics in the Twentieth Century*, trans. Dieter Pevsner (New York: Norton, 1967); Fritz Fischer, *War of Illusions: German Policies from 1911 to 1914*, trans. Marian Jackson (New York: Norton, 1975); Paul M. Kennedy, *The Rise of the Anglo-German Antagonism, 1860–1914* (London: Allen and Unwin, 1980), chap. 18; Hans Kohn, *The Mind of Germany: The Education of a Nation* (New York: Harper Torchbook, 1965), chaps. 7–12; and Louis L. Snyder, *German Nationalism: The Tragedy of a People* (Harrisburg, Pa.: Telegraph Press, 1952).
38. There is a voluminous literature on the German killing machine in World War II. Among the best overviews of the subject are Ian Kershaw, *The Nazi Dictatorship: Problems and Perspectives of Interpretation*, 2nd ed. (London: Arnold, 1989), chaps. 5, 8, 9; Henry L. Mason, "Imponderables of the Holocaust," *World Politics*, Vol. 34, No. 1 (October 1981), pp. 90–113; and Mason, "Implementing the Final Solution: The Ordinary Regulating of the Extraordinary," *World Politics*, Vol. 40, No. 4 (July 1988), pp. 542–569.

world wars. The policy of murder arose chiefly from domestic sources; the wars arose mainly from aspects of the distribution and character of power in Europe.

THE COLD WAR RECORD. The European state system abruptly shifted from multipolar to bipolar after 1945. Three factors were responsible: the near-complete destruction of German power, the growth of Soviet power, and the permanent American commitment to the European Continent. The weakening of the German Reich was accomplished by allied occupation and dismemberment. Silesia, Pomerania, East Prussia, and parts of West Prussia and Brandenburg were given to other countries, the Sudetenland was returned to Czechoslovakia, and Austria was restored to independence. The rest of the German Reich was divided into two countries, East and West Germany, which became enemies. This reduction of German power, coupled with the physical presence of American and Soviet military might in the heart of Europe, eliminated the threat of German aggression.[39]

Meanwhile the Soviet Union extended its power westward, becoming the dominant power on the Continent and one of the two strongest powers in the world. There is no reason to think that the Soviets would not have reached for continental hegemony, as the Spanish, French, and Germans did earlier, had they believed they could win a hegemonic war. But the Soviets, unlike their predecessors, made no attempt to gain hegemony by force, leaving Europe in peace.

Bipolarity supplies part of the reason. Bipolarity made Europe a simpler place in which only one point of friction—the East-West conflict—had to be managed to avoid war. The two blocs encompassed most of Europe, leaving few unprotected weak states for the Soviets to conquer. As a result the Soviets have had few targets to bully. They have also been unable to gang up on the few states that are unprotected, because their West-bloc adversary has been their only potential ganging-up partner.

Bipolarity also left less room for miscalculation of both resolve and capability. During the first fifteen years of the Cold War, the rules of the road for the conflict were not yet established, giving rise to several serious crises. However, over time each side gained a clear sense of how far it could push the other, and what the other would not tolerate. A set of rules came to be agreed upon: an understanding on the division of rights in Austria, Berlin,

---

39. See Anton W. DePorte, *Europe between the Superpowers: The Enduring Balance,* 2nd ed. (New Haven: Yale University Press, 1986).

and elsewhere in Europe; a proscription on secret unilateral re-deployment of large nuclear forces to areas contiguous to the opponent; mutual toleration of reconnaissance satellites; agreement on rules of peacetime engagement between naval forces; and so forth. The absence of serious crises during 1963–90 was due in part to the growth of such agreements on the rights of both sides, and the rules of conduct. These could develop in large part because the system was bipolar in character. Bipolarity meant that the same two states remained adversaries for a long period, giving them time to learn how to manage their conflict without war. By contrast, a multipolar world of shifting coalitions would repeatedly have forced adversaries to re-learn how their opponents defined interests, reach new accords on the division of rights, and establish new rules of competitive conduct.

Bipolarity also left less room to miscalculate the relative strength of the opposing coalitions. The composition of possible war coalitions has been clear because only two blocs have existed, each led by an overwhelmingly dominant power that could discipline its members. Either side could have miscalculated its relative military strength, but bipolarity removed ambiguity about relative strength of adversarial coalitions arising from diplomatic uncertainties.

The East-West military balance in Europe has been roughly equal throughout the Cold War, which has further bolstered stability. This approximate parity strengthened deterrence by ensuring that no state was tempted to use force to exploit a power advantage. Parity resulted partly from bipolarity: because the two blocs already encompassed all the states of Europe, both sides have balanced mainly by internal rather than external means. These more efficient means have produced a more nearly equal balance.

Nuclear weapons also played a key role in preventing war in post–World War II Europe.

Western elites on both sides of the Atlantic quickly recognized that nuclear weapons were vastly destructive and that their widespread use in Europe would cause unprecedented devastation. The famous *Carte Blanche* exercises conducted in Germany in 1955 made it manifestly clear that a nuclear war in Europe would involve far greater costs than another World War II.[40] Accordingly, Western policymakers rarely suggested that nuclear war could be "won," and instead emphasized the horrors that would attend nuclear war.

---

40. See Hans Speier, *German Rearmament and Atomic War: The Views of German Military and Political Leaders* (Evanston, Ill.: Row, Peterson, 1957), chap. 10.

Moreover, they have understood that conventional war could well escalate to the nuclear level, and have in fact based NATO strategy on that reality.

Soviet leaders also recognized the horrendous results that a nuclear war would produce.[41] Some Soviet military officers have asserted that victory is possible in nuclear war, but even they have acknowledged that such a victory would be Pyrrhic. Soviet civilians have generally argued that victory is impossible. Furthermore, the Soviets long maintained that it was not possible to fight a purely conventional war in Europe, and that conventional victory would only prompt the loser to engage in nuclear escalation.[42] The Soviets later granted more possibility that a conventional war might be controlled, but still recognized that escalation is likely.[43] Under Gorbachev, Soviet military thinking has placed even greater emphasis on the need to avoid nuclear war and devoted more attention to the dangers of inadvertent nuclear war.[44]

Official rhetoric aside, policymakers on both sides have also behaved very cautiously in the presence of nuclear weapons. There is not a single case of a leader brandishing nuclear weapons during a crisis, or behaving as if nuclear war might be a viable option for solving important political problems. On the contrary, policymakers have never gone beyond nuclear threats of a very subtle sort, and have shown great caution when the possibility of nuclear confrontation has emerged.[45] This cautious conduct has lowered the risk of war.

Nuclear weapons also imposed an equality and clarity on the power relations between the superpowers. This equality and clarity represented a

41. See Robert L. Arnett, "Soviet Attitudes Towards Nuclear War: Do They Really Think They Can Win?" *Journal of Strategic Studies*, Vol. 2, No. 2 (September 1979), pp. 172–191; and David Holloway, *The Soviet Union and the Arms Race* (New Haven: Yale University Press, 1983).

42. Thus Nikita Khrushchev explained, "Now that the big countries have thermonuclear weapons at their disposal, they are sure to resort to those weapons if they begin to lose a war fought with conventional means. If it ever comes down to a question of whether or not to face defeat, there is sure to be someone who will be in favor of pushing the button, and the missiles will begin to fly." Nikita Khrushchev, *Khrushchev Remembers: The Last Testament*, trans. and ed. by Strobe Talbott (New York: Bantam, 1976), pp. 603–604.

43. See James M. McConnell, "Shifts in Soviet Views on the Proper Focus of Military Development," *World Politics*, Vol. 37, No. 3 (April 1985), pp. 317–343.

44. See Stephen M. Meyer, "The Sources and Prospects of Gorbachev's New Political Thinking on Security," *International Security*, Vol. 13, No. 2 (Fall 1988), pp. 134–138.

45. See Hannes Adomeit, *Soviet Risk-taking and Crisis Behavior: A Theoretical and Empirical Analysis* (London: Allen and Unwin, 1982); Richard K. Betts, *Nuclear Blackmail and Nuclear Balance* (Washington, D.C.: Brookings, 1987); and McGeorge Bundy, *Danger and Survival: Choices about the Bomb in the First Fifty Years* (New York: Random House, 1988). Also see Joseph S. Nye, Jr., "Nuclear Learning and U.S.-Soviet Security Regimes," *International Organization*, Vol. 41, No. 3 (Summer 1987), pp. 371–402.

marked change from the earlier non-nuclear world, in which sharp power inequalities and miscalculations of relative power were common.[46]

During the Cold War, the United States and the Soviet Union have exhibited markedly less hyper-nationalism than did the European powers before 1945. After World War II, nationalism declined sharply within Europe, partly because the occupation forces took active steps to dampen it,[47] and also because the European states, no longer providing their own security, now lacked the incentive to purvey hyper-nationalism in order to bolster public support for national defense. More importantly, however, the locus of European politics shifted to the United States and the Soviet Union—two states that, each for its own reasons, had not exhibited nationalism of the virulent type found earlier in Europe. Nor has nationalism become virulent in either superpower during the Cold War. In part this reflects the greater stability of the postwar order, arising from bipolarity, military equality, and nuclear weapons; with less expectation of war, neither superpower has faced the need to mobilize its population for war. It also reflects a second effect of nuclear weapons: they have reduced the importance of mass armies for preserving sovereignty, thus diminishing the importance of maintaining a hyper-nationalized pool of manpower.

THE CAUSES OF THE LONG PEACE: COMPETING EXPLANATIONS

The claim that bipolarity, equality, and nuclear weapons have been largely responsible for the stability of the past 45 years is further strengthened by the absence of persuasive competing explanations. Two of the most popular theories of peace—*economic liberalism* and *peace-loving democracies*—are not relevant to the issue at hand.

Economic liberalism, which posits that a liberal economic order bolsters peace (discussed in more detail below), cannot explain the stability of postwar Europe, because there has been little economic exchange between the Soviet Union and the West over the past 45 years. Although economic flows be-

---

46. Some experts acknowledge that nuclear weapons had deterrent value in the early decades of the Cold War, but maintain that they had lost their deterrent value by the mid-1960s when the Soviets finally acquired the capability to retaliate massively against the American homeland. I reject this argument and have outlined my views in John J. Mearsheimer, "Nuclear Weapons and Deterrence in Europe," *International Security*, Vol. 9, No. 3 (Winter 1984/85), pp. 19–46.
47. See Paul M. Kennedy, "The Decline of Nationalistic History in the West, 1900–1970," *Journal of Contemporary History*, Vol. 8, No. 1 (January 1973), pp. 77–100; and E.H. Dance, *History the Betrayer* (London: Hutchinson, 1960).

tween Eastern and Western Europe have been somewhat greater, in no sense has all of Europe been encompassed by a liberal economic order.

The peace-loving democracies theory (also discussed below) holds that democracies do not go to war against other democracies, but concedes that democracies are not especially pacific when facing authoritarian states. This theory cannot account for post–World War II stability because the Soviet Union and its allies in Eastern Europe have not been democratic over the past 45 years.

A third theory of peace, *obsolescence of war*, proposes that modern conventional war had become so deadly by the twentieth century that it was no longer possible to think of war as a sensible means to achieve national goals.[48] It took the two world wars to drive this point home, but by 1945 it was clear that large-scale conventional war had become irrational and morally unacceptable, like institutions such as slavery and dueling. Thus, even without nuclear weapons, statesmen in the Cold War would not seriously have countenanced war, which had become an anachronism. This theory, it should be emphasized, does not ascribe the absence of war to nuclear weapons, but instead points to the horrors of modern conventional war.

This argument probably provides the most persuasive alternative explanation for the stability of the Cold War, but it is not convincing on close inspection. The fact that World War II occurred casts serious doubt on this theory; if any war could have convinced Europeans to forswear conventional war, it should have been World War I, with its vast casualties. There is no doubt that conventional war among modern states could devastate the participants. Nevertheless, this explanation misses one crucial difference between nuclear and conventional war, a difference that explains why war is still a viable option for states. Proponents of this theory assume that all conventional wars are protracted and bloody wars of attrition, like World War I on the Western front. However, it is possible to score a quick and decisive victory in a conventional war and avoid the devastation that usually attends a protracted conventional war.[49] Conventional war can be won; nuclear war cannot be, since neither side can escape devastation by the other, regardless of the outcome on the battlefield. Thus, the incentives to avoid

---

48. This theory is most clearly articulated by John E. Mueller, *Retreat from Doomsday: The Obsolescence of Major War* (New York: Basic Books, 1989). See also Carl Kaysen, "Is War Obsolete? A Review Essay," *International Security,* Vol. 14, No. 4 (Spring 1990), pp. 42–64.
49. See Mearsheimer, *Conventional Deterrence,* chaps. 1–2.

war are far greater in a nuclear than a conventional world, making nuclear deterrence much more robust than conventional deterrence.[50]

Predicting the Future: The Balkanization of Europe?

What new order will emerge in Europe if the Soviets and Americans withdraw to their homelands and the Cold War order dissolves? What characteristics will it have? How dangerous will it be?

It is certain that bipolarity will disappear, and multipolarity will emerge in the new European order. The other two dimensions of the new order—the distribution of power among the major states, and the distribution of nuclear weapons among them—are not pre-determined, and several possible arrangements could develop. The probable stability of these arrangements would vary markedly. This section examines the scope of the dangers that each arrangement would present, and the likelihood that each will emerge.

The distribution and deployment patterns of nuclear weapons in the new Europe is the least certain, and probably the most important, element of the new order. Accordingly, this section proceeds by exploring the character of the four principal nuclear worlds that might develop: a denuclearized Europe, continuation of the current patterns of nuclear ownership, and nuclear proliferation either well- or ill-managed.

The best new order would incorporate the limited, managed proliferation of nuclear weapons. This would be more dangerous than the current order, but considerably safer than 1900–45. The worst order would be a non-nuclear Europe in which power inequities emerge between the principal poles of power. This order would be more dangerous than the current world, perhaps almost as dangerous as the world before 1945. Continuation of the current

---

50. German decision-making in the early years of World War II underscores this point. See Mearsheimer, *Conventional Deterrence*, chap. 4. The Germans were well aware from their experience in World War I that conventional war among major powers could have devastating consequences. Nevertheless, they decided three times to launch major land offensives: Poland (1939); France (1940); and the Soviet Union (1941). In each case, the Germans believed that they could win a quick and decisive victory and avoid a costly protracted war like World War I. Their calculations proved correct against Poland and France. They were wrong about the Soviets, who thwarted their blitzkrieg and eventually played the central role in bringing down the Third Reich. The Germans surely would have been deterred from attacking the Soviet Union if they had foreseen the consequences. However, the key point is that they saw some possibility of winning an easy and relatively cheap victory against the Red Army. That option is not available in a nuclear war.

pattern, or mismanaged proliferation, would be worse than the world of today, but safer than the pre-1945 world.

EUROPE WITHOUT NUCLEAR WEAPONS

Some Europeans and Americans seek to eliminate nuclear weapons from Europe, and would replace the Cold War order with a wholly non-nuclear order. Constructing this nuclear-free Europe would require Britain, France and the Soviet Union to rid themselves of nuclear weapons. Proponents believe that a Europe without nuclear weapons would be the most peaceful possible arrangement; in fact, however, a nuclear-free Europe would be the most dangerous among possible post–Cold War orders. The pacifying effects of nuclear weapons—the security they provide, the caution they generate, the rough equality they impose, and the clarity of relative power they create— would be lost. Peace would then depend on the other dimensions of the new order—the number of poles, and the distribution of power among them. However, the new order will certainly be multipolar, and may be unequal; hence the system may be very prone to violence. The structure of power in Europe would look much like it did between the world wars, and it could well produce similar results.

The two most powerful states in post–Cold War Europe would probably be Germany and the Soviet Union. They would be physically separated by a band of small, independent states in Eastern Europe. Not much would change in Western Europe, although the states in that area would have to be concerned about a possible German threat on their eastern flank.

The potential for conflict in this system would be considerable. There would be many possible dyads across which war might break out. Power imbalances would be commonplace as a result of the opportunities this system would present for bullying and ganging up. There would be considerable opportunity for miscalculation. The problem of containing German power would emerge once again, but the configuration of power in Europe would make it difficult to form an effective counterbalancing coalition, for much the same reason that an effective counterbalancing coalition failed to form in the 1930s. Eventually the problem of containing the Soviet Union could also re-emerge. Finally, conflicts may erupt in Eastern Europe, providing the vortex that could pull others into a wider confrontation.

A reunified Germany would be surrounded by weaker states that would find it difficult to balance against German aggression. Without forces stationed in states adjacent to Germany, neither the Soviets nor the Americans would be in a good position to help them contain German power. Furthermore, those small states lying between Germany and the Soviet Union might fear the Soviets as much as the Germans, and hence may not be disposed to cooperate with the Soviets to deter German aggression. This problem in fact arose in the 1930s, and 45 years of Soviet occupation in the interim have done nothing to ease East European fears of a Soviet military presence. Thus, scenarios in which Germany uses military force against Poland, Czechoslovakia, or even Austria become possible.

The Soviet Union also might eventually threaten the new status quo. Soviet withdrawal from Eastern Europe does not mean that the Soviets will never feel compelled to return to Eastern Europe. The historical record provides abundant instances of Russian or Soviet involvement in Eastern Europe. Indeed, the Russian presence in Eastern Europe has surged and ebbed repeatedly over the past few centuries.[51] Thus, Soviet withdrawal now hardly guarantees a permanent exit.

Conflict between Eastern European states is also likely to produce instability in a multipolar Europe. There has been no war among the states in that region during the Cold War because the Soviets have tightly controlled them. This point is illustrated by the serious tensions that now exist between Hungary and Romania over Romanian treatment of the Hungarian minority in Transylvania, a region that previously belonged to Hungary and still has roughly 2 million Hungarians living within its borders. Were it not for the Soviet presence in Eastern Europe, this conflict could have brought Romania and Hungary to war by now, and it may bring them to war in the future.[52] This will not be the only danger spot within Eastern Europe if the Soviet empire crumbles.[53]

Warfare in Eastern Europe would cause great suffering to Eastern Europeans. It also might widen to include the major powers, because they would

51. See, inter alia: Ivo J. Lederer, ed., *Russian Foreign Policy: Essays in Historical Perspective* (New Haven: Yale University Press, 1962); Andrei Lobanov-Rostovsky, *Russia and Europe, 1825–1878* (Ann Arbor, Mich.: George Wahr Publishing, 1954); and Marc Raeff, *Imperial Russia, 1682–1825: The Coming of Age of Modern Russia* (New York: Knopf, 1971), chap. 2.
52. To get a sense of the antipathy between Hungary and Romania over this issue, see *Witnesses to Cultural Genocide: First-Hand Reports on Romania's Minority Policies Today* (New York: American Transylvanian Federation and the Committee for Human Rights in Romania, 1979). The March 1990 clashes between ethnic Hungarians and Romanians in Tîrgu Mures (Romanian Transylvania) indicate the potential for savage violence that is inherent in these ethnic conflicts.
53. See Zbigniew Brzezinski, "Post-Communist Nationalism," *Foreign Affairs*, Vol. 68, No. 5 (Winter 1989/1990), pp. 1–13; and Mark Kramer, "Beyond the Brezhnev Doctrine: A New Era in Soviet-East European Relations?" *International Security*, Vol. 14, No. 3 (Winter 1989/90), pp. 51–54.

be drawn to compete for influence in that region, especially if disorder created fluid politics that offered opportunities for wider influence, or threatened defeat for friendly states. During the Cold War, both superpowers were drawn into Third World conflicts across the globe, often in distant areas of little strategic importance. Eastern Europe is directly adjacent to both the Soviet Union and Germany, and has considerable economic and strategic importance; thus trouble in Eastern Europe could offer even greater temptations to these powers than past conflicts in the Third World offered the superpowers. Furthermore, because the results of local conflicts will be largely determined by the relative success of each party in finding external allies, Eastern European states will have strong incentives to drag the major powers into their local conflicts.[54] Thus both push and pull considerations would operate to enmesh outside powers in local Eastern European wars.

Miscalculation is also likely to be a problem in a multipolar Europe. For example, the new order might well witness shifting patterns of conflict, leaving insufficient time for adversaries to develop agreed divisions of rights and agreed rules of interaction, or constantly forcing them to re-establish new agreements and rules as old antagonisms fade and new ones arise. It is not likely that circumstances would allow the development of a robust set of agreements of the sort that have stabilized the Cold War since 1963. Instead, Europe would resemble the pattern of the early Cold War, in which the absence of rules led to repeated crises. In addition, the multipolar character of the system is likely to give rise to miscalculation regarding the strength of the opposing coalitions.

It is difficult to predict the precise balance of conventional military power that would emerge between the two largest powers in post–Cold War Europe, especially since the future of Soviet power is now hard to forecast. The Soviet Union might recover its strength soon after withdrawing from Central Europe; if so, Soviet power would overmatch German power. Or centrifugal national forces may pull the Soviet Union apart, leaving no remnant state that is the equal of a united Germany.[55] What seems most likely is that

---

54. The new prime minister of Hungary, Jozsef Antall, has already spoken of the need for a "European solution" to the problem of Romania's treatment of Hungarians in Transylvania. Celestine Bohlen, "Victor in Hungary Sees '45 as the Best of Times," *New York Times*, April 10, 1990, p. A8.

55. This article focuses on how changes in the strength of Soviet power and retraction of the Soviet empire would affect the prospects for stability in Europe. However, the dissolution of the Soviet Union, a scenario not explored here in any detail, would raise dangers that would be different from and in addition to those discussed here.

Germany and the Soviet Union might emerge as powers of roughly equal strength. The first two scenarios, with their marked inequality between the two leading powers, would be especially worrisome, although there is cause for concern even if Soviet and German power are balanced.

Resurgent hyper-nationalism will probably pose less danger than the problems described above, but some nationalism is likely to resurface in the absence of the Cold War and may provide additional incentives for war. A non-nuclear Europe is likely to be especially troubled by nationalism, since security in such an order will largely be provided by mass armies, which often cannot be maintained without infusing societies with hyper-nationalism. The problem is likely to be most acute in Eastern Europe, but there is also potential for trouble in Germany. The Germans have generally done an admirable job combatting nationalism over the past 45 years, and in remembering the dark side of their past. Nevertheless, worrisome portents are now visible; of greatest concern, some prominent Germans have lately advised a return to greater nationalism in historical education.[56] Moreover, nationalism will be exacerbated by the unresolved border disputes that will be uncovered by the retreat of American and Soviet power. Especially prominent is that of the border between Germany and Poland, which some Germans would change in Germany's favor.

However, it seems very unlikely that Europe will actually be denuclearized, despite the present strength of anti-nuclear feeling in Europe. For example, it is unlikely that the French, in the absence of America's protective cover and faced with a newly unified Germany, would get rid of their nuclear weapons. Also, the Soviets surely would remain concerned about balancing the American nuclear deterrent, and will therefore retain a deterrent of their own.

THE CURRENT OWNERSHIP PATTERN CONTINUES

A more plausible order for post–Cold War Europe is one in which Britain, France and the Soviet Union keep their nuclear weapons, but no new nuclear powers emerge in Europe. This scenario sees a nuclear-free zone in Central Europe, but leaves nuclear weapons on the European flanks.

---

56. Aspects of this story are recounted in Richard J. Evans, *In Hitler's Shadow: West German Historians and the Attempt to Escape from the Nazi Past* (New York: Pantheon, 1989). A study of past German efforts to mischaracterize history is Holger H. Herwig, "Clio Deceived: Patriotic Self-Censorship in Germany After the Great War," *International Security*, Vol. 12, No. 2 (Fall 1987), pp. 5–44.

This scenario, too, also seems unlikely, since the non-nuclear states will have substantial incentives to acquire their own nuclear weapons. Germany would probably not need nuclear weapons to deter a conventional attack by its neighbors, since neither the French nor any of the Eastern European states would be capable of defeating a reunified Germany in a conventional war. The Soviet Union would be Germany's only legitimate conventional threat, but as long as the states of Eastern Europe remained independent, Soviet ground forces would be blocked from a direct attack. The Germans, however, might not be willing to rely on the Poles or the Czechs to provide a barrier and might instead see nuclear weapons as the best way to deter a Soviet conventional attack into Central Europe. The Germans might choose to go nuclear to protect themselves from blackmail by other nuclear powers. Finally, given that Germany would have greater economic strength than Britain or France, it might therefore seek nuclear weapons to raise its military status to a level commensurate with its economic status.

The minor powers of Eastern Europe would have strong incentives to acquire nuclear weapons. Without nuclear weapons, these Eastern European states would be open to nuclear blackmail from the Soviet Union and, if it acquired nuclear weapons, from Germany. No Eastern European state could match the conventional strength of Germany or the Soviet Union, which gives these minor powers a powerful incentive to acquire a nuclear deterrent, even if the major powers had none. In short, a continuation of the current pattern of ownership without proliferation seems unlikely.

How stable would this order be? The continued presence of nuclear weapons in Europe would have some pacifying effects. Nuclear weapons would induce greater caution in their owners, give the nuclear powers greater security, tend to equalize the relative power of states that possess them, and reduce the risk of miscalculation. However, these benefits would be limited if nuclear weapons did not proliferate beyond their current owners, for four main reasons.

First, the caution and the security that nuclear weapons impose would be missing from the vast center of Europe. The entire region between France and the Soviet Union, extending from the Arctic in the north to the Mediterranean in the south, and comprising some eighteen significant states, would become a large zone thereby made "safe" for conventional war. Second, asymmetrical power relations would be bound to develop, between nuclear and non-nuclear states and among non-nuclear states, raising the dangers that attend such asymmetries. Third, the risk of miscalculation would rise, reflecting the multipolar character of this system and the absence of nuclear weapons from a large portion of it. A durable agreed political order would be hard to build because political coalitions would tend to shift over time, causing miscalculations of resolve between adversaries. The relative strength of potential war coalitions would be hard to calculate because coalition strength would depend heavily on the vagaries of diplomacy. Such uncertainties about relative capabilities would be mitigated in conflicts that arose among nuclear powers: nuclear weapons tend to equalize power even among states or coalitions of widely disparate resources, and thus to diminish the importance of additions or defections from each coalition. However, uncertainty would still be acute among the many states that would remain non-nuclear. Fourth, the conventionally-armed states of Central Europe would depend for their security on mass armies, giving them an incentive to infuse their societies with dangerous nationalism in order to maintain public support for national defense efforts.

NUCLEAR PROLIFERATION, WELL-MANAGED OR OTHERWISE

The most likely scenario in the wake of the Cold War is further nuclear proliferation in Europe. This outcome is laden with dangers, but also might provide the best hope for maintaining stability on the Continent. Its effects depend greatly on how it is managed. Mismanaged proliferation could produce disaster, while well-managed proliferation could produce an order nearly as stable as the current order. Unfortunately, however, any proliferation is likely to be mismanaged.

Four principal dangers could arise if proliferation is not properly managed. First, the proliferation process itself could give the existing nuclear powers strong incentives to use force to prevent their non-nuclear neighbors from gaining nuclear weapons, much as Israel used force to preempt Iraq from acquiring a nuclear capability.

Second, even after proliferation was completed, a stable nuclear competition might not emerge between the new nuclear states. The lesser European powers might lack the resources needed to make their nuclear forces survivable; if the emerging nuclear forces were vulnerable, this could create first-strike incentives and attendant crisis instability. Because their economies are far smaller, they would not be able to develop arsenals as large as those of the major powers; arsenals of small absolute size might thus be vulnerable. Furthermore, their lack of territorial expanse deprives them of possible basing modes, such as mobile missile basing, that would secure their deterrents.

Several are landlocked, so they could not base nuclear weapons at sea, the most secure basing mode used by the superpowers. Moreover, their close proximity to one another deprives them of warning time, and thus of basing schemes that exploit warning to achieve invulnerability, such as by the quick launch of alert bombers. Finally, the emerging nuclear powers might also lack the resources required to develop secure command and control and adequate safety procedures for weapons management, thus raising the risk of accidental launch, or of terrorist seizure and use of nuclear weapons.

Third, the elites and publics of the emerging nuclear European states might not quickly develop doctrines and attitudes that reflect a grasp of the devastating consequences and basic unwinnability of nuclear war. There will probably be voices in post–Cold War Europe arguing that limited nuclear war is feasible, and that nuclear wars can be fought and won. These claims might be taken seriously in states that have not had much direct experience with the nuclear revolution.

Fourth, widespread proliferation would increase the number of fingers on the nuclear trigger, which in turn would increase the likelihood that nuclear weapons could be fired due to accident, unauthorized use, terrorist seizure, or irrational decision-making.

If these problems are not resolved, proliferation would present grave dangers. However, the existing nuclear powers can take steps to reduce these dangers. They can help deter preventive attack on emerging nuclear states by extending security guarantees. They can provide technical assistance to help newly nuclear-armed powers to secure their deterrents. And they can help socialize emerging nuclear societies to understand the nature of the forces they are acquiring. Proliferation managed in this manner can help bolster peace.

How broadly should nuclear weapons be permitted to spread? It would be best if proliferation were extended to Germany but not beyond.[57] Germany has a large economic base, and can therefore sustain a secure nuclear force. Moreover, Germany will feel insecure without nuclear weapons; and Germany's great conventional strength gives it significant capacity to disturb Europe if it feels insecure. Other states—especially in Eastern Europe—may also want nuclear weapons, but it would be best to prevent further proliferation. The reasons are, as noted above, that these states may be unable to

---

57. See David Garnham, "Extending Deterrence with German Nuclear Weapons," *International Security*, Vol. 10, No. 1 (Summer 1985), pp. 96–110.

secure their nuclear deterrents, and the unlimited spread of nuclear weapons raises the risk of terrorist seizure or possession by states led by irrational elites. However, if the broader spread of nuclear weapons proves impossible to prevent without taking extreme steps, the existing nuclear powers should let the process happen, while doing their best to channel it in safe directions.

However, even if proliferation were well-managed, significant dangers would remain. If all the major powers in Europe possessed nuclear weapons, history suggests that they would still compete for influence among the lesser powers and be drawn into lesser-power conflicts. The superpowers, despite the security that their huge nuclear arsenals provide, have competed intensely for influence in remote, strategically unimportant areas such as South Asia, Southeast Asia, and Central America. The European powers are likely to exhibit the same competitive conduct, especially in Eastern Europe, even if they possess secure nuclear deterrents.

The possibility of ganging up would remain: several nuclear states could join against a solitary nuclear state, perhaps aggregating enough strength to overwhelm its deterrent. Nuclear states also might bully their non-nuclear neighbors. This problem is mitigated if unbounded proliferation takes place, leaving few non-nuclear states subject to bullying by the nuclear states, but such widespread proliferation raises risks of its own, as noted above.

Well-managed proliferation would reduce the danger that states might miscalculate the relative strength of coalitions, since nuclear weapons clarify the relative power of all states, and diminish the importance of unforeseen additions and defections from alliances. However, the risk remains that resolve will be miscalculated, because patterns of conflict are likely to be somewhat fluid in a multipolar Europe, thus precluding the establishment of well-defined spheres of rights and rules of conduct.

Unbounded proliferation, even if it is well-managed, will raise the risks that appear when there are many fingers on the nuclear trigger—accident, unauthorized or irrational use, or terrorist seizure.

In any case, it is not likely that proliferation will be well-managed. The nuclear powers cannot easily work to manage proliferation while at the same time resisting it; there is a natural tension between the two goals. But they have several motives to resist. The established nuclear powers will be reluctant to give the new nuclear powers technical help in building secure deterrents, because it runs against the grain of state behavior to transfer military power to others, and because of the fear that sensitive military technology could be turned against the donor state if that technology were further transferred to its adversaries. The nuclear powers will also be reluctant to undermine the legitimacy of the 1968 Nuclear Non-Proliferation Treaty by allowing any signatories to acquire nuclear weapons, since this could open the floodgates to the wider proliferation that they seek to avoid, even if they would otherwise favor very limited proliferation. For these reasons the nuclear powers are more likely to spend their energy trying to thwart the process of proliferation, rather than managing it.

Proliferation can be more easily managed if it occurs during a period of relative international calm. Proliferation that occurred during a time of crisis would be especially dangerous, since states in conflict with the emerging nuclear powers would then have a strong incentive to interrupt the process by force. However, proliferation is likely not to begin until the outbreak of crisis, because there will be significant domestic opposition to proliferation within the potential nuclear powers, as well as significant external resistance from the established nuclear powers. Hence it may require a crisis to motivate the potential nuclear powers to pay the domestic and international costs of moving to build a nuclear force. Thus, proliferation is more likely to happen under disadvantageous international conditions than in a period of calm.

Finally, there are limits to the ability of the established nuclear powers to assist small emerging nuclear powers to build secure deterrents. For example, small landlocked powers cannot be given access to sea-based deterrents or land-mobile missile systems requiring vast expanses of land; these are geographic problems that technology cannot erase. Therefore even if the existing nuclear powers move to manage the proliferation process early and wisely, that process still may raise dangers that they cannot control.

Alternative Theories that Predict Peace

Many students of European politics will reject my pessimistic analysis of post–Cold War Europe and instead argue that a multipolar Europe is likely to be at least as peaceful as the present order. Three specific scenarios for a peaceful future have been advanced. Each rests on a well-known theory of international relations. However, each of these theories is flawed and thus cannot serve as the basis for reliable predictions of a peaceful order in a multipolar Europe; hence the hopeful scenarios they support lack plausibility.

Under the first optimistic scenario, even a non-nuclear Europe would remain peaceful because Europeans recognize that even a conventional war would be horrific. Sobered by history, national leaders will take great care to avoid war. This scenario rests on the "obsolescence of war" theory.

Although modern conventional war can certainly be very costly, there are several flaws in this argument. There is no systematic evidence demonstrating that Europeans believe war is obsolete. However, even if it were widely believed in Europe that war is no longer thinkable, attitudes could change. Public opinion on national security issues is notoriously fickle and responsive to elite manipulation and world events. Moreover, only one country need decide war is thinkable to make war possible again. Finally, it is possible that a conventional war could be fought and won without suffering grave losses, and elites who saw this possibility could believe war is a viable option.

Under the second optimistic scenario, the existing European Community (EC) grows stronger with time, a development heralded by the Single European Act, designed to create a unified Western European market by 1992. A strong EC then ensures that this economic order remains open and prosperous, and the open and prosperous character of the European economy keeps the states of Western Europe cooperating with each other. In this view, the present EC structure grows stronger, but not larger. Therefore, while conflict might emerge in Eastern Europe, the threat of an aggressive Germany would be removed by enmeshing the newly unified German state deeply in the EC. The theory underpinning this scenario is "economic liberalism."

A variant of this second scenario posits that the EC will spread to include Eastern Europe and possibly the Soviet Union, bringing prosperity and peace to these regions as well.[58] Some also maintain that the EC is likely to be so successful in the decade ahead that it will develop into a state apparatus: a unified Western European super-state would emerge and Germany would be subsumed in it. At some future point, the remainder of Europe would be incorporated into that super-state. Either way, suggest the proponents of this second scenario and its variants, peace will be bolstered.

Under the third scenario, war is avoided because many European states have become democratic since the early twentieth century, and liberal democracies simply do not fight against each other. At a minimum, the presence of liberal democracies in Western Europe renders that half of Europe free from armed conflict. At a maximum, as democracy spreads to Eastern Europe and the Soviet Union, it bolsters peace among these states, and between

---

58. Jack Snyder, "Averting Anarchy in the New Europe," *International Security*, Vol. 14, No. 4 (Spring 1990), pp. 5–41.

these states and Western Europe. This scenario is based on the theory that can be called "peace-loving democracies."

ECONOMIC LIBERALISM

THE LOGIC OF THE THEORY. Economic liberalism rejects the notion that the prospects for peace are tightly linked to calculations about military power, and posits instead that stability is mainly a function of international economic considerations. It assumes that modern states are primarily motivated by the desire to achieve prosperity, and that national leaders place the material welfare of their publics above all other considerations, including security. This is especially true of liberal democracies, where policymakers are under special pressure to ensure the economic well-being of their populations.[59] Thus, the key to achieving peace is establishment of an international economic system that fosters prosperity for all states.

The taproot of stability, according to this theory, is the creation and maintenance of a liberal economic order that allows free economic exchange between states. Such an order works to dampen conflict and enhance political cooperation in three ways.[60]

First, it makes states more prosperous; this bolsters peace because prosperous states are more economically satisfied, and satisfied states are more

59. This point about liberal democracies highlights the fact that economic liberalism and the theory of peace-loving democracies are often linked in the writings of international relations scholars. The basis of the linkage is what each theory has to say about peoples' motives. The claim that individuals mainly desire material prosperity, central to economic liberalism, meshes nicely with the belief that the citizenry are a powerful force against war, which, as discussed below, is central to the theory of peace-loving democracies.

60. The three explanations discussed here rest on three of the most prominent theories advanced in the international political economy (IPE) literature. These three are usually treated as distinct theories and are given various labels. However, they share important common elements. Hence, for purposes of parsimony, I treat them as three strands of one general theory: economic liberalism. A caveat is in order. The IPE literature often fails to state its theories in a clear fashion, making them difficult to evaluate. Thus, I have construed these theories from sometimes opaque writings that might be open to contrary interpretations. My description of economic liberalism is drawn from the following works, which are among the best of the IPE genre: Richard N. Cooper, "Economic Interdependence and Foreign Policies in the Seventies," *World Politics*, Vol. 24, No. 2 (January 1972), pp. 158–181; Ernst B. Haas, "Technology, Pluralism, and the New Europe," in Joseph S. Nye, Jr., ed., *International Regionalism* (Boston: Little, Brown, 1968), pp. 149–176; Robert O. Keohane and Joseph S. Nye, Jr., *Power and Interdependence: World Politics in Transition* (Boston: Little, Brown, 1977); Robert O. Keohane, *After Hegemony: Cooperation and Discord in the World Political Economy* (Princeton: Princeton University Press, 1984); David Mitrany, *A Working Peace System* (Chicago: Quadrangle Press, 1966); Edward L. Morse, "The Transformation of Foreign Policies: Modernization, Interdependence, and Externalization," *World Politics*, Vol. 22, No. 3 (April 1970), pp. 371–392; and Richard N. Rosecrance, *The Rise of the Trading State: Commerce and Conquest in the Modern World* (New York: Basic Books, 1986).

peaceful. Many wars are waged to gain or preserve wealth, but states have less motive for such wars if they are already wealthy. Wealthy societies also stand to lose more if their societies are laid waste by war. For both reasons they avoid war.

Moreover, the prosperity spawned by economic liberalism feeds itself, by promoting international institutions that foster greater liberalism, which in turn promotes still greater prosperity. To function smoothly, a liberal economic order requires international regimes or institutions, such as the EC, the General Agreement on Tariffs and Trade (GATT), and the International Monetary Fund (IMF). These institutions perform two limited but important functions. First, they help states to verify that partners keep their cooperative commitments. Second, they provide resources to governments experiencing short-term problems arising from their exposure to international markets, and by doing so they allow states to eschew beggar-thy-neighbor policies that might otherwise undermine the existing economic order. Once in place, these institutions and regimes bolster economic cooperation, hence bolster prosperity. They also bolster themselves: once in existence they cause the expansion of their own size and influence, by proving their worth and selling themselves to states and publics. And as their power grows they become better able to promote cooperation, which promotes greater prosperity, which further bolsters their prestige and influence. In essence, a benevolent spiral-like relationship sets in between cooperation-promoting regimes and prosperity, in which each feeds the other.

Second, a liberal economic order fosters economic interdependence among states. Interdependence is defined as a situation in which two states are mutually vulnerable; each is a hostage of the other in the economic realm.[61] When interdependence is high, this theory holds, there is less temptation to cheat or behave aggressively towards other states because all states could retaliate. Interdependence allows states to compel each other to cooperate on economic matters, much as mutual assured destruction allows nuclear powers to compel each other to respect their security. All states are forced by the others to act as partners in the provision of material comfort for their home publics.

Third, some theorists argue that with ever-increasing political cooperation, international regimes will become so powerful that they will assume an

---

61. See Kenneth N. Waltz, "The Myth of National Interdependence," in Charles P. Kindelberger, ed., *The International Corporation* (Cambridge: MIT Press, 1970), pp. 205–223.

independent life of their own, eventually growing into a super-state. This is a minority view; most economic liberals do not argue that regimes can become so powerful that they can coerce states to act against their own narrow interests. Instead most maintain that regimes essentially reflect the interests of the states that created and maintain them, and remain subordinate to other interests of these states. However, the "growth to super-statehood" view does represent an important strand of thought among economic liberals.

The main flaw in this theory is that the principal assumption underpinning it—that states are primarily motivated by the desire to achieve prosperity—is wrong. States are surely concerned about prosperity, and thus economic calculations are hardly trivial for them. However, states operate in both an international political environment and an international economic environment, and the former dominates the latter in cases where the two systems come into conflict. The reason is straightforward: the international political system is anarchic, which means that each state must always be concerned to ensure its own survival. Since a state can have no higher goal than survival, when push comes to shove, international political considerations will be paramount in the minds of decision-makers.

Proponents of economic liberalism largely ignore the effects of anarchy on state behavior and concentrate instead on economic considerations. When this omission is corrected, however, their arguments collapse, for two reasons.

First, competition for security makes it very difficult for states to cooperate. When security is scarce, states become more concerned about relative gains than absolute gains.[62] They ask of an exchange not, "will both of us gain?" but instead, "who will gain more?"[63] When security is scarce, they reject even cooperation that would yield an absolute economic gain, if the other state would gain more of the yield, from fear that the other might convert its gain to military strength, and then use this strength to win by coercion in later rounds.[64] Cooperation is much easier to achieve if states worry only about absolute gains, as they are more likely to do when security is not so

---

62. See Joseph M. Grieco, "Anarchy and the Limits of Cooperation: A Realist Critique of the Newest Liberal Institutionalism," *International Organization*, Vol. 42, No. 3 (Summer 1988), pp. 485–507; and Grieco, *Cooperation among Nations: Europe, America and Non-Tariff Barriers to Trade* (Ithaca: Cornell University Press, 1990).
63. Waltz, *Theory of International Politics*, p. 105.
64. It is important to emphasize that because military power is in good part a function of economic might, the consequences of economic dealings among states sometimes have important security implications.

scarce. The goal then is simply to insure that the overall economic pie is expanding and each state is getting at least some part of the resulting benefits. However, anarchy guarantees that security will often be scarce; this heightens states' concerns about relative gains, which makes cooperation difficult unless gains can be finely sliced to reflect, and thus not disturb, the current balance of power.

In contrast to this view, economic liberals generally assume that states worry little about relative gains when designing cooperative agreements, but instead are concerned mainly about absolute gains. This assumption underlies their optimism over the prospects for international cooperation. However, it is not well-based: anarchy forces states to reject agreements that result in asymmetrical payoffs that shift the balance of power against them.

Second, interdependence is as likely to lead to conflict as cooperation, because states will struggle to escape the vulnerability that interdependence creates, in order to bolster their national security. States that depend on others for critical economic supplies will fear cutoff or blackmail in time of crisis or war; they may try to extend political control to the source of supply, giving rise to conflict with the source or with its other customers. Interdependence, in other words, might very well lead to greater competition, not to cooperation.[65]

Several other considerations, independent of the consequences of anarchy, also raise doubts about the claims of economic liberals.

First, economic interactions between states often cause serious frictions, even if the overall consequences are positive. There will invariably be winners and losers within each state, and losers rarely accept defeat gracefully. In modern states, where leaders have to pay careful attention to their constit-

---

65. There are numerous examples in the historical record of vulnerable states pursuing aggressive military policies for the purpose of achieving autarky. For example, this pattern of behavior was reflected in both Japan's and Germany's actions during the interwar period. On Japan, see Michael A. Barnhart, *Japan Prepares for Total War: The Search for Economic Security, 1919–1941* (Ithaca: Cornell University Press, 1987); and James B. Crowley, *Japan's Quest for Autonomy* (Princeton: Princeton University Press, 1966). On Germany, see William Carr, *Arms, Autarky and Aggression: A Study in German Foreign Policy, 1933–39* (New York: Norton, 1973). It is also worth noting that during the Arab oil embargo of the early 1970s, when it became apparent that the United States was vulnerable to OPEC pressure, there was much talk in America about using military force to seize Arab oil fields. See, for example, Robert W. Tucker, "Oil: The Issue of American Intervention," *Commentary*, January 1975, pp. 21–31; Miles Ignotus [said to be a pseudonym for Edward Luttwak], "Seizing Arab Oil," *Harpers*, March 1975, pp. 45–62; and U.S. Congress, House Committee on International Relations, *Report on Oil Fields as Military Objectives: A Feasibility Study*, prepared by John M. Collins and Clyde R. Mark, 94th Cong., 1st sess. (Washington, D.C.: U.S. Government Printing Office [U.S. GPO], August 21, 1975).

uents, losers can cause considerable trouble. Even in cases where only winners are involved, there are sometimes squabbles over how the spoils are
divided. In a sense, then, expanding the network of contacts among states
increases the scope for international disagreements among them. They now
have more to squabble about.

Second, there will be opportunities for blackmail and for brinkmanship in
a highly dynamic economic system where states are dependent on each other.
For example, although mutual vulnerabilities may arise among states, it is
likely that the actual levels of dependence will not be equal. The less vulnerable states would probably have greater bargaining power over the more
dependent states and might attempt to coerce them into making extravagant
concessions. Furthermore, different political systems, not to mention individual leaders, have different capacities for engaging in tough bargaining
situations.

THE HISTORICAL RECORD. During two periods in the twentieth century,
Europe witnessed a liberal economic order with high levels of interdependence. Stability should have obtained during those periods, according to economic liberalism.

The first case clearly contradicts the theory. The years between 1890 and
1914 were probably the time of greatest economic interdependence in Europe's history. Yet World War I broke out following this period.[66]

The second case covers the Cold War years. During this period there has
been much interdependence among the EC states, while relations among
these states have been very peaceful. This case, not surprisingly, is the
centerpiece of the economic liberals' argument.

The correlation in this second case does not mean, however, that interdependence has *caused* cooperation among the Western democracies. It is
more likely that the prime cause was the Cold War, and that this was the
main reason that intra-EC relations have flourished.[67] The Cold War caused
these results in two different but mutually reinforcing ways.

First, old-fashioned balance of power logic mandated cooperation among
the Western democracies. A powerful and potentially dangerous Soviet

---

66. See Richard N. Rosecrance, et al., "Whither Interdependence?" *International Organization*,
Vol. 31, No. 3 (Summer 1977), pp. 432–434.
67. This theme is reflected in Barry Buzan, "Economic Structure and International Security: The
Limits of the Liberal Case," *International Organization*, Vol. 38, No. 4 (Autumn 1984), pp. 597–
624; Robert Gilpin, *U.S. Power and the Multinational Corporation: The Political Economy of Foreign
Direct Investment* (New York: Basic Books, 1975); and Robert A. Pollard, *Economic Security and the
Origins of the Cold War, 1945–1950* (New York: Columbia University Press, 1985).

Union forced the Western democracies to band together to meet the common threat. Britain, Germany, and France no longer worried about each other, because all faced a greater menace from the Soviets. This Soviet threat muted concerns about relative gains arising from economic cooperation among the EC states by giving each Western democracy a vested interest in seeing its alliance partners grow powerful, since each additional increment of power helped deter the Soviets. The Soviet threat also muted relative-gains fears among Western European states by giving them all a powerful incentive to avoid conflict with each other while the Soviet Union loomed to the east, ready to harvest the gains of Western quarrels. This gave each Western state greater confidence that its Western partners would not turn their gains against it, as long as these partners behaved rationally.

Second, America's hegemonic position in NATO, the military counterpart to the EC, mitigated the effects of anarchy on the Western democracies and facilitated cooperation among them.[68] As emphasized, states do not trust each other in anarchy and they have incentives to commit aggression against each other. America, however, not only provided protection against the Soviet threat, but also guaranteed that no EC state would aggress against another. For example, France did not have to fear Germany as it rearmed, because the American presence in Germany meant that the Germans were not free to attack anyone. With the United States serving as night watchman, relative-gains concerns among the Western European states were mitigated and, moreover, those states were willing to allow their economies to become tightly interdependent.

In effect, relations among EC states were spared the effects of anarchy—fears about relative gains and an obsession with autonomy—because the United States served as the ultimate arbiter within the Alliance.

If the present Soviet threat to Western Europe is removed, and American forces depart for home, relations among the EC states will be fundamentally altered. Without a common Soviet threat and without the American night watchman, Western European states will begin viewing each other with greater fear and suspicion, as they did for centuries before the onset of the Cold War. Consequently, they will worry about the imbalances in gains as well as the loss of autonomy that results from cooperation.[69] Cooperation in

---

68. See Josef Joffe, "Europe's American Pacifier," *Foreign Policy*, No. 54 (Spring 1984), pp. 64–82.

69. Consider, for example, a situation where the European Community is successfully extended

this new order will be more difficult than it has been in the Cold War. Conflict will be more likely.

In sum, there are good reasons for looking with skepticism upon the claim that peace can be maintained in a multipolar Europe on the basis of a more powerful EC.

PEACE-LOVING DEMOCRACIES

The peace-loving democracies theory holds that domestic political factors, not calculations about military power or the international economic system, are the principal determinant of peace. Specifically, the argument is that the presence of liberal democracies in the international system will help to produce a stable order.[70] The claim is not that democracies go to war less often than authoritarian states. In fact, the historical record shows clearly that such is not the case.[71] Instead, the argument is that democracies do not go to war against other democracies. Thus, democracy must spread to Eastern Europe and the Soviet Union to insure peace in post–Cold War Europe.

It is not certain that democracy will take root among the states of Eastern Europe or in the Soviet Union. They lack a strong tradition of democracy; institutions that can accommodate the growth of democracy will have to be built from scratch. That task will probably prove to be difficult, especially in an unstable Europe. But whether democracy takes root in the East matters

---

to include Eastern Europe and the Soviet Union, and that over time all states achieve greater prosperity. The Germans, however, do significantly better than all other states. Hence their relative power position, which is already quite strong, begins to improve markedly. It is likely that the French and the Soviets, just to name two states, would be deeply concerned by this situation.

70. This theory has been recently articulated by Michael Doyle in three articles: "Liberalism and World Politics," *American Political Science Review*, Vol. 80, No. 4 (December 1986), pp. 1151–1169; "Kant, Liberal Legacies, and Foreign Affairs," *Philosophy and Public Affairs*, Vol. 12, No. 3 (Summer 1983), pp. 205–235; and "Kant, Liberal Legacies, and Foreign Affairs, Part 2," *Philosophy and Public Affairs*, Vol. 12, No. 4 (Fall 1983), pp. 323–353. Doyle draws heavily on Immanuel Kant's classic writings on the subject. This theory also provides the central argument in Francis Fukuyama's widely publicized essay on "The End of History?" in *The National Interest*, No. 16 (Summer 1989), pp. 3–18. For an excellent critique of the theory, see Samuel P. Huntington, "No Exit: The Errors of Endism," *The National Interest*, No. 17 (Fall 1989), pp. 3–11.

71. There is a good empirical literature on the relationship between democracy and war. See, for example, Steve Chan, "Mirror, Mirror on the Wall . . . Are the Freer Countries More Pacific?" *Journal of Conflict Resolution*, Vol. 28, No. 4 (December 1984), pp. 617–648; Erich Weede, "Democracy and War Involvement," in ibid., pp. 649–664; Bruce M. Russett and R. Joseph Monsen, "Bureaucracy and Polyarchy As Predictors of Performance," *Comparative Political Studies*, Vol. 8, No. 1 (April 1975), pp. 5–31; and Melvin Small and J. David Singer, "The War-Proneness of Democratic Regimes, 1816–1965," *The Jerusalem Journal of International Relations*, Vol. 1, No. 4 (Summer 1976), pp. 50–69.

little for stability in Europe, since the theory of peace-loving democracies is unsound.

THE LOGIC OF THE THEORY. Two explanations are offered in support of the claim that democracies do not go to war against one another.

First, some claim that authoritarian leaders are more prone to go to war than leaders of democracies, because authoritarian leaders are not accountable to their publics, which carry the main burdens of war. In a democracy, by contrast, the citizenry that pays the price of war has greater say in the decision-making process. The people, so the argument goes, are more hesitant to start trouble because it is they who pay the blood price; hence the greater their power, the fewer wars.

The second argument rests on the claim that the citizens of liberal democracies respect popular democratic rights—those of their fellow countrymen, and those of individuals in other states. As a result they are reluctant to wage war against other democracies, because they view democratic governments as more legitimate than others, and are loath to impose a foreign regime on a democratic state by force. This would violate their own democratic principles and values. Thus an inhibition on war is introduced when two democracies face each other that is missing in other international relationships.

The first of these arguments is flawed because it is not possible to sustain the claim that the people in a democracy are especially sensitive to the costs of war and therefore less willing than authoritarian leaders to fight wars. In fact, the historical record shows that democracies are every bit as likely to fight wars as are authoritarian states.

Furthermore, mass publics, whether democratic or not, can become deeply imbued with nationalistic or religious fervor, making them prone to support aggression, regardless of costs. The widespread public support in post-revolutionary France for Napoleon's wars of aggression is just one example of this phenomenon. On the other hand, authoritarian leaders are just as likely as democratic publics to fear going to war, because war tends to unleash democratic forces that can undermine the regime.[72] War can impose high costs on authoritarian leaders as well as on their citizenries.

The second argument, which emphasizes the transnational respect for democratic rights among democracies, rests on a weaker factor that is usually

---

72. See, for example, Stanislav Andreski, "On the Peaceful Disposition of Military Dictatorships," *Journal of Strategic Studies*, Vol. 3, No. 3 (December 1980), pp. 3–10.

overridden by other factors such as nationalism and religious fundamentalism. There is also another problem with the argument. The possibility always exists that a democracy will revert to an authoritarian state. This threat of backsliding means that one democratic state can never be sure that another democratic state will not change its stripes and turn on it sometime in the future. Liberal democracies must therefore worry about relative power among themselves, which is tantamount to saying that each has an incentive to consider aggression against the other to forestall future trouble. Lamentably, it is not possible for even liberal democracies to transcend anarchy.

THE HISTORICAL RECORD. Problems with the deductive logic aside, the historical record seems to offer strong support for the theory of peace-loving democracies. There appears to have been no case where liberal democracies fought against each other. Although this evidence looks impressive at first glance, closer examination shows it to be indecisive. In fact, history provides no clear test of the theory. Four evidentiary problems leave the issue in doubt.

First, democracies have been few in number over the past two centuries, and thus there have not been many cases where two democracies were in a position to fight with each other. Only three prominent cases are usually cited: Britain and the United States (1832–present); Britain and France (1832–49, 1871–1940); and the Western democracies since 1945.

Second, there are other persuasive explanations for why war did not occur in those three cases, and these competing explanations must be ruled out before the peace-loving democracies theory can be accepted. While relations between the British and the Americans during the nineteenth century were hardly free of conflict,[73] their relations in the twentieth century were quite harmonious, and thus fit closely with how the theory would expect two democracies to behave towards each other. That harmony, however, can easily be explained by the presence of a common threat that forced Britain and the United States to work closely together.[74] Both faced a serious German threat in the first part of the century, and a Soviet threat later. The same basic argument applies to France and Britain. While Franco-British relations

---

73. For a discussion of the hostile relations that existed between the United States and Britain during the nineteenth century, see H.C. Allen, *Great Britain and the United States: A History of Anglo-American Relations, 1783–1952* (London: Odhams, 1954).
74. For a discussion of this rapprochement, see Stephen R. Rock, *Why Peace Breaks Out: Great Power Rapprochement in Historical Perspective* (Chapel Hill: University of North Carolina Press, 1989), chap. 2.

were not the best throughout most of the nineteenth century,[75] they improved significantly around the turn of the century with the rise of a common threat: Germany.[76] Finally, as noted above, the Soviet threat can explain the absence of war among the Western democracies since 1945.

Third, it bears mention that several democracies have come close to fighting one another, which suggests that the absence of war may be due simply to chance. France and Britain approached war during the Fashoda crisis of 1898. France and Weimar Germany might have come to blows over the Rhineland during the 1920s, had Germany possessed the military strength to challenge France. The United States has clashed with a number of elected governments in the Third World during the Cold War, including the Allende regime in Chile and the Arbenz regime in Guatemala.

Lastly, some would classify Wilhelmine Germany as a democracy, or at least a quasi-democracy; if so, World War I becomes a war among democracies.[77]

Conclusion

This article argues that bipolarity, an equal military balance, and nuclear weapons have fostered peace in Europe over the past 45 years. The Cold War confrontation produced these phenomena; thus the Cold War was principally responsible for transforming a historically violent region into a very peaceful place.

There is no doubt that the costs of the Cold War have been substantial. It inflicted oppressive political regimes on the peoples of Eastern Europe, who were denied basic human rights by their forced membership in the Soviet

---

75. For a good discussion of Franco-British relations during the nineteenth century, see P.J.V. Rolo, *Entente Cordiale: The Origins and Negotiation of the Anglo-French Agreements of 8 April 1904* (New York: St. Martins, 1969), pp. 16–109.

76. Stephen Rock, who has examined the rapprochement between Britain and France, argues that the principal motivating force behind their improved relations derived from geopolitical considerations, not shared political beliefs. See Rock, *Why Peace Breaks Out,* chap. 4.

77. Doyle recognizes this problem and thus has a lengthy footnote that attempts to deal with it. See "Kant, Liberal Legacies, and Foreign Affairs [Part One]," pp. 216–217, n. 8. He argues that "Germany was a liberal state under republican law for domestic issues," but that the "emperor's active role in foreign affairs . . . made imperial Germany a state divorced from the control of its citizenry in foreign affairs." However, an examination of the decision-making process leading to World War I reveals that the emperor (Wilhelm II) was not a prime mover in foreign affairs and that he was no more bellicose than other members of the German elite, including the leading civilian official, Chancellor Bethmann-Hollweg.

empire. It consumed national wealth, by giving rise to large and costly defense establishments in both East and West. It spawned bloody conflicts in the Third World; these produced modest casualties for the superpowers, but large casualties for the Third World nations. Nevertheless, the net human and economic cost of the Cold War order has been far less than the cost of the European order of 1900–45, with its vast violence and suffering.

A Cold War order without confrontation would have been preferable to the order that actually developed; then the peace that the Cold War order produced could have been enjoyed without its attendant costs. However, it was East-West enmity that gave rise to the Cold War order; there would have been no bipolarity, no equality, and no large Soviet and American nuclear forces in Europe without it. The costs of the Cold War arose from the same cause—East-West confrontation—as did its benefits. The good could not be had without the bad.

This article further argues that the demise of the Cold War order is likely to increase the chances that war and major crises will occur in Europe. Many observers now suggest that a new age of peace is dawning; in fact the opposite is true.

The implications of my analysis are straightforward, if paradoxical. The West has an interest in maintaining peace in Europe. It therefore has an interest in maintaining the Cold War order, and hence has an interest in the continuation of the Cold War confrontation; developments that threaten to end it are dangerous. The Cold War antagonism could be continued at lower levels of East-West tension than have prevailed in the past; hence the West is not injured by relaxing East-West tension, but a complete end to the Cold War would create more problems than it would solve.

The fate of the Cold War, however, is mainly in the hands of the Soviet Union. The Soviet Union is the only superpower that can seriously threaten to overrun Europe; it is the Soviet threat that provides the glue that holds NATO together. Take away that offensive threat and the United States is likely to abandon the Continent, whereupon the defensive alliance it has headed for forty years may disintegrate. This would bring to an end the bipolar order that has characterized Europe for the past 45 years.

The foregoing analysis suggests that the West paradoxically has an interest in the continued existence of a powerful Soviet Union with substantial military forces in Eastern Europe. Western interests are wholly reversed from those that Western leaders saw in the late 1940s: instead of seeking the retraction of Soviet power, as the West did then, the West now should hope that the Soviet Union retains at least some military forces in the Eastern European region.

There is little the Americans or the Western Europeans can or are likely to do to perpetuate the Cold War, for three reasons.

First, domestic political considerations preclude such an approach. Western leaders obviously cannot base national security policy on the need to maintain forces in Central Europe for the purpose simply of keeping the Soviets there. The idea of deploying large forces in order to bait the Soviets into an order-keeping competition would be dismissed as bizarre, and contrary to the general belief that ending the Cold War and removing the Soviet yoke from Eastern Europe would make the world safer and better.[78]

Second, the idea of propping up a declining rival runs counter to the basic behavior of states. States are principally concerned about their relative power position in the system; hence, they look for opportunities to take advantage of each other. If anything, they prefer to see adversaries decline, and thus will do whatever they can to speed up the process and maximize the distance of the fall. In other words, states do not ask which distribution of power best facilitates stability and then do everything possible to build or maintain such an order. Instead, they each tend to pursue the more narrow aim of maximizing their power advantage over potential adversaries. The particular international order that results is simply a byproduct of that competition, as illustrated by the origins of the Cold War order in Europe. No state intended to create it. In fact, both the United States and the Soviet Union worked hard in the early years of the Cold War to undermine each other's position in Europe, which would have ended the bipolar order on the Continent. The remarkably stable system that emerged in Europe in the late 1940s was the unintended consequence of an intense competition between the superpowers.

Third, even if the Americans and the Western Europeans wanted to help the Soviets maintain their status as a superpower, it is not apparent that they could do so. The Soviet Union is leaving Eastern Europe and cutting its

---

78. This point is illustrated by the 1976 controversy over the so-called "Sonnenfeldt Doctrine." Helmut Sonnenfeldt, an adviser to Secretary of State Henry Kissinger, was reported to have said in late 1975 that the United States should support Soviet domination of Eastern Europe. It was clear from the ensuing debate that whether or not Sonnenfeldt in fact made such a claim, no administration could publicly adopt that position. See U.S. Congress, House Committee on International Relations, *Hearings on United States National Security Policy Vis-à-Vis Eastern Europe (The "Sonnenfeldt Doctrine")*, 94th Cong., 2nd sess. (Washington, D.C.: U.S. GPO, April 12, 1976).

military forces largely because its economy is foundering. It is not clear that the Soviets themselves know how to fix their economy, and there is little that Western governments can do to help them solve their economic problems. The West can and should avoid doing malicious mischief to the Soviet economy, but at this juncture it is difficult to see how the West can have significant positive influence.[79]

The fact that the West cannot sustain the Cold War does not mean that the United States should abandon all attempts to preserve the current order. The United States should do what it can to direct events toward averting a complete mutual superpower withdrawal from Europe. For instance, the American negotiating position at the conventional arms control talks should aim toward large mutual force reductions, but should not contemplate complete mutual withdrawal. The Soviets may opt to withdraw all their forces unilaterally anyway; there is little the United States could do to prevent this.

POLICY RECOMMENDATIONS

If complete Soviet withdrawal from Eastern Europe proves unavoidable, the West faces the question of how to maintain peace in a multipolar Europe. Three policy prescriptions are in order.

First, the United States should encourage the limited and carefully managed proliferation of nuclear weapons in Europe. The best hope for avoiding war in post–Cold War Europe is nuclear deterrence; hence some nuclear proliferation is necessary to compensate for the withdrawal of the Soviet and American nuclear arsenals from Central Europe. Ideally, as I have argued, nuclear weapons would spread to Germany, but to no other state.

Second, Britain and the United States, as well as the Continental states, will have to balance actively and efficiently against any emerging aggressor to offset the ganging up and bullying problems that are sure to arise in post–Cold War Europe. Balancing in a multipolar system, however, is usually a problem-ridden enterprise, either because of geography or because of significant coordination problems. Nevertheless, two steps can be taken to maximize the prospects of efficient balancing.

The initial measure concerns Britain and the United States, the two prospective balancing states that, physically separated from the Continent, may

---

79. For an optimistic assessment of how the West can enhance Gorbachev's prospects of succeeding, see Jack Snyder, "International Leverage on Soviet Domestic Change," *World Politics*, Vol. 42, No. 1 (October 1989), pp. 1–30.

thus conclude that they have little interest in what happens there. They would then be abandoning their responsibilities and, more importantly, their interests as off-shore balancers. Both states' failure to balance against Germany before the two world wars made war more likely in each case. It is essential for peace in Europe that they not repeat their past mistakes, but instead remain actively involved in maintaining the balance of power in Europe.

Specifically, both states must maintain military forces that can be deployed to the Continent to balance against states that threaten to start a war. To do this they must also socialize their publics to support a policy of continued Continental commitment. Support for such a commitment will be more difficult to mobilize than in the past, because its principal purpose would be to preserve peace, rather than to prevent an imminent hegemony, and the latter is a simpler goal to explain publicly. Moreover, it is the basic nature of states to focus on maximizing relative power, not on bolstering stability, so this prescription asks them to take on an unaccustomed task. Nevertheless, the British and American stake in peace is real, especially since there is a sure risk that a European war might involve large-scale use of nuclear weapons. It should therefore be possible for both countries to lead their publics to recognize this interest and support policies that protect it.[80]

The other measure concerns American attitudes and actions toward the Soviet Union. The Soviets may eventually return to their past expansionism and threaten to upset the status quo. If so, we are back to the Cold War; the West should respond as quickly and efficiently as it did the first time. However, if the Soviets adhere to status quo policies, Soviet power could play a key role in balancing against Germany and in maintaining order in Eastern Europe. It is important that, in those cases where the Soviets are acting in a balancing capacity, the United States recognize this, cooperate with its former adversary, and not let residual distrust from the Cold War interfere with the balancing process.

Third, a concerted effort should be made to keep hyper-nationalism at bay, especially in Eastern Europe. This powerful force has deep roots in Europe and has contributed to the outbreak of past European conflicts. Nationalism has been contained during the Cold War, but it is likely to reemerge once

---

80. Advancing this argument is Van Evera, "Why Europe Matters, Why the Third World Doesn't."

Soviet and American forces leave the heart of Europe.[81] It will be a force for trouble unless it is curbed. The teaching of honest national history is especially important, since the teaching of false chauvinist history is the main vehicle for spreading virulent nationalism. States that teach a dishonestly self-exculpating or self-glorifying history should be publicly criticized and sanctioned.[82]

On this count it is especially important that relations between Germany and its neighbors be handled carefully. Many Germans rightly feel that Germany has behaved very responsibly for 45 years, and has made an honest effort to remember and make amends for an ugly period of its past. Therefore, Germans quickly tire of lectures from foreigners demanding that they apologize once again for crimes committed before most of the current German population was born. On the other hand, peoples who have suffered at the hands of the Germans cannot forget their enormous suffering, and inevitably ask for repeated assurance that the past will not be repeated. This dialogue has the potential to spiral into mutual recriminations that could spark a renewed sense of persecution among Germans, and with it, a rebirth of German-nationalism. It is therefore incumbent on all parties in this discourse to proceed with understanding and respect for one another's feelings and experience. Specifically, others should not ask today's Germans to apologize for crimes they did not commit, but Germans must understand that others' ceaseless demands for reassurance have a legitimate basis in history, and should view these demands with patience and understanding.

None of these tasks will be easy to accomplish. In fact, I expect that the bulk of my prescriptions will not be followed; most run contrary to powerful strains of domestic American and European opinion, and to the basic nature of state behavior. Moreover, even if they are followed, this will not guarantee the peace in Europe. If the Cold War is truly behind us, the stability of the past 45 years is not likely to be seen again in the coming decades.

---

81. On the evolution of nationalistic history-teaching in Europe see Kennedy, "The Decline of Nationalistic History," and Dance, *History the Betrayer.*
82. My thinking on this matter has been influenced by conversations with Stephen Van Evera.

The Unipolar Illusion | *Christopher Layne*

Why New Great Powers Will Rise

The Soviet Union's collapse transformed the international system from bipolarity to unipolarity. To be sure, the United States has not imposed a "universal monarchy" on the international system. There are other states that are formidable militarily (Russia) or economically (Japan and Germany).[1] However, because only the United States possesses imposing strength in all categories of great power capability, it enjoys a preeminent role in international politics.[2] Following the Gulf War and the Soviet Union's collapse, many commentators suggested that America should adopt a new grand strategy that would aim at perpetuating unipolarity.[3] Belief that unipolarity favors the United States, and hence should be maintained, resonated in official Washington as well. This became apparent in March 1992, when the initial draft of the Pentagon's Defense

Christopher Layne teaches international politics at UCLA.

I am grateful to the following for their perceptive and helpful comments on the drafts of this article: John Arquilla, Ted Galen Carpenter, Kerry Andrew Chase, John Mearsheimer, Ben Schwarz, Alan Tonelson, Kenneth Waltz, and an anonymous reviewer. I am also indebted to Harry Kreisler (Institute of International Studies, UC Berkeley) and Jed Snyder (Washington Strategy Seminar) for providing stimulating intellectual forums that helped refine my thinking about unipolarity and prompted me to write this article.

1. Germany, Japan and Russia certainly have the potential to be great powers. Germany and Japan cannot today be considered great powers, however, because they lack the requisite military capabilities, especially strategic nuclear arsenals that would give them deterrence self-sufficiency. Notwithstanding Russia's still formidable nuclear and conventional military capabilities, economic difficulties and domestic political uncertainties have undercut its great power status. China will be a strong contender for great power status if it can maintain its internal cohesion. Buoyed by its vibrant economy, China has embarked on a major modernization and expansion of its air, naval, and ground forces, including its power-projection capabilities. Nicholas D. Kristof, "China Builds Its Military Muscle, Making Some Neighbors Nervous," *New York Times*, January 11, 1993, p. A1.
2. I define a unipolar system as one in which a single power is geopolitically preponderant because its capabilities are formidable enough to preclude the formation of an overwhelming balancing coalition against it.
3. Analysts of such diverse views as the liberal internationalist Joseph S. Nye, Jr., and neoconservatives Charles Krauthammer and Joshua Muravchick agree that a unipolar world is highly conducive to American interests. See Joseph S. Nye, Jr., *Bound to Lead: The Changing Nature of American Power* (New York: Basic Books, 1990); Charles Krauthammer, "The Unipolar Moment," *Foreign Affairs: America and the World*, Vol. 70, No. 1 (1990/91) and "What's Wrong With The 'Pentagon Paper'?" *Washington Post*, March 13, 1992; Joshua Muravchick, "At Last, Pax Americana," *New York Times*, January 24, 1991, p. A19.

International Security, Vol. 17, No. 4 (Spring 1993)
© 1993 by the President and Fellows of Harvard College and the Massachusetts Institute of Technology.

Planning Guidance (DPG) for Fiscal Years 1994–99 was leaked to the *New York Times*.[4] Specifically, the document stated that, "We must account sufficiently for the interests of the large industrial nations to discourage them from challenging our leadership or seeking to overturn the established political or economic order" and that "we must maintain the mechanisms for *deterring potential competitors from even aspiring to a larger regional or global role*."[5]

The initial draft of the DPG was controversial, and a subsequent draft deleted the language referring to the goal of preserving unipolarity.[6] Nevertheless, the available evidence suggests that the DPG accurately reflected official views about unipolarity. For example, the 1991 Summer Study organized by the Pentagon's Director of Net Assessment defined a "manageable" world as one in which there is no threat to America's superpower role.[7] The main risk to American security, the study argued, is that of "Germany and/or Japan disconnecting from multilateral security and economic arrangements and pursuing an independent course."[8] During late 1992 and early 1993, the Pentagon's Joint Staff was preparing a "new NSC 68" intended to establish an intellectual framework for America's post–Cold War grand strategy. One of this document's key themes is that a multipolar world is, by definition, dangerously unstable. There is as yet no evidence that the Clinton administration's view of unipolarity will differ from the Bush administration's.[9]

Although there are shadings of difference among the various proposals for perpetuating unipolarity, it is fair to speak of a single strategy of predomi-

---

4. Patrick E. Tyler, "U.S. Strategy Plan Calls for Insuring No Rivals Develop," *New York Times*, March 8, 1992, p. A1.

5. "Excerpts From Pentagon's Plan: 'Prevent the Re-emergence of a New Rival'," *New York Times*, March 8, 1992, p. A14 (emphasis added).

6. See Leslie H. Gelb, "They're Kidding," *New York Times*, March 9, 1992, p. A15; William Pfaff, "Does America Want to Lead Through Intimidation?" *Los Angeles Times*, March 11, 1992, p. B7; and the comments of Senator Joseph Biden (D-Del.) and the Brookings Institution's John D. Steinbruner quoted in Melissa Healy, "Pentagon Cool to Sharing Its Power," *Los Angeles Times*, March 9, 1992, p. A8; Patrick E. Tyler, "Pentagon Drops Goal of Blocking New Superpowers," *New York Times*, May 24, 1992, p. A1; Melissa Healy, "Pentagon Maps Post–Cold War Defense Plans," *Los Angeles Times*, May 24, 1992, p. A1; Barton Gellman, "On Second Thought, We Don't Want to Rule the World," *Washington Post National Weekly Edition*, June 1–7, 1992, p. 31.

7. Undersecretary of Defense (Policy), *1991 Summer Study*, Organized by the Director, Net Assessment, held at Newport, R.I., August 5–13, 1991, p. 17.

8. Ibid., p. 73.

9. Post-election analyses stressed the likelihood of substantial continuity between the Clinton and Bush foreign policies. At his first post-election news conference, President-elect Clinton referred to the responsibilities imposed on the United States by virtue of its position as the "sole superpower." "Excerpts from President-Elect's News Conference in Arkansas," *New York Times*, November 13, 1992, p. A8.

nance. This strategy is not overtly aggressive; the use of preventive measures to suppress the emergence of new great powers is not contemplated. It is not, in other words, a strategy of heavy-handed American dominance. Rather the strategy of preponderance seeks to preserve unipolarity by persuading Japan and Germany that they are better off remaining within the orbit of an American-led security and economic system than they would be if they became great powers. The strategy of preponderance assumes that rather than balancing against the United States, other states will bandwagon with it. Important benefits are thought to flow from the perpetuation of unipolarity. In a unipolar system, it is argued, the United States could avoid the unpredictable geopolitical consequences that would attend the emergence of new great powers. Unipolarity would, it is said, minimize the risks of both strategic uncertainty and instability. In effect, the strategy of preponderance aims at preserving the Cold War status quo, even though the Cold War is over.

In this article, I use neorealist theory to analyze the implications of unipolarity. I argue that the "unipolar moment" is just that, a geopolitical interlude that will give way to multipolarity between 2000–2010. I start with a very simple premise: states balance against hegemons, even those like the United States that seek to maintain their preeminence by employing strategies based more on benevolence than coercion. As Kenneth N. Waltz says, "In international politics, overwhelming power repels and leads other states to balance against it."[10] In a unipolar world, systemic constraints—balancing, uneven growth rates, and the sameness effect—impel eligible states (i.e., those with the capability to do so) to become great powers. I use neorealist theory to explain the process of great power emergence.

My theoretical argument is supported by an extensive historical discussion. A unipolar world is not *terra incognita*. There have been two other comparable unipolar moments in modern international history. The evidence from those two eras confirms the expectations derived from structural realism: (1) unipolar systems contain the seeds of their own demise because the hegemon's unbalanced power creates an environment conducive to the emergence of new great powers; and (2) the entry of new great powers into the international system erodes the hegemon's relative power and, ultimately, its preeminence. In the final section of this article, I consider the policy implications,

---

10. Kenneth N. Waltz, "America as a Model for the World? A Foreign Policy Perspective," *PS*, December 1991, p. 669.

and I argue that the strategy of preponderance is unlikely to be successful.[11] It will be difficult for the United States to maintain the Cold War status quo because structural change has destroyed the bipolar foundation of the post-1945 international system. I conclude by outlining a new grand strategy that could accomplish the two main geopolitical tasks facing the United States in the years ahead: (1) managing the potentially difficult transition from unipolarity to multipolarity; and (2) advancing American interests in the multipolar world that inevitably will emerge.

Why Great Powers Rise—The Role of Systemic Constraints

Whether the United States can maintain its standing as the sole great power depends largely on whether new great powers will rise. To answer that question, we need to understand why states become great powers.[12] This is

---

11. In a sense, this article extends Mearsheimer's examination of post–Cold War Europe's geopolitical future to the global level. See John Mearsheimer, "Back to the Future: Instability in Europe After the Cold War," *International Security*, Vol. 15, No. 1 (Summer 1990), pp. 5–56. It should be noted that Mearsheimer and I come to very different policy conclusions regarding the American military commitment to Europe (and no doubt we would not agree on some of the other policy recommendations made in this article), notwithstanding the similarity of our analyses.

12. As Kenneth Waltz writes, great powers are defined by capabilities: "States, because they are in a self-help system, have to use their combined capabilities in order to serve their interests. The economic, military, and other capabilities of nations cannot be sectored and separately weighed. States are not placed in the top rank because they excel in one way or another. Their rank depends on how they score on all of the following items: size of population and territory; resource endowment; military strength; political stability; and competence." Kenneth N. Waltz, *Theory of International Politics* (Reading, Mass.: Addison-Wesley, 1979), p. 131. Because of their capabilities, great powers tend to behave differently than other states. Jack Levy writes that great powers are distinguished from others by: 1) a high level of military capability that makes them relatively self-sufficient strategically and capable of projecting power beyond their borders; 2) a broad concept of security that embraces a concern with regional and/or global power balances; and 3) a greater assertiveness than lesser powers in defining and defending their interests. Jack Levy, *War and the Modern Great Power System, 1495–1975* (Lexington: University Press of Kentucky, 1983), pp. 11–19.

Recently there have been several questionable attempts to redefine great power status. For example, Joseph S. Nye, Jr., and Samuel P. Huntington argue that only the United States has the "soft" power resources (socio-cultural and ideological attractiveness to other states) that Nye and Huntington claim are a prerequisite of great power status. Nye, *Bound to Lead*; Huntington, "The U.S.—Decline or Renewal?" *Foreign Affairs*, Vol. 67, No. 2 (Winter 1988/89), pp. 90–93. This argument has three weaknesses. First, it is far from clear that others view U.S. culture and ideology in the same positive light that Nye and Huntington do. America's racial, economic, educational, and social problems have eroded others' admiration for the United States. Second, it is not unusual for great powers to see themselves as cultural or ideological role models; examples include nineteenth-century Britain and France, pre-1914 Germany and, of course, the Soviet Union. Finally, when it comes to setting great powers apart from others, soft power may

a critical issue because the emergence (or disappearance) of great powers can have a decisive effect on international politics; a consequential shift in the number of great powers changes the international system's structure. Waltz defines a "consequential" shift as "variations in number that lead to different expectations about the effect of structure on units."[13] Examples are shifts from: bipolarity to either unipolarity or multipolarity; unipolarity to bipolarity or multipolarity; multipolarity to bipolarity or unipolarity; from a multipolar system with three great powers to one of four or more (or vice versa).[14]

Throughout modern international history, there has been an observable pattern of great power emergence. Although neorealism does not, and cannot, purport to predict the foreign policies of specific states, it can account for outcomes and patterns of behavior that happen recurrently in international politics. Great power emergence is a structually driven phenomenon. Specifically, it results from the interaction of two factors: (1) differential growth rates and (2) anarchy.

Although great power emergence is shaped by structural factors, and can cause structural effects, it results from unit-level actions. In other words, a feedback loop of sorts is at work: (1) structural constraints press eligible states to become great powers; (2) such states make unit-level decisions whether to pursue great power status in response to these structural constraints; (3) if a unit-level decision to seek great power status produces a consequential shift in polarity, it has a structural impact. Rising states have choices about whether to become great powers. However, a state's freedom to choose whether to seek great power status is in reality tightly constrained by structural factors. Eligible states that fail to attain great power status are predictably punished. If policymakers of eligible states are socialized to the inter-

---

be a helpful supplement to the other instruments of statecraft, but states with the requisite hard power capabilities (per Waltz's definition) are great powers regardless of whether they "stand for an idea with appeal beyond [their] borders."

Another popular intellectual fashion holds that Japan and Germany will carve out niches in international politics as the first "global civilian powers." Hanns Maull, "Germany and Japan: The New Civilian Powers," *Foreign Affairs*, Vol. 69, No. 5 (Winter 1990/91), pp. 91–106. As civilian powers, it is argued, they will eschew military strength in favor of economic power, work through international institutions to promote global cooperation, and "furnish international public goods, such as refugee resettlement, national disaster relief, development of economic infrastructure, and human resources improvements." Yoichi Funabashi, "Japan and America: Global Partners," *Foreign Policy*, No. 86 (Spring 1992), p. 37. In the real world, however, one does not find traditional great powers and "civilian" great powers. One finds only states that are great powers and those that are not.

13. Waltz, *Theory of International Politics*, p. 162.
14. Ibid., pp. 163–170.

national system's constraints, they understand that attaining great power status is a prerequisite if their states are to be secure and autonomous.[15] The fate that befell nineteenth-century China illustrates what can happen to an eligible state when its leaders ignore structural imperatives. But nineteenth-century China is a rather singular exception to the pattern of great power emergence. Far more typical is post-1860 Italy, a state that tried hard to attain great power status notwithstanding that it "had more in common with . . . a small Balkan state or a colony than a Great Power" in that it was economically backward, financially weak, and resource-poor.[16]

DIFFERENTIAL GROWTH RATES

The process of great power emergence is underpinned by the fact that the economic (and technological and military) power of states grows at differential, not parallel rates. That is, in relative terms, some states are gaining power while others are losing it. As Robert Gilpin notes, over time, "the differential growth in the power of various states in the system causes a fundamental redistribution of power in the system."[17] The result, as Paul Kennedy has shown, is that time and again relative "economic shifts heralded the rise of new Great Powers which one day would have a decisive impact on the military/territorial order."[18] The link between differential growth rates

15. Kenneth N. Waltz, "A Reply to My Critics" in Robert O. Keohane, ed., *Neorealism and Its Critics* (New York: Columbia University Press, 1986), p. 343.
16. R.J.B. Bosworth, *Italy, the Least of the Great Powers: Italian Foreign Policy before the First World War* (Cambridge: Cambridge University Press, 1979), p. 2. In mid to late nineteenth-century China, some attempts were made at "self-strengthening"—adoption of Western industrial, technological, and military innovations. However, the initiative for such efforts came more from regional strongmen like Li Hongzang than from the central government in Peking. Economic problems resulting from unfavorable demographics, and social and cultural factors, especially Peking's inability to mobilize the elite for a centrally-directed reform program, undercut the modernization effort. "Late imperial China experienced a profound structural breakdown brought on by traditional forces that propelled dynastic cycles. At this unfortunate juncture between dynastic breakdown and foreign intrusion, the leadership simply lacked the internal resources to protect China from other expansive nations in search of wealth and glory." June Grasso, Jay Corrin, and Michael Kort, *Modernization and Revolution in China* (Armonk, N.Y.: M.E. Sharpe, 1991), p. 69.
17. Robert Gilpin, *War and Change in World Politics* (Cambridge: Cambridge University Press, 1981), p. 13. The role of uneven growth rates in the rise of great powers is closely connected to long cycle explanations. See Joshua S. Goldstein, *Long Cycles: Prosperity and War in the Modern Age* (New Haven: Yale University Press, 1988); George Modelski, *Long Cycles in World Politics* (Seattle: University of Washington Press, 1987); and William R. Thompson, "Dehio, Long Cycles, and the Geohistorical Context of Structural Transition," *World Politics*, Vol. 45, No. 1 (October 1992), pp. 127–152.
18. Paul Kennedy, *The Rise and Fall of Great Powers: Economic Change and Military Conflict From 1500 to 2000* (New York: Random House, 1987), p. xxii.

and great power emergence has important implications for unipolarity. Unipolarity is likely to be short-lived because new great powers will emerge as the uneven growth process narrows the gap between the hegemon and the eligible states that are positioned to emerge as its competitors.

There are at least three other respects in which great power emergence is affected by differential growth rates. First, as eligible states gain relative power, they are more likely to attempt to advance their standing in the international system. As Gilpin points out, "The critical significance of the differential growth of power among states is that it alters the cost of changing the international system and therefore the incentives for changing the international system."[19] Second, Gilpin observes, rising power leads to increasing ambition. Rising powers seek to enhance their security by increasing their capabilities and their control over the external environment.[20] Third, as Kennedy explains, rising power leads also to increased international interests and commitments. Oftentimes for great powers, geopolitical and military capabilities are the consequence of a process that begins with economic expansion. Economic expansion leads to new overseas obligations (access to markets and raw materials, alliances, bases), which then must be defended.[21]

THE CONSEQUENCES OF ANARCHY: BALANCING AND SAMENESS

Because it is anarchic, the international political system is a self-help system in which states' foremost concern must be with survival.[22] In an anarchic system, states must provide for their own security and they face many real or apparent threats.[23] International politics thus is a competitive realm, a fact that in itself constrains eligible states to attain great power status. Specifically, there are two manifestations of this competitiveness that shape great power emergence: balancing and the "sameness effect."[24]

BALANCING. The competitiveness of international politics is manifested in the tendency of states to balance.[25] Balancing has especially strong explana-

---

19. Gilpin, *War and Change*, p. 95.
20. Ibid., pp. 94–95. As Gilpin notes, rising power can tempt a state to seek change in the international system, which can trigger "hegemonic war." This problem is discussed in more detail in the conclusion.
21. Kennedy, *Rise and Fall of Great Powers*, p. xxiii.
22. Waltz, *Theory of International Politics*, pp. 107, 127.
23. Kenneth N. Waltz, "The Origins of War in Neorealist Theory," in Robert I. Rotberg and Theodore K. Rabb, eds., *The Origin and Prevention of Major Wars* (Cambridge: Cambridge University Press, 1989), p. 43.
24. The phrase "sameness effect" is from Waltz, *Theory of International Politics*, p. 128.
25. For discussion of the differences between bandwagoning and balancing behavior, see Waltz,

tory power in accounting for the facts that unipolarity tends to be short-lived and that would-be hegemons invariably fail to achieve lasting dominance. Structural realism leads to the expectation that hegemony should generate the rise of countervailing power in the form of new great powers.

The reason states balance is to correct a skewed distribution of relative power in the international system. States are highly attentive to changes in their relative power position because relative power shifts have crucial security implications.[26] It is the interaction of differential growth rates—the main cause of changes in the relative distribution of power among states— and anarchy that produces important effects. In an anarchic, self-help system, states must always be concerned that others will use increased relative capabilities against them. By enhancing their own relative capabilities or diminishing those of an adversary, states get a double payoff: greater security and a wider range of strategic options.[27] The reverse is true for states that remain indifferent to relative power relationships. Thus, as Gilpin says, the international system's competitiveness "stimulates, and may compel, a state to increase its power; at the least, it necessitates that the prudent state prevent relative increase in the powers of competitor states."[28] By definition, the distribution of relative power in a unipolar system is extremely unbalanced. Consequently, in a unipolar system, the structural pressures on eligible states to increase their relative capabilities and become great powers should be overwhelming. If they do not acquire great power capabilities, they may be exploited by the hegemon. Of course, an eligible state's quest for security may give rise to the security dilemma because actions intended to bolster its own security may have the unintended consequence of threatening others.[29]

It can be argued on the basis of hegemonic stability theory and balance of threat theory that a "benign" hegemon might be able to prevent new great powers from emerging and balancing against it.[30] These arguments are unpersuasive. Although hegemonic stability theory is usually employed in the

---

Theory of International Politics, pp. 125–126; Stephen M. Walt, *The Origins of Alliances* (Ithaca: Cornell University Press, 1987), pp. 17–33.

26. Waltz, *Theory of International Politics*, p. 126.

27. Gilpin, *War and Change*, pp. 86–87.

28. Ibid., pp. 87–88.

29. John Herz, "Idealist Internationalism and the Security Dilemma," *World Politics*, Vol. 2, No. 2 (January 1950), pp. 157–180.

30. On balance of threat theory, see Walt, *The Origins of Alliances*, pp. 17–26. For an overview of the benevolent and coercive strands of hegemonic stability theory, see Duncan Snidal, "The Limits of Hegemonic Stability Theory," *International Organization*, Vol. 39, No. 4 (Autumn 1985), pp. 579–614.

context of international political economy, it can be extended to other aspects of international politics. The logic of collective goods underlying the notion of a benign hegemon assumes that all states will cooperate because they derive absolute benefit from the collective goods the hegemon provides. Because they are better off, the argument goes, others should willingly accept a benign hegemon and even help to prop it up if it is declining. However, as Michael C. Webb and Stephen D. Krasner point out, the benign version of hegemonic stability theory assumes that states are indifferent to the distribution of relative gains.[31] This is, as noted, a dubious assumption. As Joseph Grieco points out, because states worry that today's ally could become tomorrow's rival, "they pay close attention to how cooperation might affect relative *capabilities* in the future."[32] Moreover, if stability is equated with the dominant state's continuing preeminence, the stability of hegemonic systems is questionable once the hegemon's power begins to erode noticeably. As Gilpin points out, over time a hegemon declines from its dominant position because: (1) the costs of sustaining its preeminence begin to erode the hegemon's economic strength, thereby diminishing its military and economic capabilities; and (2) the hegemonic paradox results in the diffusion of economic, technological, and organizational skills to other states, thereby causing the hegemon to lose its "comparative advantage" over them.[33] Frequently, these others are eligible states that will rise to great power status and challenge the hegemon's predominance.

This last point suggests that in unipolar systems, states do indeed balance against the hegemon's unchecked power. This reflects the fact that in unipolar systems there is no clear-cut distinction between balancing against threat and balancing against power. This is because the threat inheres in the hegemon's power.[34] In a unipolar world, others must worry about the he-

---

31. Michael C. Webb and Stephen D. Krasner, "Hegemonic Stability Theory: An Empirical Assessment," *Review of International Studies*, Vol. 15, No. 2 (April 1989), pp. 184–185.
32. Joseph M. Grieco, "Anarchy and the Limits of Cooperation: A Realist Critique of the Newest Liberal Institutionalism," *International Organization*, Vol. 42, No. 3 (Summer 1988), p. 500 (emphasis in original).
33. Gilpin, *War and Change*, pp. 156–210.
34. Traditional balance-of-power theory postulates that states align against others that are excessively powerful. Stephen Walt refined balance of power theory by arguing that states actually balance against threats rather than against power *per se*. However, Walt's balance-of-threat analysis is more ambiguous than it might seem at first glance. For example, he admits that every post-1648 bid for European hegemony was repulsed by a balancing coalition. *Origins of Alliances*, pp. 28–29. Why? Because would-be hegemons were powerful or because they were threatening? He does not say directly but one suspects that his answer would be "both." Walt

gemon's capabilities, not its intentions. The preeminent power's intentions may be benign today but may not be tomorrow. Robert Jervis cuts to the heart of the matter when he notes, "Minds can be changed, new leaders can come to power, values can shift, new opportunities and dangers can arise."[35] Unless they are prepared to run the risk of being vulnerable to a change in the hegemon's intentions, other states must be prepared to counter its capabilities. Moreover, even a hegemon animated by benign motives may pursue policies that run counter to others' interests. Thus, as Waltz says, "Balance-of-power theory leads one to expect that states, if they are free to do so, will flock to the weaker side. The stronger, not the weaker side, threatens them if only by pressing its preferred policies on other states."[36]

Invariably, the very fact that others believe a state is excessively powerful redounds to its disadvantage by provoking others to balance against it. It was precisely for this reason that, responding to Sir Eyre Crowe's 1907 "German danger" memorandum, Lord Thomas Sanderson counseled that London should try hard to accommodate rising great powers while simultaneously moderating its own geopolitical demands. Showing commendable empathy for other states' views of Britain's policies and its power, he observed that it would be unwise for Britain to act as if every change in international politics menaced its interests. "It has sometimes seemed to me that to a foreigner . . . the British Empire must appear in the light of some huge giant sprawling over the globe, with gouty fingers and toes stretching in every direction, which cannot be approached without eliciting a scream."[37]

does not downplay the importance of power as a factor in inducing balancing behavior; he simply says it is not the *only* factor (p. 21). Indeed, power and threat blend together almost imperceptibly. Note that two of his threat variables, geographic proximity and offensive capabilities, correlate closely with military *power*. When Walt says that states do not necessarily balance against the most powerful actor in the system he essentially is equating power with GNP. When he says that states balance against threat he is saying that they balance against military power (coupled with aggressive intentions). Obviously, power is more than just GNP. What states appear to balance against in reality is actual or latent military capabilities. In a unipolar world, the hegemon's possession of actual or latent military capabilities will result in balancing regardless of its intentions. If, in a unipolar world, capabilities matter more than intentions, the U.S. monopoly on long-range power-projection capabilities—that is, its preponderance of military power—probably will be viewed by others as threatening.
35. Robert Jervis, "Cooperation Under the Security Dilemma," *World Politics*, Vol. 30, No. 2 (January 1978), p. 105.
36. Kenneth N. Waltz, "The Emerging Structure of International Politics," paper presented at the annual meeting of the American Political Science Association, San Francisco, California, August 1990, p. 32.
37. "Memorandum by Lord Sanderson," in G.P. Gooch and Harold Temperley, eds., *British Documents on the Origins of the War, 1898–1914*, Volume III (London: His Majesty's Stationery Office [HMSO], 1928), p. 430.

It is unsurprising that counter-hegemonic balancing has occurred even during periods of *perceived* unipolarity. After the 1962 Cuban missile crisis, for instance, French policy was driven by the belief that the scales of power in the U.S.-Soviet competition were weighted too heavily in America's favor. French President DeGaulle said that the United States had become the greatest power and that it was driven "automatically" to extend its influence and "to exercise a preponderant weight, that is to say, a hegemony over others."[38] DeGaulle's policy was animated by the need to redress this perceived imbalance. As Edward Kolodziej observes, "In the closing years of Gaullist rule, *the possible development of a unipolar system became one of the major concerns of the French government.*"[39] One of the most important questions concerning international politics today is whether this pattern of balancing against the dominant power in a unipolar system (actual or perceived) will recur in the post–Cold War world.

SAMENESS. As Waltz points out, "competition produces a tendency toward sameness of the competitors"; that is, toward imitating their rivals' successful characteristics.[40] Such characteristics include not only military strategies, tactics, weaponry, and technology, but also administrative and organizational techniques. If others do well in developing effective instruments of competition, a state must emulate its rivals or face the consequences of falling behind. Fear drives states to duplicate others' successful policies because policymakers know that, as Arthur Stein observes, "failure in the anarchic international system can mean the disappearance of their states."[41] From this standpoint, it is to be expected that in crucial respects, great powers will look and act very much alike. It is also to be expected that sameness-effect imperatives will impel eligible states to become great powers and to acquire all the capabilities attendant to that status. As Waltz observes, "In a self-help system, the possession of most but not all of the capabilities of a great power leaves a state vulnerable to others who have the instruments that the lesser state lacks."[42]

Additional light is shed on the sameness effect by the "second image reversed" perspective, which posits a linkage between the international sys-

---

38. Quoted in Edward A. Kolodziej, *French International Policy Under DeGaulle and Pompidou: The Politics of Grandeur* (Ithaca: Cornell University Press, 1974), p. 91.
39. Ibid., pp. 90–91 (emphasis added).
40. Waltz, *Theory of International Politics*, p. 127.
41. Arthur Stein, *Why Nations Cooperate: Circumstance and Choice in International Relations* (Ithaca, New York: Cornell University Press, 1990), pp. 115–116.
42. Waltz, "Emerging Structure," p. 21.

tem's structural constraints and a state's domestic structure. Charles Tilly's famous aphorism, "War made the state, and the state made war" neatly captures the concept.[43] Tilly shows how the need to protect against external danger compelled states in early modern Europe to develop administrative and bureaucratic structures to maintain, supply, and finance permanent military establishments. But there is more to it than that. As is discussed below, the evidence from 1660–1713 and 1860–1910 suggests that great power emergence reflects an eligible state's adjustment to the international system's structural constraints. Otto Hinze observed that the way in which states are organized internally reflects "their position relative to each other and their overall position in the world" and that "throughout the ages pressure from without has been a determining influence on internal structure."[44]

Great powers are similar because they are not, and cannot be, functionally differentiated. This is not to say that great powers are identical. They may adopt different strategies and approaches; however, ultimately they all must be able to perform satisfactorily the same security-related tasks necessary to survive and succeed in the competitive realm of international politics. The sameness effect reflects the enormous pressure that the international system places on great powers to imitate the successful policies of others. Hinze's discussion of Prussia-Germany and England is illustrative. Their respective domestic, political and economic systems developed dissimilarly, in large part because each was affected differently by international pressures. (Maritime England was far more secure than continental Germany.) But, as is true for all great powers, in other crucial respects Prussia-Germany and England were very much alike. That is, both were organized for war and trade in order to maximize their security in a competitive international environment.

Response to Unipolarity: 1660–1714

In this and the following section, I use historical evidence to test my hypotheses about great power emergence. Such a test should be especially useful because there have been two prior occasions in history similar to

43. Charles Tilly, "Reflections on the History of European State Making," in Charles Tilly, ed., *The Formation of National States in Western Europe* (Princeton: Princeton University Press, 1975), p. 42.
44. Otto Hinze, "Military Organization and the Organization of the State," in Felix Gilbert, ed., *The Historical Essays of Otto Hinze* (Princeton: Princeton University Press, 1975), p. 183.

today's unipolar moment. France in 1660 and Great Britain in 1860 were as dominant in the international system as the United States is today. In neither case, however, did unipolarity last beyond fifty years. France's unipolar moment ended when Britain and Austria emerged as great powers; Britain's when Germany, Japan and the United States ascended to great power status. If the emergence of those great powers correlates strongly with uneven growth rates, the sameness effect, and balancing against hegemonic power, it can be expected that the present unipolar moment will be displaced by multipolarity within a reasonably short time.

FRENCH HEGEMONY IN A UNIPOLAR WORLD

It is generally agreed that in 1660, when Louis XIV ascended the French throne, France was Europe's sole great power, "the strongest and richest state in the world"; it was "a rare situation of preeminence."[45] France's dominant position reflected her own strength and the relative weakness of Europe's other states. In 1660, France was Europe's most populous state, had Europe's most efficient centralized administration, was (by the standards of the age) rich agriculturally, and had the potential to develop a dynamic industrial base.[46] In contrast, France's rivals were declining powers (Spain), or beset by internal troubles (England), or lacked France's capabilities or the means to mobilize them (Habsburg Austria).[47]

France achieved hegemonic standing by developing the means to mobilize its assets and convert them into effective diplomatic, military, and economic power.[48] France under Louis XIV was responsible for what G.R.R. Treasure calls the "*étatisation*" of war: "the mobilization of the total resources of the state, of the economy, as well as of manpower."[49] Under War Minister Michel Le Tellier, and his son and successor Louvois, the army was brought under the administrative control of the central government and a standing professional military force was created. The Military Revolution was completed and the French army was drastically altered and improved in such areas as

---

45. G.R.R. Treasure, *Seventeenth Century France* (London: Rivingtons, 1966), pp. 257–258. Agreeing that France was Europe's only great power in 1660 are Derek McKay and H.M. Scott, *The Rise of the Great Powers, 1648–1815* (London: Longman, 1983); John B. Wolf, *Toward a European Balance of Power, 1620–1715* (Chicago: Rand McNally, 1970), p. 1.
46. McKay and Scott, *Rise of the Great Powers*, pp. 14–15.
47. Treasure, *Seventeenth Century France*, pp. 210–215, surveys the relative weakness of France's European rivals.
48. McKay and Scott, *Rise of the Great Powers*, pp. 14–15.
49. Treasure, *Seventeenth Century France*, pp. 219–220.

selection of officers, recruitment, weapons, tactics, training and logistics. Finance Minister Colbert labored to strengthen France's financial and economic base to provide the wherewithal to support its enhanced military capabilities. These military, economic, and financial initiatives were made possible by the administrative reforms that strengthened the central government's power and made it more efficient.[50]

Although France was Europe's only great power in 1660, by 1713 England and Habsburg Austria, as well as Russia, had emerged as great powers. The rise of England and Habsburg Austria—that is, the international system's transformation from unipolarity to multipolarity—is directly traceable to anarchy and its consequences: the sameness effect and balancing. Because French dominance threatened their security and autonomy, England and Austria responded by: (1) organizing the Grand Alliances that, in the Nine Years' War and War of the Spanish Succession, sought to contain France and counter its power; and (2) reorganizing themselves administratively, military, and economically to acquire great power capabilities comparable to France's. Treasure observes that, "France's example forced change on other states"; Derek McKay and H.M. Scott point out that, to compete with France, France's opponents "had begun to copy the French model."[51] The increasing power of governments was a response to external danger: "International competition and war," says William Doyle, "were the main spur to domestic innovation."[52] The danger to their security posed by French hegemony forced England and Austria to emulate France and to develop the capabilities that would enable them to stand on an equal geopolitical footing with France.

England's rise to great power status was a direct response to France's preeminent position in international politics. The English King William III was concerned with maintaining England's security by establishing a balance of power to preserve "the peace, liberties, and well-being of Europe, which happened in his lifetime to be threatened by overgrown French power."[53] In

---

50. For brief discussions of the administrative, military, and economic bases of French power, see John B. Wolf, *The Emergence of the Great Powers, 1685–1715* (New York: Harper and Brothers, 1951), pp. 97–103, pp. 181–187; Treasure, *Seventeenth Century France*, pp. 231–244, 288–320; and William Doyle, *The Old European Order, 1660–1800* (Oxford: Oxford University Press, 1978), pp. 244–245. Ultimately, of course, fiscal reforms were only partially successful and France was unable to bear the huge financial costs of the Nine Years' War and War of the Spanish Succession.
51. Treasure, *Seventeenth Century France*, p. 241; McKay and Scott, *Rise of the Great Powers*, pp. 41–42.
52. Doyle, *The Old Order*, p. 265.
53. G.C. Gibbs, "The Revolution in Foreign Policy," in Geoffrey Holmes, ed., *Britain After the Glorious Revolution, 1689–1714* (London: Macmillan, 1989), p. 61.

rising to great power status, England was balancing at least as much against France's hegemonic power as against the French threat. Indeed, the distinction between power and threat was blurred.[54] After 1688, England was at war with France almost continuously for twenty-five years and the extent of its military involvement on the continent increased dramatically. England maintained a sizeable standing army and the largest and most powerful navy in the world. The imperatives of war meant that the state had to improve its ability to extract and mobilize the nation's wealth and, as in France, England's administrative capabilities were greatly expanded for this purpose between 1688 and 1713. France's hegemonic challenge was the most powerful stimulus to the growth of power of the English state: England "became, like her main rivals, a fiscal-military state, one dominated by the task of waging war."[55]

Habsburg Austria, too, emerged as a great power in response to France's hegemonic power, and also the Ottoman threat to Austria's eastern interests. The goals of Austria's western policy were "establishment of a recognized great power position and the fight against the supremacy of France."[56] In this context, for Austria, the stakes in the War of the Spanish Succession were survival and emergence as a great power.[57] Like Britain and France, Austria undertook administrative reforms aimed at increasing the state's warmaking capabilities. "The centralizing drive of the Habsburg government, latent in the sixteenth and conscious in the seventeenth centuries, was based upon a desire to consolidate power for the purpose of state security."[58]

---

54. Secretary of State Charles Hedges said, "We are awake and sensible to the too great growth of our dangerous neighbor, and are taking vigorous measures for the preservation of ourselves, and the peace of Europe." And in June 1701, King William III instructed the Duke of Marlborough to commence negotiations for an anti-French coalition "for the Preservation of the Liberties of Europe, the Property and Peace of England, and for reducing the Exorbitant Power of France." Quoted in John B. Hattendorf, "Alliance, Encirclement, and Attrition: British Grand Strategy in the War of the Spanish Succession," in Paul Kennedy, ed., *Grand Strategy in War and Peace* (New Haven: Yale University Press, 1991), p. 16.
55. John Brewer, *The Sinews of Power: War, Money, and the English State, 1688–1783* (London: Unwin Hyman, 1989), p. 27.
56. Robert A. Kann, *A History of the Habsburg Empire* (Berkeley: University of California Press, 1974), pp. 77–78.
57. Ibid., pp. 84–85.
58. Thomas M. Barker, *Double Eagle and Crescent: Vienna's Second Turkish Siege and Its Historical Setting* (Albany: State University of New York Press, 1967), p. 19. In the administrative sphere, efforts were stepped up to subject Hungary (the bulk of which only came under firm Austrian control after the Ottomans were defeated in 1683) to Vienna's control so that Austria could draw upon its resources; a central organ, the *Hofkanzlei*, was established to conduct foreign and domestic affairs; the *Hofkammer* was established to exert central control over the finances of Habsburg Austria's possessions; and the *Hofkriegsrat* was created to administer Austria's army centrally and remodel it as a standing professional army on French lines. See Wolf, *Emergence*

Austria was considerably less successful than France and England in creating administrative mechanisms for the efficient mobilization of national resources. Nevertheless, it remains the case that the need for security in the face of French hegemony forced Austria (like England) both to emulate France and to balance against it in order to attain great power status.[59]

Response to Unipolarity: 1860–1910

In 1860, Britain was in a position of apparently unequaled dominance in an international system that has been characterized as unipolar.[60] Because it was Europe's arbiter and possessor of a worldwide and unchallenged colonial empire, "Britain could not have been met with an overwhelming balancing coalition."[61] Indeed, Britain's dominance was so pronounced that it was able in the early 1860s largely to turn its back on European security affairs and withdraw into a "splendid isolation" that lasted until the turn of the century. Britain's hegemony was a function of its naval power, its colonial empire, and its overwhelming economic and financial strength.[62] The Royal Navy was as strong as those of the next three or four naval powers combined. Britain's level of per capita industrialization was more than twice that of the

of the Great Powers, pp. 126–137; R.J.W. Evans, *The Making of the Habsburg Monarchy* (Oxford: Clarendon Press, 1979), pp. 148–150.

59. Although Russia's rise to great power status paralleled England's and Austria's, I do not discuss it at length because it was unconnected to the wars against French hegemony.

60. The phrase "unequaled dominance" is from Paul Kennedy, *Rise and Fall of Great Powers*, p. 152. Michael Doyle describes the international system in 1860 as "unipolar-peripheral"; that is, in the extra-European world, Britain's power was unchallenged. Doyle, *Empires* (Ithaca: Cornell University Press, 1986), p. 236. Building on Doyle, Fareed Zakaria drops the qualifier and describes the mid-nineteenth century international system as unipolar. Zakaria, "Realism and Domestic Politics: A Review Essay," *International Security*, Vol. 17, No. 1 (Summer 1992), pp. 186–187.

61. Zakaria, "Realism and Domestic Politics," p. 187. There is empirical support for Zakaria's statement. William B. Moul's measurement of the power capability shares of Europe's great powers confirms Britain's hegemonic standing. In 1860, Britain's share was 43.8 percent, while the combined shares of Prussia, France, Austria, Russia and Italy was 56.2 percent. France was the second-ranked power at 19.7 percent. Moul, "Measuring the 'Balances of Power': A Look at Some Numbers," *Review of International Studies*, Vol. 15, No. 2 (April 1989), p. 120.

62. This discussion, and the figures cited, are based on Kennedy, *Rise and Fall of Great Powers*, pp. 152–157. In the United States there is a spirited debate about the contemporary implications of Britain's decline. For contrasting views in a policy context, see Nye, *Bound to Lead*, pp. 49–68, which rejects the British analogy's relevance; and David P. Calleo, *Beyond American Hegemony: The Future of the Western Alliance* (New York: Basic Books, 1987), pp. 129–149, which sees a strong parallel between the *Pax Britannica*'s demise and the likely demise of the post-1945 *Pax Americana*.

next ranking power (France), and Britain in 1860 accounted for 53.2 percent of world manufacturing output (a bit more than America's share in 1945).

In the following discussion, I look at the great power emergence of Germany, the United States, and Japan (but not Italy's attempted rise to great power status), and analyze how each was affected by relative power shifts and the consequences of anarchy. Germany's rise to world power status was most obviously a direct response to Britain's hegemony, while in the American and Japanese cases the connection between unipolarity and great power emergence, though less direct, is still discernible.

BRITISH HEGEMONY IN A UNIPOLAR WORLD

Britain's preeminence cast a shadow over the international system. By 1880, it was widely (and correctly) perceived that the European great power system was evolving into a system of three or four "world" powers (what today are called superpowers).[63] International politics was profoundly affected by this trend, which alerted policymakers to the security and economic consequences of the relative distribution of power in the international system. After 1880, there was among statesmen "a prevailing view of the world order which stressed struggle, change, competition, the use of force and the organization of national resources to enhance state power."[64] Britain was the first world power and it was the model that other rising powers sought to imitate as they climbed to great power status. In other words, the sameness effect was very much in evidence. Speaking of Germany, Japan, and Italy, Paul Kennedy says:

In all three societies there were impulses to emulate the established powers. By the 1880s and 1890s each was acquiring overseas territories; each, too, began to build a modern fleet to complement its standing army. Each was a significant element in the diplomatic calculus of the age and, at the least by 1902, had become an alliance partner of an older power.[65]

---

63. See Kennedy, *Rise and Fall of Great Powers*, pp. 194–202. This transformation is illustrated by the great powers' respective shares of total industrial potential and world manufacturing output. In 1880 Germany, France, and Russia were tightly bunched and well behind both Britain and the United States in terms of both total industrial potential and shares of world manufacturing output. However, by 1913 Britain, the United States, and Germany had widely distanced themselves from the rest of the great power pack. In terms of total industrial potential and share of world manufacturing output, third-place Germany held nearly a 2:1 advantage over Russia, the next ranking power.
64. Ibid., p. 196.
65. Ibid., pp. 202–203.

Kennedy does not mention the United States in this passage but he could have. Although the United States did not need a large army and was able to refrain from joining a great power alliance, it followed the same pattern of building a powerful modern navy, acquiring overseas colonies, and becoming a major factor in great power diplomacy.

GERMANY'S RISE TO WORLD POWER

The effect of differential growth rates was an important factor in Germany's rise to great power status. As Paul Kennedy has pointed out, Germany's economic growth after 1860 was "explosive."[66] Between 1860 and 1913, Germany's share of world manufacturing output rose from 4.9 percent to 14.8 percent and its share of world trade from 9.7 percent to 13 percent.[67] In 1913, Germany's share of world exports was 13 percent (compared to Britain's 14 percent).[68] Germany's rising power facilitated Berlin's decision to seek change in the international system. As Kennedy observes, Germany "either already possessed the instruments of power to alter the status quo or had the material resources to create such instruments."[69] As Kurt Reiszler, political confidant of pre–World War I Chancellor Bethmann Hollweg, observed, *Weltpolitik* was tightly linked to the dynamic growth of Germany's export-driven economy.[70] Reiszler also noted how Germany's demands for power and prestige increased in proportion to its rising strength.[71] Predictably, Germany's increasing ambition reflected Berlin's concern with protecting its deepening stakes in the international system. For a rising power such behavior is typical: "In order to increase its own security, it will try to expand its political, economic and territorial control; it will try to change the international system in accordance with its particular interests."[72]

Germany's rise to world power status was a direct response to Britain's preeminence in international politics. "The Germans came to resent British power and even British efforts to maintain their position unimpaired."[73] *Weltpolitik*—Germany's push for a big navy, colonies, and equality with Brit-

66. Ibid., p. 210.
67. Ibid., pp. 149, 202; Paul Kennedy, *The Rise of the Anglo-German Antagonism, 1860–1914* (London: George Allen and Unwin, 1980), pp. 44, 292.
68. Kennedy, *Anglo-German Antagonism*, p. 292.
69. Kennedy, *Rise and Fall of Great Powers*, p. 211.
70. Quoted in Imanuel Geiss, *German Foreign Policy, 1871–1914* (London: Routledge and Kegan Paul, 1976), p. 9.
71. Ibid., p. 81.
72. Gilpin, *War and Change*, pp. 94–95.
73. William L. Langer, *The Diplomacy of Imperialism, 1890–1902*, 2d ed. (New York: Alfred A. Knopf, 1965), p. 416.

ain in political influence and prestige—was driven by security concerns and was a clear manifestation of the sameness effect. German leaders were concerned that unless Germany developed countervailing naval power, its independence and interests in international politics would be circumscribed by Britain.[74] Chancellor Chlodwig Hohenlohe-Schillingfurst said in 1896: "Unless we are prepared to yield at all times and to give up the role of world power, then we must be respected. Even the most friendly word makes no impression in international relations if it is not supported by adequate material strength. Therefore, a fleet is necessary in the face of other naval powers." Notwithstanding the consequences, in an anarchic world Germany had little choice but to emulate Britain by building a powerful navy.[75]

Germany's rise to world power status and the resulting Anglo-German antagonism were structurally determined. Unless Germany acquired world power capabilities, it would have been vulnerable to states like Britain that did have them.[76] William L. Langer points out that Germany's increasing international interests and the need to defend them in the face of Britain's

---

74. Grand Admiral Alfred von Tirpitz believed Germany could not remain a great power unless it developed into a first-rank maritime power. Volker R. Berghahn, *Germany and the Approach of War in 1914* (London: MacMillan, 1973), p. 29. "Naval power," Tirpitz said, "is essential if Germany does not want to go under"; Ivor Lambi, *The Navy and German Power Politics, 1862–1914* (Boston: George Allen and Unwin, 1984), p. 139.

75. Quotation from Lambi, *The Navy and German Power Politics*, p. 114. Even Sir Eyre Crowe, the British Foreign Office's leading anti-German hardliner, recognized this in his famous 1907 memorandum. Crowe conceded that it was for Berlin, not London, to determine the size of the navy necessary to defend German interests. Crowe also understood that British opposition to Germany's naval buildup would serve only to accentuate Berlin's security dilemma: "Apart from the question of right and wrong, it may also be urged that nothing would be more likely than an attempt at such dictation, to impel Germany to persevere with her shipbuilding programs." "Memorandum by Mr. [Sir] Eyre Crow," in Gooch and Temperley, *Documents on the Origins of the War*, p. 418.

76. In the late nineteenth and early twentieth century, Germany's international behavior differed little from Britain's or America's. But unlike Britain, Germany's outward thrust did not go into a geopolitical vacuum, and unlike the United States, Germany lacked a secure strategic and economic base of continental dimension. Germany was hemmed in and its rise to great power status was too rapid, and too freighted with implications for others' interests, to be accommodated. David Calleo, *The German Problem Reconsidered: Germany and the World Order, 1870 to the Present* (Cambridge: Cambridge University Press, 1978), pp. 83–84. As W.E. Mosse observes, Germany's rise to great power status "could not but affect the interests and policies of all others. It was bound to frustrate and arouse the opposition of some at least of the older powers." W.E. Mosse, *The European Powers and the German Question, 1848–1871: With Special Reference to England and Russia* (Cambridge: Cambridge University Press, 1958), p. 2. In a real sense, therefore, Germany was born encircled. Merely by existing, it posed a threat to others. There is an important lesson here. A state must decide for itself whether to strive for great power status, but success hinges on how others react. Some states (such as pre-1914 Germany) may face a difficult path to great power status, while for others (e.g., the United States) the going is relatively easy. Environmental factors, such as geographic positioning, have a lot to do with the difficulties that may confront an eligible state as it attempts to rise to great power status.

preeminence meant that Berlin was "virtually driven" into imitating London by pursuing a policy of naval and colonial expansion. Given these circumstances, "it is hard to see how Germany could have avoided colliding with England."[77] The Anglo-German rivalry was a textbook example of the security dilemma. Because Germany's rise to world power status challenged a *status quo* that primarily reflected Britain's predominance and interests, *Weltpolitik* made Britain less secure and prompted London to take counteraction. Thus, the Anglo-German rivalry illustrates that the process of great power emergence can trigger a Hertz/Avis dynamic if a rising great power emerges as the clear challenger to a preeminent state's position.[78]

Such states are fated to engage in intense competition. The effect of Germany's emergence to great power status on Anglo-German relations is suggestive. In 1880, for example, Germany's power position (measured by share of world manufacturing output and total industrial potential) was similar to that of France and Russia.[79] While London and Berlin were on close terms during the 1880s (which at times verged on *de facto* alliance), France and Russia were Britain's main rivals.[80] By 1900, however, the Anglo-German rivalry had heated up and Germany had by a decisive margin established

---

77. Langer, *Diplomacy of Imperialism*, p. 794.

78. The competition between the largest and second-largest U.S. automobile rental companies (Hertz and Avis, respectively) became famous when Avis ran an advertising campaign with the slogan, "We're number two; we try harder." The analogy of the Anglo-German rivalry to commercial competition was apparent to Tirpitz, who wrote, "the older and stronger firm inevitably seeks to strangle the new and rising one before it is too late." Paul Kennedy, "The Kaiser and German *Weltpolitik*: Reflexions on Wilhelm II's Place in the Making of German Foreign Policy," in John C.G. Röhl and Nicolaus Sombart, *Kaiser Wilhelm II: New Interpretations* (Cambridge: Cambridge University Press, 1982), p. 149.

79. In 1880, the total industrial potential of the four powers was: Britain (73.3, where Britain in 1900 is the index benchmark of 100), Germany (27.4), France (25.1), Russia (24.5). The four powers' shares of world manufacturing output were: Britain (22.9 percent), Germany (8.5 percent), France (7.8 percent), Russian (7.6 percent). Kennedy, *Rise and Fall of Great Powers*, pp. 201–202.

80. This does not contradict my argument that Germany's rise to world power status was a balancing response to Britain's hegemony. On the contrary: during the 1880s, Berlin and London were able to mantain a cordial relationship because Germany's relative power had not risen to a point that thrust Germany into the challenger's role. It should also be noted that during the 1880s the Anglo-German relationship was indirect. London was aligned not with Berlin itself but with Germany's allies, Austria-Hungary and Italy. This alignment was part of Bismarck's intricate alliance scheme and was meant to counter Russian ambitions in the Near East and Mediterranean, an objective that overlapped Britain's interests. Bismarck's system also was intended to isolate France while simultaneously keeping Berlin on friendly terms with Europe's other great powers. After 1890, the stunning rise in Germany's relative power became manifest. Inexorably, Germany was pushed down the path to world power status, and to confrontation with Britain.

itself as Europe's second-ranking power. Indeed, Germany was closing in on Britain in terms of share of world manufacturing output and total industrial potential, and by 1913, Germany would pass Britain in these two categories.[81] The dramatic change in the two states' relative power positions fueled the deterioration in Anglo-German relations, and led to a shift in European geopolitical alignments as London sought ententes with its erstwhile rivals, France and Russia, as counterweights to German power.

EMBRYONIC SUPERPOWER: AMERICA'S RISE TO WORLD POWER

It has been argued that the United States did not seek to become a great power but rather had that status thrust upon it.[82] This view does not hold up, however. By the mid-1870s, the United States was contemplating a new role in world affairs, however tentatively.[83] This outward thrust was underpinned by the effect of differential growth rates. In the decades after the War Between the States, the United States acquired enormous economic capabilities including a rapidly expanding manufacturing and industrial base, leadership in advanced technology, a highly productive agricultural sector, abundant raw materials, ample foreign (and later internally generated) capital.[84] In 1880, the United States (at 14.7 percent) ranked second behind Great Britain (at 22.9 percent) in world manufacturing output. By 1913, the United States (at 32 percent) held a commanding advantage in share of world manufacturing production over Germany (14.8 percent) and Britain (13.6 percent).[85] As Kennedy has observed, given the economic, technological, and

---

81. In 1900, the total industrial potential of the four powers was: Britain, 100; Germany, 71.3; Russia, 47.6; France, 36.8. The four powers' shares of world manufacturing output were: Britain, 18.5 percent, Germany, 13.2 percent, Russia, 8.8 percent, France, 6.8 percent. Kennedy, *Rise and Fall of Great Powers*, pp. 201–202.
82. Ernest R. May, *Imperial Democracy: The Emergence of America as a Great Power* (New York: Harcourt, Brace and World, 1961), pp. 269–270.
83. Milton Plesur, *America's Outward Thrust: Approaches to Foreign Affairs, 1865–1890* (DeKalb: Northern Illinois University Press, 1971). "Whether great power status came in the 1890s or earlier, it is certain that the United States did not make the decision for colonialism and world involvement in a sudden movement which caught the national psyche offguard. The new departure had its roots in the quiet years of the Gilded Age." Ibid., pp. 9–10. Edward P. Crapol has recently surveyed the state of the historiography of late nineteenth-century American foreign policy. Many recent works take the view that the United States consciously sought world power status. Crapol, "Coming to Terms with Empire: The Historiography of Late Nineteenth Century American Foreign Relations," *Diplomatic History*, Vol. 16, No. 4 (Fall 1992), pp. 573–597.
84. See Kennedy, *Rise and Fall of Great Powers*, pp. 178–182, 242–249.
85. Ibid., pp. 201–202.

resource advantages the United States enjoyed, there "was a virtual inevitability to the whole process" of its rise to great power status.[86]

In the late nineteenth century, the historian Frederick Jackson Turner noted that because states develop significant international political interests as their international economic interests deepen, the United States was already on the way to becoming a great power.[87] During the Benjamin Harrison administration, the United States began engaging in what Secretary of State James G. Blaine (echoing William Pitt the younger) called "the annexation of trade."[88] Focusing first on Latin America, U.S. overseas economic interests expanded later to encompass Asia and Europe as well. Like Germany, as America's overseas economic stakes grew (or were perceived to grow), its international political interests also increased.[89] Paul Kennedy observes that the "growth of American industrial power and overseas trade was accompanied, perhaps inevitably, by a more assertive diplomacy and by an American-style rhetoric of *Weltpolitik*."[90]

Again like Germany, as America's stakes in the international system deepened, Washington began acquiring the capabilities to defend its interests. As early as the 1870s, proponents of naval expansion argued that, lacking an enlarged and modernized fleet, the United States would be vulnerable and powerless to defend its interests.[91] In the 1880s, Alfred Thayer Mahan argued that attainment of world power status was the key to America's security. His arguments about the "influence of sea power upon history" displayed an intuitive understanding of the sameness effect and he presciently argued that, to become a world power, the United States would have to emulate Britain's naval, colonial, and trade policies.[92] America's naval buildup began during the Harrison administration (1889–93) when Navy Secretary Tracy

86. Kennedy, *Rise and Fall of Great Powers*, p. 242.

87. Quoted in Walter LaFeber, *The New Empire: An Interpretation of American Expansion, 1860–1898* (Ithaca: Cornell University Press, 1963), pp. 69–70.

88. Quoted in ibid., p. 106.

89. American policymakers believed that overseas markets were more crucial to the nation's economic health than in fact was true. By 1913, foreign trade accounted for only 8 percent of GNP, compared with 26 percent for Britain. Kennedy, *Rise and Fall of Great Powers*, p. 244.

90. Kennedy, *Rise and Fall of Great Powers*, p. 246.

91. J.A.S. Grenville and George B. Young, *Politics, Strategy, and American Diplomacy: Studies in American Foreign Policy, 1873–1917* (New Haven: Yale University Press, 1966), pp. 5–6.

92. On Mahan's views, see Harold and Margaret Sprout, *The Rise of American Naval Power, 1776–1918* (Princeton: Princeton University Press, 1944), pp. 202–222; LaFeber, *The New Empire*, pp. 80–95.

persuaded Congress to authorize construction of a modern battleship fleet.[93] This building program signalled a break with the navy's traditional strategy of protecting American commerce, in favor of one challenging rivals for command of the sea. Responding to an increasingly competitive international environment, the navy chose "to make itself into a European-style force ready for combat with the navies of the other major powers."[94] America's naval buildup was underpinned by its rising economic power. Naval expenditures as a percentage of federal spending rose from 6.9 percent in 1890 to 19 percent in 1914 and Kennedy recounts the shock of a famous British warship designer when he discovered during a 1904 visit that America's industrial capabilities were such that the United States was simultaneously building 14 battleships and 13 armored cruisers.[95]

The extent to which America's great power emergence was a direct response to unipolarity is unclear. It is apparent, however, that Britain's preeminence was at least an important factor. The impetus for America's naval buildup and growing geopolitical assertiveness was deepening apprehension about the Western hemisphere's vulnerabilty to European encroachment, especially if the European great powers shifted the focus of their colonial rivalries from Asia to the Americas.[96] Policymakers became convinced that "American claims in Latin America would only be as strong as the military force behind them. Consequently, as American stakes in Central and South America increased, so did American military [i.e., naval] strength."[97] Thus, America's rise to great power status was a defensive reaction to the threat posed by others to its expanding overseas interests. Until 1898, the United States regarded Britain as the main danger to its strategic and commercial interests in the Western hemisphere.[98] No doubt, American feelings toward

---

93. For a brief discussion, see Kenneth J. Hagan, *This People's Navy: The Making of American Sea Power* (New York: The Free Press, 1991), pp. 194–197.
94. Ibid., p. 186.
95. Kennedy, *Rise and Fall of Great Powers*, pp. 243, 247.
96. The relationship between security worries and American foreign and strategic policy is explored in Richard D. Challener, *Admirals, Generals and Foreign Policy, 1898–1914* (Princeton: Princeton University Press, 1973); and Grenville and Young, *Politics, Strategy and American Diplomacy.*
97. LaFeber, *New Empire*, p. 229.
98. Kinley J. Brauer has argued that between 1815 and 1860, American leaders were concerned about the implications of Britain's expanding global interests, and various strategies were contemplated to counter the threat posed by Britain's naval and economic power and its formal and informal empire. Although these proposed strategic responses to British power did not

Britian were ambivalent because not only was the United States threatened by Britain's hegemony but simultaneously it was also a major beneficiary of London's preeminence. Nevertheless, Britain's predominance was tolerated only until the United States was strong enough to challenge it. Backed by growing naval power and unlimited industrial potential, in the mid-1890s the United States launched a diplomatic offensive against Britain. In 1895–96, the United States provoked a crisis with Britain over the seemingly obscure boundary dispute between Venezuela and British Guiana.[99] London was compelled to back down and to acknowledge America's hemispheric primacy. By 1903, Britain had given in completely to American demands concerning control over the proposed isthmian canal and the boundary between Alaska and Canada. Shortly thereafter, Britain bowed to the reality of America's overwhelming regional power and withdrew its naval and military forces from North America.

JAPAN: EXTERNAL THREAT, INTERNAL RESPONSE

Japan's great power emergence differed from Germany's and America's. The effect of differential growth rates was not a factor. Between 1860 and 1938, comparative measures of great power capabilities put Japan at or near the bottom of the list. For example, between 1860 and 1938, Japan's share of world manufacturing output rose only from 2.6 percent to 3.8 percent.[100] Japan's great power emergence was, rather, driven by its extreme vulnerability. Indeed, in the 1860s, Japan's very existence as a nation-state was at risk.

Although Japan's security-driven great power emergence was not a direct response to unipolarity, here too Britain's preeminence had its effect. Specifically, it was Britain's defeat of China in the Opium Wars, and China's consequent loss of independence, that provided an object lesson for the

---

come to fruition before the War Between the States, they nevertheless laid the groundwork for America's subsequent rise to world power status. Kinley J. Brauer, "The United States and British Imperial Expansion," *Diplomatic History*, Vol. 12, No. 1 (Winter 1988), pp. 19–38.
99. For brief discussions of the Venezuela crisis, see J.A.S. Grenville, *Lord Salisbury and Foreign Policy at the Close of the Nineteenth Century* (London: Athlone Press, 1964), pp. 54–73; May, *Imperial Democracy*, pp. 35–55; LaFeber, *The New Empire*, pp. 242–283; and "The Background of Cleveland's Venezuelan Policy: A Reconsideration," *American Historical Review*, Vol. 66, No. 4 (July 1961), pp. 947–967.
100. Kennedy, *Rise and Fall of Great Powers*, pp. 198–209.

reformers who led the Meiji Restoration.[101] They were determined that Japan would not suffer China's fate. As Shumpei Okamoto notes, the Meiji reformers shared a common purpose: "Throughout the Meiji period, the aspiration and resolve shared by all those concerned with the fate of the nation were that Japan strive to maintain its independence in a world dominated by the Western powers."[102] The reformers' aim was neatly expressed in the slogan *fukoku kyohei*—"enrich the country, strengthen the army"—which "became the official program of the Meiji government, geared to achieving the strength with which Japan could resist the West."[103]

Driven by security concerns, Japan's great power emergence reflected the sameness effect. To be secure Japan needed to develop the kind of military and economic capabilities that would enable it to compete with the West. In Meiji Japan, therefore, domestic politics was shaped by foreign policy concerns.[104] The era's governmental and administrative reforms, for example, were intended to reorganize Japan's central governmental structure along Western lines; centralized government was seen to be necessary if Japan were to organize itself to defend its interests from foreign encroachment.[105] Similarly, the Imperial Edict abolishing the feudal domains (1871) justified the action by observing that Japan needed a strong central government if it was "to stand on an equal footing with countries abroad."[106]

Recognizing the link between economics and national power, the Meiji era reformers worked hard to expand Japan's industrial and commercial strength. Toshimichi Okubo said in 1874:

A country's strength depends on the prosperity of its people . . . [which] in turn depends upon their productive capacity. And although the amount of production is determined in large measure by the diligence of the people

---

101. The intellectual background of the Meiji Restoration is discussed in W.G. Beasley, *The Meiji Restoration* (Stanford: Stanford University Press, 1972), pp. 74–139.
102. Shumpei Okamoto, *The Japanese Oligarchy and the Russo-Japanese War* (New York: Columbia University Press, 1960), p. 43.
103. Beasley, *The Meiji Restoration*, p. 379.
104. See James B. Crowley, "Japan's Military Foreign Policies," in James W. Morley, ed., *Japan's Foreign Policy, 1868–1941: A Research Guide* (New York: Columbia University Press, 1974). Also see W.G. Beasley, *The Rise of Modern Japan* (London: Weidenfeld and Nicolson, 1990), p. 21, where it is similarly pointed out that the Meiji Restoration, and its consequent reforms, were based on the assumption that a causal relationship existed between modernization at home and success in foreign policy.
105. See Beasley, *Rise of Modern Japan*, pp. 68–69; and *The Meiji Restoration*, pp. 303–304.
106. Quoted in Beasley, *The Meiji Restoration*, p. 347.

engaged in manufacturing industries, a deeper probe for the ultimate determinate reveals no instance when a country's productive power was increased without the patronage and encouragement of the government and its officials.[107]

Okubo, a key figure in the early Restoration governments, had visited Europe, including Bismarckian Germany. His travels underscored for Okubo the competitive nature of international politics and "convinced him that he must establish for Japan the same bases upon which the world powers of the day had founded their wealth and strength."[108] Under his direction, the government supported the expansion of manufacturing, trade, and shipping. At all times, there was a sense of urgency about Japan's internal efforts to enhance its national security by becoming a great power. Field Marshal Aritomo Yamagata, one of the Meiji era's towering political and military figures, said in 1898 that if Japan wanted to avoid lagging behind the West, "we cannot relax for even a day from encouraging education, greater production, communications and trade."[109]

From the beginning, almost every aspect of Meiji policy was directed toward safeguarding Japan's security and to vindicating its claim to equal status with the Western powers. To this end, Field Marshal Yamagata stressed, no effort must be spared to expand Japan's army and navy and to revise the post-1853 unequal treaties that the Western powers had forced upon Tokyo. These goals had largely been accomplished by 1890. A rising Japan then began to project its power outwards. The fear that the European powers would try to deny Japan economic access to China led the Japanese leadership to conclude that Japan must establish its own sphere of influence on the mainland.[110] Japan "found that a concern with defense led easily to arguments for expansion."[111] Japan's policy led to the Sino-Japanese War of 1894–95 and eventually to the Russo-Japanese War of 1904–05. Japan's mili-

---

107. Quoted in Masakazu Iwata, *Okubo Toshimichi: The Bismarck of Modern Japan* (Berkeley: University of California Press, 1964), p. 236.
108. Ibid., p. 175.
109. Quoted in Roger F. Hackett, *Yamagata Aritomo and the Rise of Modern Japan, 1838–1922* (Cambridge: Harvard University Press, 1971), p. 195.
110. Crowley, "Japan's Military Foreign Policies," p. 14.
111. Beasley, *Rise of Modern Japan*, p. 140. Beasley's observation seems entirely correct. Fear begets expansion. And expansion has its own consequences. As John Lewis Gaddis comments, "the principal occupational hazard as a general rule of being a great power is paranoia . . . and the exhaustion it ultimately produces." "Toward the Post–Cold War World," in John Lewis Gaddis, *The United States and the End of the Cold War: Implications, Reconsiderations, Provocations* (New York: Oxford University Press, 1992), p. 215.

tary successes in these conflicts established it as the leading power in Northeast Asia, and Japan's victory over Russia "secured her recognition as a major world power."[112]

HISTORY, UNIPOLARITY AND GREAT POWER EMERGENCE
There is a strong correlation between unipolarity and great power emergence. Late seventeenth-century England and Austria and late nineteenth-century Germany balanced against the dominant pole in the system. Moreover, even when great power emergence was not driven primarily by the need to counterbalance the hegemon's power, the shadow of preeminence was an important factor.[113] This is illustrated by the rise of the United States and Japan to great power status in the late nineteenth century. It is, therefore, apparent that a general tendency exists during unipolar moments: several new great powers simultaneously enter the international system. The events of the late nineteenth century also illustrate how competition from established great powers combined with challenges from rising great powers to diminish Britain's relative power and erode its primacy. During the last years of the nineteenth century, Britain, the most powerful state in the system, was the target of others' balancing policies. "The story of European international relations in the 1890s is the story of the assault of Russia and France upon the territorial position of Britain in Asia and Africa, and the story of the great economic duel between England and her all-too-efficient German rival."[114]

In the late nineteenth century, the growth of American, German, and Japanese naval power compelled Britain to forgo its policy of maintaining global naval supremacy.[115] Indeed, Britain was pressed hard by its rivals on all fronts. By 1900, it was apparent that London could not simultaneously meet the German challenge across the North Sea, defend its imperial and colonial interests from French and Russian pressure, and preserve its position in the Western hemisphere. Britain withdrew from the Western hemisphere

---

112. Ian Nish, *Japanese Foreign Policy, 1869–1942* (London: Routledge and Kegan Paul, 1977), p. 78.
113. The shadow effect is a consequence of anarchy. The unbalanced distribution of power in the hegemon's favor implicitly threatens others' security. This is because states must react to the hegemon's capabilities rather than to its intentions. In a unipolar system, concern with security is a compelling reason for eligible states to acquire great power capabilities, even if they are not immediately menaced by the hegemon.
114. Langer, *The Diplomacy of Imperialism*, p. 415.
115. See Aaron L. Friedberg, *The Weary Titan: Britain and the Experience of Relative Decline, 1895–1905* (Princeton: Princeton University Press, 1988), pp. 135–208.

because London realized it lacked the resources to compete successfully against the United States and that the naval forces deployed in North American waters could better be used elsewhere.[116] The Anglo-Japanese alliance was driven, from London's standpoint, by the need to use Japanese naval power to protect Britain's East Asian interests and thereby allow the Royal Navy units in the Far East to be redeployed to home waters. Like the rapproachment with Washington and the alliance with Tokyo, the ententes with France and Russia also evidenced Britain's declining relative power. By 1907, Britain's geopolitical position "depended upon the kindness of strangers." Over the longer term, the great power emergence of the United States and Japan paved the way for Britain's eclipse, first as hegemon and then as a great power. In the 1930s, Japanese power cost Britain its Far Eastern position, and America's relative power ultimately rose to a point where it could displace Britain as hegemon. Such was the result of Britain's policy of benign hegemony, a policy that did not merely abstain from opposing, but actually had the effect of facilitating the emergence of new great powers.

After the Cold War: America in a Unipolar World?

The historical evidence from 1660–1714 and 1860–1914 strongly supports the hypothesis derived from neorealist theory: unipolar moments cause geopolitical backlashes that lead to multipolarity. Nevertheless, in principle, a declining hegemon does have an alternative to a policy of tolerating the rise of new great powers: it can actively attempt to suppress their emergence. Thus, if Washington were prepared to contemplate preventive measures (including the use of force), it might be able to beat back rising challengers.[117] But, although prevention may seem attractive at first blush, it is a stop-gap measure. It may work once, but over time the effect of differential growth rates ensures that other challengers will subsequently appear. Given its probable costs and risks, prevention is not a strategy that would lend itself to repetition.

---

116. See C.J. Lowe and M.L. Dockrill, *The Mirage of Power*, Vol. I: *British Foreign Policy, 1902–14* (London: Routledge and Kegan Paul, 1972), pp. 96–106.
117. When a hegemon finds its primacy threatened, the best strategy is "to eliminate the source of the problem." Gilpin, *War and Change*, p. 191.

THE STRATEGY OF PREPONDERANCE

In any event, the United States has chosen a somewhat different strategy to maintain its primacy. Essentially the United States is trying to maintain intact the international order it constructed in World War II's aftermath. As Melvyn Leffler points out, after 1945 American strategy aimed at achieving a "preponderance of power" in the international system.[118] Washington sought to incorporate Western Europe, West Germany, and Japan into an American-led alliance; create an open global economy that would permit the unfettered movement of goods, capital and technology; and create an international environment conducive to America's democratic values. While committed to reviving Western Europe, Germany, and Japan economically and politically, Washington also believed that "neither an integrated Europe nor a united Germany nor an independent Japan must be permitted to emerge as a third force or a neutral bloc."[119] To maintain its preeminence in the non-Soviet world, American strategy used both benevolent and coercive incentives.

In attempting to perpetuate unipolarity, the United States is pursuing essentially the same goals, and using the same means to achieve them, that it pursued in its postwar quest for preponderance.[120] The "new NSC 68" argues that American grand strategy should actively attempt to mold the international environment by creating a secure world in which American interests are protected. American alliances with Japan and Germany are viewed as an integral part of a strategy that seeks: (1) to prevent multipolar rivalries; (2) to discourage the rise of global hegemons; and (3) to preserve a cooperative and healthy world economy. The forward deployment of U.S. military forces abroad is now viewed primarily as a means of preserving unipolarity. If the United States continues to extend security guarantees to Japan and Germany, it is reasoned, they will have no incentive to develop great power capabilities. Indeed, fear that Japan and Germany will acquire independent capabilities—that is, that they will become great powers—per-

---

118. Melvyn P. Leffler, *A Preponderance of Power: National Security, the Truman Administration, and the Cold War* (Stanford: Stanford University Press, 1992).
119. Ibid., p. 17. For second-image theorists, America's rejection of a preventive war strategy is unsurprising. It has been argued that in addition to not fighting other democracies, declining democratic powers also do not engage in preventive war against rising challengers. Randall Schweller, "Domestic Structure and Preventive War: Are Democracies More Pacific?" *World Politics*, Vol. 44, No. 2 (January 1992), pp. 235–269.
120. As I discuss below, it was the bipolar structure of the postwar system that allowed Washington to pursue a strategy of preponderance successfully and thereby smother the re-emergence of Japan and Germany as great powers.

vades the thinking of American strategists. For example, a recent RAND study of American strategy in the Pacific says that Washington must manage relations with Tokyo to maintain "the current alliance and reduce Japanese incentives for major rearmament."[121] A RAND study of the future of U.S. forces in Europe suggests that American withdrawal from Europe could result in Germany reemerging as "a heavy handed rogue elephant in Central Europe" because it would drive Germany in the "direction of militarization, nuclearization, and chronically insecure policies."[122]

Inevitably, a strategy of preponderance will fail. A strategy of more or less benign hegemony does not prevent the emergence of new great powers. The fate of nineteenth-century Britain, which followed such a strategy, is illustrative. A strategy of benign hegemony allows others to free-ride militarily and economically. Over time, the effect is to erode the hegemon's preeminence. A hegemon tends to overpay for security, which eventually weakens the internal foundation of its external position. Other states underpay for security, which allows them to shift additional resources into economically productive investments. Moreover, benign hegemony facilitates the diffusion of wealth and technology to potential rivals. As a consequence, differential growth rates trigger shifts in relative economic power that ultimately result in the emergence of new great powers. No doubt, the strategy of preponderance could prolong unipolarity somewhat, as long as eligible states calculate that the benefits of free riding outweigh the constraints imposed on them by American hegemony. Over time, however, such a policy will accelerate the hegemon's relative decline.

There is another reason why a strategy of preponderance will not work. Such a strategy articulates a vision of an American-led international order. George Bush's New World Order and Bill Clinton's apparent commitment to assertive projection of America's democratic and human rights values reflect America's desire to "press its preferred policies" on others.[123] But there is more to it than that. Other states can justifiably infer that Washington's

---

121. James A. Winnefeld, et al., *A New Strategy and Fewer Forces: The Pacific Dimension*, R-4089/1-USDP (Santa Monica, Calif.: RAND 1992), p. 111.
122. Richard L. Kugler, *The Future U.S. Military Presence in Europe: Forces and Requirements for the Post–Cold War Era*, R-4194-EUCOM/NA (Santa Monica, Calif.: RAND, 1992), pp. 11, 16.
123. As Waltz points out, other states cannot trust an excessively powerful state to behave with moderation. The United States may believe it is acting for the noblest of reasons. But, he notes, America's definition of peace, justice, and world order reflects American interests and may conflict with the interests of other states. "With benign intent, the United States has behaved, and until its power is brought into some semblance of balance, will continue to behave in ways that frighten and annoy others." Waltz, "America as a Model?" p. 669.

unipolar aspirations will result in the deliberate application of American power to compel them to adhere to the United States' policy preferences. For example, in a February 1991 address to the New York Economic Club, Bush said that because the United States had taken the leader's role in the Gulf militarily, America's renewed credibility would cause Germany and Japan to be more forthcoming in their economic relations with Washington.[124] Several weeks later, Harvard professor Joseph S. Nye, Jr. suggested that the deployment of United States forces in Europe and Japan could be used as a bargaining chip in trade negotiations with those countries.[125] Such a "leverage strategy" is no mere abstraction. In February 1992, then–Vice President Dan Quayle linked the continuance of America's security commitment to NATO with West European concessions in the GATT negotiations.[126]

The leverage strategy is the hegemonic stability theory's dark side. It calls for the United States to use its military power to compel other states to give in on issue areas where America has less power. It is a coercive strategy that attempts to take advantage of the asymmetries in great power capabilities that favor the United States. The leverage strategy is not new. Washington employed it from time to time in intra-alliance relations during the Cold War. However, American policies that others found merely irritating in a bipolar world may seem quite threatening in a unipolar world. For example, Japan almost certainly must realize that its lack of power projection capability renders it potentially vulnerable to leverage policies based on America's present ability to control the flow of Persian Gulf oil. Proponents of America's preponderance have missed a fundamental point: other states react to the threat of hegemony, not to the hegemon's identity. American leaders may regard the United States as a benevolent hegemon, but others cannot afford to take such a relaxed view.

REACTION TO UNIPOLARITY: TOWARDS A MULTIPOLAR WORLD

There is ample evidence that widespread concern exists today about America's currently unchallenged dominance in international politics.[127] In Sep-

---

124. Quoted in Norman Kempster, "U.S., Allies Might Help Iraq Rebuild After War, Baker Says," *Los Angeles Times*, February 17, 1991, p. A1.
125. William J. Eaton, "Democrats Groping For Image Building Issues," *Los Angeles Times*, March 9, 1991, p. A14.
126. William Tuohy, "Quayle Remarks Spark European Alarm on Trade vs. Security," *Los Angeles Times*, February 11, 1992, p. A4; Craig R. Whitney, "Quayle, Ending European Trip, Lobbies for New Trade Accord," *New York Times*, February 12, 1992, p. A4.
127. It has been suggested that the Persian Gulf War demonstrates that other states welcome, rather than fear, America's post–Cold War preeminence. However, this simply is not the case.

tember 1991, French Foreign Minister Roland Dumas warned that American "might reigns without balancing weight" and he and European Community Commission President Jacques Delors called for the EC to counterbalance the United States.[128] Some European policy analysts have said that the Soviet Union's collapse means that Europe is now threatened mainly by unchallenged American ascendancy in world politics.[129] This viewpoint was echoed in Japan in the Gulf War's aftermath. A number of commentators worried that the United States—a "fearsome" country—would impose a Pax Americana in which other states would be compelled to accept roles "as America's underlings."[130] China, too, has reacted adversely to America's post–Cold War preeminence. "Chinese analysts reacted with great alarm to President George Bush's 'New World Order' proclamations, and maintained that this was a ruse for extending U.S. hegemony throughout the globe. From China's perspective, unipolarity was a far worse state of affairs than bipolarity."[131] Similar sentiments have been echoed in the Third World. Although the reactions of these smaller states are not as significant as those of potential new great powers, they confirm that unipolarity has engendered general unease throughout the international system. At the September 1992 Nonaligned Movement Meeting, Indonesian President Suharto warned that the New World Order cannot be allowed to become "a new version of the same old

---

First, it was *after* the Persian Gulf crisis began that others began voicing their concerns about unipolarity. Second, to the extent that the Gulf War is an example of states bandwagoning with the United States, it is easily explainable. As Walt points out, weak powers threatened by a powerful neighbor will often turn to an outside great power for defensive support. Walt, *Origins of Alliances*, p. 266. Third, as Jean Edward Smith points out, the United States had to exert considerable pressure on both Egypt and Saudi Arabia to get these nations to accept the Bush administration's decision to confront Iraq militarily after the invasion of Kuwait. Jean Edward Smith, *George Bush's War* (New York: Henry Holt and Company, 1992), pp. 63–95. Finally, it should be remembered that during the war, the Arab coalition partners restrained the United States from overthrowing Saddam Hussein and that, in July and August 1992, Egypt, Turkey and Syria restrained the United States when it appeared that the Bush administration was going to provoke a military showdown over the issue of UN weapons inspectors' access to Iraq's Agricultural Ministry.

128. Quoted in "France to U.S.: Don't Rule," *New York Times*, September 3, 1991, p. A8.
129. Rone Tempest, "French Revive Pastime Fretting About U.S. 'Imperialism'," *Los Angeles Times*, February 15, 1989, p. A9.
130. See the views of Waseda University Professor Sakuji Yoshimura, quoted in Paul Blustein, "In Japan, Seeing The War On A Five-Inch Screen," *Washington Post National Weekly Edition*, February 25–March 3, 1991, and of Tokyo University Professor Yasusuke Murakami and Opposition Diet Member Masao Kunihiro, in Urban C. Lehner, "Japanese See A More 'Fearsome' U.S. Following American Success in the Gulf," *Wall Street Journal*, March 14, 1991.
131. David Shambaugh, "China's Security Policy in the Post–Cold War Era," *Survival*, Vol. 34, No. 2 (Summer 1992), p. 92.

patterns of domination of the strong over the weak and the rich over the poor." At this same meeting, UN Secretary General Boutros-Ghali warned that "the temptation to dominate, whether worldwide or regionally, remains"; Malaysian Prime Minister Mahathir Mohammed pointedly stated that a "unipolar world is every bit as threatening as a bipolar world."[132]

As has been shown, the post–Cold War world's geopolitical constellation is not unique. Twice before in international history there have been "unipolar moments." Both were fleeting. On both occasions, the effect of the entry of new great powers in the international system was to redress the one-sided distribution of power in the international system. There is every reason to expect that the pattern of the late seventeenth and nineteenth centuries will recur. The impact of differential growth rates has increased the relative power of Japan and Germany in a way that clearly marks them as eligible states. As their stakes in the international system deepen, so will their ambitions and interests. Security considerations will cause Japan and Germany to emulate the United States and acquire the full spectrum of great power capabilities, including nuclear weapons.[133] It can be expected that both will seek recognition by others of their great power status. Evidence confirming the expectation of Japan's and Germany's great power emergence already exists.

Germany is beginning to exert its leadership in European security affairs. It has assumed primary responsibility for providing economic assistance to the former Soviet Union and Eastern Europe, and took the lead in securing EC recognition of the breakaway Yugoslav republics of Croatia and Slovenia. In a sure sign that the scope of German geopolitical interests is expanding, Defense Minister Volker Rühe is advocating acquisition of large military transport aircraft.[134] Chancellor Kohl's decision to meet with outgoing Austrian President Kurt Waldheim suggests that Germany is rejecting the external constraints heretofore imposed on its behavior. Germany is also insisting that henceforth its diplomats (who had previously spoken in French or

---

132. Quoted in Charles B. Wallace, "Nonaligned Nations Question New World Order," *Los Angeles Times,* September 2, 1992, p. A4.

133. The nuclear issue is being debated, albeit gingerly, in Japan but not in Germany (or at least not openly). Nevertheless it seems to be widely understood, in the United States and in Germany and Japan, that their accession to the nuclear club is only a matter of time. See Doyle McManus, "Thinking the Once Unthinkable: Japan, Germany With A-Bombs," *Los Angeles Times* (Washington D.C. ed.), June 10, 1992, p. A8. For a discussion of a nuclear Germany's strategic implications, see Mearsheimer, "Back to the Future."

134. Terrence Roth, "New German Defense Chief Is Redefining Agency's Role," *Wall Street Journal,* August 14, 1992, p. A10.

English) will use only German when addressing international conferences.[135] Finally, Germany's open expression of interest in permanent membership on the UN Security Council is another indication that Berlin is moving toward great power status. In making Germany's position known, Foreign Minister Klaus Kinkel pointedly noted that the Security Council should be restructured because as now constituted it reflects, not the present distribution of power, but the international order that existed at the end of World War II.[136]

Notwithstanding legal and historical inhibitions, Japan is beginning to seek strategic autonomy. An important step is the decision to develop the capability to gather and analyze politico-military and economic intelligence independently of the United States.[137] Japan has also begun importing huge amounts of plutonium from Europe. The plutonium is to be used by Japan's fast breeder reactors, thereby enabling Tokyo to free itself of dependence on Persian Gulf oil and American uranium. Plutonium imports plus the acquisition of other materials in recent years mean that Japan has the capability of moving quickly to become a nuclear power.[138] After prolonged debate, Japan has finally authorized unarmed Japanese military personnel to participate in UN peacekeeping operations. This may well be the opening wedge for Japan to develop military capabilities commensurate with great power status. As a special panel of the Liberal Democratic Party argued in February 1992, "Now that we have become one of the very few economic powerhouses, it would fly in the face of the world's common sense if we did not play a military role for the maintenance and restoration of global peace."[139] As Japan becomes more active on the international stage, military power will be needed to support its policies and ensure it is not at a bargaining disadvantage in its dealings with others. Unsurprisingly, Japan has plans to build a full-spectrum

---

135. Stephen Kinzer, "Thus Sprake Helmut Kohl Auf Deutsch," New York Times, February 23, 1992, p. A4.

136. "Germany Seeks a Permanent Council Seat," Los Angeles Times, September 24, 1992, p. A9; Paul Lewis, "Germany Seeks Permanent UN Council Seat," New York Times, September 24, 1992, p. A1.

137. David E. Sanger, "Tired of Relying on U.S., Japan Seeks to Expand Its Own Intelligence Efforts," New York Times, January 1, 1992, p. A6.

138. Jim Mann, "Japan's Energy Future Linked to Risky Cargo," Los Angeles Times, February 23, 1992, p. A1. The initial plutonium shipment left for Japan from Cherbourg, France, in early November 1992 and arrived in Japan in early January 1993. There has been speculation that the mere fact that Japan will possess a substantial plutonium stockpile may serve as a deterrent even if Tokyo does not acquire nuclear weapons. See David Sanger, "Japan's Atom Fuel Shipment Is Worrying Asians," New York Times, November 9, 1992, p. A3.

139. Quoted in Teresa Watanabe, "Shift Urged on Sending Japan's Troops Abroad," Los Angeles Times, February 22, 1992, p. A10.

navy (including aircraft carriers) capable of operating independently of the American Seventh Fleet.[140] In January 1993, Foreign Minister Michio Watanabe openly called for Japan to acquire long-range air and naval power-projection capabilities. Japan is also showing signs of diplomatic assertiveness, and its leading role in the UN effort to rebuild Cambodia is viewed by Tokyo as the beginning of a more forceful and independent foreign policy course now that Japan no longer is constrained to "obey U.S. demands."[141] Japan's policies toward Russia, China, and Iran demonstrate a growing willingness to follow an independent course, even if doing so leads to open friction with Washington. It is suggestive of Japan's view of the evolving international system that its recently appointed ambassador to the United States has spoken of the emergence of a "multipolar world in which the United States could no longer play the kind of dominant role it used to play."[142] That Japan is measuring itself for a great power role is reflected in its expressed desire for permanent membership of the UN Security Council.[143]

Back to the Future: The Political Consequences of Structural Change

Since 1945, the West has enjoyed a Long Peace.[144] During the post–World War II era, American leadership has been maintained, Germany and Japan have been prevented from becoming great powers, a cooperative economic order has been established, and the spread of democratic values has been

---

140. This information provided by John Arquilla based on his discussions with Japanese defense analysts. See also David E. Sanger, "Japanese Discuss an Expanded Peacekeeping Role for the Military," *New York Times*, January 10, 1993, p. A9. The issue of constitutional reform and elimination of the "peace clause" has been raised again recently; Jacob M. Schlesinger, "Japan's Ruling Party Will Seek a Review of 1946 Constitution," *Wall Street Journal*, January 14, 1993, p. A13; David E. Sanger, "Japanese Debate Taboo Topic of Military's Role," *New York Times*, January 17, 1993, p. A7.

141. Quoted in Teresa Watanabe, "Putting Cambodia Together Again," *Los Angeles Times*, March 3, 1992, p. HI.

142. Quoted in Sam Jameson, "Japan's New Envoy to U.S. Sees 'Crucial Period' Ahead," *Los Angeles Times*, February 18, 1992, p. A4.

143. Sam Jameson, "Japan to Seek U.N. Security Council Seat," *Los Angeles Times*, January 29, 1992, p. A1.

144. See John Lewis Gaddis, "The Long Peace: Elements of Stability in the Postwar International System," *International Security*, Vol. 10, No. 4 (Spring 1986), pp. 99–142, where Gaddis probed for an explanation of the absence of great power war during the Cold War rivalry between the Soviet Union and the United States. Gaddis has revisited the issue and asked whether certain factors (nuclear weapons, polarity, hegemonic stability, "triumphant" liberalism, and long cycles) have implications for the possible prolongation of the Long Peace into the post–Cold War era. Gaddis, "Great Illusions, the Long Peace, and the Future of the International System," in *The United States and the End of the Cold War*.

promoted. The strategy of preponderance seeks to maintain the geopolitical status quo that the Long Peace reflects. American strategic planners and scholars alike believe the United States can successfully perpetuate this status quo. This sanguine outlook is predicated on the belief that second-image factors (economic interdependence, common democratic institutions) militate against the reappearance of traditional forms of great power competition while promoting new forms of international cooperation.[145] Neorealists, however, believe that the Long Peace was rooted primarily in the bipolar structure of the international system, although the unit-level factor of nuclear deterrence also played a role.[146] Because they expect structural change to lead to changed international political outcomes, neorealists are not sanguine that the Long Peace can endure in the coming era of systemic change. Neorealist theory leads to the expectation that the world beyond unipolarity will be one of great power rivalry in a multipolar setting.

During the Cold War era, international politics was profoundly shaped by the bipolar competition between the United States and the Soviet Union.[147] The Soviet threat to their common security caused the United States, Western Europe, and Japan to form an anti-Soviet coalition. Because of America's military preeminence in a bipolar system, Western Europe and Japan did not have to internalize their security costs because they benefited from the protective mantle of Washington's containment policy. At the same time, because Western Europe's and Japan's political and economic stability were critical to containment's success, the United States resolved the "hegemon's dilemma"

---

145. For scholarly elaborations of this viewpoint, see John Mueller, *Retreat from Doomsday: The Obsolescence of Major War* (New York: Basic Books, 1989); Richard Rosecrance, *The Rise of the Trading State: Commerce and Conquest in the Modern World* (New York: Basic Books, 1986); Robert Jervis, "The Future of World Politics: Will It Resemble the Past?" *International Security*, Vol. 16, No. 3 (Winter 1991/92), pp. 39–73; Carl Kaysen, "Is War Obsolete?" *International Security*, Vol. 14, No. 4 (Spring 1990), pp. 42–64; Charles Kupchan and Clifford Kupchan, "Concerts, Collective Security and the Future of Europe," *International Security*, Vol. 16, No. 1 (Summer 1991), pp. 114–161; Richard Rosecrance, "A New Concert of Powers," *Foreign Affairs*, Vol. 71, No. 2 (Spring 1992), pp. 64–82; James M. Goldgeier and Michael McFaul, "A Tale of Two Worlds: Core and Periphery in the Post–Cold War Era," *International Organization*, Vol. 46, No. 3 (Spring 1992), pp. 467–491. The Defense Planning Guidance and similar documents also stress that the spread of democracy and economic interdependence are crucial to the success of the strategy of preponderance. The classic discussion of the second and third images of international politics is Kenneth N. Waltz, *Man, the State, and War* (New York: Columbia University Press, 1958).
146. This argument is presented in the European context in Mearsheimer, "Back to the Future."
147. For a different view, see Ted Hopf, "Polarity, the Offense-Defense Balance, and War," *American Political Science Review*, Vol. 81, No. 3 (June 1991), pp. 475–494. Hopf argues that the international system's stability during the Cold War era was attributable to nuclear deterrence and that bipolarity was an irrelevant factor.

by forgoing maximization of its relative gains and pursuing instead a policy of promoting absolute gains for all members of the anti-Soviet coalition.[148] For strategic reasons, the United States encouraged Western Europe's economic integration and Japan's discriminatory trade and foreign investment policies, even though the inevitable consequence of these policies was to enhance Western Europe's and Japan's relative power at America's expense.

Bipolarity was the decisive variable in the West's Long Peace because it removed the security dilemma and the relative gains problem from the agenda of relations among the Western powers. Even non-neorealists implicitly acknowledge the salience of structural factors in securing the postwar "liberal peace." Michael Doyle, for example, admits that American military leadership was crucial because it dampened the need for Western Europe and Japan to become strategically independent (which would rekindle the security dilemma) and reinforced the bonds of economic interdependence (thereby alleviating the relative gains problem). Doyle says the erosion of American preeminence could imperil the liberal peace "if independent and substantial military forces were established" by Western Europe and Japan.[149] In other words, if liberated from the bipolar structural constraints that, with Washington's help, smothered their great power emergence, states like Germany and Japan might respond to new international systemic constraints by becoming—*and acting like*—great powers. Here, Doyle is correct and that is precisely the point: structure affects outcomes.

AMERICA IN A MULTIPOLAR WORLD: IMPLICATIONS AND RECOMMENDATIONS

The Cold War structure has been swept away. American policymakers must now think about international politics from a wholly new analytical framework. This will not be easy. Richard Rosecrance observed in 1976, when it was already apparent that the bipolar system was beginning to erode, that

---

148. Arthur A. Stein, "The Hegemon's Dilemma: Great Britain, the United States, and the International Economic Order," *International Organization*, Vol. 38, No. 2 (Spring 1984), pp. 355–386. Stein delineates the hegemon's dilemma as follows:

A hegemonic power's decision to enrich itself is also a decision to enrich others more than itself. Over time, such policies will come at the expense of the hegemon's relative standing and will bring forth challengers. Yet choosing to sustain its relative standing . . . is a choice to keep others impoverished at the cost of increasing its own wealth. Maintaining its relative position has obvious costs not only to others but to itself. Alternatively, maximizing its absolute wealth has obvious benefits but brings even greater ones to others.

Stein, *Why Nations Cooperate*, p. 139.

149. Michael Doyle, "Kant, Liberal Legacies and Foreign Affairs," Part 1, *Philosophy and Public Affairs*, Vol. 12, No. 3 (Summer 1983), p. 233.

Washington has, since 1945, always had difficulty in understanding how Western Europe and Japan could have different interests than the United States.[150] More recently, Stephen Krasner has observed that "U.S. policymakers have paid little attention to the possibility that a loss of power *vis-à-vis* friends could present serious and unforeseen difficulties, either because friends can become enemies or because managing the international system may be more difficult in a world in which power is more evenly distributed."[151] The impending structural shift from unipolarity to multipolarity means that the security dilemma and the relative gains problem will again dominate policymakers' concerns. As Japan and Germany become great powers, the quality of their relations with the United States will be profoundly altered.[152] Relations will become significantly more competitive, great power security rivalries and even war will be likely, and cooperation will correspondingly become more difficult.

The implications of multipolarity will be especially evident in the United States-Japan relationship.[153] Summarizing his incisive analysis of the pre-1914 Anglo-German antagonism, Paul Kennedy states that the "most profound cause, surely, was *economic*."[154] By this, Kennedy does not mean the commercial competition between British and German firms, but rather that economic shifts had radically transformed the relative power relationship between Britain and Germany. Kennedy asks if the relative power relationship of two great powers has ever changed so remarkably with the span of a single lifetime. The answer may now be "yes."

There is a very good chance that early in the next decade Japan's GNP may equal or surpass America's.[155] Such an economic change would be a fact

---

150. Richard Rosecrance, "Introduction," in Rosecrance, ed., *America as an Ordinary Country* (Ithaca: Cornell University Press, 1976), p. 12.
151. Stephen Krasner, "Trade Conflicts and the Common Defense: The United States and Japan," *Political Science Quarterly*, Vol. 101, No. 5 (1986), pp. 787–806.
152. Others have argued that America's relations with Japan and Germany will become more competitive in the post–Cold War era. A notable example is Jeffrey E. Garten, *A Cold Peace: America, Japan, Germany and the Struggle for Supremacy* (New York: Times Books, 1992). Garten's argument differs from mine in two critical respects. First, Garten pinpoints the locus of rivalry in second-image factors; specifically the different cultural, political, and economic traditions of the three countries. Second, he discounts the possibility of war or of security competitions and argues that the rivalry will be primarily economic.
153. An interesting albeit flawed attempt to consider the geopolitical consequences of the altered relative power relationship of Japan and the United States is George Friedman and Meredith Lebard, *The Coming War With Japan* (New York: St. Martin's Press, 1991).
154. Kennedy, *Anglo-German Antagonism*, p. 464.
155. This is C. Fred Bergsten's projection based on the following assumptions: Japan's annual

of enormous geopolitical significance. Should this relative power shift occur, no doubt Japan would demand that power and prestige in the international system be redistributed to reflect its new status. Besides demands for UN Security Council membership, Tokyo might: (1) insist on the decisive vote in international economic institutions; (2) demand that the yen become the international economy's primary reserve currency; (3) exploit advantageous technological, economic, and fiscal asymmetries to advance its strategic interests; and (4) become a much more assertive actor geopolitically.

Whether the United States could comfortably accommodate a Japan of equal or greater power is an open question. The answer would depend on the moderation, and the moderate tone, of Japan's *desiderata* and on the willingness of the United States to make reasonable concessions gracefully. But even skillful and patient diplomacy on both sides could fail to avert conflict. In that case, the question is not so much who as *what* would be responsible for conflict between the United States and Japan: I argue that it would be the international political system's structure and the constraints it exerts on great power behavior.

Again, history may provide insight. At the turn of the century, Great Britain was able to reach an accommodation with the United States because America's ambitions did not immediately seem to threaten London's most vital security concerns.[156] On the other hand, Germany's rising power did appear to present such a threat. It is worrisome that the changing relative power relationship between the United States and Japan contains the same Hertz/Avis dynamic that fueled the Anglo-German antagonism. Thus once again, the prospect of hegemonic war, thought to have been banished from international politics, must be reckoned with even as we hope to avoid it. Indeed, it must be reckoned with *especially* if we hope to avoid it. The main point of the hegemonic war theory is that:

there is incompatibility between crucial elements of the existing international system and the changing distribution of power among the states within the system. . . . The resolution of the disequilibrium between the superstructure of the system and the underlying distribution of power is

---

growth is about 4 percent, the United States' is 2 to 2½ percent, and the yen appreciates to 100 to 1 against the dollar. Bergsten, "Primacy of Economics," *Foreign Policy*, No. 87 (Summer 1992), p. 6.

156. See Charles S. Campbell, *Anglo-American Understanding, 1898–1903* (Baltimore: The Johns Hopkins University Press, 1957); Dexter Perkins, *The Great Rapprochement: England and the United States, 1895–1914* (New York: Atheneum, 1968).

found in the outbreak and intensification of what becomes a hegemonic war.[157]

Great power war is not a certainty, because some factors could reduce the war-proneness of the coming multipolar system. At the unit level, nuclear deterrence could maintain the peace among the great powers in a multipolar system where each has nuclear weapons.[158] In such a system, great power conflict might be played out in the economic, rather than the military, arena.[159] Still, the shadow of war will loom over a multipolar system. Consequently, the United States will have to rethink the answer it gave in the late 1940s to "the hegemon's dilemma." Put another way, Washington will have to come to grips with the *declining* hegemon's dilemma. Precisely because major shifts in relative economic power presage change in the relative distribution of power geopolitically, the United States must begin to concern itself with maintaining its relative power rather than pursuing absolute gains for itself and those who are its partners today but may become its rivals tomorrow. Although states can cooperate readily to promote absolute gains

---

157. Robert Gilpin, "The Theory of Hegemonic War," in Rotberg and Rabb, *Origin and Prevention of Major Wars*, pp. 25–26.

158. Kenneth N. Waltz, "Nuclear Myths and Political Realities," *American Political Science Review*, Vol. 81, No. 3 (September 1991), pp. 731–746; *The Spread of Nuclear Weapons: More May Be Better*, Adelphi Paper No. 171 (London: International Institute for Strategic Studies, 1981). For a more pessimistic view of the possible consequences of the spread of nuclear weapons, see Barry R. Posen, *Inadvertent Escalation: Conventional War and Nuclear Weapons* (Ithaca: Cornell University Press, 1991).

159. If deterrence holds among the great powers in a multipolar world, the prevailing conventional wisdom is that economic competitions would replace security competitions as the primary means of great power rivalry. Under the shadow of war, trade wars that improve a state's relative position by inflicting more pain on a rival could become a rational strategy. States in a position to do so could also use their financial power or control over access to key technologies to advance their interests relative to rivals. For a suggestive first cut at the possible role of "economic statecraft" in great power relations in the emerging multipolar system, see Aaron L. Friedberg, "The Changing Relationship Between Economics and National Security," *Political Science Quarterly*, Vol. 106, No. 2 (1991), pp. 272–274.

One should be careful about assuming that economics will entirely displace military power. Deterrence rests on military strength. Moreover, it could be expected that arms races and tests of resolve would be employed by the great powers as substitutes for actual fighting. A great power nuclear stalemate could have two other important military effects. Just as the Cold War superpowers did in Korea, Vietnam, Angola and Afghanistan, the great powers in a multipolar system could wage war through proxies. Also, deterrence at the nuclear level could, notwithstanding the risk of escalation, cause the great powers to fight (or attempt to fight) limited conventional wars. Here, it may be useful to revisit the early Cold War literature on limited war. See Henry Kissinger, *Nuclear Weapons and Foreign Policy* (New York: Harper and Row, 1957); Robert E. Osgood, *Limited War* (Chicago: University of Chicago Press, 1957).

for all when the shadow of war is absent from their relations, the barriers to cooperation become formidable when the shadow of war is present.[160]

STRATEGIC INDEPENDENCE IN A MULTIPOLAR WORLD

Because multipolarity is inevitable, it is pointless to debate the comparative merits of unipolar, bipolar, and multipolar systems. Rather than vainly and counterproductively pursuing a strategy of preponderance, the United States needs to design a strategy that will (1) safeguard its interests during the difficult transition from unipolarity to multipolarity; and (2) enable the United States to do as well as possible in a multipolar world. America's optimal strategy is to make its power position similar to Goldilocks' porridge: not too strong, which would frighten others into balancing against the United States; not too weak, which would invite others to exploit American vulnerabilities; but just right—strong enough to defend American interests, without provoking others.

The transition from unipolarity to multipolarity will challenge the United States to devise a policy that will arrest its relative decline while minimizing the chances that other states will be provoked into balancing against the United States. Relative decline has internal and external causes. Relative decline can be addressed by policies that focus on either or both of these causes. It would be counterproductive for the United States to attempt to maintain its relative power position by attempting to suppress the emergence of new great powers. This approach would heighten others' concerns about the malign effects of unchecked American power, which probably would accelerate the rise of new great powers, and increase the probability that balancing behavior would be directed against the United States. American policymakers need to remember that other states balance against hegemons

---

160. Robert Powell, "The Problem of Absolute and Relative Gains in International Relations Theory," *American Political Science Review*, Vol. 81, No. 4 (December 1991), pp. 1303–1320. Joanne Gowa points out that free trade is more likely to prevail in bipolar international systems than in multipolar ones. Because the risk of exit from a bipolar alliance is less than from an alliance in a multipolar system, bipolar alignments are more stable. Consequently, bipolar alliances are better able to internalize the security externalities of free trade (the members do not need to be concerned with relative gains because today's ally is unlikely to be tomorrow's rival). Moreover, in a bipolar alliance, the dominant partner has incentives to act altruistically towards its allies because it benefits when they do. All of these incentives are reversed in multipolar systems where exit risks (i.e., defection of allies) and buck passing/free rider tendencies force states to ponder the relative gains problem and to think hard about the wisdom of acting unselfishly. Free trade thus is problematic in a multipolar system. Gowa, "Bipolarity, Multipolarity and Free Trade," *American Political Science Review*, Vol. 79, No. 4 (December 1989), pp. 1245–1266.

and they should not want the United States to be seen by others as a "sprawling giant with gouty fingers and toes." A policy that concentrates U.S. energies on redressing the internal causes of relative decline would be perceived by others as less threatening than a strategy of preponderance. Although vigorous internal renewal might cause frictions with others over economic policy, it is less likely to have negative geopolitical repercussions than a policy that aims at perpetuating unipolarity.

Washington also needs to remember that while the United States may regard its hegemony as benign, others will have different perceptions. The international order objectives embedded in a strategy of preponderance reinforce others' mistrust of American preeminence. The more the United States attempts to press its preferences and values on others, the more likely it is that they will react against what is, in their view, overweening American power. Moreover, policies that arouse others' fear of America today could carry over into the emerging multipolar system. It makes no sense to alienate needlessly states (such as China) that could be strategically useful to the United States in a multipolar world. To avoid frightening others, the United States should eschew a value-projection policy and moderate both its rhetoric and its ambitions.[161]

The United States must adjust to the inevitable emergence of new great powers. The primary role of forward-deployed American forces now is to dissuade Japan and Germany from becoming great powers. There are three reasons why American forward deployments in Europe and Northeast Asia should be phased out soon. First, a policy of forward deployment could unnecessarily entangle the United States in overseas conflicts where the stakes are more important to others than to itself. Second, because the United States faces severe fiscal and economic constraints, the opportunity costs of such a strategy are high. Third, such a policy cannot work. Indeed, the strategy of preponderance is probably the worst option available to the United States because it is not coercive enough to prevent Japan and Germany from becoming great powers, but it is coercive enough to antagonize them and cause them to balance against the United States. If the analysis presented in this article is correct, a policy of attempting to smother Germany's and Japan's great power emergence would be unavailing because

---

161. For a discussion of value projection as a grand strategic option see Terry L. Deibel, "Strategies Before Containment: Patterns for the Future," *International Security*, Vol. 16, No. 4 (Spring 1992), pp. 79–108.

structural pressures will impel them to become great powers regardless of what the United States does or does not do. Simply stated, the declining hegemon's dilemma is acute: neither benign nor preventive strategies will prevent the emergence of challengers and the consequent end of the hegemon's predominance in the international system.

American grand strategy must be redesigned for a multipolar world. In a multipolar system, the United States should follow a policy of strategic independence by assuming the posture of an offshore balancer.[162] Traditionally, America's overriding strategic objective has been to ensure that a hegemon does not dominate Eurasia.[163] That objective would not change under strategic independence, but the means of attaining it would. Rather than assuming primary responsibility for containing the rise of a potential hegemon, the United States would rely on global and regional power balances to attain that goal. Strategic independence is not an isolationist policy that rules out the use of American power abroad.[164] Strategic independence also differs from the selective-commitment variant of offshore balancing articulated by John Mearsheimer and Stephen Van Evera, whereby the United States would be relatively indifferent to Third World events but would remain militarily engaged in Europe and Northeast Asia in order to preserve "stability."[165] Strategic independence is a hedging strategy that would commit the United States militarily if, but only if, other states failed to balance effectively against a rising Eurasian hegemon. The United States would need to remain alert to

---

162. I first used the term "strategic independence" in 1983 and I elaborated on it in 1989. Christopher Layne, "Ending the Alliance," *Journal of Contemporary Studies*, Vol. 6, No. 3 (Summer 1983), pp. 5–31; and Layne, "Realism Redux: Strategic Independence in a Multipolar World," *SAIS Review*, Vol. 9, No. 2 (Summer–Fall 1989), pp. 19–44. Ted Galen Carpenter, who has also embraced a form of strategic independence, has acknowledged that I was the first to articulate the concept and to so name it. Ted Galen Carpenter, "Introduction," in Carpenter, ed., *Collective Defense of Strategic Independence: Alternative Strategies for the Future* (Washington, D.C.: Cato Institute, 1989), p. xx, n. 7. The most recent explication of his views on strategic independence is Carpenter, *A Search for Enemies: America's Alliances After the Cold War* (Washington, D.C.: Cato Institute, 1992).
163. See John Lewis Gaddis, *Strategies of Containment* (New York: Oxford University Press, 1982), chap. 2; George F. Kennan, *Realities of American Foreign Policy* (Princeton: Princeton University Press, 1954), pp. 63–65; Hans Morgenthau, *In Defense of the National Interest* (Lanham, Md.: University Press of America, 1982, reprint of 1951 edition), pp. 5–7; Nicholas Spykman, *America's Strategy in World Politics: The United States and the Balance of Power* (New York: Harcourt, Brace, 1942), part 1.
164. For the isolationist approach to post–Cold War American grand strategy, see Earl C. Ravenal, "The Case For Adjustment," *Foreign Policy*, No. 81 (Winter 1990/91), pp. 3–19.
165. Mearsheimer, "Back to the Future"; Stephen Van Evera, "Why Europe Matters, Why the Third World Doesn't: American Grand Strategy After the Cold War," *Journal of Strategic Studies*, Vol. 13, No. 2 (June 1990), pp. 1–51.

the events that would require a more engaged policy: (1) the appearance of a "careful" challenger able to cloak its ambitions and ward off external balancing against it; (2) a dramatic narrowing of America's relative power margin over Japan; or (3) the inability of other states to act as effective counterweights due to internal difficulties.[166]

Strategic independence aims to capitalize on America's inherent geopolitical advantages.[167] First, in a relative sense, the United States is probably the most secure great power in history because of the interlocking effects of geography, nuclear weapons, and capabilities which, although diminished relatively, are still formidable in absolute terms. Such "strategic security enables the balancer to stay outside the central balance until the moment when its intervention can be decisive."[168] America's insularity means that it can benefit strategically from geography in another way, as well. Because America is distant from the likely theaters of great power conflict, in a multipolar world others are unlikely to view it as a threat to their security. Indeed distance would enhance America's attractiveness as an ally. (In a unipolar world the United States loses this advantage because hegemons repel others rather than attracting them). Finally, because of its still considerable great power capabilities, in a multipolar world America's intervention would decisively tip the scales against an aspiring hegemon.

---

166. For a discussion of the "careful" challenger, see John Arquilla, "Balances Without Balancing," paper presented at the annual meeting of the American Political Science Association, Chicago, Illinois, September 1992.

167. It is not neorealist heresy to suggest that the United States can play an offshore balancer's role. I do not claim that there is a functionally differentiated role for a balancer in the international system. Rather, like Waltz, I am saying that under "narrowly defined and historically unlikely conditions," certain states can play this role because of their unit-level attributes (especially geography and capabilities). The United States today meets Waltz's criteria: (1) American strength added to a weaker coalition would redress the balance; (2) America has (or ought to have) no positive ends—its goal is the negative one of thwarting an aspiring hegemon; (3) America's power for the foreseeable future will be at least the equal of any other state's. Waltz, *Theory of International Politics*, pp. 163–164. It should also be noted that balancers often are attractive allies precisely because they do not have ambitions that threaten others. As George Liska notes, Britain benefited from its "attractiveness in Europe whenever she was ready to meet an actual or potential hegemonical threat" from Europe. To win allies, "Britain had only to abstain from direct acquisitions on the continent and, when called, limit voluntarily her wartime gains overseas." George Liska, *The Quest for Equilibrium: America and the Balance of Power on Land and Sea* (Baltimore: The John Hopkins University Press, 1977), p. 13. For additional discussion of the criteria that a state should meet to be an effective balancer, see Michael Sheehan, "The Place of the Balancer in Balance of Power Theory," *Review of International Studies*, Vol. 15, No. 2 (April 1989), pp. 123–133.

168. Sheehan, "The Place of the Balancer," p. 128.

An insular great power in a multipolar system enjoys a wider range of strategic options than less fortunately placed states.[169] This would certainly be true for the United States. Because of its relative immunity from external threat, in a multipolar world the United States could stand by and could rationally adopt buck-passing strategies that force others to "go first."[170] The emerging great powers are located in regions where other potentially powerful actors are present (Ukraine, Russia, China, and Korea, which probably will be reunified in the next decade) and where the potential for intense security competitions also exists. The emerging great powers (and these other actors) are likely to be kept in check by their own rivalries. There are three reasons why this situation could be beneficial to the United States. First, the fact that the emerging great powers are involved in regional rivalries will have the effect of enhancing America's relative power.[171] Second, Japan, America's most likely future geopolitical rival, could be contained by others without the United States having to risk direct confrontation. Third, if the emerging great powers are compelled to internalize their security costs, they no longer will be free to concentrate primarily on trading-state strategies that give them an advantage in their economic competition with the United States.

Strategic independence is responsive to the constraints of the impending structural changes in the international system. It is a strategy that would serve America's interests in the emerging multipolar system. It is, admittedly, a competitive strategy. But such a strategy is needed in a world where great power rivalries, with both security and economic dimensions, will be a fact of international life. At the same time, strategic independence is a restrained

---

169. Liska, *Quest for Equilibrium*, p. 12.
170. For a discussion of the "buck-passing" phenomenon see Thomas J. Christensen and Jack Snyder, "Chain Gangs and Passed Bucks: Predicting Alliance Patterns in Multipolarity," *International Organization*, Vol. 44, No. 2 (Spring 1990), pp. 137–168; Waltz, *Theory of International Politics*, p. 165. John Arquilla defines "bystanding" as a state's propensity to avoid conflicts, if it can do so, for self-preservation reasons. Arquilla, "Balances Without Balancing."
171. An offshore balancer can benefit from others' rivalries: by the mid-1890s, America's navy was powerful, though still smaller than Britain's and those of Europe's lending powers. But "such equality was not necessary. The growing instability of the European political equilibrium seriously tied the hands of the Great Powers of that Continent, and rendered progressively improbable any determined aggression from that quarter against the interests of the United States in the northern part of the Western Hemisphere. European instability, in short, enhanced the *relative* power and security of the United States." Harold and Margaret Sprout, *Rise of American Naval Power*, p. 222 (emphasis in original). Similarly, during the nineteenth century, Britain was able to enjoy a relatively high degree of security while spending proportionately less on defense than the European powers, precisely because the European states were preoccupied with security competitions among themselves.

and prudent policy that would (1) avoid provocative actions that would cause others to regard the United States as an overpowerful hegemon; (2) minimize the risks of open confrontation with the emerging great powers; and (3) attempt to enhance America's relative power indirectly through skillful manipulation of the dynamics of multipolarity.

Strategic independence is also a more realistic policy than the strategy of preponderance, which is based on preserving the status quo and on maintaining stability. "Stability" is defined as a world where the United States is unchallenged by rivals and its interests are undisturbed by international political unheaval.[172] The strategy of preponderance aims at attaining a condition that approximates absolute security for the United States. In this respect, it is another form of American exceptionalism. It is a transcendant strategy that seeks nothing less than the end of international politics. However, unwanted and unanticipated events happen all the time in international politics; in this respect, "instability" is normal. War, the security dilemma, the rise and fall of great powers, the formation and dissolution of alliances,

---

172. For a devastating critique of America's stability obsession, see Benjamin C. Schwarz, "Rights and Foreign Policy: Morality is No Mantra," *New York Times*, November 20, 1992, p. A19. The focus on instability means that the strategy of preponderance leads inexorably to the open-ended proliferation of American commitments, all of which are seen as "interdependent." The United States must, under this strategy, worry about both the rise of new great powers and turmoil in strategically peripheral areas. The latter, it is feared, could set off a cascading series of effects that would spill over and affect important American interests. There is particular concern that American economic interests could be harmed by instability. As Bush's Secretary of Defense Dick Cheney said: "We are a trading nation, and our prosperity is linked to peace and stability in the world. . . . Simply stated, the worldwide market that we're part of cannot thrive where regional violence, instability, and aggression put it at peril." Dick Cheney, "The Military We Need in the Future," *Vital Speeches of the Day*, Vol. 59, No. 1 (October 15, 1992), p. 13. For a similar argument see Van Evera, "Why Europe Matters," pp. 10–11.

This line of thinking is an ironic twist on the interdependence/trading state concept, which holds that territorial conquest does not pay because the most effective means of increasing national power is through trade, and that war is too costly to be a viable option for economically powerful states. Rather than being a stimulus for peace, under the strategy of preponderance economic interdependence means that the United States must maintain a forward military presence and be prepared to wage war, in order to ensure that it is not cut off from the markets with which it has become economically interconnected. Here, two flaws of the stability-oriented strategy of preponderance become clear. First, there is a failure to consider whether the benefits of maintaining stability outweigh the costs of attempting to do so. Admittedly, instability abroad conceivably could harm the United States. The issue, however, is whether this harm would exceed the certain costs of maintaining American forward-deployed forces and the possible costs if commitment leads to involvement in a conflict. Second, there is no consideration of alternative strategies. For example, by relying on its large domestic market (which will get bigger if the North American Free Trade Agreement goes into effect) and diversifying its overseas markets, the United States could minimize the economic disruption that could accompany possible geopolitical disturbances in Europe and East Asia.

and great power rivalries are enduring features of international politics. The goal of a unipolar world in which the United States is unthreatened and able to shape the international environment is alluring but it is a chimera. No state can achieve absolute security because no state, not even the United States, can rise above the international political system's structural constraints.

THE COMING TEST

The coming years will be ones of turmoil in international politics. Systemic change occasioned by the rise and fall of great powers has always been traumatic. No doubt neorealism's critics will continue to point to second-image factors as reasons to take an optimistic view of the future. No doubt, too, the debate between neorealists and their critics will continue. But this one is not fated to drag on inconclusively. In coming years, the international system will provide a definitive field test of the contending views of international politics offered by neorealists and their critics. Fifty years from now, and probably much sooner, we will know who was right and who was wrong. Structural realists can be confident that events will vindicate their predictions: (1) Because of structural factors, an American strategy of preponderance or an attempt to perpetuate unipolarity is doomed to failure; (2) unipolarity will stimulate the emergence of eligible states as great powers; (3) unipolarity will cause other states to balance against the United States; (4) in a multipolar system, traditional patterns of great power competition will reemerge notwithstanding the effect of second-image factors; and (5) if differential growth rate effects allow Japan to challenge America's leading position, the United States–Japan relationship will become highly competitive and the possibility of hegemonic war will be present.

Part II:
Realism on the Sources of
Alignment and Aggression

The Spoils of Conquest | *Peter Liberman*

$\mathbf{D}$oes conquest pay in
the modern era? Are industrial economies "cumulative resources" that can
be mobilized by foreign conquerors? This question lies at the root of important international relations debates. Realists have claimed that conquest pays,
especially the conquest of modern industrial societies, but liberals argue that
the conquest of modern societies is economically futile. These opposing
viewpoints represent different theories about the way the world works, and
support divergent foreign policies.

Since conquest pays, according to the realist view, the more you conquer,
the more wealthy and powerful you become. Rulers have economic and
security incentives to expand. Status-quo states must rely more heavily on
threats of war to contain expansionists, and on war itself if threats fail to
deter. Unless they are contained, imperial rulers will swallow up weaker
nations, growing stronger and more invincible with each new conquest.
Realists conclude that only the vigilance of defensive coalitions stands in the
way of an Orwellian nightmare of huge clashing despotisms, or even a single
world empire.

In the liberal view, we live in a more benign world. Since conquest is
unprofitable, rulers have no economic incentive to expand and are thus less
covetous of neighboring real estate. Expansionists would only weaken themselves by blundering into costly quagmires, falling behind more economically
dynamic nation-states, and eventually collapsing from imperial deficits and
rebellion. Since aggressors are rare and less dangerous, status-quo states can
more safely afford disarmament and isolation. According to liberals, the
unprofitability of conquest strengthens the harmony of interests among
states, and thus strengthens international peace and cooperation.

Peter Liberman is Assistant Professor of Political Science at Tulane University.

This article draws on my "Does Conquest Pay? The Exploitation of Occupied Industrial Economies" (Ph.D dissertation, Massachusetts Institute of Technology, February 1992). Among the
many teachers and colleagues who have given me invaluable suggestions, I would like to thank
Douglass Forsyth, Kenneth Oye, Stephen Van Evera, and most of all Barry Posen. Support for
this work was provided by MIT's Defense and Arms Control Studies Program, the MacArthur
Foundation, the Ford Foundation, and the John M. Olin Institute for Strategic Studies at Harvard
University.

International Security, Vol. 18, No. 2 (Fall 1993), pp. 125–153

In fact, however, as this article shows, conquerors *have* made conquest pay in modern times. The explanation, I argue, lies in basic facts of modernization, illuminated by theories of coercion and collective action. Modernization makes societies wealthy, and thus increases the social surplus potentially mobilized by conquerors. Modernization also increases the efficiency of coercion and repression. The result is that coercive and repressive conquerors can make defeated modern societies pay a large share of their economic surplus in tribute.

This conclusion has important implications for our understanding of international politics. First, it reaffirms the age-old realist dictum that it is wise to contain expansionists, especially those that threaten industrial heartlands. A second implication is that the international system is more war-prone than liberals claim. If conquest and empire have become less common in the modern age, we should be thankful for other causes of peace, such as effective balancing behavior, nuclear deterrence, and spreading liberal democracy. Third, guerrilla-based and civilian-based defenses are unlikely to work or even to be implemented against coercive and repressive conquerors.

The following section describes the realist-liberal debate over the profitability of conquest. The article next explains in more detail the argument behind the liberal position, and then shows that conquest still pays, with an explanation based on the realist theory of coercion, collective goods theory, and basic observations about modernization. The concluding section explores the implications of this for international relations theory and practice.

The Debate

Imperial rulers and propagandists, unsurprisingly, have typically believed that conquest pays. Thucydides observed that Athenian imperialism was fueled by its demand for tribute, mines, and foreign markets.[1] Indeed, the rise of all nation-states can be seen as a cycle of conquest, consolidation, and resource extraction.[2] But the notion that conquest pays also informs a venerable tradition of balance-of-power thinking by realist statesmen and scholars. From Thucydides on, realists have argued that security requires not only

---

1. See Thucydides, *The Peloponnesian Wars*, trans. Rex Warner (New York: Penguin Books, 1954), I., paragraphs 100–101.
2. Charles Tilly, "War Making and State Making as Organized Crime," in Peter B. Evans, Dietrich Rueschemeyer, and Theda Skocpol, eds., *Bringing the State Back In* (New York: Cambridge University Press, 1985), pp. 169–191.

cultivating one's own power, but also making sure that no other single state becomes powerful enough to dominate the rest. They typically have focused, moreover, on conquest as the prime threat to balances of power, on the assumption that seized territories add to the conquerors' wealth and military power.[3]

This assumption is especially clear in the writings of geopolitical realists, such as the British geographer Halford Mackinder. Mackinder wrote in 1904 that the political consolidation of the Eurasian continent (the "World Island") "would permit the use of vast continental resources for fleet-building, and the empire of the world would then be in sight." He later concluded that "who rules eastern Europe commands the Heartland; who rules the Heartland commands the World Island; and who rules the World Island commands the World."[4] German domination of Europe during World War II led Yale political scientist Nicholas Spykman to reformulate Mackinder's dictum: "who controls the rimland rules Eurasia; who rules Eurasia controls the destinies of the world."[5] The underlying logic, that control of territory allows the full use of its material and human resources, regardless of national loyalties, was the same. As Spykman explained, successful conquerors throughout history made "each new conquest the stepping stone for further enlargement. Power tends to grow and diffuse through wider areas, and the states in the vicinity have the choice between collective defense and ultimate absorption."[6]

American realists' arguments for joining the war against Hitler were based on this premise as well, especially after the fall of France in the summer of 1940 focused their attention on the geopolitical significance of a Nazi-dominated Europe. As one economist calculated in the pages of *Foreign Affairs:*

---

3. Seminal realist balance-of-power works include Hans J. Morgenthau, *Politics Among Nations: The Struggle for Power and Peace* (New York: Knopf, 1948); and Kenneth N. Waltz, *Theory of International Politics* (New York: Random House, 1979).
4. Halford Mackinder, "The Geographical Pivot of History," *Geographic Journal*, Vol. 23, No. 4 (April 1904), p. 436; Mackinder, *Democratic Ideals and Reality* (New York: Henry Holt, 1919), p. 150. Mackinder's view of the malleability of human loyalties is further revealed in his 1904 paper (p. 437): "Were the Chinese . . . organized by the Japanese, to overthrow the Russian Empire and conquer its territory, they might constitute the yellow peril to the world's freedom just because they would add an oceanic frontage to the resources of the great continent, an advantage as yet denied to the Russian tenant of the pivot region."
5. Nicholas J. Spykman, *The Geography of the Peace*, ed. Helen R. Nicholl (New York: Harcourt, Brace & Company, 1944; repr., Hamden, Conn.: Archon Books, 1969), p. 43.
6. Spykman, *America's Strategy in World Politics: The United States and the Balance of Power* (New York: Harcourt, Brace, 1942), p. 24.

The estimated annual shipbuilding capacity of countries now under Nazi rule . . . plus that of Japan, plus that of Italy, was about 2,300,000 gross tons at the outbreak of the war. Nazi conquest of the British Isles [would add] about 2,500,000 gross tons . . . If that is a good estimate, it would take us more than four years to overtake totalitarian shipbuilding capacity, *supposing that they stood still.*[7]

For at least a year before Pearl Harbor and Hitler's declaration of war, President Roosevelt had been itching to join the European struggle because, "if Great Britain goes down, the Axis powers will control the continents of Europe, Asia, Africa, Australia, and the high seas—and they will . . . bring enormous military and naval resources against this hemisphere."[8] Similarly, the influential journalist Walter Lippmann argued that the United States had to defeat Hitler because "the potential military strength of the Old World is enormously greater than that of the New World."[9]

After the war, Stalin's domination of Eastern and Central Europe provoked fears that he had replaced Hitler as a contender for European hegemony. Advocates of containment also assumed that the Soviet Union could mobilize conquered industrial economies for war against the United States. George Kennan, an architect of containment, explained that the United States had to assure "that no single Continental land power should come to dominate the entire Eurasian land mass . . . become a great sea power as well as land power . . . and enter . . . on an overseas expansion hostile to ourselves and supported by the immense resources of the interior of Europe and Asia."[10] Likewise, a 1948 National Security Council report stated that "there are in Europe and Asia areas of great potential power which if added to the . . . Soviet world would enable the latter to become so superior in manpower, resources and territory that the prospect for the survival of the United States

---

7. Eugene Staley, "The Myth of the Continents," *Foreign Affairs*, Vol. 19, No. 3 (April 1941), p. 488 (emphasis in original).
8. Quoted in Alton Frye, *Nazi Germany and the American Hemisphere, 1933–1941* (New Haven: Yale University Press, 1967), p. 190.
9. Walter Lippmann, *U.S. Foreign Policy: Shield of the Republic* (Boston: Little, Brown, 1943), p. 109. See also William Langer and S. Everett Gleason, *The Challenge to Isolation* and *The Undeclared War* (New York: Harper, 1952 and 1953); Robert Dallek, *Franklin D. Roosevelt and American Foreign Policy, 1932–1945* (New York: Oxford University Press, 1979), esp. pp. 173, 181, 214–215, 219, 228, 231, 256, 266. According to Sumner Welles (quoted in ibid., p. 321), Roosevelt's grasp of geopolitics was "almost instinctive."
10. George F. Kennan, *American Diplomacy 1900–1950* (Chicago: University of Chicago Press, 1951), p. 5.

as a free nation would be slight."[11] Containment, like the U.S. participation in the war against Hitler, was inspired by moral and economic motives as well. But even at the end of the Cold War, the chief goal of containment remained, in President George Bush's words, "to prevent any hostile power or group of powers from dominating the Eurasian land mass."[12]

This focus on the Eurasian land mass, from Mackinder to Bush, stemmed from the geopolitical axiom that the wealthier the conquest, the more wealth and power gained. Kennan thus argued for limiting containment to the protection of only those "centers of industrial and military power"—Great Britain, Germany and Central Europe, and Japan—which have the "requisite conditions of climate, of industrial strength, of population and of tradition" capable of generating significant "amphibious power."[13] In 1951, Secretary of State Dean Acheson justified the deployment of additional U.S. troops to Europe by noting that "outside our own country, free Europe has the greatest number of scientists, the greatest industrial production, and the largest pool of skilled manpower in the world. It has a tremendous shipbuilding capacity, essential to control of the seas."[14] International relations theorist Kenneth Waltz makes a similar point when he writes that "only Japan, Western Europe, and the Middle East are prizes that if won by the Soviet Union would alter the balance of GNPs and the distribution of resources enough to be a danger."[15]

But the notion that GNPs can be transferred between capitals like money wired between banks has long had its critics. Adam Smith's *The Wealth of Nations* (published in 1776, as the American colonists declared their independence) concluded with a diatribe against maintaining the "showy equipage"

---

11. NSC 7, reprinted in *Foreign Relations of the United States, 1948*, Vol. 1: *General: The United Nations*, part 2 (Washington, D.C.: U.S. Government Printing Office [GPO], 1976), p. 546. Similar claims appear in NSC 20/4 (ibid., p. 665), which Truman approved in November 1948.
12. George Bush, *National Security Strategy of the United States, 1990–1991* (New York: Brassey's, 1990), p. 5. See also John Lewis Gaddis, *Strategies of Containment: A Critical Appraisal of Postwar American National Security Policy* (Oxford: Oxford University Press, 1982); Melvyn P. Leffler, "The American Conception of National Security," and replies, *American Historical Review*, No. 89 (April 1984), pp. 346–400.
13. Quoted in Gaddis, *Strategies of Containment*, p. 30; see also Kennan, *The Realities of American Foreign Policy* (Princeton: Princeton University Press, 1954), pp. 63–65; Barry Posen and Stephen Van Evera, "Departure from Containment," *International Security*, Vol. 8, No. 1 (Summer 1983), pp. 3–45; and Stephen Walt, "The Case for Finite Containment: Analyzing U.S. Grand Strategy," *International Security*, Vol. 14, No. 1 (Summer 1989), pp. 17–18.
14. Quoted in Eliot A. Cohen, "Do We Still Need Europe?" *Commentary*, Vol. 81, No. 1 (January 1986), p. 29.
15. Waltz, *Theory of International Politics*, p. 172.

of colonies "which contribute neither revenue nor military force towards the support of an empire."[16] Smith thought that empire often drained the mother country because the costs of seizing and defending colonies from imperial rivals typically exceeded the low revenues collected from them. Nineteenth- and twentieth-century writers have advanced a more ambitious claim, that even cheap and unopposed conquest among modern states did not pay. The British free-trade advocate, Richard Cobden, pronounced in 1849 that where "one empire will take possession, by force of arms, of its neighbor's territory . . . the accession of territory would be a source of weakness, not of strength."[17] On the eve of World War I, Norman Angell's *The Great Illusion* popularized the notion that "it is a logical fallacy and an optical illusion in Europe to regard a nation as increasing its wealth when it increases its territory."[18] Postwar theorists have since resuscitated Angell's claims. Klaus Knorr argues that "the conquest of territory for economic reasons has become an anachronism."[19] Carl Kaysen agrees that "the extent to which the conquest of new territory added to the economic strength of the conqueror is questionable."[20] Martin McGuire concludes that "much of the surplus that accrues to modern populations is simply not available to a conqueror."[21] Other political scientists and economists have made similar claims.[22]

---

16. Adam Smith, *The Wealth of Nations* (1776; repr. New York: Modern Library, 1937), p. 899; for Smith's general critique of empire, see pp. 557–596. For other early liberal views of conquest, see Donald Winch, *Classical Political Economy and Colonies* (London: G. Bell and Sons, 1965); and Alan Milward, *The New Order and the French Economy* (Oxford: Clarendon, 1970), pp. 3–17.

17. Richard Cobden, *Speeches on Questions of Public Policy*, John Bright and James Rogers, eds. (London: Macmillan, 1870), Vol. 1, p. 484. See also Cobden, *Political Writings* (New York: D. Appleton, 1867), Vol. 1, pp. 191–198, 244–252, 262–266, 463.

18. Norman Angell, *The Great Illusion: A Study of the Relation of Military Power to National Advantage*, 4th rev. and enl. ed. (New York: G.P. Putnam's Sons, 1913), p. 34; cf. pp. 107–130. For a contemporary critique, see J.H. Jones, *The Economics of War and Conquest: An Examination of Mr. Norman Angell's Economic Doctrines* (London: P.S. King & Son, 1915). On Angell's impact, see J.D.B. Miller, *Norman Angell and the Futility of War* (London: Macmillan, 1986), esp. pp. 4–10, 37–39.

19. Klaus M. Knorr, *The Power of Nations: The Political Economy of International Relations* (New York: Basic Books, 1975), pp. 124–125. Knorr originally presented this argument in *On the Uses of Military Power in the Nuclear Age* (Princeton: Princeton Unversity Press, 1966), pp. 21–34.

20. Carl Kaysen, "Is War Obsolete? A Review Essay," *International Security*, Vol. 14, No. 4 (Spring 1990), p. 54.

21. Martin C. McGuire, "The Revolution in International Security," *Challenge* (March–April 1990), p. 8.

22. Raymond Aron, *Peace and War: A Theory of International Relations*, trans. Richard Howard and Annette Baker Fox (New York: Praeger, 1968), p. 257; Kenneth Boulding, "The Economics and Noneconomics of the World War Industry," *Contemporary Policy Issues*, Vol. 4, No. 4 (October 1986), pp. 12–21; Alastair Buchan, "Technology and World Politics," in Brian Porter, ed., *The Aberystwyth Papers: International Politics 1919–1969* (Oxford: Oxford University Press, 1972),

This "liberal" view of conquest has been used not only to criticize empire and imperialism, but also to challenge traditional realist arguments about power-balancing and the likelihood of war. If the conquest of modern societies is economically futile, balancing—including the use of force to stop conquerors—becomes less important and less likely. Cobden used this idea as ammunition against British intervention against Russia in the Crimea, and Angell's *Great Illusion* served as the bible of interwar British isolationists. Similarly, opponents of the U.S. entry into World War II argued that internal resistance by the occupied societies would have minimized German and Japanese gains from conquest.[23] And critics of containment argued that the Soviet Union could not mobilize a conquered Western Europe for war against the United States.[24]

The liberal view of conquest has also been used to explain an apparent secular decline in war over the course of modern history and to predict peace among developed nations.[25] This idea is distinct from—though typically advanced as part of—the more general "war-does-not-pay" argument, which also includes the high costs of modern warfare. When conquest paid, it was

---

pp. 160–182; Robert Gilpin, *War and Change in World Politics* (New York: Cambridge University Press, 1981), pp. 106–185, 221–223; John Mueller, *Retreat from Doomsday: The Obsolescence of Major War* (New York: Basic Books, 1989), pp. 222–223; and especially Richard Rosecrance, *The Rise of the Trading State: Commerce and Conquest in the Modern World* (New York: Basic Books, 1986).

23. Bruce Russett, *No Clear and Present Danger: A Skeptical View of the United States Entry into World War II* (New York: Harper & Row, 1972), pp. 33–34, 62. See also Lawrence Dennis, "The Economic Consequences of American Intervention," in Justus D. Doenecke, ed., *In Danger Undaunted: The Anti-Interventionist Movement of 1940–1941 as Revealed in the Papers of the America First Committee* (Stanford: Hoover Institution Press, 1990), pp. 200–205. Most isolationists, however, stressed the difficulty of intercontinental power projection, rather than of economic mobilization. See Manfred Jonas, *Isolationism in America, 1935–1941* (Ithaca: Cornell University Press, 1966).

24. Christopher Layne, "Atlanticism Without NATO," *Foreign Policy*, No. 67 (Summer 1987), p. 38; Earl C. Ravenal, "Europe Without America: The Erosion of NATO," *Foreign Affairs*, Vol. 63, No. 5 (Summer 1985), p. 1034; Jerry Sanders, "Security and Choice," *World Policy Journal*, No. 1 (Summer 1984), p. 713; and Sherle Schwenninger and Jerry Sanders, "The Democrats and a New Grand Strategy," *World Policy Journal*, No. 3 (Summer 1986), p. 400. One who favored containment on moral grounds nevertheless agreed: Stanley Kober, "Can NATO Survive?" *International Affairs*, No. 59 (Summer 1983), pp. 343–345.

25. Kaysen, "Is War Obsolete?"; McGuire, "Revolution in International Security"; Mueller, *Retreat from Doomsday*, pp. 221–223; Gilpin, *War and Change*, pp. 219–223; Robert Jervis, "The Future of World Politics; Will it Resemble the Past?" *International Security*, Vol. 16, No. 3 (Winter 1991/92), pp. 48–50; and—relating to the postindustrial era—Stephen Van Evera, "Primed for Peace: Europe After the Cold War," *International Security*, Vol. 15, No. 3 (Winter 1990/91), pp. 14–16. Ted Hopf emphasizes the cumulativity of resources in a general theory of the causes of war in "Polarity, the Offense-Defense Balance, and War," *American Political Science Review*, Vol. 85, No. 2 (June 1991), pp. 477–478.

only natural that, as Frederick the Great put it, "at all times it was the principle of great states to subjugate all whom they could and to extend their power continuously."[26] But now that conquest no longer pays, goes this argument, even power-hungry despots have lost their appetite for neighboring territory, eliminating an age-old cause of war.

A variant of the liberal view has been advanced in support of civilian- and guerrilla-based defense policies. Guerrilla-warfare strategists argue that local knowledge and popular support enable a committed few to impose high costs on occupying armies and disrupt economic collaboration.[27] Advocates of non-violent, civilian-based defenses argue that preparation and training in civil disobedience could economically and politically paralyze invaded countries, and thus deny a conqueror any gains.[28] Rather than claim that conquest is always unprofitable, proponents argue that preparation and training in these "porcupine" strategies can make it so. But arguments for their effectiveness share liberal assumptions about the power potential of civil society, and provide support for the liberal view of conquest.

Not all realists think that conquest pays, and not all liberals think that it does not. The defining principle of political realism, that the international system is an anarchic arena governed by distributions of power, rests upon no inherent assumptions about the sources of power. But the assumption that conquest pays strengthens the realist argument that states should and will balance against conquerors. Where realists admit that conquest might

---

26. Quoted in Gerhard Ritter, *Frederick the Great* (Berkeley: University of California Press, 1968), p. 66. See also Martin Wight, *Power Politics*, H. Bull and C. Holbraad, eds. (New York: Holmes & Meier, 1978), pp. 144–156.

27. Kennan proposed in a controversial 1957 radio talk that Europe adopt Swiss-type paramilitary forces whose "function should be primarily internal rather than external," and which should be trained to "offer whatever overt resistance might be possible to a foreign invader but also to constitute the cores of a civil resistance movement on any territory . . . overrun by the enemy." George F. Kennan, *Russia, the Atom and the West* (New York: Harper & Bros., 1958), p. 63. See also Walter Lacqueur, ed., *The Guerrilla Reader: A Historical Anthology* (Philadelphia: Temple University Press, 1977). For a critical review of recent proposals, see Stephen J. Flanagan, "Nonprovocative and Civilian-Based Defenses," in Joseph S. Nye, Jr., Graham T. Allison, and Albert Carnesale, eds., *Fateful Visions: Avoiding Nuclear Catastrophe* (Cambridge, Mass.: Ballinger, 1988), pp. 393–410.

28. Gene Sharp, *Civilian-Based Defense* (Princeton: Princeton University Press, 1990); Gene Sharp, *Making Europe Unconquerable: The Potential of Civilian-Based Deterrence and Defense* (Cambridge, Mass.: Ballinger, 1985); Gene Keyes, "Strategic Non-Violent Defense," *Journal of Strategic Studies*, Vol. 4, No. 2 (June 1981), pp. 125–151; Adam Roberts, ed., *Civilian Resistance as a National Defence: Non-Violent Action against Aggression*, 2nd ed. (Harmondsworth: Penguin Books, 1969); Anders Boserup and Andrew Mack, *War Without Weapons: Non-Violence in National Defense* (New York: Schocken, 1975); Stephen King Hall, *Defense in the Nuclear Age* (London: Victor Gallancz, 1958), pp. 145–159.

not pay (as when Waltz claims that "force is always on the side of the governed"), they weaken the deductive strength of balance-of-power strategy and theory.[29] Likewise, the liberal doctrine that free trade maximizes wealth entails no presumptions about the profitability of conquest, allowing astute liberals like Jeremy Bentham to distinguish between profitless overseas colonies and profitable continental conquests.[30] It is difficult to do full justice to the variety of opinion within schools of thought as broad as realism and liberalism. But these labels provide a useful way to distinguish between two contending sets of assumptions, predictions, and prescriptions.

The Liberal Argument

Four reasons have been advanced to support the liberal view of conquest. First, modern societies are inherently nationalistic and thus will oppose foreign rule with unremitting hostility. Second, the maintenance of control over politically hostile societies is expensive. Third, economic resistance and the stultifying effects of repression would withhold or reduce modern societies' social surplus. Fourth, conquest results in opportunity costs because gains in trade with free and prosperous nations are forgone.

Nationalism, the desire to be governed by members of one's own culture, provides an explanation for the hostility of developing and developed societies to foreign rule. Robert Gilpin claims that "the imperial game of territorial conquest for the sake of exploitation [was] discovered by Napoleonic France to be costly in an age of nationalism."[31] Richard Rosecrance and others think that it was only in the nineteenth century that nationalism had become

---

29. Waltz explains that foreign "governors, being few in number, depend for the exercise of their rule on the more or less willing assent of their subjects. If sullen disregard is the response to every command, no government can rule." Waltz, *Theory of International Politics*, p. 188. Kennan falls into the same inconsistency when he writes that "one must not be too frightened of those who aspire to world domination" because of "the continued and undiminished relevance in the modern world of Gibbon's assertion that 'there is nothing more contrary to nature than the attempt to hold in obedience distant provinces'." Kennan, *Memoirs 1925–1950* (New York: Pantheon Books, 1967), pp. 129–130.
30. According to Bentham, "the new property, being contiguous, is laid on his old property . . . the inhabitants, as many as he thinks fit to set his mark on, go to increase his armies; their substance, as much as he thinks fit to squeeze from them, goes into his own purse." Bentham, "A Plan for a Universal and Perpetual Peace," in *The Works of Jeremy Bentham*, Sir John Bowring, ed., (London: Russell and Russell, 1962), Vol. II, p. 557. On overseas colonies, see ibid., p. 457, and "Emancipate Your Colonies! Shewing the Uselessness and Mischievousness of Distant Dependencies to an European State," in ibid., Vol. IV, pp. 407–418.
31. Gilpin, *War and Change*, p. 142.

sufficiently virulent to make "foreign rule impracticable."[32] Liberals would agree that nationalism is pervasive in twentieth-century industrial societies, nearly impossible to eradicate, and a potent motivation for struggle against foreign domination.[33]

Political hostility reduces the profits of conquest both by raising the costs of empire and by reducing its revenues. The costs are increased by the fact that nationalistic populations will rebel absent an expensive and permanent repressive apparatus, which even then may not be able to contain assassinations, riots, insurgencies, and wars of independence. The European overseas empires, imposed cheaply on backward, pre-nationalistic societies, saw pacification costs soar after those societies caught fire with nationalism. As Knorr points out, "the French required only thirty thousand men to subdue Algeria in 1830. In 1962, they could not subdue her with a force twenty times as large."[34]

Liberals also contend that, as Angell put it, "the exaction of tribute from a conquered people has become an economic impossibility."[35] Modern societies will withhold, reduce, or eliminate their economic surpluses from detested rulers. This is possible, according to Rosecrance, because "highly developed economies are much more dependent upon social cooperation and obedience to the rulers of the state than are primitive or transitional economic systems."[36] In other words, modernization itself provides nationalistic populations with unique possibilities for economic noncooperation.

There are three plausible justifications for this claim. First, modernization increases the potential for political and economic collective action. International relations theorists may have borrowed this idea from research in comparative politics. Robert Dahl's *Polyarchy* contends that "economic develop-

---

32. Rosecrance, *Rise of the Trading State*, p. 34; cf. pp. 135, 176. Kaysen, "Is War Obsolete?" p. 52.

33. Ernest Gellner's *Nations and Nationalism* (Ithaca: Cornell University Press, 1983), provides a persuasive explanation for the link between development and nationalism. Peasants living in small, isolated, agrarian communities have little contact with their rulers and care little about their cultural credentials. But these communities dissolve as modernization creates "a mobile, literate, culturally standardized, interchangeable population." This occurs because states provide mass education to create a basically literate and numerate work-force, while the population seeks education to compete for the growing number of industrial and service jobs. Because non-agricultural workers depend on their proficiency in a shared culture for economic advancement, they prefer rulers who share their language and other traits subject to discrimination. Thus modern peoples identify with the state, or potential state, that promises to protect their cultures.

34. Knorr, *Power of Nations*, p. 112.

35. Angell, *Great Illusion*, p. 45.

36. Rosecrance, *Rise of the Trading State*, pp. 36–37; cf. pp. 128, 135, 176.

ment itself generates the conditions of a pluralistic social order," in part because advanced economies "automatically distribute political resources and political skills to a vast variety of individuals, groups, and organizations."[37] Just as important is the increased population densities which facilitate social self-organization. As Marx and Engels argued in the *Communist Manifesto*, "the improved means of communication that are created by modern industry and that place the workers of different localities in contact with one another" are essential "to centralize the numerous local struggles, all of the same character, into one national struggle between classes."[38] Political skills and resources, combined with easy and rapid communication, invest modern societies with the potential to bargain collectively, boycott, and strike, and thus to withhold resources from illegitimate regimes.

Second, skilled labor may be inherently more difficult to exploit than unskilled labor. McGuire has this in mind when he argues that:

the costs to a tyrant of extracting a surplus out of a conquered territory will increase as more and more of the indigenous product of the territory is attributable to human capital. Seizing gold, rubber, minerals, lumber, or other natural resources must be surely less costly than enlisting sufficient cooperation from an enslaved population to produce electronic parts, computer programs, or reliable transportation.[39]

Economic transaction-cost analyses support this argument.[40] Monitoring the performance of complex tasks requires considerable attention and expertise, making it difficult to detect and penalize slack working. Sabotage is easier too, and potentially more damaging since manufacturing relies on valuable and often delicate equipment. If the exploitability of work is inversely related to its complexity, then higher levels of development should provide greater

---

37. Robert Dahl, *Polyarchy: Participation and Opposition* (New Haven: Yale University Press, 1971), p. 77. Dahl points out, however, that development is neither necessary nor sufficient for polyarchy; pp. 68–71.
38. From Robert C. Tucker, ed., *The Marx-Engels Reader*, 2nd ed. (New York: W.W. Norton, 1978), pp. 480–481.
39. McGuire, "Revolution in International Security," p. 8; Kaysen, "Is War Obsolete?" p. 53.
40. Stefano Fenoaltea, "Slavery and Supervision in Comparative Perspective: A Model," *The Journal of Economic History*, Vol. 44, No. 3 (September 1984), esp. pp. 635–668. Economists have also argued that performance is motivated by identification with ultimate goals as well as by pay, at least after one's salary has reached the point of diminishing returns. John K. Galbraith, *The New Industrial State*, 4th ed. (Boston: Houghton Mifflin, 1985), pp. 136–147. Experimental studies have shown that morale and motivation have a slight effect on assembly-line productivity, but morale would surely suffer more from national subjugation than, say, not enough coffee breaks. Charles Perrow, *Complex Organizations*, 3rd ed. (New York: Random House, 1986), pp. 86–87.

opportunities for economic resistance by nationalist populations. Dahl agrees, noting that "compulsion and coercion are often damaging to incentives. In an advanced economy, long-run performance under threat or coercion is less productive at all levels than a more willing performance based on voluntary compliance."[41]

Third, foreign control may interfere with other requisites of productivity. Foreign domination automatically impoverishes modern industrial economies, it is argued, by precluding subversive yet economically critical communication practices and technologies. According to Stephen Van Evera, the productivity of highly developed societies depends on free access to information, which in turn:

requires a free domestic press, and access to foreign publications, foreign travel, personal computers, and photocopiers. But police measures needed to subdue a conquered society require that these technologies and practices be forbidden, because they also carry subversive ideas. Thus critical elements of the economic fabric now must be ripped out to maintain control over conquered polities.[42]

Van Evera applies this argument to post-industrial economies, but they should apply to a lesser extent to "smokestack" economies as well. In sum, modernization enhances modern societies' social power by facilitating collective action and by making their economic productivity dependent on uncoerceable skilled labor and politically dangerous practices and technologies.

Finally, an old liberal criticism of empire stresses the opportunity costs of conquest: conquerors lose the gains from trade and investment that they would have enjoyed had they opted for peace over aggression.[43] Contemporary theorists claim that this was more true than ever after the Industrial Revolution because "there was no sense in using military force to acquire power and wealth when they could be obtained more efficiently through peaceful economic development and trade."[44] Conquest can result in three

---

41. Dahl, *Polyarchy*, p. 77.
42. Van Evera, "Primed for Peace," pp. 14–15.
43. Jean-François Melon, a French liberal economist, wrote in 1734: "To encourage marriages, to grant assistance to fathers burdened with large families, to take charge of the education of orphans and foundlings is to strengthen the State much more than conquest would. In so far as what the capture of a town ordinarily costs in men and money, compared to its value, there is always a loss for the conqueror, who is certain to meet with subsequent resistance." Quoted in Milward, *New Order*, p. 3.
44. Rosecrance, *Rise of the Trading State*, p. 139. Also making this claim are Aron, *Peace and War*, p. 257; Boulding, "Economics and Noneconomics," pp. 14–17; Buchan, "Technology and World Politics," p. 177; Gilpin, *War and Change*, pp. 106–185; Kaysen, "Is War Obsolete?" pp. 56–57; and Knorr, *Uses of Military Power*, pp. 21–34.

sorts of opportunity costs: those arising from war costs, from loss of trade outside the empire, and from loss of trade with conquered nations. Since the first two are predicted by realist balance-of-power theory, only the third is properly part of the liberal critique. After all, realists hold that it is precisely high war costs which deter conquest. If war costs are low (a situation that realists aim to prevent), the smallest imperial profits would provide the conqueror with *additional* investment capital for domestic use. Opportunity costs arising from third-party economic sanctions, such as the British blockade of Germany during both world wars, or the UN embargo of Iraq after the latter invaded Kuwait, also depend upon international rather than intra-imperial politics. But a third opportunity cost can arise from nationalistic resistance. Both Angell's *Great Illusion* and John Maynard Keynes' *The Consequences of the Peace* (a 1920 critique of the heavy reparations the Allies demanded from Germany) stressed that free and thriving trading partners are more economically useful than taxed but withering appendages.[45] This assumes that free trade is the norm, because trade barriers decrease trading gains. But if free trade is given, and if conquest does in fact ruin modern economies, then conquerors will suffer opportunity costs from forgone trade with their possessions.

In sum, the liberal view of conquest holds that modernization increases nationalism, collective action potential, and the dependence of individual productivity on worker goodwill and freely-flowing information. Together, these factors increase the costs and diminish the benefits of conquest, and result in long-term losses from forgone trade.

A Realist Argument

While most realists assume that the conquest of modern societies pays, they have never tried systematically to prove it. Still, a good argument can be marshalled from the realist theory that the strong can coerce the weak. In addition, basic observations about modernization provide three reasons to think that as countries industrialize they become tastier and easier prey for ruthless conquerors. First, and requiring little further argument: modernization vastly increases the economic surplus produced. The richer a country, the more that can be stolen from it, so nationalistic resistance would have to

---

45. Angell, *Great Illusion*, pp. 50–67; John M. Keynes, *The Economic Consequences of the Peace* (New York: Harcourt, Brace and Howe, 1920).

be very effective to make conquest unprofitable. Second, modernization increases the efficiency of coercion because it centralizes control over coercive resources, facilitates the quick deployment of this power over expansive regions, and gives hostage societies more to lose from resistance. Third, a relatively low-cost investment in repression prevents most people in modern societies from contributing to the collective good of resistance.

If there is a distinctively realist theory about the profitability of conquest, it is that coercion works. Realists habitually use theories of coercion to explain why sovereign states bend to threats and demands.[46] Coercion is typically a weapon of the strong against the weak because strong states can effectively threaten weak ones without fear of retaliation. It is for this reason that realists predict that small, vulnerable countries without effective allies will form alliances (i.e., bandwagon) with powerful neighbors.[47] Coercion then should be especially easy against defeated and occupied countries, which can neither protect their populations from harm nor retaliate. Thus Hans Morgenthau claimed in *Politics Among Nations* that conquest "without prospects for speedy recovery usually breaks the will to resist of the conquered people."[48]

Obviously, great powers, especially irresolute ones, have not always been successful in coercing weak Third World countries.[49] But history shows that merciless conquerors have in fact successfully pacified and exploited modern industrial societies. The Soviet Union, for example, extracted about 6 billion marks in reparations from a passive East Germany each year between 1947 and 1953; this was 33 percent, falling to 18 percent of East German GNP as the base economy recovered from World War II.[50] Even if the costs of all 400,000 Soviet troops deployed in East Germany—a force designed to battle the entire West—are counted, the control costs were roughly only a quarter

---

46. For an especially lucid explication of coercion theory, see Thomas C. Schelling, *Arms and Influence* (New Haven: Yale University Press, 1966), pp. 1–34, 69–91, 170–184.
47. Stephen M. Walt, *The Origins of Alliances* (Ithaca: Cornell University Press, 1987), pp. 28–33; 172–178.
48. Morgenthau, *Politics among Nations*, p. 81. For discussion of coercion between victor and vanquished, see Paul Kecskemeti, *Strategic Surrender: The Politics of Victory and Defeat* (Stanford: Stanford University Press, 1958); and Schelling, *Arms and Influence*, chap. 1.
49. Andrew Mack, "Why Big Nations Lose Small Wars: The Politics of Asymmetric Conflict," *World Politics*, Vol. 27, No. 2 (January 1975), pp. 175–200.
50. These figures, which do not count technology and deported labor taken from Germany, are from Heinz Köhler, *Economic Integration in the Soviet Bloc with an East German Case Study* (New York: Praeger, 1965), chap. 1. Paul Marer accepts these figures, and provides additional data on the lesser exactions from other Eastern European nations, in "Soviet Economic Policy in Eastern Europe," in U.S. Congress, Joint Economic Committee, *Reorientation and Commercial Relations of the Economies of Eastern Europe* (Washington, D.C.: U.S. GPO, 1974), pp. 135–163.

of the total gains.[51] Finally, although reparations were terminated soon after the June 17, 1953, demonstrations in East Germany, this was probably due more to the recognition that this new ally would remain in the Soviet orbit indefinitely, and should thus be fattened for future use.[52]

Western Europe under German domination during World War II provides further compelling examples. In stark contrast to liberal predictions, nationalistic and industrialized nations failed to withhold, eliminate, or significantly reduce their economic surpluses, nor did they impose enough costs to take a bite out of the conqueror's gains. Through financial transfers alone, Germany was able to mobilize an annual average of 30 percent of French national incomes, 42–44 percent of Dutch, Belgian, and Norwegian prewar national income, and at least 25 percent of Czech prewar national income.[53] This does not include the value of the booty and the surprisingly productive slave labor Germany also gained from its new empire.[54] And the fact that continental coal shortages sharply limited industrial production in these countries makes German success all the more astonishing.[55] Control costs could not have

---

51. Based on average East German wage data for 1951, from Wolfgang F. Stolper, *The Structure of the East German Economy* (Cambridge: Harvard University Press, 1960), p. 431.

52. As Margaret Levi argues in *Of Rule and Revenue* (Berkeley: University of California Press, 1988), rulers choose extraction rates according to their time horizons. On Soviet policy, see Ann L. Phillips, *Soviet Policy Toward East Germany Reconsidered: The Postwar Decade* (Westport, Conn.: Greenwood Press, 1986).

53. Mobilization data for the Czech Protectorate (which do not include goods and services Germany consumed within its borders, and therefore understate the Czech contribution) from Jaroslav Krejčí, "The Bohemian-Moravian War Economy," in M.C. Kaser and E.A. Radice, eds., *The Economic History of Eastern Europe, 1919–1975*, Vol. 2: *Interwar Policy, the War, and Reconstruction* (Oxford, U.K.: Clarendon, 1986), pp. 452–492. All other financial transfer data (which take into account purchasing-power parities and black market rates) from Oberkommando der Wehrmacht, Forschungsstelle für Wehrwirtschaft [German Supreme Command's Research Office for War Economy], "Die finanziellen Leistungen der besetzten Gebiete bis Ende März 1944," October 1944, reproduced with commentary in Christoph Buchheim, "Die besetzten Länder im Dienste der deutschen Kriegswirtschaft während des Zweiten Weltkriegs," *Vierteljahrshefte für Zeitgeschichte*, No. 34 (April 1986), pp. 117–145. Income data (net national product) from Colin Clark, *The Conditions of Economic Progress*, 3rd ed. (London: Macmillan, 1957), with French income reduced 5 percent to compensate for the wartime separation of Alsace-Lorraine. Income data converted into Reichsmarks according to the 1940 "real" exchange rates used in the above-cited German study.

54. Plunder was especially extensive in France; see Milward, *New Order*; and France, Présidence du Conseil, Commission Consultative des Dommages et des Reparations, *Dommages subis par la France et l'Union Française du fait de la guerre et de l'occupation ennemie (1939–1945)*, Part imputable à l'Allemagne, 9 vols. (Paris: Imprimerie Nationale, 1947–1951). On slave labor, see Edward L. Homze, *Foreign Labor in Nazi Germany* (Princeton: Princeton University Press, 1967).

55. John R. Gillingham, *Industry and Politics in the Third Reich: Ruhr Coal, Hitler and Europe* (London: Methuen, 1985). The distribution of coal helps to explain the difference in mobilization rates within occupied Western Europe, according to coal allocation data in Sven-Olof Olsson,

exceeded several percent of German gains, because few German troops, police, and administrators were needed to suppress all outward signs of resistance. In France in late 1941, for example, a half-million German soldiers (for the most part training or manning the coastal perimeter), 6,000 German police, and 1,500 officials proved sufficient to pacify a country of 42 million.[56]

To put the European mobilization rates in perspective, consider that military spending in France had reached 23 percent of national income in 1939.[57] Thus the Nazis mobilized French resources at least as fully as had the Third Republic on the eve of war. This fell short of the levels of military spending reached by the United States, Britain, and Germany (54 percent, 47 percent, and 60 percent of national income, respectively), but these belligerents did not face the same raw-material bottlenecks.[58] Hitler's "hostile takeover" of European nations enabled him to mobilize a European war economy for the duration of the war.

Germany profited from Europe's skilled technicians and high-tech industries as well as its farmers, miners, builders, railway workers, and craftsmen. The Dutch corporation Philips provided radios to the Luftwaffe, and the German Navy even placed a development contract for new submarine components in Rotterdam.[59] The collaboration of the Belgian electronics industry was so extensive that the German conglomerate AEG fretted about the expansion of its competition there.[60] Almost all European production was useful to the German war economy, and although many firms drew the line at arms production, even this was usually an empty gesture. In Belgium, for example, the Fabrique Nationale agreed to produce its famous small arms on the condition that the Germans "take over" its Liège plant with 79 supervisors,

---

German Coal and Swedish Fuel 1939–1945 (Göteborg: Institute of Economic History of Göteborg University, 1975), pp. 120–123, 135–141.

56. France, Commission Consultative des Dommages et des Reparations, *Dommages*, Vol. 2, p. 375. Data on officials and police from Werner Best (a high German official in occupied France and later Denmark), "Die deutschen Aufsichtsverwaltungen in Frankreich, Belgien, den Niederlanden, Norwegen, Dänemark, und im Protektorat Böhmen und Mähren," September 1941, Records of German Field Commands, U.S. National Archives, T501/101/1367; and Norman Rich, *Hitler's War Aims*, Vol. 2: *The Establishment of the New Order* (New York: Norton, 1974), p. 208.

57. British and German mobilization rates were about the same. Anthony Adamthwaite, *France and the Coming of the Second World War, 1936–1939* (London: Cass, 1977), p. 164.

58. Mark Harrison, "Resource Mobilization for World War II," *Economic History Review*, 2nd ser., No. 41 (1988), pp. 184–185.

59. Gerhard Hirschfeld, *Nazi Rule and Dutch Collaboration: The Netherlands under German Occupation 1940–1945*, trans. L. Willmot (New York: Berg, 1988), pp. 183–192.

60. John Gillingham, *Belgian Business in the Nazi New Order* (Ghent: Jan Dhondt Stichting, 1977), p. 151.

and Cockerill Steel rejected a German Navy order for gun barrels until they were renamed "tubes."[61] Throughout the war, construction companies built air bases, coastal fortifications, and submarine pens, all to be used to prevent the Allied liberation of "Fortress Europe."[62]

Comparing Germany's industrial conquests with its agrarian conquests provides further evidence for the realist view that modernization makes conquest more profitable rather than less. Table 1 ranks the occupied countries by their level of modernization, and compares the average yearly amount that citizens of the occupied countries were compelled to contribute (under the rubric of "occupation costs" and "clearing deficits") to the German war economy. As the table makes clear, Germany was able to mobilize the more modern economies—Norway, Belgium, the Netherlands, and France—

Table 1. European Modernization Levels and Contributions to the German War Economy During World War II.

Country	GNP/capita, 1938 (Germany=100)	Average annual burden per capita (Reichsmarks)
Norway	115	447
Belgium	90	306
Netherlands	82	360
France	76	228
Greece	52	27
Poland (General-Government)	33	108
Serbia	30	45

SOURCES: GNP per capita from Paul Bairoch, "Europe's Gross National Product: 1800–1975," *Journal of European Economic History*, Vol. 5, No. 2 (Fall 1976), p. 297. Financial transfer data from Oberkommando der Wehrmacht, Forschungsstelle für Wehrwirtschaft [German Supreme Command's Research Office for War Economy], "Die finanziellen Leistungen der besetzten Gebiete bis Ende März 1944," October 1944, reproduced with commentary in Christoph Buchheim, "Die besetzten Länder im Dienste der deutschen Kriegswirtschaft während des Zweiten Weltkriegs," *Vierteljahrshefte für Zeitgeschichte*, No. 34 (April 1986, pp. 117–145. Population data from B.R. Mitchell, *European Historical Statistics, 1750–1970*, 2nd rev. ed (New York: Facts on File, 1981); and E.A. Radice, "Territorial Changes, Population Movements and Labor Supplies," in M.C. Kaser and E.A. Radice, eds., *The Economic History of Eastern Europe, 1919–1975*, Vol. 2: *Interwar Policy, the War, and Reconstruction* (Oxford, U.K.: Clarendon, 1986), pp. 309–328.

61. For several such examples, see Peter F. Klemm, "German Economic Policies in Belgium from 1940 to 1944" (Ph.D. diss., University of Michigan, 1973), pp. 213–232.
62. Hirschfeld, *Nazi Rule*, pp. 189n, 211–213; Milward, *New Order*, pp. 134, 278.

much more intensively than the less modern ones—Greece, Poland, and Serbia.

Table 1 does not take into account Germany's control costs, but it appears that modernization helped minimize these as well. Armed guerrillas were virtually non-existent in Denmark, the Netherlands, Belgium, and Czechoslovakia, only marginally active in the mountainous regions of France and upper Italy, and greatest in the Balkans.[63] In the Netherlands, active resisters numbered around a thousand, or less than a tenth of one percent of the population.[64] At their peak, French partisans numbered only around 400,000, or just 1 percent of the French population: most of these were unarmed and joined just before the liberation.[65] In February 1944, Yugoslav partisans totalled 250,000, or 1.7 percent of the Yugoslav population; moreover, they tied down several German divisions and their numbers continued to grow until the end of the war.[66]

Modernization makes nations easy to coerce for three reasons. One is that modernization allows tyrants to monopolize coercive resources more easily.[67] The division of labor in modern societies grants the state a real monopoly on violence, legitimate or not. In the eighteenth century, a population armed with rifles, like the American colonists, could do considerable damage to an occupying army. But after centuries of relying entirely on their state to protect them, from criminals as well as from conquerors, ordinary people's skills and tools for violence have not kept pace with those of modern militaries, police, and paramilitary forces. In World War II, the few active European resistance fighters were poorly armed, and depended almost entirely on Allied air-drops (most of which were intercepted by the Germans) for sup-

---

63. Walter Laqueur, *Guerrilla: A Historical and Critical Study* (Boston: Little Brown, 1976), pp. 202–238. For overviews of European resistance, see Henri Michel, *The Shadow War: European Resistance, 1939–1945* (London: 1972); M.R.D. Foot, *Resistance: European Resistance to Nazism, 1940–1945* (New York: McGraw-Hill, 1977); and Jørgen Haestrup, *European Resistance Movements, 1939–1945: A Complete History* (Westport, Conn.: Meckler, 1981).
64. Werner Warmbrunn, *The Dutch under German Occupation, 1940–1945* (Stanford: Stanford University Press, 1963), p. 266, states that there were 1,200 full-time resisters.
65. Robert O. Paxton, *Vichy France: Old Guard and New Order, 1940–1944* (New York: Columbia University Press, 1972), pp. 294–295; and Gordon Wright, "Reflections on the French Resistance," *Political Science Quarterly*, Vol. 77, No. 3 (1962), p. 337–339.
66. Haestrup, *European Resistance Movements*, p. 474.
67. Morgenthau makes this point in *Politics Among Nations*, p. 299. For elaboration, see Stanislav Andreski, *Military Organization and Society* (Berkeley: University of California Press, 1968), pp. 35–36; and Anthony Giddens, *The Nation-State and Violence* (Berkeley: University of California Press, 1987), pp. 181–197.

plies.[68] They had little chance to impose high costs on, much less defeat, Nazi troops equipped with artillery, machine guns, armored vehicles, and radio-locating systems.

A second reason is that the rapid communication and mobility permitted by modernization allows conquerors to use their coercive resources efficiently. Communication links and technologies make surveillance easier.[69] And since urbanization, roads, and mechanized forms of transport permit rapid and sequential responses to outbreaks of resistance, despots no longer have to distribute forces throughout their dominions. Morgenthau astutely observed, "Today the government of a world empire, appraised . . . by radio, would send within a few hours a squadron of bombers and a score of transports loaded with parachutists, mortars, and tanks, weapons of which it has a monopoly or near monopoly, to the revolting city and squelch the revolt with ease."[70] Studies of guerrilla warfare typically conclude that modern societies, and particularly urban areas, do not provide a hospitable environment for armed resistance.[71]

Modern societies' very wealth provides a third vulnerability to coercion. It is easier to coerce an industrial society than an agrarian one because their wealth can be held hostage for compliance. While all conquerors can resort to the age-old terror tactics of murder, rape, and slavery, cunning ones can also threaten modern societies' plentiful industrial capital, national treasures, market networks, or centralized services. Modernization provides a wide range of vulnerable and highly valued property and freedoms; even the threat of administrative mismanagement can appear ominous to complex, service-dependent societies. And, despite liberal claims to the contrary, the fact that modern societies' cooperation is needed to maintain economic production does not give them much bargaining leverage against rulers. By taking a

---

68. The Allied Command concluded that "without the organization, communications, material, training and leadership which SOE [the British Special Operations Executive] supplied, . . . 'resistance' would have been of no military value." Quoted in M.R.D. Foot, *S.O.E. in France: An Account of the Work of the British Special Operations Executive in France, 1940–44* (London: Her Majesty's Stationery Office [HMSO], 1966), p. 442.
69. Studies of totalitarianism, e.g., Carl J. Friedrich and Zbigniew K. Brzezinski, *Totalitarian Dictatorship and Autocracy* (New York: Praeger, 1956), stressed the political implications of modern surveillance. See also Nathan Leites and Charles Wolf, Jr., *Rebellion and Authority: An Analytic Essay on Insurgent Conflicts* (Chicago: Markham, 1970), pp. 132–148; and Giddens, *Nation-State and Violence*, pp. 295–310.
70. Morgenthau, *Politics Among Nations*, p. 299.
71. Edward E. Rice, *Wars of the Third Kind: Conflict in Underdeveloped Countries* (Berkeley and Los Angeles: University of California Press, 1988), ch. 2; Laqueur, *Guerrilla*, pp. 395 and passim.

fixed percentage of production, a conqueror provides powerful incentives for the population to perform and thus reap at least some of the benefits of their own labors. The people themselves would face the gravest consequences of their own nonproductivity. Liberals are right about the importance of social collaboration to modern productivity, but they draw the wrong conclusion. Defeated societies will collaborate when their welfare depends on it.

Even if a modern nation were willing to sacrifice everything above subsistence to deny gains to a conqueror, it would find it impossible to do so. Agrarian societies can eliminate their surpluses by reverting to subsistence farming, but modern societies must work to eat. During World War II, while farmers in the more developed areas of Europe continued to produce and sell their commercial crops, Serbian and Polish farmers consumed much of their own declining production. Modern urban workers do not have backyard gardens to fall back on, and the ingrained division between industrial and agricultural production in modern societies makes a return to the land difficult even without the interference of a repressive conqueror. All durable strikes depend on some form of strike pay, but that is rarely feasible for conquered societies.[72] The few historical cases of massive, nationalistic general strikes by modern societies involved atypically restrained conquerors. During World War I, Germany had no foodstuffs to spare for a normally grain-importing occupied Belgium, so it permitted an international relief effort to feed the Belgians rather than allowing them to starve.[73] Occupied Luxembourg did not gain access to this relief, and unlike Belgium it collaborated fully with the Germans.[74] Similarly, the strike-sustaining funds smuggled into the occupied Ruhr valley in 1923 were tolerated by the French because they feared Britain's reaction to more draconian economic countermeasures. The importance of these funds was revealed by the fact that when they dried up in the autumn of 1923, the Germans went back to work.[75] In most cases, a conqueror will be able to make a "work or starve" threat, and thereby compel economic collaboration.

---

72. E.A. Radice, "Agriculture and Food," in Kaser and Radice, *Economic History of Eastern Europe*, Vol. 2, pp. 366–397; Colin Crouch, *Trade Unions: The Logic of Collective Action* (Glasgow: Fontana, 1982), pp. 89–93.
73. Henri Pirenne, *La Belgique et la Guerre Mondiale* (Paris: Presses Universitaires Français, 1928).
74. Carlo Hemmer, *L'économie du Grand-Duché de Luxembourg*, Vol. 1 (Luxembourg: Beffort, 1948); Gilbert Trausch, *Contributions à l'histoire sociale de la question du Luxembourg, 1914–1922* (Luxembourg: Saint-Paul, 1974).
75. See Walter A. McDougall, *France's Rhineland Diplomacy, 1914–1924* (Princeton: Princeton University Press, 1978); and Marc Trachtenberg, *Reparation in World Politics* (New York: Columbia University Press, 1980).

Thus, societies confronted by ruthless conquerors will generally decide that collaboration is a lesser evil than resistance. The remnants of their administrative bodies and elites, recognizing this, will agree. Pre-modern colonies were often ruled through the help of corrupt, class-based local elites.[76] But even modern "satellite" or "puppet" governments will collaborate simply because they believe it is in the interest of their society as a whole to do so, regardless of selfish or ideological opportunism.[77] Nazi-occupied Europe was, for the most part, administered not by Quislings, but by politically mainstream officials. Thus, although Holland's chief economics official recognized that Germany planned to exploit Dutch productive capacity ruthlessly, he believed that extensive collaboration was the only way "to secure essential supplies for the population and maintain the country's economic and social structure."[78] He defended his own actions after the war (and indeed was pardoned and pensioned) by pointing out that refusal would have led much earlier to the kind of chaos and suffering experienced during the 1944–45 "hunger winter," brought on in part by a Dutch railway strike.[79] Dutch police collaboration was likewise justified on the grounds that resisters:

have obviously not understood the gravity of the current situation. In their blindness they believe they can damage the occupying power by acts of sabotage, although in reality they can only damage the *interests of the Dutch people.* This cannot be permitted. Understand that the German authorities cannot tolerate incorrect conduct on the part of the Dutch population and

---

76. On pre-modern collaboration see Ronald Robinson, "Non-European Foundations of European Imperialism: Sketch for a Theory of Collaboration," in Roger Owen and Bob Sutcliff, eds., *Studies in the Theory of Imperialism* (London: Longman, 1972), pp. 117–142; and Michael Doyle, *Empires* (Ithaca: Cornell University Press, 1986).

77. A seminal work distinguishing collaboration for *raison d'état* from ideological "collaborationism" is Stanley Hoffmann, *Decline or Renewal: France Since the 1930s* (New York: Viking Press, 1974), chap. 2. Some liberals have claimed that collaboration depended on right-wing "fifth columns" in occupied Europe. But the mainstream political backgrounds and public justifications of most administrative collaborators, their reliance on prewar directives, and their popular support all suggest that financial and police collaboration was a rational response to German coercion.

78. Hirschfeld, *Nazi Rule*, p. 205. The motivation of the Belgian Secretaries-General was the same; see Marc Van Den Wijngaert, "La politique du moindre mal. La politique du Comité des Secrétaires Généraux en Belgique sous l'occupation allemande, 1940–1944," *Revue du Nord*, special ser. no. 2 (1987), pp. 63–72.

79. Hirschfeld, *Nazi Rule*, pp. 141–142, 150–154. Warmbrunn, *Dutch under German Occupation*, pp. 121–127, 267–275. On the final traumatic winter, in which 20,000 Dutch perished of starvation, see Henri Van Der Zee, *The Hunger Winter: Occupied Holland 1944–45* (London: Jill Norman & Hobhouse, 1982).

realize above all that the life of many people is brought into great danger by
. . . the actions of reckless and criminal elements.[80]

Modern societies will resist even less than coercion theory suggests they
would, because atomizing repression reduces their ability to bargain and to
act collectively. While collaborating regimes can act in the national interest,
multitudes of individuals face coordination problems, which will further
minimize resistance. Rational choice theorists point out that individuals try
to shirk paying for public goods, goods which all will share regardless of
whether they contributed or not. National liberation may be fervently desired, but as a public good it will be underprovided by "free-riding" individuals. Organizations or close-knit social communities that reward resisters
and punish free-riders can surmount the collective action problem, which
explains their historic importance in rebellions and revolutions.[81] Crowds
also facilitate collective action by helping in coordination and by providing
safety in numbers.[82]

Modernization has a double-edged effect on the likelihood of collective
action. As mentioned above, high population densities in cities and factories
facilitate the formation of opposition organizations and crowds. But high
population density and modern technology also enhance state surveillance
and policing capabilities, allowing the efficient repression of organization
and preventing the formation of crowds.[83] Atomizing repression efficiently
counteracts modern societies' increased *potential* for collective action. Even
when resistance is in the national interest, self-interested individuals will
shirk their duty.

The efficiency of repression has implications for the feasibility of economic
as well as political resistance. Strikes, sabotage, boycotts, and foot-dragging
must be practiced on a mass scale to frustrate a conqueror economically. Yet

---

80. Quoted in Hirschfeld, *Nazi Rule*, p. 149. Emphasis in original.
81. On collective goods theory, see Mancur Olson, Jr., *The Logic of Collective Action*, 2nd ed.
(Cambridge: Harvard University Press, 1971); and Russell Hardin, *Collective Action* (Baltimore:
Johns Hopkins University Press, 1982). Gordon Tullock noted the relevance of the collective
action problem to revolutions in "The Paradox of Revolution," *Public Choice*, Vol. 11 (Fall 1971),
pp. 89–99. See also Samuel L. Popkin, *The Rational Peasant: The Political Economy of Revolution in
Vietnam* (Berkeley: University of California Press, 1979), chap. 6; Michael Taylor, "Rationality
and Revolutionary Collective Action," in Taylor, ed., *Rationality and Revolution* (Cambridge:
Cambridge University Press, 1988), pp. 63–97.
82. Mark Granovetter, "Threshold Models of Collective Behavior," *American Journal of Sociology*,
Vol. 83 (May 1978), pp. 1420–1443; Pamela E. Oliver, "Bringing the Crowd Back In: The Non-
organizational Elements of Social Movements," in Louis Kriesberg, ed., *Research in Social Movements, Conflict and Change*, Vol. 11 (Greenwich, Conn.: JAI Press, 1989).
83. See Leites and Wolf, *Rebellion and Authority*, pp. 132–148; Giddens, *Nation-State and Violence*,
pp. 295–310; Brian Chapman, *Police State* (New York: Praeger, 1970), pp. 81–94.

economic resistance by individual firms and workers involves bearing costs and risks for the greater good, costs which will be quite high—especially to those who stick their necks out first—without the support of unions, relief networks, or opposition parties. Stripped of independent organization, firms and workers are unable to provide a united front against exploitation, even if all would be better off turning down orders or sabotaging output. The same competition for profits and salaries that, with its inevitable free-riding, prevents price-setting collusion under normal conditions also prevents collusion against exploitation.[84]

During World War II, for example, Vichy's attempts to negotiate limits on German procurement of bauxite, iron, and aircraft components were outflanked by French companies' eagerness to cut individual deals with German agencies and firms.[85] The French automotive industry provides additional examples of profit-maximizing and competitive behavior. After an Allied bombing raid in 1943, Renault's director-general argued that the factories must rapidly resume producing tank parts and trucks for the German Army because otherwise "their labor and material will little by little be removed and put at the disposition of more active factories. Our activity will be progressively reduced to the profit of other enterprises ready to do work."[86] Another leading truck manufacturer, Marius Berliet, explained after the war that the possibilities for German gain from his energetic truck production "were subtleties I didn't consider. In any case we were not at war since there was an armistice. I saw matters only as an industrial leader."[87] Nor was labor immune to the incentives to work. Strikes and sabotage were rare, and had little impact on the occupied economies.[88] In the French automobile industry overall, according to historian Patrick Fridenson, "absenteeism, turnover, lack of discipline, and resistance (including even a few strikes) had a conspicuous likeness to those of the prewar period."[89]

---

84. This argument parallels that of Mancur Olson that social cartelization decreases national economic efficiency. See Olson, *The Rise and Decline of Nations: Economic Growth, Stagflation, and Social Rigidities* (New Haven: Yale University Press, 1982).

85. Milward, *New Order*, pp. 75, 82, 87–88.

86. Quoted in Gilbert Hatry, *Louis Renault, patron absolu* (Paris: Éditions Lafourcade, 1982), p. 390.

87. Quoted in Ted Morgan, *An Uncertain Hour: The French, the Germans, the Jews, the Barbie Trial, and the City of Lyon, 1940–1945* (New York: William Morrow, 1990), p. 119. See also Gérard Declas, "Les usines Berliet, 1895–1949," Part 2, *De Renault Frères*, Vol. 3 (December 1979), pp. 326–333.

88. Haestrup, *European Resistance Movements*, pp. 92–131.

89. Patrick Fridenson, "Automobile Workers in France and Their Work, 1914–83," in Steven L. Kaplan and Cynthia J. Koepp, eds., *Work in France: Representations, Meaning, Organization, and Practice* (Ithaca: Cornell University Press, 1986), p. 529; Fernand Picard, *L'épopée de Renault* (Paris: Albin Michel, 1976), pp. 198, 208.

The overall lack of political resistance in occupied Europe may also have been due to free-riding. A hint of this is the fact that in all of Nazi-occupied France, the most courageous examples of resistance to the deportation of Jews occurred in small, close-knit villages of the kind where social ties generate collective action. The isolated Protestant communes of the Haute Loire, the Hautes Alpes, and the Tarn—the most celebrated being Chambon-sur-Lignon, the "safest place for Jews in Europe"—were unique in the risks they took to offer shelter and aid to Jewish refugees. Even when the Gestapo arrived to "clean out" Chambon, the villagers maintained a solid front.[90]

Since conquest does not immediately ruin the productivity of modern societies, there are no opportunity costs from forgone trade with the conquered economy, at least in the short term. In fact, where there existed high barriers to trade between two countries, conquest of one by the other will increase the level of trade between them. Exactly this occurred between Germany and the countries it occupied during World War II.[91] But whatever the gains of trade were, Germany profited far beyond that, by extorting tribute.

The probable liberal reply is that conquered economies wither gradually, decreasing imperial revenues and increasing opportunity costs in trade over the long run, but this is not very persuasive. Even supposing that productivity depends on freedom of information, there is no reason to think that despotic regimes cannot promote the communication of economic and scientific data while suppressing political organization and dissent. The subversive potential of personal computers and photocopiers, furthermore, must be weighed against their contribution to state surveillance. Bar codes, magnetic stripes, miniature microphones, video cameras, and computerized data banks all have Orwellian implications in the hands of a repressive secret police.

History does not provide much evidence for either side on this point. Most industrial conquests were quickly liberated by balancing coalitions. Japan achieved high rates of growth in Taiwan, Korea, and Manchuria in the 1930s, but these colonies remained at a relatively early stage of industrialization (metallurgical and chemical industries were only just getting under way).[92]

---

90. On Chambon-sur-Lignon, see Phillip Hallie, *Lest Innocent Blood Be Shed* (New York: Harper & Row, 1979).
91. Mitchell, *European Historical Statistics*, p. 548.
92. Samuel Pao-San Ho, "Colonialism and Development: Korea, Taiwan, and Kwantung," in Ramon H. Myers and Mark R. Peattie, eds., *The Japanese Colonial Empire, 1895–1945* (Princeton: Princeton University Press, 1984), pp. 347–398; Katsuji Nakagane, "Manchukuo and Economic

Under Russian hegemony, Eastern Europe (and the non-Russian republics of the USSR) grew rapidly in the 1950s and 1960s.[93] Subsequently, however, the entire Soviet bloc began to stagnate, and some contend that this forced Moscow to provide politically stabilizing trade subsidies, estimated at $196 billion (1984 dollars) between 1970 and 1984.[94] But the fact that unstable Poland received less than half the per-capita subsidies of glacially quiescent East Germany or Czechoslovakia casts doubt on the subsidy-for-stability thesis; furthermore, the total subsidies amount to less than half of East European spending on militaries that were ostensibly under Soviet control.[95] Above all, Soviet and East European stagnation is weak evidence for the liberal view of conquest because it was due to the imposition of inefficient centrally planned economies rather than nationalistic resistance or repression, and thus should not be considered an inherent consequence of foreign rule.[96] Computers and photocopiers failed to proliferate in the Soviet bloc more because of their cost than because of their subversive potential.[97]

Development," in Peter Duus, Ramon H. Myers, and Mark R. Peattie, eds., *The Japanese Informal Empire in China, 1895–1937* (Princeton: Princeton University Press, 1989), pp. 133–157.

93. Thad P. Alton, "Economic Structure and Growth in Eastern Europe," in U.S. Congress, Joint Economic Committee, *Economic Developments in Countries of Eastern Europe* (Washington, D.C.: U.S. GPO, 1970), pp. 41–67; Romuald Misiunas and Rein Taagepera, *Baltic States: Years of Dependence, 1940–1980* (Berkeley and Los Angeles: University of California Press, 1983).

94. On the economic slowdown, see Paul Marer, "The Economies and Trade of Eastern Europe," in William E. Griffith, ed., *Central and Eastern Europe: The Opening Curtain?* (Boulder: Westview Press, 1989), pp. 37–73. Valerie Bunce advances the subsidy-for-stability thesis in "The Empire Strikes Back: The Evolution of the Eastern Bloc from a Soviet Asset to a Soviet Liability," *International Organization*, Vol. 39, No. 1 (Winter 1985), pp. 235–267. Trade subsidy estimates are those of Michael Marrese and Jan Vanous, "The Content and Controversy of Soviet Trade Relations with Eastern Europe, 1970–1984," in Josef C. Brada, Ed A. Hewlett, and Thomas A. Wolf, eds., *Economic Adjustment and Reform in Eastern Europe and the Soviet Union* (Durham: Duke University Press, 1988), p. 203; they interpret the subsidies as loyalty bribes. Other studies have argued that the subsidies amounted to no more than $30–40 billion. Kazimierz Poznanski, "Opportunity Cost in Soviet Trade with Eastern Europe: Discussion of Methodology and New Evidence," *Soviet Studies*, Vol. 40, No. 2 (April 1988), pp. 290–307; Raimund Dietz, "Soviet Foregone Gains in Trade with the CMEA Six: A Reappraisal," *Comparative Economic Studies*, Vol. 27, No. 2 (Summer 1986), pp. 69–94.

95. For per-capita subsidy distributions, see Marrese and Vanous, "Content and Controversy." For East European military spending, see U.S. Arms Control and Disarmament Agency, *World Military Expenditures and Arms Transfers, 1986* (Washington, D.C.: U.S. GPO, 1987), pp. 72, 75, 78, 90.

96. See Ronald Amman and Julian Cooper, eds., *Industrial Innovation in the Soviet Union* (New Haven: Yale University Press, 1982); and Paul R. Gregory and Robert C. Stuart, *Soviet Economic Structure and Performance*, 3rd ed. (New York: Harper & Row, 1986), esp. chaps. 7, 8, 11.

97. Paul Snell, "Soviet Microprocessors and Microcomputers," in Ronald Amann and Julian Cooper, eds., *Technical Progress and Soviet Economic Development* (New York: Basil Blackwell, 1986), pp. 62–63; Seymour Goodman, "Information Technologies and the Citizen: Toward a 'Soviet-Style Information Society'?" in Loren R. Graham, ed., *Science and the Soviet Social Order* (Cambridge: Harvard University Press, 1990), pp. 371–372 fn. 10.

The Japanese and Soviet empires do support the realist view that modern societies are easily pacified. Rapid industrialization over the course of many years failed to incubate Taiwanese, Korean, or Manchurian resistance to Japanese rule.[98] The Soviet Empire faced only sporadic and weak rebellions, and the two largest (the abortive Hungarian and Czechoslovak revolutions of 1956 and 1968) resulted from rare periods of liberalization. Its two most developed satellites, East Germany and Czechoslovakia, were also the most passive in the last decades of Soviet domination.[99] Finally, the empire collapsed only after Gorbachev reversed the Brezhnev doctrine by ending Soviet coercion and allowing East European regime liberalization (i.e., a decline in repression). It took a revolution from above to break over forty years of enforced submission to Soviet hegemony.[100]

In summary, realists are justified in assuming that industrial economies are highly cumulative. The nationalism of conquered states matters, to be sure, and conquerors that are morally or otherwise restrained from engaging in ruthless repression do face massive political and economic resistance. But coercion and repression can put a lid on nationalism, if not eradicate it. And control measures, though necessarily protracted, are inexpensive compared to the massive resources that can be extorted from wealthy nations. Because modernization at once increases nations' economic surplus, the efficiency of coercion, and the efficiency of repression, the conquest of modern societies can pay.

Conclusions

The fact that conquest still pays confirms an important premise of power-balancing grand strategies. The German conquest of Europe had to be halted

---

98. Edward I-Te Chen, "Formosan Political Movements Under Japanese Colonial Rule, 1914–1937," *Journal of Asian Studies*, Vol. 31, No. 3 (May 1972), pp. 477–497; Chong-sik Lee, *The Politics of Korean Nationalism* (Berkeley and Los Angeles: University of California Press, 1965); and Lee, *Revolutionary Struggle in Manchuria: Chinese Communists and Soviet Interest, 1922–1945* (Berkeley and Los Angeles: University of California Press, 1983).

99. Paul Kecskemeti, *The Unexpected Revolution: Social Forces in the Hungarian Uprising* (Stanford: Stanford University Press, 1961); H. Gordon Skilling, *Czechoslovakia's Interrupted Revolution* (Princeton: Princeton University Press, 1976); J.M. Montias, "Economic Conditions and Political Instability in Communist Countries: Observations on Strikes, Riots, and Other Disturbances," *Studies in Comparative Communism*, Vol. 13, No. 4 (Winter 1980), pp. 283–299.

100. J.F. Brown, *Surge to Freedom: The End of Communist Rule in Eastern Europe* (Durham: Duke University Press, 1991). For a rational-choice explanation, see Timur Kuran, "Now Out of Never: The Element of Surprise in the East European Revolution of 1989," *World Politics*, Vol. 44, No. 1 (October 1991), pp. 7–48.

because it did in fact greatly augment German geopolitical might. And the Soviet Union, as the architects of containment correctly recognized, could have mobilized much, if not all, of Eurasia's military-industrial potential, especially if it had avoided the mistake of imposing inefficient centrally-planned economies.[101] If the Soviet Union had conquered Japan and NATO Europe in the last decade of the Cold War, and gained the equivalent of half their (and Eastern Europe's) GNPs, NATO North America would have found itself outstripped in economic potential by a fifth. (Without the discount, the ratio increases to two-to-one.) A "contained" Soviet Union, by contrast, commanded less GNP than either the United States or Western Europe, not to mention the two combined.[102] In retrospect, the Soviet Union appears never to have had much interest in conquering Western Europe or Japan, but U.S. planners were wise to play it safe.

Of course, any broad assessment of containment must consider other factors. Gaining economic resources is not the only worrisome result of conquest; a conqueror's gain of bases alone, or the loss of potential allies, may warrant a reaction. On the other hand, the liberal view of conquest is not the only or even the most potent argument against containment. Post–World War II isolationists have argued that the nuclear revolution rendered GNP calculations obsolete. If nuclear-armed Davids can deter invasion by geopolitical Goliaths, then the United States had no need to fear a Soviet takeover of France and Britain; even if they had capitulated, the United States still could have deterred or defended against direct attacks on North America.[103] Analyzing the robustness of nuclear deterrence is beyond the scope of this study.[104] But even if nuclear weapons have made geopolitics obsolete,

---

101. One could argue that communist economics were necessary for maintaining political control, whether because communist ideology was necessary to maintain legitimacy or because private capital would inevitably gain political power. But Soviet hegemony over Eastern Europe did not depend on legitimacy (which anyway might have been greater with better-performing capitalist economies). See, e.g., Kuran, "Surprise in the East European Revolution." Moreover, the bargaining leverage of private capital, when atomized by political repression, amounted to little in Nazi-occupied Europe.
102. Central Intelligence Agency, *Handbook of Economic Statistics, 1987* (Washington: U.S. GPO, 1987), pp. 34–35.
103. Robert J. Art, "A Defensible Defense: America's Grand Strategy After the Cold War," *International Security*, Vol. 15, No. 4 (Spring 1991), pp. 18–23.
104. For the argument that nuclear stand-offs permit conventional war (the "stability-instability paradox"), see Glenn Snyder, "The Balance of Power and the Balance of Terror," in Paul Seabury, ed., *The Balance of Power* (San Francisco: Chandler, 1965), pp. 184–201. For a critique see Robert Jervis, *The Illogic of American Nuclear Strategy* (Ithaca: Cornell University Press, 1984), pp. 148–157.

there remain regions of the world without nuclear weapons that may fall outside of the great powers' spheres of interest. The lessons drawn here should encourage the containment of would-be regional expansionists, such as a Serbia bent on the conquest of Bosnia, the military-industrial core of the former Yugoslavia.[105]

Since coercive and repressive regimes can still make conquest pay, it is unlikely that nationalism by itself has rendered war among developed nations obsolete. It is true that twentieth-century conquerors appear to have sought raw materials and territory more than industrial capacity per se.[106] But those ruthless enough to apply coercion and repression found that they could pacify and mobilize modern societies. The fact that modernization increases the profitability of conquest suggests that the world should be thankful for other causes of peace, such as balancing alliances, nuclear weapons, and the spread of democracy. In fact, realists would contend that the international system automatically compensates at least partially for changes in the profitability of conquest.[107]

Finally, this study suggests that violent or non-violent "porcupine" defenses are unlikely to work or even be attempted against coercive and repressive conquerors. The risks and costs of engaging in resistance will almost always outweigh the chances of success, a difficulty exacerbated by free-

---

105. Bosnia-Herzegovina contains 60 percent of the former Yugoslavia's military industries, according to Misha Glenny, "Yugoslavia: The Revenger's Tragedy," *New York Review of Books*, August 13, 1992, p. 38.

106. Wilhelmine Germany developed ambitions for continental aggrandizement only during World War I, and even then economic aims focused more on raw material supplies and markets than on acquiring industrial capacity. French territorial ambitions prior, during, and after the war appear to have been even more strongly moderated by a lack of interest in acquiring German-speaking citizens. Both Japanese and Nazi imperialism were motivated largely by geopolitical hunger, but for farmland and raw materials rather than for industrial capacity. Japan's victims were all pre-industrial and potentially assimilable; Hitler's long-range solutions to nationalism—Germanization or extermination—were hardly calculated to maximize German-controlled GNP. It is possible that Stalin seized Eastern Europe for its industry as well as its territory, but he risked only a "cold" war in doing so.

107. The argument would go like this: If states believe that expansion pays, they may be more likely to try it themselves, but they will also try harder to deter the expansion of rivals. The more valuable the real estate, the fancier the security system to catch burglars. But states can bolster deterrence only as far as their resources permit. If conquest pays, those lacking the necessary resources or alliances to deter are more likely to be gobbled up. Weak states are often sheltered by alliances, but these alliances will not be extended and strengthened in direct proportion to the profitability of conquest. States balance inadequately, because they tend to buck-pass in multipolar systems, because they sometimes fail to recognize threats in time to deter them, and because even prompt balancing can fail to deter. The uncertainties, misperceptions, and inefficiencies in international politics make it unlikely that balancing behavior would fully compensate for the temptation of easily exploitable territories.

riding. Advocates claim that preparation and training would produce "an effective power (conservatively estimated) at least ten times greater than that demonstrated in the most powerful of the past cases of improvised nonviolent struggle."[108] But preparation and training are unlikely to make a difference because they would not affect the principal determinants of the success or failure of resistance. No amount of training can put food in the mouths of the hungry families of striking workers. A system that distributed food to cities, or allowed for a mass return to the land, would be a prerequisite for successful resistance, but it is hard to imagine this working in the face of a conqueror's determined opposition. Furthermore, neither preparation nor training can overcome the collective action problem because organizations, no matter how well trained, will be dismantled by repressive conquerors. Indeed, prior preparation would probably only lengthen the arrest lists, as was the case for a Czech resistance organization based on the prewar secret police. Given the vulnerability of societies once occupied, it appears that the best passive strategy to prevent resource extraction by an invader is to sabotage one's industrial base before an occupation is complete.[109]

---

108. Sharp, *Civilian-Based Defense*, p. 83.
109. For example, Stalin's scorched-earth policy in 1941 reduced Hitler's economic gains from occupied Russia, and Sweden's threat to blow up its iron-ore mines (along with its willingness to sell ore at a discount) may have deterred German invasion during World War II.

Alliance Formation and the Balance of World Power

Stephen M. Walt

The question "what causes alignment?" is a central issue in debates on American foreign policy, and the choices that are made often turn on which hypotheses of alliance formation are endorsed. In general, those who believe that American security is fragile most often assume that Soviet allies are reliable and America's are prone to defect, while those who believe it is robust tend to view American allies as stronger and more reliable than those of the U.S.S.R. These divergent beliefs clash over a variety of specific issues. For example, should the U.S. increase its commitment to NATO, to prevent the growth of Soviet military power from leading to the "Finlandization" of Europe? Alternatively, should the U.S. do less in the expectation that its allies will do more? Should the U.S. oppose leftist regimes in the developing world because their domestic ideology will lead them to ally with the Soviet Union, or can a policy of accommodating radical nationalist regimes lead to good relations with them? Can Soviet or American military aid create reliable proxies in the Third World? Is it worth the effort and expense? Each of these questions carries important implications for American national security policy, and the answers ultimately turn upon which hypotheses of alliance formation are believed to be most valid.

Despite the obvious importance of understanding how states select their partners, most scholarly research on alliances has ignored or obscured these questions.[1] This article is intended to correct these omissions by outlining

---

I would like to thank Robert Art, George Breslauer, Lynn Eden, Charles Glaser, Lori Gronich, Fen Hampson, John Mearsheimer, Kenneth Oye, Glenn Snyder, Jack Snyder, Marc Trachtenberg, and Kenneth Waltz for their thoughtful comments on earlier drafts of this article.

Stephen M. Walt is an Assistant Professor of Politics and International Affairs in the Department of Politics and the Woodrow Wilson School at Princeton University.

---

1. For representative examples of typical scholarly efforts, consult: Robert Rood and Patrick McGowan, "Alliance Behavior in Balance of Power Systems," *American Political Science Review*, Vol. 69, No. 3 (September 1975); George T. Duncan and Randolph Siverson, "Flexibility of Alliance Partner Choice in Multipolar Systems," *International Studies Quarterly*, Vol. 26, No. 4 (December 1982); R.P.Y. Li and W.R. Thompson, "The Stochastic Process of Alliance Formation Behavior," *American Political Science Review*, Vol. 72, No. 3 (December 1978). More traditional

---

International Security, Spring 1985 (Vol. 9, No. 4)

some of the most important hypotheses of alliance formation, and by exploring the policy implications of each. The first section explores the competing propositions that states either balance against strong or threatening states or, alternatively, that they "bandwagon" with them. I shall also consider the sharply different foreign and defense policies that each proposition implies. The second section develops the contrasting hypotheses that ideological or cultural similarities can either bind states together or drive them apart. The third section examines the ability of states to create allies or proxies by military and economic aid, propaganda, or political penetration. Finally, the last section demonstrates how these hypotheses, taken together, can explain the current structure of world power, and suggests what they imply for American national security policy.

Balancing Versus Bandwagoning: Alliances as a Response to Threat

Alliances are most commonly viewed as a response to threats, yet there is sharp disagreement as to what that response will be. When entering an alliance, states may either *balance* (ally in opposition to the principal source of danger) or *bandwagon* (ally with the state that poses the major threat).[2] These contrasting hypotheses depict very different worlds, and the policies that follow from each are equally distinct. In the simplest terms, if balancing is more common than bandwagoning, then states are more secure because aggressors will face combined opposition. Status quo states should therefore avoid provoking countervailing coalitions by eschewing threatening foreign and defense policies. But if bandwagoning is the dominant tendency, then security is scarce because aggression is rewarded. A more belligerent foreign

---

works on alliances are: George Liska, *Nations in Alliance* (Baltimore: Johns Hopkins University Press, 1962), and Robert L. Rothstein, *Alliances and Small Powers* (New York: Columbia University Press, 1968). Useful summaries of the literature on alliances may be found in: Ole Holsti, P. Terrence Hopmann, and John D. Sullivan, *Unity and Disintegration in International Alliances* (New York: Wiley–Interscience, 1973), Chapter 1 and Appendix C; Bruce Bueno de Mesquita and J. David Singer, "Alliance, Capabilities, and War," *Political Science Annual*, Vol. 4 (1974); Philip Burgess and David Moore, "Inter-nation Alliances: An Inventory and Appraisal of Propositions," *Political Science Annual*, Vol. 3 (1973); and Michael Don Ward, "Research Gaps in Alliance Dynamics," *Monograph Series in International Affairs*, Vol. 19, No. 1 (Denver: University of Denver, Graduate School of International Studies, 1982).

2. My use of the terms "balancing" and "bandwagoning" follows that of Kenneth Waltz in his *Theory of International Politics* (Reading, Mass.: Addison-Wesley, 1979). Arnold Wolfers uses a similar terminology in his essay "The Balance of Power in Theory and Practice," in *Discord and Collaboration* (Baltimore: Johns Hopkins University Press, 1962), pp. 122–124.

policy and a more capable military establishment are the logical policy choices.

Although both of these hypotheses have been examined by scholars and embraced by statesmen, important details have been neglected. Accordingly, I shall first present each hypothesis in its simplest (and most common) form, and then indicate how they should be revised. That task accomplished, I shall then consider which hypothesis describes the dominant tendency in international politics.

BALANCING BEHAVIOR

The proposition that states will join alliances in order to avoid domination by stronger powers lies at the heart of traditional balance of power theory.[3] According to this hypothesis, states join alliances to protect themselves from states or coalitions whose superior resources could pose a threat. States will choose to balance for two main reasons.

First, states risk their own survival if they fail to curb a potential hegemon before it becomes too strong. To ally *with* the dominant power means placing one's trust in its continued benevolence. The safer strategy is to join with those who cannot readily dominate their allies, in order to avoid being dominated by those who can.[4] As Winston Churchill explained Britain's traditional alliance policy:

For four hundred years the foreign policy of England has been to oppose the strongest, most aggressive, most dominating power on the Continent. . . . it would have been easy . . . and tempting to join with the stronger and

---

3. For impressive analyses of the classical writings on the balance of power, see: Edward V. Gulick, *Europe's Classical Balance of Power* (New York: W.W. Norton, 1955), Part I; F.H. Hinsley, *Power and the Pursuit of Peace: Theory and Practice in the History of Relations between States* (Cambridge: Cambridge University Press, 1963), Part I; Inis L. Claude, *Power and International Relations* (New York: Random House, 1962), Chapters 2 and 3; Robert Osgood and Robert Tucker, *Force, Order, and Justice* (Baltimore: Johns Hopkins University Press, 1967), pp. 96–104 and *passim*; and Martin Wight, "The Balance of Power," in Martin Wight and Herbert Butterfield, eds., *Diplomatic Investigations* (London: Allen and Unwin, 1966). For modern versions of the theory, see Waltz, *Theory of International Politics*, Chapter 6; Morton Kaplan, *System and Process in International Politics* (New York: John Wiley, 1957); and Hans J. Morgenthau, *Politics Among Nations*, 5th ed. (New York: Alfred A. Knopf, 1978), Part IV.

4. As Vattel wrote several centuries ago: "The surest means of preserving this balance of power would be to bring it about that no State should be much superior to the others . . . but this could not be realized without injustice and violence. . . . [It] is simpler, easier, and more just . . . to form alliances in order to make a stand against a very powerful sovereign and prevent him from dominating." Quoted in Gulick, *Europe's Classical Balance of Power*, pp. 61–62.

share the fruits of his conquest. However, we always took the harder course, joined with the less strong Powers, . . . and thus defeated the Continental military tyrant whoever he was. . . .[5]

In the same way, Henry Kissinger advocated *rapprochement* with China rather than the Soviet Union because he believed that, in a triangular relationship, it was better to align with the weaker side.[6]

Second, joining the more vulnerable side increases the new member's influence, because the weaker side has greater need for assistance. Joining the stronger side, by contrast, reduces the new member's influence (because it adds relatively less to the coalition) *and* leaves it vulnerable to the whims of its new partners. Alignment with the weaker side is thus the preferred choice.[7]

The appeal of balance of power theory as an explanation for alliance formation is unsurprising, given the numerous examples of states joining together to resist a threatening state or coalition.[8] Yet despite the powerful evidence that history provides in support of this hypothesis, it is often suggested that the opposite response is more likely, that states will prefer to ally with the strongest power. Who argues that bandwagoning is the dominant tendency in international politics, and why do they think so?

BANDWAGONING BEHAVIOR

The belief that states will tend to ally *with* rather than against the dominant side is surprisingly common. According to one scholar,

[In international politics] momentum accrues to the gainer and accelerates his movement. The appearance of irreversibility in his gains enfeebles one side and stimulates the other all the more. The bandwagon collects those on the sidelines.[9]

---

5. Winston S. Churchill, *The Second World War: Volume I, The Gathering Storm* (Boston: Houghton Mifflin, 1948), pp. 207–208.
6. Henry A. Kissinger, *White House Years* (Boston: Little, Brown, 1979), p. 178.
7. In the words of Kenneth Waltz: "Secondary states, if they are free to choose, flock to the weaker side; for it is the stronger side that threatens them. On the weaker side, they are both more appreciated and safer, provided, of course, that the coalition they join achieves enough defensive or deterrent strength to dissuade adversaries from attacking." See his *Theory of International Politics*, p. 127.
8. This theme is explored in Ludwig Dehio, *The Precarious Balance* (New York: Vintage, 1965); Hinsley, *Power and the Pursuit of Peace*; and Gulick, *Europe's Classical Balance of Power*.
9. W. Scott Thompson, "The Communist International System," *Orbis*, Vol. 20, No. 4 (Winter 1977), p. 843.

Scholars are not alone in this conception. For example, the German Admiral Alfred von Tirpitz's famous "risk theory" implied such a view. By building a great battle fleet, Tirpitz argued, Germany could force England into neutrality or alliance with it by posing a threat to England's vital maritime supremacy.[10] More recently, American officials have repeatedly embraced the bandwagoning hypothesis in justifying American foreign policy commitments. John F. Kennedy claimed that, "if the United States were to falter, the whole world . . . would inevitably begin to move toward the Communist bloc."[11] Although the *rapprochement* with China showed his own willingness to balance, Henry Kissinger also revealed his belief that most states tend to bandwagon by suggesting that "if leaders around the world . . . assume that the U.S. lacked either the forces or the will . . . they will accommodate themselves to the dominant trend."[12] And Ronald Reagan has endorsed the same beliefs in his claim that "if we cannot defend ourselves [in Central America] . . . then we cannot expect to prevail elsewhere . . . our credibility will collapse and our alliances will crumble."[13]

Statements like these reveal a common theme: states are attracted to strength. The more powerful you are and the more clearly this is demonstrated, the more likely others are to ally with you. By contrast, a decline in relative position will lead one's allies to opt for neutrality at best or to defect to the other side at worst.

What is the logic behind the bandwagoning hypothesis? Two distinct motives can be identified. First, bandwagoning may be adopted as a form of

---

10. See William L. Langer, *The Diplomacy of Imperialism* (New York: Alfred A. Knopf, 1953), pp. 434–435; and Gordon L. Craig, *Germany: 1866–1945* (London: Oxford University Press, 1978), pp. 303–314. This view was not confined to military circles in Germany. In February 1914, Secretary of State Jagow predicted that Britain would remain neutral in the event of a Continental war, expressing the widespread view that drove German policy prior to World War I. As he told the German Ambassador in London: "We have not built our fleet in vain, and in my opinion, people in England will seriously ask themselves whether it will be just that simple and without danger to play the role of France's guardian angel against us." Quoted in Imanuel Geiss, *July 1914* (New York: W.W. Norton, 1967), pp. 24–25.

11. Quoted in Seyom Brown, *The Faces of Power* (New York: Columbia University Press, 1968), p. 217.

12. Quoted in Committee on International Relations, "The Soviet Union and the Third World: Watershed in Great Power Policy?," U.S. House of Representatives, 97th Congress, 1st session (Washington, D.C.: U.S. Government Printing Office, 1977), pp. 157–158.

13. "President Reagan's Address to a Joint Session of Congress on Central America," *The New York Times*, April 28, 1983, p. A-12. In the same speech, Reagan also said, "if Central America were to fall, what would the consequences be for our position in Asia and Europe and for alliances such as NATO. . . . Which ally, which friend would trust us then?"

appeasement. By aligning with the threatening state or coalition, the band-wagoner may hope to avoid an attack on himself by diverting it elsewhere. Second, a state may align with the dominant side in war in order to share the spoils of victory. Mussolini's declaration of war on France and Russia's entry into the war against Japan in 1945 illustrate this type of bandwagoning, as do Italian and Rumanian alliance choices in World War I.[14] By joining what they believed was the stronger side, each hoped to make territorial gains at the end of the fighting.

Stalin's decision to ally with Hitler in 1939 illustrates *both* motives nicely. The Nazi–Soviet Pact led to the dismemberment of Poland and may have deflected Hitler's ambitions westward. Stalin was thus able to gain both time and territory by bandwagoning with Hitler.[15] In general, however, these two motives for bandwagoning are quite different. In the first, bandwagoning is chosen for *defensive* reasons, as a means of maintaining independence in the face of a potential threat. In the second, a bandwagoning state chooses the leading side for *offensive* reasons, in order to acquire territory. Regardless of the specific motive, however, bandwagoning behavior stands in sharp con-trast to the predictions of balance of power theory. The two hypotheses thus offer mutually exclusive explanations for how states will make their alliance choices.

DIFFERENT SOURCES OF THREAT

Balancing and bandwagoning are usually framed solely in terms of power. Balancing is alignment with the weaker side; bandwagoning means to choose the stronger.[16] This view is seriously flawed, however, because it ignores the other factors that statesmen will consider when identifying potential threats and prospective allies. Although power is an important factor in their cal-culations, it is not the only one. Rather than allying in response to power alone, it is more accurate to say that states will ally with or against the most

---

14. See Denis Mack Smith, *Mussolini* (New York: Alfred A. Knopf, 1982), pp. 234–235, 246–250; Adam B. Ulam, *Expansion and Coexistence* (New York: Praeger, 1972), pp. 394–398; and A.J.P. Taylor, *The First World War* (New York: Perigee Books, 1980), pp. 88–90, 153.
15. See Ulam, *Expansion and Coexistence*, pp. 276–277; Isaac Deutscher, *Stalin: A Political Biography* (London: Pelican Books, 1966), pp. 437–443; and Joachim Fest, *Hitler* (New York: Vintage, 1974), pp. 583–584, 592–593.
16. The preeminent example of balance of power theory focusing exclusively on the distribution of capabilities is Waltz, *Theory of International Politics*, Chapter 6. For examples of theorists who acknowledge that other factors can be important, see Gulick, *Europe's Classical Balance of Power*, pp. 25, 45–47, 60–62.

threatening power. For example, states may *balance* by allying with other strong states, if a weaker power is more dangerous for other reasons. Thus the coalitions that defeated Germany in World Wars I and II were vastly superior in total resources, but united by their common recognition that German expansionism posed the greater danger.[17] Because balancing and bandwagoning are more accurately viewed as a response to threats, it is important to consider all the factors that will affect the level of threat that states may pose. I shall therefore discuss the impact of: 1) aggregate power; 2) proximity; 3) offensive capability; and 4) offensive intentions.

AGGREGATE POWER. The greater a state's total resources (i.e., population, industrial and military capability, technological prowess, etc.), the greater a potential threat it can pose to others. Recognizing this, Walter Lippmann and George Kennan defined the aim of American grand strategy to be preventing any single state from controlling the combined resources of industrial Eurasia, and they advocated U.S. intervention on whichever side was weaker when this prospect emerged.[18] Similarly, Lord Grey, British Foreign Secretary in 1914, justified British intervention against the Dual Alliance by saying:

To stand aside would mean the domination of Germany; the subordination of France and Russia; the isolation of Britain, . . . and ultimately Germany would wield the whole power of the continent.[19]

In the same way, Castlereagh's aim to create a "just distribution of the forces in Europe" reveals his own concern for the distribution of aggregate power, as does Bismarck's dictum that "in a system of five great powers, the goal

---

17. In World War I, the alliance of Great Britain, France, and Russia controlled 27.9 percent of world industrial production, while Germany and Austria together controlled only 19.2 percent. With Russia out of the war but the United States joining Britain and France, the percentage opposing the Dual Alliance reached 51.7 percent, an advantage of more than 2 to 1. In World War II, the defense expenditures of the U.S., Great Britain, and the Soviet Union exceeded those of Germany by roughly 4.5 to 1. Even allowing for Germany's control of Europe and the need to fight Japan, the Grand Alliance possessed an enormous advantage in latent capabilities. Thus balancing against *power* was not the sole explanation for these alliances. For these and other statistics on the relative power in these two wars, see: Paul M. Kennedy, "The First World War and the International Power System," *International Security*, Vol. 9, No. 1 (Summer 1984), pp. 7–40; and *The Rise and Fall of British Naval Mastery* (London: Macmillan, 1983), pp. 309–315.
18. For a summary of these ideas, see John Lewis Gaddis, *Strategies of Containment* (New York: Oxford University Press, 1982), pp. 25–88. Kennan's own thoughts are found in his *Realities of American Foreign Policy* (New York: New American Library, 1951), p. 10. Lippmann's still compelling analysis is found in his *The Cold War: A Study of U.S. Foreign Policy* (New York: Harper Brothers, 1947).
19. Quoted in Bernadotte Schmitt, *The Coming of the War in 1914* (New York: Howard Fertig, 1968), Vol. 2, p. 115.

must always be to be in a group of three or more."[20] The overall power that states can wield is thus an important component of the threat they can pose to others.

If power can be threatening, however, it can also be prized. States with great power have the capacity either to punish enemies or reward friends. By itself, therefore, another state's aggregate power may be a motive for either balancing or bandwagoning.

PROXIMATE POWER. States will also align in response to threats from proximate power. Because the ability to project power declines with distance, states that are nearby pose a greater threat than those that are far away.[21] For example, the British Foreign Office explained why Britain was especially sensitive to German naval expansion by saying:

If the British press pays more attention to the increase of Germany's naval power than to a similar movement in Brazil . . . this is no doubt due to the proximity of the German coasts and the remoteness of Brazil.[22]

As with aggregate power, proximate threats can produce either a balancing or a bandwagoning response. When proximate threats trigger a balancing response, alliance networks that resemble checkerboards are the likely result. Students of diplomatic history have long been told that "neighbors of neighbors are friends," and the tendency for encircling states to align against a central power has been known since Kautilya's writings in the 4th century.[23] Examples include: France and Russia against Wilhelmine Germany; France

---

20. Castlereagh's policy is described in Harold Nicolson, *The Congress of Vienna* (New York: Harcourt, Brace, Jovanovich, 1946), pp. 205–206. Bismarck's statement is quoted in William L. Langer, *European Alliances and Alignments*, 2nd ed. (New York: Random House, 1950), p. 197.

21. See Harvey Starr and Benjamin A. Most, "The Substance and Study of Borders in International Relations Research," *International Studies Quarterly*, Vol. 20 (1976). For a discussion of the relationship between power and distance, see Kenneth A. Boulding, *Conflict and Defense: A General Theory* (New York: Harper Torchbooks, 1962), pp. 229–230, 245–247. For an interesting practical critique, see Albert Wohlstetter, "Illusions of Distance," *Foreign Affairs*, Vol. 46, No. 2 (Fall 1968).

22. Quoted in Paul M. Kennedy, *The Rise of the Anglo–German Antagonism* (London: Allen and Unwin, 1980), p. 421.

23. Kautilya's analysis ran as follows: "The king who is situated anywhere immediately on the circumference of the conqueror's territory is termed the enemy. The king who is likewise situated close to the enemy, but separated from the conqueror only by the enemy is termed the friend (of the conqueror). . . . In front of the conqueror and close to the enemy, there happened to be situated kings such as the conqueror's friend, next to him the enemy's friend, and next to the last the conqueror's friend's friend, and next, the enemy's friend's friend." See "Arthasastra" (Science of Politics), in Paul A. Seabury, ed., *Balance of Power* (San Francisco: Chandler, 1965), p. 8.

and the "Little Entente" in the 1930s; the Soviet Union and Vietnam against China and Cambodia in the 1970s; the U.S.S.R. and India against the U.S. and Pakistan presently; and the tacit alignment between Iran and Syria against Iraq and its various Arab supporters. When a threat from proximate power leads to bandwagoning, by contrast, the familiar phenomenon of a "sphere of influence" is created. Small states bordering a great power may be so vulnerable that they choose to bandwagon rather than balance, especially if their powerful neighbor has demonstrated its ability to compel obedience. Thus Finland, whose name has become synonymous with bandwagoning, chose to do so only after losing two major wars against the Soviet Union within a five-year period.

OFFENSIVE POWER. All else being equal, states with large offensive capabilities are more likely to provoke an alliance than those who are either militarily weak or capable only of defending.[24] Once again, the effects of this factor vary. On the one hand, the immediate threat that such capabilities pose may lead states to balance by allying with others.[25] Tirpitz's "risk strategy" backfired for precisely this reason. England viewed the German battle fleet as a potent offensive threat, and redoubled its own naval efforts while reinforcing its ties with France and Russia.[26] On the other hand, when offensive power permits rapid conquest, vulnerable states may see little hope in resisting. Balancing may seem unwise because one's allies may not be able to provide assistance quickly enough. This is another reason why "spheres of influence" may form: states bordering those with large offensive capabilities (and who are far from potential allies) may be forced to bandwagon because balancing alliances are simply not viable.[27]

---

24. The best discussions of the implications of offense and defense are: Robert Jervis, "Cooperation Under the Security Dilemma," *World Politics,* Vol. 30, No. 2 (January 1978); Stephen W. Van Evera, "Causes of War" (Ph.D. dissertation, University of California, Berkeley, 1984); and George H. Quester, *Offense and Defense in the International System* (New York: Wiley, 1977).
25. See Langer, *European Alliances and Alignments,* pp. 3–5; Raymond J. Sontag, *European Diplomatic History, 1871–1932* (New York: Appleton-Century Crofts, 1933), pp. 4–5; Jervis, "Cooperation Under the Security Dilemma," p. 189; and Quester, *Offense and Defense in the International System,* pp. 105–106.
26. As Imanuel Geiss notes: "Finding an agreement with Britain along German lines without a substantial naval agreement thus amounted to squaring the circle." See his *German Foreign Policy* (London: Routledge and Kegan Paul, 1977), p. 131. See also Kennedy, *The Rise of the Anglo–German Antagonism,* pp. 416–423.
27. Thus alliance formation becomes more *frenetic* when the offense is believed to have the advantage: great powers will balance more vigorously while weak states seek protection by bandwagoning more frequently. A world of tight alliances and few neutral states is the likely result.

OFFENSIVE INTENTIONS. Finally, states that appear aggressive are likely to provoke others to balance against them. As I noted earlier, Nazi Germany provoked an overwhelming coalition against itself because it combined substantial power with extremely offensive ambitions. Indeed, even states with rather modest capabilities may trigger a balancing response if they are perceived as especially aggressive. Thus Libya under Colonel Qaddafi has prompted Egypt, Israel, France, the U.S., Chad, and the Sudan to coordinate political and military responses in order to defend against Libyan activities.[28]

Perceptions of intent play an especially crucial role in alliance choices. In addition to the factors already mentioned, for example, changing perceptions of German aims helped create the Triple Entente. Whereas Bismarck had followed a careful policy of defending the status quo after 1870, the expansionist ambitions of his successors provoked steadily increasing alarm among the other European powers.[29] Although the growth of German power played a major role, the importance of German intentions should not be ignored. This is nicely revealed by Eyre Crowe's famous 1907 memorandum defining British policy towards Germany. The analysis is all the more striking because Crowe obviously has few objections to the growth of German power *per se:*

It cannot for a moment be questioned that the mere existence and healthy activity of a powerful Germany is an undoubted blessing for all. . . . *So long, then, as Germany competes for an intellectual and moral leadership of the world in reliance on its own natural advantages and energies* England cannot but admire. . . . [So] long *as Germany's action does not overstep the line of legitimate protection of existing rights it can always count upon the sympathy and good will,* and even the moral support of England. . . . It would be of real advantage if the determination not to bar Germany's *legitimate and peaceful expansion* were made as patent and pronounced as authoritatively as possible, provided that care was taken at the same time to make it quite clear that *this benevolent attitude will give way to determined opposition at the first sign* of British or allied interests being adversely affected.[30]

---

28. For a discussion of Libya's international position, see Claudia Wright, "Libya and the West: Headlong Into Confrontation?," *International Affairs* (London), Vol. 58, No. 1 (Winter 1981–82), pp. 13–41.

29. See Craig, *Germany: 1866–1945*, pp. 101, 242–247, and Chapter 10; Geiss, *German Foreign Policy*, pp. 66–68; and Kennedy, *The Rise of the Anglo–German Antagonism*, Chapters 14 and 20.

30. "Memorandum by Sir Eyre Crowe on the Present State of British Relations with France and Germany, January 1, 1907," in G.P. Gooch and Harold Temperley, eds., *British Documents on the Origins of the War, 1898–1914* (London: British Foreign Office, 1928), Volume 3, pp. 403 and *passim* (emphasis added). See also G.W. Monger, *The End of Isolation: British Foreign Policy 1900–1907* (London: Thomas Nelson, 1963), pp. 313–315.

In short, Britain will oppose Germany only if Germany seeks to expand through conquest. Intentions, not power, are crucial.

When a state is believed to be unalterably aggressive, others are unlikely to bandwagon. After all, if an aggressor's intentions are impossible to change, then balancing with others is the best way to avoid becoming a victim. Thus Prime Minister de Broqueville of Belgium rejected the German ultimatum of August 2, 1914 by saying:

If die we must, better death with honor. We have no other choice. Our submission would serve no end . . . if Germany is victorious, Belgium, *whatever her attitude*, will be annexed to the Reich.[31]

In short, the more aggressive or expansionist a state appears, the more likely it is to trigger an opposing coalition.

By refining the basic hypotheses to consider several sources of threat, we gain a more complete picture of the factors that statesmen will consider when making alliance choices. However, one cannot say a priori which sources of threat will be most important in any given case, only that all of them are likely to play a role. The next step is to consider which—balancing or bandwagoning—is the dominant tendency in international affairs.

THE IMPLICATIONS OF BALANCING AND BANDWAGONING

The two hypotheses I have just elaborated paint starkly contrasting pictures of international politics. Resolving the question of which picture is more accurate is especially important because the two hypotheses imply very different policy prescriptions. What are the worlds that each depicts, and what policies are implied?

If balancing is the dominant tendency, then threatening states will provoke others to align against them. Because those who seek to dominate others will attract widespread opposition, status quo states can take a relatively sanguine view of threats. Credibility is less important in a balancing world because one's allies will resist threatening states out of their own self-interest, not because they expect others to do it for them. Thus the fear that allies will defect declines. Moreover, if balancing is the norm *and* if statesmen understand this tendency, aggression is discouraged because those who contemplate it will anticipate resistance.

---

31. Quoted in Luigi Albertini, *The Origins of the War in 1914* (London: Oxford University Press, 1952), Volume 3, p. 458 (emphasis added).

In a balancing world, policies that demonstrate restraint and benevolence are best. Strong states may be valued as allies because they have much to offer their partners, but they must take particular care to avoid appearing aggressive. Foreign and defense policies that minimize the threat one poses to others make the most sense in such a world.

By contrast, a bandwagoning world is much more competitive. If states tend to ally with the strongest and most threatening state, then great powers will be rewarded if they appear both strong and potentially dangerous. International rivalries will be more intense, because a single defeat may signal the decline of one side and the ascendancy of the other. This is especially alarming in a bandwagoning world, because additional defections and a further decline in the loser's position are to be expected. Moreover, if statesmen believe that bandwagoning is widespread, they will be more inclined to use force to resolve international disputes. This is because they will both fear the gains that others may make by demonstrating *their* power or resolve, and because they will assume that others will be unlikely to balance against them.[32]

Finally, misperceiving the relative propensity to balance or bandwagon is dangerous, because the policies that are appropriate for one situation will backfire *completely* in the other. If statesmen follow the balancing prescription in a bandwagoning world, their moderate responses and relaxed view of threats will encourage their allies to defect, leaving them isolated against an overwhelming coalition. Conversely, following the bandwagoning prescription (employing power and threats frequently) in a world of balancers will merely lead others to oppose you more and more vigorously.[33]

These concerns are not just theoretical. In the 1930s, France failed to recognize that its allies in the "Little Entente" were prone to bandwagon, a

---

32. Thus both Napoleon and Hitler underestimated the costs of aggression by assuming their potential enemies would bandwagon. After Munich, for example, Hitler dismissed the likelihood he would be opposed by claiming that the leaders of France and Britain were "little worms." Napoleon apparently believed that "England cannot reasonably make war on us unaided," and assumed that England would remain pacified after the Peace of Amiens. On these points, see Fest, *Hitler*, pp. 594–595; Liska, *Nations in Alliance*, p. 45; and Geoffrey Bruun, *Europe and the French Imperium* (New York: Harper Torchbooks, 1938), p. 118. Because Hitler and Napoleon believed in a bandwagoning world, they were unwisely eager to go to war.

33. This situation is analogous to Robert Jervis's distinction between the spiral model and the deterrence model. The former calls for appeasement, the latter for opposition to a suspected aggressor. Balancing and bandwagoning are the alliance equivalents of deterring and appeasing. See Jervis, *Perception and Misperception in International Politics* (Princeton: Princeton University Press, 1976), Chapter 3.

tendency that French military and diplomatic policies reinforced. By contrast, Soviet attempts to intimidate Turkey after World War II backfired by provoking a greater U.S. commitment in the area and by cementing Turkey's interest in a formal alliance with the West.[34] Likewise, the self-encircling bellicosity of Wilhelmine Germany and Imperial Japan reflected the assumption, prevalent in both states, that bandwagoning was the dominant tendency in international affairs.

WHY BALANCING IS MORE COMMON THAN BANDWAGONING
Which of these two worlds most resembles reality? Which hypothesis describes the dominant tendency in international politics? Although statesmen frequently justify their actions by invoking the bandwagoning hypothesis, history provides little evidence for this assertion. On the contrary, balance of power theorists from Ranke forward have persistently and persuasively shown that states facing an external threat overwhelmingly prefer to balance against the threat rather than bandwagon with it. This is primarily because an alignment that preserves most of a state's freedom of action is preferable to accepting subordination under a potential hegemon. Because intentions can change and perceptions are unreliable, it is safer to balance against potential threats than to hope that strong states will remain benevolent.

The overwhelming tendency for states to balance rather than bandwagon defeated the hegemonic aspirations of Spain under Philip II, France under Louis XIV and Napoleon, and Germany under Wilhelm II and Hitler. Where the bandwagoning hypothesis predicts that these potential hegemons should have attracted more and more support as they expanded, the actual response of the powers that they threatened was precisely the opposite. The more clearly any one state sought to dominate the rest, the more reliably the others combined to counter the threat.[35]

---

34. The French attempt to contain Germany after World War I was undermined both by the Locarno Treaty (which guaranteed the French border with Germany but failed to provide similar guarantees for its allies) and by the French adoption of a defensive military doctrine, which made it impossible for it come to the aid of its allies. See Telford Taylor, *Munich: The Price of Peace* (New York: Vintage, 1980), pp. 111–112; and Richard D. Challener, *The French Theory of the Nation in Arms* (New York: Columbia University Press, 1969), pp. 264–265. For the effects of Soviet pressure on Turkey, see: George Lenczowski, *The Middle East in World Affairs* (Ithaca: Cornell University Press, 1980), pp. 134–138; and Bruce R. Kuniholm, *The Origins of the Cold War in the Near East* (Princeton: Princeton University Press, 1980), pp. 355–378.
35. See Jack S. Levy, "Theories of General War," unpublished ms., 1984. (An extensively revised version of this paper will be published in *World Politics*, April 1985.)

Nor is this tendency confined to Europe, as a few examples will illustrate. The American defeat in Indochina, rather than inviting bandwagoning throughout Southeast Asia, brought renewed cooperation among the ASEAN states and permitted the traditional animosity between China and Vietnam to burst forth anew. In the 1950s, the long-standing rivalry between the House of Saud in Saudi Arabia and the Hashemite dynasties in Iraq and Jordan gave way to the "King's Alliance" when Nasser's Egypt emerged as the dominant power in the region. The desire to balance against regional threats has also inspired most Middle Eastern states to align with one or the other superpower, just as the superpower rivalry itself made the Soviet Union and the United States willing to support these regional clients.[36] In the same way, the threat from revolutionary Iran has provoked the formation of the Gulf Cooperation Council, led by Saudi Arabia. Whatever one may think of the *efficacy* of these various arrangements, the *tendency* that they illustrate is striking.[37] Even in widely different contexts, the strong tendency for states to balance when making alliance choices is confirmed.

Scholars or statesmen who argue the opposite view—whether in the guise of "Finlandization," the "domino theory," or other variations on bandwagoning logic—are placing themselves in direct opposition to the most widely accepted theory in the field of international relations. Just as clearly, their predictions about expected state behavior are contrary to most of international history. The effects of this disregard for evidence are severe: 1) such views exaggerate American insecurity by portraying U.S. allies as excessively prone to defect; 2) they distort American security priorities by inflating the perceived benefits of large military forces and "get-tough" policies; and 3) they make it easier for allies to "free-ride," by encouraging the U.S. to do too much. Thus the U.S. pays a high price for its failure to appreciate the dominant tendency for others to balance. Indeed, the erroneous fear that bandwagoning was likely has probably been the principal intellectual error underlying the most counterproductive excesses in postwar American foreign policy.

This is not to say that bandwagoning never occurs. Three conditions may increase somewhat the generally low tendency for states to bandwagon. First,

---

36. For evidence and analysis on this point, see Stephen M. Walt, "The Origins of Alliances" (Ph.D. dissertation, University of California, Berkeley, 1983), especially Chapter 6.
37. See Mahnaz Zehra Ispahani, "Alone Together: Regional Security Arrangements in Southern Africa and the Arabian Gulf," *International Security*, Vol. 8, No. 4 (Spring 1984), pp. 152–175.

especially weak states will be more likely to bandwagon, both because they are more vulnerable to pressure and because the capabilities they can add to either side are unlikely to make much difference. Because they can do little to affect the outcome, they are more likely to opt for the winning side.[38] Thus King Leopold of Belgium and Urho Kekkonen of Finland justified their own alliance policies with reference to the special vulnerabilities of small states bordering upon great powers.[39] A further deduction is that weak states may balance against other weak states, but may be relatively more likely to bandwagon when confronted by a great power.

Second, weak states are more likely to bandwagon when allies are simply unavailable. Even weak states may be persuaded to balance when they are confident of allied support; in its absence, however, accommodation with the threatening power may be the only viable alternative. Thus a further prerequisite for effective balancing behavior is an active system of diplomatic communication, permitting potential allies to recognize their shared interests and coordinate their responses.[40] If weak states see no possibility of external assistance, accommodation through alignment with the threatening power may be chosen as a last resort. Thus the first Shah of Iran took the British withdrawal from Kandahar in 1881 as a signal to bandwagon with Russia. As he told the British representative, all he had received from Britain was "good advice and honeyed words—nothing else."[41] Finland's foreign policy suggests the same lesson. Finland's bandwagoning alliance with the Soviet Union after World War II was encouraged by the fact that Finland's *balancing*

---

38. See Rothstein, *Alliances and Small Powers*, p. 11.
39. As King Leopold explained Belgian neutrality after World War I, "an alliance, even if purely defensive, does not lead to the goal [of security], for no matter how prompt the help of an ally might be, it would not come until after the invader's attack which will be overwhelming. . . ." Quoted in Rothstein, *Alliances and Small Powers*, pp. 111–112. Kekkonen of Finland argued for accommodation with the U.S.S.R. by saying: "A small state cannot stand forever armed to the teeth . . . the first to be overrun by the enemy, and devoid of political importance to lend any significance to its word when decisions over war and peace are being taken. . . ." See Urho Kekkonen, *A President's View*, trans. Gregory Coogan (London: Heinemann, 1982), pp. 42–43.
40. One reason for Rome's durable hegemony in the ancient world was the fact that its various opponents lacked the diplomatic means to coordinate opposition against Rome effectively. See Edward N. Luttwak, *The Grand Strategy of the Roman Empire* (Baltimore: Johns Hopkins University Press, 1976), pp. 192, 199–200. When a workable diplomatic system was established in the Renaissance, prospects for European hegemony declined drastically. On this point, see Gulick, *Europe's Classical Balance of Power*, p. 16; Hedley Bull, *The Anarchical Society* (New York: Columbia University Press, 1977), p. 106 and Chapter 7; Garrett Mattingly, *Renaissance Diplomacy* (Boston: Houghton Mifflin, 1971), Chapters 13–16; and Harold Nicolson, *Diplomacy* (London: Oxford University Press, 1963), Chapter 1.
41. Quoted in C.J. Lowe, *The Reluctant Imperialists* (New York: Macmillan, 1967), p. 85.

alliance with Nazi Germany during the war had alienated the potential allies it might have sought against Soviet pressure.[42]

This means that a concern for credibility is not entirely mistaken. Those who argue for American isolation ignore the possibility that weak states might be forced to bandwagon with other powers, were the prospect of American support eliminated entirely. Yet the opposite error is more common: the exaggerated fear that bandwagoning is likely leads the U.S. to squander resources in strategically meaningless conflicts (e.g., Vietnam) in order to reassure allies who are likely to remain loyal in any event.

Taken together, these two factors help explain why great powers are occasionally able to create spheres of influence. Although strong neighbors will balance, small and weak states in close proximity to a great power are the most likely candidates for bandwagoning. Because they will be the first victims of an attack, because potential allies may be scarce or distant, and because they lack the capabilities to stand alone or alter the balance significantly, accommodating a neighboring great power may occasionally make more sense.

Such circumstances, however, are rare; and such alliances will decay when the disparities that produce them erode.[43] Moreover, even if weak states do bandwagon on occasion, their decisions will have little impact on the global balance of power. For the states that matter, balancing is the rule: they will join forces against the threats posed by the power, proximity, offensive capabilities, and intentions of others.

Of course, statesmen do not live by threat assessments alone. It is therefore necessary to consider another influential hypothesis: that ideological solidarity provides a powerful force for alignment.

"Birds of a Feather Flocking Together" (and Flying Apart): Ideology and Alliance Formation

"Ideological solidarity" (to use Hans Morgenthau's term) refers to alliances that result between states sharing political, cultural, or other traits. According

---

42. See Fred Singleton, "The Myth of Finlandisation," *International Affairs* (London), Vol. 57, No. 2 (Spring 1981), especially pp. 276–278. Singleton points out that the Western allies approved the 1944 armistice between Finland and the U.S.S.R. (which established Soviet predominance there) in 1947.

43. This seems to be true both in Latin America and Eastern Europe. As the relative power of both superpowers has declined, the ability of states in their respective spheres to defy the

to this hypothesis, the more similar two or more states are, the more likely they are to ally. Although most scholars believe that this is at best a secondary explanation for alliances,[44] the belief that ideological affinities are crucial often appears in the rhetoric of statesmen seeking to justify alignment with one side or opposition to another. Thus Samora Machel of Mozambique explained his close relationship with the U.S.S.R. by describing the two states as "natural socialist allies."[45] Lord Palmerston of Britain, despite his assertion that England had "no permanent friends . . . only permanent interests," also believed in the natural affinity of democracies. In a statement that also reveals a belief that weak states will bandwagon, Palmerston said:

Our policy ought now to be to form a Western confederacy of free states as a counterpoise to the Eastern League of arbitrary governments. England, France, Spain, and Portugal . . . will form a political and moral power in Europe. . . . We shall be on the advance, they on the decline, and all the smaller planets in Europe will have a natural tendency to gravitate towards our system.[46]

More recently, John Foster Dulles justified American support for Chiang Kaishek and Synghman Rhee by proclaiming that these leaders "were Christian gentlemen . . . who have suffered for their faith."[47] In the same spirit, Ronald Reagan has praised the fact that the U.S. and its allies have "rediscovered their democratic values," values that "unite us in a stewardship of peace and freedom with our allies and friends."[48] And throughout the Cold War, American opposition to leftist movements in the Third World has been based on

---

hegemonic power has increased. Obviously, this tendency is more pronounced in the Western Hemisphere than in Eastern Europe, because geography makes it easier for the Soviets to enforce their control.

44. For scholarly discussions that question the importance of ideology in alliance formation, see: Edwin Fedder, "The Concept of Alliance," *International Studies Quarterly*, Vol. 12 (1968), p. 86; Morgenthau, *Politics Among Nations*, pp. 183–184; Ernst B. Haas and Allen Whiting, *Dynamics of International Relations* (New York: McGraw-Hill, 1956), pp. 167–168; Robert E. Osgood, *Alliances and American Foreign Policy* (Baltimore: Johns Hopkins University Press, 1968), p. 20; and Harold Guetzkow, "Isolation and Collaboration: A Partial Theory of International Relations," *Journal of Conflict Resolution*, Vol. 1, No. 1 (1957), p. 158.

45. Quoted in Committee on International Relations, "The Soviet Union and the Third World," pp. 46–48. Under pressure from South Africa, Machel has recently moderated his pro-Soviet stance.

46. Quoted in Charles K. Webster, *The Foreign Policy of Palmerston* (London: G. Bell and Sons, 1951), Vol. 1, p. 390.

47. Quoted in Townsend Hoopes, *The Devil and John Foster Dulles* (Boston: Little, Brown, 1973), pp. 77–78.

48. "State of the Union Message," *The New York Times*, January 26, 1983.

the belief that such regimes were naturally inclined towards alignment with the Soviet Union because they shared similar ideological traits.[49]

What is the logic behind such beliefs? Several possibilities can be identified. First, alignment with similar states may be viewed as a way of defending one's own political principles. After all, if statesmen believe their own system is inherently good, then protecting states with a similar system must be considered good as well. Second, states with similar traits may fear each other less, because they will find it harder to imagine an inherently "good" state deciding to attack them. Third, alignment with similar states may enhance the legitimacy of a weak regime, by demonstrating that it is part of a large popular movement.[50] Fourth, the ideology itself may prescribe alignment, as Marxism–Leninism explicitly does.[51]

In addition to logic, there are many examples to support this hypothesis. Australia fought Germany in both World Wars, despite the fact that Germany posed no direct threat to it. According to one account, the colonies' loyalty to Great Britain was "not one of all to one but all to all, to the British ideal and way of life wherever it was to be found."[52] In the 19th century, the "Holy Alliance" that followed Napoleon's defeat and Bismarck's "League of the Three Emperors" united similar states in opposition to alternative systems, although considerations of power and security played an important role as well.[53] The same could also be said for the Treaty of Munchengratz in 1833 and the Quadruple Alliance of 1834, which divided Europe neatly along ideological lines (notwithstanding important rifts within the two coalitions).[54]

---

49. See Richard Barnet, *Intervention and Revolution* (New York: Meridien, 1968); Richard E. Feinberg and Kenneth A. Oye, "After the Fall: U.S. Policy Toward Radical Regimes," *World Policy Journal*, Vol. 1, No. 1 (Fall 1983); and Gaddis, *Strategies of Containment*, pp. 96, 136–144, 175–182, 284–288.
50. On this point see Liska, *Nations in Alliance*, p. 37.
51. For a discussion of the centralizing character of Marxism–Leninism and a general history of the World Communist Movement, see Richard Lowenthal, *World Communism: The Disintegration of a Secular Faith* (New York: Oxford University Press, 1964).
52. See James A. Williamson, *Great Britain and the Commonwealth* (London: Adam and Charles Black, 1965), pp. 180–181.
53. The "Holy Alliance" began with a declaration by the principal European sovereigns to refrain from using force against each other. By 1820, England had withdrawn over the issue of intervention against liberal movements, leaving Austria–Hungary, Russia, and Prussia in an alliance against the threat of liberal revolution. See Nicolson, *The Congress of Vienna*, pp. 242–243, 245–251, and Chapter 16. On the League of Three Emperors, see Geiss, *German Foreign Policy*, pp. 29–30; and Craig, *Germany: 1866–1945*, pp. 103–104.
54. See Webster, *The Foreign Policy of Palmerston*, Vol. 1, pp. 386–410; and Hinsley, *Power and the Pursuit of Peace*, pp. 215–217.

Two issues remain. First, we must consider an alternative hypothesis: that certain ideological types promote conflict among similar states rather than cooperation. Second, we should ask how large a role ideology plays in alliance formation, and what factors either increase or decrease its significance.

"BIRDS OF A FEATHER FLYING APART": DIVISIVE IDEOLOGIES

Although a common ideology can help create effective alliances, certain types of ideology are more likely to produce conflict than cooperation among adherents. When the ideology calls for the members to form a centralized hierarchical movement obeying a single authoritative leadership, the likelihood of conflict is increased. This somewhat paradoxical result occurs for several reasons.

First, because the ideology is a source of legitimacy for each member regime, each must at a minimum affirm its universal validity. But when the ideology calls for a single leader, then all regimes save the one that emerges on top will find their autonomy threatened *by the other members of the same movement*.[55]

Second, because the authority of the leadership rests on its interpretation of the common ideology, ideological quarrels are quite likely. They are also likely to be intense, because rival factions can defend their own interpretation only by portraying rivals as traitors or heretics.

The history of international Communism provides a striking example of these dynamics. According to an authoritative Soviet source, "ideological cohesion on the basis of Marxism–Leninism is the foundation of [Communist] international cohesion."[56] But as a number of scholars have shown, the cohesion of the Communist International lasted only as long as foreign Communist Parties were dependent on Moscow's support. Once self-sufficient Communist states emerged, the unchallenged role of the Communist Party of the Soviet Union was a thing of the past.[57] Since World War II,

---

55. Richard Lowenthal, "Factors of Unity and Factors of Conflict," *The Annals*, Vol. 349 (1963), p. 107; Rothstein, *Alliances and Small Powers*, p. 178; Liska, *Nations in Alliance*, pp. 170–171; and Fedder, "The Concept of Alliance," p. 83.
56. V.V. Zagladin, *The World Communist Movement: Outline of Strategy and Tactics* (Moscow: Progress Publishers, 1973), p. 465.
57. See Lowenthal, *World Communism*, pp. 234–235, 247–252, 256; Zbigniew Brzezinski, *The Soviet Bloc: Unity and Conflict* (Cambridge: Harvard University Press, 1967), pp. 51–58; and Franz Borkenau, *World Communism: A History of the Communist International* (Ann Arbor: University of Michigan Press, 1971), pp. 196–207.

rivalries *between* Communist states have been among the world's most viru-lent quarrels. The "natural" cohesion of the movement was guaranteed only in Eastern Europe, and there only by force.

The history of Pan-Arabism provides an even more striking illustration. Despite the many attempts to translate the Arab world's common ethnic character and ideological vision into workable political cohesion, the ideology of Pan-Arabism has led to repeated rivalries.[58] And the more serious the commitment to unity, the more intense the conflict. Thus the bitterest rival-ries in the Arab world took place between Nasser (the leading Pan-Arab figure) and the transnational, explicitly Pan-Arab Ba'ath party. And the Ba'ath Party itself eventually split into rival Syrian and Iraqi factions in 1966, a schism that persists to this day.[59]

The explanation for these rivalries lies in the contradictory premises of Pan-Arab ideology. Although support for Arab unity was an important com-ponent of regime legitimacy after 1955,[60] *implementation* of the ideal threat-ened the existence of each separate regime. If unity were ever achieved, all elites save the one that emerged on top would be eliminated. The various attempts at formal union thus quickly became struggles for power, in which the ideology was used to justify extreme measures against rivals.[61] As one member of the Ba'ath explained: "the rupture [of the United Arab Republic] . . . was caused by *a certain Egyptian hegemonic view of the union.*"[62] After the split, Nasser himself seemed to recognize the fundamental contradiction:

---

58. For analyses of the various rifts between the Arabs, see: Malcolm Kerr, *The Arab Cold War: Gamal 'Abdel Nasser and His Rivals* (London: Oxford University Press, 1971); Nadav Safran, "Arab Politics: Peace and War," *Orbis*, Vol. 18, No. 2 (Summer 1974); and *From War to War* (New York: Dial Press, 1969), Chapter 2; and Walt, "The Origins of Alliances," Chapter 7.
59. For discussions of the split within the Ba'ath Party, see: John F. Devlin, *The Ba'ath Party* (Stanford, Calif.: Hoover Institute Press, 1968), pp. 313–315; and Itamar Rabinovich, *Syria Under the Ba'ath, 1963–1966: The Army–Party Symbiosis* (New York: Halsted Press, 1974), pp. 207–208.
60. For a discussion of the role of Pan-Arabism in the legitimacy formula of Arab regimes, see Michael Hudson, *Arab Politics: The Search for Legitimacy* (New Haven: Yale University Press, 1977), Chapter 2 and p. 242.
61. As the Egyptian National Charter stated: "Egypt is bound to spread its mission and put the principles upon which it rests at the disposal of all the Arabs, disregarding the worn-out notion that in doing so it is interfering in other people's affairs." Quoted in Adeed Dawisha, *Egypt in the Arab World* (London: Macmillan, 1976), p. 35. "Spreading its mission" involved military intervention in the Yemeni civil war, assassination attempts against other Arab leaders, support for Nasserist groups in other countries, and continuous propaganda over Radio Cairo.
62. Quoted in Robert Stephens, *Nasser: A Political Biography* (London: Allen Lane/The Penguin Press, 1971), p. 343. Emphasis added.

Nowadays the concept of union is itself in crisis. . . . This kind of multiplicity of nationalist activities seems to lead us to clashes. . . . While every Arab country boasts a [revolutionary] party . . . union seems utterly impossible. True political opposition would generate into regionalism, with Syria at odds with Egypt, Iraq at odds with Syria, and so forth.[63]

By contrast, Anwar Sadat's success in achieving effective Arab cooperation between 1971 and 1975 was due both to the fact that he lacked the stature to lead a unity movement and the fact that he viewed effective alliances as more important to Egypt than formal unity.[64]

Significantly, these problems do not afflict either democracies or monarchies when they ally with a similar state. Both types of states rest upon bases of legitimacy that do not extend beyond their borders. For democracies, it is popular support as expressed through elections. For monarchies, it is the traditional or "divine" right of kings. Because the ruling principles of a monarchical or democratic regime grant legitimacy over one's own domain *but imply no such authority over the domain of others*, alliances between monarchies or between democracies are not torn by ideological conflicts. Moreover, their interest in collaborating to oppose alternative ideologies that *do* threaten their legitimacy provides a further incentive for allying together.[65] Thus it is not surprising that the monarchies in Jordan and Saudi Arabia joined forces to guard against Nasser's Egypt, or that Russia, Prussia, and Austria–Hungary allied together against liberal movements in the 1820s.[66] And, as Michael

---

63. Gamal 'Abdel Nasser, "Speech on the 11th Anniversary of the July 23 Revolution," *Arab Political Documents 1963* (Beirut: American University of Beirut, 1964), pp. 333 and *passim*.

64. For Sadat's views and useful analyses, see: Raphael Israeli, ed., *The Public Diary of President Sadat* (Leiden: E.J. Brill, 1978), Volume 1, pp. 369, 403; Kerr, *Arab Cold War*, p. 129; Hudson, *Arab Politics*, pp. 248–249; Mohamed Heikal, "Egyptian Foreign Policy," *Foreign Affairs*, Vol. 56, No. 4 (July 1978), p. 720, and *The Road to Ramadan* (New York: Quadrangle Books, 1975), pp. 133–134; Raymond J. Baker, *Egypt's Uncertain Revolution Under Nasser and Sadat* (Cambridge: Harvard University Press, 1978), p. 126; and Fouad Ajami, "The End of Pan-Arabism," *Foreign Affairs*, Vol. 47, No. 2 (Winter 1978–79), pp. 360–373.

65. Of course, liberalism can pose a threat to monarchical systems. We would therefore not expect to find monarchies and democracies cooperating as a result of ideological solidarity, except against regimes that they both found even more repugnant or dangerous.

66. For a discussion of the Saudi–Jordanian alliance, see: David Holden and Richard Johns, *The House of Saud* (New York: Holt, Rinehart, and Winston, 1981), pp. 194–195; Lenczowski, *The Middle East in World Affairs*, p. 288; and "Chronology," *Middle East Journal*, Vol. 17, No. 1 (1963), p. 117. On the Holy Alliance in the 1820s, see: William L. Langer, *Political and Social Upheaval: 1832–1852* (New York: Harper Torchbooks, 1969), pp. 290–295; and Walter Alison Philips, *The Confederation of Europe* (London: Longmans, Green, 1920), pp. 202–203, 208–209, and passim. This is merely a variation on the general tendency for states to balance against significant threats.

Doyle has shown, the extraordinary absence of warfare between democratic or republican regimes suggests that their domestic orders help to reduce conflicts between them as well.[67]

THE IMPORTANCE OF IDEOLOGICAL SOLIDARITY

Is ideological solidarity an important cause of alliances? Under what conditions does it play a greater or lesser role? These questions are difficult because ideology is but one factor among many. Nonetheless, several conclusions can be stated with confidence.

First, states are more likely to follow their ideological preferences when they are already fairly secure. When faced by great danger, one takes whatever allies one can get. Winston Churchill captured this in his famous statement that "if Hitler invaded Hell, I should at least make a favorable reference to the Devil in the House of Commons," a sentiment that Franklin D. Roosevelt shared.[68] These reactions may be compared with earlier British and American policies. In the 1920s, Germany's weakness made it possible for Britain, France, and the United States to treat the Soviet Union with disdain, a revulsion based largely on ideology and echoed by the Soviets. Only when Nazi Germany began to pose a significant threat did these ideological preferences lose their power.[69] In other words, security considerations take precedence over ideological preferences, and ideologically based alliances are unlikely to survive when more pragmatic interests intrude.

Several interesting implications follow from this conclusion. In particular, those factors which tend to make states more secure should increase the importance of ideological considerations in alliance choices. If Kenneth Waltz is correct that bipolar worlds are the most stable, then the impact of ideology may increase because all states are more secure. Not only will the bipolar rivalry encourage both superpowers to support third parties freely (giving third parties the option to choose the ideologically most compatible side), but the caution that bipolarity imposes on superpower conduct may permit most other states to follow ideological preferences rather than security re-

---

67. Michael Doyle, "Kant, Liberal Legacies, and Foreign Affairs," *Philosophy and Public Affairs*, Vol. 17, Nos. 3 and 4 (Summer/Fall 1983).
68. Winston S. Churchill, *The Second World War: Volume III, The Grand Alliance* (Boston: Houghton Mifflin, 1950), p. 370.
69. See John Lewis Gaddis, *Russia, the Soviet Union, and the United States: An Interpretive History* (New York: John Wiley, 1978), Chapters 4 and 5.

quirements.[70] Bipolarity may also be a permissive cause of neutralism, as third parties will be more confident both that the superpowers will restrain each other and that at least one of them will be available if a great power ally is needed. Thus Prince Sihuanouk, while proclaiming Cambodia to be neutral, also stated that "in the event of a Viet Minh invasion we will count on the aid . . . of the United States."[71]

Furthermore, other factors that make defense easy and conquest difficult should render ideological considerations more important. Thus a permissive cause of the ideological alliances of the 1820s and 1830s may have been the condition of defense dominance that resulted from the small standing armies that the European states preferred at that time.[72] In the same way, the existence of nuclear weapons, by inhibiting warfare among the great powers, may make ideology somewhat more important now than previously. Because nuclear weapons make it more difficult for great powers to threaten weaker states (and give them incentives to moderate the conduct of others as well), third parties both need formal alliances less and can pay greater attention to ideological factors when choosing alliance partners. As Nasser pointed out in rejecting American requests to join the Baghdad Pact: "there would be no [Soviet] aggression . . . for the simple reason that . . . nuclear weapons have changed the whole art of war, and rendered any foreign aggression a remote possibility."[73]

A second conclusion is that the apparent importance of ideology can be exaggerated by the perceptions of statesmen and the policies that they adopt as a result. If statesmen *believe* that ideology determines international alignments, they will view similar states as potential friends and dissimilar ones

---

70. See Kenneth N. Waltz, "The Stability of a Bipolar World," *Daedalus*, Vol. 93, No. 3 (Summer 1964); and *Theory of International Politics*, Chapter 8; Glenn Snyder and Paul Diesing, *Conflict Among Nations: Bargaining, System Structure, and Decisionmaking in International Crises* (Princeton: Princeton University Press, 1977), pp. 419–429; and Herbert Dinerstein, "The Transformation of Alliance Systems," *American Political Science Review*, Vol. 59, No. 3 (1965), p. 596.

71. Quoted in Rothstein, *Alliances and Small Powers*, p. 247. Gamal Nasser expressed a similar view by saying that "Egypt's great strength lies in the rival interests of America and Russia in the Middle East area . . . each of the superpowers will protect her from the other." Quoted in Anthony Nutting, *Nasser* (London: Constable, 1972), p. 271.

72. On this point, see: Osgood and Tucker, *Force, Order, and Justice*, pp. 52–53, 78–81; Quester, *Offense and Defense in the International System*, pp. 73–76; Robert Jervis, "Security Regimes," in Stephen Krasner, ed., *International Regimes* (Ithaca: Cornell University Press, 1983), pp. 178–184; and Stanislav Andreski, *Military Organization and Society* (Berkeley: University of California Press, 1968), pp. 68–69.

73. Quoted in Patrick Seale, *The Struggle for Syria: A Study of Postwar Arab Politics 1945–1958* (London: Oxford University Press, 1965), p. 188.

as potential enemies. Reacting positively towards the former and harshly towards the latter will encourage good relations with one and drive the others to cling together more tightly in opposition. The hypothesis thus becomes self-fulfilling, and the result is then used to prove that the original belief was correct. Thus American beliefs in a Communist "monolith" led the U.S. to behave in ways that may have made the alliance of the Soviet Union and other leftist forces far more cohesive than it would otherwise have been. As the behavior of Yugoslavia, China, and Zimbabwe suggests, the *apparent* importance of ideology in determining Cold War alignments may be less the result of "natural" Marxist solidarity than the naïve American assumption that this was the case.

Third, the importance of ideology may also be exaggerated by taking the rhetoric of statesmen too seriously. For both internal and external reasons, statesmen are likely to emphasize this factor when discussing national commitments. Not only does this help convince adversaries that the alliance is a viable one, but domestic support will be enhanced if the public believes that one's allies share its goals and values. The whitewashing that Joseph Stalin received during World War II (in which the former tyrant became the paternal "Uncle Joe") provides a superb example, as does Vice President Bush's commendation of Phillippine President Ferdinand Marcos's commitment to democracy.[74] Thus the tendency for "birds of a feather to flock together" will be overstated if we look solely at the rhetoric of national leaders.

In sum, although ideology does play a role in alliance choices, it is usually a subordinate one. Moreover, despite the pervasive fear that Marxist regimes form natural allies, reality may actually be just the opposite. The more seriously such regimes pursue the Leninist imperative to follow an international vanguard, the more likely they are to quarrel among themselves. What solidarity does exist is only enhanced by the American perception that such ideologies pose a threat that must be met by relentless opposition. This is not to say that ideological factors play no role in the cohesion of America's opponents, only that we have generally failed to exploit the inevitable tensions to the fullest. Worse than that, we have acted in ways that give them few incentives to cooperate with us, and many reasons not to.

---

74. See Robert Dallek, *Franklin D. Roosevelt and American Foreign Policy: 1932–1945* (London: Oxford University Press, 1979), pp. 296–298. On the general tendency for allies to exaggerate their level of agreement, see Robert Jervis, "Hypotheses on Misperception," *World Politics*, Vol. 20, No. 3 (April 1968), p. 463.

The Instruments of Alliance Formation: "Bribery" and Penetration

States seeking allies will employ specific policy instruments to attract others to their side. The use of such instruments (or the interpretation placed on their use by others) rests upon implicit hypotheses about the relative effectiveness of such tactics. The most important of these hypotheses concerns the instruments of "bribery" and penetration. What are these hypotheses, and how seriously should we take them?

"INTERNATIONAL BRIBERY": FOREIGN AID AND ALLIANCE FORMATION
According to this hypothesis, the provision of economic or military assistance will create effective allies, either by demonstrating one's own favorable intentions, by evoking a sense of gratitude, or because the recipient will become dependent on the donor. Simply stated, the hypothesis is: the more aid, the tighter the resulting alliance. This hypothesis lies at the heart of most economic and military assistance programs, as well as American concern over Soviet arms shipments to various Third World countries. For example, U.S. Undersecretary of Defense Fred C. Iklé has warned that Soviet arms assistance to Cuba and Nicaragua threatens to turn Central America into "another Eastern Europe," just as earlier U.S. officials saw Soviet military aid to other areas as a reliable tool of influence.[75] Via the same logic, Undersecretary of State James Buckley has suggested that increasing American arms transfers will help "revitalize American alliances."[76] Regardless of the context, the argument is the same: the provision of military or economic assistance is believed to give suppliers significant leverage over the recipient.

The belief that such sidepayments play a role in alliance formation is not without some justification. Throughout history, states have often offered material inducements to attract allies. Louis XIV purchased English neutrality during his campaign for hegemony in Europe by dispensing subsidies to the impoverished court of James II.[77] In World War I, Britain and France obtained the support of various Arab leaders by promising them territory after the war and by providing a gold subsidy immediately. Similar promises brought Italy into the war as well.[78] Historians generally agree that French loans to

---

75. *The New York Times*, March 15, 1983.
76. "Arms Transfers and the National Interest," *Current Policy #279*, May 21, 1981, Bureau of Public Affairs (Washington, D.C.: U.S. Department of State, 1981), p. 2.
77. See John Wolf, *The Emergence of the Great Powers* (New York: Harper Torchbooks, 1962), pp. 18, 26, 103.
78. See Lenczowski, *The Middle East in World Affairs*, p. 81; Howard M. Sachar, *The Emergence*

Russia played a role in encouraging the Franco–Russian alliance of 1892.[79] Sidepayments are thus frequently part of the process of alliance formation. To conclude that they are the principal cause of alignment or a powerful tool of influence, however, is erroneous. The simplistic notion that "aid creates allies" ignores the fact that military or economic assistance is offered and accepted only when both parties feel it is in their interest to do so. In other words, offering or accepting aid is one way that states with different capabilities can respond to a common threat. Thus a large aid relationship is more often the *result* of alignment than a *cause* of it. For example, no one would claim that the Grand Alliance in World War II was "caused" by American Lend–Lease aid to Great Britain and the Soviet Union. Rather, Lend–Lease was a means by which American industrial productivity could be applied more effectively against the common enemy.[80] Yet those who now argue that Soviet or American military aid can create reliable proxies are in effect making just such a claim: they are focusing solely on the means by which an alliance is implemented, and ignoring the common interests that inspired the relationship in the first place.

Accordingly, it is more appropriate to consider the conditions under which the use of military or economic assistance will have powerful *independent* effects on the recipient's conduct. If we are worried about Soviet military assistance, for example, we want to know if and when this will enable Moscow to direct recipients for its own purposes. The question thus becomes: when does "bribery" give suppliers effective political leverage? The answer is: not very often. This is true for several reasons.[81]

First, unless the supplier is the only available source of economic or military aid, leverage will be limited because the recipient can always obtain it else-

of the Middle East: 1914–1924 (New York: Alfred A. Knopf, 1969), pp. 125–130, 136; Bernadotte Schmitt and Harold M. Vedeler, *The World in the Crucible: 1914–1918* (New York: Harper and Row, 1984), pp. 92–94.

79. Jacob Viner, "International Finance and Balance of Power Diplomacy, 1881–1914," in Viner, *International Economics: Studies* (Glencoe, Ill.: Free Press, 1952); George F. Kennan, *The Decline of Bismarck's European Order* (Princeton: Princeton University Press, 1978), pp. 342–346; and Fritz Stern, *Gold and Iron: Bismarck, Bleichroder, and the Building of the German Empire* (New York: Vintage, 1979), pp. 439–447.

80. See Gaddis, *Strategies of Containment*, Chapter 1; and William H. McNeill, *America, Britain, and Russia: Their Cooperation and Conflict, 1941–1946* (London: Oxford University Press, 1953), pp. 137–155 and *passim*.

81. There is an extensive literature on the sources and conditions of economic leverage. I have found the following works especially helpful: Ariel Levite and Athanassios Platias, "Evaluating Small States' Dependence on Arms Imports: An Alternative Perspective" (Ithaca: Cornell Peace Studies Program, 1983); Albert O. Hirschman's classic *State Power and the Structure of International*

where. With two superpowers capable of providing assistance, client states can usually threaten to shift suppliers if their interests are not being served.[82]

Second, because recipients are usually weaker than suppliers, they will bargain harder because they have more at stake. At the same time, suppliers will be reluctant to cut off supplies if they feel it will leave their allies vulnerable. This limits their effective leverage still further.

Third, the more important the recipient is to the donor, the more aid it is likely to receive. But if a recipient is that important, then the donor will be even more reluctant to pressure it too severely. This tendency will be increased by the fact that the provision of aid also commits the donor's own prestige. The client's threats to realign if its interests are not served will be all the more effective once its patron has already invested heavily. If the recipient decides to realign or suffers a defeat, the patron's own prestige is likely to suffer.[83] A supplier's ability to enforce obedience by restricting supplies thus declines even more. In fact, large aid programs, far from providing suppliers with effective leverage, may actually indicate that the client has successfully manipulated the patron into providing ever-increasing amounts of support.

Finally, the provision of aid can be self-defeating, because it strengthens the recipient's position and thus reduces the need to follow its patron's wishes. As Henry Kissinger described the bargaining process with Israel during his "step-by-step" diplomacy:

I ask [Israeli Prime Minister] Rabin to make concessions, and he says he can't because Israel is weak. So I give him more arms, and he says he doesn't need to make concessions because Israel is strong.[84]

Trade (Berkeley: University of California Press, 1945), especially pp. 29–40; James A. Caporaso, "Dependence, Dependency, and Power in the Global System: A Structural and Behavioral Analysis," *International Organization*, Vol. 32, No. 1 (Winter 1978); Klaus Knorr, *The Power of Nations* (New York: Basic Books, 1975), and "Is International Coercion Waning or Rising?," *International Security*, Vol. 1, No. 4 (Spring 1977), pp. 92–110; and Steven E. Miller, "Arms and Impotence: Arms Transfers and Superpower Influence" (paper delivered at the IISS Young Scholars Conference in Bellagio, Italy, 1979).

82. For example, Jordan was able to obtain a variety of advanced weaponry (e.g., tanks and surface-to-air missiles) from the United States by threatening to turn to the Soviet Union in 1963, 1964, and again in 1975–76. In the same way, Nasser persuaded a reluctant Soviet leadership to send air defense troops and equipment to Egypt during the War of Attrition by threatening to resign in favor of a pro-American president.

83. During the October War, for example, Henry Kissinger reportedly argued that the United States "could not permit Soviet clients to defeat a traditional [American] friend." See his *Years of Upheaval* (Boston: Little, Brown, 1981), p. 468.

84. Quoted in Edward R.F. Sheehan, *The Arabs, Israelis, and Kissinger* (Pleasantville: Reader's Digest Press, 1976), p. 199.

For all these reasons, the provision of military or economic assistance is likely to be a rather weak tool of superpower influence. The historical record supports this conclusion. Not only have superpower clients demonstrated a remarkable ability to defy their patrons on important issues,[85] but earlier great powers derived equally evanescent benefits. Although Britain financed and equipped the coalition that defeated Napoleon, for example, it found its allies to be an unruly coalition in which British leverage was at best erratic.[86]

In sum, the common assertion that Soviet or American military assistance will create reliable proxies is misleading at best and wrongheaded at worst, because the hypothesis that "bribery" can create reliable allies does not take the context within which aid is provided into account. Rather than being a tool through which the great powers gain reliable allies, the provision of aid is a means by which recipients can deal with their own problems through external assistance. Obviously, a large aid program does indicate that the states involved share certain common interests. Thus Nicaragua, Cuba, and the Soviet Union all oppose U.S. intervention in Central America, just as Saudi Arabia and the United States fear Soviet meddling in the Middle East. But it is wrong to conclude that recipients become Soviet (or, for that matter, American) minions, because aid can provide substantial leverage only over the most helpless (and therefore inconsequential) recipients. Foreign aid can make an existing alliance more effective, but it rarely creates one in the absence of shared political interests.

PENETRATION

The last hypothesis concerns the effects of political penetration, defined as the covert or indirect manipulation of one state's political system by another. This may take many forms: 1) public officials whose loyalties are divided may use their positions to move one state closer to another; 2) lobbying organizations may be used to alter policy decisions and public perceptions regarding a potential ally; or 3) foreign propaganda may be used to sway elite and mass attitudes. This hypothesis predicts that alliances can be readily formed by manipulating foreign governments through these indirect means.

---

85. For an analysis of the historical record, see Walt, "The Origins of Alliances," Chapter 8. See also Robert O. Keohane, "The Big Influence of Small Allies," *Foreign Policy*, Number 2 (Spring 1971), pp. 161–182.
86. See Robert Sherwig, *Guineas and Gunpowder: British Foreign Aid in the Wars with France* (Cambridge: Harvard University Press, 1969), pp. 311–313, 350–355.

Although penetration has received relatively little attention in recent scholarly research,[87] examples are easy to find. The Turkish decision to ally with Germany in World War I was due in part to the influence of Liman von Sanders, a German officer commanding the Turkish Army in Constantinople.[88] During the war itself, Britain conducted an effective propaganda campaign in the United States, which played a significant role in the U.S. decision to enter.[89] During the 1950s, the "China Lobby" exerted a substantial influence over American policy in the Far East by manipulating public opinion and influential American officials.[90] Finally, the belief that penetration may be an effective tool of alliance-building has inspired the political indoctrination programs that accompanied American military training for various developing countries, not to mention American concern over similar Soviet educational and military assistance programs.[91]

The circumstances in which penetration will have a significant effect, however, are limited. First, it is more likely to succeed in open societies, where influential elites are more accessible to foreign ideas. Second, if the effort to penetrate is viewed by the target state as subversive or illegitimate, it is likely to react by moving away from the state seeking to enhance its influence and the penetration will therefore be counterproductive. This possibility implies that penetration will be safest (i.e., have the best chance of success) when there are already strong incentives for the two states to align, so that the activities to encourage the alliance via penetration will not appear as dangerous. Of course, this implies that penetration is at best serving to supplement the incentives for alignment that already exist.

---

87. Exceptions include: K.J. Holsti, *International Politics: A Framework for Analysis* (Englewood Cliffs, N.J.: Prentice-Hall, 1967), Chapter 8; Andrew M. Scott, *The Revolution in Statecraft: Informal Penetration* (New York: Random House, 1965); Nicholas O. Berry, "The Management of Foreign Penetration," *Orbis*, Vol. 17, No. 3 (Summer 1973); and Knorr, *The Power of Nations*.

88. Schmitt and Vedeler, *The World in the Crucible*, pp. 98–102; A.J.P. Taylor, *The Struggle for Mastery in Europe: 1848–1945* (London: Oxford University Press, 1952), pp. 508–511, 533–534.

89. See Horace C. Peterson, *Propaganda for War: The British Campaign Against American Neutrality, 1914–1918* (Norman: University of Oklahoma Press, 1939).

90. See Ross Y. Koen, *The China Lobby in American Politics* (New York: Harper and Row, 1974); and Stanley Bachrack, *The Committee for One Million* (New York: Columbia University Press, 1976).

91. Miles D. Wolpin, "External Political Socialization as a Source of Conservative Military Behavior in the Third World," in Kenneth Fidel, ed., *Militarism in Developing Countries* (New Brunswick: Transaction Books, 1975); Anthony Cordesman, "U.S. and Soviet Competition in Arms Exports and Military Assistance," *Armed Forces Journal International*, August 1981, pp. 66–67; and U.S. Department of Defense, *Soviet Military Power* (Washington, 1983), pp. 86–90.

In addition, to infer that penetration plays a strong causal role in contemporary international alliances is to reverse the likely causal relationship between the decision to ally and the development of extensive contacts between two states. As with foreign aid, a large military or educational training program is one *effect* of good political relations, but it is rarely an independent *cause*.[92]

Several examples will illustrate these considerations. The ethnic lobbies that affect American alliance policy are effective precisely because: 1) they are operating within an open political system; 2) their aims are limited to a narrow range of issues; and 3) their actions are viewed as consistent with the interest group traditions of American politics. Thus the likelihood of a counterproductive backlash is reduced. Recognizing this, the Chairman of the American–Israeli Public Affairs Committee has commented: "unless you can always translate this in terms of what's in America's interest, you're lost."[93] By contrast, several accounts report that Soviet interference in Egypt's internal affairs was instrumental in Sadat's decision to expel his Russian advisors in 1972. Similar events have apparently taken place in Syria and Iraq, albeit with less severe repercussions.[94]

Thus where penetration does contribute to an alliance, it will be where the *means* are perceived as legitimate and where tangible incentives for alignment already exist, so that the campaign will be viewed as less intrusive and the relevant targets will be inclined to view the message favorably. But this means that penetration is unlikely to do more than reinforce existing pressures for

---

92. Thus the Soviet military presence in Egypt and Syria soared after the Six Day War, at the request of the two host countries. Similarly, the number of Jordanians receiving military training in the U.S. tripled after the Jordan Crisis in 1970. Prior political alignments and changing external circumstances determine the level of contact between influential elites, not the reverse.

93. Quoted in "Lobbying and the Middle East," *Congressional Quarterly*, August 22, 1981, p. 1529. See also Charles McC. Mathias, "Ethnic Groups and Foreign Policy," *Foreign Affairs*, Vol. 59, No. 5 (Summer 1981), pp. 975–998; Seth P. Tillman, *The United States in the Middle East* (Bloomington: Indiana University Press, 1982), Chapter 2; and I.L. Kenen, *Israel's Defense Line* (Buffalo: Prometheus Books, 1981).

94. On the Soviet expulsion from Egypt, see: Alvin Z. Rubinstein, *Red Star on the Nile: The Soviet–Egyptian Influence Relationship Since the June War* (Princeton: Princeton University Press, 1975), pp. 195–196; Anwar Sadat, *In Search of Identity* (New York: Harper and Row, 1978), pp. 230–231; and Steven David, "The Realignment of Third World Regimes from One Superpower to the Other: Ethiopia's Mengistu, Somalia's Siad, and Egypt's Sadat" (Ph.D. dissertation, Harvard University, 1980), pp. 297–299, 319–320, 328–329. On the tensions caused by Soviet interference within Syria, see *Middle East Record 1969–70* (Jerusalem: Israel Universities Press, 1977), pp. 427–429, 431–432. In 1978, Iraq executed 21 Communists discovered forming cells in the armed forces. See Francis Fukuyama, *The Soviet Union and Iraq*, Research Note N-1524-AF (Santa Monica, Calif.: Rand Corporation, 1980), pp. 56–61.

alignment. In short, penetration may preserve or enhance an existing alliance, but it rarely creates one by itself.

Finally, the cases where penetration has had a strong independent effect reinforce these conclusions. Penetration will be most effective when the central authority of the target state is extremely weak. In such circumstances, penetration may provide a foreign power with de facto control. For example, the Warsaw Pact presence in South Yemen has enabled the U.S.S.R. to protect the alliance by ensuring that pro-Soviet factions remain in power. This was demonstrated in 1978, when Cuban and East German forces supported a violent coup ousting a moderate faction led by Rubay Ali.[95] Similar events seem to have occurred in Afghanistan as well. Of course, states that are this vulnerable to outside interference are rarely important players on the international stage. As with foreign aid, therefore, penetration is by itself most useful for acquiring allies that don't really matter very much, or in cementing ties between states whose interests are already highly compatible.

Conclusion: Alliance Formation and the Balance of World Power

The analysis above may be summarized as follows. First, states form alliances to balance against threats rather than bandwagon with them. Threats, in turn, are the product of several different sources. Second, ideology is a weaker cause of alliance formation, and ideological movements that strive for tight central authority are more likely to lead to conflict than cooperation. Third, the instruments of "bribery" and penetration are by themselves weak determinants of alignment; they make existing alliances more effective, but rarely create them in the absence of common interests.

These propositions tell us a great deal about America's global position and the optimal strategies for maintaining it. To demonstrate this, I shall conclude by considering the following question: what explains the current balance of world power between the Soviet and American alliance systems? In other words, why have third parties aligned with one or the other superpower? I make two claims. First, in contrast to the prevailing American wisdom, the present balance greatly favors the United States and its allies. Second, this favorable *imbalance* of power can be explained by the central propositions

---

95. See J.B. Kelly, *Arabia, the Gulf, and the West* (New York: Basic Books, 1980), pp. 470–473; Laurie A. Mylroie, *The Soviet Presence in the People's Democratic Republic of Yemen: Internal Vulnerabilities and Regional Challenges*, Research Note N-2052-AF (Santa Monica, Calif.: Rand Corporation, 1983); and *Middle East Contemporary Survey, 1977–78* (London: Holmes and Meier, 1979), pp. 655–660, 662–666.

advanced in this essay. To support these claims, I shall first offer a rough assessment of the present balance. I shall then show how these hypotheses provide a persuasive explanation of this situation, and draw out several important policy implications from these results.

THE PRESENT (IM)BALANCE OF WORLD POWER

Measuring the power of states or coalitions precisely is complicated and difficult. Fortunately, a detailed "net assessment" is not necessary here. A rough but reliable comparison of the Soviet and American alliance systems can be obtained by considering the following items: population, gross national product (GNP), size of armed forces, and defense expenditure.[96] I have categorized alliance members either by the existence of a formal security treaty or by the presence of a significant level of security cooperation between the ally and the superpower in question. The Soviet system thus includes the Warsaw Pact and Moscow's principal regional clients; the American system includes NATO, Japan, and the other regional powers with obvious and longstanding ties to the U.S. The current distribution of capabilities between these two systems is shown in Table 1.

Not only does the American alliance system outnumber that of the Soviet Union, but these figures reveal a striking Western advantage in overall resources. Moreover, the disparity is especially pronounced on the indicators

Table 1. Ratios of Capabilities Between the American and Soviet Alliance Networks

Coalitions	Population	GNP	Size of Armed Forces	Defense $
U.S. + Allies / U.S.S.R. + Allies	2.25	3.26	0.99	1.17
U.S. + Allies + PRC / U.S.S.R. + Allies + India	1.81	3.30	1.32	1.30
U.S. + Allies + PRC / U.S.S.R. + Allies	4.08	3.52	1.49	1.32

Note: See Appendices for the data used to prepare this table.

---

96. On the problems of estimating national power, see: Knorr, *The Power of Nations*, Chapters 3 and 4; Harold and Margaret Sprout, *Foundations of International Politics* (Princeton: Van Nostrand, 1962); Morgenthau, *Politics Among Nations*, Part 3; and Ray S. Cline, *World Power Assessment 1977: A Calculus of Strategic Drift* (Washington: Georgetown, 1978).

that reflect latent power. Significantly, the worst case for the U.S.S.R.—China allied with the U.S. and India neutral—is probably the most likely case as well. The Soviets face a ratio of more than 3:1 in population and GNP, to say nothing of their technological disadvantages.[97] The gap is smaller in terms of *mobilized* power, because the Soviets and their allies have sought to compensate for their relative weakness by devoting a larger percentage of GNP to defense. Despite this disproportionate effort, the Soviet alliance system still trails the U.S. and its allies by a considerable margin on these items as well.

At first glance, this result would seem to contradict the assertion that states choose alliance partners in order to balance against the strongest. Focusing solely on aggregate power would lead us to expect more states to ally with the Soviet Union, in order to prevent the United States from using its superior overall resources in harmful ways. Judging from the preponderance of aggregate power favoring the West, many states appear to have "bandwagoned" rather than balanced by aligning with the U.S. This is even more striking when one remembers that the United States was overwhelmingly the world's most powerful country in the immediate postwar period, yet was able to bring most of the other industrial powers into alignment with rather than against it.[98]

This apparent anomaly can be resolved by considering the central propositions developed above. In particular, we should recall that states balance against *threats*, of which aggregate power is only one component. By considering the effects of each separate source of threat, as well as the less important but still significant effects of ideology, a persuasive account of the current structure of world power can be obtained. Let us consider each element in turn.

First, not to belabor the obvious, the Soviet–American rivalry is itself determined by the tendency for states to balance against aggregate power.

---

97. According to the U.S. Undersecretary of Defense for Research and Engineering, in 1982 the U.S. led the U.S.S.R. in 15 out of 23 basic technology areas, with 6 even, and with the U.S.S.R. ahead in 2. In deployed military systems, U.S. technology was superior in 12, even in 11, and inferior in 6. See Statement by the Hon. Richard E. Delauer, U.S. House of Representatives, "The FY1983 Department of Defense Program for Research, Development, and Acquisition," 97th Congress, 2nd session (Washington, D.C.: U.S. Government Printing Office, 1982), pp. II-21 and II-22.

98. In 1950, the United States produced approximately 40 percent of Gross World Product, while the Soviet Union managed only 13.5 percent. American naval and air power were far superior, and the U.S. had a clear advantage in deliverable atomic weaponry.

Because each is the other's greatest potential threat, the two superpowers devote their primary attention to the actions of the other. For the Soviets, this is an especially daunting prospect. The rigid logic of bipolarity has locked them into a competition with history's wealthiest and most technologically advanced society. Even before we consider the allies that each superpower has attracted, it is clear that the Soviet Union begins from a relatively weaker position.

Second, the effects of proximity help explain why the alliance choices of other important states make the Soviet situation even worse. Because the Soviet Union is the largest power on the Eurasian land mass, it poses a significant threat to the many states on or near its borders. As a result, Soviet relations with neighboring countries are generally either imperial or hostile: those countries are either under *de facto* Soviet control or allied with the U.S. Although geographic proximity may in some cases make it easier for the Soviet Union to use military power against its neighbors, this situation also provides the independent states of Eurasia with a powerful incentive to seek allies elsewhere to deter such an attempt or to defeat it should it occur.

The United States, by contrast, has only two countries on its borders. Neither is especially powerful.[99] Because American policy towards both has been benign in recent years (and because their own weakness and isolation from potential allies makes resistance futile), both have chosen to bandwagon with the U.S. Even more important, the United States is separated by two oceans from the other vital centers of world power. For the medium powers of Western Europe and Asia, the U.S. is the perfect ally. It is sufficiently powerful to contribute substantially to their defense, it is driven by its own concerns to oppose Soviet expansion, and yet it is sufficiently distant from those allies so that it does not itself pose a significant threat. Thus the United States is *geographically* isolated but *politically* popular, while the Soviet Union is *politically* isolated as a consequence of *geographic proximity*. More than any other factor, geography explains why so many of the world's significant powers have chosen to ally with the U.S.[100]

---

99. Were Canada and Mexico to ally against the U.S., they would trail in GNP by seven to one and in population by almost 2.5 to one.
100. This analysis stands many familiar notions of geopolitics on their heads. For example, Halford Mackinder suggested that Russia gained great advantages from its geographic position at the center of the world "Heartland." The implications of alliance theory are that while this may provide some military advantages, it also greatly increases the number of potential enemies the centrally placed power will face. For analyses of Mackinder's ideas, see Robert E. Harkavy, *Great Power Competition for Overseas Bases: The Geopolitics of Access Diplomacy* (New York: Perga-

Third, the Soviet response to this situation is both predictable and self-defeating. Faced with an encircling coalition of far greater overall resources, the Soviets have responded by devoting considerable efforts to defense. For this and other reasons, their force posture and military doctrine emphasize offensive capabilities and operations. In the event of war, the Soviet Union aims to fight an offensive battle of conquest rather than a defensive battle on its borders, regardless of how the war actually begins. This *offensive* capability, however, merely reinforces the cohesion of the alliance that already opposes them, because it increases the level of threat that Soviet neighbors perceive.[101]

Fourth, the final source of threat—perceived intentions—works against the U.S.S.R. as well. Actions like the invasion of Afghanistan, periodic interventions in Eastern Europe, support for terrorist organizations and revolutionary movements abroad, all reinforce global opposition to the Soviet Union. Although these actions may attract the support of radical forces around the globe, they have also increased the already strong tendency for the world's wealthiest and most stable regimes to ally together for mutual defense.[102]

Significantly, these factors have been largely reversed in the Third World, which explains why the Soviets have done better there while the U.S. has done worse. The Soviet capacity for global power projection has been and remains distinctly inferior to that of the United States, and the U.S.S.R. has generally adopted a much more favorable attitude towards the aspirations of the non-aligned movement and revolutionary forces throughout the world.[103]

---

mon, 1982), Chapter 6; and Paul M. Kennedy, "Mahan Versus Mackinder: Two Views on Naval Strategy," in his *Strategy and Diplomacy: Collected Essays* (London: Allen and Unwin, 1983).

101. According to the IISS, the U.S.S.R. now leads the world in total defense spending. On the offensive nature of Soviet military doctrine, see: Benjamin Lambeth, *How to Think About Soviet Military Doctrine*, Rand Paper P-5939 (Santa Monica, Calif.: Rand Corporation, 1978); and Jack L. Snyder, "Civil-Military Relations and the Cult of the Offensive, 1914 and 1984," *International Security*, Vol. 9, No. 1 (Summer 1984), pp. 108–146.

102. Recent examples of balancing behavior by the West include: the *rapprochement* with China in the 1970s; the modernization of Norwegian coastal and air defenses and the pre-positioning of equipment for a U.S. marine battalion in Norway itself; the NATO decision and deployment of intermediate range nuclear missiles in Europe; the 1976 agreement for an annual 3 percent real increase in alliance spending; and continued discussions for coordinated action in areas outside of NATO. These responses habitually fall short of American desires, a phenomenon still best explained by the theory of collective goods. On the latter point, see Mancur Olson and Richard Zeckhauser's classic "An Economic Theory of Alliances," *Review of Economics and Statistics* (1966); and Robert J. Art, "Fixing Transatlantic Bridges," *Foreign Policy*, Number 46 (Spring 1982), pp. 69–70.

103. See Andrew Marshall, "Sources of Soviet Power: The Military Potential in the 1980s," in Christoph Bertram, ed., *Prospects of Soviet Power in the 1980s* (Hamden, Conn.: Archon Books, 1980), pp. 65–66; Stephen S. Kaplan, *Diplomacy of Power: Soviet Armed Forces as a Political Instrument* (Washington, D.C.: Brookings Institution, 1981), Chapter 5.

By contrast, the United States denounced neutralism as immoral, was usually hostile to leftist nationalist movements, and employed its considerable military capabilities against a variety of developing countries on several occasions.[104] Thus where Soviet power and perceived intentions threatened the developed world but not the former colonies, American power and American *actions* did just the opposite. U.S. interventionism in the developing world drove more Third World regimes to the Soviet side than it attracted to its own, and undermined relations with its other allies as well. Thus the same factors that explain America's close ties with the industrial states of Eurasia also account for its relatively poorer standing throughout much of the rest of the world.[105]

Fifth, these tendencies are reinforced by the effects of ideology. The *divisive* character of Soviet Marxism–Leninism—an ideology calling for the authoritative leadership of the Socialist system by Moscow—contributes to Soviet isolation. Indeed, every Communist state that has been physically able to establish an independent position from Moscow has done so, at the price of a severe quarrel with the U.S.S.R. Ideological disagreements are not the only source of intra-Communist conflicts, but they have clearly exacerbated these relations.

America's democratic system provides an advantage here as well. As I described in the second section, democratic regimes enjoy unusually good relations because these systems do not tend to engage in ideological disputes with one another. Moreover, the world's democracies are wealthy, technologically advanced, and militarily capable, while most Marxist states (and especially those in the developing world) are economically weak. As a result, the American alliance system is both impressive in its capabilities and unusually cohesive, especially by historical standards.[106]

---

104. See Barnet, *Intervention and Revolution*; and Barry M. Blechman and Stephen S. Kaplan, *Force Without War: The Use of American Military Forces as a Political Instrument* (Washington, D.C.: Brookings Institution, 1978).
105. Predictably, as Soviet military activity in the Third World has grown, the popularity of the Soviet Union among these developing countries has declined. For the basic trends since the beginning of the Cold War, the best source is still: Center for Defense Information, "Soviet Geopolitical Momentum: Myth or Menace?," *The Defense Monitor*, Vol. 9, No. 1 (January 1980).
106. Despite the perennial predictions of NATO's impending collapse, it is still remarkable that a coalition of fifteen nations has endured for more than thirty years. For a pessimistic view of the future, see Eliot A. Cohen, "The Long-Term Crisis of the Alliance," *Foreign Affairs*, Vol. 61, No. 2 (Winter 1982–83), pp. 325–343. For more optimistic visions, see: Bruce Russett and Donald R. Deluca, "Theatre Nuclear Forces: Public Opinion in Western Europe," *Political Science Quarterly*, Vol. 98, No. 2 (Summer 1983); and Richard Eichenberg, "The Myth of Hollanditis," *International Security*, Vol. 8, No. 2 (Fall 1983), pp. 143–159.

Finally, neither bribery nor penetration is likely to alter this situation very much. The provision of economic and military assistance will not sway the policies of Western Europe or Japan, and the U.S.S.R. has already shown its inability to provide competitive economic benefits to the developing world.[107] Although the Soviets can and do provide large amounts of military equipment, their "proxies" have shown a striking ability to follow their own interests rather than those of the U.S.S.R. Similarly, Soviet efforts to penetrate the West have failed to unravel Western cohesion significantly, and their attempts to create a network of loyal Third World allies through subversion or educational assistance has provided few tangible benefits save in a small number of rather backward and weak countries. Indeed, the U.S. and its allies retain the dominant position in providing economic assistance and in educating emerging Third World elites.[108] In any case, the durable forces of nationalism are likely to limit the overall importance of these instruments as independent causes of alignment, for the reasons already noted.

America's global position is thus doubly reassuring. Not only is it the leading member of an anti-Soviet coalition possessing superior latent and mobilized capabilities, but this alliance is bound together by many durable and powerful forces. The current balance of world power, viewed in light of these ideas, is likely to be extremely stable. The task of American foreign and defense policy is to exploit these fundamental tendencies to the fullest. This can best be accomplished by the following steps.

First, because balancing is the dominant tendency in international politics, the United States should worry less about its allies defecting and worry more about how it provokes opposition through misplaced belligerence. As the balancing hypothesis implies, the less threatening the U.S. appears, the more popular it is likely to be. This means that intervention in peripheral areas for the sake of "credibility" should usually be rejected. Instead, a policy of appeasement in the Third World is often the more promising approach. By patiently and persistently demonstrating that American power is directed by benevolent rather than aggressive intentions, the likelihood that others will embrace the Soviet Union is reduced. Even if they occasionally do, it will

---

107. See Committee on International Relations, "The Soviet Union and the Third World," pp. 170 and *passim*; and Henry Bienen, "Soviet Political Relations with Africa," *International Security*, Vol. 6, No. 4 (Spring 1982), pp. 153–173. Significantly, less than 1 percent of all global development assistance comes from the U.S.S.R. See the Central Intelligence Agency, *Communist Aid Activites in Non-Communist LDCs: 1979 and 1954–1979*, pp. 8–9.

108. On this point, see: CIA, *Communist Aid Activities*, p. 9; and Committee on International Relations, "The Soviet Union and the Third World," pp. 82–90.

have little effect on America's overall position. Given the tendency for states to balance, America's other allies will be more likely to do more.

Second, the present U.S. military program should be revised. It is based on two related errors: 1) that the Soviet buildup has brought significant political advantages; and 2) that a unilateral U.S. response will preserve its own commitments efficiently. Although the Western Alliance suffers from important military deficiencies, they are more the result of spending money unwisely than in spending too little. Moreover, a major U.S. buildup is hardly likely to spur its allies to greater efforts. Via the logic of balancing, they are far more likely to free-ride. Thus the Carter Administration's efforts to fashion a more equitable and efficient NATO defense program made far more sense than the Reagan Administration's attempts to solve Western military deficiencies by spending more and more American dollars. The U.S. can expect its allies to do more against their common foes if those allies were less confident that the U.S. was trying to do it all.

Third, America's knee-jerk opposition to leftist forces in the developing world should be abandoned. Not only is ideology generally a weak force for alignment, but the Marxist doctrines that Americans are so fearful of are as likely to lead to intra-Communist conflict as they are to produce unity. The examples of Mao, Tito, Togliatti, Mugabe, Berlinguer, Carillo, and Pol Pot all demolish the myth of Marxist solidarity, a fact that has somehow escaped the grasp of those responsible for American foreign policy. As George Kennan's original formulation of containment prescribed, the U.S. should seek to exploit these divisions, not work to reinforce the fragile unity of leftist regimes by its own actions.[109]

Fourth, the U.S. should reject the simplistic assumption that Soviet arms recipients are reliable agents of the Kremlin. Providing large arms shipments did not give the Soviet Union reliable influence in Yugoslavia, Egypt, Indonesia, Somalia, China, or Zimbabwe, to name but a few examples. At the same time, the U.S. should recognize that its own aid policies will not provide it with much leverage either. After all, Israel, the country that is probably most dependent on American support, is also one of the more independent in its behavior. Aid may strengthen allies whose political aims parallel our own, but it hardly creates reliable satellites. By exaggerating the effectiveness of this instrument, U.S. leaders exaggerate the size of the Soviet bloc and

---

109. See Gaddis, *Strategies of Containment*, Chapter 2; and Oye and Feinberg, "After the Fall."

ignore the possibility of weaning clients away from Moscow through appropriate political incentives. The U.S. is also likely to provide its own allies with too much, in the mistaken view that this will cement their allegiance and enhance American control.

The arguments advanced in this paper do not mean that the American alliance network is indestructible, that isolationism is preferable, or that Western defense capabilities could not be improved.[110] What they do mean is that Americans could hardly ask for much more. The principal causes of alliance formation work to America's advantage, and isolate the Soviet Union from virtually all of the world's strategically significant states. If Americans recognize this fact, the task of formulating appropriate national security policies should be greatly simplified. Even more important, the policies that emerge will reinforce—rather than undermine—the considerable advantages the United States already enjoys.

---

110. For analyses of the military problems facing the West along with various solutions, see: Barry R. Posen and Stephen W. Van Evera, "Reagan Administration Defense Policy: Departure from Containment," *International Security*, Vol. 8, No. 1 (Summer 1983), pp. 3–45; Carnegie Endowment for International Peace, *Challenges for U.S. National Security: Assessing the Balance: Defense Spending and Conventional Forces, Part II* (Washington, D.C.: Carnegie Endowment, 1982); William W. Kaufmann, "Non-nuclear Deterrence," in John Steinbruner and Leon V. Sigal, eds., *Alliance Security: NATO and the No-First-Use Question* (Washington, D.C.: Brookings Institution, 1984); Asa Clark et al., *The Defense Reform Debate* (Baltimore: Johns Hopkins University Press, 1984); Report of the European Security Study, *Strengthening Conventional Deterrence in Europe: Proposals for the 1980s* (New York: St. Martin's, 1983); and Barry R. Posen, "Measuring the European Conventional Balance: Coping with Complexity in Threat Assessment," *International Security*, Vol. 9, No. 3 (Winter 1984–85), pp. 47–88.

Appendix 1. The Balance of World Power: The Soviet Alliance Network (All Data 1982)

Country	Population (millions)	GNP ($ m)	# in Armed Forces (1000s)	Defense $ ($ m)
U.S.S.R.	270.0	1715000	4400	257000
Bulgaria	8.9	37451	175	3761
Czechoslovakia	15.4	147065	213	7634
East Germany	16.7	175522	233	10236
Hungary	10.7	69111	112	3108
Poland	36.2	186823	429	13494
Rumania	22.5	104827	237	4793
Afghanistan	14.2	2900	30	165
Angola	7.4	7634	47	90
Cuba	9.8	21971	230	1109
Ethiopia	30.6	4635	250	455
Iraq	14.0	25177	450	11689
North Korea	18.7	16200	710	3500
Laos	3.6	320	57	30
Libya	3.3	23986	55	2800
Mongolia	1.7	1100	36	113
Mozambique	12.7	4786	20	163
Nicaragua	2.7	2515	75	169
Syria	9.4	17583	290	2528
Vietnam	55.8	7750	1000	1000
P.D.R. Yemen	2.0	956	23	120
Finland	4.8	51232	36	897
TOTAL	571.1	2624544	9108	324854
% of World Total	12.4	19.3	33.1	39.7
India	715.1	178141	1120	6223
TOTAL WITH INDIA	1286.2	2802685	10228	331077
% of World Total (with India)	27.8	20.6	37.0	40.5

Source: U.S. Arms Control and Disarmament Agency, *World Military Expenditures and Arms Transfers, 1972–1982* (Washington: April 1984).

Appendix 2. The Balance of World Power: The American Alliance Network

Country	Population (millions)	GNP ($ m)	# in Armed Forces (1000s)	Defense $ ($ m)
United States	232.1	3071400	2108	196345
Belgium	9.9	101721	85	3507
Canada	24.6	276706	82	6139
China (Taiwan)	18.5	50583	504	3660
Denmark	5.1	61192	31	1575
Egypt	44.6	29375	447	2395
France	54.4	607429	485	25612
West Germany	61.6	720485	480	24351
Greece	9.8	40209	186	2782
Italy	56.3	374162	391	9778
Japan	118.4	1226951	241	12159
South Korea	40.7	69539	600	4783
Netherlands	14.3	146305	108	4755
Norway	4.1	58521	37	1823
Spain	38.0	197175	353	4123
Turkey	48.1	65252	638	3375
United Kingdom	56.0	531606	322	27368
Thailand	49.7	38695	241	1562
Australia	15.1	180057	73	4415
Philippines	51.8	41830	155	1033
New Zealand	3.1	25817	13	543
Brazil	128.3	295648	460	1850
Saudi Arabia	10.1	16118	55	24754
Somalia	6.1	1985	54	160
Israel	3.9	22917	180	5838
Jordan	3.3	4615	65	984
Mexico	73.8	243677	145	1261
Pakistan	92.1	33598	478	2033
Portugal	10.0	24522	68	900
TOTAL	1283.8	8558090	9085	379863
% of World Total	27.7	62.8	33.0	46.5
P.R. China	1044.8	698000	4490	49500
TOTAL WITH P.R.C.	2328.6	9256090	13575	429363
% of World Total	50.4	67.9	49.3	52.5

Bandwagoning for Profit

Randall L. Schweller

Bringing the Revisionist State Back In

$\mathbf{D}$o states ally more often with the weaker or with the stronger side in a conflict? In the parlance of international relations theory: do states tend to balance against or bandwagon with a rising state or coalition? The answer to this question is critical to the formulation of grand strategy and the definition of vital interests. If states resist the gains of their neighbors by drawing together to redress the balance, then conquest does not pay[1] and interventions to defend far-flung commitments are not only unnecessary, but often counterproductive in causing local states to unite against the meddling great power and its protegé. Conversely, if states gravitate to expanding power, then bandwagons will roll, dominoes will fall, and great powers will find it wise, even at the cost of blood and treasure, to defend remote areas of little or no intrinsic value to their national interests.[2]

While international relations scholars have traditionally accepted the view that states balance against threatening increases of power, paradoxically, practitioners through the ages have held a bandwagoning image of international politics. As Jack Snyder remarks, "most imperial strategists defending far-flung commitments have feared falling dominoes, and most rising chal-

Randall L. Schweller is a John M. Olin Post-Doctoral Fellow in National Security at the Center for International Affairs, Harvard University. In August 1994 he will join the faculty of the Department of Political Science at The Ohio State University.

The author is grateful to Richard Betts, Marc Busch, Thomas Christensen, Dale Copeland, Michael Desch, Richard Herrmann, Robert Jervis, Ethan Kapstein, James McAllister, Gideon Rose, David Schweller, Jack Snyder, Kimberly Marten Zisk, and the members of the Olin National Security Group at Harvard's CFIA for their comments on earlier drafts of this essay.

1. A leading proponent of the "balancing predominates" view, Kenneth N. Waltz, remarks: "In international politics, success leads to failure. The excessive accumulation of power by one state or coalition of states elicits the opposition of others." Waltz, "The Origins of War in Neorealist Theory," in Robert I. Rotberg and Theodore K. Rabb, eds., *The Origin and Prevention of Major Wars* (Cambridge: Cambridge University Press, 1988), p. 49.
2. The bandwagoning image of international politics pictures the global order as a complex machine of wheels within wheels. In this highly interconnected world, small local disruptions quickly grow into large disturbances as their effects cascade and reverberate throughout the system. In contrast, the balancing image sees a world composed of many discrete, self-regulating balance-of-power systems. Because balancing is the prevailing tendency among states, prudent powers should limit their commitments to places where their core interests are at stake.

International Security, Vol. 19, No. 1 (Summer 1994), pp. 72–107
© 1994 by the President and Fellows of Harvard College and the Massachusetts Institute of Technology.

lengers have anticipated bandwagon effects."[3] Dean Acheson, for example, expressed the bandwagoning image that underlay American containment strategy, warning the U.S. cabinet in 1947 that, "if Greece fell within the Russian orbit, not only Turkey would be affected but also Italy, France, and the whole of Western Europe."[4] Similarly, in 1635, the count-duke of Olivares predicted that, in the coming war with France, small losses for Spain would lead to more far-ranging ones: "The first and most fundamental dangers threaten Milan, Flanders and Germany. Any blow against these would be fatal to this monarchy; and if any one of them were to go, the rest of the monarchy would follow, for Germany would be followed by Italy and Flanders, Flanders by the Indies, and Milan by Naples and Sicily."[5]

The bandwagoning belief that "nothing succeeds like success" in war has been at the heart of every bid for world mastery. Napoleon asserted: "My power depends on my glory and my glories on the victories I have won. My power will fail if I do not feed it on new glories and new victories. Conquest has made me what I am, and only conquest can enable me to hold my position."[6] Likewise, Hitler declared: "We shall yet have to engage in many fights, but these will undoubtedly lead to magnificent victories. Thereafter the way to world domination is practically certain."[7]

---

3. Jack Snyder, "Introduction," to Robert Jervis and Jack Snyder, eds., *Dominoes and Bandwagons: Strategic Beliefs and Great Power Competition in the Eurasian Rimland* (New York: Oxford University Press, 1991), p. 3.
4. Quoted in Deborah Welch Larson, "Bandwagoning Images in American Foreign Policy: Myth or Reality?" in ibid., p. 95.
5. Quoted in J.H. Elliott, "Managing Decline: Olivares and the Grand Strategy of Imperial Spain," in Paul Kennedy, ed., *Grand Strategies in War and Peace* (New Haven, Conn.: Yale University Press, 1991), p. 97.
6. Quoted in Paul Kennedy, *The Rise and Fall of the Great Powers: Economic Change and Military Conflict From 1500 to 2000* (New York: Random House, 1987), p. 133. Napoleon often spoke in terms of bandwagoning dynamics. In 1794, he said: "It is necessary to overwhelm Germany; that done, Spain and Italy fall of themselves"; in 1797: "Let us concentrate all our activity on the side of the navy, and destroy England; this done, Europe is at our feet"; and in 1811, "In five years, I shall be the master of the world; there only remains Russia, but I shall crush it." Quoted in R.B. Mowat, *The Diplomacy of Napoleon* (New York: Russell & Russell, [1924] 1971), pp. 22, 53, 243. Not all French strategists of the period viewed the world in these terms, however. After his remarkable victory over the First Coalition in 1794, Carnot feared that France might become drunk with victory: "The rapidity of our military successes . . . do not permit us to doubt that we could . . . reunite to France all the ancient territory of the Gauls. But however seductive this system may be, it will be found perhaps that it is wise to renounce it, and that France would only enfeeble herself and prepare an interminable war by aggrandizement of this kind." Quoted in ibid., p. 11.
7. Adolf Hitler in a speech to Gauleiters on May 8, 1943. Quoted in J. Noakes and G. Pridham, eds., *Nazism, 1919–1945: A History in Documents and Eyewitness Accounts*, Vol. II: *Foreign Policy, War and Racial Extermination* (New York: Schocken Books, 1988), p. 857.

Recently, the issue of how states choose sides in a conflict has sparked a rich and somewhat heated theoretical debate. The view that "balancing predominates" has been most forcefully articulated by Stephen Walt.[8] Offering balance-of-threat theory to explain the causes of alignment, Walt claims that under most conditions balancing is far more common than bandwagoning. Some of his critics, however, point to numerous historical examples of bandwagoning and claim that balancing is the exception, not the rule.[9] Others argue that Walt's theory downplays the importance of domestic factors in alliance decisions. They suggest that illegitimate elites and states that are weak *vis-à-vis* their societies bandwagon more often than balance-of-threat theory predicts.[10]

In this article, I argue that all sides in the debate have mistakenly assumed that bandwagoning and balancing are opposite behaviors motivated by the same goal: to achieve greater security. As a result, the concept of bandwagoning has been defined too narrowly—as giving in to threats—as if it were simply the opposite of balancing. In practice, however, states have very different reasons to choose balancing or bandwagoning. The aim of balancing is self-preservation and the protection of values already possessed, while the goal of bandwagoning is usually self-extension: to obtain values coveted. Simply put, balancing is driven by the desire to avoid losses; bandwagoning by the opportunity for gain.[11] The presence of a significant external threat, while required for effective balancing, is unnecessary for states to bandwagon.

---

8. For his most comprehensive statement on the subject, see Stephen M. Walt, *The Origins of Alliances* (Ithaca, N.Y.: Cornell University Press, 1987).

9. See Robert G. Kaufman, "To Balance or to Bandwagon? Alignment Decisions in 1930s Europe," *Security Studies*, Vol. 1, No. 3 (Spring 1992), pp. 417–447; and Paul W. Schroeder, "Neo-Realist Theory and International History: An Historian's View," paper presented at the War and Peace Institute, Columbia University, June 11, 1993.

10. The domestic-sources school of alliance formation includes Deborah Welch Larson, Stephen R. David, and Jack S. Levy and Michael M. Barnett. See Larson, "Bandwagoning Images in American Foreign Policy," pp. 85–111; Steven R. David, "Explaining Third World Alignment," *World Politics*, Vol. 43, No. 2 (January 1991), pp. 233–256; David, "Why the Third World Still Matters," *International Security*, Vol. 17, No. 3 (Winter 1992/93), pp. 127–159; David, *Choosing Sides: Alignment and Realignment in the Third World* (Baltimore, Md.: The Johns Hopkins University Press, 1991); and Jack S. Levy and Michael M. Barnett, "Alliance Formation, Domestic Political Economy, and Third World Security," *The Jerusalem Journal of International Relations*, Vol. 14, No. 4 (December 1992), pp. 19–40; Levy and Barnett, "Domestic Sources of Alliances and Alignments: The Case of Egypt, 1962–1973," *International Organization*, Vol. 45, No. 3 (Summer 1991), pp. 369–395.

11. As will be discussed, when its purpose is profit and not security, bandwagoning is the opposite of defensive buck-passing, not of balancing. We might call this type of bandwagoning "predatory buck-passing": riding free on the *offensive* efforts of others to gain unearned spoils.

I adopt a different definition of bandwagoning—one that accords with common usage of the term—and argue that it is far more widespread than Walt suggests. To see this, however, we must focus on two factors that have been overlooked: the opportunistic aspect of bandwagoning, and the alliance choices of states that pose threats as well as those of states that respond to threats. In short, the theoretical literature on alliances must bring the revisionist state back in.

The article begins by outlining the various positions in the "balancing versus bandwagoning" debate. In the next section, I offer a different critique of balance-of-threat theory that centers on Walt's definition of bandwagoning and the limitations of his theory as an explanation of alliances. This is followed by a discussion of rewards and bandwagoning, which underscores the opportunistic aspect of bandwagoning that has gone overlooked. Next, I examine the various reasons why states bandwagon other than as a form of appeasement. Finally, I propose an alternative theory of alliances based on the political goals of states.

Balance-of-Threat Theory and Its Critics

In *The Origins of Alliances* and several other works,[12] Stephen Walt offers a refinement of balance-of-power theory, called balance-of-threat theory. Like structural balance-of-power theorists, Walt concludes that states usually balance and rarely bandwagon; unlike them, however, he argues that states do not align solely or even primarily in response to the distribution of capabilities. States' alliance choices are driven instead, Walt argues, by imbalances of threat, when one state or coalition is especially dangerous.[13] The level of threat that a state poses to others is the product of its aggregate power, geographic proximity, offensive capability, and the perceived aggressiveness of its intentions.

---

12. See Stephen M. Walt, "Alliance Formation and the Balance of World Power," *International Security*, Vol. 9, No. 4 (Spring 1985), pp. 3–43; Walt, "Testing Theories of Alliance Formation: The Case of Southwest Asia," *International Organization*, Vol. 43, No. 2 (Spring 1988), pp. 275–316; Walt, "The Case for Finite Containment: Analyzing U.S. Grand Strategy," *International Security*, Vol. 14, No. 1 (Summer 1989), pp. 5–49; Walt, "Alliance Formation in Southwest Asia: Balancing and Bandwagoning in Cold War Competition," in Jervis and Snyder, *Dominoes and Bandwagons*, pp. 51–84; Walt, "Alliances, Threats, and U.S. Grand Strategy: A Reply to Kaufman and Labs," *Security Studies*, Vol. 1, No. 3 (Spring 1992), pp. 448–482.
13. Walt, *The Origins of Alliances*, p. 265; Walt, "Alliance Formation in Southwest Asia," p. 54.

Walt claims that his theory "improves on traditional balance of power theory by providing greater explanatory power with equal parsimony."[14] Because aggregate power is only one of several components defining a threat, Walt's theory explains, *inter alia*, the formation of overlarge winning coalitions in World Wars I and II, and "alliance choices when a state's potential allies are roughly equal in power. In such circumstances, a state will ally with the side it believes is least dangerous."[15]

Walt's theory is an impressive and convincing amendment of traditional balance-of-power theory. Walt builds on existing theory in a critical and constructive way, and he presents a clear and compelling set of ideas backed by a comprehensive survey of alliance formation in several regional universes of cases. While the evidence appears to support Walt's central claims, however, his theory has not been without its critics.

THE CHALLENGERS: THE DOMESTIC SOURCES OF ALLIANCES

Robert Kaufman argues that democracies do not behave as balance-of-threat theory predicts because various domestic constraints imposed by the democratic process delay balancing behavior and dilute its effectiveness.[16] As evidence, Kaufman points to the appeasement policies and the slow pace of balancing by the Western democracies in response to Hitler, who, he asserts, "gave ample warning that he would lead a powerful, extremely dissatisfied Germany . . . down a path . . . that made conflict with other states inevitable." Given the clear danger presented by Nazi Germany, Europe during the 1930s is an "easy case" for Walt's theory; yet, Kaufman claims, it fails the test.[17]

Deborah Larson's central charge against Walt's theory is that it cannot explain why similarly situated states behave in opposite ways and contrary to the theory's predictions, i.e., why strong states sometimes bandwagon

---

14. Walt, *The Origins of Alliances*, p. 263.
15. Ibid., p. 264. This is a somewhat curious claim, however, since balance-of-power theory already has a commonly known phrase for this situation, called "holding the balance." When a state occupies this enviable position, it can play the role of balancer or that of kingmaker. As balancer, it seeks to preserve a stalemate between the two rivals. As kingmaker, it sells its services to the highest bidder. The motto of the kingmaker is: "*Cui adhaereo prae est,*" translated as "the one that I join is the one which will turn the scales" or "the party to which I adhere getteth the upper hand." See Herbert Butterfield, "The Balance of Power," p. 138; and Martin Wight, "The Balance of Power," p. 159; both in Butterfield and Wight, eds., *Diplomatic Investigations: Essays in the Theory of International Politics* (Cambridge, Mass.: Harvard University Press, 1966).
16. Kaufman, "To Balance or to Bandwagon?" pp. 423, 436, 438.
17. Ibid., pp. 419–420.

and weak states sometimes balance.[18] To explain these empirical anomalies, Larson offers an institutionalist approach that measures state strength by the nature of its state-society relations.[19] Positing that elites' primary concern is to preserve their rule, Larson concludes that bandwagoning can help a weak regime retain authority by ending external subversion, undermining domestic rivals, and providing economic assistance and "an aura of invincibility by association with the great power's victories."[20]

Steven David argues that realism's state-centric perspective ignores the "often fatal nature of the international and *domestic* political environment that characterizes the Third World."[21] To explain Third World alliances, David introduces the concept of omnibalancing, so-called because it "incorporates the need of leaders to appease secondary adversaries, as well as to balance against both internal and external threats in order to survive in power."[22] Like Larson, David suggests that fragile Third World elites often bandwagon with hostile powers to balance more dangerous domestic or foreign threats.[23]

Similarly, Jack Levy and Michael Barnett maintain that realism is "relatively silent concerning Third World alliances in general or how state-society relations in particular might give rise to distinctive patterns of alignment behavior."[24] Stressing the resource-providing function of alliances and the impact of the domestic political economy on Third World alignments,[25] they conclude that Third World leaders form alliances "to secure urgently needed economic and military resources to promote domestic goals, respond to external and internal security threats, and consolidate their domestic political positions."[26]

Despite these attempts to discredit balance-of-threat theory's explanation of alliance formation, Walt has been able to respond effectively for several

---

18. Larson, "Bandwagoning Images."
19. Specifically, Larson measures the strength of a state not only by its size and capabilities but also by its level of institutional identity and elite legitimacy.
20. Ibid., p. 103. For a similar argument, see J.W. Burton, *International Relations: A General Theory* (London: Cambridge University Press, 1965), pp. 173–185.
21. David, "Explaining Third World Alignment," p. 235. See also David, "Why the Third World Still Matters;" David, *Choosing Sides.*
22. David, "Explaining Third World Alignment," p. 236.
23. David asserts, "Third World leaders will bandwagon to a superpower threatening them in order to balance against the principal threats" being backed by that superpower. David, *Choosing Sides*, p. 25. But he claims that Egypt's realignment with the United States and Ethiopia's realignment with the Soviet Union during the 1970s are examples of omnibalancing rather than bandwagoning, because neither state appeased its primary threat. Ibid., pp. 184, 186.
24. Levy and Barnett, "Alliance Formation," p. 22. See also Levy and Barnett, "Domestic Sources of Alliances and Alignments."
25. Levy and Barnett, "Alliance Formation," p. 23.
26. Ibid., p. 35.

reasons. First, his theory predicts most of the cases of bandwagoning that his critics attribute to domestic sources. According to the measures of power described by both Walt and Kenneth Waltz,[27] states with illegitimate leaders, weak governmental institutions, and/or little ability to mobilize economic resources are weak states that are likely to bandwagon anyway.[28] As for Kaufman's claim that democracies tend to bandwagon and cannot balance as effectively as balance-of-threat theory predicts, Walt convincingly refutes this argument by pointing out the ambiguity of Hitler's intentions prior to Munich and the vigorous democratic response after March 1939.[29]

Second, the claim that fragile elites often bandwagon with secondary adversaries to counter their principal domestic threats is consistent with Walt's general argument that states balance against the most dangerous threat to their survival.[30] Third, Walt has an advantage in the debate because no one else has undertaken as extensive a survey of alliance formation in the Middle East and Southwest Asia, both Third World regions. This undercuts the claim by Walt's critics that realist theory cannot explain and is "relatively silent concerning" Third World alliances. As for the "resource-providing" function of alliances raised by Levy and Barnett, Walt indeed tests the hypothesis that "states select alliance partners in order to obtain side payments cf material assistance, such as economic or military aid,"[31] and finds little support for it.[32] Finally, Walt's critics have not proposed a comprehensive alternative theory to challenge balance-of-threat theory. Thus it holds up fairly well as an explanation of alliance choices.

---

27. Waltz lists economic capability and political stability and competence as measures of state capabilities. Kenneth N. Waltz, *Theory of International Politics* (Reading, Mass.: Addison-Wesley, 1979), p. 131. Walt defines power as the product of several different components, including economic capability and political cohesion. In his discussion of Soviet penetration of South Yemen in the mid-1970s, Walt also cites the lack of established government institutions as a source of state weakness. Walt, *The Origins of Alliances*, pp. 250, 265.

28. Walt, *The Origins of Alliances*, pp. 29–31, 263. Similarly, Waltz writes: "The power of the strong may deter the weak from asserting their claims, not because the weak recognize a kind of rightfulness of rule on the part of the strong, but simply because it is not sensible to tangle with them." Waltz, *Theory of International Politics*, p. 113.

29. See Walt, "Alliance, Threats, and U.S. Grand Strategy," pp. 449–469.

30. For instance, David suggests that omnibalancing theory "explains why what is thought to be bandwagoning is really consistent with balancing behavior (albeit against internal threats)." David, *Choosing Sides*, p. 191.

31. Walt, *The Origins of Alliances*, p. 218. For Walt's test of this hypothesis, see ibid., pp. 219–242.

32. Walt's analysis of superpower foreign aid to the Middle East throughout the Cold War "suggests that, by itself, economic and military assistance has relatively little impact on alliance choices." Ibid., p. 241.

Walt has so far won the debate because his critics, with the exception of Levy and Barnett, have accepted his premise that alliance choices are best examined as a response to threat, though some have broadened the focus to include internal as well as external threats. Consequently, the "domestic sources" challengers have not questioned Walt's definition of bandwagoning as giving in to the most menacing threat.

I argue instead that the central premise of balance-of-threat theory stacks the deck in favor of disproportionately finding balancing over bandwagoning behavior. Defining bandwagoning as a form of capitulation, and thus examining only those alliances formed as a response to significant external threats, Walt not surprisingly finds that balancing is more common than bandwagoning. This is especially true among strong states, when credible allies are available, and in wartime prior to its becoming a "mopping-up" operation.[33]

Alliance choices, however, are often motivated by opportunities for gain as well as danger, by appetite as well as fear. Balance-of-threat theory is designed to consider only cases in which the goal of alignment is security, and so it systematically excludes alliances driven by profit. Yet, as Walt himself claims, one of the primary motivations for bandwagoning is to share in the spoils of victory. When profit rather than security drives alliance choices, there is no reason to expect that states will be threatened or cajoled to climb aboard the bandwagon; they do so willingly. The bandwagon gains momentum through the promise of rewards, not the threat of punishment. Thus, we will not observe cases of bandwagoning for profit by examining alliances as a response to threats. We must look instead at alliance choices made in the expectation of gain, unfettered by a desire for greater security.

Bandwagoning in Balance-of-Threat Theory

There are several problems with Walt's definition of bandwagoning: it departs from conventional usage; it excludes common forms of bandwagoning for profit rather than security; and it reflects a status-quo bias. His conclusion that balancing is more common than bandwagoning is therefore somewhat misleading.

---

33. The absence of any one of these three conditions "may increase somewhat the likelihood of bandwagoning." Walt, "Alliance, Threats, and U.S. Grand Strategy," pp. 450–451; Walt, *The Origins of Alliances*, pp. 29–31.

CONVENTIONAL USAGE

The term "bandwagoning" as a description of international alliance behavior first appeared in Kenneth Waltz's *Theory of International Politics*.[34] In his structural model of balance-of-power theory, Waltz uses "bandwagoning" to serve as the opposite of balancing: bandwagoning refers to joining the stronger coalition, balancing means allying with the weaker side.[35]

Walt re-defines these terms to suit balance-of-threat theory: "When confronted by a significant external threat, states may either balance or bandwagon. *Balancing* is defined as allying with others against the prevailing threat; *bandwagoning* refers to alignment with the source of danger."[36] By these definitions, Walt, like Waltz before him, intends to place the concepts of balancing and bandwagoning in polar opposition: bandwagoning is meant to serve as the opposite of balancing. Without exception, the literature on alliance behavior in international relations theory has accepted Walt's definition of bandwagoning as aligning with the most menacing threat to a state's independence.[37]

In a later work, Walt fleshes out his definition of bandwagoning:

Bandwagoning involves *unequal exchange;* the vulnerable state makes asymmetrical concessions to the dominant power and accepts a subordinate role. . . . Bandwagoning is an accommodation to pressure (either latent or manifest). . . . Most important of all, bandwagoning suggests a willingness to support or tolerate illegitimate actions by the dominant ally.[38]

---

34. Waltz credits the term to Stephen Van Evera. Waltz, *Theory of International Politics,* p. 126. Arnold Wolfers earlier mentioned the term "bandwagoning" to mean the opposite of balancing, but only in a passing reference. Arnold Wolfers, "The Balance of Power in Theory and Practice," in Wolfers, *Discord and Collaboration: Essays on International Politics* (Baltimore, Md.: The Johns Hopkins University Press, 1962), p. 124.
35. Waltz, *Theory of International Politics,* p. 126.
36. Walt, *The Origins of Alliances,* p. 17. See also Walt, "Alliance Formation and the Balance of World Power," p. 4.
37. Walt's definition of bandwagoning is used by all of the authors in Jervis and Snyder, *Dominoes and Bandwagons.* Likewise, Eric J. Labs, Robert G. Kaufman, and Stephen M. Walt define bandwagoning as aligning with the source of danger in their essays for "Balancing vs. Bandwagoning: A Debate," *Security Studies,* Vol. 1, No. 3 (Spring 1992). Stephen Van Evera also defines balancing as aligning against the the greatest threat to a state's independence, while bandwagoning means "to give in to threats." See Stephen Van Evera, "Primed for Peace: Europe After the Cold War," *International Security,* Vol. 15, No. 3 (Winter 1990/91), p. 20.
38. Walt, "Alliance Formation in Southwest Asia", p. 55. In a later passage (on p. 75), however, Walt seems to contradict himself when he states that dominoes may fall because, among other reasons, "one side's victories convince other states to shift their alignment to the winning side *voluntarily.* Strictly speaking, only the last variant should be viewed as bandwagoning" (emphasis added).

One of several criteria for selecting a taxonomy is the "avoidance of unnecessary departures from common usage."[39] In borrowing the terms "balancing" and "bandwagoning" from balance-of-power theory, Walt wants to retain the original idea that "bandwagoning" should serve as the opposite of "balancing." But in so doing, he violates the rule of common usage with respect to the concept of bandwagoning.[40]

Conventional usage defines a bandwagon as a candidate, side, or movement that attracts adherents or amasses power by its momentum. The phrase "to climb aboard the bandwagon" implies following a current or fashionable trend or joining the side that appears likely to win. Bandwagoning may be freely chosen, or it can be the result of resignation to an inexorable force. By this standard, balance-of-power theory's definition of bandwagoning as "joining the stronger coalition" is faithful to common usage. Balance-of-threat theory's definition as "aligning with the source of danger" or "giving in to threats" only encompasses the coercive or compulsory aspect of the concept captured by the phrase: "If you can't beat 'em, join 'em."

In fact, the behavior Walt defines as bandwagoning comes very close to the concept of capitulation, defined as "the act of surrendering or of yielding (as to a dominant influence)."[41] In keeping with ordinary language, bandwagoning should not assume involuntary support gained through coercion, which is instead capitulation. This distinction is not simply a matter of semantic taste. To see why, we must examine the motives Walt ascribes to bandwagoning:

What is the logic behind the bandwagoning hypothesis? Two distinct motives can be identified. First, bandwagoning may be adopted as a form of appeasement. By aligning with the threatening state or coalition, the bandwagoner may hope to avoid an attack on himself by diverting it elsewhere. Second, a state may align with the dominant side in war in order to share the spoils of victory. Mussolini's declaration of war on France and Russia's entry into the war against Japan in 1945 illustrate this type of bandwagoning, as do Italian and Rumanian alliance choices in World War I. By joining what they believed

---

39. David A. Baldwin, *Economic Statecraft* (Princeton, N.J.: Princeton University Press, 1985), p. 12.

40. For a discussion of "ordinary language" and conceptual definitions, see Felix E. Oppenheim, "The Language of Political Inquiry: Problems of Clarification," in Fred I. Greenstein and Nelson W. Polsby, eds., *Handbook of Political Science*, Vol. 1: *Political Science: Scope and Theory* (Reading, Mass.: Addison-Wesley, 1975), pp. 283–335, especially, pp. 307–309. See also Baldwin, *Economic Statecraft*, chap. 3.

41. *Webster's Ninth New Collegiate Dictionary* (Springfield, Mass.: Merriam-Webster, 1986), p. 204.

was the stronger side, each hoped to make territorial gains at the end of the fighting.[42]

Walt correctly points out that states bandwagon both out of fear of being despoiled and out of the desire to despoil others. But both motives for bandwagoning may be present even when there is no imbalance of threat, that is, when neither side is perceived as significantly more dangerous than the other.

Consider Walt's first motive for bandwagoning: to avoid attack.[43] For him, this means appeasing the most dangerous side. This need not be the case, however. Suppose war is coming, and a state caught in the crossfire must choose sides, but there is no imbalance of threat. Seeking shelter from the storm, the state may align with the stronger coalition because there is safety in numbers and its survival depends on its being on the winning side. Here, the source of greatest danger to the state does not come from one side or the other but from the consequences of being on the losing side, whichever that may be.[44] Thus power, not threat, drives the state's choice.

Walt's second motive for bandwagoning—to share the spoils of victory— is certainly correct, but it is not consistent with his claim that "balancing and bandwagoning are more accurately viewed as a response to threats" rather than power imbalances.[45] Security from Germany was not the primary motivation for Italy's declaration of war against France in 1940, or Japan's decision to bandwagon with the Axis later in the year. Similarly, Stalin's eagerness to fight Japan in 1945 was driven more by the prospect of gaining unearned spoils than a desire for greater security from the United States or Japan. The opportunistic aspect of bandwagoning is especially important for

---

42. Walt, "Alliance Formation and the Balance of World Power," pp. 7–8.
43. When the goal is to divert attack, bandwagoning is virtually indistinguishable from buck-passing behavior. Consider, for instance, the Nazi-Soviet pact. Were the Soviets bandwagoning to divert attack or passing the balancing buck to France and Britain? Are not these goals one and the same?
44. The Italians employed this strategy to survive the initial stage of the War of the Spanish Succession. Emperor Leopold of Austria opened the hostilities against the Franco-Spanish forces by attacking Italy, which he believed had been loyal to the Spanish regime of Louis XIV's grandson King Philip V, the seventeen-year-old Duke of Anjou. In truth, the "people of Italy had no particular love for either Bourbon or Hapsburg; they only wanted to be on the winning side." Thus, when the Imperial army led by Prince Eugene of Savoy smashed Louis's forces under the command of General Villeroi at Chiari, Italy jumped on the Austrian bandwagon. Bitter over the pro-Imperial behavior of the Italians, Louis wrote: "You should be cautious and risk nothing with people who know how to profit by everything and who entrench themselves before you." John B. Wolf, *Louis XIV* (New York: W.W. Norton, 1968), pp. 516 and 518.
45. Walt, "Alliance Formation," p. 9.

assessing the alliance choices of revisionist states. Walt identifies this motive but then overlooks it because the logic of his theory forces him to conflate the various forms of bandwagoning into one category: giving in to threats.

CASE SELECTION

To determine whether balancing or bandwagoning is the dominant tendency, Walt considers only cases involving a significant external threat.[46] Walt's causal scheme for alliance behavior may be diagrammed as in Table 1.

Holding constant the initial condition of a clear external threat in selecting his cases,[47] Walt finds strong evidence that balancing is the preferred response. But the theory thus only tests for balancing and appeasement-type bandwagoning among threatened states, while it ignores the behavior of unthreatened states that align for reasons other than security and that present the threats that drive Walt's theory. In short, Walt does not offer a theory of alliances so much as a theory of how states respond to external threats.

The hard case for confirming the balancing hypothesis is a situation in which a state is not directly menaced by a predatory state but decides to balance against it anyway to protect its long-term security interests. In Walt's words, "when examining the historical record, we should focus not only on what states did, but even more important, on what they preferred to do."[48] But his cases are not designed to do this.

When confronted by a dire and unmistakable threat to national survival, statesmen "can be said to act under external compulsion rather than

Table 1. Walt's Causal Scheme for Alliance Behavior.

Causal Variable	Dependent Variable
Significant External Threat (initial condition held constant) $\longrightarrow$	Balancing or Bandwagoning (hypothesized behavior)

46. Each of the states in the two regions he examines, the Middle East and Southwest Asia since World War II, have at all times confronted external threats.
47. The level of threat does vary in the cases Walt considers. But when the state in question does not perceive a significant external threat, it cannot engage in either balancing or bandwagoning, since, by Walt's own definitions, both behaviors are responses to the most dangerous threat to the state's survival. For this reason, cases that do not involve significant external threats cannot be used to test for balancing versus bandwagoning behavior, as Walt defines these terms.
48. Ibid., p. 55.

in accordance with their preferences."[49] This is the logic behind Arnold Wolfers's well-known metaphor of a house on fire: With rare exceptions, we expect individuals inside a burning house to feel an irresistible compulsion to run toward the exits.[50] Similarly, when statesmen are confronted by a dangerous imbalance of threat, we would expect them to "rush to enhance or maximize national power,"[51] especially under the conditions that Walt identifies as most favorable for balancing: when the threatened state is strong enough to affect the balance of power, allies are available, and the outcome of the war remains in doubt.

The problem is that the security literature has tended to overgeneralize Walt's findings by not specifying the conditions required for his theory to operate.[52] Thus, it is commonly asserted, without supporting evidence, that "balancing behavior is the prevalent tendency of states."[53] Walt himself declares, "as I have argued at length elsewhere, balancing behavior predominates in international politics. . . . These results expose the poverty of much of the justification for U.S. foreign policy since World War II."[54] Similarly, Stephen Van Evera claims that bandwagoning is a "rare event" and "history indicates that such cases are the exception, not the rule."[55] Yet Van Evera's own argument in support of the 1990–91 Persian Gulf deployment rests almost entirely on bandwagoning logic:

Had Iraq gone unchecked, its seizure of Kuwait might have foreshadowed its seizure of the rest of the Arab Gulf states (Saudi Arabia, the United Arab Emirates, Qatar, Bahrain, and Oman). . . . Syria, Jordan, Yemen, and Lebanon would then be vastly outmatched by Iraqi power, and might succumb to it.[56]

---

49. Arnold Wolfers, "The Actors in International Politics," in *Discord and Collaboration*, p. 13.
50. Ibid., pp. 13–16.
51. Ibid., p. 14.
52. For instance, Eric Labs defines bandwagoning as giving into threats and admits without explanation that he does not consider cases of "bandwagoning to share in the spoils of conquest." Labs, "Do Weak States Bandwagon?" *Security Studies*, Vol. 1, No. 3 (Spring 1992), p. 409. Consequently, Labs's claim that bandwagoning places last among small states' choices is misleading. He arrives at this conclusion by substituting "capitulation" for "bandwagoning" and by focusing on the alliance choices of only small states seeking to maintain what they have, excluding unthreatened, small states with irredenta that choose to align for profit.
53. Van Evera, "Primed for Peace," p. 36.
54. Walt, "The Case for Finite Containment," p. 35.
55. Van Evera, "Primed for Peace," pp. 36–37. Also see Van Evera, "The Cult of the Offensive and the Origins of the First World War," *International Security*, Vol. 9, No. 1 (Summer 1984), p. 62.
56. Stephen Van Evera, "American Intervention in the Third World: Less Would Be Better," *Security Studies*, Vol. 1, No. 1 (Autumn 1991), pp. 12 and 14.

In another reference to bandwagoning, Van Evera says "militaries exaggerate the tendency of other states to give in to threats—to 'bandwagon' with the threat instead of 'balancing' against it. Such myths bolster the military's arguments for larger forces by reinforcing claims that a bigger force can be used to make diplomatic gains."[57] Focusing exclusively on the threatened target of the military buildup, Van Evera does not consider how this signal affects other unthreatened states that may see themselves as beneficiaries of the larger military force. Historically, military buildups have sometimes served to encourage untargeted states to bandwagon with the "bigger force" for profit or for protection from other more threatening states. Dissatisfied states or those states that lack internal strength and stability tend to gravitate away from declining powers and towards a rising power.[58]

THE STATUS-QUO BIAS

At bottom, balance-of-threat theory suffers from a problem that plagues all contemporary realist theory: it views the world solely through the lens of a satisfied, status-quo state.[59] Unlike traditional realists such as E.H. Carr and Hans Morgenthau, modern realists typically assume that states are willing to pay high costs and take great risks to protect the values they possess, but will only pay a small price and take low risks to improve their position in the system. Waltz writes:

In anarchy, security is the highest end. Only if survival is assured can states safely seek such other goals as tranquility, profit, and power. Because power is a means and not an end, states prefer to join the weaker of two

---

57. Van Evera, "Primed for Peace," p. 20.
58. Martin Wight, *Power Politics*, edited by Hedley Bull and Carsten Holbraad (New York: Holmes and Meier, 1978), p. 163. As Napoleonic France grew in power, it gained alliances with Spain, Russia, Austria, and Prussia; likewise, the expansion of Nazi Germany's military power secured for Hitler pacts with Poland, Rumania, Italy, Hungary, Japan, and Russia, among others.
59. In contrast, postwar realists invariably distinguished two types of states: Morgenthau called them imperialistic and status-quo powers; Schuman employed the terms satiated and unsatiated powers; Kissinger referred to revolutionary and status-quo states; Carr distinguished satisfied from dissatisfied Powers; Johannes Mattern, among other geopoliticians, divided the world into "have" and "have-nots," and Wolfers referred to status-quo and revisionist states. See Hans J. Morgenthau, *Politics Among Nations: The Struggle for Power and Peace* (New York: Alfred A. Knopf, 1948), esp. chaps. 2, 3, 9, 10, and p. 156; Frederick L. Schuman, *International Politics: The Destiny of the Western State System*, 4th ed. (New York: McGraw-Hill, 1948), pp. 377–380; Edward Hallett Carr, *The Twenty Years' Crisis: 1919–1939: An Introduction to the Study of International Relations* (New York: Harper & Row, 1946); Henry A. Kissinger, *A World Restored: Castlereagh, Metternich, and the Problem of Peace, 1812–22* (Boston: Houghton Mifflin, 1957); Johannes Mattern, *Geopolitics: Doctrine of National Self-Sufficiency and Empire* (Baltimore, Md.: The Johns Hopkins University Press, 1942); Wolfers, "The Balance of Power in Theory and Practice," pp. 125–126.

coalitions. . . . If states wished to maximize power, they would join the stronger side . . . this does not happen because balancing, not bandwagoning, is the behavior induced by the system. The first concern of states is not to maximize power but to maintain their positions in the system.[60]

Waltz is right to say that states seeking to maximize their power will bandwagon, not balance. But it is simply not true that the first concern of *all* states is security.[61] Here, he takes a distinctly status-quo perspective.[62] Only in reference to satisfied countries can it be said that the primary goal is "to maintain their positions in the system."[63] In contrast, classical realists described the "true interests" of states as "a continuous striving for greater power and expansion." For them, the goal of diplomacy was "to evaluate

---

60. Waltz, *Theory of International Politics*, p. 126.
61. In this regard, Joseph M. Grieco has coined the term "defensive positionality," which essentially posits that the primary goal of states is to prevent relative losses. He argues that "it is a defensively positional concern that partners might do better—not an offensively oriented interest in doing better oneself—that drives the relative-gains problem for cooperation." Grieco, "The Relative-Gains Problem for International Cooperation," *American Political Science Review*, Vol. 87, No. 3 (September 1993), p. 742 (emphasis in original). See also Grieco, *Cooperation Among Nations: Europe, America, and Non-Tariff Barriers to Trade* (Ithaca, N.Y.: Cornell University Press, 1990); and Grieco, "Anarchy and the Limits of Cooperation: A Realist Critique of the Newest Liberal Institutionalism," *International Organization*, Vol. 42, No. 3 (Summer 1988), p. 498. Similarly, Robert Gilpin says international competition "stimulates, and may compel, a state to increase its power; at the least, it necessitates that the prudent state prevent relative increase in the powers of competitor states." Gilpin, *War and Change in World Politics* (Cambridge: Cambridge University Press, 1981), pp. 87–88.
62. For a more recent example of neorealism's status-quo bias, see Thomas J. Christensen and Jack Snyder, "Chain Gangs and Passed Bucks: Predicting Alliance Patterns in Multipolarity," *International Organization*, Vol. 44, No. 2 (Spring 1990), pp. 137–168. By combining two "top-shelf" realist theories, Christensen and Snyder purport to explain alliance patterns in Europe prior to World Wars I and II. Absent from their discussion, however, are the alliance choices of the members of the revisionist coalitions: Austria-Hungary and Turkey prior to World War I, and Italy and Japan prior to World War II. Moreover, they examine Hitler's strategy of piecemeal aggression but do not mention Germany's alliance choices.
63. Waltz admits that states may seek profit and power, but he says that they must pursue them "safely" and only "if survival is assured." This view of state preferences is aptly described by Arthur Stein: "States that place preeminent weight on security and do not gamble with it regardless of temptation to do so may, for example, act to maximize assured security rather than expected payoffs. Such states would undertake attractive gambles only when assured of survival." Arthur A. Stein, *Why Nations Cooperate: Circumstance and Choice in International Relations* (Ithaca, N.Y.: Cornell University Press, 1990), p. 90. In rational-choice terminology, this is known as lexicographic preferences: actors have a hierarchy of objectives and maximize in sequence rather than making trade-offs. See Charles W. Ostrom, Jr., "Balance of Power and the Maintenance of 'Balance': A Rational-Choice Model With Lexical Preferences," in Dina A. Zinnes and John V. Gillespie, eds., *Mathematical Models in International Relations* (New York: Praeger, 1976), pp. 318–332.

correctly the interplay of opposing forces and interests and to create a constellation favorable to conquest and expansion."[64]

This aside, preventing relative losses in power and prestige is sound advice
for satisfied states that seek, above all, to keep what they have. But staying
in place is not the primary goal of revisionist states. They want to increase,
not just preserve, their core values and to improve their position in the
system. These goals cannot be achieved simply by ensuring that everyone
else does not gain relative to them. They must gain relative to others. Arnold
Wolfers recognized this when he wrote: "[Revisionist states] can accept balanced power only with utter resignation since they know that only in quite
exceptional cases can the established order be seriously modified without
the threat of force so preponderant that it will overcome the resistance of
the opposing side."[65]

Calling for a "new order," dissatisfied states are attracted to expanding
revisionist powers. Waltz overlooks such states when he asserts: "Secondary
states, if they are free to choose, flock to the weaker side; for it is the stronger
side that threatens them. On the weaker side they are both more appreciated
and safer."[66] That states are safer on the weaker side is a curious claim. Are
they also more appreciated by the weaker side? Consider, for instance, the
case of Italy in 1936. Mussolini believed that he would be more appreciated
and politically autonomous as Hitler's satellite than as a member of the
weaker Anglo-French coalition. Unlike Britain and France, Nazi Germany
supported Mussolini's goal of turning the Mediterranean into an "Italian
Lake."[67] Moreover, Mussolini's decision to hitch Italy's wagon to the rising

---

64. Felix Gilbert, *To the Farewell Address: Ideas of Early American Foreign Policy* (Princeton, N.J.:
Princeton University Press, 1961), pp. 95–96. Of contemporary realists, Fareed Zakaria, Samuel
P. Huntington, and John J. Mearsheimer come closest in their views of state interest to that of
eighteenth-century power politics. See Zakaria, "Realism and Domestic Politics: A Review
Essay," *International Security*, Vol. 17, No. 1 (Summer 1992), pp. 177–198; Huntington, "Why
International Primacy Matters," *International Security*, Vol. 17, No. 4 (Spring 1993), pp. 68–83;
and Mearsheimer, "Back to the Future: Instability in Europe After the Cold War," *International
Security*, Vol. 15, No. 1 (Summer 1990), p. 12.
65. Wolfers, "The Balance of Power," p. 126.
66. Waltz, *Theory of International Politics*, p. 127. I am grateful to Michael Desch for drawing my
attention to this point. For more on balancing behavior and the goal of autonomy, see Barry R.
Posen, *The Sources of Military Doctrine: France, Britain, and Germany Between the World Wars* (Ithaca,
N.Y.: Cornell University Press, 1984), p. 17; Posen, "Nationalism, the Mass Army, and Military
Power," *International Security*, Vol. 18, No. 2 (Fall 1993), p. 82; Kenneth N. Waltz, "The Emerging
Structure of International Politics," *International Security*, Vol. 18, No. 2 (Fall 1993), p. 74.
67. "Any future modifications of the Mediterranean balance of power," Hitler told Ciano in

Nazi star was motivated by his raw Social-Darwinist predilections. As Alan Cassels asserts, "Fascists worshipped strength, and what Mussolini called a fascist foreign policy meant in effect siding with the strongest power."[68]

In the end, Italy paid a high price for siding with Germany. This did not prove to be the safer choice, but it was not because Italy joined the stronger coalition, as Waltz's logic would have us believe. To the contrary, Italy was crushed because, after the United States actively entered the war, it was on the weaker side.

The general point is that most states, even of the Great-Power variety, must ultimately serve someone; only top dogs can expect otherwise. And because members of military alliances always sacrifice some foreign-policy autonomy, the most important determinant of alignment decisions is the compatibility of political goals, not imbalances of power or threat.[69] Satisfied powers will join the status-quo coalition, even when it is the stronger side; dissatisfied powers, motivated by profit more than security, will bandwagon with an ascending revisionist state.

Bandwagoning for Rewards

As mentioned, Walt associates bandwagoning with giving in to threats, unequal exchange favoring the dominant power, acceptance of illegitimate actions by the stronger ally, and involuntary compliance. This view of the concept illustrates the tendency among political scientists to ignore the role of positive inducements in the exercise of power. Yet, positive sanctions are the most effective means to induce bandwagoning behavior. States, like delegates at party conventions, are lured to the winning side by the promise

---

1936, "must be in Italy's favour." Count Galeazzo Ciano, *Ciano's Diplomatic Papers*, edited by Malcolm Muggeridge (London: Odhams Press, 1948), p. 57.

68. Alan Cassels, "Switching Partners: Italy in A.J.P. Taylor's *Origins of the Second World War*," in Gordon Martel, ed., *"The Origins of the Second World War" Reconsidered: The A.J.P. Taylor Debate After Twenty-Five Years* (Boston: Allen & Unwin, 1986), p. 82.

69. For example, in 1940, the British ambassador, Sir Stafford Cripps, was sent to Moscow to persuade Stalin that German expansion in Western Europe endangered Russia as well as Britain. "'Therefore both countries,' he argued, 'ought to agree on a common policy of self-protection against Germany and on the re-establishment of the European balance of power.' Stalin replied that he did not see any danger of Europe being engulfed by Germany. 'The so-called European balance of power,' he said, 'had hitherto oppressed not only Germany but also the Soviet Union. Therefore the Soviet Union would take all measures to prevent the re-establishment of the old balance of power in Europe.'" Wight, "The Balance of Power," p. 155.

of future rewards.[70] By contrast, relying on force to coerce states to band-wagon involuntarily often backfires for the dominant partner. Seeking revenge, the unwilling bandwagoner becomes a treacherous ally that will bolt from the alliance the first chance it gets.

During the Italian Wars of 1494 to 1517, for instance, Venice "recklessly chang[ed] over to the side of the French, lured by the prospect of gaining more territory on the Italian mainland,"[71] namely, half of Lombardy. Later, by the secret Treaty of Granada of November 11, 1500, Spain's Ferdinand of Aragon bandwagoned with Louis XII of France to rob the king of Naples of his kingdom.[72] Then, in 1508, the allies of the League of Cambrai—France, Spain, and Austria—bandwagoned to cut up the Venetian territories.[73] Finally, in 1513, Henry VIII of England bandwagoned with the Holy League against the weaker Franco-Venetian side to gain provinces in Northern France.[74]

During the period 1667–79, Louis XIV's France achieved hegemonic status in Europe largely by promising rewards to attract bandwagoners. For example, in the War of Devolution (1667–68), Emperor Leopold I of the Austrian Hapsburgs bandwagoned with France to partition Spain. By the secret Franco-Austrian treaty of 1668, the French Bourbons were to inherit Spanish Navarre, the Southern Netherlands, Franche-Comté, Naples and Sicily, and

---

70. "Delegates wish to be on bandwagons because support of the nominee at the convention will be a basic criterion for the later distribution of Presidential favors and patronage." Gerald Pomper, *Nominating the President: The Politics of Convention Choice* (Evanston, Ill.: Northwestern University Press, 1963), p. 144.
71. R.B. Mowat, *A History of European Diplomacy, 1451–1789* (New York: Longmans, Green and Co., 1928), p. 28.
72. Ibid., p. 31; Garrett Mattingly, *Renaissance Diplomacy* (Boston: Houghton Mifflin, 1955), pp. 165–166. After capturing Naples, Spain and France quarreled over the spoils, unleashing the Franco-Spanish wars for Italy that lasted with only occasional breaks for nearly sixty years.
73. "All princes who had any claims upon Venice, or rather upon its lands and possessions, were to be invited to join in the operations. The frontiers of Milan and Naples were to be readjusted in favour of Louis and Ferdinand, those of the Empire and Austria in favour of Maximilian, and those of the States of the Church in favour of the Pope." Mowat, *History of European Diplomacy*, pp. 33–34. For the precise territorial arrangements contained in the secret Treaty of Blois, see Francesco Guicciardini, *The History of Italy*, trans. and ed. by Sidney Alexander (New York: Macmillan, [1561] 1969), book 8, pp. 191–207, esp. p. 196.
74. Mowat, *European Diplomacy*, p. 39; Guicciardini, *The History of Italy*, Books 10 and 11, especially pp. 243 and 276. In the partitions of the Milanese between France and Venice, Naples between France and Spain, and Venice among the allies of the League of Cambrai, the governing principle was "the biggest dog gets the meatiest bone, and others help themselves in the order of size." Mattingly, *Renaissance Diplomacy*, p. 163. Dismembering the victim's territory according to the relative size of the conquerers supports classical realism's stress on power as the determining factor in international relations, but it contradicts the "defensive positionalist" tenet of avoiding gains gaps for security reasons.

the Philippines, in exchange for which Louis ceded his rights to the Spanish Crown.[75]

In preparation for the Dutch War (1672–79), Louis offered rewards to gain the support of virtually all the powers that had previously opposed him. Charles II of England signed the June 1670 Treaty of Dover, with plans for a joint Anglo-French attack against the Dutch in 1672, in exchange for Louis's agreement to provide England subsidies of £225,000 a year and territorial gains around the Scheldt estuary. In April\1672, Sweden, too, abandoned what was left of the Triple Alliance and jumped on the French bandwagon against the Dutch. Between 1670 and 1672, Louis offered the payment of French subsidies to gain alliances with many of the former members of the defunct League of the Rhine, including the Rhenish archbishop-electors, Saxony, the Palatinate, Bavaria, the Archbishop-Elector of Cologne, and the Bishop of Münster. And while he did not ally with France, Leopold I signed a neutrality agreement in November 1671.[76]

The peace of Nijmegen that ended the Dutch War in 1679 proved that Louis could take on all his enemies and still dictate the peace. A contemporary statesman declared: "France has already become the arbiter of Europe . . . , henceforth no prince will find security or profit except with the friendship and alliance of the King of France."[77]

Like his predecessor, Napoleon Bonaparte used territorial rewards and spectacular military victories to attract bandwagoners. For example, in creating the Confederation of the Rhine (1806) as a counterweight to Prussia and Austria, Napoleon strengthened Bavaria, Baden, Hesse-Darmstadt, and Württemberg at the expense of the tiny German states. Lured by the promise of aggrandizement, these middle-sized German states voluntarily climbed aboard Napoleon's bandwagon.[78]

75. David Kaiser, *Politics and War: European Conflict from Philip II to Hitler* (Cambridge, Mass.: Harvard University Press, 1990), pp. 149 and 172. Derek McKay and H.M. Scott, *The Rise of the Great Powers, 1648–1815* (London: Longman, 1983), pp. 14–23.

76. McKay and Scott, *The Rise of the Great Powers*, pp. 23–35.

77. Quoted in ibid., p. 36. For a detailed account of Louis's preparations for the Dutch War, see Paul G. Sonnino, *Louis XIV and the Origins of the Dutch War* (New York: Cambridge University Press, 1988).

78. David G. Chandler, *The Campaigns of Napoleon* (New York: Macmillan, 1966), pp. 449–450; Mowat, *The Diplomacy of Napoleon*, chap. 16. In Article 1 of the Franco-Bavarian treaty of alliance (August 24, 1805), Napoleon pledged "to seize all occasions which present themselves to augment the power and splendour of the House of Bavaria," in return for support by 20,000 Bavarian troops. See ibid., p. 152. Likewise, greed not security, Mowat claims, animated Baden's decision to bandwagon with France: "The Elector of Baden, in the preamble of the treaty, gives

Similarly, Alexander I bandwagoned with the French Empire in 1807, when Napoleon not only used his decisive victory over the tsar's army at Friedland to force an alliance, but coupled it with the reward of the Vistula as the new expanded frontier of Russia. Napoleon also offered Russia control over European Turkey and Finland, and he encouraged further Russian conquests in Asia. In exchange, the tsar was asked to join the Continental System against England, use his influence to compel Denmark and Sweden to follow suit, and send the Russian Navy to aid France in the capture of Gibraltar.[79] As the historian R.B. Mowat put it: "Thus a prospect was held out to the defeated autocrat not merely of keeping what he possessed, but actually of gaining more territory: a strange sequel to the *débâcle* of Russia at Friedland!"[80]

Saying, "I will be your second against England," Alexander quickly accepted the proffered alliance with France, which "put the Continent of Europe at the disposal of the two Powers of France and Russia, with, however, the balance distinctly in favour of France."[81] During the Franco-Austrian war of 1809, Alexander proved his loyalty to Napoleon by "fail[ing] to avail himself of the opportunity to 'hold the balance' between the antagonists, with the result that France once more defeated Austria, added more territory to her already bulging empire, and threw the European system still further out of balance."[82] The defeated Austrian state was shorn of most of its possessions in Italy, Illyria, and Germany.

Napoleon's amiability toward Russia at Tilsit did not carry over to Prussia. After crushing the Prussian army at Jena, Napoleon was determined to exact his pound of flesh from King William Frederick for inciting war against him. By the Prussian Treaty of Tilsit, William suffered the humiliating loss of one-third of his territory,[83] nearly half of his subjects and, most stinging of all,

---

the curious reason for making it, that 'the renewal of hostilities threatened the independence of the States of the German Empire'; therefore he joined with that Empire's enemy. The real reason is . . . that the Elector of Baden, through the support of France in 1802–03, had gained greatly in territory." Ibid., p. 154.

79. Chandler, *The Campaigns of Napoleon*, p. 588; Mowat, *The Diplomacy of Napoleon*, chap. 18; Georges Lefebvre, *Napoleon: From 18 Brumaire to Tilsit, 1799–1807*, trans. Henry F. Stockhold (New York: Columbia University Press, 1969), pp. 272–275.

80. Mowat, *The Diplomacy of Napoleon*, p. 176.

81. Ibid., pp. 177, 182.

82. Edward Vose Gulick, *Europe's Classical Balance of Power: A Case History of the Theory and Practice of One of the Great Concepts of European Statecraft* (New York: W.W. Norton, 1955), p. 106.

83. Virtually all of Prussia's possessions west of the Elbe were torn away and incorporated into the new Kingdom of Westphalia or merged into a Grand Duchy of Warsaw ruled by the King of Saxony.

the occupation of French garrisons on Prussian soil pending full payment of a war indemnity.[84]

Ironically, it was the Prussian foreign minister, Karl von Hardenberg, who, at Tilsit, had advised Alexander "to offer Napoleon a three-cornered alliance whose purpose would be to fight England and to redraw the map of Europe." Agreeing in principle to Hardenberg's plan, the tsar did his best to defend his Prussian ally in his private meetings with the French emperor, but to no avail. Napoleon held all of Prussia by right of conquest and would not consider admitting Frederick William as a third party.[85]

Prussia and Austria got their revenge in June of 1813, when they joined England and Russia to form the Fourth Coalition that defeated France. But the victory of the Allies over the would-be hegemon was not as inevitable as the "balancing predominates" view would have us believe. The Allied coalition, whose forces doubled those of France by February of 1814, would never have come together in the first place, much less held together, had Napoleon not attacked his own allies and neutrals. By repeatedly thwarting the bandwagoning strategies of Russia, Prussia, Spain, and Austria, Napoleon finally succeeded where the British had failed in creating a coalition with the strength and resolve to defeat Imperial France.[86]

Why States Bandwagon

Bandwagoning dynamics move the system in the direction of change. Like a ball rolling down an incline, initial success generates further success, not greater resistance. In the language of systems theory, bandwagoning is a form of positive feedback. By contrast, the purpose of balancing behavior is

---

84. Chandler, *The Campaigns of Napoleon*, pp. 589ff; Lefebvre, *Napoleon*, pp. 273–274; Mowat, *The Diplomacy of Napoleon*, pp. 175–187. In practice, the indemnity, which was of an undefined amount, meant that Napoleon could defer the evacuation forever by imposing payments beyond Prussia's capacity. Mowat writes: "Simple, dishonest, cynical, Napoleon's method of veiled annexation was put in practice, and French troops remained in Prussia until driven out by force in 1813." Ibid., p. 186.
85. Lefebvre, *Napoleon*, p. 272.
86. For more on this point, see Paul W. Schroeder, "Napoleon's Foreign Policy: A Criminal Enterprise," *Journal of Military History*, Vol. 54, No. 2 (April 1990), pp. 147–162; and Schroeder, "The Collapse of the Second Coalition," *Journal of Modern History*, Vol. 59 (1987), pp. 244–290. Holland, Italy, and the maritime states of Scandinavia, Denmark, and Portugal were similarly coerced into bandwagoning with the French Empire.

to prevent systemic disequilibrium or, when deterrence fails, to restore the balance. Balancing is a form of negative feedback.[87]

This is not to suggest that bandwagoning effects are always undesirable; this depends on the nature of the existing order. If it is characterized by conflict, bandwagoning behavior may enhance the prospects for a more durable peace. In this regard, the bandwagon's *raison d'être* also matters. "Jackal" bandwagoning, with a rising expansionist state or a coalition that seeks to overthrow the status quo, decreases system stability. Conversely, "piling on" bandwagoning with the stronger status-quo coalition enhances system stability. Other forms of bandwagoning may have varying effects on system stability. What all these forms of bandwagoning have in common, however, is that they are motivated by the prospect of making gains. Herein lies the fundamental difference between bandwagoning and balancing. Balancing is an extremely costly activity that most states would rather not engage in, but sometimes must to survive and protect their values. Bandwagoning rarely involves costs and is typically done in the expectation of gain. This is why bandwagoning is more common, I believe, than Walt and Waltz suggest.

JACKAL BANDWAGONING

Just as the lion attracts jackals, a powerful revisionist state or coalition attracts opportunistic revisionist powers.[88] The goal of "jackal bandwagoning" is profit. Specifically, revisionist states bandwagon to share in the spoils of victory.[89] Because unlimited-aims revisionist powers cannot bandwagon (they *are* the bandwagon), offensive bandwagoning is done exclusively by lesser aggressors, which I call limited-aims revisionist states. Typically, the lesser aggressor reaches an agreement with the unlimited-aims revisionist leader

---

87. See Robert Jervis, "Systems Theory and Diplomatic History," in Paul Gordon Lauren, ed., *Diplomacy: New Approaches in History, Theory, and Policy* (New York: Free Press, 1979), pp. 220–222; Jervis, "Domino Beliefs and Strategic Behavior," in Jervis and Snyder, *Dominoes and Bandwagons*, pp. 22–23; Lisa L. Martin, "Coalition Dynamics: Bandwagoning in International Politics," paper presented at Columbia University, Seminar on International Political Economy, October, 29, 1993.

88. "In a style less grave than that of history, I should perhaps compare the emperor Alexius to the jackal, who is said to follow the steps, and to devour the leavings, of the lion. Whatever had been his fears and toils in the passage of the first crusade, they were amply recompensed by the subsequent benefits which he derived from the exploits of the Franks." Edward Gibbon, *The History of the Decline and Fall of the Roman Empire*, Vol. 6 (New York: Macmillan, 1914), p. 335.

89. For this motivation for bandwagoning, see Larson, "Bandwagon Images," pp. 85–87; Jervis, "Systems Theory," p. 220; and Walt, "Alliance Formation," p. 8. None of these authors specifically refer to jackal behavior.

on spheres of influence, in exchange for which the junior partner supports the revisionist leader in its expansionist aims.

Aside from the desire to acquire additional territory, the motivation for jackal bandwagoning may also be security from the lion itself. As Roy Douglas remarks, "Stalin merits Churchill's famous epithet, 'Hitler's jackal' as richly as does Mussolini, to whom it was applied. Pickings from the lion's kill were succulent and satisfying for lesser beasts; but they also afforded these creatures strength to resist the greater predator should he later turn his attentions to them."[90]

Sometimes the revisionist leader is stronger than the opposing status-quo coalition. In such cases, the revisionist leader does not require the active assistance of the junior partner. Instead, it seeks to prevent or block the formation of a powerful status-quo coalition.[91] When blocking is the goal, the revisionist leader often allows the limited-aims revisionist state to gain unearned spoils in exchange for a pledge not to join the adversarial coalition. Because the jackal is a scavenger and not a true predator, this type of bandwagoning is a form of predatory buck-passing: the jackal seeks to ride free on the offensive efforts of others.

Exemplifying this strategy, Hitler encouraged Italy, the Soviet Union, Japan, Hungary, and Bulgaria to feed on the pickings of the Nazi lion's kill, in order to block the formation of a dangerous rival coalition.[92] In this way, the Reich became master of Europe by 1941. But just as Napoleon had gratuitously destroyed the source of his own success by attacking his allies, Hitler brought Germany to ruin by declaring war against his Soviet ally and the United States, "two World powers who asked only to be left alone."[93] In so

---

90. Roy Douglas, *New Alliances, 1940–41* (London: Macmillan, 1982), p. 40. Walt makes this point in "Alliance Formation," p. 8.
91. See George Liska, *Nations in Alliance: The Limits of Interdependence* (Baltimore, Md.: The Johns Hopkins University Press, 1962), p. 33.
92. For example, Mussolini and Hitler successfully played on Hungary's and Bulgaria's revisionist aspirations to lure these states into the Axis camp. As part of the Munich agreement of September 30, 1938, a German-Italian court of arbitration pressured the Czech government to grant a broad strip of southern Slovakia and Ruthenia to Hungary. Then, when the Germans carved up the rest of Czechoslovakia in March 1939, Hitler, in a deliberate attempt to gain further favor with the Hungarian government, ceded the remainder of Ruthenia (Carpatho-Ukraine) to Hungary. In exchange for these territorial rewards, Hungary pledged its unshakable support for the Nazi cause, and its "foreign policy was brought into line with that of the Reich. On February 24, 1939, Hungary joined the Anti-Comintern Pact, on April 11 it left the League of Nations." Norman Rich, *Hitler's War Aims: Ideology, the Nazi State, and the Course of Expansion* (London: W.W. Norton, 1973), p. 184.
93. A.J.P. Taylor, *The Origins of the Second World War* (New York: Atheneum, 1961), p. 278.

doing, the Führer forced into creation the only coalition powerful enough to prevent a German victory in Europe.

PILING ON

"Piling-on bandwagoning" occurs when the outcome of a war has already been determined. States typically bandwagon with the victor to claim an unearned share of the spoils. When this is the motive, piling on is simply jackal bandwagoning that takes place at the end of wars. Contrariwise, states may pile on because they fear the victors will punish them if they do not actively side against the losers. Whatever the motivation, either opportunity or fear, piling on is a form of predatory buck-passing with regard to the winning coalition.

Historically, most major wars have ended with piling-on behavior. In the War of the Spanish Succession, for instance, Louis XIV watched his waning hopes for victory vanish when two of his staunchest allies, Portugal and the Duke of Savoy, deserted the Franco-Spanish coalition and bandwagoned with the Grand Alliance to make gains at Spain's expense.[94] The Napoleonic Wars ended when Sweden, Austria, Spain, and certain German and Italian states sided with Prussia, Britain, and Russia at the precise moment that Napoleon's defeat appeared certain.[95]

During the First World War, Japan bandwagoned with the Entente powers because it coveted German possessions in Asia, while China bandwagoned to gain Anglo-French protection from Japan and Imperial Russia. For its part Italy, expecting to gain unearned spoils at Austria's expense, declared war against its former friends in May of 1915.[96] In 1916, Russia's decisive victory over Austria persuaded Rumania to enter the war on the Allied side.

In World War II, the Soviets wanted a fight to the finish with Japan to get in on the kill and thereby share in occupying Japan. In contrast, Turkey wanted to remain neutral but was coerced by the Allies into declaring war against Germany and Japan on February 23, 1945. Ankara did so because of the Allied decision to exclude from the organizing conference for the United

---

94. Wolf, *Louis XIV*, pp. 526–529. For similar reasons, on August 16, 1703, Sweden also acceded to the Grand Alliance. Thus, by October of 1703, "France was left with no allies except Spain, and the Electorates of Cologne and Bavaria . . .; and when one by one the other satellites of Louis dropped off, in 1702 and 1703, Bavaria alone kept to her engagements." Mowat, *A History of European Diplomacy*, p. 166.
95. Gulick, *Europe's Classical Balance of Power*, p. 88.
96. The Allies were not impressed, however, and awarded Italy a loser's share at Versailles.

Nations any country that had not entered the war against the Axis by March 1, 1945. More recently, the overwhelmingly superior coalition arrayed against Iraq in the Gulf War exemplifies piling-on bandwagoning behavior.

WAVE OF THE FUTURE

States may bandwagon with the stronger side because they believe it represents the "wave of the future." During the Cold War era, for example, many less-developed countries viewed communism in this way. Consequently, they did not have to be coerced or bribed to join the Sino-Soviet bloc; they did so voluntarily. Third World elites as well as the masses were attracted to communism for rational reasons: they thought they could profit by it, as had the Chinese and the Soviets. This type of bandwagoning most concerned George Kennan in 1947, as he understood that "a given proportion of the adherents to the [communist] movement are drawn to it . . . primarily by the belief that it is the coming thing, the movement of the future . . . and that those who hope to survive—let alone to thrive—in the coming days will be those who have the foresight to climb on the bandwagon when it was still the movement of the future."[97] And indeed, the Soviet success with Sputnik caused more dominoes to fall than Soviet military pressure ever could.

Likewise, states across the globe have recently abandoned communism in favor of the newest wave of the future, liberal democracy. Van Evera points out that "the chain of anti-communist upheavals in Eastern Europe during 1989" is "the only widespread domino effect on record."[98] But the definition of bandwagoning as "giving in to threats," which he endorses, does not cover this voluntary global epidemic. The same can be said about the massive decolonization of the 1950s and 1960s. Both trends are instances of benign positive feedback; that is, they altered the course of international politics in a more stabilizing direction.

Wave-of-the-future bandwagoning is typically induced by charismatic leaders and dynamic ideologies, especially when buoyed by massive propaganda

---

97. Quoted in Jervis, "Domino Beliefs," p. 33.
98. Stephen Van Evera, "Why Europe Matters, Why the Third World Doesn't: American Grand Strategy After the Cold War," *The Journal of Strategic Studies*, Vol. 13, No. 2 (June 1990), p. 23. On this latest domino effect, see Harvey Starr, "Democratic Dominoes: Diffusion Approaches to the Spread of Democracy in the International System," *Journal of Conflict Resolution*, Vol. 35, No. 2 (June 1991), pp. 356–381; Timur Kuran, "Now Out of Never: The Element of Surprise in the East European Revolution of 1989," *World Politics*, Vol. 44, No. 1 (October 1991), pp. 7–48.

campaigns and demonstrations of superiority on the battlefield. Here, the bandwagon becomes a "mass orgy feeling that sweeps with the fervor of a religious revival."[99] For example, Germany's stunning military victories in May of 1940 convinced Japan to reverse its neutralist policy and bandwagon with the Axis. Hosoya writes:

The rising prestige of Germany in the eyes of the Japanese resulted in resurrecting pro-Nazi sentiment from its demise following the conclusion of the Nonaggression Pact. This change in public opinion naturally affected the balance of power between the Anglo-American and Axis factions in Japan. Second, the existence of the French and Dutch colonies in Indochina and the East Indies now swam into the ken of the Japanese people, and a mood to seize the opportunity to advance into Southeast Asia spread to all strata of society.[100]

In this case, the Japanese public's psychological desire to support a winner dovetailed with their more rational interest in jackal opportunism. Both goals were captured by Japan's catch-phrase of the day, "Don't miss the bus."[101]

In its rarest form, wave-of-the-future bandwagoning may be the result of leaders and their publics simply enjoying "the feeling of 'going with the winner'—even a winner about whose substantive qualities they have no illusions."[102] Recognizing this effect, Machiavelli pointed to the results of the Venetians having foolishly invited King Louis "to plant his foot in Italy":

The king, then, having acquired Lombardy, immediately won back the reputation lost by Charles. Genoa yielded, the Florentines became his friends, the Marquis of Mantua, the Dukes of Ferrara and Bentivogli, the Lady of Forli, the Lords of Faenza, Pesaro, Rimini, Camerino, and Piombino, the inhabitants of Lucca, of Pisa, and of Siena, all approached him with offers of friendship. The Venetians might then have seen the effects of their te-

---

99. Ralph G. Martin, *Ballots and Bandwagons* (Chicago: Rand McNally, 1964), p. 444. Also see Steven J. Brams, *The Presidential Election Game* (New Haven, Conn.: Yale University Press, 1978), p. 43.
100. Hosoya Chihiro, "The Tripartite Pact, 1939–1940," in James William Morley, ed., *Deterrent Diplomacy: Japan, Germany, and the USSR, 1935–1940* (New York: Columbia University Press, 1976), p. 206.
101. Sumio Hatano and Sadao Asada, "The Japanese Decision to Move South (1939–1941)," in Robert Boyce and Esmonde M. Robertson, eds., *Paths to War: New Essays on the Origins of the Second World War* (New York: St. Martin's Press, 1989), p. 387; Michael A. Barnhart, *Japan Prepares for Total War: The Search for Economic Security, 1919–1941* (Ithaca, N.Y.: Cornell University Press, 1987), p. 158; Hosoya "The Tripartite Pact," p. 207.
102. Bartels, *Presidential Primaries*, pp. 111–112.

merity, how to gain a few cities in Lombardy they had made the king ruler over two-thirds of Italy.[103]

Other examples of supporting-the-winner bandwagoning include the near-unanimous enthusiasm with which the southern German states joined Prussia after its defeat of France in 1871, and the Austrians' embrace of the *Anschluss* with Germany in 1938.

THE CONTAGION OR DOMINO EFFECT

Throughout the Cold War era, the metaphors of "spreading desease" and "falling dominoes" were used interchangeably by U.S. officials to support the policy of containing communism. The Truman administration employed the contagion metaphor to justify intervening in Greece in 1947: "Like apples in a barrel infected by one rotten one, the corruption of Greece would infect Iran and all to the East. It would also carry infection to Africa through Asia Minor and Egypt, to Europe and France."[104] The same argument became known as the "domino theory" when President Eisenhower used the metaphor in reference to Southeast Asia: "You have a row of dominoes set up, you knock over the first one, and what will happen to the last one is the certainty that it will go over very quickly. So you could have a beginning of a disintegration that would have the most profound influences."[105] More recently, President Reagan argued that if we "ignore the malignancy in Managua," it will "spread and become a mortal threat to the entire New World."[106]

Whether the metaphor is infection or falling dominoes, the underlying dynamic is the same. In each case, the bandwagon is set in motion by an external force, which touches off a chain reaction, fueling the bandwagon at ever-greater speeds. Thus, the domino theory posits revolutions as "essen-

---

103. Niccolò Machiavelli, *The Prince and The Discourses* (New York: Random House, 1950), p. 12.
104. Dean Acheson, *Present at the Creation* (New York: W.W. Norton, 1969), p. 219. Also quoted in Jerome Slater, "Dominos in Central America: Will They Fall? Does It Matter?" *International Security*, Vol. 12, No. 2 (Fall 1987), p. 106. Studies in American politics also use the metaphor of spreading disease to describe bandwagoning effects among voters. See Larry M. Bartels, *Presidential Primaries and the Dynamics of Public Choice* (Princeton, N.J.: Princeton University Press, 1988), p. 111.
105. Quoted in Ross Gregory, "The Domino Theory," in Alexander DeConde, ed., *Encyclopedia of American Foreign Policy*, Vol. 1 (New York: Charles Scribner's Sons, 1978), p. 275. Also quoted in Slater, "Dominoes in Central America," p. 105.
106. Quoted in Slater, "Dominos in Central America," p. 106. For a similar critique of the domino theory, see Robert H. Johnson, "Exaggerating America's Stakes in Third World Conflicts," *International Security*, Vol. 10, No. 3 (Winter 1985/86), pp. 39–40.

tially external events" that spread quickly because countries within a region are tightly linked and "because revolutions actively seek to export themselves."[107] Similarly, the contagion effect proposes tight regional linkages and cascading alliances as explanations for the spread of war.[108]

Although associated with the spread of revolution and war, this type of bandwagoning dynamic can also exert a positive influence on the stability of the international system. Consider, for instance, the 1993 land-for-peace accord between the Palestine Liberation Organization and Israel. In response to the agreement, Jordan, Syria, and Lebanon are each reportedly seeking similar arrangements with Israel. In the words of Uri Savir, director general of the Israeli Foreign Ministry who led the Israeli team in the secret negotiations with the PLO in Norway, "With all the progress around, everybody in the region seems to make an effort to jump on this new bandwagon."[109] In what appears to be the latest aftershock of the historic earthquake that ended the Cold War, a peculiar domino effect is unfolding in the Middle East—peculiar in that it is being welcomed by most scholars and practitioners of international relations.

An Alternative Theory of Alliances: Balance of Interests

I have argued that states tend to bandwagon for profit rather than security and that contemporary realist theory, because of its status-quo bias, has underestimated the extent of bandwagoning behavior. In order to bring the revisionist state back in to the study of alliances, I propose a theory of balance-of-interests. The concept of balance of interests has a dual meaning, one at the unit level, the other at the systemic level. At the unit level, it refers to the costs a state is willing to pay to defend its values relative to the costs it is willing to pay to extend its values. At the systemic level, it refers to the relative strengths of status quo and revisionist states.

---

107. Slater, "Dominos in Central America," p. 107.
108. For a good overview of the empirical literature on the spread of wars through diffusion or contagion effects, see Benjamin A. Most, Harvey Starr, and Randolph M. Siverson, "The Logic and Study of the Diffusion of International Conflict," in Manus I. Midlarsky, ed., *Handbook of War Studies* (Boston: Unwin Hyman, 1989), pp. 111–139.
109. Quoted in Clyde Haberman, "Israel and Syria Reported Ready To Negotiate About Golan Heights," *New York Times*, September, 6, 1993, p. A3.

BALANCE OF INTERESTS AT THE UNIT LEVEL

By relaxing neorealism's assumption that states value what they possess more than what they covet, the full range of state interest emerges: some states value what they covet more than what they have; others are entirely satisfied with their possessions; still others value what they have only slightly more than what they covet, and vice versa; some states consider their possessions meager but are not envious of others.

We may conceptualize this range of state interest in the following way. Let x be the costs a given state is willing to pay to increase its values; and y be the costs the same state is willing to pay to defend the values it already has.[110] Let x and y range from 0 to n. The state's interest can then be represented as $x-y$ and will fall somewhere on the line shown in Figure 1.

Figure 1. State Interest (n) = (value of revision) − (value of status quo).

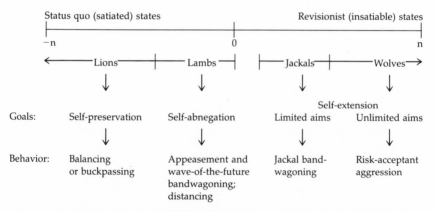

NOTE: *The top line represents the state's calculation of its relative interests in the values of revision and of the status quo. Where the status quo outweighs revision (where n is negative), states are satiated; where revision outweighs the status quo (n is positive), states are revisionist.*

---

110. For this conceptualization, see Robert Jervis, *Perception and Misperception in International Politics* (Princeton, N.J.: Princeton University Press, 1976), p. 51. Jervis calls this the state's "basic intention." For a similar scheme, see Charles L. Glaser, "Political Consequences of Military Strategy: Expanding and Refining the Spiral and Deterrence Models," *World Politics*, Vol. 44, No. 4 (July 1992), pp. 497–538. Glaser uses the concepts of myopia and greed.

LIONS. Lions are states that will pay high costs to protect what they possess but only a small price to increase what they value. The primary goal of these states is consistent with contemporary realism's assumption of actors as defensive positionalists and security-maximizers. As extremely satisfied states, they are likely to be status-quo powers of the first rank.

The choice of the lion to represent these states is partly motivated by Machiavelli's famous discussion of the lion and the fox: "A prince being thus obliged to know well how to act as a beast must imitate the fox and the lion, for the lion cannot protect himself from traps, and the fox cannot defend himself from wolves. One must therefore be a fox to recognize traps, and a lion to frighten wolves."[111]

Just as lions are the king of the jungle, satisfied Great Powers rule and manage the international system. After all, states that find the status quo most agreeable are usually the ones that created the existing order; as the principal beneficiaries of the status quo, they more than anyone else have a vested interest in preserving it.[112] And just as lions "frighten wolves," status-quo Great Powers must deter powerful revisionist states from aggression or, if that fails, bear the brunt of the fighting in order to defeat them. They take on these responsibilities not primarily in the expectation of gain or for altruistic reasons, but rather for self-preservation and to maintain their relative positions and prestige in the system.[113] Providing for the common defense is a dirty job, but someone has to do it, and only Great Powers can.[114] As Walter Lippmann put it: "Only a great power can resist a great power. Only a great power can defeat a great power."[115] If they believe that others will provide these collective goods for them, however, they will be tempted to pass the buck.

LAMBS. Lambs are countries that will pay only low costs to defend or extend their values. In a world of predators and prey, these states are prey.

111. Machiavelli, The Prince and The Discourses, p. 64.
112. This argument is consistent with the power-transition model. See A.F.K. Organski and Jacek Kugler, The War Ledger (Chicago: University of Chicago Press, 1980), chap. 1, especially pp. 19–23; and Gilpin, War and Change.
113. Great-power cooperation to manage the system is often achieved by spheres of interest and informal empires. See Jan Triska, ed., Dominant Powers and Subordinate States (Durham, N.C.: Duke University Press, 1986).
114. See Inis L. Claude, Jr., "The Common Defense and Great-Power Responsibilities," Political Science Quarterly, Vol. 101, No. 5 (1986), pp. 719–732, especially p. 725.
115. Walter Lippmann, U.S. Foreign Policy: Shield of the Republic (Boston: Little, Brown, 1943), p. 100. Quoted in Michael C. Desch, "The Keys that Lock Up the World: Identifying American Interests in the Periphery," International Security, Vol. 14, No. 1 (Summer 1989), p. 87.

Lambs are weak states in that they possess relatively few capabilities, or suffer from poor state-society relations for a variety of reasons: their elites and institutions may lack legitimacy with the masses; they may be internally divided along ethnic, political, class, religious, or tribal lines; the state's ideology may conflict with and be imposed on the popular culture; or they may be what Samuel Huntington calls torn countries: states "that have a fair degree of cultural homogeneity but are divided over whether their society belongs to one civilization or another."[116]

Because lambs are unwilling to sacrifice to extend their values, their foreign policy is not driven by irredentist aims. This distinguishes them from jackals, which may also be weak states. Lambs often bandwagon, as Walt implies, to divert and appease threats. But some, especially torn countries, engage in wave-of-the-future and domino bandwagoning. Others ally with the stronger side for protection from more pressing dangers, or out of fear of being despoiled if they wind up on the losing side. Examples of lambs are Czechoslovakia, Rumania, Austria, Yugoslavia, and France during the 1930s. Except for Rumania,[117] the decision of each to bandwagon with Hitler was facilitated by the successful penetration by Nazi fifth columns into the state and large segments of society.[118]

In addition to bandwagoning, lambs may choose not to align with either side but instead to distance themselves from more directly threatened states. In adopting a policy of distancing,[119] they seek the boon Odysseus sought

---

116. Samuel P. Huntington, "The Clash of Civilizations?" *Foreign Affairs*, Vol. 72, No. 3 (Summer 1993), p. 42. Huntington offers Turkey, Mexico, and Russia as examples of torn countries. See ibid., pp. 42–45.
117. Rumania bandwagoned with the Axis for protection from Russia, Hungary, and Bulgaria, which viewed Russia's territory as irredenta.
118. See Larson, "Bandwagon Images." For historical works on this subject, see Piotr S. Wandycz, *The Twilight of French Eastern Alliances: 1926–1936* (Princeton, N.J.: Princeton University Press, 1988); J.B. Hoptner, *Yugoslavia in Crisis: 1939–1941* (New York: Columbia University Press, 1962); Joseph Rothschild, *East Central Europe Between the Wars* (Seattle: University of Washington Press, 1974); C.A. Macartney and A.W. Palmer, *Independent Eastern Europe* (New York: St. Martin's Press, 1966); Anthony Tihamer Komjathy, *The Crises of France's East Central European Diplomacy: 1933–1938* (New York: Columbia University Press, 1976); and Hugh Seton-Watson, *Eastern Europe Between the Wars: 1918–1941* (Cambridge: Cambridge University Press, 1945).
119. For a discussion of distancing, see Randall L. Schweller, "Tripolarity and the Second World War," *International Studies Quarterly*, Vol. 37, No. 1 (March 1993), pp. 84, 87–92. Paul Schroeder calls this "hiding"; and John Arquilla introduces the term "bystanding," defined as a state's propensity to avoid conflicts for reasons of self-preservation. See Schroeder, "Neo-Realist Theory and International History"; and Arquilla, "Balances Without Balancing," paper presented at the annual meeting of the American Political Science Association, Chicago, Illinois, September 1992.

so successfully from Cyclops: to be eaten last.[120] There are several good reasons for doing this. First, the distancing state can hope that, before its number comes up, the aggressor will exhaust itself or satisfy its appetite for expansion. As Winston Churchill remarked about the behavior of Europe's small powers: "Each one hopes that if he feeds the crocodile enough, the crocodile will eat him last. All of them hope that the storm will pass before their turn comes to be devoured."[121]

Second, as the predatory state or coalition gains in strength with each conquest, the threat to other powerful status-quo states that have hitherto remained on the sidelines grows. Consequently, they are more likely to unite against the aggressor, switching from neutrality or twilight belligerence to active balancing. Third, the status-quo power can hope that, as time goes by, the opposing revisionist coalition will fall apart because of disputes over the division of military burdens or over the spoils of victory. And finally, the state may seek to be eaten last because it believes that the expansionist policies of the predator state will prove too costly for the latter's own domestic public. The hope is that the hostile and expansionist government will be replaced by a more friendly one.

JACKALS. Jackals are states that will pay high costs to defend their possessions but even greater costs to extend their values. Like wolves, jackals are dissatisfied powers, but they value their possessions and so as expanders they tend to be risk-averse and opportunistic. To use a biblical metaphor: the jackal trails the lion to scavenge the scraps it leaves behind.[122] While jackals are often found trailing wolves (revisionist leaders), they will also trail lions (status-quo leaders) who are on the verge of victory. Both forms of bandwagoning are examples of predatory buck-passing: attempts to ride free on the offensive efforts of others.

WOLVES. Wolves are predatory states. They value what they covet far more than what they possess. Like terminally ill patients, very hungry states are willing to take great risks—even if losing the gamble means extinction—to

---

120. Robert L. Rothstein, *Alliances and Small Powers* (New York: Columbia University Press, 1968), p. 26.
121. Winston Churchill, *Blood, Sweat and Tears* (New York: G.P. Putnam's, 1941), p. 215.
122. The jackal principle is usually associated with Italy's traditionally opportunistic foreign policy. See A.J.P. Taylor, *The Struggle for Mastery in Europe, 1848–1918* (Oxford: Oxford University Press, 1954), p. 286; Robert Rothstein, *Alliances and Small Powers* (New York: Columbia University Press, 1968), p. 227.

improve their condition, which they consider to be intolerable. Uninhibited by the fear of loss, they are free to pursue reckless expansion. As Hitler told his commanders in chief on the eve of war: "It is easy for us to make decisions. We have nothing to lose; we have everything to gain. . . . We have no other choice, we must act. Our opponents will be risking a great deal and can gain only a little."[123]

The historical record is replete with examples of states that sought to maximize or significantly increase their power, and put their own survival at risk to improve, not merely to maintain, their positions in the system. Alexander the Great, Rome, the Arabs in the seventh and eighth centuries, Charles V, Philip II, Frederick the Great, Louis XIV, Napoleon I, and Hitler all lusted for universal empire and waged all-or-nothing, apocalyptic wars to attain it. Seeking to conquer the world or a large portion of it, wolves do not balance or bandwagon; they *are* the bandwagon.

BALANCE OF INTERESTS AT THE SYSTEMIC LEVEL

At the systemic level, balance-of-interest theory suggests that the distribution of capabilities, by itself, does not determine the stability of the system. More important are the goals and means to which those capabilities or influence are put to use: whether power and influence is used to manage the system or destroy it; whether the means employed to further such goals threaten other states or make them feel more secure. In other words, the stability of the system depends on the balance of revisionist and conservative forces. When status-quo states are far more powerful than revisionist states, the system will be stable. When a revisionist state or coalition is stronger than the defenders of the status quo, the system will eventually undergo change; only the questions of when, how, and to whose advantage remain undecided.

Because the terms status quo and revisionist are somewhat nebulous and difficult to operationalize, it is necessary to define them as precisely as possible. Status-quo powers seek self-preservation and the protection of values they already possess; they are security-maximizers, not power-maximizers.[124] For status-quo states, the potential gains from nonsecurity expan-

---

123. Hitler speech to the Commanders in Chief on August 22, 1939, *Documents on German Foreign Policy, 1918–1945*, Series D, Vol. VII (Washington, D.C.: U.S. Government Printing Office, 1956), p. 201.

124. It is often pointed out that power-maximizing is a somewhat murky concept. But the same can be said of security-maximizing. Some argue that absolute security requires universal empire. But this is just a semantic solution, as external insecurity becomes internal insecurity.

sion are outweighed by the costs of war. While they may seek to extend their values, status-quo states do not employ military means to achieve this end. For this reason, their interest in military power varies with the level of threat to their values.[125]

In contrast, revisionist states value what they covet more than what they currently possess, although this ratio may vary considerably among their ranks; they will employ military force to change the status quo and to extend their values. For revisionist states, the gains from nonsecurity expansion exceed the costs of war. Needing preponderant power to overturn the status quo, dissatisfied states band together precisely when it appears that they will thus be stronger than the conservative side, for it is only then that they can expect to succeed in their expansionist aims.

Generally, revisionist powers are the prime movers of alliance behavior; status-quo states are the "reactors." Once again, Wolfers writes: "Because self-extension almost invariably calls for additional power, countries that seek self-extension tend to be the initiators of power competition and the resort to violence. Herein lies the significant kernel of truth in the idealist theory of aggression."[126] Aggressor states must exert initial pressure (that is, present a significant external threat) before satisfied powers will respond with counterpressure, which is often slow and reluctant. The vernacular of modern realism refers to this reaction as "balancing behavior," which the theory generalizes to apply to all states. But what, then, is the initial pressure exerted by the revisionist states called? In this light, it can be seen that the opposite of balancing is not bandwagoning, as today's realists claim, but rather aggression. In the absence of a reasonable external threat, states need not, and typically do not, engage in balancing. It is not surprising, therefore, that the Concert of Europe replaced the balance-of-power system in 1815, when all the war-weary Great Powers accepted and embraced the status-quo order.[127]

---

125. On this point, Wolfers writes: "Self-preservation calls forth . . . a variety of attitudes toward power because countries which are satisfied to let things stand as they are have no immediate incentive for valuing power or for wishing to enhance it. Whether they become interested in power at all, and the extent to which they do, depends on the actions they expect from others. It is a responsive interest which takes its cue from the threats, real or imagined, directed at things possessed and valued. If policy is rationally decided, the quest for power here increases or decreases in proportion to these external threats." Arnold Wolfers, "The Pole of Power and the Pole of Indifference," in Wolfers, *Discord and Collaboration*, p. 97.
126. Ibid., p. 96.
127. Conversely, the system did not go from balance to concert after either world war this century because, in each case, some of the major powers did not view the new order as legitimate. For a different view, see Robert Jervis, "From Balance to Concert: A Study of

The balance-of-power system returned with the outbreak of the Crimean War, when a revitalized France no longer accepted the status quo and instead sought to reestablish its prior hegemony over the Continent.

In short, the presence of Great Powers that are all known to accept the status quo and are unlikely to pursue unilaterally expansionist goals is a necessary and sufficient explanation for a Concert system; balance-of-power systems simply cannot survive under such conditions. Because in today's world "all major powers are coming to hold a common view of what constitutes an acceptable status quo," the current system is likely to go from balance to Concert.[128] Balance-of-interest theory, by focusing on variations in actors' preferences, can account for this change; structural balance-of-power theory and balance-of-threat theory cannot.

Conclusion

The question of whether balancing is more common than bandwagoning is a misleading one. They are not opposite behaviors. The motivation for bandwagoning is fundamentally different from that of balancing. Bandwagoning is commonly done in the expectation of making gains; balancing is done for security and it always entails costs. In practice, even Great Powers have chosen to remain on the sidelines in the hope of avoiding the high costs of balancing aggressively against powerful predatory states.[129] Many would not actively fight the aggressors until they were actually attacked. Conversely, bandwagoners, whether they are partners in crime or simply followers of a fashionable trend, do not attach high costs to their behavior. Instead, they

---

International Security Cooperation," in Kenneth A. Oye, ed., *Cooperation Under Anarchy* (Princeton, N.J.: Princeton University Press, 1986), pp. 58–79.

128. Charles A. Kupchan and Clifford A. Kupchan, "A New Concert for Europe," in Graham Allison and Gregory F. Treverton, eds., *Rethinking America's Security: Beyond Cold War to New World Order* (New York: W.W. Norton, 1992), p. 251. Also see Kupchan and Kupchan, "Concerts, Collective Security, and the Future of Europe," *International Security*, Vol. 16, No. 1 (Summer 1991), pp. 114–161.

129. In this regard, Churchill praises Britain for its traditional role of balancer precisely because, as such, it was the exception, not the rule: "Faced by Philip II of Spain, against Louis XIV under William II and Marlborough, against Napoleon, against William II of Germany, it would have been easy and must have been very tempting to join with the stronger and share the fruits of his conquest. However, we always took the harder course, joined with the less strong Powers, made a combination among them, and thus defeated and frustrated the Continental military tyrant, whoever he was, whatever nation he led." Winston S. Churchill, *The Gathering Storm* (New York: Bantam, 1961), pp. 186–187.

anticipate the advantages of being on the winning side. For them, alliances are a positive-sum game.

Rather than being opposite behaviors, bandwagoning and balancing are associated with opposite systemic conditions: balancing with stasis; bandwagoning with change. Accordingly, bandwagons roll when the system is in flux; either when the status-quo order starts to unravel or when a new order is being imposed. In the first instance, the rise of an unlimited-aims expansionist power will attract a following of lambs—vassal states too weak and frightened to defend their autonomy—and of jackal states, with their own revisionist aims to pursue. Sometimes, the status-quo order is destroyed by the decline of a dominant power, such as the demise of the Soviet Union and the wave of democratic revolutions that followed in 1989.

In the second instance, states pile on to the winning coalition at the end of large-scale wars to claim shares of the spoils or to escape the wrath of the victors. Here, states bandwagon to benefit from—or, at least, to avoid being damaged by—the peace settlement. Occasionally, a new order arises through peaceful means. Although it is perhaps too early to tell, the 1993 accord between Israel and the Palestine Liberation Organization has produced a bandwagon effect among the neighboring Arab states, each seeking its own settlement with Israel. As this last example shows, bandwagoning is not always, as the literature implies, a cowed response to an evil regime; it is often done voluntarily. Like change itself, bandwagon effects are feared by those who are content with the status quo and welcomed by those that are not.

Part III:
Realism and the Causes of Peace

Kant or Cant | *Christopher Layne*

The Myth of the Democratic Peace

$\mathbf{T}$he theory of the "Democratic Peace" raises important theoretical issues:[1] the contention that democratic states behave differently toward each other than toward non-democracies cuts to the heart of the international relations theory debate about the relative salience of second-image (domestic politics) and of third-image (systemic structure) explanations of international political outcomes. Democratic peace theory has also come to have a real-world importance as well: Policymakers who have embraced democratic peace theory see a crucial link between America's security and the spread of democracy, which is viewed as the antidote that will prevent future wars. Indeed some democratic peace theorists, notably Bruce Russett, believe that in an international system comprising a critical mass of democratic states, "It may be possible in part to supersede the 'realist' principles (anarchy, the security dilemma of states) that have dominated practice to the exclusion of 'liberal' or 'idealist' ones since at least the seventeenth century."[2] Because of its theoretical claims and

Christopher Layne of Los Angeles is an unaffiliated scholar. He is presently a consultant to the government contracts practice group of the law firm of Hill, Wynne, Troop and Meisinger, which represents major firms in the defense industry.

I am extremely grateful to the following colleagues who reviewed various drafts of this paper and offered helpful criticisms: John Arquilla, Ted Galen Carpenter, Kerry Andrew Chase, Jeffry Frieden, John Mearsheimer, Benjamin C. Schwarz, Jack Snyder, Stephen Walt, and Kenneth Waltz. I also thank Stephen Van Evera and David Spiro for providing me copies of, and permission to quote from, their unpublished works.

1. I use the term "democratic peace theory" because it is a convenient shorthand term. However, strictly speaking, the claim that democracies do not fight democracies is a proposition, or hypothesis, rather than a theory. Democratic peace "theory" proposes a causal relationship between an independent variable (democratic political structures at the unit level) and the dependent variable (the asserted absence of war between democratic states). However, it is not a true theory because the causal relationship between the independent and dependent variables is neither proven nor, as I demonstrate in this article, adequately explained. See Stephen Van Evera, "Hypotheses, Laws and Theories: A User's Guide," unpub. memo, Department of Political Science, MIT.
2. Bruce Russett, *Grasping the Democratic Peace: Principles for a Post–Cold War World* (Princeton: Princeton University Press, 1993), chap. 7; and Russett, "Can A Democratic Peace Be Built?" *International Interactions*, Vol. 18, No. 3 (Spring 1993), pp. 277–282.

International Security, Vol. 19, No. 2 (Fall 1994), pp. 5–49
© 1994 by the President and Fellows of Harvard College and the Massachusetts Institute of Technology.

policy implications, the democratic peace theory merits careful examination.[3] In this article, I focus primarily on a critique of the persuasiveness of democratic peace theory's causal logic and ask whether democratic peace theory or realism is a better predictor of international outcomes. I then briefly assess the robustness of democratic peace theory's empirical evidence in light of my conclusions about the strength of its explanatory power.

I begin by reviewing the explanations of the Democratic Peace advanced by democratic peace theorists. There are two strands to the theory's causal logic. One attributes the absence of war between democracies to institutional constraints: the restraining effects of public opinion, or of the checks and balances embedded in a democratic state's domestic political structure. The other posits that it is democratic norms and culture—a shared commitment to the peaceful adjudication of political disputes—that accounts for the absence of war between democratic states. As I demonstrate, the institutional-constraints argument fails to provide a compelling explanation for the absence of war between democracies. Thus, democratic peace theory's explanatory power rests on the persuasiveness of the contention that democratic norms and culture explain why, although democratic states fight with non-democracies, they do not go to war with each other.

This article's centerpiece is a test of the competing explanations of international outcomes offered by democratic peace theory and by realism. This test is based on case studies of four "near misses"—crises where two democratic states almost went to war with each other. These four cases are well-documented instances of democratic great powers going to the brink of war without going over it. As such, they present an opportunity to determine which of the competing hypotheses advanced respectively by democratic peace theory and realism best account for international political outcomes.[4]

---

3. In this article, I build upon and expand the criticisms of democratic peace theory found in John J. Mearsheimer, "Back to the Future: Instability in Europe After the Cold War," *International Security*, Vol. 15, No. 1 (Summer 1990), pp. 5–56; and Kenneth N. Waltz, "America as Model for the World? A Foreign Policy Perspective," *PS* (December 1991), pp. 667–670.
4. Other cases of crises between democratic great powers that might be studied include Anglo-French relations during the Liberal *entente cordiale* of 1832–48, Franco-Italian relations during the late 1880s and early 1890s and, if Wilhelmine Germany is classified as a democracy, the Moroccan crises of 1905–06 and 1911 and the Samoan crises of 1889 and 1899. These cases would support my conclusions. For example, from 1832 to 1848, the Foxite legacy disposed England's Whigs to feel a strong commitment to France based on a shared liberal ideology. Yet Anglo-French relations during this period were marked by intense geopolitical rivalry over Belgium, Spain, and the Near East, and the threat of war was always a factor in the calculations of policymakers in both London and Paris. Foreign Minister Lord Palmerston profoundly distrusted French ambitions and constantly urged that England maintain sufficient naval power to defend its

Moreover, they present an easy case for democratic peace theory and a hard case for realism. The selected cases favor democratic peace theory because, in each, the pacifying effect of democratic norms and culture was bolstered by complementary factors (e.g., economic interdependence, or special ties linking the disputants). I deduce, from both the democratic norms and culture argument and from realism, sets of indicators—testable propositions— that should be present if a crisis's outcome is explained by either of the two theories. Using a process-tracing approach, I examine each crisis in detail.

I conclude that realism is superior to democratic peace theory as a predictor of international outcomes. Indeed, democratic peace theory appears to have extremely little explanatory power in the cases studied. Doubts about the validity of its causal logic suggest that the empirical evidence purporting to support democratic peace theory should also be revisited. Democratic peace theorists contend that the theory is validated by a large number of cases. However, a powerful argument can be made that the universe of cases from which it can be tested is actually quite small. This is a crucial issue, because if the theory's empirical support is based on a small-N universe, this magnifies the importance of possible exceptions to the rule that democracies do not fight each other (for example, World War I, the War between the States, the War of 1812). I conclude by discussing democratic peace theory's troublesome implications for post–Cold War American foreign policy.

The Case for a Democratic Peace: Its Claims and its Logic

Democratic peace theory does not contend that democratic states are less war-prone than non-democracies; they are not. The theory does, however, make two important claims, first, that democracies never (or rarely; there is

---

interests against a French challenge. See Kenneth Bourne, *Palmerston: The Early Years, 1784–1841* (New York: Macmillan, 1982), p. 613. Also see Roger Bullen, *Palmerston, Guizot and the Collapse of the Entente Cordiale* (London: Athlone Press, 1974); and Sir Charles Webster, *The Foreign Policy of Palmerston*, Vol. I: *1830–1841, Britain, The Liberal Movement and The Eastern Question* (London: G. Bell & Sons, 1951). Italy challenged France for Mediterranean ascendancy although the two nations were bound by liberalism, democracy, and a common culture. The two states engaged in a trade war and came close to a real war. France apparently was dissuaded from attacking Italy in 1888 when the British Channel Fleet was sent to the Italian naval base of La Spezia. Italy was prevented from attacking France by its military and economic weakness. See C.J. Lowe and F. Marzari, *Italian Foreign Policy, 1870–1940* (London: Routledge & Kegan Paul, 1975), chap. 4; C.J. Lowe, *The Reluctant Imperialists: British Foreign Policy 1879–1902* (London: Routledge & Kegan Paul, 1974), Vol. I, pp. 147–150; John A.C. Conybeare, *Trade Wars: The Theory and Practice of International Commercial Rivalry* (New York: Columbia University Press, 1987), pp. 183–188.

a good deal of variation about this) go to war with other democracies.[5] As Jack S. Levy observes, the "absence of war between democracies comes as close as anything we have to an empirical law in international relations."[6] Second, when democracies come into conflict with one another, they only rarely threaten to use force, because it is "illegitimate" to do so.[7] Democratic peace theory explicitly holds that it is the very nature of democratic political systems that accounts for the fact that democracies do not fight or threaten other democracies.

THE CAUSAL LOGIC

Democratic peace theory must explain an anomaly: democracies are no less war-prone than non-democratic states. Yet, while they will readily threaten and fight non-democracies, they do not threaten or fight other democracies. The key challenge for the theory, then, is to identify the special characteristics of democratic states that restrain them from using coercive threats against, or actually going to war with, other democracies. The theory advances two alternative explanations: (1) institutional constraints; and (2) democratic norms and cultures.[8]

There are two major variants of the institutional constraints argument. Michael Doyle, building on Immanuel Kant, explains that democratic governments are reluctant to go to war because they must answer to their

5. Melvin Small and J. David Singer first observed the pattern of democracies not fighting democracies in a 1976 article: Small and Singer, "The War-proneness of Democratic Regimes, 1816–1865," *Jerusalem Journal of International Relations*, Vol. 1, No. 4 (Summer 1976), pp. 50–69. Their finding has been the subject of extensive further empirical testing which has produced a consensus around the propositions stated in the text. See Stuart A. Bremer, "Dangerous Dyads: Conditions Affecting the Likelihood of Interstate War, 1816–1865," *Journal of Conflict Resolution*, Vol. 36, No. 2 (June 1992), pp. 309–341; Steve Chan, "Mirror, Mirror on the Wall . . . Are the Freer Countries More Pacific?" *Journal of Conflict Resolution*, Vol. 28, No. 4 (December 1984), pp. 617–648; Zeev Maoz and Nasrin Abdolali, "Regime Type and International Conflict," *Journal of Conflict Resolution*, Vol. 33, No. 1 (March 1989), pp. 3–35; R.J. Rummel, "Libertarianism and International Violence," *Journal of Conflict Resolution*, Vol. 27, No. 1 (March 1983), pp. 27–71; Erich Weede, "Democracy and War Involvement," *Journal of Conflict Resolution*, Vol. 28, No. 4 (December 1984), pp. 649–664.
6. Jack S. Levy, "Domestic Politics and War," in Robert I. Rotberg and Theodore K. Rabb, eds., *The Origin and Prevention of Major Wars* (Cambridge: Cambridge University Press, 1989), p. 88.
7. Russett, *Grasping the Democratic Peace*, p. 33; Michael W. Doyle, "Kant, Liberal Legacies and Foreign Affairs," Part I, *Philosophy and Public Affairs*, Vol. 12, No. 3 (Summer 1983), p. 213.
8. This is the terminology employed by Russett, *Grasping the Democratic Peace*; also see Bruce Russett and Zeev Maoz, "Normative and Structural Causes of Democratic Peace," *American Political Science Review*, Vol. 87, No. 3 (September 1993), pp. 624–638. Russett points out (pp. 40–42) that, although analytically distinct, these two explanations are intertwined.

citizens.[9] Citizens pay the price for war in blood and treasure; if the price of conflict is high, democratic governments may fall victim to electoral retribution. Moreover, in democratic states, foreign policy decisions carrying the risk of war are debated openly and not made behind closed doors, which means that both the public and policymakers are sensitized to costs of fighting. A second version of the institutional constraints argument focuses on "checks and balances"; it looks at three specific features of a state's domestic political structure: executive selection, political competition, and the pluralism of the foreign policy decisionmaking process.[10] States with executives answerable to a selection body, with institutionalized political competition, and with decisionmaking responsibility spread among multiple institutions or individuals, should be more highly constrained and hence less likely to go to war.

The democratic norms explanation holds that "the *culture, perceptions, and practices* that permit compromise and the peaceful resolution of conflicts without the threat of violence *within countries* come to apply across national boundaries toward other democratic countries."[11] Democratic states assume both that other democracies also subscribe to pacific methods of regulating political competition and resolving disputes, and that others will apply these norms in their external relations with fellow democracies. In other words, democratic states develop positive perceptions of other democracies. Consequently, Doyle says, democracies, "which rest on consent, presume foreign republics to be also consensual, just and therefore deserving of accommodation."[12] Relations between democratic states are based on mutual respect

---

9. Doyle, "Kant, Liberal Legacies, and Foreign Affairs," pp. 205–235. See also Doyle, "Liberalism and World Politics," *American Political Science Review*, Vol. 80, No. 4 (December 1986), pp. 1151–1169; Russett, *Grasping the Democratic Peace*, pp. 38–40.
10. T. Clifton Morgan and Sally H. Campbell, "Domestic Structure, Decisional Constraints and War: So Why Kant Democracies Fight?" *Journal of Conflict Resolution*, Vol. 35, No. 2 (June 1991), pp. 187–211; and T. Clifton Morgan and Valerie L. Schwebach, "Take Two Democracies and Call Me in the Morning: A Prescription for Peace?" *International Interactions*, Vol. 17, No. 4 (Summer 1992), pp. 305–420.
11. Russett, *Grasping the Democratic Peace*, p. 31 (second emphasis added).
12. Doyle, "Kant, Liberal Legacies, and Foreign Affairs," p. 230. It is also argued that the predisposition of democratic states to regard other democracies favorably is reinforced by the fact that liberal democratic states are linked by mutually beneficial ties of economic interdependence. Democracies thus have strong incentives to act towards each other in a manner that enhances cooperation and to refrain from acting in a manner that threatens their stake in mutually beneficial cooperation. Ibid., pp. 230–232; Rummel, "Libertarianism and International Violence," pp. 27–28. For the "interdependence promotes peace" argument see Richard Rosecrance, *The Rise of the Trading State* (New York: Basic Books, 1986). In fact, however, for great powers economic interdependence, rather than promoting peace, creates seemingly important

rooted in the fact that democracies perceive each other as dovish (that is, negotiation or the status quo are the only possible outcomes in a dispute). This perception, it is argued, is based on a form of learning. Democratic states benefit from cooperative relations with one another and they want to expand their positive interactions. In turn, this desire predisposes them to be responsive to the needs of other democratic states, and ultimately leads to creation of a community of interests. As democracies move towards community, they renounce the option to use (or even to threaten to use) force in their mutual interactions.[13]

The democratic ethos—based on "peaceful competition, persuasion and compromise"—explains the absence of war and war-like threats in relations between democratic states.[14] Conversely, the absence of these norms in relations between democracies and non-democracies, it is said, explains the paradox that democracies do not fight each other even though in general they are as war-prone as non-democracies: "When a democracy comes into conflict with a nondemocracy, it will not expect the nondemocratic state to be restrained by those norms [of mutual respect based on democratic culture]. It may feel obliged to adapt to the harsher norms of international conduct of the latter, lest it be exploited or eliminated by the nondemocratic state that takes advantage of the inherent moderation of democracies."[15] Thus it is a fundamental postulate of democratic peace theory that democracies behave in a qualitatively different manner in their relations with each other than they do in their relations with non-democracies.

The Realist Case: The Same Things Over and Over Again

If history is "just one damn thing after another," then for realists international politics is the same damn things over and over again: war, great power security and economic competitions, the rise and fall of great powers, and the formation and dissolution of alliances. International political behavior is characterized by continuity, regularity, and repetition because states are con-

---

interests that must be defended by overseas military commitments (commitments that carry with them the risk of war). See Christopher Layne and Benjamin C. Schwarz, "American Hegemony—Without an Enemy," *Foreign Policy*, No. 92 (Fall 1993), pp. 5–23.
13. Doyle, "Kant, Liberal Legacies, and Foreign Affairs"; and Harvey Starr, "Democracy and War: Choice, Learning and Security Communities," *Journal of Peace Research*, Vol. 29, No. 2 (1992), pp. 207–213.
14. Maoz and Russett, "A Statistical Artifact?" p. 246.
15. Russett, *Grasping the Democratic Peace*, p. 33.

strained by the international system's unchanging (and probably unchangeable) structure.

The realist paradigm explains why this is so.[16] International politics is an anarchic, self-help realm. "Anarchy," rather than denoting chaos or rampant disorder, refers in international politics to the fact that there is no central authority capable of making and enforcing rules of behavior on the international system's units (states). The absence of a rule-making and enforcing authority means that each unit in the system is responsible for ensuring its own survival and also that each is free to define its own interests and to employ means of its own choice in pursuing them. In this sense, international politics is fundamentally competitive. And it is competitive in a manner that differs crucially from domestic politics in liberal societies, where the losers can accept an adverse outcome because they live to fight another day and can, therefore, ultimately hope to prevail. In international politics, states that come out on the short end of political competition face potentially more extreme outcomes, ranging from constraints on autonomy to occupation to extinction.

It is anarchy that gives international politics its distinctive flavor. In an anarchic system, a state's first goal is to survive. To attain security, states engage in both internal and external balancing for the purpose of deterring aggressors, and of defeating them should deterrence fail. In a realist world, cooperation is possible but is hard to sustain in the face of the competitive pressures that are built into the international political system's structure. The imperative of survival in a threatening environment forces states to focus on strategies that maximize their power relative to their rivals. States have powerful incentives both to seek the upper hand over their rivals militarily and to use their edge not only for self-defense but also to take advantage of others. Because military power is inherently offensive rather than defensive in nature, states cannot escape the security dilemma: measures taken by a state as self-defense may have the unintended consequence of threatening others. This is because a state can never be certain that others' intentions are benign; consequently its policies must be shaped in response to others' capabilities. In the international system, fear and distrust of other states is the normal state of affairs.

---

16. Classic explications of realism are Kenneth N. Waltz, *Theory of International Politics* (Reading, Mass.: Addison-Wesley, 1979) and Hans J. Morgenthau, rev. by Kenneth W. Thompson, *Politics Among Nations: The Struggle for Power and Peace*, 6th ed. (New York: Knopf, 1985).

Here democratic peace and realism part company on a crucial point. The former holds that changes within states can transform the nature of international politics. Realism takes the view that even if states change internally, the structure of the international political system remains the same. As systemic structure is the primary determinant of international political outcomes, structural constraints mean that similarly placed states will act similarly, regardless of their domestic political systems. As Kenneth Waltz says: "In self-help systems, the pressures of competition weigh more heavily than ideological preferences or internal political pressures."[17] Changes at the unit level do not change the constraints and incentives imbedded at the systemic level. States respond to the logic of the situation in which they find themselves even though this may result in undesirable outcomes, from the breakdown of cooperation to outright war. States that ignore the imperatives of a realist world run the risk of perishing. In a realist world, survival and security are always at risk, and democratic states will respond no differently to democratic rivals than to non-democratic ones.

Testing Democratic Peace Theory

Institutional constraints do not explain the democratic peace. If democratic public opinion really had the effect ascribed to it, democracies would be peaceful in their relations with all states, whether democratic or not. If citizens and policymakers of a democracy were especially sensitive to the human and material costs of war, that sensitivity should be evident whenever their state is on the verge of war, regardless of whether the adversary is democratic: the lives lost and money spent will be the same. Nor is democratic public opinion, *per se*, an inhibitor of war. For example, in 1898 it was public opinion that impelled the reluctant McKinley administration into war with Spain; in 1914 war was enthusiastically embraced by public opinion in Britain and France. Domestic political structure—"checks and balances"— does not explain the democratic peace either. "This argument," as Morgan and Schwebach state, "does not say anything directly about the war-proneness of democracies," because it focuses on an independent variable—decisional constraints embedded in a state's domestic political structure—that is associated with, but not exclusive to, democracies.

---

17. Kenneth N. Waltz, "A Reply to My Critics," in Robert O. Keohane, ed., *Neorealism and Its Critics* (New York: Columbia University Press, 1986), p. 329.

Because these explanations fall short, the democratic norms and culture explanation must bear the weight of the democratic peace theory's causal logic. It is there we must look to find that "something in the internal makeup of democratic states" that explains the democratic peace.[18]

Democratic peace theory not only predicts a specific outcome—no war between democracies—but also purports to explain why that outcome will occur. It is thus suited to being tested by the case study method, a detailed look at a small number of examples to determine if events unfold and actors act as the theory predicts. The case study method also affords the opportunity to test the competing explanations of international political outcomes offered by democratic peace theory and by realism. To test the robustness of democratic peace theory's causal logic, the focus here is on "near misses," specific cases in which democratic states had both opportunity and reason to fight each other, but did not.

The case studies in this article use the process-tracing method (opening up the "black box") to identify the factors to which decisionmakers respond, how those factors influence decisions, the actual course of events, and the possible effect of other variables on the outcome.[19] As Stephen Van Evera says, if a theory has strong explanatory power, process-tracing case studies provide a robust test because decisionmakers "should speak, write, and otherwise behave in a manner consistent with the theory's predictions."[20]

Democratic peace theory, if valid, should account powerfully for the fact that serious crises between democratic states ended in near misses rather than in war. If democratic norms and culture explain the democratic peace, in a near-war crisis, certain indicators of the democratic peace theory should be in evidence: First, public opinion should be strongly pacific. Public opinion is important not because it is an institutional constraint, but because it is an indirect measure of the mutual respect that democracies are said to have for each other. Second, policymaking elites should refrain from making military threats against other democracies and should refrain from making preparations to carry out threats. Democratic peace theorists waffle on this point by

---

18. Maoz and Russett, "Normative and Structural Causes," p. 624.
19. Alexander L. George and Timothy J. McKeown, "Case Studies and Theories of Organizational Decision Making," in Robert F. Coulam and Richard A. Smith, eds., *Advances in Information Processing in Organizations*, Vol. 2 (Greenwich, Conn.: JAI Press, 1985), p. 35.
20. Stephen Van Evera, "What Are Case Studies? How Should They Be Performed?" unpub. memo, September 1993, Department of Political Science, MIT, p. 2.

suggesting that the absence of war between democracies is more important than the absence of threats. But this sets the threshold of proof too low. Because the crux of the theory is that democracies externalize their internal norms of peaceful dispute resolution, then especially in a crisis, one should not see democracies threatening other democracies. And if threats are made, they should be a last-resort option rather than an early one. Third, democracies should bend over backwards to accommodate each other in a crisis. Ultimata, unbending hard lines, and big-stick diplomacy are the stuff of *Realpolitik*, not the democratic peace.

A realist explanation of near misses would look at a very different set of indicators. First, realism postulates a ratio of national interest to democratic respect: in a crisis, the more important the interests a democracy perceives to be at stake, the more likely that its policy will be shaped by realist imperatives rather than by democratic norms and culture. When vital interests are on the line, democracies should not be inhibited from using threats, ultimata, and big-stick diplomacy against another democracy. Second, even in a crisis involving democracies, states should be very attentive to strategic concerns, and the relative distribution of military capabilities between them should crucially—perhaps decisively—affect their diplomacy. Third, broader geopolitical considerations pertaining to a state's position in international politics should, if implicated, account significantly for the crisis's outcome. Key here is what Geoffrey Blainey calls the "fighting waterbirds' dilemma," involving concerns that others watching from the sidelines will take advantage of a state's involvement in war; that war will leave a state weakened and in an inferior relative power position *vis-à-vis* possible future rivals; and that failure to propitiate the opposing state in a crisis will cause it to ally with one's other adversaries or rivals.[21]

I have chosen to study four modern historical instances in which democratic great powers almost came to blows: (1) the United States and Great Britain in 1861 ("the *Trent* affair"); (2) the United States and Great Britain in 1895–96 (the Venezuela crisis); France and Great Britain in 1898 (the Fashoda crisis); and France and Germany in 1923 (the Ruhr crisis).[22] I focus on great

---

21. Geoffrey Blainey, *The Causes of War*, 3rd ed. (South Melbourne: Macmillan Co. of Australia, 1988), pp. 57–67. As the parable goes, while the waterbirds fight over the catch, the fisherman spreads his net.
22. My classification of the United States in 1861 and 1895 and of Germany in 1923 as great powers might be challenged. By the mid-nineteenth century British policymakers viewed the United States, because of its size, population, wealth, and growing industrial strength (and

powers for several reasons. First, international relations theory is defined by great powers: they are the principal components of the international system, and their actions—especially their wars—have a greater impact on the international system than do those of small powers.[23] Moreover, while democratic peace theory should apply to both great and small powers, realist predictions about great power behavior are not always applicable to small powers, because the range of options available to the latter is more constrained.[24] Crises between democratic great powers are a good head-to-head test because democratic peace theory and realism should both be applicable.[25]

The cases selected should favor democratic peace theory for more than the obvious reason that none of them led to war. In each crisis, background factors were present that should have reinforced democratic peace theory's predictions. In the two Anglo-American crises, a common history, culture and language, and economic interdependence were important considerations.[26] In the Fashoda crisis, the factors that led to the 1904 Anglo-French entente were already present and both countries benefited significantly from their economic relations.[27] The Franco-German Ruhr crisis tested both the Wilsonian prescription for achieving security in post–World War I Europe and the belief (increasingly widespread among French and German business elites, and to a lesser extent the political elites) that the prosperity of both states hinged on their economic collaboration.

---

latent military power), as "a great world power," notwithstanding the fact that it was not an active participant in the European state system. Ephraim Douglass Adams, *Great Britain and the American Civil War* (New York: Russell and Russell, 1924), Vol. I, p. 10. In 1895 the perception of American power had heightened in Britain and in other leading European powers. In 1923, Germany, although substantially disarmed pursuant to Versailles, remained Europe's most economically powerful state. As most statesmen realized, it was, because of its population and industry, a latent continental hegemon. Democratic peace theorists have classified all eight states as having been democracies at the time of their involvement in the crises under discussion. See Doyle, "Kant, Liberal Legacies, and Foreign Affairs," part I, pp. 214–215. Russett, *Grasping the Democratic Peace*, pp. 5–9, briefly discusses the Venezuela and Fashoda crises, but his bibliography has few historical references to these two crises (and related issues), and omits most standard sources.
23. Waltz, *Theory of International Politics*, pp. 72–73.
24. See Robert L. Rothstein, *Alliances and Small Powers* (New York: Columbia University Press, 1968), especially chap. 1.
25. As noted above, other such crises also support my argument.
26. For a brief discussion of the cultural, social, and economic bonds between Britain and the United States during the mid-nineteenth century, see Martin Crawford, *The Anglo-American Crisis of the Mid-Nineteenth Century: The Times and America, 1850–1862* (Athens: University of Georgia Press, 1987), pp. 39–55.
27. Stephen R. Rock, *Why Peace Breaks Out: Great Power Rapprochement in Historical Perspective* (Chapel Hill: University of North Carolina Press, 1989), pp. 91–119.

ANGLO-AMERICAN CRISIS I: THE *TRENT* AFFAIR, 1861

In 1861, tensions arising from the War Between the States brought the Union and Britain to the brink of war. The most important causes of Anglo-American friction stemmed from the Northern blockade of Confederate ports and the consequent loss to Britain of the cotton upon which its textile industry depended. The immediate precipitating cause of the Anglo-American crisis, however, was action of the *USS San Jacinto* which, acting without express orders from Washington, intercepted the British mail ship *Trent* on November 8, 1861. The *Trent* was transporting James M. Mason and John Slidell, the Confederacy's commissioners-designate to Great Britain and France; they had boarded the *Trent*, a neutral vessel, in Havana, Cuba, a neutral port. A boarding party from the *San Jacinto*, after searching the *Trent*, placed Mason and Slidell under arrest. The *Trent* was allowed to complete its voyage while the *San Jacinto* transported Mason and Slidell to Fort Warren in Boston harbor, where they were incarcerated.

When word was received in Britain, the public was overcome with war fever. "The first explosion of the Press, on receipt of the news of the *Trent*, had been a terrific one."[28] An American citizen residing in England reported to Secretary of State William H. Seward, "The people are frantic with rage, and were the country polled I fear 999 men out of 1000 would declare for war."[29] From Edinburgh, another American wrote, "I have never seen so intense a feeling of indignation in my life."[30]

The British government was hardly less bellicose than the public and the press. Fortified by legal opinions holding that Mason and Slidell had been removed from the *Trent* in contravention of international law, the Cabinet adopted a hard-line policy that mirrored the public mood. Prime Minister Lord Palmerston's first reaction to the news of the *Trent* incident was to write to the Secretary of State for War that, because of Britain's "precarious" relations with the United States, the government reconsider cuts in military expenditures planned to take effect in 1862.[31] At the November 29 Cabinet meeting, Palmerston reportedly began by flinging his hat on the table and

---

28. Adams, *Britain and the Civil War*, Vol. I, p. 216.
29. Quoted in Gordon H. Warren, *Fountain of Discontent: The Trent Affair and Freedom of the Seas* (Boston: Northeastern University Press, 1981), p. 105.
30. Quoted in Adams, *Britain and the Civil War*, Vol. I, p. 217.
31. Quoted in Norman B. Ferris, *The Trent Affair: A Diplomatic Crisis* (Knoxville: University of Tennessee Press, 1977), p. 44.

declaring to his colleagues, "I don't know whether you are going to stand this, but I'll be damned if I do!"[32]

The Cabinet adopted a dual-track approach towards Washington: London used military threats to coerce the United States into surrendering diplomatically, while on the diplomatic side, Foreign Secretary Lord John Russell drafted a note to the Union government in which, while holding firm to the demand that Mason and Slidell be released, he offered Washington an avenue of graceful retreat by indicating that London would accept, as tantamount to an apology, a declaration that the *San Jacinto* had acted without official sanction. Nevertheless, the note that was actually transmitted to Washington was an ultimatum. Although the British minister in Washington, Lord Lyons, was instructed to present the communication in a fashion calculated to maximize the chances of American compliance, his charge was clear: unless within seven days of receipt the Union government unconditionally accepted Britain's demands, Lyons was to ask for his passports and depart the United States. As Russell wrote to Lyons: "What we want is a plain Yes or a plain No to our very simple demands, and we want that plain Yes or No within seven days of the communication of the despatch."[33]

Although some, notably including Russell, hoped that the crisis could be resolved peacefully, the entire Cabinet recognized that its decision to present an ultimatum to Washington could lead to war. The British believed that there was one hope for peace: that Washington, overawed by Britain's military power and its readiness to go to war, would bow to London's demands rather than resisting them.[34] As the Undersecretary of State for Foreign Affairs stated, "Our only chance of peace is to be found in working on the fears of the Government and people of the United States."[35]

Driven by the belief that Washington would give in only to the threat of force, London's diplomacy was backed up by ostentatious military and naval preparations. Anticipating a possible conflict, the Cabinet embargoed the export to the United States of saltpeter (November 30) and of arms and ammunition (December 4). Underscoring the gravity of the crisis, for only

---

32. Ibid., p. 109; Howard Jones, *Union in Peril: The Crisis Over British Intervention in the Civil War* (Chapel Hill: University of North Carolina Press, 1992), pp. 84–85.
33. Quoted in Jones, *Union in Peril*, p. 85.
34. Jenkins, *War for the Union*, p. 214.
35. Quoted in Kenneth Bourne, *Britain and the Balance of Power in North America, 1815–1908* (Berkeley: University of California Press, 1967), p. 219.

the fourth time in history the Cabinet created a special war committee to oversee strategic planning and war preparations. Urgent steps were taken to reinforce Britain's naval and military contingents in North America. Beginning in mid-December, a hastily organized sealift increased the number of regular British army troops in Canada from 5,000 to 17,658, and Royal Navy forces in North American waters swelled from 25 to forty warships, with 1,273 guns (compared to just 500 before the crisis).[36] These measures served two purposes: they bolstered London's diplomacy and, in the event diplomacy failed, they positioned Britain to prevail in a conflict.

London employed big-stick diplomacy because it believed that a too-conciliatory policy would simply embolden the Americans to mount increasingly serious challenges to British interests.[37] Moreover, British policymakers believed that England's resolve, credibility, and reputation were at stake internationally, not just in its relations with the United States. The comments of once and future Foreign Secretary Lord Clarendon were typical: "What a figure . . . we shall cut in the eyes of the world, if we lamely submit to this outrage when all mankind will know that we should unhesitatingly have poured our indignation and our broadsides into any weak nation . . . and what an additional proof it will be of the universal . . . belief that we have two sets of weights and measures to be used according to the power or weakness of our adversary."[38] Thus "the British were prepared to accept the cost of an Anglo-American war . . . rather than sacrifice their prestige as a great power by headlong diplomatic defeat."[39]

London's hard-line policy was fortified by its "general optimism about the ultimate outcome" of an Anglo-American war.[40] Queen Victoria said a war would result in "utter destruction to the North Americans" and Secretary of

---

36. The figures are from Warren, *Fountain of Discontent*, pp. 130, 136. For an overview of British military and naval activities during the Trent crisis see Kenneth Bourne, "British Preparations for War with the North, 1861–1862," *English Historical Review*, Vol. 76, No. 301 (October 1961), pp. 600–632.

37. Ferris, *Trent Affair*, p. 56; Wilbur Devereux Jones, *The American Problem in British Diplomacy, 1841–1861* (London: Macmillan, 1974), p. 203. In international relations theory terms, London's view of Anglo-American relations was based on a deterrence model rather than a spiral model. See Robert Jervis, *Perception and Misperception in International Politics* (Princeton: Princeton University Press, 1976), pp. 58–111. Coexisting uneasily with the positive view of an Anglo-American community was the British image of the United States as a vulgar "mobocracy" that, unless firmly resisted, would pursue a rapacious and bullying foreign policy. Warren, *Fountain of Discontent*, pp. 47–51.

38. Quoted in Bourne, *Balance of Power*, p. 247.

39. Bourne, "British Preparations," p. 631.

40. Bourne, *Balance of Power*, p. 247.

State for War George Cornewall Lewis said "we shall soon *iron the smile* out of their face."[41] Palmerston was therefore untroubled by the discomfiture imposed on the Union by London's uncompromising policy. In his view, regardless of whether the crisis was resolved peacefully or resulted in war, Britain's interests would be upheld. He wrote to Queen Victoria:

If the Federal Government comply with the demands it will be honorable to England and humiliating to the United States. If the Federal Government refuse compliance, Great Britain is in a better state than at any former time to inflict a severe blow upon, and to read a lesson to the United States which will not soon be forgotten.[42]

In late 1861, the war against the Confederacy was not going well for Washington and the one major engagement, the first Battle of Manassas, had resulted in a humiliating setback for the Union army. Whipped up by Secretary of State Seward, who was a master at "twisting the lion's tail" for maximum domestic political effect, Northern opinion was hostile in London and resented especially Queen Victoria's May 1861 neutrality proclamation, which Northerners interpreted as *de facto* British recognition of Southern independence. News of the seizure of Mason and Slidell had a double effect on Northern public opinion. First, it was a tonic for sagging Northern morale. Second, it was seen as a warning to Britain to refrain from interfering with the Union's prosecution of the war against the Confederacy. Thus, although some papers (notably the *New York Times* and the *New York Daily Tribune*) urged that Washington should placate the British, public opinion strongly favored a policy of standing up to London and refusing to release Mason and Slidell.[43] In response to Britain's hard line, "a raging war cry reverberated across the Northern states in America."[44] Charles Francis Adams, Jr., whose father was U.S. minister in London at the time, wrote later of the affair: "I do not remember in the whole course of the half-century's retrospect . . . any occurrence in which the American people were so completely swept off their feet, for the moment losing possession of their senses, as during the weeks which immediately followed the seizure of Mason and Slidell."[45]

41. Quoted in ibid., pp. 245–246, emphasis in original.
42. Quoted in Jenkins, *War for the Union*, p. 216.
43. Ferris, *Trent Affair*, pp. 111–113.
44. Norman B. Ferris, *Desperate Diplomacy: William H. Seward's Foreign Policy, 1861* (Knoxville: University of Tennessee, 1976), p. 194.
45. Quoted in Adams, *Britain and the Civil War*, Vol. I, p. 218.

The Lincoln administration was aware of the strength of anti-British sentiment among the public and in Congress (indeed, in early December, Congress passed a resolution commending the *San Jacinto's* captain for his action). There is some evidence that in order to placate public opinion, President Lincoln was inclined toward holding on to Mason and Slidell, notwithstanding the obvious risks of doing so.[46] Nevertheless, after first toying with the idea of offering London arbitration in an attempt to avoid the extremes of war or a humiliating climb-down, the United States elected to submit to Britain's demands. Given that Washington "could not back down easily," it is important to understand why it chose to do so.

The United States bowed to London because, already fully occupied militarily trying to subdue the Confederacy, the North could not also afford a simultaneous war with England, which effectively would have brought Britain into the War Between the States on the South's side.[47] This was clearly recognized by the Lincoln administration when the cabinet met for two days at Christmas to decide on the American response to the British note. The cabinet had before it two critical pieces of information. First, Washington had just been informed that France supported London's demands (ending American hopes that Britain would be restrained by its own "waterbird" worries that France would take advantage of an Anglo-American war).[48] Second, Washington had abundant information about the depth of the pro-war sentiment of the British public. The American minister in London, Charles Francis Adams, wrote that the English "were now all lashed up into hostility" and that: "The leading newspapers roll out as much fiery lava as Vesuvius is doing, daily. The Clubs and the army and the navy and the people in the streets generally are raving for war."[49] Senator Charles Sumner passed on to the Lincoln administration letters from the noted Radical members of parliament, Richard Cobden and John Bright. While deploring their government's policy and the tenor of British public opinion, both Cobden and Bright

---

46. Warren, *Fountain of Discontent*, pp. 184–185; Adams, *Britain and the Civil War*, p. 231. Howard Jones, however, suggests that Lincoln probably intended to give up Mason and Slidell and that he may have been posturing in order to shift to other members of his cabinet the onus of advancing the argument for surrendering them. Jones, *Union in Peril*, pp. 91–92.

47. Ferris, *Trent Affair*, pp. 177–182; Jenkins, *War for the Union*, pp. 223–226; Warren, *Fountain of Discontent*, pp. 181–182.

48. See Jenkins, *War for the Union*, pp. 225–226.

49. Quoted in Ferris, *Trent Affair*, pp. 154, 147 and see also pp. 66–67, 139–141; Jones, *Union in Peril*, p. 89.

stressed that war would result unless the United States gave in to London. Cobden observed:

Formerly England feared a war with the United States as much from the dependence on your cotton as from a dread of your power. *Now* the popular opinion (however erroneous) is that a war would give us cotton. And we, of course, consider your power weakened by your Civil War.[50]

Facing the choice of defying London or surrendering to its demands, Washington was compelled to recognize both that Britain was serious about going to war and that such a war almost certainly would result in the Union's permanent dissolution. During the cabinet discussions, Attorney General Edward Bates suggested that Britain was seeking a war with the United States in order to break the Northern blockade of Southern cotton ports and he worried that London would recognize the Confederacy. The United States, he said, "cannot afford such a war." He went on to observe, "In such a crisis, with such a civil war upon our hands, we cannot hope for success in a . . . war with England, backed by the assent and countenance of France. We must evade it—with as little damage to our own honor and pride as possible."[51] Secretary of State Seward concurred, stating that it was "no time to be diverted from the cares of the Union into controversies with other powers, even if just causes for them could be found."[52] When the United States realized that Britain's threat to go to war was not a bluff, strategic and national interest considerations—the "waterbird dilemma"—dictated that Washington yield to Britain.

The *Trent* affair's outcome is explained by realism, not democratic peace theory. Contrary to democratic peace theory's expectations, the mutual respect between democracies rooted in democratic norms and culture had no influence on British policy. Believing that vital reputational interests affecting its global strategic posture were at stake, London played diplomatic hardball, employed military threats, and was prepared to go to war if necessary. Both the public and the elites in Britain preferred war to conciliation. Across the Atlantic, public and governmental opinion in the North was equally bellicose. An Anglo-American conflict was avoided only because the Lincoln admin-

---

50. Quoted in ibid., p. 172 (emphasis in original). Bright's letter warned: "If you are resolved to succeed against the South, *have no war with England.*" Quoted in Adams, *Britain and the Civil War*, p. 232 (emphasis in original).
51. Quoted in ibid., p. 182.
52. Quoted in Jenkins, *War for the Union*, p. 224.

istration came to understand that diplomatic humiliation was preferable to a war that would have arrayed Britain with the Confederacy and thus probably have secured the South's independence.

ANGLO-AMERICAN CRISIS II: VENEZUELA, 1895–96

In 1895–96, the United States and Great Britain found themselves embroiled in a serious diplomatic confrontation arising out of an obscure long-standing dispute between London and Caracas over the Venezuela–British Guiana boundary. By 1895, Caracas was desperately beseeching Washington to pressure London to agree to arbitrate the dispute. The Cleveland administration decided to inject the United States diplomatically into the Anglo-Venezuelan disagreement, but not out of American solicitude for Venezuela's interests or concern for the issue's merits.[53] For the United States, the Anglo-Venezuelan affair was part of a larger picture. By 1895, American policymakers, conscious of the United States's status as an emerging great power, were increasingly concerned about European political and commercial intrusion into the Western Hemisphere.[54] For Washington, the controversy between London and Caracas was a welcome pretext for asserting America's claim to geopolitical primacy in the Western hemisphere. It was for this reason that the United States provoked a showdown on the Anglo-Venezuelan border dispute.[55]

The American position was set forth in Secretary of State Richard Olney's July 20, 1895, note to the British government.[56] The United States stated that its "honor and its interests" were involved in the Anglo-Venezuelan dispute, "the continuance of which it cannot regard with indifference." Washington demanded that London submit the dispute to arbitration. In grandiloquent terms, Olney asserted that the Monroe Doctrine not only gave the United

---

53. Walter LaFeber demonstrates that the United States injected itself into the crisis to protect its own interests, not Venezuela's. LaFeber, *The New Empire: An Interpretation of American Expansion, 1860–1898* (Ithaca: Cornell University Press, 1963), chap. 6.
54. The relationship between security concerns and American foreign and strategic policy is discussed in Richard D. Challener, *Admirals, General and Foreign Policy, 1898–1914* (Princeton: Princeton University Press, 1973) and J.A.S. Grenville and George B. Young, *Politics, Strategy, and American Diplomacy: Studies in American Foreign Policy, 1873–1917* (New Haven: Yale University Press, 1966).
55. Walter LaFeber, "The Background of Cleveland's Venezuelan Policy: A Reinterpretation," *American Historical Review*, Vol. 66 No. 4 (July 1961), p. 947; Ernest R. May, *Imperial Democracy: The Emergence of America as a Great Power* (New York: Harcourt, Brace and World, 1961), p. 34.
56. The full text of the note can be found in *Foreign Relations of the United States, 1895* (Washington, D.C.: U.S. Government Printing Office), Vol. I, pp. 542–576.

States the right to intervene in the Venezuela affair but also a more general right to superintend the affairs of the Western hemisphere.

In challenging Britain, President Grover Cleveland and his secretary of state realized they were taking a serious step. Although they almost certainly hoped to score a peaceful diplomatic victory, their strategy was one that could have led instead to an armed confrontation. Olney's July 20 note (praised by Cleveland as "the best thing of the kind I have ever read") was deliberately brusque and, as Henry James pointed out, under prevailing diplomatic custom, London could justifiably have regarded it as an ultimatum.[57] Moreover, Washington intended Olney's note for publication. Olney and Cleveland believed that their strong language would get London's attention and that, by using the Monroe Doctrine as a lever, the United States could ram a diplomatic settlement down Britain's throat.[58] Cleveland and Olney expected London to back down and agree to arbitration and they hoped that Britain's positive response could be announced when Congress reconvened in December.

To the administration's consternation, however, London refused to give in to Washington's demands. British Prime Minister and Foreign Secretary Salisbury's unyielding reply prompted Cleveland's December 17, 1895, message to Congress. While acknowledging that the prospect of an Anglo-American war was an unhappy one to contemplate, the president declared there was "no calamity which a great nation can invite which equals that which follows a supine submission to wrong and injustice and the consequent loss of national self-respect and honor beneath which are shielded and defended a people's safety and greatness." Cleveland strongly defended the validity of the Monroe Doctrine, which he described as vital to America's national security and to the integrity of its domestic political institutions. He asserted that London's exercise of jurisdiction over any territory that the United States determined to belong properly to Venezuela was "willful aggression upon [America's] rights and interests."

In taking this position, Cleveland declared that he was "fully alive to the responsibility incurred and keenly realize[d] all the consequences that may follow." Notwithstanding his strong rhetoric, however, Cleveland did leave

---

57. Henry James, *Richard Olney and His Public Service* (New York: DaCapo Press, 1971, reprint ed.), p. 109. President Cleveland quoted in May, *Imperial Democracy*, p. 40.
58. Gerald C. Eggert, *Richard Olney: Education of a Statesman* (University Park: Pennsylvania State University Press, 1974), pp. 202, 212–213.

the British with some maneuvering room. Before acting against Britain, he said, the United States would set up a commission to investigate the Anglo-Venezuelan dispute and Washington would take no steps until the commission's report was made and accepted. Nevertheless, the import of Cleveland's message was clear: the United States was willing to fight Britain if necessary in order to establish America's primacy in the Western hemisphere.[59]

As Kenneth Bourne points out, during the Venezuela crisis the risk of war was quite real.[60] Salisbury flatly rejected the terms for resolving the crisis set out in Olney's July 20 note. J.A.S. Grenville wrote: "nothing could be plainer than Salisbury's rejoinder to Olney: the United States had no business interfering in the dispute, the Monroe Doctrine had no standing as an international treaty and did not in any case apply to the controversy; the British government would accordingly continue to refuse arbitration of the Venezuelan claims as a whole."[61] Salisbury understood the risk that Washington would maintain its stance and that the crisis would escalate. But as Grenville points out, he was willing to run this risk because "he did not believe the danger to Britain would be serious. The country and empire would have united in defence of British possessions, and in the face of their determination he believed the United States would give way."[62] Either Washington would understand the significance of the disparity between its military power and Britain's, or the United States would be defeated.

In late 1895 Britain and the United States clearly were on a collision course, and conflict almost certainly would have occurred had Britain held fast to the policy line adopted by Salisbury in November 1895. London did not do so, however, and by late January 1896 London and Washington had embarked upon a diplomatic process that culminated in November 1896 in an amicable settlement of Anglo-American differences. The crucial question is, why did Britain suddenly reverse course at the beginning of 1896?

---

59. Both Walter LaFeber and Ernest May come to this conclusion. See LaFeber, *The New Empire*, p. 268 and May, *Imperial Democracy*, p. 42.
60. Kenneth Bourne, *Balance of Power*, p. 319. It should be noted that not all historians agree with Bourne. For example, J.A.S. Grenville has argued that the Venezuelan crisis was synthetic and that there was no real risk of war during the crisis; Grenville, *Lord Salisbury and Foreign Policy at the Close of the Nineteenth Century* (London: Athlone Press, 1964), p. 55. However, in later work, Grenville wrote: "Given the mood of the British Cabinet . . . a serious Anglo-American conflict seemed inevitable." Grenville and Young, *Politics, Strategy and American Diplomacy*, p. 169.
61. Grenville, *Lord Salisbury*, p. 63.
62. Ibid., p. 65.

Although there is no "smoking gun," compelling circumstantial evidence supports the historians' consensus opinion that Britain was constrained from going to war in 1896 by an unfavorable distribution of military capabilities *vis-à-vis* the United States and by a deteriorating international situation. London, Lord Salisbury excepted, had become concerned about the outcome of an Anglo-American war because of Britain's inability, due to threats elsewhere, to spare warships to reinforce its naval presence in North American waters; fears that Canada would be conquered by the United States; and fears that in a prolonged war, the United States would be able to force a stalemate and possibly even prevail because of its enormous economic strength.[63] Moreover, between November 1895 and mid-January 1896, Britain's international position took a sharp turn for the worse: "England stood completely isolated at the beginning of 1896. Her position was scarcely endurable."[64] Anglo-German relations had been plunged into crisis by the Krueger telegram that Kaiser Wilhelm II had dispatched in the wake of the Jameson raid on the Transvaal. Elsewhere, the threats from Britain's main rivals, Russia and France, seemed only slightly less menacing.

Britain concluded that it must settle with Washington because it could not afford yet another enemy. At the critical January 11, 1896, Cabinet meeting, Salisbury remained steadfastly committed to his November "no negotiations" policy, but his colleagues decided to resolve the crisis with Washington peacefully. As Grenville and Young point out: "In November they believed that Britain held all the trump cards [but] the mood was no longer confident. The Cabinet was now inclined to cut Britain's losses in a world which appeared to have become suddenly hostile."[65] Overruled by the Cabinet, Salisbury—who believed that eventual war with the United States was "some-

---

63. See Bourne, *The Balance of Power in North America*, p. 340–341; A.E. Campbell, *Britain and the United States*, pp. 29–40; Eggert, *Richard Olney*, pp. 232–233; Paul Kennedy, *The Realities Behind Diplomacy: Background Influences on British External Policy, 1865–1980* (London: George Allen & Unwin, 1981), pp. 107–109; Arthur J. Marder, *The Anatomy of British Sea Power: A History of British Naval Policy in the Pre-Dreadnought Era, 1880–1905* (New York: Knopf, 1940), pp. 254–257. In an early January 1896 letter to Theodore Roosevelt, Lord Bryce said that nothing could be farther from his countrymen's minds than interfering with America's rights or the hemispheric balance of power because: "Our hands are more than sufficiently full elsewhere." Quoted in A.E. Campbell, *Britain and the United States*, pp. 59–60.
64. Marder, *Anatomy of British Sea Power*, p. 257.
65. Grenville and Young, *Politics, Strategy and American Diplomacy*, p. 170; Grenville, *Lord Salisbury*, pp. 67–69.

thing more than a possibility"—apparently considered resigning the premiership.[66]

There is virtually no evidence that supports a democratic peace theory explanation of the Venezuela crisis's outcome. Although the crisis ended before either London or Washington could make war-like threats, both the United States and Britain began planning militarily for a possible conflict.[67] This suggests that both British and American policymakers considered that war, or at least the preparation for it, was a legitimate component of their diplomatic strategies.

It does not appear, either, that public opinion affected policy on either side of the Atlantic. In Britain, the Cleveland administration's demands initially were greeted with hostility. Nevertheless, even before January 1896, British public opinion overwhelmingly favored a peaceful settlement of the Anglo-American crisis. There is, however, no evidence in the historical record that public opinion had any effect on the Cabinet's January 11 decision to resolve the crisis peacefully. Indeed, during the Venezuela crisis, Britain's policy-making elite had a different view of Anglo-American relations than did the British public. At the time of the Venezuela crisis there was still "an enormous gulf" between the advocates of an Anglo-American rapprochement based on racial kinship "and the hard-headed realism of the school of professional politicians and strategists headed by Salisbury."[68]

On the American side of the Atlantic, Cleveland's bellicose December 17 message elicited widespread public support. As Walter LaFeber notes, "Expansionist-minded Americans heartily endorsed the President's message, though most of them also fully shared his hopes that no war would result."[69] However the public's enthusiasm rather quickly subsided, and important groups, especially the churches and some elements of the financial and manufacturing sectors, recoiled at the prospect of an Anglo-American war. Nevertheless, if war had occurred, the public would probably have united behind the Cleveland administration. American public opinion viewed the prospect of war with England "not with enthusiasm but as, though regret-

---

66. See J.L. Garvin, *Life of Joseph Chamberlain* (London: Macmillan, 1934), Vol. III, p. 161; Salisbury quoted in Bourne, *The Balance of Power in North America*, p. 339.
67. Both London and Washington planned for a North American war during early 1896. American planning focused on invading Canada, Britain's on defending it. See Bourne, *The Balance of Power in North America*, pp. 319–331.
68. Bourne, *Balance of Power*, p. 340. Marder, *Anatomy of British Sea Power*, pp. 254–255, shows that Britain's national security elites took a very hard-line stance during the Venezuela crisis.
69. LaFeber, *New Empire*, p. 270.

table, necessary if there were no other way of establishing the paramount position of the United States in the western hemisphere."[70]

Recent generations have come to regard the Anglo-American "special relationship" as an immutable fact of international life. Indeed, in some ways it is considered an archetype of relations between democratic states. The "great rapprochement" upon which the special relationship was built was the epilogue to the Venezuelan crisis. But whatever Anglo-American relations arguably have become, the impetus for the rapprochement between London and Washington (like the impetus for the settlement of the Venezuelan crisis itself) was, as C.S. Campbell points out, rooted in geostrategic concerns and not in the considerations that underlie democratic peace theory.[71]

By 1898, the effects of Britain's by then not-so-splendid isolation were being painfully felt, and London's overtures to Washington must be viewed as part of the dramatic "end of isolation" process of strategic and diplomatic readjustment that London undertook after the Boer War.[72] The British did not welcome the rapid expansion of American power; rather they reconciled themselves to something they could not prevent and which, unlike the German, Russian and French challenges, did not seem immediately threatening to vital British interests. The Anglo-American rapprochement was possible because on every issue in dispute between them, London yielded to Washington's demands. As Bourne dryly observes, "All this was not simply or even perhaps at all significant of any special goodwill towards the United States."[73] Britain could not afford to make any more enemies, and least of all could London afford to incur the enmity of the United States, with which the British knew they could no longer compete geopolitically. For London, the "special relationship" was a myth devised "to enable Britain

---

70. A.E. Campbell, *Britain and the United States*, p. 41.
71. Charles S. Campbell, *Anglo-American Understanding, 1898–1903* (Baltimore: Johns Hopkins University Press, 1957), pp. 8–24. Kenneth Bourne and Paul Kennedy both point out that many of the same non-strategic factors underlying the Anglo-American rapprochement ("Anglo-Saxonism," economic interdependence) had been strongly present since at least 1850. They did not, however, noticeably mitigate Anglo-American hostility. These factors only came into play *after* the changing international situation forced London to reassess its grand strategy. Bourne, *Balance of Power*, p. 343; Kennedy, *Realities Behind Diplomacy*, p. 118.
72. There is strong consensus on this point among diplomatic historians. Bourne, *Balance of Power*, pp. 409–410; A.E. Campbell, *Britain and the United States*, p. 208; C.S. Campbell, *Anglo-American Understanding*, p. 346, 184–185; Bradford Perkins, *The Great Rapprochement: England and the United States, 1895–1914* (New York: Atheneum, 1968) pp. 156–157; Kennedy, *Realities Behind Diplomacy*, pp. 118–119.
73. Bourne, *Balance of Power*, p. 343.

to withdraw gracefully" from those areas where British interests clashed with Washington's, and its function was to make the "pill" of appeasing the United States "more palatable to swallow."[74]

The outcome of the Venezuelan crisis is better explained by realism than by democratic peace theory. Consistent with realist expectations, both Britain and the United States began planning for war. Although, as democratic peace theory would predict, there was no war fever in either Britain or the United States, there is no evidence that public opinion played any role in London's decision-making process. It was London's decision to reverse its initially uncompromising stance and instead seek an amicable diplomatic solution with Washington that allowed Britain and the United States to avoid war. All available evidence supports the realist explanation that London made this decision solely for strategic reasons.

THE ANGLO-FRENCH STRUGGLE FOR CONTROL OF THE NILE: FASHODA, 1898

The Fashoda crisis marked the culmination of the Anglo-French struggle for supremacy over Egypt and the headwaters of the Nile.[75] Until 1882 Egypt, although nominally part of the Ottoman Empire, had been administered by an Anglo-French condominium. In 1882, Britain intervened unilaterally to suppress a nationalist revolt. Because the Suez canal was the vital artery linking Britain with India and its other far eastern imperial interests, strategic considerations overrode London's initial inclination to withdraw quickly from Egypt after the 1882 intervention. By the early 1890s, Lord Salisbury and other British policymakers had determined that in order to safeguard Egypt, Britain had to exert control over the Nile's source and its entire valley.

For France, Britain's post-1882 Egyptian primacy was an affront and, spurred by France's colonial party, Paris periodically looked for ways in which it could compel London to honor its pledge to withdraw from Egypt.

---

74. Ronald Hyam, *Britain's Imperial Century, 1815–1914: A Study of Empire and Expansion* (London: B.T. Batsford, 1976), pp. 202, 205; C.J. Lowe and M.L. Dockrill, *The Mirage of Power: British Foreign Policy, 1902–1914*, Vol. I (London: Routledge and Kegan Paul, 1972), p. 99.
75. For accounts of the Fashoda crisis and its background, the following are excellent sources: William L. Langer, *The Diplomacy of Imperialism, 1890–1902*, 2d ed. (New York: Knopf, 1965), pp. 101–144, 259–302; Ronald Robinson and John Gallagher with Alice Denny, *Africa and the Victorians: The Official Mind of Imperialism* (London: Macmillan, 1981, rev. ed.), pp. 76–159, 290–306; G.N. Sanderson, *England, Europe, and the Upper Nile, 1882–1899* (Edinburgh: Edinburgh University Press, 1965), chaps. 12–15; and Sanderson, "The Origins and Significance of the Anglo-French Confrontation at Fashoda," in Prosser Gifford and William Roger Louis, eds., *France and Britain in Africa: Imperial Rivalry and Colonial Rule* (New Haven: Yale University Press, 1971), pp. 285–332.

The immediate impetus for the French expedition to Fashoda appears to have come from a January 1893 talk given by the hydraulic engineer Victor Prompt at the Egyptian Institute in Paris, which suggested that the flow of water to Egypt could be restricted by damming the Upper Nile. After reviewing Prompt's speech, President of the French Republic Sadi Carnot exclaimed, "we must occupy Fashoda!"[76]

The plan to advance on Fashoda was eagerly embraced by Theophile Delcassé during his 1893–95 tenure first as undersecretary and then as minister for colonies. As a journalist and as a politician, he had been obsessed by the Egyptian question. For Delcassé and other French colonialists, France's prestige and its Mediterranean interests required an end to Britain's occupation of Egypt.[77] In 1896, a plan by marine captain Jean-Baptiste Marchand for an overland expedition to establish French control at Fashoda was approved by Foreign Minister Gabriel Hanotaux and Colonial Minister Emile Chautemps. They did not seek to precipitate an armed confrontation with Britain; they favored an eventual Anglo-French rapprochement and entente. However, they were convinced that French opinion would not accept an entente unless the two powers could reach settlement on the points of dispute between them, including Egypt. Thus, for Hanotaux and Delcassé, the Fashoda expedition was conceived as a lever to force the British to negotiate the Egyptian question and thus to increase France's great-power prestige.

In September 1898, Delcassé was foreign minister. As the conflict loomed, he hoped that it might be averted by Marchand's failure to reach his objective or, if the French expedition did run into British forces, by an agreement that the crisis would be settled diplomatically by London and Paris, not militarily by the opposing forces at Fashoda. Apparently relying on Salisbury's reputation for making "graceful concessions," Delcassé hoped to defuse the crisis by exchanging Marchand's withdrawal for Britain's agreement to reopen the Egyptian question and to discuss giving France an outlet on the Nile.[78] The British, however, had no intention of negotiating. London's position was simple: "Marchand should go, without quibbles or face saving."[79]

---

76. Quoted in A.J.P. Taylor, "Prelude to Fashoda: The Question of the Upper Nile, 1894–5," *English Historical Review*, Vol. 65, No. 254 (January 1950), p. 54.

77. Christopher Andrew, *Theophile Delcassé and the Making of the Entente Cordiale: A Reappraisal of French Foreign Policy, 1898–1905* (New York: Macmillan, 1968), pp. 21–25.

78. Ibid., p. 100; Roger Glenn Brown, *Fashoda Reconsidered: The Impact of Domestic Politics on French Policy in Africa* (Baltimore: Johns Hopkins University Press, 1970), pp. 92–93.

79. Robinson and Gallagher, *Africa and the Victorians*, p. 371.

French policymakers "deluded themselves" into thinking that by taking Fashoda they could force London to negotiate the Egyptian issue.[80] As early as March 1895, when London had its first intimations about French designs on the upper Nile, Sir Edward Grey, then parliamentary undersecretary for foreign affairs, had stated bluntly that such a move "would be an unfriendly act and would be so viewed in England."[81] In spring 1898, responding to reports that France was driving on the upper Nile, London decided on an all-out reconquest of Sudan.

After victory at Khartoum, Field Marshal Lord Kitchener was ordered to advance to Fashoda and instructed, in the event he encountered French forces, to do nothing that "would in any way imply a recognition on behalf of Her Majesty's Government of a title on behalf of France . . . to any portion of the Nile Valley."[82] On September 19, 1898, Kitchener's forces reached Fashoda, where they were greeted by Marchand's band. Although the opposing forces treated each other with elaborate military courtesy, their meeting plunged London and Paris into a deep diplomatic crisis. The Anglo-French "quarrel was not about Fashoda, or about the fate of the Sudan, or even about the security of the Nile waters and of Egypt; it was about the relative status of France and Britain as Powers."[83]

Once the crisis began, Delcassé quickly recognized that France was in an untenable position. The British ambassador in Paris reported that Delcassé was "prepared to retreat . . . if we can build him a golden bridge."[84] Delcassé believed his maneuvering room was seriously circumscribed by the potentially volatile domestic political situation in France stemming from the Dreyfus affair. To accept a humiliating diplomatic defeat would probably mean the Brisson cabinet's fall and, it was widely feared, even a military coup.[85] Delcassé reportedly begged London, "Do not drive me into a corner."[86] On October 11, he told the British ambassador that if London made it easy for

---

80. Langer, *Diplomacy of Imperialism*, pp. 550–551.
81. Quoted in James Goode, *The Fashoda Crisis: A Survey of Anglo-French Imperial Policy on the Upper Nile Question, 1882–1899* (Ph.D. diss., North Texas State University, 1971), p. 150; and Darrell Bates, *The Fashoda Incident of 1898: Encounter on the Nile* (New York: Oxford University Press, 1984), p. 24.
82. Lord Salisbury's instructions quoted in Robinson and Gallagher, *Africa and the Victorians*, p. 368.
83. Sanderson, "Origins and Significance of Fashoda," p. 289.
84. Quoted in Sanderson, *The Upper Nile*, p. 346.
85. Brown, *Fashoda Reconsidered*, pp. 99–100, 127.
86. Quoted in T.W. Riker, "A Survey of British Policy in the Fashoda Crisis," *Political Science Quarterly*, Vol. 44, No. 1 (March 1929), p. 63.

him "in form he would be conciliatory in substance."[87] On October 27 the French ambassador to London, telling Salisbury that Marchand would soon leave Fashoda, pleaded for Britain to make some concession in return.[88]

Meanwhile, notwithstanding both the pleading tone of French diplomacy and the possible repercussions of Britain's stance on French internal politics, London adamantly refused to give Paris an alternative to the bleak choice of ordering Marchand's humiliating withdrawal or going to war. On September 18, the British ambassador in Paris told Delcassé "categorically" that London would not consent to any compromise of the Fashoda dispute.[89] On September 30, responding to Delcassé's statement that France would fight rather than submit to a British ultimatum, the British ambassador reiterated that there could be no discussions until Marchand withdrew from Fashoda. Salisbury was determined "to compel, rather than persuade, the French to withdraw."[90]

London's hard-line diplomacy was overwhelmingly supported by bellicose public opinion. Even before Fashoda, because of the tensions engendered by the Anglo-French colonial rivalry, "war with France was not exactly desired in England, but it would be accepted without hesitation if the occasion arose."[91] Once the crisis began, the press overwhelmingly supported the government's decision to refuse negotiations with France, and during the crisis "the British popular press indulged in an orgy of scurrility."[92] "There was plenty of warlike spirit in the country," and British public opinion was "aggressively jingoistic" over Fashoda.[93] "The unequivocal expression of British opinion" was solidly behind the Cabinet's hard-line policy.[94] This no doubt was true because the British public believed England's prestige was at stake and consequently was "in a mood to respond vigorously" to the French challenge.[95]

The public mood was matched by that of Britain's political elite. As Chancellor of the Exchequer Michael Hicks Beach said on October 19, "The country

---

87. Quoted in Keith Eubank, "The Fashoda Crisis Re-examined," *The Historian*, Vol. 22, No. 2 (February 1960), p. 152.
88. Quoted in ibid., p. 154.
89. Quoted in Robinson and Gallagher, *Africa and the Victorians*, p. 370.
90. Sanderson, *The Upper Nile*, p. 334.
91. Ibid., p. 372.
92. Ibid.; Riker, "British Policy in the Fashoda Crisis," pp. 65–67; Sanderson, *The Upper Nile*, p. 348.
93. Robinson and Gallagher, *Africa and the Victorians*, p. 376; Sanderson, *The Upper Nile*, p. 354.
94. Riker, "British Policy in the Fashoda Crisis," pp. 66–67.
95. Sanderson, "Origins and Significance of Fashoda," pp. 295, 300.

has put its foot down."[96] The government's uncompromising stance was supported strongly by the opposition Liberal Imperialists, notably Lord Rosebery, H.H. Asquith, and Sir Edward Grey.[97] Rosebery, a former prime minister and foreign secretary, recalled that his Cabinet had warned the French away from the Upper Nile in 1895 and declared that any Cabinet that showed signs of conciliating Paris over Fashoda would be replaced within a week. Indeed when, in the crucial October 27 Cabinet meeting, Salisbury left the impression in some minds that he was leaning towards compromise with Paris, the majority of ministers quickly poured cold water on that idea and the Admiralty was ordered to put the navy on a war footing.

The British knew that if Paris did not capitulate, armed conflict would ensue. London regarded that prospect with equanimity and, indeed, confidence. Because they believed both Britain's credibility and its reputation as a great power to be at stake, the British felt they had no alternative to forcing a showdown with the French: "Had Britain followed a less intransigent policy in the circumstances of October 1898, there would certainly have been a temptation, not only in Paris but also in St. Petersburg and Berlin, to write her off as a Power who would never risk a war, however great the provocation."[98]

In October 1898 the British navy enjoyed a decisive superiority over the French fleet in both numbers and quality, and the outcome of an Anglo-French war was a foregone conclusion.[99] London manifested no reluctance in pressing its strategic advantage. During October, the Royal Navy made preparations for a war with France.[100] On October 15, the Channel fleet was assembled. By October 26, the Royal Navy had drawn up detailed war plans. On October 28 the reserve squadron was activated and concentrated at Portland; soon the Channel fleet was deployed to Gibraltar and the Mediterranean fleet was moved to Malta. As these measures became known in Paris from intelligence reports and stories in the British press, they made a strong impression on French policymakers.

There is no question that France was finally compelled to accept a crushing diplomatic defeat because of its military inferiority *vis-à-vis* Britain. The Royal

---

96. Quoted in Langer, *Diplomacy of Imperialism*, p. 553.
97. Langer, *Diplomacy of Imperialism*, pp. 552–553; Robinson and Gallagher, *Africa and the Victorians*, pp. 376–378; Riker, "British Policy in the Fashoda Crisis," p. 67; Sanderson, *The Upper Nile*, p. 347.
98. Sanderson, "Origin and Significance of Fashoda," pp. 301–302.
99. On the Royal Navy's advantages and London's confidence in British sea power, see Marder, *Anatomy of British Sea Power*, pp. 320–331; Langer, *Diplomacy of Imperialism*, pp. 559–560.
100. Marder, *Anatomy of British Sea Power*, pp. 321–328.

Navy's power contrasted sharply with the numerical and qualitative deficiencies, and unpreparedness, of the French fleet. When Paris calculated the prevailing Anglo-French military balance, an embarrassing diplomatic climbdown emerged as a more attractive alternative than decisive defeat in a war.[101] As Delcassé admitted, he and President of the Republic Fauré were compelled to order Marchand's withdrawal by "the necessity of avoiding a naval war which we are absolutely incapable of carrying on, even with Russian help."[102] In the end, "Delcassé had no real alternative but to yield; except as an irrational gesture of defiance, war with England was not a possible choice."[103] The Fashoda crisis's outcome was, as Grenville says, "a demonstration of British power and French weakness."[104]

The outcome of the Fashoda crisis is explained by realism, not by democratic peace theory. Believing that vital strategic and reputational interests were at stake, the British ruled out diplomatic accommodation with Paris notwithstanding Delcassé's pleas to be given a face-saving way to extricate France from the crisis. Britain's intransigence runs directly counter to democratic peace theory's expectation that relations between democratic states are governed by mutual respect based on democratic norms and culture. Backed strongly by public and elite opinion, London adopted a policy that left Paris with two stark choices: diplomatic humiliation or military defeat in a war. Counter to democratic peace theory's expectations, but consistent with those of realism, Britain made, and was prepared to carry out, military threats against France. Paris caved in to British demands rather than fight a war it could not win.

FRANCO-GERMAN CRISIS: THE RUHR, 1923

The Ruhr occupation, culmination of the post-1918 cold peace, "practically amounted to the renewal of war."[105] The occupation arose from the collision

---

101. Two other factors weighed heavily in Britain's favor: First, Kitchener had an enormous local superiority over Marchand on the ground at Fashoda. Second, France's Russian ally made it clear that it would not support Paris and, in any event, even if St. Petersburg had wanted to intervene there was little the Russian navy could do to offset Britain's maritime superiority. See Langer, *Diplomacy of Imperialism*, pp. 559–563; Marder, *Anatomy of British Sea Power*, pp. 323, 328–329. As Paul Kennedy observes, "all the best cards were in Britain's hands." Kennedy, *Realities Behind Diplomacy*, pp. 112–113.
102. Quoted in Andrew, *Theophile Delcassé*, pp. 102–103. Faure's reaction to Britain's naval preparations is described in Brown, *Fashoda Reconsidered*, pp. 115–116.
103. Sanderson, *The Upper Nile*, p. 362.
104. Grenville, *Lord Salisbury*, p. 218.
105. Royal J. Schmidt, *Versailles and the Ruhr: Seedbed of World War II* (The Hague: Martinus Nijhoff, 1968), p. 17; Marshall M. Lee and Wolfgang Michalka, *German Foreign Policy, 1917–1933:*

of France's policy of security and Germany's policy of seeking revision of the Versailles Treaty system. The reparations issue was the immediate cause of the Ruhr occupation, but although it had economic significance in itself, its true importance was that Paris and Berlin regarded it as symbolic of the geopolitical competition between them.[106]

For Paris, compelling Germany to adhere strictly to its reparations obligations was seen as crucial to maintaining the Versailles system. Moreover reparations were, as the Ruhr occupation demonstrated, a lever for France to revise Versailles in its favor by imposing political and territorial sanctions on Germany when Berlin defaulted on its payments. For Germany, obtaining modification of reparations was a wedge to open the issue of revising the entire Versailles framework. The "fulfillment" policies adopted by Berlin were designed to force revision by demonstrating that strict compliance with reparations obligations was beyond Germany's capacity and would lead inevitably to Germany's financial and economic collapse.[107]

Although Germany had been defeated and its short-term power constrained by the Versailles settlement, the underlying sources of its geopolitical strength—its industrial base and population—remained intact. French policymakers were obsessed about the resurgence of a German security threat and determined to prevent it by imposing military, territorial and economic restrictions on Germany.

France's postwar German policy was rooted in the aims that Paris had pursued during the war. As early as 1915, Foreign Minister Delcassé had envisioned breaking up the German Reich into a number of small states, coupled with annexation by France, Holland, and Belgium of the Rhine's left bank.[108] By late 1917, Paris had decided to leave a truncated Reich intact while annexing Alsace-Lorraine and the Saar, and creating an independent

---

Continuity or Break? (Leamington Spa, U.K.: Berg, 1987), p. 47; Detlev J.K. Peukert, *The Weimar Republic: The Crisis of Classical Modernity*, trans. Richard Deveson (New York: Hill and Wang, 1992), p. 61; Hermann J. Rupieper, *The Cuno Government and Reparations, 1922–1923: Politics and Economics* (The Hague: Martinus Nijhoff, 1979) p. 96.

106. Peukert, *Weimar Republic*, p. 55; Marc Trachtenberg, *Reparation in World Politics: France and European Economic Diplomacy, 1916–1923* (New York: Columbia University Press, 1980), p. 122; Stephen A. Schuker, *The End of French Predominance in Europe: The Financial Crisis of 1924 and the Adoption of the Dawes Plan* (Chapel Hill: University of North Carolina Press, 1976), p. 6.

107. On Berlin's strategy of seeking revision through fulfillment, see David Felix, *Walther Rathenau and the Weimar Republic: The Politics of Reparations* (Baltimore: Johns Hopkins University Press); and Rupieper, *The Cuno Government*.

108. D. Stevenson, *French War Aims Against Germany, 1914–1919* (Oxford: Clarendon Press, 1982), pp. 26–27.

French satellite state in the Rhineland.[109] France's military and economic security would be enhanced by imposing reparations on Germany and by giving France control of the iron and coal that were crucial to West European industrial supremacy.

After the war, France's objectives did not change. Paris sought military security, reparations, and the establishment of France as Europe's leading steel producer. At Versailles, to avoid alienating Britain and the United States, France abandoned its annexationist aspirations in the Rhineland; however, throughout the period from the Armistice to the Ruhr occupation, Paris covertly supported Rhenish separatism while continuing to harbor hopes of controlling the left bank.[110] Even while appearing to abandon France's territorial claims in the Rhineland, French Premier Clemenceau had achieved much of their essence by coupling the reparations and security issues: under the Versailles Treaty's provisions, as long as Germany remained in default on reparations, French troops could remain in the Rhineland.

The government's German policy was strongly supported by the French public. French public opinion had demanded a peace settlement that would "impose the greatest possible restrictions on Germany's influence and power," and the French public's Germanophobia carried over into the postwar period.[111] Public and policymakers alike believed that Germany should be forced to pay all of the costs France had sustained in connection with the war (including reconstruction of German-occupied French territory), and official and public opinion were mutually reinforcing. Indeed, French public opinion, which French Prime Minister Poincaré had done much to shape, was so anti-German in late 1922 that it is doubtful that he would have survived politically had he not moved to occupy the Ruhr.[112]

The French military invasion of the Ruhr was prompted by Paris's mounting frustration with Germany's campaign to obtain a significant reduction of its reparations obligations. Although there is some disagreement as to the exact nature of Poincaré's objectives in occupying the Ruhr, the balance of

---

109. On French war aims see Walter A. McDougall, *France's Rhineland Diplomacy, 1914–1924: The Last Bid for a Balance of Power in Europe* (Princeton: Princeton University Press, 1978), p. 25; Schmidt, *Versailles to the Ruhr*, pp. 22–23; Stevenson, *French War Aims*, pp. 38–39.
110. Stevenson, *French War Aims*, pp. 195–196. The definitive account of France's Rhenish policy is McDougall, *Rhineland Diplomacy*.
111. Stevenson, *French War Aims*, pp. 135–136. Leaders such as Poincaré actively promoted anti-German attitudes, not a particularly difficult task. See Schmidt, *From Versailles to the Ruhr*, p. 231.
112. Rupieper, *The Cuno Government*, pp. 88, 96; Schmidt, *From Versailles to the Ruhr*, p. 52.

opinion is that the Ruhr occupation was undertaken in an attempt to advance France's goals of revising the Versailles system in its favor. The Ruhr occupation clearly was intended to bolster French security by crippling Germany's economy while simultaneously enabling Paris to realize its ambition of establishing France as Europe's leading economic power. At a minimum, Paris hoped that the Ruhr occupation would inflame Rhenish separatism and lead the Rhineland to break away from the Reich; there is some evidence that the Ruhr occupation was undertaken specifically to advance the French aims of annexing the Rhineland and dissolving the Reich.[113] Once the Ruhr crisis commenced, France actively abetted the Rhenish separatists.

In the Ruhr crisis, France did not hesitate to use military force against democratic Weimar Germany in pursuit of French security interests. Indeed, what leaps out from histories of the period between 1915 (when French policymakers began to think seriously about their war aims) and 1923 is the repeated French rejection of "second image" arguments that France's postwar security position would be enhanced if Germany were transformed into a democracy. Unlike the British, who soon after the war came to believe a democratic Germany was the key to maintaining the peace in Europe, France preferred to put German democracy at risk rather than abandon its strategy of protecting its security with tangible guarantees. As Walter McDougall observes:

The Quai d'Orsay perceived little connection between forms of government and foreign policies. The Wilsonian idea that democracies choose peaceful foreign policies, while authoritarian regimes are aggressive, found few disciples in the French government and military . . . . A strong united Germany, whether monarchist or republican, would pose a threat to France and surely come to dominate the economies of the Danubian and Balkan regions.[114]

The French military occupation of the Ruhr provoked a major crisis—if not a Franco-German war, at least a quasi-war. A real war was avoided only because Germany lacked the capabilities to wage it. Still the Germans resisted the occupation fiercely. If anything united the fractious Germans of the

---

113. McDougall argues that Rhenish separation from the Reich was Poincaré's hope but not his specific goal in the Ruhr operation. McDougall, *Rhineland Diplomacy*, pp. 247–249. Schmidt argues that Poincaré undertook the Ruhr occupation for the specific purpose of gaining permanent territorial control of the Ruhr and Rhineland and promoting the Reich's disintegration. Schmidt, *From Versailles to the Ruhr*, pp. 232–233.
114. McDougall, *Rhineland Diplomacy*, p. 114.

Weimar Republic, it was hatred for the Versailles system and a determination to overturn it. The Germans believed that the French move was designed to bring about the dissolution of the Reich. Because of Germany's military weakness, the Reichswehr ruled out a policy of active resistance to the French occupation; however, steps were taken to facilitate military resistance in the event the French attempted to advance beyond the Ruhr.[115] Although unable to oppose France militarily, the Berlin government did adopt a policy of resistance to the French occupation, based on the noncooperation of German workers, civil servants, and railway personnel with French occupation authorities. The resistance was not entirely passive; the Reichswehr coordinated an active campaign of sabotage against the French occupation forces.[116] To sustain the resistance, the Berlin government provided the Ruhr population with food and unemployment subsidies. Passive resistance was financed by printing money, a practice that triggered Germany's financial collapse (due to hyperinflation and the concomitant collapse of the mark); this ultimately compelled Berlin to abandon its resistance to the Ruhr occupation. Over the long term, the Ruhr occupation had even more important effects on German domestic politics and public opinion: France's hard line policies strengthened the position of the right-wing nationalist parties in Germany and served to discredit the Weimar democracy.

The Ruhr crisis strongly disconfirms democratic peace theory. In World War I's aftermath, both the public and the elites in France perceived Germany as a dangerous threat to France's security and its great power status, even though Weimar Germany was a democracy. What mattered to the French was Germany's latent power, not its domestic political structure. Contrary to democratic peace theory's predictions, French policy toward democratic Germany reflected none of the mutual respect based on democratic norms and culture that democracies are supposed to display in their relations with each other. On the contrary, driven by strategic concerns, the French used military power coercively to defend the Versailles system upon which they believed their safety depended, rather than entrust their national security to

---

115. See F.L. Carsten, *The Reichswehr and Politics, 1918 to 1933* (Oxford: Clarendon Press, 1966) pp. 154–155. German preparations included mobilization of reserve units (whose existence was illegal under the terms of Versailles), the purchase of fighter aircraft from Holland and seaplanes from Sweden, and the training of secret units to conduct guerrilla operations behind the lines of any French advance beyond the Ruhr.
116. Ibid., pp. 154–155.

the hope that Germany's postwar democratic institutions would mitigate the geopolitical consequences flowing from the underlying disparity between German and French power.

Theoretical Conclusions

Proponents have made sweeping theoretical claims for, and have drawn important policy conclusions from, democratic peace theory. These claims rest on a shaky foundation, however. The case studies presented above subject both democratic peace theory and realism to a robust test. It is striking that in each of these four cases realism, not democratic peace theory, provides the more compelling explanation of why war was avoided. Indeed, the democratic peace theory indicators appear not to have played *any* discernible role in the outcome of these crises.

In each of these crises, at least one of the democratic states involved was prepared to go to war (or, in the case of France in 1923, to use military force coercively) because it believed it had vital strategic or reputational interests at stake. In each of these crises, war was avoided only because one side elected to pull back from the brink. In each of the four crises, war was avoided not because of the "live and let live" spirit of peaceful dispute resolution at democratic peace theory's core, but because of realist factors. Adverse distributions of military capabilities explain why France did not fight over Fashoda, and why Germany resisted the French occupation of the Ruhr passively rather than forcibly. Concerns that others would take advantage of the fight (the "waterbirds dilemma") explain why Britain backed down in the Venezuela crisis, and the Union submitted to Britain's ultimatum in the *Trent* affair. When one actually looks beyond the *result* of these four crises ("democracies do not fight democracies") and attempts to understand *why* these crises turned out as they did, it becomes clear that democratic peace theory's causal logic has only minimal explanatory power.

Although democratic peace theory identifies a correlation between domestic structure and the absence of war between democracies, it fails to establish a causal link. Because democratic peace theory's deductive logic lacks explanatory power, a second look at the theory's empirical support is warranted to see if the evidence is as strong as is commonly believed. The statistical evidence that democracies do not fight each other seems impressive but in fact, it is inconclusive, because the universe of cases providing empirical support for democratic peace theory is small, and because several important cases of wars between democratic states are not counted for reasons that are not persuasive.

QUANTITATIVE SUPPORT FOR THE THEORY: HOW BIG AN N?
Democratic peace theory purports to be validated by a large number ("N") of cases. A large N is achieved by aggregating the number of possible democratic dyads. Thus Switzerland and Sweden, or Austria and Israel, count as democratic dyads validating democratic peace theory. The result is the appearance of a large number of interactions with little or no conflict between democracies. Notwithstanding the theory's claim, however, the universe of supporting cases is small. There are three reasons why this is so. First, between 1815 and 1945 there were very few democracies (and the N would shrink further if only dyads involving democratic great powers are considered). Second, the possibility of *any* dyad (whether democratic, mixed, or non-democratic) becoming involved in a war is small, because wars are a relatively rare occurrence. States, even great powers, do not spend most of their time at war.[117] As David Spiro points out, if all nations are unlikely to fight wars, the claim that democracies do not fight each other loses much of its power. He states that if nations are rarely at war, and liberal dyads are a small proportion of all possible pairings of nation-states, then perhaps we should be surprised if democracies ever do go to war, but not at the absence of wars among democracies.[118]

Third, not all dyads are created equal. For the purposes of testing democratic peace theory, a dyad is significant only if it represents a case where there is a real possibility of two states going to war. To fight, states need both the *opportunity* (that is, the ability to actually project their power to reach an opponent) and a *reason* to do so. Only dyads meeting these preconditions are part of the appropriate universe of cases from which democratic peace theory can be tested.

---

117. On the striking decline in the frequency of great power war during the past two centuries see Jack S. Levy, *War and the Modern Great Power System, 1495–1975* (Lexington: University Press of Kentucky, 1983), chap. 6.
118. David E. Spiro, "The Insignificance of the Liberal Peace," *International Security*, Vol. 19, No. 2 (Fall 1994), pp. 50–86. Spiro concludes that the statistical evidence for the liberal peace is weak: either the data are ambiguous, or random chance would predict the absence of wars between democracies. Spiro is sympathetic to the democratic peace theory. He suggests that the tendency of liberal states to ally with, instead of opposing, each other is important and probably is rooted in liberal norms.

WARS BETWEEN DEMOCRACIES: BIG EXCEPTIONS IN A SMALL-N WORLD. The size of the N is an important question. If the effective universe of cases from which democratic peace theory can be tested is a small N, the importance of exceptions to the rule that democracies do not fight each other is heightened. Here, by their own admissions, democratic peace theorists are on thin ice. For example, referring specifically to the classification of the War of 1812 as one not involving two democracies, Bruce Russett acknowledges that this decision "may seem like a cheap and arbitrary escape" but asserts it is not.[119] It is only intellectual suppleness—the continual tinkering with definitions and categories—that allows democratic peace theorists to deny that democratic states have fought each other.[120]

An important example of this is the War Between the States, which the democratic peace theorists generally rule out on the grounds that it was an internal conflict within a state rather an international conflict between sovereign states.[121] Yet the events of 1861–65 seem especially relevant because the theory is based explicitly on the premise that the norms and culture that operate within democracies are externalized by them in their relations with other democratic states.[122] Democratic peace theory itself makes relevant the

---

119. Russett, *Grasping the Democratic Peace*, p. 16. However, sometimes things *are* exactly as they seem. Russett excludes the War of 1812 on the grounds that, prior to the Reform Bill of 1832, Britain was not a democracy. Yet, until the "revolution" that followed Andrew Jackson's 1828 election to the presidency, the United States was not appreciably more democratic than Britain. *The Federalist* and the Constitution itself, in its provision for an Electoral College and indirect election of senators, reflect the desire of the framers to circumscribe egalitarian democratic impulses. In early nineteenth-century America, suffrage was significantly restricted by property and other qualifications imposed at the state level. See Clinton Williamson, *American Suffrage: From Property to Democracy, 1750 to 1860* (Princeton: Princeton University Press, 1960); Paul Kleppner, et al., *The Evolution of American Electoral Systems* (Westport, Conn.: Greenwood Press, 1981).

120. A good example is James L. Ray, "Wars Between Democracies: Rare, or Nonexistent?" *International Interactions*, Vol. 18, No. 3 (1993), pp. 251–276. After readjusting the definition of democracy, Ray takes a brief look at five of the nineteen alleged exceptions to the rule that democratic states do not fight each other and concludes that over the last 200 to 250 years there are no exceptions to the rule.

121. Russett's comments (*Grasping the Democratic Peace*, p. 17) notwithstanding, after secession the War Between the States did take on the cast of an international conflict between two sovereign democratic entities. It certainly was so regarded by contemporaneous observers (and had the Confederacy prevailed, it certainly would be so regarded today). For example, no less a figure than Prime Minister William Gladstone, the arch-apostle of British Liberalism, observed that: "Jefferson Davis and other leaders of the South have made an army; they are making, it appears, a navy; and they have made what is more than either: they have made a nation." Quoted in James M. McPherson, *Battle Cry of Freedom: The Civil War Era* (New York: Oxford University Press, 1988), p. 552.

122. Democratic peace theory "*extends to the international arena* the cultural norms of live-and-let-

issue of whether democratic norms and culture do, in fact, result in the peaceful resolution of disputes within democracies. The War Between the States cuts to the heart of the democratic peace theory's causal logic: if democratic norms and culture fail to prevent the outbreak of civil war within democracies, what reason is there to believe that they will prevent the outbreak of interstate wars between democracies?

In the case of the Union and the Confederacy, the characteristics at the heart of democratic peace theory—the democratic ethos of respect for other democracies, a political culture that emphasizes the non-violent dispute resolution, the shared benefits of cooperation, the restraining effect of open debate and public opinion—failed conspicuously to assure a peaceful result. Indeed, if a democracy as tightly knit—politically, economically, culturally—as the United States was in 1861 could split into two warring successor states, we should have little confidence that democracy will prevent great power conflicts in an anarchic, competitive, self-help realm like international politics.

An even more important example is the issue of whether Wilhelmine Germany was a democracy. Even if World War I were the only example of democracies fighting each other, it would be so glaring an exception to democratic peace theory as to render it invalid. As even Michael Doyle concedes, the question of whether Wilhelmine Germany was a democracy presents a "difficult case."[123] Indeed, it is such a difficult case that, in a footnote, Doyle creates a new category in which to classify Wilhelmine Germany—that of a bifurcated democracy: pre-1914 Germany was, he says, democratic with respect to domestic politics but not in the realm of foreign policy.[124] Doyle does not consider Imperial Germany to have been a democracy for foreign policy purposes because the executive was not responsible to the Reichstag and, consequently, the foreign policy making process remained, he argues, autocratic.

---

live and peaceful conflict resolution that operate *within* democracies." Ibid., p. 19 (emphasis added).
123. Doyle, "Kant, Liberal Legacies and Foreign Affairs," part I, p. 216, fn 8.
124. Ibid. I do not address the issue of whether any state can in fact have such a tightly compartmentalized political system that it can be democratic in domestic politics but not in foreign policy. I know of no other example of a bifurcated democracy. If this concept of bifurcated democracy were accepted, proponents of democratic peace theory could defend their argument by asserting that, while democratic in the realm of domestic policy, in 1914 Britain and France, like Wilhelmine Germany, also were non-democratic in terms of foreign policy.

In fact, however, with respect to foreign policy, Wilhelmine Germany was as democratic as France and Britain. In all three countries, aristocratic or upper-middle-class birth and independent wealth were prerequisites for service in the diplomatic corps and the key political staffs of the foreign office.[125] In all three countries, foreign policy was insulated from parliamentary control and criticism because of the prevailing view that external affairs were above politics.

In democratic France, the Foreign Minister enjoyed virtual autonomy from the legislature, and even from other members of the cabinet.[126] As Christopher Andrew notes, "On the rare occasions when a minister sought to raise a question of foreign policy during a cabinet meeting, he was accustomed to the remark: 'Don't let us concern ourselves with that, gentlemen, it is the business of the foreign minister and the President of the Republic.'"[127] Treaties and similar arrangements were ratified by the president of the Republic (that is, by the cabinet) and the legislature played no role in the treaty making process (although the Senate did have the right to ask to be informed of treaty terms insofar as national security permitted).[128] Notwithstanding the formal principle of ministerial responsibility, the French legislature possessed no mechanisms for effectively supervising or reviewing the government's conduct of foreign policy.[129] Even in democratic France, the executive enjoyed unfettered power in the realm of foreign policy. This concentration of foreign policy-making power in the executive had a profound effect on the chain of events leading to World War I. The terms of the Franco-Russian alliance and military convention—the "fateful alliance" that ensured that an Austro-Russian war in the Balkans could not remain localized—were kept secret from the French legislature, public, and press.[130]

In democratic Britain, too, as in France and Germany, crucial foreign policy decisions were taken without consulting Parliament. Notwithstanding the

---

125. See Lamar Cecil, *The German Diplomatic Service, 1871–1914* (Princeton: Princeton University Press, 1976); Paul Gordon Lauren, *Diplomats and Bureaucrats: The First Institutional Responses to Twentieth Century Diplomacy in France and Germany* (Stanford: Hoover Institution Press, 1976), pp. 27–29; Frederick L. Schuman, *War and Diplomacy in the French Republic: An Inquiry into Political Motivations and the Control of Foreign Policy* (New York: Whittlesy House, 1931); Zara S. Steiner, *The Foreign Office and Foreign Policy, 1898–1914* (Cambridge: Cambridge University Press, 1969); and Steiner, "The Foreign Office under Sir Edward Grey," in F.H. Hinsley, ed., *British Foreign Policy Under Sir Edward Grey* (Cambridge: Cambridge University Press, 1977), pp. 22–69.
126. Schuman, *War and Diplomacy*, pp. 21, 28–32.
127. Andrew, *Theophile Delcassé*, p. 64.
128. Ibid., p. 22; Lauren, *Diplomats and Bureaucrats*, p. 29.
129. Lauren, *Diplomats and Bureaucrats*, p. 29.
130. Schuman, *War and Diplomacy*, p. 143.

profound implications of the Anglo-French staff talks, which began in January 1906, Foreign Secretary Sir Edward Grey and Prime Minister H.H. Asquith did not inform the Cabinet of their existence.[131] Grey and Asquith feared (and rightly so) that a Cabinet majority would oppose the staff talks and indeed the very idea of more intimate Anglo-French strategic relations. When questioned in Parliament in 1910, 1911, and 1913 about the Anglo-French military discussions, Grey and Asquith consistently gave false or evasive answers that kept hidden both the nature and the implications of the strategic agreements between London and Paris.[132] Even when Grey and Asquith had to account to the Cabinet, after it learned in November 1911 of the existence of staff talks, they left their colleagues with the incorrect impression that London had undertaken no binding obligations to France.[133] Notwithstanding Grey's and Asquith's constant reiteration (to the French, to Cabinet, and to Parliament) that London retained unimpaired freedom of maneuver, they had, in fact, undertaken a portentous commitment through a constitutionally doubtful process. In the Cabinet's debates about whether Britain should go to war in August 1914, Grey's argument that the Entente, and the concomitant military and naval agreements, had morally obligated Britain to support France proved decisive.[134]

It is apparent that before World War I, the most important and consequential grand strategic decisions made by both Paris (on the Russian alliance) and London (on the entente and military arrangements with France) were made without any legislative control or oversight, notwithstanding both countries' democratic credentials. Form should not be confused with substance. In the realm of foreign policy, France and Britain were no more and no less democratic than the Second Reich.[135]

---

131. See Samuel R. Williamson, *The Politics of Grand Strategy: Britain and France Prepare for War, 1904–1914* (Cambridge: Harvard University Press, 1969).
132. Ibid., pp. 134, 137–138, pp. 202–204, 330–331.
133. Ibid., pp. 198–200.
134. Grey threatened to resign from the Cabinet unless it agreed to take Britain into the war on France's side. Grey's resignation threat was determinative because the non-interventionist Cabinet Radicals realized that their refusal to declare war would lead to the Cabinet's replacement either by a Conservative-Unionist government or by a coalition between the Conservatives and the Liberal Imperialists. See K.M. Wilson, "The British Cabinet's Decision for War, 2 August 1914," *British Journal of International Studies*, Vol. 1, No. 2 (July 1975), pp. 148–159.
135. The classification of Wilhelmine Germany as a democracy is also supported by an analysis of the foreign policy making process of its successor, the Weimar Republic. Although the Weimar Republic invariably is classified as a democracy, in crucial respects, it closely resembled the Second Reich. During the Weimar Republic, the Foreign Office and the Army collaborated to ensure that the processes of formulating foreign policy and grand strategy were insulated from

The case of Wilhelmine Germany suggests that democratic great powers indeed have gone to war against one another (and could do so again in the future). Yet the prevailing view that the Second Reich was not a democracy has powerfully influenced the international relations–theory debate both on the broad question of how domestic political structure affects international outcomes and the specific issue of whether there is a "democratic peace." However, the received wisdom about pre–World War I Germany has been badly distorted by a combination of factors: the liberal bias of most Anglo-American accounts of German history between 1860–1914; the ideologically tinged nature of post-1960 German studies of the Wilhelmine era; and the residual effects of Allied propaganda in World War I, which demonized Germany.[136] The question of whether Wilhelmine Germany should be classified as a democracy is an important one and it deserves to be studied afresh.

AN ALTERNATIVE HYPOTHESIS: THE SECOND IMAGE REVERSED

From a realist perspective, democratic peace theory has mistakenly reversed the linkage between international systemic constraints and domestic political institutions. Otto Hintze made the realist argument that a state's internal political structure is highly influenced by external factors.[137] This creates a selection process that explains why some states become democracies while others do not. States that enjoy a high degree of security, like Britain and the United States at the beginning of the twentieth century, can afford the more minimalist state political structures of classical Anglo-American liber-

the Reichstag's oversight and control. The leading study is Gaines Post, Jr., *The Civil-Military Fabric of Weimar Foreign Policy* (Princeton: Princeton University Press, 1973). Post observes (p. 358) that the Weimar Republic stands as a "model for the virtual exclusion of the parliamentary or legislative level from politico-military activity in a representative system of government." If Weimar Germany is considered to be a democracy, then how can Wilhelmine Germany be classified as a non-democracy?

136. For a discussion of the leftist ideological biases that color the writings of Fritz Fischer's disciples and a critique of Fischer, Berghahn, Kehr, and Wehler, see Wolfgang J. Mommsen, "Domestic Factors in German Foreign Policy before 1914," *Central European History*, Vol. 6, No. 1 (March 1973), pp. 4–18. An insightful critique of the "failure of liberalism" school is Klaus P. Fischer, "The Liberal Image of German History," *Modern Age*, Vol. 22, No. 4 (Fall 1978), pp. 371–383.

137. This thesis is developed in Otto Hintze, "The Formation of States and Constitutional Development: A Study in History and Politics"; Hintze, "Military Organization and the Organization of the State"; and Hintze, "The Origins of the Modern Ministerial System: A Comparative Study," in Felix Gilbert, ed., *The Historical Essays of Otto Hintze* (New York: Oxford University Press, 1975).

alism, because there is no imminent external threat that necessitates a powerful governmental apparatus to mobilize resources for national security purposes. States that live in a highly threatening external environment are more likely to choose either more statist forms of democracy or even authoritarian structures, precisely because national security concerns require that the state have available to it the instruments for mobilizing national power resources.[138] The greater the external threat a state faces (or believes it does), the more "autocratic" its foreign policymaking process will be, and the more centralized its political structures will be.

If this hypothesis is true, it suggests that democratic peace theory is looking through the wrong end of the telescope. States that are, or that believe they are, in high-threat environments are less likely to be democracies because such states are more likely to be involved in wars, and states that are likely to be involved in wars tend to adopt autocratic governmental structures that enhance their strategic posture.[139] Thus, as realist theory would predict, international systemic structure is not only the primary determinant of a state's external behavior but may also be a crucial element in shaping its domestic political system. This hypothesis may provide a more useful approach than democratic peace theory to investigating the links between domestic structure and foreign policy.

Policy Conclusions: Why It Matters

The validity of democratic peace theory is not a mere academic concern. Democratic peace theory has been widely embraced by policymakers and foreign policy analysts alike and it has become a lodestar that guides Amer-

---

138. This argument is developed in Brian M. Downing, *The Military Revolution and Political Change: Origins of Democracy and Political Change* (Princeton: Princeton University Press, 1992).
139. There is another way of visualizing this phenomenon. The more threatened a state is (or believes it is) the more it will move toward more centralized domestic structures. A state may move so far that it ceases to be democratic and becomes autocratic. This hypothesis conforms with the experience of liberal democratic great powers in this century. In both World Wars, the exigencies of conflict resulted in such a concentration of state power in both the United States and Britain that, for a time, arguably, both became autocratic. The Cold War, similarly, impelled the United States to become a "national security state," still a democracy but one where the power of the state was vastly enhanced and the executive's predominance over the legislature in the sphere of foreign policy was decisively established. Quincy Wright came to a similar conclusion about the effect of external environment on domestic political structure and observed that "autocracy, at least in the handling of foreign affairs, has been the prevailing constitutional form." Wright, *A Study of War* (Chicago: University of Chicago Press, 1964, abridged ed.), p. 158.

ica's post–Cold War foreign policy. Michael Doyle's 1983 conception of a democratic "zone of peace" is now routinely used in both official and unofficial U.S. foreign policy pronouncements. Following the Cold War, a host of commentators have suggested that the export or promotion of democracy abroad should become the central focus of American's post–Cold War foreign policy.[140] From Haiti to Russia, America's interests and its security have been identified with democracy's success or failure. National Security Adviser Anthony Lake said that America's post–Cold War goal must be to expand the zone of democratic peace and prosperity because, "to the extent democracy and market economics hold sway in other nations, our own nation will be more secure, prosperous and influential."[141]

Those who want to base American foreign policy on the extension of democracy abroad invariably disclaim any intention to embark on a "crusade," and profess to recognize the dangers of allowing policy to be based on excessive ideological zeal.[142] These reassurances are the foreign-policy version of "trust me." Because it links American security to the nature of other states' internal political systems, democratic peace theory's logic inevitably pushes the United States to adopt an interventionist strategic posture. If democracies are peaceful but non-democratic states are "troublemakers" the conclusion is inescapable: the former will be truly secure only when the latter have been transformed into democracies, too.

Indeed, American statesmen have frequently expressed this view. During World War I, Elihu Root said that, "To be safe democracy must kill its enemy when it can and where it can. The world cannot be half democratic and half autocratic."[143] During the Vietnam War, Secretary of State Dean Rusk claimed that the "United States cannot be secure until the total international environment is ideologically safe." These are not isolated comments; these views reflect the historic American propensity to seek absolute security and to

---

140. See for example Joshua Muravchik, *Exporting Democracy: Fulfilling America's Destiny* (Washington, D.C.: AEI Press, 1991); and Larry Diamond, "Promoting Democracy," *Foreign Policy*, No. 87 (Summer 1992), pp. 25–46.

141. "Remarks of Anthony Lake," Johns Hopkins School of Advanced International Studies, Washington, D.C., September 21, 1993 (Washington, D.C.: National Security Council Press Office).

142. Lake stated that the Clinton administration does not propose to embark on a "democratic crusade." Both Doyle and Russett acknowledge that democratic peace theory could encourage democratic states to pursue aggressive policies toward non-democracies, and both express worry at this. Doyle, "Kant, Liberal Legacies, and Foreign Affairs," part II; Russett, *Grasping the Democratic Peace*, p. 136.

143. Quoted in Russett, *Grasping the Democratic Peace*, p. 33.

define security primarily in ideological (and economic) terms. The political culture of American foreign policy has long regarded the United States, because of its domestic political system, as a singular nation. As a consequence, American policymakers have been affected by a "deep sense of being alone" and they have regarded the United States as "perpetually beleaguered."[144] Consequently, America's foreign and defense policies have been shaped by the belief that the United States must create a favorable ideological climate abroad if its domestic institutions are to survive and flourish.[145]

Democratic peace theory panders to impulses which, however noble in the abstract, have led to disastrous military interventions abroad, strategic overextension, and the relative decline of American power. The latest example of the dangers of Wilsonianism is the Clinton administration's Partnership for Peace. Under this plan, the asserted American interest in projecting democracy into East Central Europe is advanced in support of NATO security guarantees and eventual membership for Poland, Hungary, and the Czech Republic (and some form of U.S. security guarantee for Ukraine). The underlying argument is simple: democratic governments in these countries will guarantee regional peace in the post–Cold War era, but democracy cannot take root unless these countries are provided with the "reassurance" of U.S. or NATO security guarantees.

In fact, however, East Central Europe is bound to be a highly volatile region regardless of whether NATO "moves east." The extension of NATO guarantees eastward carries with it the obvious risk that the United States will become embroiled in a future regional conflict, which could involve major powers such as Germany, Ukraine, or Russia. There is little wisdom in assuming such potentially risky undertakings on the basis of dubious assumptions about the pacifying effects of democracy.[146]

---

144. William Appleman Williams, *Empire As A Way of Life: An Essay on the Causes and Character of America's Present Predicament Along With a Few Thoughts About An Alternative* (New York: Oxford University Press, 1980), p. 53.

145. Lloyd C. Gardner, *A Covenant With Power: America and World Order from Wilson to Reagan* (New York: Oxford University Press, 1984), p. 27. For an excellent critique of the notion that America's domestic ideology must be validated by its foreign policy, see Michael H. Hunt, *Ideology and U.S. Foreign Policy* (New Haven: Yale University Press, 1987).

146. It could be argued that if Hintze's argument is correct (that secure states are more likely to become, or remain, democratic), then extending security guarantees to states like Ukraine, or preserving extant alliances with states like Germany, Japan, and South Korea, is precisely what the United States should do. Indeed, the Bush and Clinton administrations have both subscribed to a worldview that holds that the United States, as the sole remaining superpower, must take responsibility for maintaining regional power balances in Europe and East Asia. By

Democratic peace theory is dangerous in another respect, as well: it is an integral component of a new (or more correctly, recycled) outlook on international politics. It is now widely believed that the spread of democracy and economic interdependence have effected a "qualitative change" in international politics, and that war and serious security competitions between or among democratic great powers are now impossible.[147] There is therefore, it is said, no need to worry about future great power challenges from states like Japan and Germany, or to worry about the relative distribution of power between the United States and those states, unless Japan or Germany were to slide back into authoritarianism.[148] The reason the United States need not be concerned with the great-power emergence of Japan and Germany is said to be simple: they are democracies and democracies do not fight democracies.

Modern-day proponents of a liberal theory of international politics have constructed an appealing vision of perpetual peace within a zone of democracy and prosperity. But this "zone of peace" is a peace of illusions. There is no evidence that democracy at the unit level negates the structural effects of anarchy at the level of the international political system. Similarly, there is no evidence that supports the sister theory: that economic interdependence leads to peace. Both ideas have been around for a long time. The fact that they are so widely accepted as a basis for international relations theory shows that for some scholars, "theories" are confirmed by the number of real-world tests that they fail. Proponents of liberal international relations theory may contend, as Russett does, that liberal approaches to international politics have not failed, but rather that they have not been tried.[149] But this is what disappointed adherents of ideological worldviews always say when belief is overcome by reality.

---

preventing the "renationalization" of other states' security policies and by foreclosing the possibility of regional power vacuums, the United States, it is argued, can preserve the kind of international environment that is conducive to the spread of democracy and economic interdependence. For critiques of this policy see Christopher Layne, "The Unipolar Illusion: Why New Great Powers Will Rise," *International Security*, Vol. 17, No. 4 (Spring 1993), pp. 5–51; Layne, "American Grand Strategy After the Cold War: Primacy or Blue Water?" in Charles F. Hermann, ed., *American Defense Annual* (New York: Lexington Books, 1994); and Layne and Schwarz, "American Hegemony."

147. Robert Jervis, "The Future of World Politics: Will It Resemble the Past?" *International Security*, Vol. 16, No. 3 (Winter 1991/92), pp. 39–73.

148. For an example of this argument see James M. Goldgeier and Michael McFaul, "A Tale of Two Worlds: Core and Periphery in the Post–Cold War Era," *International Organization*, Vol. 46, No. 3 (Spring 1992), pp. 467–491.

149. Russett, *Grasping the Democratic Peace*, p. 9, says that Kantian and Wilsonian principles have not been given a real chance to operate in international politics.

If American policymakers allow themselves to be mesmerized by democratic peace theory's seductive—but false—vision of the future, the United States will be ill prepared to formulate a grand strategy that will advance its interests in the emerging world of multipolar great power competition. Indeed, as long as the Wilsonian worldview underpins American foreign policy, policymakers will be blind to the need to have such a grand strategy, because the liberal theory of international politics defines out of existence (except with respect to non-democracies) the very phenomena that are at the core of strategy: war, the formation of power balances, and concerns about the relative distribution of power among the great powers. But in the end, as its most articulate proponents admit, liberal international relations theory is based on hope, not on fact.[150] In the final analysis, the world remains what it always has been: international politics continues to occur in an anarchic, competitive, self-help realm. This reality must be confronted, because it cannot be transcended. Given the stakes, the United States in coming years cannot afford to have either its foreign policy, or the intellectual discourse that underpins that policy, shaped by theoretical approaches that are based on wishful thinking.

---

150. Russett, *Grasping the Democratic Peace*, p. 136, argues that, "understanding the sources of democratic peace can have the effect of a self-fulfilling prophecy. Social scientists sometimes create reality as well as analyze it. Insofar as norms do guide behavior, repeating those norms helps to make them effective. *Repeating the norms as descriptive principles can help to make them true.*" (Emphasis added.)

The False Promise of International Institutions

John J. Mearsheimer

Since the Cold War ended, Western policymakers have sought to create security arrangements in Europe, as well as in other regions of the globe, that are based on international institutions. In doing so, they explicitly reject balance-of-power politics as an organizing concept for the post–Cold War world. During the 1992 presidential campaign, for example, President Clinton declared that, "in a world where freedom, not tyranny, is on the march, the cynical calculus of pure power politics simply does not compute. It is ill-suited to a new era." Before taking office, Anthony Lake, the president's national security adviser, criticized the Bush administration for viewing the world through a "classic balance of power prism," whereas he and Mr. Clinton took a "more 'neo-Wilsonian' view."[1]

This approach to international politics rests on the belief that institutions are a key means of promoting world peace.[2] In particular, Western policymakers claim that the institutions that "served the West well" before the Soviet Union collapsed must be reshaped to encompass Eastern Europe as well.[3] "There is no reason," according to Secretary of State Warren Christopher, "why our institutions or our aspirations should

John J. Mearsheimer is a professor in the Political Science Department at the University of Chicago.

This article emerged from a working paper written for "The Changing Security Environment and American National Interests," a project of the John M. Olin Institute for Strategic Studies at Harvard University. I am grateful to Robert Art, Benjamin Frankel, Markus Fischer, Charles Glaser, Hein Goemans, Joseph Grieco, Robert Jervis, Christopher Layne, Eric Lopez, Robert Pape, Ashley Tellis, Bradley Thayer, Ivan Toft, Stephen Van Evera, Stephen Walt, and especially Michael Desch for their most helpful comments.

1. Bill Clinton, "American Foreign Policy and the Democratic Ideal," Campaign speech, Pabst Theater, Milwaukee, Wisconsin, October 1, 1992; Steven A. Holmes, "Choice for National Security Adviser Has a Long-Awaited Chance to Lead," *New York Times*, January 3, 1993.
2. The other prominent theme in Western policymaking circles is the importance of spreading democracy and capitalism across the globe. Prosperous democracies, so the argument goes, do not fight each other. Thus, the aim is to increase the number of stable democracies in the international system. This line of argument is not examined here. For conciseness, international institutions are henceforth referred to simply as institutions.
3. Douglas Hurd, "A New System of Security in Europe," Speech to the Diplomatic and Commonwealth Writers' Association, London, June 2, 1992. Hurd, the British Foreign Secretary, said in this speech: "We have in Western Europe, in the West as a whole, a set of international institutions which have proved their worth for one set of problems—the problems for which they were set up, and now have to be adapted for another. That is the key, the necessary changes in all these institutions are the key to getting the right help, the right reassurance to the countries of central and Eastern Europe." Even Margaret Thatcher, with all her reservations about European institutions, has adopted this theme. She argued days after Iraq invaded Kuwait that, "We must bring the new democracies of Eastern Europe into closer association with the institutions of Western Europe. . . . The European Community has reconciled antagonisms within Western Europe; it

International Security, Winter 1994/95 (Vol. 19, No. 3)
© 1995 by the President and Fellows of Harvard College and of the Massachusetts Institute of Technology.

stop at [the] old frontiers of the Cold War."[4] The institutions he has in mind include the European Community (EC), the North Atlantic Treaty Organization (NATO), the Conference on Security and Cooperation in Europe (CSCE), and the Western European Union (WEU). No single institution is expected to play a dominating role in Europe, however; instead, the aim is to create "a framework of complementary, mutually reinforcing" institutions.[5] "We can promote more durable European security," Christopher claims, "through interlocking structures, each with complementary roles and strengths."[6]

No other region of the world has institutions as extensive and as well-developed as those in Europe. Consequently, Western policymakers trumpet the importance of creating webs of overlapping institutions outside of Europe. Special emphasis is placed on Asia, where there are only a few weak institutions, and where fear of Japan, coupled with the rise of China and the prospect of a further reduction in the American presence, has observers worried about future stability in the region.[7]

There has also been a recent wave of academic interest in institutions. Academic institutionalists, not surprisingly, consider institutions to be a powerful force for stability.[8] Robert Keohane, for example, declares that, "avoiding military conflict in Europe after the Cold War depends greatly on whether the next decade is characterized by a continuous pattern of institutionalized cooperation."[9] Commenting on the aftermath of the Soviet collapse and the end of the Cold War, John Ruggie maintains that "there seems little doubt that multilateral norms and institutions have helped stabilize their international consequences. Indeed, such norms and institutions appear to be playing

---

should now help to overcome divisions between East and West in Europe." Margaret Thatcher, "Shaping A New Global Community," Speech to the Aspen Institute, Aspen, Colorado, August 5, 1990.

4. Warren Christopher, "Toward a More Integrated World," Statement at the Organization for Economic Cooperation and Development (OECD) Ministerial Meeting, Paris, June 8, 1994. President Clinton and German Chancellor Helmut Kohl share the same view, as Clinton made clear when describing his private talks with Kohl in July 1994: "We know from our experience how half of Europe was integrated through NATO and other institutions that built stability after World War II. At the heart of our discussion today was what we have to do to integrate Europe's other half, the new independent nations." Thomas L. Friedman, "Clinton Sees Germany as Main Partner of the U.S. in Europe," *New York Times,* July 12, 1994.

5. "Interlocking Institutions: The Conference on Security and Cooperation in Europe (CSCE)," NATO Basic Fact Sheet No. 6 (Brussels, June 1994). Also see Jacques Delors, "European Unification and European Security," in *European Security after the Cold War,* Part 1, Adelphi Paper No. 284 (London: International Institute for Strategic Studies [IISS], January 1994), pp. 3–14.

6. Warren Christopher, "The CSCE Vision: European Security Rooted in Shared Values," Statement to the Plenary Session of the Conference on Security and Cooperation in Europe, Rome, November 30, 1993.

7. See Stephen J. Blank, *Helsinki in Asia?* (Carlisle Barracks, Pa.: Strategic Studies Institute, U.S. Army War College, 1993).

8. Stability is simply the absence of wars and major crises.

9. Robert O. Keohane, "The Diplomacy of Structural Change: Multilateral Institutions and State Strategies," in Helga Haftendorn and Christian Tuschhoff, eds., *America and Europe in an Era of Change* (Boulder, Colo.: Westview Press, 1993), p. 53.

a significant role in the management of a broad array of regional and global changes in the world system today."[10]

This article examines the claim that institutions push states away from war and promote peace. I concentrate on assessing the major international relations theories that employ institutions as a core concept: liberal institutionalism, collective security, and critical theory.[11] I begin, however, with a brief review of realism, because of the "institutionalist" theories is largely a response to realism, and each directly challenges realism's underlying logic.[12] Realists and institutionalists particularly disagree about whether institutions markedly affect the prospects for international stability. Realists say no; institutionalists say yes. Realists maintain that institutions are basically a reflection of the distribution of power in the world. They are based on the self-interested calculations of the great powers, and they have no independent effect on state behavior. Realists therefore believe that institutions are not an important cause of peace. They matter only on the margins. Institutionalists directly challenge this view of institutions, arguing instead that institutions can alter state preferences and therefore change state behavior. Institutions can discourage states from calculating self-interest on the basis of how every move affects their relative power positions. Institutions are independent variables, and they have the capability to move states away from war.

Although institutionalists are united in their opposition to realist claims about institutions, each institutionalist theory makes a different argument about how institutions work to alter state behavior. My goal is to evaluate these three theories to determine whether the claim that institutions cause peace is persuasive. That task involves answering four questions: 1) What are institutions? 2) How do they work to cause peace? Specifically, what is the causal logic that underpins each theory? 3) Are these different logics that explain how institutions work compelling? 4) Does the evidence support these theories?

My central conclusion is that institutions have minimal influence on state behavior, and thus hold little promise for promoting stability in the post–Cold War world. The three theories on which the case for institutions is based are all flawed. Each has problems in its causal logic, and all three institutionalist theories find little support in the historical record.

The remainder of this article is organized as follows. I begin with a brief definition of institutions and a discussion of realism, because each of the institutionalist theories takes its bearings from realism. In the main body of the article, I describe and evaluate

---

10. John G. Ruggie, "Multilateralism: The Anatomy of an Institution," *International Organization*, Vol. 46, No. 3 (Summer 1992), p. 561.

11. Prescriptions about how best to maintain peace should rest on general theories about the causes of war and peace. This point is true for both academics and policymakers. Although policymakers are seldom self-conscious in their use of theory, their views about institutions are nevertheless shaped by their implicit preferences for one theory of international relations over another.

12. Keohane, for example, writes, "Institutionalist thinking has focused its critical fire on realism." Robert O. Keohane, "Institutional Theory and the Realist Challenge After the Cold War," in David A. Baldwin, ed., *Neorealism and Neoliberalism: The Contemporary Debate* (New York: Columbia University Press, 1993), p. 271.

liberal institutionalism, collective security, and critical theory. The concluding section considers why institutions are so highly regarded by policymakers and academics, when there is so little evidence that they are an important cause of peace.

What Are Institutions?

There is no widely-agreed upon definition of institutions in the international relations literature.[13] The concept is sometimes defined so broadly as to encompass all of international relations, which gives it little analytical bite.[14] For example, defining institutions as "recognized patterns of behavior or practice around which expectations converge" allows the concept to cover almost every regularized pattern of activity between states, from war to tariff bindings negotiated under the General Agreement on Tariffs and Trade (GATT), thus rendering it largely meaningless.[15] Still, it is possible to devise a useful definition that is consistent with how most institutionalist scholars employ the concept.

I define institutions as a set of rules that stipulate the ways in which states should cooperate and compete with each other.[16] They prescribe acceptable forms of state behavior, and proscribe unacceptable kinds of behavior. These rules are negotiated by states, and according to many prominent theorists, they entail the mutual acceptance of higher norms, which are "standards of behavior defined in terms of rights and obligations."[17] These rules are typically formalized in international agreements, and are

---

13. Regimes and institutions are treated as synonymous concepts in this article. They are also used interchangeably in the institutionalist literature. See Robert O. Keohane, "International Institutions: Two Approaches," *International Studies Quarterly*, Vol. 32, No. 4 (December 1988), p. 384; Robert O. Keohane, *International Institutions and State Power: Essays in International Relations Theory* (Boulder, Colo.: Westview Press, 1989), pp. 3–4; and Oran R. Young, *International Cooperation: Building Regimes for Natural Resources and the Environment* (Ithaca, N.Y.: Cornell University Press, 1989), chaps. 1 and 8. The term "multilateralism" is also virtually synonymous with institutions. To quote John Ruggie, "the term 'multilateral' is an adjective that modifies the noun 'institution.' Thus, multilateralism depicts a *generic institutional form* in international relations. . . . [Specifically,] multilateralism is an institutional form which coordinates relations among three or more states on the basis of 'generalized' principles of conduct." Ruggie, "Multilateralism," pp. 570–571.
14. For discussion of this point, see Arthur A. Stein, *Why Nations Cooperate: Circumstance and Choice in International Relations* (Ithaca, N.Y.: Cornell University Press, 1990), pp. 25–27. Also see Susan Strange, "*Cave! Hic Dragones*: A Critique of Regime Analysis," in Stephen D. Krasner, ed., *International Regimes*, special issue of *International Organization*, Vol. 36, No. 2 (Spring 1982), pp. 479–496.
15. Oran R. Young, "Regime Dynamics: The Rise and Fall of International Regimes," in Krasner, *International Regimes*, p. 277.
16. See Douglass C. North and Robert P. Thomas, "An Economic Theory of the Growth of the Western World," *The Economic History Review*, 2nd series, Vol. 23, No. 1 (April 1970), p. 5.
17. Krasner, *International Regimes*, p. 186. Non-realist institutions are often based on higher norms, while few, if any, realist institutions are based on norms. The dividing line between norms and rules is not sharply defined in the institutionalist literature. See Robert O. Keohane, *After Hegemony: Cooperation and Discord in the World Political Economy* (Princeton, N.J.: Princeton University Press, 1984), pp. 57–58. For example, one might argue that rules, not just norms, are concerned with rights and obligations. The key point, however, is that for many institutionalists, norms, which are core beliefs about standards of appropriate state behavior, are the foundation on which more specific rules are constructed. This distinction between norms and rules applies in a rather straightforward

usually embodied in organizations with their own personnel and budgets.[18] Although rules are usually incorporated into a formal international organization, it is not the organization *per se* that compels states to obey the rules. Institutions are not a form of world government. States themselves must choose to obey the rules they created. Institutions, in short, call for the "decentralized cooperation of individual sovereign states, without any effective mechanism of command."[19]

To answer the three remaining questions about how institutions do or do not work, we must examine the different institutionalist theories separately. However, a brief discussion of realism is in order first.

Realism

Realism paints a rather grim picture of world politics.[20] The international system is portrayed as a brutal arena where states look for opportunities to take advantage of each other, and therefore have little reason to trust each other.[21] Daily life is essentially a struggle for power, where each state strives not only to be the most powerful actor in the system, but also to ensure that no other state achieves that lofty position.

International relations is not a constant state of war, but it is a state of relentless security competition, with the possibility of war always in the background. The intensity of that competition varies from case to case. Although it might seem counterintuitive, states do frequently cooperate in this competitive world. Nevertheless, cooperation among states has its limits, mainly because it is constrained by the dominating logic of security competition, which no amount of cooperation can eliminate. Genuine peace, or a world where states do not compete for power, is not likely, according to realism.

---

way in the subsequent discussion. Both collective security and critical theory challenge the realist belief that states behave in a self-interested way, and argue instead for developing norms that require states to act more altruistically. Liberal institutionalism, on the other hand, accepts the realist view that states act on the basis of self-interest, and concentrates on devising rules that facilitate cooperation among states.

18. International organizations are public agencies established through the cooperative efforts of two or more states. These administrative structures have their own budget, personnel, and buildings. John Ruggie defines them as "palpable entities with headquarters and letterheads, voting procedures, and generous pension plans." Ruggie, "Multilateralism," p. 573. Once rules are incorporated into an international organization, "they may seem almost coterminous," even though they are "distinguishable analytically." Keohane, *International Institutions and State Power*, p. 5.

19. Charles Lipson, "Is the Future of Collective Security Like the Past?" in George W. Downs, ed., *Collective Security beyond the Cold War* (Ann Arbor: University of Michigan Press), p. 114.

20. Although realist scholars agree about many aspects of international politics, there are important intellectual disagreements among them. Consider Hans Morgenthau and Kenneth Waltz, probably the two most influential realists over the past fifty years. Morgenthau maintains that states have a will to power, while Waltz begins his theory with the assumption that states merely want to survive and are therefore driven to maximize security. See Hans J. Morgenthau, *Politics Among Nations: The Struggle for Power and Peace*, 5th ed. (New York: Knopf, 1973); and Kenneth N. Waltz, *Theory of International Politics* (Reading, Mass.: Addison-Wesley, 1979). The discussion in this section is based on my own thinking about realism, which is closer to Waltz than to Morgenthau.

21. See Stephen Van Evera, "The Hard Realities of International Politics," *Boston Review*, Vol. 17, No. 6 (November/December 1992), p. 19.

This pessimistic view of how the world works can be derived from realism's five assumptions about the international system. The first is that the international system is anarchic. This does not mean that it is chaotic or riven by disorder.[22] It is easy to draw that conclusion, since realism depicts a world characterized by security competition and war. However, "anarchy" as employed by realists has nothing to do with conflict; rather it is an ordering principle, which says that the system comprises independent political units (states) that have no central authority above them. Sovereignty, in other words, inheres in states, because there is no higher ruling body in the international system. There is no "government over governments."[23]

The second assumption is that states inherently possess some offensive military capability, which gives them the wherewithal to hurt and possibly to destroy each other. States are potentially dangerous to each other. A state's military power is usually identified with the particular weaponry at its disposal, although even if there were no weapons, the individuals of a state could still use their feet and hands to attack the population of another state.

The third assumption is that states can never be certain about the intentions of other states. Specifically, no state can be certain another state will not use its offensive military capability against the first. This is not to say that states necessarily have malign intentions. Another state may be reliably benign, but it is impossible to be certain of that judgment because intentions are impossible to divine with 100 percent certainty. There are many possible causes of aggression, and no state can be sure that another state is not motivated by one of them. Furthermore, intentions can change quickly, so a state's intentions can be benign one day and malign the next. Uncertainty is unavoidable when assessing intentions, which simply means that states can never be sure that other states do not have offensive intentions to go with their offensive military capability.

The fourth assumption is that the most basic motive driving states is survival. States want to maintain their sovereignty. The fifth assumption is that states think strategically about how to survive in the international system. States are instrumentally rational. Nevertheless, they may miscalculate from time to time because they operate in a world of imperfect information, where potential adversaries have incentives to misrepresent their own strength or weakness and to conceal their true aims.

None of these assumptions alone mandates that states will behave competitively. In fact, the fundamental assumption dealing with motives says that states merely aim to survive, which is a defensive goal.[24] When taken together, however, these five assump-

---

22. See Waltz, *Theory of International Politics*, pp. 88–93. Also see Robert J. Art and Robert Jervis, eds., *International Politics: Anarchy, Force, Imperialism* (Boston: Little, Brown, 1973), part 1; and Helen Milner, "International Theories of Cooperation among Nations: Strengths and Weaknesses," *World Politics*, Vol. 44, No. 3 (April 1992), p. 468.

23. Inis L. Claude, Jr., *Swords Into Plowshares: The Problems and Progress of International Organization*, 4th ed. (New York: Random House, 1971), p. 14.

24. Morgenthau, as emphasized, maintains that states have an innate will to power, and are therefore inherently offensive in their outlook. The argument here is that states begin with a defensive motive, but are forced to think and sometimes act offensively because of the structure of the international system.

tions can create incentives for states to think and sometimes to behave aggressively. Specifically, three main patterns of behavior result.

First, states in the international system fear each other. They regard each other with suspicion, and they worry that war might be in the offing. They anticipate danger. There is little room for trust among states. Although the level of fear varies across time and space, it can never be reduced to a trivial level.[25] The basis of this fear is that in a world where states have the capability to offend against each other, and might have the motive to do so, any state bent on survival must be at least suspicious of other states and reluctant to trust them. Add to this the assumption that there is no central authority that a threatened state can turn to for help, and states have even greater incentive to fear each other. Moreover, there is no mechanism—other than the possible self-interest of third parties—for punishing an aggressor. Because it is often difficult to deter potential aggressors, states have ample reason to take steps to be prepared for war.

The possible consequences of falling victim to aggression further illustrate why fear is a potent force in world politics. States do not compete with each other as if international politics were simply an economic marketplace. Political competition among states is a much more dangerous business than economic intercourse; it can lead to war, and war often means mass killing on the battlefield and even mass murder of civilians. In extreme cases, war can even lead to the total destruction of a state. The horrible consequences of war sometimes cause states to view each other not just as competitors, but as potentially deadly enemies.

Second, each state in the international system aims to guarantee its own survival. Because other states are potential threats, and because there is no higher authority to rescue them when danger arises, states cannot depend on others for their security. Each state tends to see itself as vulnerable and alone, and therefore it aims to provide for its own survival. As Kenneth Waltz puts it, states operate in a "self-help" system. This emphasis on self-help does not preclude states from forming alliances.[26] But alliances are only temporary marriages of convenience, where today's alliance partner might be tomorrow's enemy, and today's enemy might be tomorrow's alliance partner. States operating in a self-help world should always act according to their own self-interest, because it pays to be selfish in a self-help world. This is true in the short term as well as the long term, because if a state loses in the short run, it may not be around for the long haul.

Third, states in the international system aim to maximize their relative power positions over other states.[27] The reason is simple: the greater the military advantage one

---

25. This point is illustrated by the reaction of Britain and France to German reunification at the end of the Cold War. Despite the fact that these three states had been close allies for almost forty-five years, both Britain and France immediately began thinking about the dangers of a united Germany. See David Garnham, "European Defense Cooperation: The 1990s and Beyond," in Dale L. Smith and James Lee Ray, eds., *The 1992 Project and the Future of Integration In Europe* (Armonk, N.Y.: M.E. Sharpe, 1993), pp. 203–205; and Margaret Thatcher, *The Downing Street Years* (New York: HarperCollins, 1993), chaps. 25–26.
26. See Stephen M. Walt, *The Origins of Alliances* (Ithaca, N.Y.: Cornell University Press, 1987).
27. There is disagreement among realists on this point. Some realists argue that states are principally interested in maintaining the existing balance of power, not maximizing relative power. For

state has over other states, the more secure it is. Every state would like to be the most formidable military power in the system because this is the best way to guarantee survival in a world that can be very dangerous. This logic creates strong incentives for states to take advantage of one another, including going to war if the circumstances are right and victory seems likely. The aim is to acquire more military power at the expense of potential rivals. The ideal outcome would be to end up as the hegemon in the system. Survival would then be almost guaranteed.

All states are influenced by this logic, which means not only that they look for opportunities to take advantage of one another, but also that they work to insure that other states do not take advantage of them.[28] States are, in other words, both offensively-oriented and defensively-oriented. They think about conquest themselves, and they balance against aggressors; this inexorably leads to a world of constant security competition, with the possibility of war always in the background. Peace, if one defines that concept as a state of tranquility or mutual concord, is not likely to break out in this world.

COOPERATION IN A REALIST WORLD

Although realism envisions a world that is fundamentally competitive, cooperation between states does occur. It is sometimes difficult to achieve, however, and always difficult to sustain. Two factors inhibit cooperation: relative-gains considerations, and concern about cheating.[29]

States contemplating cooperation must consider how the profits or gains will be distributed among them. They can think about the division in two different ways. They can think in terms of absolute gains, which means each side focuses on maximizing its own profit, and cares little about how much the other side gains or loses in the deal. Each side cares about the other only to the extent that the other side's behavior affects its own prospects for achieving maximum profits. Alternately, states can think in terms of relative gains, which means each side not only considers its individual gain, but also how well it does compared to the other side.

Because states in a realist world are concerned about the balance of power, they must be motivated primarily by relative gains concerns when considering cooperation. While each state wants to maximize its absolute gains, it is more important to make sure that it does better, or at least no worse, than the other state in any agreement. However, cooperation is more difficult to achieve when states are attuned to relative-gains logic, rather than absolute-gains logic. This is because states concerned about absolute gains

---

examples of this "defensive realism," which contrasts with my "offensive realism," see: Joseph M. Grieco, "Anarchy and the Limits of Cooperation: A Realist Critique of the Newest Liberal Institutionalism," *International Organization*, Vol. 42, No. 3 (Summer 1988), pp. 498–500; Jack L. Snyder, *Myths of Empire: Domestic Politics and International Ambition* (Ithaca, N.Y.: Cornell University Press, 1991), pp. 10–13; and Waltz, *Theory of International Politics*, pp. 126–127. Also see Fareed Zakaria, "Realism and Domestic Politics: A Review Essay," *International Security*, Vol. 17, No. 1 (Summer 1992), pp. 190–196. Morgenthau is also an offensive realist. This disagreement notwithstanding, all realists do believe that states care greatly about the relative balance of power.
28. See Walt, *Origins of Alliances*.
29. See Grieco, "Anarchy and the Limits of Cooperation."

need only make sure that the pie is expanding and that they are getting at least some portion of the increase, while states that worry about relative gains must care also about how the pie is divided, which complicates cooperative efforts.

Concerns about cheating also hinder cooperation. States are often reluctant to enter into cooperative agreements for fear that the other side will cheat on the agreement and gain a relative advantage. There is a "special peril of defection" in the military realm, because the nature of military weaponry allows for rapid shifts in the balance of power. Such a development could create a window of opportunity for the cheating state to inflict a decisive defeat on the victim state.[30]

These barriers to cooperation notwithstanding, states do cooperate in a realist world. For example, balance-of-power logic often causes states to form alliances and cooperate against common enemies. States sometimes cooperate to gang up on a third state, as the Germans and the Soviets did against Poland in 1939.[31] Rivals as well as allies cooperate. After all, deals can be struck that roughly reflect the distribution of power, and satisfy concerns about cheating. The various arms control agreements signed by the superpowers during the Cold War illustrate this point.

The bottom line, however, is that cooperation takes place in a world that is competitive at its core—one where states have powerful incentives to take advantage of other states. This point is graphically highlighted by European politics in the forty years before World War I. There was much cooperation among the great powers during this period, but that did not stop them from going to war in 1914.[32]

INSTITUTIONS IN A REALIST WORLD

Realists also recognize that states sometimes operate through institutions. However, they believe that those rules reflect state calculations of self-interest based primarily on the international distribution of power. The most powerful states in the system create and shape institutions so that they can maintain their share of world power, or even increase it. In this view, institutions are essentially "arenas for acting out power relationships."[33] For realists, the causes of war and peace are mainly a function of the balance of power, and institutions largely mirror the distribution of power in the system. In short, the balance of power is the independent variable that explains war; institutions are merely an intervening variable in the process.

NATO provides a good example of realist thinking about institutions. NATO is an institution, and it certainly played a role in preventing World War III and helping the

---

30. Lipson, "International Cooperation," p. 14.
31. Randall L. Schweller, "Bandwagoning for Profit: Bringing the Revisionist State Back In," *International Security*, Vol. 19, No. 1 (Summer 1994), pp. 72–107.
32. See John Maynard Keynes, *The Economic Consequences of the Peace* (New York: Penguin Books, 1988), chap. 2; and J.M. Roberts, *Europe, 1880–1945* (London: Longman, 1970), pp. 239–241. There was also significant cooperation between the United States and the Soviet Union during World War II, but that cooperation did not prevent the outbreak of the Cold War shortly after Germany and Japan were defeated.
33. Tony Evans and Peter Wilson, "Regime Theory and the English School of International Relations: A Comparison," *Millennium: Journal of International Studies*, Vol. 21, No. 3 (Winter 1992), p. 330.

West win the Cold War. Nevertheless, NATO was basically a manifestation of the bipolar distribution of power in Europe during the Cold War, and it was that balance of power, not NATO *per se*, that provided the key to maintaining stability on the continent. NATO was essentially an American tool for managing power in the face of the Soviet threat. Now, with the collapse of the Soviet Union, realists argue that NATO must either disappear or reconstitute itself on the basis of the new distribution of power in Europe.[34] NATO cannot remain as it was during the Cold War.

Varieties of Institutionalist Theories

There are three institutionalist theories, and each offers a different argument about how institutions push states away from war and help foster stability.[35] Liberal institutionalism is the least ambitious of the three theories. It does not directly address the important question of how to prevent war, but focuses instead on explaining why economic and environmental cooperation among states is more likely than realists recognize. Increased cooperation in those realms is presumed to reduce the likelihood of war, although liberal institutionalists do not explain how. The theory is predicated on the belief that cheating is the main inhibitor of international cooperation, and that institutions provide the key to overcoming that problem. The aim is to create rules that constrain states, but not to challenge the fundamental realist claim that states are self-interested actors.

Collective security directly confronts the issue of how to prevent war. The theory starts with the assumption that force will continue to matter in world politics, and that states will have to guard against potential aggressors. However, the threat of war can be greatly reduced, according to the theory, by challenging realist thinking about state behavior, and substituting in its place three anti-realist norms. First, states should reject the idea of using force to change the status quo. Second, to deal with states that violate that norm and threaten (or start) a war, responsible states must not act on the basis of their own narrow self-interest. Rather, they must suppress the temptation to respond in whatever way would maximize their individual gains, and instead automatically join together to present the aggressor with the threat of overwhelming force. Third, states must trust each other to renounce aggression and to mean that renunciation. They must also be confident that other states will come to their rescue, should they become the target of aggression.

Critical theory is the most ambitious of the theories, as its ultimate aim is to transform the fundamental nature of international politics and to create a world where there is not just increased cooperation among states, but the possibility of genuine peace. Like collective security, but unlike liberal institutionalism, critical theory directly challenges

---

34. See Gunther Hellmann and Reinhard Wolf, "Neorealism, Neoliberal Institutionalism, and the Future of NATO," *Security Studies*, Vol. 3, No. 1 (Autumn 1993), pp. 3–43.
35. Despite these differences among institutionalist theories, proponents of each theory occasionally make favorable reference to the other theories, and thus seem to recognize that all three theories are part of an institutionalist body of literature that takes anti-realism as its main point of reference. See, for example: Charles A. Kupchan and Clifford A. Kupchan, "Concerts, Collective Security, and the Future of Europe," *International Security*, Vol. 16, No. 1 (Summer 1991), pp. 114–161; and Ruggie, "Multilateralism," pp. 561–598.

realist thinking about the self-interested behavior of states. The theory is predicated on the assumption that ideas and discourse—how we think and talk about international politics—are the driving forces behind state behavior. It utterly rejects realism's claim that state behavior is largely a function of the given structure of the external world. For critical theorists, ideas shape the material world in important ways, and thus the way to revolutionize international politics is to change drastically the way individuals think and talk about world politics. Intellectuals, especially the critical theorists themselves, are believed to play a key role in that process.

LIBERAL INSTITUTIONALISM

Liberal institutionalism does not directly address the question of whether institutions cause peace, but instead focuses on the less ambitious goal of explaining cooperation in cases where state interests are not fundamentally opposed.[36] Specifically, the theory looks at cases where states are having difficulty cooperating because they have "mixed" interests; in other words, each side has incentives both to cooperate and not to cooperate.[37] Each side can benefit from cooperation, however, which liberal institutionalists define as "goal-directed behavior that entails mutual policy adjustments so that all sides end up better off than they would otherwise be."[38] The theory is of little relevance in situations where states' interests are fundamentally conflictual and neither side thinks it has much to gain from cooperation. In these circumstances, states aim to gain advantage over each other. They think in terms of winning and losing, and this invariably leads to intense security competition, and sometimes war. But liberal institutionalism does not deal directly with these situations, and thus says little about how to resolve or even ameliorate them.

Therefore, the theory largely ignores security issues and concentrates instead on economic and, to a lesser extent, environmental issues.[39] In fact, the theory is built on the assumption that international politics can be divided into two realms—security and

---

36. Among the key liberal institutionalist works are: Robert Axelrod and Robert O. Keohane, "Achieving Cooperation under Anarchy: Strategies and Institutions," *World Politics*, Vol. 38, No. 1 (October 1985), pp. 226–254; Keohane, *After Hegemony*; Keohane, "International Institutions: Two Approaches," pp. 379–396; Keohane, *International Institutions and State Power*, chap. 1; Charles Lipson, "International Cooperation in Economic and Security Affairs," *World Politics*, Vol. 37, No. 1 (October 1984), pp. 1–23; Lisa L. Martin, "Institutions and Cooperation: Sanctions During the Falkland Islands Conflict," *International Security*, Vol. 16, No. 4 (Spring 1992), pp. 143–178; Lisa L. Martin, *Coercive Cooperation: Explaining Multilateral Economic Sanctions* (Princeton, N.J.: Princeton University Press, 1992); Kenneth A. Oye, "Explaining Cooperation Under Anarchy: Hypotheses and Strategies," *World Politics*, Vol. 38, No. 1 (October 1985), pp. 1–24; and Stein, *Why Nations Cooperate*.
37. Stein, *Why Nations Cooperate*, chap. 2. Also see Keohane, *After Hegemony*, pp. 6–7, 12–13, 67–69.
38. Milner, "International Theories of Cooperation," p. 468.
39. For examples of the theory at work in the environmental realm, see Peter M. Haas, Robert O. Keohane, and Marc A. Levy, eds., *Institutions for the Earth: Sources of Effective International Environmental Protection* (Cambridge, Mass.: MIT Press, 1993), especially chaps. 1 and 9. Some of the most important work on institutions and the environment has been done by Oran Young. See, for example, Young, *International Cooperation*. The rest of my discussion concentrates on economic, not environmental issues, for conciseness, and also because the key theoretical works in the liberal institutionalist literature focus on economic rather than environmental matters.

political economy—and that liberal institutionalism mainly applies to the latter, but not the former. This theme is clearly articulated by Charles Lipson, who writes that "significantly different institutional arrangements are associated with international economic and security issues."[40] Moreover, the likelihood of cooperation is markedly different within these two realms: when economic relations are at stake, "cooperation can be sustained among several self-interested states," whereas the prospects for cooperation are "more impoverished . . . in security affairs."[41] Thus, the theory's proponents pay little attention to the security realm, where questions about war and peace are of central importance.

Nevertheless, there are good reasons to examine liberal institutionalism closely. Liberal institutionalists sometimes assert that institutions are an important cause of international stability. Moreover, one might argue that if the theory shows a strong causal connection between institutions and economic cooperation, it would be relatively easy to take the next step and link cooperation with peace.[42] Some proponents of the theory maintain that institutions contribute to international stability; this suggests that they believe it is easy to connect cooperation and stability.[43] I doubt this claim, mainly because proponents of the theory define cooperation so narrowly as to avoid military issues. Let us assume, however, that liberal institutionalists are attempting to take a giant step toward developing a theory that explains how institutions push states away from war.

CAUSAL LOGIC. Liberal institutionalists claim to accept realism's root assumptions while arguing that cooperation is nevertheless easier to achieve than realists recognize. Robert Keohane, for example, writes in *After Hegemony* that he is "adopting the realist model of rational egoism." He continues: "I propose to show, on the basis of their own assumptions, that the characteristic pessimism of realism does not necessarily follow. I seek to demonstrate that realist assumptions about world politics are consistent with the formation of institutionalized arrangements . . . which promote cooperation."[44] In particular, liberal institutionalists emphasize that states "dwell in perpetual anarchy," and must therefore act as rational egoists in what is a self-help world.[45]

---

40. Lipson, "International Cooperation," pp. 2, 12. Also see Axelrod and Keohane, "Achieving Cooperation Under Anarchy," pp. 232–233; and Keohane, *After Hegemony,* pp. 39–41.
41. Lipson, "International Cooperation," p. 18.
42. I have suggested a possible line of argument in John J. Mearsheimer, "Back to the Future: Instability in Europe After the Cold War," *International Security,* Vol. 15, No. 1 (Summer 1990), pp. 42–44. Also, Charles Glaser makes the connection between cooperation and peace in "Realists as Optimists: Cooperation as Self-Help," *International Security,* Vol. 19, No. 3 (Winter 1994/95), pp. 50–90.
43. Liberal institutionalists assume that cooperation is a positive goal, although they recognize it has a downside as well. See Keohane, *After Hegemony,* pp. 10–11, 247–257; and Keohane, "International Institutions: Two Approaches," p. 393. The virtues and vices of cooperation are not explored in any detail in the liberal institutionalist literature.
44. Keohane, *After Hegemony,* p. 67; also see p. 29. Similarly, Arthur Stein claims that, "Despite the different conclusions that they draw about the cooperative or conflictual nature of international politics, realism and liberalism share core assumptions." Stein, *Why Nations Cooperate,* p. 8.
45. Oye, "Explaining Cooperation Under Anarchy," p. 1.

According to liberal institutionalists, the principal obstacle to cooperation among states with mutual interests is the threat of cheating.[46] The famous "prisoners' dilemma," which is the analytical centerpiece of most of the liberal institutionalist literature, captures the essence of the problem that states must solve to achieve cooperation.[47] Each of two states can either cheat or cooperate with the other. Each side wants to maximize its own gain, but does not care about the size of the other side's gain; each side cares about the other side only so far as the other side's chosen strategy affects its own prospects for maximizing gain. The most attractive strategy for each state is to cheat and hope the other state pursues a cooperative strategy. In other words, a state's ideal outcome is to "sucker" the other side into thinking it is going to cooperate, and then cheat. But both sides understand this logic, and therefore both sides will try to cheat the other. Consequently, both sides will end up worse off than if they had cooperated, since mutual cheating leads to the worst possible outcome. Even though mutual cooperation is not as attractive as suckering the other side, it is certainly better than the outcome when both sides cheat.

The key to solving this dilemma is for each side to convince the other that they have a collective interest in making what appear to be short-term sacrifices (the gain that might result from successful cheating) for the sake of long-term benefits (the substantial payoff from mutual long-term cooperation). This means convincing states to accept the second-best outcome, which is mutual collaboration. The principal obstacle to reaching this cooperative outcome will be fear of getting suckered, should the other side cheat. This, in a nutshell, is the problem that institutions must solve.

To deal with this problem of "political market failure," institutions must deter cheaters and protect victims.[48] Three messages must be sent to potential cheaters: you will be caught, you will be punished immediately, and you will jeopardize future cooperative efforts. Potential victims, on the other hand, need early warning of cheating to avoid serious injury, and need the means to punish cheaters.

Liberal institutionalists do not aim to deal with cheaters and victims by changing fundamental norms of state behavior. Nor do they suggest transforming the anarchical nature of the international system. They accept the assumption that states operate in an anarchic environment and behave in a self-interested manner.[49] In this regard, their approach is less ambitious than collective security and critical theory, which aim to alter

---

46. Cheating is basically a "breach of promise." Oye, "Explaining Cooperation Under Anarchy," p. 1. It usually implies unobserved non-compliance, although there can be observed cheating as well. Defection is a synonym for cheating in the institutionalist literature.
47. The centrality of the prisoners' dilemma and cheating to the liberal institutionalist literature is clearly reflected in virtually all the works cited in footnote 36. As Helen Milner notes in her review essay on this literature: "The focus is primarily on the role of regimes [institutions] in solving the defection [cheating] problem." Milner, "International Theories of Cooperation," p. 475.
48. The phrase is from Keohane, *After Hegemony*, p. 85.
49. Kenneth Oye, for example, writes in the introduction to an issue of *World Politics* containing a number of liberal institutionalist essays: "Our focus is on non-altruistic cooperation among states dwelling in international anarchy." Oye, "Explaining Cooperation Under Anarchy," p. 2. Also see Keohane, "International Institutions: Two Approaches," pp. 380–381; and Keohane, *International Institutions and State Power*, p. 3.

important international norms. Liberal institutionalists instead concentrate on showing how rules can work to counter the cheating problem, even while states seek to maximize their own welfare. They argue that institutions can change a state's calculations about how to maximize gains. Specifically, rules can get states to make the short-term sacrifices needed to resolve the prisoners' dilemma and thus to realize long-term gains. Institutions, in short, can produce cooperation.

Rules can ideally be employed to make four major changes in "the contractual environment."[50] First, rules can increase the number of transactions between particular states over time.[51] This *institutionalized iteration* discourages cheating in three ways. It raises the costs of cheating by creating the prospect of future gains through cooperation, thereby invoking "the shadow of the future" to deter cheating today. A state caught cheating would jeopardize its prospects of benefiting from future cooperation, since the victim would probably retaliate. In addition, iteration gives the victim the opportunity to pay back the cheater: it allows for reciprocation, the tit-for-tat strategy, which works to punish cheaters and not allow them to get away with their transgression. Finally, it rewards states that develop a reputation for faithful adherence to agreements, and punishes states that acquire a reputation for cheating.[52]

Second, rules can tie together interactions between states in different issue areas. *Issue-linkage* aims to create greater interdependence between states, who will then be reluctant to cheat in one issue area for fear that the victim—and perhaps other states as well—will retaliate in another issue area. It discourages cheating in much the same way as iteration: it raises the costs of cheating and provides a way for the victim to retaliate against the cheater.

Third, a structure of rules can increase the amount of *information* available to participants in cooperative agreements so that close monitoring is possible. Raising the level of information discourages cheating in two ways: it increases the likelihood that cheaters will be caught, and more importantly, it provides victims with early warning of cheating, thereby enabling them to take protective measures before they are badly hurt.

Fourth, rules can reduce the *transaction costs* of individual agreements.[53] When institutions perform the tasks described above, states can devote less effort to negotiating and monitoring cooperative agreements, and to hedging against possible defections. By increasing the efficiency of international cooperation, institutions make it more profitable and thus more attractive for self-interested states.

Liberal institutionalism is generally thought to be of limited utility in the security realm, because fear of cheating is considered a much greater obstacle to cooperation

---

50. Haas, Keohane, and Levy, *Institutions for the Earth*, p. 11. For general discussions of how rules work, which inform my subsequent discussion of the matter, see Keohane, *After Hegemony*, chaps. 5–6; Martin, "Institutions and Cooperation," pp. 143–178; and Milner, "International Theories of Cooperation," pp. 474–478.
51. See Axelrod and Keohane, "Achieving Cooperation Under Anarchy," pp. 248–250; Lipson, "International Cooperation," pp. 4–18.
52. Lipson, "International Cooperation," p. 5.
53. See Keohane, *After Hegemony*, pp. 89–92.

when military issues are at stake.[54] There is the constant threat that betrayal will result in a devastating military defeat. This threat of "swift, decisive defection" is simply not present when dealing with international economics. Given that "the costs of betrayal" are potentially much graver in the military than the economic sphere, states will be very reluctant to accept the "one step backward, two steps forward" logic which underpins the tit-for-tat strategy of conditional cooperation. One step backward in the security realm might mean destruction, in which case there will be no next step—backward or forward.[55]

FLAWS IN THE CAUSAL LOGIC.   There is an important theoretical failing in the liberal institutionalist logic, even as it applies to economic issues. The theory is correct as far as it goes: cheating can be a serious barrier to cooperation. It ignores, however, the other major obstacle to cooperation: relative-gains concerns. As Joseph Grieco has shown, liberal institutionalists assume that states are not concerned about relative gains, but focus exclusively on absolute gains.[56] Keohane acknowledged this problem in 1993: "Grieco has made a significant contribution by focusing attention on the issue of relative gains, a subject that has been underemphasized, especially by liberal or neoliberal commentators on the world economy."[57]

This oversight is revealed by the assumed order of preference in the prisoners' dilemma game: each state cares about how its opponent's strategy will affect its own (absolute) gains, but not about how much one side gains relative to the other. In other words, each side simply wants to get the best deal for itself, and does not pay attention to how well the other side fares in the process.[58] Nevertheless, liberal institutionalists

---

54. This point is clearly articulated in Lipson, "International Cooperation," especially pp. 12–18. The subsequent quotations in this paragraph are from ibid. Also see Axelrod and Keohane, "Achieving Cooperation Under Anarchy," pp. 232–233.
55. See Roger B. Parks, "What if 'Fools Die'? A Comment on Axelrod," Letter to *American Political Science Review*, Vol. 79, No. 4 (December 1985), pp. 1173–1174.
56. See Grieco, "Anarchy and the Limits of Cooperation." Other works by Grieco bearing on the subject include: Joseph M. Grieco, "Realist Theory and the Problem of International Cooperation: Analysis with an Amended Prisoner's Dilemma Model," *The Journal of Politics*, Vol. 50, No. 3 (August 1988), pp. 600–624; Grieco, *Cooperation among Nations: Europe, America, and Non-Tariff Barriers to Trade* (Ithaca, N.Y.: Cornell University Press, 1990); and Grieco, "Understanding the Problem of International Cooperation: The Limits of Neoliberal Institutionalism and the Future of Realist Theory," in Baldwin, *Neorealism and Neoliberalism*, pp. 301–338. The telling effect of Grieco's criticism is reflected in ibid., which is essentially organized around the relative gains vs. absolute gains debate, an issue given little attention before Grieco raised it in his widely cited 1988 article. The matter was briefly discussed by two other scholars before Grieco. See Joanne Gowa, "Anarchy, Egoism, and Third Images: *The Evolution of Cooperation* and International Relations," *International Organization*, Vol. 40, No. 1 (Winter 1986), pp. 172–179; and Oran R. Young, "International Regimes: Toward a New Theory of Institutions," *World Politics*, Vol. 39, No. 1 (October 1986), pp. 118–119.
57. Robert O. Keohane, "Institutional Theory and the Realist Challenge," in Baldwin, *Neorealism and Neoliberalism*, p. 283. When liberal institutionalists developed their theory in the mid-1980s, they did not explicitly assume that states pursue absolute gains. There is actually little evidence that they thought much about the distinction between relative gains and absolute gains. However, the assumption that states pursue absolute but not relative gains is implicit in their writings.
58. Lipson writes: "The Prisoner's Dilemma, in its simplest form, involves two players. Each is assumed to be a self-interested, self-reliant maximizer of his own utility, an assumption that clearly parallels the Realist conception of sovereign states in international politics." Lipson, "International

cannot ignore relative-gains considerations, because they assume that states are self-interested actors in an anarchic system, and they recognize that military power matters to states. A theory that explicitly accepts realism's core assumptions—and liberal institutionalism does that—must confront the issue of relative gains if it hopes to develop a sound explanation for why states cooperate.

One might expect liberal institutionalists to offer the counterargument that relative-gains logic applies only to the security realm, while absolute-gains logic applies to the economic realm. Given that they are mainly concerned with explaining economic and environmental cooperation, leaving relative-gains concerns out of the theory does not matter.

There are two problems with this argument. First, if cheating were the only significant obstacle to cooperation, liberal institutionalists could argue that their theory applies to the economic, but not the military realm. In fact, they do make that argument. However, once relative-gains considerations are factored into the equation, it becomes impossible to maintain the neat dividing line between economic and military issues, mainly because military might is significantly dependent on economic might. The relative size of a state's economy has profound consequences for its standing in the international balance of military power. Therefore, relative-gains concerns must be taken into account for security reasons when looking at the economic as well as military domain. The neat dividing line that liberal institutionalists employ to specify when their theory applies has little utility when one accepts that states worry about relative gains.[59]

Second, there are non-realist (i.e., non-security) logics that might explain why states worry about relative gains. Strategic trade theory, for example, provides a straightforward economic logic for why states should care about relative gains.[60] It argues that states should help their own firms gain comparative advantage over the firms of rival states, because that is the best way to insure national economic prosperity. There is also a psychological logic, which portrays individuals as caring about how well they do (or their state does) in a cooperative agreement, not for material reasons, but because it is human nature to compare one's progress with that of others.[61]

Another possible liberal institutionalist counterargument is that solving the cheating problem renders the relative-gains problem irrelevant. If states cannot cheat each other, they need not fear each other, and therefore, states would not have to worry about relative power. The problem with this argument, however, is that even if the cheating problem were solved, states would still have to worry about relative gains because gaps

---

Cooperation," p. 2. Realists, however, do not accept this conception of international politics and, not surprisingly, have questioned the relevance of the prisoners' dilemma (at least in its common form) for explaining much of international relations. See Gowa, "Anarchy, Egoism, and Third Images"; Grieco, "Realist Theory and the Problem of International Cooperation"; and Stephen D. Krasner, "Global Communications and National Power: Life on the Pareto Frontier," *World Politics*, Vol. 43, No. 3 (April 1991), pp. 336–366.

59. My thinking on this matter has been markedly influenced by Sean Lynn-Jones, in his June 19, 1994, correspondence with me.

60. For a short discussion of strategic trade theory, see Robert Gilpin, *The Political Economy of International Relations* (Princeton, N.J.: Princeton University Press, 1987), pp. 215–221. The most commonly cited reference on the subject is Paul R. Krugman, ed., *Strategic Trade Policy and the New International Economics* (Cambridge, Mass.: MIT Press, 1986).

61. See Robert Axelrod, *The Evolution of Cooperation* (New York: Basic Books, 1984), pp. 110–113.

in gains can be translated into military advantage that can be used for coercion or aggression. And in the international system, states sometimes have conflicting interests that lead to aggression.

There is also empirical evidence that relative-gains considerations mattered during the Cold War even in economic relations among the advanced industrialized democracies in the Organization for Economic Cooperation and Development (OECD). One would not expect realist logic about relative gains to be influential in this case: the United States was a superpower with little to fear militarily from the other OECD states, and those states were unlikely to use a relative-gains advantage to threaten the United States.[62] Furthermore, the OECD states were important American allies during the Cold War, and thus the United States benefited strategically when they gained substantially in size and strength.

Nonetheless, relative gains appear to have mattered in economic relations among the advanced industrial states. Consider three prominent studies. Stephen Krasner considered efforts at cooperation in different sectors of the international communications industry. He found that states were remarkably unconcerned about cheating but deeply worried about relative gains, which led him to conclude that liberal institutionalism "is not relevant for global communications." Grieco examined American and EC efforts to implement, under the auspices of GATT, a number of agreements relating to non-tariff barriers to trade. He found that the level of success was not a function of concerns about cheating but was influenced primarily by concern about the distribution of gains. Similarly, Michael Mastanduno found that concern about relative gains, not about cheating, was an important factor in shaping American policy towards Japan in three cases: the FSX fighter aircraft, satellites, and high-definition television.[63]

I am not suggesting that relative-gains considerations make cooperation impossible; my point is simply that they can pose a serious impediment to cooperation and must therefore be taken into account when developing a theory of cooperation among states. This point is apparently now recognized by liberal institutionalists. Keohane, for example, acknowledges that he "did make a major mistake by underemphasizing distributive issues and the complexities they create for international cooperation."[64]

CAN LIBERAL INSTITUTIONALISM BE REPAIRED? Liberal institutionalists must address two questions if they are to repair their theory. First, can institutions facilitate

---

62. Grieco maintains in *Cooperation among Nations* that realist logic should apply here. Robert Powell, however, points out that "in the context of negotiations between the European Community and the United States . . . it is difficult to attribute any concern for relative gains to the effects that a relative loss may have on the probability of survival." Robert Powell, "Absolute and Relative Gains in International Relations Theory," *American Political Science Review*, Vol. 85, No. 4 (December 1991), p. 1319, footnote 26. I agree with Powell. It is clear from Grieco's response to Powell that Grieco includes non-military logics like strategic trade theory in the realist tent, whereas Powell and I do not. See Grieco's contribution to "The Relative-Gains Problem for International Relations," *American Political Science Review*, Vol. 87, No. 3 (September 1993), pp. 733–735.

63. Krasner, "Global Communications and National Power," pp. 336–366; Grieco, *Cooperation among Nations*; and Michael Mastanduno, "Do Relative Gains Matter? America's Response to Japanese Industrial Policy," *International Security*, Vol. 16, No. 1 (Summer 1991), pp. 73–113. Also see Jonathan B. Tucker, "Partners and Rivals: A Model of International Collaboration in Advanced Technology," *International Organization*, Vol. 45, No. 1 (Winter 1991), pp. 83–120.

64. Keohane, "Institutional Theory and the Realist Challenge," p. 292.

cooperation when states seriously care about relative gains, or do institutions only matter when states can ignore relative-gains considerations and focus instead on absolute gains? I find no evidence that liberal institutionalists believe that institutions facilitate cooperation when states care deeply about relative gains. They apparently concede that their theory only applies when relative-gains considerations matter little or hardly at all.[65] Thus the second question: when do states not worry about relative gains? The answer to this question would ultimately define the realm in which liberal institutionalism applies.

Liberal institutionalists have not addressed this important question in a systematic fashion, so any assessment of their efforts to repair the theory must be preliminary. What exists are a lengthy response by Keohane to Grieco's original work on relative gains, and two studies responding to Grieco's writings by Robert Powell and Duncan Snidal, which Keohane and other liberal institutionalists point to as exemplars of how to think about the relative-gains problem.[66]

Powell and Snidal offer different arguments about when relative-gains considerations are slight. Nevertheless, both are essentially realist arguments.[67] Neither study discusses how institutions might facilitate cooperation, and both explanations are built around familiar realist concepts.

At the root of Powell's argument is the well-known offense-defense balance made famous by Robert Jervis, George Quester, Jack Snyder, and Stephen Van Evera.[68] Powell maintains that relative-gains considerations matter little, and that states act in accordance with liberal institutionalism when the threat of aggressive war is low and "the use of force is no longer at issue."[69] That situation obtains when the cost of aggression is high, which is, in turn, a function of the "constraints imposed by the underlying technology of war."[70] In other words, when the prevailing military weaponry favors

---

65. For example, Keohane wrote after becoming aware of Grieco's argument about relative gains: "Under specified conditions—where mutual interests are low and relative gains are therefore particularly important to states—neoliberal theory expects neorealism to explain elements of state behavior." Keohane, *International Institutions and State Power,* pp. 15–16.
66. Keohane, "Institutional Theory and the Realist Challenge," pp. 269–300; Powell, "Absolute and Relative Gains," pp. 1303–1320; and Duncan Snidal, "Relative Gains and the Pattern of International Cooperation," *American Political Science Review,* Vol. 85, No. 3 (September 1991), pp. 701–726. Also see Powell, "Anarchy in International Relations Theory: The Neorealist-Neoliberal Debate," *International Organization,* Vol. 48, No. 2 (Spring 1994), pp. 313–344; Snidal, "International Cooperation among Relative Gains Maximizers," *International Studies Quarterly,* Vol. 35, No. 4 (December 1991), pp. 387–402; and Powell and Snidal's contributions to "The Relative-Gains Problem for International Cooperation," pp. 735–742.
67. On this point, see Sean Lynn-Jones, "Comments on Grieco, 'Realist Theory and the Relative Gains Problem for International Cooperation: Developments in the Debate and the Prospects for Future Research'," unpublished memorandum, December 10, 1992.
68. Robert Jervis, "Cooperation under the Security Dilemma," *World Politics,* Vol. 30, No. 2 (January 1978), pp. 167–214; George H. Quester, *Offense and Defense in the International System* (New York: John Wiley, 1977); Jack Snyder, *The Ideology of the Offensive: Military Decision Making and the Disasters of 1914* (Ithaca, N.Y.: Cornell University Press, 1984); and Stephen Van Evera, "The Cult of the Offensive and the Origins of the First World War," *International Security,* Vol. 9, No. 1 (Summer 1984), pp. 58–107.
69. Powell, "Absolute and Relative Gains," p. 1314; also see p. 1311.
70. Ibid., p. 1312. Powell does not use the term "offense-defense" balance in his article.

the offense, then the cost of war is low, and relative-gains considerations will be intense. Institutions can do little to facilitate cooperation in such circumstances. However, when defensive technology dominates, the cost of initiating aggression is high and the relative-gains problem is subdued, which allows institutions to cause cooperation.

Snidal maintains that relative-gains concerns might not matter much to states even if they face a serious threat of war. The root concept in his argument is the distribution of power in the international system.[71] Specifically, he maintains that in a multipolar system where more than a small number of states have roughly equal power, states will not worry much about relative gains. Increasing the number of states in the system decreases concern for relative gains. "The reason is that more actors enhance the possibilities of protecting oneself through forming coalitions; and, generally, the less well united one's potential enemies, the safer one is."[72] However, he concedes that "the relative gains hypothesis . . . has important consequences for two-actor situations and, where there are small numbers or important asymmetries among larger numbers, it may modify conclusions obtained from the absolute gains model."[73]

I draw three conclusions from this discussion of the liberal institutionalists' efforts to deal with the relative-gains problem. First, even if one accepts Powell and Snidal's arguments about when states largely ignore relative-gains concerns, those conditions are rather uncommon in the real world. Powell would look for a world where defensive military technologies dominate. However, it is very difficult to distinguish between offensive and defensive weapons, and Powell provides no help on this point.[74] Nuclear weapons are an exception; they are defensive weapons in situations of mutual assured destruction.[75] Still, the presence of massive numbers of nuclear weapons in the arsenals of the superpowers during the Cold War did not stop them from engaging in an intense security competition where relative-gains considerations mattered greatly. Very importantly, Powell provides no historical examples to illustrate his central argument. Snidal

---

71. Although Snidal's basic arguments about distribution of power fit squarely in the realist tradition (in fact, Grieco made them in abbreviated form in "Anarchy and the Limits of Cooperation," p. 506), the formal model he develops rests on the non-realist assumption that "gains from cooperation are proportional to the size of the involved states and are shared equally between them." Snidal, "Relative Gains," p. 715. This assumption essentially eliminates the possibility of gaps in gains and thus erases the relative-gains problem. For discussion of this matter, see Grieco's contribution to "The Relative-Gains Problem for International Cooperation," pp. 729–733.
72. Snidal, "Relative Gains," p. 716.
73. Ibid., p. 702.
74. There is general agreement that defensive weapons make conquest difficult and costly, while offensive weapons make conquest cheap and easy. However, there is no recognized set of criteria for assigning specific weapons either offensive or defensive status. See Marion Boggs, *Attempts to Define and Limit "Aggressive" Armament in Diplomacy and Strategy* (Columbia: University of Missouri, 1941); Jack Levy, "The Offensive/Defensive Balance of Military Technology: A Theoretical and Historical Analysis," *International Studies Quarterly*, Vol. 28, No. 2 (June 1984), pp. 219–238; John J. Mearsheimer, *Conventional Deterrence* (Ithaca, N.Y.: Cornell University Press, 1983), pp. 25–27; and Jonathan Shimshoni, "Technology, Military Advantage, and World War I: A Case for Military Entrepreneurship," *International Security*, Vol. 15, No. 3 (Winter 1990/1991), pp. 187–215.
75. See Shai Feldman, *Israeli Nuclear Deterrence: A Strategy for the 1980s* (New York: Columbia University Press, 1982), pp. 45–49; Charles L. Glaser, *Analyzing Strategic Nuclear Policy* (Princeton, N.J.: Princeton University Press, 1990); Jervis, "Cooperation under the Security Dilemma"; and Stephen Van Evera, *Causes of War*, Vol. II: *National Misperception and the Origins of War*, forthcoming), chap. 13.

would look for a multipolar world with large numbers of roughly equal-sized great powers. However, historically we find multipolar systems with small numbers of great powers—usually five or six—and very often significant power asymmetries within them. Snidal offers no historical examples of multipolar systems in which the great powers largely ignored relative-gains considerations.[76]

Second, liberal institutionalism itself has little new to say about when states worry about relative gains. Proponents of the theory have instead chosen to rely on two realist explanations to answer that question: the offense-defense balance and the distribution of power in the system. Thus, liberal institutionalism can hardly be called a theoretical alternative to realism, but instead should be seen as subordinate to it.[77]

Third, even in circumstances where realist logic about relative gains does not apply, non-military logics like strategic trade theory might cause states to think in terms of relative gains. Liberal institutionalist theory should directly confront those logics.

PROBLEMS WITH THE EMPIRICAL RECORD.   Although there is much evidence of cooperation among states, this alone does not constitute support for liberal institutionalism. What is needed is evidence of cooperation that would not have occurred in the absence of institutions because of fear of cheating, or its actual presence. But scholars have provided little evidence of cooperation of that sort, nor of cooperation failing because of cheating. Moreover, as discussed above, there is considerable evidence that states worry much about relative gains not only in security matters, but in the economic realm as well.

This dearth of empirical support for liberal institutionalism is acknowledged by proponents of that theory.[78] The empirical record is not completely blank, however, but the few historical cases that liberal institutionalists have studied provide scant support for the theory. Consider two prominent examples.

---

76. Keohane actually discusses the prospects for stability in post–Cold War Europe in his response to Grieco; see Keohane, "Institutional Theory and the Realist Challenge," pp. 284–291. Surprisingly, his optimistic assessment pays no attention to either Powell or Snidal's arguments, although earlier in that response, he relies on their arguments to "delimit the scope of both realist and institutionalist arguments." See ibid., p. 276.

77. Liberal institutionalists have not always been clear about the relationship between their theory and realism. For example, Keohane makes the modest claim in *After Hegemony* (p. 14) that his theory is a "modification of Realism. Realist theories. . . . need to be supplemented, though not replaced." He made a somewhat bolder claim a few years later, writing that, "despite [certain] affinities with neorealism, neoliberal institutionalism should be regarded as a distinct school of thought." Keohane, *International Institutions and State Power*, p. 8. In that same piece, however, he makes the very bold argument that "we must understand that neoliberal institutionalism is not simply an alternative to neorealism, but, in fact, claims to subsume it." Ibid., p. 15.

78. For example, Lisa Martin writes that "scholars working in the realist tradition maintain a well-founded skepticism about the empirical impact of institutional factors on state behavior. This skepticism is grounded in a lack of studies that show precisely how and when institutions have constrained state decision-making." According to Oran Young, "One of the more surprising features of the emerging literature on regimes [institutions] is the relative absence of sustained discussions of the significance of . . . institutions, as determinants of collective outcomes at the international level." Martin, "Institutions and Cooperation," p. 144; Young, *International Cooperation*, p. 206.

Keohane looked at the performance of the International Energy Agency (IEA) in 1974–81, a period that included the 1979 oil crisis.[79] This case does not appear to lend the theory much support. First, Keohane concedes that the IEA failed outright when put to the test in 1979: "regime-oriented efforts at cooperation do not always succeed, as the fiasco of IEA actions in 1979 illustrates."[80] He claims, however, that in 1980 the IEA had a minor success "under relatively favorable conditions" in responding to the outbreak of the Iran-Iraq War. Although he admits it is difficult to specify how much the IEA mattered in the 1980 case, he notes that "it seems clear that 'it [the IEA] leaned in the right direction'," a claim that hardly constitutes strong support for the theory.[81] Second, it does not appear from Keohane's analysis that either fear of cheating or actual cheating hindered cooperation in the 1979 case, as the theory would predict. Third, Keohane chose the IEA case precisely because it involved relations among advanced Western democracies with market economies, where the prospects for cooperation were excellent.[82] The modest impact of institutions in this case is thus all the more damning to the theory.

Lisa Martin examined the role that the European Community (EC) played during the Falklands War in helping Britain coax its reluctant allies to continue economic sanctions against Argentina after military action started.[83] She concludes that the EC helped Britain win its allies' cooperation by lowering transaction costs and facilitating issue linkage. Specifically, Britain made concessions on the EC budget and the Common Agricultural Policy (CAP); Britain's allies agreed in return to keep sanctions on Argentina.

This case, too, is less than a ringing endorsement for liberal institutionalism. First, British efforts to maintain EC sanctions against Argentina were not impeded by fears of possible cheating, which the theory identifies as the central impediment to cooperation. So this case does not present an important test of liberal institutionalism, and thus the cooperative outcome does not tell us much about the theory's explanatory power. Second, it was relatively easy for Britain and her allies to strike a deal in this case. Neither side's core interests were threatened, and neither side had to make significant sacrifices to reach an agreement. Forging an accord to continue sanctions was not a difficult undertaking. A stronger test for liberal institutionalism would require states to cooperate when doing so entailed significant costs and risks. Third, the EC was not essential to an agreement. Issues could have been linked without the EC, and although the EC may have lowered transaction costs somewhat, there is no reason to think these

---

79. Keohane, *After Hegemony*, chap. 10.
80. Ibid., p. 16.
81. Ibid., p. 236. A U.S. Department of Energy review of the IEA's performance in the 1980 crisis concluded that it had "failed to fulfill its promise." Ethan B. Kapstein, *The Insecure Alliance: Energy Crises and Western Politics Since 1944* (New York: Oxford University Press, 1990), p. 198.
82. Keohane, *After Hegemony*, p. 7.
83. Martin, "Institutions and Cooperation." Martin looks closely at three other cases in *Coercive Cooperation* to determine the effect of institutions on cooperation. I have concentrated on the Falklands War case, however, because it is, by her own admission, her strongest case. See ibid., p. 96.

costs were a serious impediment to striking a deal.[84] It is noteworthy that Britain and America were able to cooperate during the Falklands War, even though the United States did not belong to the EC.

There is also evidence that directly challenges liberal institutionalism in issue areas where one would expect the theory to operate successfully. The studies discussed above by Grieco, Krasner, and Mastanduno test the institutionalist argument in a number of different political economy cases, and each finds the theory has little explanatory power. More empirical work is needed before a final judgment is rendered on the explanatory power of liberal institutionalism. Nevertheless, the evidence gathered so far is unpromising at best.

In summary, liberal institutionalism does not provide a sound basis for understanding international relations and promoting stability in the post–Cold War world. It makes modest claims about the impact of institutions, and steers clear of war and peace issues, focusing instead on the less ambitious task of explaining economic cooperation. Furthermore, the theory's causal logic is flawed, as proponents of the theory now admit. Having overlooked the relative-gains problem, they are now attempting to repair the theory, but their initial efforts are not promising. Finally, the available empirical evidence provides little support for the theory.

COLLECTIVE SECURITY

The theory of collective security deals directly with the issue of how to cause peace.[85] It recognizes that military power is a central fact of life in international politics, and is likely to remain so for the foreseeable future. The key to enhancing stability in this world of armed states is the proper management of military power. As Inis Claude notes, "the problem of power is here to stay; it is, realistically, not a problem to be

---

84. Martin does not claim that agreement would not have been possible without the EC. Indeed, she appears to concede that even without the EC, Britain still could have fashioned "separate bilateral agreements with each EEC member in order to gain its cooperation, [although] this would have involved much higher transaction costs." Martin, "Institutions and Cooperation," pp. 174–175. However, transaction costs among the advanced industrial democracies are not very high in an era of rapid communications and permanent diplomatic establishments.
85. The works that best articulate the case for collective security are: Inis L. Claude, Jr., *Power And International Relations* (New York: Random House, 1966), chaps. 4–5; Claude, *Swords Into Plowshares*, chap. 12; and Kupchan and Kupchan, "Concerts and Collective Security." Also see Inis L. Claude, Jr., "Collective Security After the Cold War," in Gary L. Guertner, ed., *Collective Security In Europe and Asia* (Carlisle Barracks, Pa.: Strategic Studies Institute, U.S. Army War College, 1992), pp. 7–27; and Downs, *Collective Security beyond the Cold War*. The best critiques of collective security include: Richard K. Betts, "Systems for Peace or Causes of War? Collective Security, Arms Control, and the New Europe," *International Security*, Vol. 17, No. 1 (Summer 1992), pp. 5–43; Josef Joffe, "Collective Security and the Future of Europe: Failed Dreams and Dead Ends," *Survival*, Vol. 34, No. 1 (Spring 1992), pp. 36–50; Morgenthau, *Politics Among Nations*, pp. 293–306, 407–418; and Arnold Wolfers, *Discord And Collaboration: Essays on International Politics* (Baltimore, Md.: The Johns Hopkins Press, 1962), chap. 12. For a very useful source on collective security, see Maurice Bourquin, ed., *Collective Security*, A Record of the Seventh and Eighth International Studies Conferences (Paris: International Institute of Intellectual Cooperation, 1936).

eliminated but a problem to be managed."[86] For advocates of collective security, institutions are the key to managing power successfully.

Although the theory emphasizes the continuing importance of military force, it is explicitly anti-realist. Its proponents express a distaste for balance-of-power logic and traditional alliances, as well as a desire to create a world where those realist concepts have no role to play.[87]

In the early twentieth century, Woodrow Wilson and others developed the theory of collective security, which formed the basis for the League of Nations. Despite the well-known failings of that particular institution, the theory's popularity remains high. In fact, there has been much interest in collective security in the aftermath of the Cold War.[88] Claude notes, "Whatever their failures, the Wilsonians clearly succeeded in establishing the conviction that collective security represents a brand of international morality vastly superior to that incorporated in the balance of power system."[89]

Curiously, however, it is difficult to find scholarly work that makes the case for collective security without simultaneously expressing major reservations about the theory, and without expressing grave doubts that collective security could ever be realized in practice. Consider the writings of Claude, who is sympathetic to collective security, and has produced some of the most important work on the subject. He wrote in *Power and International Relations,* "I would regard the epithet *unrealistic* as fairly applicable to the theory of collective security." In *Swords into Plowshares,* he maintained that for "men involved in . . . establishing a collective security system . . . their devotion to the ideal has been more a manifestation of their yearning for peace and order as an end than as an expression of conviction that the theory of collective security provides a workable and acceptable means to that end." Finally, Claude wrote in 1992, "I reached the conclusion some thirty years ago that . . . the implementation of collective security theory is not a possibility to be taken seriously."[90]

---

86. Claude, *Power And International Relations,* p. 6.
87. Consider, for example, how Woodrow Wilson describes pre–World War I Europe: "The day we left behind us was a day of alliances. It was a day of balances of power. It was a day of 'every nation take care of itself or make a partnership with some other nation or group of nations to hold the peace of the world steady or to dominate the weaker portions of the world'." Quoted in Claude, *Power and International Relations,* p. 81.
88. Some examples of recent interest in collective security include: Malcolm Chalmers, "Beyond the Alliance System: The Case for a European Security Organization," *World Policy Journal,* Vol. 7, No. 2 (Spring 1990), pp. 215–250; Downs, *Collective Security beyond the Cold War;* Gregory Flynn and David J. Sheffer, "Limited Collective Security," *Foreign Policy,* No. 80 (Fall 1980), pp. 77–101; Kupchan and Kupchan, "Concerts and Collective Security"; Gene M. Lyons, "A New Collective Security: The United Nations and International Peace," *The Washington Quarterly,* Vol. 17, No. 2 (Spring 1994), pp. 173–199; Richard H. Ullman, *Securing Europe* (Princeton, N.J.: Princeton University Press, 1991); and Brian Urquhart, "Beyond the Sheriff's Posse," *Survival,* Vol. 32, No. 3 (May/June 1990), pp. 196–205.
89. Claude, *Power And International Relations,* p. 116. Also see Wolfers, *Discord And Collaboration,* p. 197.
90. Claude, *Power And International Relations,* pp. 203–204; Claude, *Swords Into Plowshares,* p. 283; and Claude, "Collective Security After the Cold War," p. 9. The Kupchans, who are also sympa-

CAUSAL LOGIC. Collective security starts with the assumption that states behave according to the dictates of realism.[91] The aim, however, is to move beyond the self-help world of realism where states fear each other and are motivated by balance-of-power considerations, even though the theory assumes that military power will remain a fact of life in the international system. For advocates of collective security, institutions are the key to accomplishing this ambitious task. Specifically, the goal is to convince states to base their behavior on three profoundly anti-realist norms.

First, states must renounce the use of military force to alter the status quo. They must not launch wars of aggression, but instead must agree to settle all disputes peaceably. Collective security allows for changes in the status quo, but those changes must come via negotiation, not at the end of a rifle barrel. The theory, as Claude notes, "depends upon a positive commitment to the value of world peace by the great mass of states."[92]

The theory nevertheless recognizes that some states may not accept this norm: if there were universal subscription to the norm, there would be no need for a collective security system to deal with troublemakers, since there would be none.[93] However, the over-whelming majority of states must renounce wars of conquest, or else the system would collapse.

It is difficult to stipulate how many aggressors a collective security system can handle at once before it comes undone. The answer depends on the particular circumstances facing the system, such as: the number of great powers, the distribution of power among them, geography, and whether the aggressors are minor or major powers. The upper limit for aggressive major powers is probably two at any one time, but even then, the system is likely to have difficulty dealing with them. Some collective security systems might even have trouble fighting two minor powers at the same time, since minor powers today are often well-armed. Fighting simultaneous wars against Iraq and North Korea, for example, would be a very demanding task, although the great powers would win them. Ideally, a collective security system would confront only one aggressor at a time, and not too often at that. Claude sums up the matter nicely: "Collective security

---

thetic to collective security (see "Concerts and Collective Security"), apparently share Claude's doubts about the theory. After detailing the strengths (pp. 125–137) and flaws (pp. 138–140) of collective security, they abandon the theory and advocate a concert system for Europe (pp. 140–161), which, as discussed below, is fundamentally different from collective security.

91. My thinking about the logic underpinning collective security has been significantly influenced by Bradley A. Thayer, "A Theory of Security Structures," unpublished manuscript, University of Chicago, July 1994.

92. Claude, *Swords Into Plowshares*, p. 250.

93. Collective security is often criticized on the grounds that "it is feasible only when it is also unnecessary." In other words, collective security requires that "all members are willing to accept the political status quo," but if that is the case, collective security would be unnecessary since no state, by definition, would cause trouble. Charles L. Glaser, "Why NATO is Still Best: Future Security Arrangements for Europe," *International Security*, Vol. 18, No. 1 (Summer 1993), p. 28. Also see Joffe, "Collective Security and the Future of Europe," pp. 44, 46; and Kupchan and Kupchan, "Concerts and Collective Security," p. 124. This criticism is unfair, however, because the very purpose of a collective security system is to deal with aggressors. If states could be guaranteed that no other state would ever launch an aggressive war, there would be no need for collective security. The theory recognizes that such a guarantee is not possible.

assumes the *lonely* aggressor; the violator of the world's peace may be allowed an accomplice or two, but in principle the evil-doer is supposed to find himself virtually isolated in confrontation with the massive forces of the international *posse comitatus.*"[94]

Second, "responsible" states must not think in terms of narrow self-interest when they act against lonely aggressors, but must instead choose to equate their national interest with the broader interests of the international community. Specifically, states must believe that their national interest is inextricably bound up with the national interest of other states, so that an attack on any state is considered an attack on every state.[95] Thus, when a troublemaker appears in the system, all of the responsible states must automatically and collectively confront the aggressor with overwhelming military power. The aim is "to create automatic obligations of a collective character."[96]

States in a self-help world calculate each move on the basis of how it will affect the balance of power. This narrow sense of self-interest means that states are likely to remain on the sidelines if vital interests are not threatened.[97] This kind of behavior is unacceptable in a collective security world, where there must instead be "a legally binding and codified commitment on the part of all members to respond to aggression whenever and wherever it might occur."[98] A collective security system allows states little freedom of action. The practical effect of this comprehensive system of mutual assistance is that lonely aggressors are quickly confronted with a coalition of over-whelming military strength. For both deterrence and warfighting purposes, this "pre-ponderant power" is far superior to the "minimum winning coalitions" that a troublemaker faces in a balance-of-power world.[99] Once it becomes clear that aggression does not pay, even states reluctant to accept the first norm (the renunciation of aggression) will be more inclined to accept it.

Third, states must trust each other. States must not only act in accordance with the first two norms, but they must trust that other states will do likewise. If states fear each other, as they do in a realist world, collective security cannot work. States, Claude

---

94. Claude, *Power And International Relations*, p. 196.
95. Woodrow Wilson said in 1916, "We are participants, whether we would or not, in the life of the world. The interests of all nations are our own also. We are partners with the rest. What affects mankind is inevitably our affair as well as the affair of the nations of Europe and of Asia." Quoted in August Heckscher, ed., *The Politics of Woodrow Wilson: Selections from His Speeches and Writings* (New York: Harper, 1956), p. 258.
96. Morgenthau, *Politics Among Nations*, p. 296.
97. A state not at risk might fail to come to the aid of a threatened state because the risks and costs of going to war are too high, or because it has an interest in letting the combatants wear each other down, thus improving its own strategic position. A state not directly at risk might even join forces with the aggressor against the threatened state, so as to gain some of the spoils of victory.
98. Kupchan and Kupchan, "Concerts and Collective Security," p. 119.
99. Traditional alliances have no place in a collective security system. Woodrow Wilson is particu-larly eloquent on this point: "I am proposing that all nations henceforth avoid entangling alliances which would draw them into a competition of power, catch them in a net of intrigue and selfish rivalry, and disturb their own affairs with influences intruded from without. There is no entangling alliance in a concert of power. When all unite to act in the same sense and with the same purpose, all act in the common interest and are free to live their own lives under a common protection." Quoted in Frederick L. Schuman, *International Politics: An Introduction to the Western State System* (New York: McGraw-Hill, 1933), p. 254.

emphasizes, must "be willing to entrust their destinies to collective security. Confidence is the quintessential condition of the success of the system; states must be prepared to rely upon its effectiveness and impartiality."[100]

Trust is actually the most important of the three norms because it underpins the first two. Specifically, states must be very confident that almost all the other states in the system will sincerely renounce aggression, and will not change their minds at a later date. States also have to be confident that when an aggressor targets them, none of the other responsible states will get cold feet and fail to confront the troublemaker. This element of certainty is of great importance in a collective security system because if it fails to work, at least some of those states that have ignored the balance of power and eschewed alliances are going to be vulnerable to attack.

This discussion of trust raises an additional point about the problems a collective security system faces when it confronts multiple aggressors. The previous discussion focused mainly on the logistical difficulties of dealing with more than one troublemaker. However, the presence of multiple aggressors also raises the question of whether most states in the system are deeply committed to peace, and therefore, whether it makes sense to trust collective security. The more troublemakers there are in the system, the more doubts responsible states are likely to have about their investment in collective security. This same logic applies to suggestions that collective security can get by without requiring that all states join the system. Some argue that one or more states can remain on the sidelines, provided the member states can still confront any troublemakers with overwhelming military force.[101] Although these free-riders are assumed to be non-aggressors, there is no guarantee that they will not later turn to conquest, in which case their free ride might have allowed them to improve significantly their relative power position. This free-rider problem, like the multiple-aggressor problem, is likely to undermine the responsible states' trust in collective security and thus to cause its failure.

FLAWS IN THE CAUSAL LOGIC. There are two major flaws in collective security theory, and both concern the all-important component of trust. Collective security is an incomplete theory because it does not provide a satisfactory explanation for how states overcome their fears and learn to trust one another. Realists maintain that states fear one another because they operate in an anarchic world, have offensive military capabilities, and can never be certain about other states' intentions. Collective security is largely silent about the first two realist assumptions, as the theory says little about either anarchy or offensive capability.[102] However, it has something to say about intentions,

---

100. Claude, *Swords Into Plowshares*, p. 255. Also see Claude, *Power And International Relations*, p. 197.

101. See Thomas R. Cusack and Richard J. Stoll, "Collective Security and State Survival in the Interstate System," *International Studies Quarterly*, Vol. 38, No. 1 (March 1994), pp. 33–59; and George W. Downs and Keisuke Iida, "Assessing the Theoretical Case against Collective Security," in Downs, *Collective Security beyond the Cold War*, pp. 17–39.

102. Advocates of collective security usually favor widespread arms reductions, but they also recognize that states must maintain a significant offensive capability so that they can challenge an aggressor. For this reason, some scholars suggest that collective security might undermine stability. See Glaser, "Why NATO is Still Best," pp. 30–33.

because the theory's first two norms call for states not to aggress, but only to defend. States, in other words, should only have benign intentions when contemplating the use of military force.

However, the theory recognizes that one or more states might reject the norms that underpin collective security and behave aggressively. The very purpose of a collective security system, after all, is to deal with states that have aggressive intentions. In effect, collective security admits that no state can ever be completely certain about another state's intentions, which brings us back to a realist world where states have little choice but to fear each other.

There is a second reason why states are not likely to place their trust in a collective security system: it has a set of demanding requirements—I count nine—that are likely to thwart efforts to confront an aggressor with preponderant power. Collective security, as Claude notes, "assumes the satisfaction of an extraordinarily complex network of requirements."[103]

First, for collective security to work, states must be able to distinguish clearly between aggressor and victim, and then move against the aggressor. However, it is sometimes difficult in a crisis to determine who is the troublemaker and who is the victim.[104] Debates still rage about which European great power, if any, bears responsibility for starting World War I. Similar disputes have followed most other wars.

Second, the theory assumes that all aggression is wrong. But there are occasionally cases where conquest is probably warranted. For example, there are good reasons to applaud the 1979 Vietnamese invasion of Cambodia, since it drove the murderous Pol Pot from power.

Third, some states are especially friendly for historical or ideological reasons. Should a state with close friends be labeled an aggressor in a collective security system, its friends are probably going to be reluctant to join the coalition against it. For example, it is difficult to imagine the United States using military force against Britain or Israel, even if they were branded aggressors by the international community.

Fourth, historical enmity between states can also complicate collective security efforts. Consider that a European collective security system would have to depend heavily on Germany and Russia, the two most powerful states on the continent, to maintain order. However, the idea of Germany, which wrought murder and destruction across Europe in 1939–45, and Russia, which was the core of the Soviet empire, maintaining order in Europe is sure to meet significant resistance from other European states.

Fifth, even if states agree to act automatically and collectively to meet aggression, there would surely be difficulty determining how to distribute the burden. States will have strong incentives to pass the buck and get other states to pay the heavy price of confronting an aggressor.[105] During World War I, for example, Britain, France, and

---

103. Claude, *Swords Into Plowshares*, p. 250.
104. See Bourquin, *Collective Security*, pp. 295–338.
105. See Mancur Olson, Jr., and Richard Zeckhauser, "An Economic Theory of Alliances," *Review of Economics and Statistics*, Vol. 48, No. 3 (August 1966), pp. 266–279; and Barry R. Posen, *The Sources of Military Doctrine: France, Britain, and Germany between the World Wars* (Ithaca, N.Y.: Cornell University Press, 1984).

Russia each tried to get its allies to pay the blood price of defeating Germany on the battlefield.[106] Rampant buck-passing might undermine efforts to produce the preponderant military power necessary to make collective security work.

Sixth, it is difficult to guarantee a rapid response to aggression in a collective security system. Planning beforehand is problematic because "it is impossible to know what the alignment of states will be if there is an armed conflict."[107] There are also significant coordination problems associated with assembling a large coalition of states to fight a war. Rapid response becomes even more problematic if the responsible states must deal with more than one aggressor. It took more than six months for the United States to put together a coalition to liberate Kuwait from Saddam Hussein. As impressive as the American effort was, threatened states are not likely to have much faith in a security system that tells them help is likely to come, but will only arrive months after they have been conquered.

Seventh, states are likely to be reluctant to join a collective security effort because the system effectively transforms every local conflict into an international conflict. States that see conflict around the globe will surely be tempted to cordon off the troubled area and prevent further escalation, as the West has done in the former Yugoslavia.[108] Collective security, however, calls for escalation, even though it is intended for peaceful purposes.

Eighth, the notion that states must automatically respond to aggression impinges in fundamental ways on state sovereignty, and will therefore be difficult to sell. States, especially democracies, are likely to guard jealously their freedom to debate whether or not to fight an aggressor. War is a deadly business, especially if great powers are involved, and few countries want to commit themselves in advance to paying a huge blood price when their own self-interests are not directly involved.

Ninth, there is some contradiction concerning attitudes towards force that raises doubts about whether responsible states would actually come to the rescue of a threatened state. Collective security theory is predicated on the belief that war is a truly horrible enterprise, and therefore states should renounce aggression. At the same time, the theory mandates that states must be ready and willing to use force to thwart troublemakers. However, responsible states find war so repellent that they would renounce it; this raises doubts about their willingness to go to war to stop aggression. Indeed, most advocates of collective security prefer "creative diplomacy and economic sanctions" to military force when dealing with an aggressor state.[109]

In sum, states have abundant reasons to doubt that collective security will work as advertised when the chips are down and aggression seems likely. Should it fail, potential

---

106. David French, *British Strategy and War Aims, 1914–1916* (London: Allen and Unwin, 1986).

107. G.F. Hudson, "Collective Security and Military Alliances," in Herbert Butterfield and Martin Wight, eds., *Diplomatic Investigations: Essays in the Theory of International Politics* (Cambridge, Mass.: Harvard University Press, 1966), p. 177.

108. For an example of this line of thinking, see Stephen M. Walt, "Collective Security and Revolutionary Change: Promoting Peace in the Former Soviet Union," in Downs, *Collective Security beyond the Cold War*, pp. 169–195.

109. Robert C. Johansen, "Lessons For Collective Security," *World Policy Journal*, Vol. 8, No. 3 (Summer 1991), p. 562.

victims are likely to be in deep trouble if they have ignored balance-of-power considerations and placed their faith in collective security. Recognizing this, states are not likely to place their fate in the hands of other states, but will prefer instead the realist logic of self-help.

PROBLEMS WITH THE EMPIRICAL RECORD. The historical record provides little support for collective security, a point acknowledged by the theory's proponents. The great powers have seriously considered implementing collective security three times in this century: after both World Wars, and after the Cold War. The League of Nations, which was established after World War I, was a serious attempt to make collective security work.[110] It had some minor successes during the 1920s. For example, League mediation resolved the Aaland Islands dispute between Finland and Sweden in 1920, and pressure from the League forced Greek, Italian, and Yugoslav troops out of Albania one year later. The League was much less successful in handling several other conflicts during the 1920s, however: it did not prevent or stop the Greco-Turkish War of 1920–22, or the Russo-Polish War of 1920, and France refused to allow the League to consider its occupation of the Ruhr in January 1923, going so far as to threaten withdrawal from the League if it intervened in the crisis. The League had a mixed record during the 1920s, even though that decade was relatively pacific, and no great power was then bent on aggression.

The international system became increasingly unstable during the 1930s, and the League was seriously tested on six occasions: 1) the Japanese invasion of Manchuria in 1931; 2) the Chaco War of 1932–35; 3) Japan's 1937 invasion of China; 4) Italy's aggression against Ethiopia in 1935; 5) the German occupation of the Rhineland in March 1936; and 6) the Soviet invasion of Finland in 1939. The League failed each test, and was effectively useless by the late 1930s, when the great powers were making the critical decisions that led to World War II.

The United Nations was established in the waning days of World War II to provide collective security around the globe. However, the Soviet-American competition followed on the heels of that war, and the United Nations was therefore never seriously tested as a collective security apparatus during the Cold War.[111]

Since the Cold War ended, there has been much talk in the West about building a collective security system.[112] The success of the American-led coalition that pushed Iraq out of Kuwait led some experts to conclude that the UN might finally be ready to operate as a collective security institution. In Europe, experts have discussed the possibility of turning NATO, or possibly the CSCE, into a collective security system for the continent. It is too early for conclusive judgments as to whether any of these ideas about collective security will be realized. However, almost all the evidence to date

---

110. The standard history of the League is F.P. Walters, *A History Of The League Of Nations,* 2 vols. (London: Oxford University Press, 1952).

111. See Ernst B. Haas, "Types of Collective Security: An Examination of Operational Concepts," *American Political Science Review,* Vol. 49, No. 1 (March 1955), pp. 40–62; and Kenneth W. Thompson, "Collective Security Reexamined," *American Political Science Review,* Vol. 47, No. 3 (September 1953), pp. 753–772.

112. See the sources cited in footnote 88.

points to failure. Iraq was an unusual case, and no effort is underway to reform the UN so that it can perform true collective security missions.[113] Moreover, the failure of the United States and its European allies either to prevent or to stop the wars in the former Yugoslavia, coupled with NATO's January 1994 decision not to expand its membership eastward, does not bode well for establishing a collective security system in post–Cold War Europe.[114]

FALLBACK POSITIONS. Given the limits of collective security, some of its proponents argue that two less ambitious forms of the theory might be realizable: peacekeeping and concerts. Although they are portrayed as the "budget" version of collective security, some experts think that peacekeeping and concerts might still be a powerful force for international stability.[115]

Peacekeeping, as William Durch notes, "evolved as an alternative to the collective security that the UN was designed to provide but could not."[116] However, peacekeeping is not a watered-down version of collective security. It is, instead, a much less ambitious alternative strategy for promoting stability. Peacekeeping entails third party intervention in minor-power civil wars or disputes between minor powers, for the purpose of either preventing war from breaking out or stopping it once it has begun. This intervention can only be accomplished with the consent of the disputants, and third parties cannot use force to affect the behavior of the parties in dispute. Peacekeeping operations must be "expressly non-threatening and impartial."[117] In essence, peacekeeping is mainly useful for helping implement cease-fires in wars involving minor powers. However, the UN's record in performing even that quite limited task is at best mixed.

Peacekeeping has no role to play in disputes between great powers. Moreover, it forbids the use of coercion, which is essential to a collective security system. Its mission is a far cry from the ambitious goals of collective security. Peacekeeping by the UN or

---

113. See Adam Roberts, "The United Nations and International Security," *Survival*, Vol. 35, No. 2 (Summer 1993), pp. 3–30; and Claude, "Collective Security After the Cold War," pp. 15–27. For a critical discussion of the performance of the United States and the United Nations in the Gulf War, see Johansen, "Lessons For Collective Security."
114. There is still discussion about extending NATO eastward to include Poland, Hungary, and the two Czechoslovakian remnant states. Russia is deeply opposed to such a move, however, and therefore NATO is not likely to expand eastward in any meaningful way. Regardless, even if those four states joined NATO, the remnant states of the former Soviet Union would still be excluded, and their inclusion would be necessary to transform NATO into an effective collective security system for Europe. For an argument that NATO should not be transformed into a collective security system, see Glaser, "Why NATO is Still Best," pp. 26–33.
115. Regarding peacekeeping, see Mats R. Berdal, *Whither UN Peacekeeping?* Adelphi Paper No. 281 (London: IISS, October 1993), pp. 3–4, 75–77. Concerning concerts, see Kupchan and Kupchan, "Concerts and Collective Security," pp. 151–161; Richard Rosecrance, "A Concert of Powers," *Foreign Affairs*, Vol. 71, No. 2 (Spring 1992), pp. 64–82; and Philip Zelikow, "The New Concert of Europe," *Survival*, Vol. 34, No. 2 (Summer 1992), pp. 12–30.
116. William J. Durch, "Building on Sand: UN Peacekeeping in the Western Sahara," *International Security*, Vol. 17, No. 4 (Spring 1993), p. 151. Also see Berdal, *Whither UN Peacekeeping?*; and William J. Durch, ed., *The Evolution of UN Peacekeeping: Case Studies and Comparative Analysis* (New York: St. Martins, 1993).
117. Berdal, *Whither UN Peacekeeping?* p. 3.

by regional organizations like the Organization of African Unity (OAU) can enhance the prospects for world peace only on the margins.[118]

Concerts are sometimes described as an "attenuated form of collective security," or a "reasonable hybrid version of collective security."[119] Charles and Clifford Kupchan maintain that "collective security organizations can take many different institutional forms along a continuum ranging from ideal collective security to concerts."[120] However, the claim that concerts are a less ambitious version of collective security is incorrect.[121] Concerts essentially reflect the balance of power, and are thus largely consistent with realism, whereas collective security, as explained above, is a fundamentally anti-realist theory. Concerts and collective security systems, therefore, reflect different and ultimately incompatible logics. As Quincy Wright reminds us, "The fundamental assumptions of the two systems are different. A government cannot at the same time behave according to the Machiavellian assumptions of the balance of power and the Wilsonian assumptions of international organization."[122]

A concert is an arrangement in which great powers that have no incentive to challenge each other militarily agree on a set of rules to coordinate their actions with each other, as well as with the minor powers in the system, often in the establishment of spheres of influence. A concert is a great power condominium that reflects the underlying balance of power among its members. The coordinated balancing that takes place inside a concert does not violate great power self-interest. In fact, when those great powers have a dispute, self-interest determines each side's policy and the concert may collapse as a result.

Concerts are most likely to emerge in the wake of great power wars in which a potential hegemon has been defeated, and power is distributed roughly equally among the victors.[123] Four factors account for this phenomenon. First, the great powers would not have much to gain militarily by attacking each other, given the rough balance of

---

118. For a discussion of the limitations of regional organizations as conflict managers, see S. Neil MacFarlane and Thomas G. Weiss, "Regional Organizations and Regional Security," *Security Studies*, Vol. 2, No. 1 (Autumn 1992), pp. 6–37.

119. Kupchan and Kupchan, "Concerts and Collective Security," p. 120; Betts, "Systems for Peace or Causes of War?" p. 27. Also see Downs, *Collective Security beyond the Cold War.*

120. Kupchan and Kupchan, "Concerts and Collective Security," p. 119.

121. I cannot find evidence that Woodrow Wilson, Inis Claude, or Arnold Wolfers considered concerts to be a limited form of collective security. It appears that the first serious efforts to link collective security with concerts were made in post–Cold War writings on collective security, especially Kupchan and Kupchan, "Concerts and Collective Security."

122. Quincy Wright, *A Study Of War*, Vol. 2 (Chicago: University of Chicago Press, 1942), p. 781. Charles Lipson provides an example of how institutionalists try to combine these two incompatible theories. He writes: "Thus, the [post-1815] Concert is a kind of beacon to advocates of collective security . . . not only because it succeeded but because it did so . . . without transforming the self-interested behavior of states." Lipson, "Future of Collective Security," p. 119. However, a system based on the self-interested behavior of states is antithetical to collective security, and therefore, it is difficult to understand how such a system could be considered a "kind of beacon to advocates of collective security." For another example of this problem, see Kupchan and Kupchan, "Concerts and Collective Security," p. 116.

123. See Robert Jervis, "From Balance to Concert: A Study of International Security Cooperation," *World Politics*, Vol. 38, No. 1 (October 1985), pp. 58–79.

power among them. Second, the victorious powers are likely to have a significant interest in maintaining the status quo, mainly because they are in control and the potential hegemon has been subdued. Third, hegemonic wars are very costly, so the great powers are likely to be war-weary, and deeply interested in avoiding another costly war. Fourth, the victorious great powers worked together to win the war, so the notion of collective action is likely to appeal to them, and carry over into the early postwar years.

Concerts usually last only a few years. The balance of power changes. Defeated powers rise from the ashes. Victorious powers squabble among themselves, especially about how to deal with minor powers. States become less sensitive to the costs of war as time passes.

The Concert of Europe, which was established after Napoleonic France had finally been subdued, is the only case of a successful concert.[124] Not surprisingly, it is sometimes held up as a model for the post–Cold War world. The Concert worked fairly well from 1815 to 1823, although the great powers did occasionally clash over their dealings with minor powers. After 1823, however, the Concert was unable to function effectively as a coordinating device for the great powers. "The concert existed in an abortive form" until its final collapse as the Crimean War began in 1854.[125] During its heyday, the Concert of Europe reflected the balance of power; states were not compelled to behave in ways that weakened their relative power position. "Maintaining a balance of power," as Richard Betts notes, "remained an important object of the nineteenth-century Concert regime."[126]

In sum, the theory of collective security directly addresses the issue of how to push states away from war and promote peace, and it recognizes that military power plays a central role in international politics. But the theory has several important flaws. It is built on the foundational norm that states should trust each other, but it does not satisfactorily explain how this is possible in an anarchic world where states have military power and uncertain intentions. Furthermore, the historical record provides little support for the theory. The single case of an operative collective security system was the League of Nations, and it was a spectacular failure. Although peacekeeping and concerts are sometimes described as limited but promising versions of collective security, they are of marginal value in promoting peace. Moreover, both peacekeeping

---

124. Among the best works on the Concert of Europe are: Richard Elrod, "The Concert of Europe: A Fresh Look at an International System," *World Politics,* Vol. 28, No. 2 (January 1976), pp. 156–174; Edward V. Gulick, *Europe's Classical Balance of Power: A Case History of the Theory and Practice of One of the Great Concepts of European Statecraft* (New York: Norton, 1955); Jervis, "From Balance To Concert"; Harold Nicolson, *The Congress of Vienna: A Study in Allied Unity, 1812–1822* (New York: Harcourt, Brace, 1946); Paul W. Schroeder, *Austria, Great Britain, and the Crimean War: The Destruction of the European Concert* (Ithaca, N.Y.: Cornell University Press, 1972); Harold Temperley, *The Foreign Policy of Canning, 1822–1827: England, the Neo-Holy Alliance, and the New World,* 2nd ed. (London: Thomas Nelson, 1966); and Charles K. Webster, *The Foreign Policy of Castlereagh: Britain and the European Alliance, 1815–1822,* 2nd ed. (London: G. Bell, 1934).

125. The phrase is from Gulick, *Europe's Classical Balance of Power,* p. 22.

126. Betts, "Systems for Peace or Causes of War?" p. 27. The Kupchans readily accept that power politics is part of the warp and woof of daily life in a concert system. See "Concerts and Collective Security," pp. 116, 120, 141–144.

and concerts work according to different logics than collective security. In fact, concerts, like alliances, basically reflect the balance of power, and are thus consistent with a realist view of institutions.

CRITICAL THEORY

Critical theorists[127] directly address the question of how to bring about peace, and they make bold claims about the prospects for changing state behavior.[128] Specifically, they aim to transform the international system into a "world society," where states are guided by "norms of trust and sharing." Their goal is to relegate security competition and war to the scrap heap of history, and create instead a genuine "peace system."[129]

Critical theorists take ideas very seriously. In fact, they believe that discourse, or how we think and talk about the world, largely shapes practice. Roughly put, ideas are the

127. Critical theory is an approach to studying the human condition that is not tied to a particular discipline. In fact, critical theory was well-developed and employed widely in other disciplines before it began to penetrate the international relations field in the early 1980s. This article does not focus on critical theory *per se*, but examines the scholarly literature where critical theory is applied to international relations. I treat those works as a coherent whole, although there are differences, especially of emphasis, among them. For a general discussion of critical theory, see David Held, *Introduction to Critical Theory: Horkheimer to Habermas* (Berkeley: University of California Press, 1980); and Pauline M. Rosenau, *Post-Modernism And The Social Sciences: Insights, Inroads, and Intrusions* (Princeton, N.J.: Princeton University Press, 1992). Also see Pauline Rosenau, "Once Again Into the Fray: International Relations Confronts the Humanities," *Millennium: Journal of International Studies*, Vol. 19, No. 1 (Spring 1990), pp. 83–110.

128. Among the key works applying critical theory to international relations are: Richard K. Ashley, "The Poverty of Neorealism," *International Organization*, Vol. 38, No. 2 (Spring 1984), pp. 225–286; Ashley, "The Geopolitics of Geopolitical Space: Toward a Critical Social Theory of International Politics," *Alternatives*, Vol. 12, No. 4 (October 1987), pp. 403–434; Robert W. Cox, "Gramsci, Hegemony and International Relations: An Essay in Method," *Millennium: Journal of International Studies*, Vol. 12, No. 2 (Summer 1983), pp. 162–175; Cox, "Social Forces, States and World Orders: Beyond International Relations Theory," *Millennium: Journal of International Studies*, Vol. 10, No. 2 (Summer 1981), pp. 126–155; Cox, "Towards A Post-Hegemonic Conceptualization of World Order: Reflections on the Relevancy of Ibn Khaldun," in James N. Rosenau, and Ernst-Otto Czempiel, eds., *Governance Without Government: Order and Change in World Politics* (New York: Cambridge University Press, 1992), pp. 132–159; Rey Koslowski and Friedrich V. Kratochwil, "Understanding Change in International Politics: The Soviet Empire's Demise and the International System," *International Organization*, Vol. 48, No. 2 (Spring 1994), pp. 215–247; Friedrich Kratochwil and John G. Ruggie, "International Organization: A State of the Art on an Art of the State," *International Organization*, Vol. 40, No. 4 (Autumn 1986), pp. 753–775; Ruggie, "Continuity and Transformation in the World Polity: Toward a Neorealist Synthesis," *World Politics*, Vol. 35, No. 2 (January 1983), pp. 261–285; Ruggie, "Territoriality And Beyond: Problematizing Modernity in International Relations," *International Organization*, Vol. 47, No. 1 (Winter 1993), pp. 139–174; Alexander Wendt, "The Agent-Structure Problem in International Relations Theory," *International Organization*, Vol. 41, No. 3 (Summer 1987), pp. 335–370; Wendt, "Anarchy Is What States Make of It: The Social Construction of Power Politics," *International Organization*, Vol. 46, No. 2 (Spring 1992), pp. 391–425; and Wendt, "Collective Identity Formation and the International State," *American Political Science Review*, Vol. 88, No. 2 (June 1994), pp. 384–396. I use the label "critical theory" to describe this body of literature; other labels are sometimes used, among them constructivism, reflectivism, post-modernism, and post-structuralism.

129. The quotations in this paragraph are from Ashley, "Poverty of Neorealism," p. 285; and Wendt, "Anarchy Is What States Make of It," p. 431.

driving force of history. Furthermore, they recognize that realism has long been the dominant theory of international politics, and therefore, according to their account of reality, has had substantial influence on state behavior. But critical theorists intend to change that situation by challenging realism and undermining it. Richard Ashley graphically describes their intentions: "Let us then play havoc with neorealist concepts and claims. Let us neither admire nor ignore the orrery of errors, but let us instead fracture the orbs, crack them open, crack them and see what possibilities they have enclosed. And then, when we are done, let us not cast away the residue. Let us instead sweep it into a jar, shine up the glass, and place it high on the bookshelf with other specimens of past mistakes."[130] With realism shattered, the way would presumably be open to a more peaceful world.

Critical theory is well-suited for challenging realism because critical theory is, by its very nature, concerned with criticizing "hegemonic" ideas like realism, not laying out alternative futures. The central aim is "to seek out the contradictions within the existing order, since it is from these contradictions that change could emerge."[131] It is called "critical" theory for good reason. Very significantly, however, critical theory *per se* has little to say about the future shape of international politics. In fact, critical theory emphasizes that, "It is impossible to predict the future."[132] Robert Cox explains this point: "Critical awareness of potentiality for change must be distinguished from utopian planning, i.e., the laying out of the design of a future society that is to be the end goal of change. Critical understanding focuses on the process of change rather than on its ends; it concentrates on the possibilities of launching a social movement rather than on what that movement might achieve."[133]

Nevertheless, international relations scholars who use critical theory to challenge and subvert realism certainly expect to create a more harmonious and peaceful international system. But the theory itself says little about either the desirability or feasibility of achieving that particular end.

CAUSAL LOGIC. Institutions are at the core of critical theory, as its central aim is to alter the constitutive and regulative norms of the international system so that states stop thinking and acting according to realism. Specifically, critical theorists hope to create "pluralistic security communities," where states behave according to the same norms or institutions that underpin collective security.[134] States would renounce the use

---

130. Ashley, "Poverty of Neorealism," p. 286.
131. Robert W. Cox, *Production, Power, and World Order: Social Forces in the Making of World History* (New York: Columbia University Press, 1987), p. 393.
132. Cox, "Post-Hegemonic Conceptualization," p. 139.
133. Cox, *Production, Power, and World Order*, p. 393. The young Karl Marx summed up this approach in 1844: "the advantage of the new trend [is] that we do not attempt dogmatically to prefigure the future, but want to find the new world only through criticism of the old." Karl Marx, "For a Ruthless Criticism of Everything Existing," in Robert C. Tucker, ed., *The Marx-Engels Reader*, 2nd ed. (New York: Norton, 1978), p. 13. Marx's early writings have markedly influenced critical theory. See, for example, Ashley, "Poverty of Neorealism," pp. 226–230; and Cox, "Social Forces," p. 133. Critical theorists, however, disparage Marx's later writings, which lay out a structural theory of politics that has much in common with realism.
134. Emanuel Adler, "Arms Control, Disarmament, and National Security: A Thirty Year Retrospective and a New Set of Anticipations," *Daedalus*, Vol. 120, No. 1 (Winter 1991), pp. 11–18; Ashley, "Geopolitics of Geopolitical Space," pp. 428, 430; and Richard Ned Lebow, "The Long Peace, the

of military force, and there would instead be "a generally shared expectation of peaceful change."[135] Furthermore, states would "identify positively with one another so that the security of each is perceived as the responsibility of all."[136] States would not think in terms of self-help or self-interest, but would instead define their interests in terms of the international community. In this new world, "national interests are international interests."[137]

Critical theorists have a more ambitious agenda than proponents of collective security. Critical theorists aim to create a world in which all states consider war an unacceptable practice, and are not likely to change their minds about the matter. There do not appear to be any troublemaker states in a pluralistic security community, as there might be in a collective security system. In fact, military power seems to be largely irrelevant in the critical theorists' post-realist world, which has the earmarks of a true "peace system."[138]

For critical theorists, the key to achieving a "postmodern international system" is to alter state identity radically, or more specifically, to transform how states think about themselves and their relationship with other states.[139] In the jargon of the theory, "intersubjective understandings and expectations" matter greatly.[140] In practice, this means that states must stop thinking of themselves as solitary egoists, and instead develop a powerful communitarian ethos.[141] Critical theorists aim to create an international system characterized not by anarchy, but by community. States must stop thinking of themselves as separate and exclusive—i.e., sovereign—actors, and instead see themselves as mutually conditioned parts of a larger whole.[142] States, or more precisely, their inhabitants and leaders, should be made to care about concepts like "rectitude," "rights," and "obligations." In short, they should have a powerful sense of responsibility to the broader international community.

End of the Cold War, and the Failure of Realism," *International Organization*, Vol. 48, No. 2 (Spring 1994), pp. 269–277. Wendt uses the term "cooperative security system" in place of "pluralistic security community." See "Anarchy Is What States Make of It," pp. 400–401. Karl Deutsch invented the concept of a pluralistic security community. See Karl W. Deutsch, et al., *Political Community and the North Atlantic Area: International Organization in the Light of Historical Experience* (Princeton, N.J.: Princeton University Press, 1957), pp. 5–9.

135. Ashley, "Geopolitics of Geopolitical Space," p. 430. Also see Adler, "Arms Control, Disarmament, and National Security," p. 11.

136. Wendt, "Anarchy Is What States Make of It," p. 400.

137. Ibid.

138. This outcome is fully consistent with Deutsch's definition of a pluralistic security community: "there is real assurance that the members of that community will not fight each other physically, but will settle their disputes in some other way. If the entire world were integrated as a security community, wars would be automatically eliminated." Deutsch, *Political Community*, p. 5.

139. John G. Ruggie, "International Structure and International Transformation: Space, Time, and Method," in Ernst-Otto Czempiel and James N. Rosenau, eds., *Global Changes and Theoretical Challenges: Approaches to World Politics for the 1990s* (Lexington, Mass.: Lexington Books, 1989), p. 30.

140. Wendt, "Anarchy Is What States Make of It," p. 397.

141. "Critical social scientific approaches," as Ashley notes, "are inherently communitarian." See Ashley, "Geopolitics of Geopolitical Space," p. 403; also see pp. 404–407.

142. In a recent article, Alexander Wendt discusses the "emergence of 'international states,' which would constitute a structural transformation of the Westphalian states system." Wendt, "Collective Identity Formation," p. 385.

A realist might argue that this goal is desirable in principle, but not realizable in practice, because the structure of the international system forces states to behave as egoists. Anarchy, offensive capabilities, and uncertain intentions combine to leave states with little choice but to compete aggressively with each other. For realists, trying to infuse states with communitarian norms is a hopeless cause.

Critical theory, however, directly challenges the realist claim that structural factors are the main determinants of state behavior. In contrast to realism, critical theory assumes that ideas and discourse are the driving forces that shape the world, although it recognizes that structural factors have some, albeit minor, influence.[143] How individuals think about and talk about the world matters greatly for determining how states act in the international system. Ideas matter so much, according to critical theorists, because the world is socially constructed by individual human beings whose behavior is mediated by their thoughts; these thoughts, in turn, are shared by the members of a larger culture. Individuals bear responsibility for shaping the world they inhabit. The world around them is not a given that forces itself upon them. On the contrary, critical theorists argue that ideational forces or "institutions often can change environments."[144] Markus Fischer sums up this crucial point: "In essence, critical theory holds that social reality is constituted by intersubjective consciousness based on language and that human beings are free to change their world by a collective act of will."[145]

Robert Cox's description of the state illustrates how this process of thinking about the world determines how it is structured. "The state," he writes, "has no physical existence, like a building or a lamp-post; but it is nevertheless a real entity. It is a real entity because everyone acts as though it were."[146] Alexander Wendt's discussion of anarchy provides another good example: "Structure," he writes, "has no existence or causal powers apart from process."[147] States, in fact, can think about anarchy in a number of different ways. "Anarchy is what states make of it." Moreover, "self-help and power politics are institutions . . . not essential features of anarchy."

This discussion of how critical theorists think about the state and anarchy points up the fact that realism and critical theory have fundamentally different epistemologies

---

143. It is important to emphasize that critical theorists do not make a case for pure idealism, where realist structure has little bearing on state behavior. Their argument is much more sophisticated, as they maintain that structure and discourse are inextricably linked together and constantly interact in a dialectical fashion. Structure, they emphasize, both enables and constrains individual behavior. Nevertheless, the key point for critical theorists is that structure is ultimately shaped and reshaped by discourse. In other words, structure may shape our thinking about the world, but structure is ultimately shaped by our discourse. Structure is not an independent material force that shapes how we think and talk about the world. Social reality, in the end, is ultimately a construction of our minds.

144. Koslowski and Kratochwil, "Understanding Change," p. 226.

145. Markus Fischer, "Feudal Europe, 800–1300: Communal Discourse and Conflictual Practices," *International Organization,* Vol. 46, No. 2 (Spring 1992), p. 430.

146. Cox, "Post-Hegemonic Conceptualization," p. 133.

147. Wendt, "Anarchy Is What States Make of It," p. 395. The subsequent quotations in this paragraph are from ibid. Also see Richard K. Ashley, "Untying the Sovereign State: A Double Reading of the Anarchy Problematique," *Millennium: Journal of International Studies,* Vol. 17, No. 2 (Summer 1988), pp. 227–262.

and ontologies, which are the most basic levels at which theories can be compared.[148] Realists maintain that there is an objective and knowable world, which is separate from the observing individual. Critical theorists, on the other hand, "see subject and object in the historical world as a reciprocally interrelated whole," and they deny the possibility of objective knowledge.[149] Where realists see a fixed and knowable world, critical theorists see the possibility of endless interpretations of the world before them. For critical theorists, "there are no constants, no fixed meanings, no secure grounds, no profound secrets, no final structures or limits of history . . . there is only interpretation. . . . History itself is grasped as a series of interpretations imposed upon interpretation—none primary, all arbitrary."[150]

Nevertheless, critical theorists readily acknowledge that realism has been the dominant interpretation of international politics for almost seven hundred years. "Realism is a name for a discourse of power and rule in modern global life."[151] Still, critical theory allows for change, and there is no reason, according to the theory anyway, why a communitarian discourse of peace and harmony cannot supplant the realist discourse of security competition and war. In fact, change is always possible with critical theory because it allows for an unlimited number of discourses, and it makes no judgment about the merit or staying power of any particular one. Also, critical theory makes no judgment about whether human beings are "hard-wired" to be good or bad, but instead treats people as infinitely changeable. The key to how they think and behave is the particular "software program" that individuals carry around in their heads, and those can be changed. In essence, critical theorists hope to replace the widely used realist software package with new software that emphasizes communitarian norms. Once that switch has been made, states will cooperate with each other and world politics will be more peaceful.

Most critical theorists do not see ideas and discourses forming at the grass roots and then percolating up to the elites of society. Rather, theirs is a top-down theory, whereby elites play the key role in transforming language and discourse about international relations. Experts, especially scholars, determine the flow of ideas about world politics. It is especially useful, however, if this intellectual vanguard consists of individuals from different states. These transnational elites, which are sometimes referred to as "epistemic communities," are well-suited for formulating and spreading the communitarian ideals that critical theorists hope will replace realism.[152]

Finally, it is worth noting that critical theorists are likely to be quite intolerant of other discourses about international politics, especially realism.[153] Four factors combine

---

148. See Cox, "Post-Hegemonic Conceptualization," pp. 132–139; Kratochwil and Ruggie, "International Organization," pp. 763–775; Yosef Lapid, "The Third Debate: On the Prospects of International Theory in a Post-Positivist Era," *International Studies Quarterly*, Vol. 33, No. 3 (September 1989), pp. 235–254; Wendt, "The Agent-Structure Problem," pp. 335–370.
149. Cox, "Post-Hegemonic Conceptualization," p. 135.
150. Ashley, "Geopolitics of Geopolitical Space," pp. 408–409.
151. Ibid., p. 422.
152. See Adler, "Arms Control"; and Peter M. Haas, ed., *Knowledge, Power, and International Policy Coordination*, special issue of *International Organization*, Vol. 46, No. 1 (Winter 1992).
153. For example, see Ashley, "Poverty of Neorealism," *passim*.

to account for this situation. The theory is based on the belief that ideas matter greatly for shaping international politics. Also, it recognizes that particular theories triumph in the marketplace of ideas, and the result is hegemonic discourse. Moreover, although the theory itself does not distinguish between good and bad ideas, critical theorists themselves certainly make that distinction. Furthermore, critical theorists have no historical guarantee that hegemonic discourse will move toward ideas about world politics that they consider sound. Realism, for example, has been the dominant discourse in the international arena for many centuries. Therefore, it makes sense for critical theorists to try to eliminate ideas they do not like, thus maximizing the prospects that their favorite discourse will triumph. Realist thinking, in this view, is not only dangerous, but is the main obstacle critical theorists face in their effort to establish a new and more peaceful hegemonic discourse.[154]

FLAWS IN THE CAUSAL LOGIC. The main goal of critical theorists is to change state behavior in fundamental ways, to move beyond a world of security competition and war and establish a pluralistic security community. However, their explanation of how change occurs is at best incomplete, and at worst, internally contradictory.[155]

Critical theory maintains that state behavior changes when discourse changes. But that argument leaves open the obvious and crucially important question: what determines why some discourses become dominant and others lose out in the marketplace of ideas? What is the mechanism that governs the rise and fall of discourses? This general question, in turn, leads to three more specific questions: 1) Why has realism been the hegemonic discourse in world politics for so long? 2) Why is the time ripe for its unseating? 3) Why is realism likely to be replaced by a more peaceful communitarian discourse?

Critical theory provides few insights on why discourses rise and fall. Thomas Risse-Kappen writes, "Research on . . . 'epistemic communities' of knowledge-based transnational networks has failed so far to specify the conditions under which specific ideas are selected and influence policies while others fall by the wayside."[156] Not surprisingly, critical theorists say little about why realism has been the dominant discourse, and why its foundations are now so shaky. They certainly do not offer a well-defined argument that deals with this important issue. Therefore, it is difficult to judge the fate of realism through the lens of critical theory.

Nevertheless, critical theorists occasionally point to particular factors that might lead to changes in international relations discourse. In such cases, however, they usually end up arguing that changes in the material world drive changes in discourse. For example, when Ashley makes surmises about the future of realism, he claims that "a crucial issue is whether or not changing historical conditions have disabled longstanding realist

---

154. Lebow, for example, writes that "Contemporary realists' . . . theories and some of the policy recommendations based on them may now stand in the way of the better world we all seek." Lebow, "The Long Peace," p. 277.
155. My thinking on this matter has been markedly influenced by Hein Goemans.
156. Thomas Risse-Kappen, "Ideas Do Not Float Freely: Transnational Coalitions, Domestic Structures, and the End of the Cold War," *International Organization*, Vol. 48, No. 2 (Spring 1994), p. 187. Also see Koslowski and Kratochwil, "Understanding Change," p. 225.

rituals of power." Specifically, he asks whether "developments in late capitalist society," like the "fiscal crisis of the state," and the "internationalization of capital," coupled with "the presence of vastly destructive and highly automated nuclear arsenals [has] deprived statesmen of the latitude for competent performance of realist rituals of power?"[157] Similarly, Cox argues that fundamental change occurs when there is a "disjuncture" between "the stock of ideas people have about the nature of the world and the practical problems that challenge them." He then writes, "Some of us think the erstwhile dominant mental construct of neorealism is inadequate to confront the challenges of global politics today."[158]

It would be understandable if realists made such arguments, since they believe there is an objective reality that largely determines which discourse will be dominant. Critical theorists, however, emphasize that the world is socially constructed, and not shaped in fundamental ways by objective factors. Anarchy, after all, is what we make of it. Yet when critical theorists attempt to explain why realism may be losing its hegemonic position, they too point to objective factors as the ultimate cause of change. Discourse, so it appears, turns out not to be determinative, but mainly a reflection of developments in the objective world. In short, it seems that when critical theorists who study international politics offer glimpses of their thinking about the causes of change in the real world, they make arguments that directly contradict their own theory, but which appear to be compatible with the theory they are challenging.[159]

There is another problem with the application of critical theory to international relations. Although critical theorists hope to replace realism with a discourse that emphasizes harmony and peace, critical theory *per se* emphasizes that it is impossible to know the future. Critical theory, according to its own logic, can be used to undermine realism and produce change, but it cannot serve as the basis for predicting which discourse will replace realism, because the theory says little about the direction change takes. In fact, Cox argues that although "utopian expectations may be an element in stimulating people to act . . . such expectations are almost never realized in practice."[160]

---

157. Ashley, "Geopolitics of Geopolitical Space," pp. 426–427.

158. Cox, "Post-Hegemonic Conceptualization," p. 138. Also see Cox, "Social Forces," pp. 138–149. For other examples, see Ruggie, "Continuity and Transformation," pp. 281–286; and Wendt, "Collective Identity Formation," pp. 389–390.

159. Cox is apparently aware of this problem. After spending eleven pages outlining various objective factors that might shape a new world order, he notes, "It would, of course, be *logically inadmissible*, as well as imprudent, to base predictions of future world order upon the foregoing considerations." Cox, "Social Forces," p. 149, emphasis added. Nevertheless, he then emphasizes in the next few sentences how important those objective considerations are for understanding future world order prospects. He writes: "Their utility is rather in drawing attention to factors which could incline an emerging world order in one direction or another. The social forces generated by changing production processes are the starting point for thinking about possible futures. These forces may combine in different configurations, and as an exercise one could consider the hypothetical configurations most likely to lead to three different outcomes as to the future of the state system. The focus on these three outcomes is not, of course, to imply that no other outcomes or configurations of social forces are possible." In other words, Cox does rely heavily on objective factors to explain possible future world orders.

160. Cox, *Production, Power, And World Order*, p. 393.

Thus, in a sense, the communitarian discourse championed by critical theorists is wishful thinking, not an outcome linked to the theory itself. Indeed, critical theory cannot guarantee that the new discourse will not be more malignant than the discourse it replaces. Nothing in the theory guarantees, for example, that a fascist discourse far more violent than realism will not emerge as the new hegemonic discourse.

PROBLEMS WITH THE EMPIRICAL RECORD.   Critical theorists have offered little empirical support for their theory.[161] It is still possible to sketch the broad outlines of their account of the past. They appear to concede that realism was the dominant discourse from about the start of the late medieval period in 1300 to at least 1989, and that states and other political entities behaved according to realist dictates during these seven centuries. However, some critical theorists suggest that both the discourse and practice of international politics during the preceding five centuries of the feudal era or central medieval period (800–1300) was not dominated by realism and, therefore, cannot be explained by it.[162] They believe that European political units of the feudal era did not think and therefore did not act in the exclusive and selfish manner assumed by realism, but instead adopted a more communitarian discourse, which guided their actions. Power politics, so the argument goes, had little relevance in these five hundred years.

Furthermore, most critical theorists see the end of the Cold War as an important watershed in world politics. A few go so far as to argue that "the revolutions of 1989 transformed the international system by changing the rules governing superpower conflict and, thereby, the norms underpinning the international system."[163] Realism, they claim, is no longer the hegemonic discourse. "The end of the Cold War . . . undermined neorealist theory."[164] Other critical theorists are more tentative in their judgment about whether the end of the Cold War has led to a fundamental transformation of international politics.[165] For these more cautious critical theorists, the revolutions of 1989 have created opportunities for change, but that change has not yet been realized.

Three points are in order regarding the critical theorists' interpretation of history. First, one cannot help but be struck by the sheer continuity of realist behavior in the critical theorists' own account of the past. Seven centuries of security competition and war represents an impressive span of time, especially when you consider the tremen-

---

161. Wendt, for example, acknowledges that, "Relatively little empirical research has been explicitly informed by structuration [critical] theory, which might illustrate its implications for the explanation of state action." Wendt, "The Agent-Structure Problem," p. 362.

162. Ruggie, "Continuity and Transformation," pp. 273–279. Also see Robert W. Cox, "Postscript 1985," in Robert O. Keohane, ed., *Neorealism and Its Critics* (New York: Columbia University Press, 1986), pp. 244–245.

163. Koslowski and Kratochwil, "Understanding Change," p. 215. Also see Lebow, "The Long Peace"; Risse-Kappen, "Ideas Do Not Float Freely"; and Janice Gross Stein, "Political Learning By Doing: Gorbachev As Uncommitted Thinker and Motivated Learner," *International Organization*, Vol. 48, No. 2 (Spring 1994), pp. 155–183. All four of these articles are published together as a symposium on "The End of the Cold War and Theories of International Relations," in the Spring 1994 *International Organization*.

164. Koslowski and Kratochwil, "Understanding Change," p. 217.

165. See, for example, Ruggie, "Territoriality and Beyond," pp. 173–174; Wendt, "Anarchy Is What States Make of It," p. 422; and Wendt, "Collective Identity Formation," p. 393.

dous political and economic changes that have taken place across the world during that lengthy period. Realism is obviously a human software package with deep-seated appeal, although critical theorists do not explain its attraction.

Second, a close look at the international politics of the feudal era reveals scant support for the claims of critical theorists. Markus Fischer has done a detailed study of that period, and he finds "that feudal discourse was indeed distinct, prescribing unity, functional cooperation, sharing, and lawfulness."[166] More importantly, however, he also finds "that while feudal actors observed these norms for the most part on the level of form, they in essence behaved like modern states." Specifically, they "strove for exclusive territorial control, protected themselves by military means, subjugated each other, balanced against power, formed alliances and spheres of influence, and resolved their conflicts by the use and threat of force."[167] Realism, not critical theory, appears best to explain international politics in the five centuries of the feudal era.

Third, there are good reasons to doubt that the demise of the Cold War means that the millennium is here. It is true that the great powers have been rather tame in their behavior towards each other over the past five years. But that is usually the case after great-power wars. Moreover, although the Cold War ended in 1989, the Cold War order that it spawned is taking much longer to collapse, which makes it difficult to determine what kind of order or disorder will replace it. For example, Russian troops remained in Germany until mid-1994, seriously impinging on German sovereignty, and the United States still maintains a substantial military presence in Germany. Five years is much too short a period to determine whether international relations has been fundamentally transformed by the end of the Cold War, especially given that the "old" order of realist discourse has been in place for at least twelve centuries.

A close look at the sources of this purported revolutionary change in world politics provides further cause for skepticism. For critical theorists, "the Cold War was fundamentally a discursive, not a material, structure."[168] Thus, if the United States and the Soviet Union had decided earlier in the Cold War that they were no longer enemies, it would have been over sooner.[169] Mikhail Gorbachev, critical theorists argue, played the central role in ending the Cold War. He challenged traditional Soviet thinking about national security, and championed ideas about international security that sounded like they had been scripted by critical theorists.[170] In fact, critical theorists argue that Gorbachev's "new thinking" was shaped by a "transnational liberal internationalist community [epistemic community] comprising the U.S. arms control community, Western European scholars and center-left policy makers, as well as Soviet institutchiks."[171] These new ideas led Gorbachev to end the Soviet Union's "imperial relationship with

---

166. Fischer, "Feudal Europe," p. 428. Also see the subsequent exchange between Fischer and Rodney Hall and Friedrich Kratochwil in *International Organization*, Vol. 47, No. 3 (Summer 1993), pp. 479–500.
167. Fischer, "Feudal Europe," p. 428.
168. Wendt, "Collective Identity Formation," p. 389.
169. This sentence is a paraphrase of Wendt, "Anarchy Is What States Make of It," p. 397.
170. See Koslowski and Kratochwil, "Understanding Change," p. 233.
171. Risse-Kappen, "Ideas Do Not Float Freely," p. 213. Also see ibid., pp. 195–214; and Stein, "Political Learning By Doing," pp. 175–180.

Eastern Europe," which led to a fundamental change in "the norms of bloc politics and thereby the rules governing superpower relations."[172] In essence, "the changed practices of one of the major actors . . . [had] system-wide repercussions."[173] Both superpowers "repudiated the notion of international relations as a self-help system and . . . transcended the consequences of anarchy as depicted by realism."[174]

Gorbachev surely played the key role in ending the Cold War, but there are good reasons to doubt that his actions fundamentally transformed international politics. His decision to shut down the Soviet empire in Eastern Europe can very well be explained by realism. By the mid-1980s, the Soviet Union was suffering an economic and political crisis at home that made the costs of empire prohibitive, especially since nuclear weapons provided the Soviets with a cheap and effective means of defense. Many empires collapsed and many states broke apart before 1989, and many of them sought to give to dire necessity the appearance of virtue. But the basic nature of international politics remained unchanged. It is not clear why the collapse of the Soviet Union is a special case.

Furthermore, now that Gorbachev is out of office and has little political influence in Russia, the Russians have abandoned his "new thinking."[175] In fact, they now have an offensively-oriented military doctrine that emphasizes first use of nuclear weapons. More importantly, since the end of 1992, the Russians have been acting like a traditional great power toward their neighbors. The former Soviet Union seems to be an arena for power politics, and Boris Yeltsin's Russia appears to be fully engaged in that enterprise.[176]

Regarding the more modest claim that the end of the Cold War presents an opportunity to move to a world where states are guided by norms of trust and sharing, perhaps this is true. But since critical theorists acknowledge that their theory cannot predict the future, why should we believe their claim, especially when it means choosing against realism, a theory that has at least 1200 years of staying power?

Critical theorists have ambitious aims. However, critical theory also has important flaws, and therefore it will likely remain in realism's shadow. Specifically, critical theory is concerned with affecting fundamental change in state behavior, but it says little about

---

172. Koslowski and Kratochwil, "Understanding Change," pp. 228, 239.
173. Ibid., p. 227.
174. Lebow, "The Long Peace," p. 276.
175. See Charles Dick, "The Military Doctrine of the Russian Federation," in *Jane's Intelligence Review*, Special Report No. 1, January 1994, pp. 1–5; Michael C. Desch, "Why the Soviet Military Supported Gorbachev and Why the Russian Military Might Only Support Yeltsin for a Price," *Journal of Strategic Studies*, Vol. 16, No. 4 (December 1993), pp. 467–474; and Stephen Foye, "Updating Russian Civil-Military Relations," *RFE/RL Research Report*, Vol. 2, No. 46 (November 19, 1993), pp. 44–50.
176. See, for example, Thomas Goltz, "Letter from Eurasia: The Hidden Russian Hand," *Foreign Policy*, No. 92, pp. 92–116; Steven E. Miller, "Russian National Interests," in Robert D. Blackwill and Sergei A. Karaganov, eds., *Damage Limitation or Crisis? Russia and the Outside World*, CSIA Studies in International Security No. 5 (Washington, D.C.: Brassey's, 1994), pp. 77–106; Alexei K. Pushkov, "Russia and America: The Honeymoon's Over," *Foreign Policy*, No. 93 (Winter 1993–1994), pp. 77–90; and Bruce D. Porter and Carol R. Saivetz, "The Once and Future Empire: Russia and the 'Near Abroad'," *Washington Quarterly*, Vol. 17, No. 3 (Summer 1994), pp. 75–90.

how it comes about. Critical theorists do occasionally point to particular causes of change, but when they do, they make arguments that are inconsistent with the theory itself. Finally, there is little empirical evidence to support the claims of critical theorists, and much to contradict them.

Conclusion

Many policymakers as well as academics believe that institutions hold great promise for promoting international peace. This optimistic assessment of institutions is not warranted, however, mainly because the three institutionalist theories which underpin it are flawed. There are serious problems with the causal logic of each theory, and little empirical evidence for any of them. What is most impressive about institutions, in fact, is how little independent effect they seem to have had on state behavior.

We have an important paradox here: although the world does not work the way institutionalist theories say it does or should, those theories remain highly influential in both the academic and policy worlds. Given the limited impact of institutions on state behavior, one would expect considerable skepticism, even cynicism, when institutions are described as a major force for peace. Instead, they are still routinely described in promising terms by scholars and governing elites.

It is beyond the scope of this paper to attempt a detailed explanation of this paradox. Nevertheless, I would like to close with some speculative comments about this puzzle, focusing on the American context.

The attraction of institutionalist theories for both policymakers and scholars is explained, I believe, not by their intrinsic value, but by their relationship to realism, and especially to core elements of American political ideology. Realism has long been and continues to be an influential theory in the United States.[177] Leading realist thinkers such as George Kennan and Henry Kissinger, for example, occupied key policymaking positions during the Cold War. The impact of realism in the academic world is amply demonstrated in the institutionalist literature, where discussions of realism are pervasive.[178] Yet despite its influence, Americans who think seriously about foreign policy issues tend to dislike realism intensely, mainly because it clashes with their basic values. The theory stands opposed to how most Americans prefer to think about themselves and the wider world.[179]

---

177. See Michael J. Smith, *Realist Thought from Weber to Kissinger* (Baton Rouge: Louisiana State University Press, 1986), chap. 1.

178. Summing up the autobiographical essays of 34 international relations scholars, Joseph Kruzel notes that "Hans Morgenthau is more frequently cited than any other name in these memoirs." Joseph Kruzel, "Reflections on the Journeys," in Joseph Kruzel and James N. Rosenau, eds., *Journeys through World Politics: Autobiographical Reflections of Thirty-four Academic Travelers* (Lexington, Mass.: Lexington Books, 1989), p. 505. Although "Morgenthau is often cited, many of the references in these pages are negative in tone. He seems to have inspired his critics even more than his supporters." Ibid.

179. See Keith L. Shimko, "Realism, Neorealism, and American Liberalism," *Review of Politics*, Vol. 54, No. 2 (Spring 1992), pp. 281–301.

There are four principal reasons why American elites, as well as the American public, tend to regard realism with hostility. First, realism is a pessimistic theory. It depicts a world of stark and harsh competition, and it holds out little promise of making that world more benign. Realists, as Hans Morgenthau wrote, are resigned to the fact that "there is no escape from the evil of power, regardless of what one does."[180] Such pessimism, of course, runs up against the deep-seated American belief that with time and effort, reasonable individuals can solve important social problems. Americans regard progress as both desirable and possible in politics, and they are therefore uncomfortable with realism's claim that security competition and war will persist despite our best efforts to eliminate them.[181]

Second, realism treats war as an inevitable, and indeed sometimes necessary, form of state activity. For realists, war is an extension of politics by other means. Realists are very cautious in their prescriptions about the use of force: wars should not be fought for idealistic purposes, but instead for balance-of-power reasons. Most Americans, however, tend to think of war as a hideous enterprise that should ultimately be abolished. For the time being, however, it can only justifiably be used for lofty moral goals, like "making the world safe for democracy"; it is morally incorrect to fight wars to change or preserve the balance of power. This makes the realist conception of warfare anathema to many Americans.

Third, as an analytical matter, realism does not distinguish between "good" states and "bad" states, but essentially treats them like billiard balls of varying size. In realist theory, all states are forced to seek the same goal: maximum relative power.[182] A purely realist interpretation of the Cold War, for example, allows for no meaningful difference in the motives behind American and Soviet behavior during that conflict. According to the theory, both sides must have been driven by concerns about the balance of power, and must have done what was necessary to try to achieve a favorable balance. Most

---

180. Hans J. Morgenthau, *Scientific Man vs. Power Politics* (Chicago: University of Chicago Press, 1974), p. 201. Nevertheless, Keith Shimko convincingly argues that the shift within realism, away from Morgenthau's belief that states are motivated by an unalterable will to power, and toward Waltz's view that states are motivated by the desire for security, provides "a residual, though subdued optimism, or at least a possible basis for optimism [about international politics]. The extent to which this optimism is stressed or suppressed varies, but it is there if one wants it to be." Shimko, "Realism, Neorealism, and American Liberalism," p. 297. Realists like Stephen Van Evera, for example, point out that although states operate in a dangerous world, they can take steps to dampen security competition and minimize the danger of war. See Van Evera, *Causes of War.*

181. See Reinhold Niebuhr, *The Children of Light and The Children of Darkness: A Vindication of Democracy and a Critique of Its Traditional Defense* (New York: Charles Scribner's, 1944), especially pp. 153–190. See also Samuel P. Huntington, *The Soldier and the State: The Theory and Politics of Civil-Military Relations* (New York: Vintage Books, 1964).

182. It should be emphasized that many realists have strong moral preferences and are driven by deep moral convictions. Realism is not a normative theory, however, and it provides no criteria for moral judgment. Instead, realism merely seeks to explain how the world works. Virtually all realists would prefer a world without security competition and war, but they believe that goal is unrealistic given the structure of the international system. See, for example, Robert G. Gilpin, "The Richness of the Tradition of Political Realism," in Keohane, *Neorealism and Its Critics*, p. 321.

Americans would recoil at such a description of the Cold War, because they believe the United States was motivated by good intentions while the Soviet Union was not.[183]

Fourth, America has a rich history of thumbing its nose at realism. For its first 140 years of existence, geography and the British navy allowed the United States to avoid serious involvement in the power politics of Europe. America had an isolationist foreign policy for most of this period, and its rhetoric explicitly emphasized the evils of entangling alliances and balancing behavior. Even as the United States finally entered its first European war in 1917, Woodrow Wilson railed against realist thinking. America has a long tradition of anti-realist rhetoric, which continues to influence us today.

Given that realism is largely alien to American culture, there is a powerful demand in the United States for alternative ways of looking at the world, and especially for theories that square with basic American values. Institutionalist theories nicely meet these requirements, and that is the main source of their appeal to policymakers and scholars. Whatever else one might say about these theories, they have one undeniable advantage in the eyes of their supporters: they are not realism. Not only do institutionalist theories offer an alternative to realism, but they explicitly seek to undermine it. Moreover, institutionalists offer arguments that reflect basic American values. For example, they are optimistic about the possibility of greatly reducing, if not eliminating, security competition among states and creating a more peaceful world. They certainly do not accept the realist stricture that war is politics by other means. Institutionalists, in short, purvey a message that Americans long to hear.

There is, however, a downside for policymakers who rely on institutionalist theories: these theories do not accurately describe the world, hence policies based on them are bound to fail. The international system strongly shapes the behavior of states, limiting the amount of damage that false faith in institutional theories can cause. The constraints of the system notwithstanding, however, states still have considerable freedom of action, and their policy choices can succeed or fail in protecting American national interests and the interests of vulnerable people around the globe. The failure of the League of Nations to address German and Japanese aggression in the 1930s is a case in point. The failure of institutions to prevent or stop the war in Bosnia offers a more recent example. These cases illustrate that institutions have mattered rather little in the past; they also suggest that the false belief that institutions matter has mattered more, and has had pernicious effects. Unfortunately, misplaced reliance on institutional solutions is likely to lead to more failures in the future.

---

183. Realism's treatment of states as billiard balls of different sizes tends to raise the hackles of comparative politics scholars, who believe that domestic political and economic factors matter greatly for explaining foreign policy behavior.

Realists as Optimists

Cooperation as Self-Help

Charles L. Glaser

Structural realists are pessimistic about the prospects for international cooperation; they believe that competition between the major powers in the international system is the normal state of affairs. The structural-realist argument is driven by the implications of international anarchy, that is, the lack of an international authority capable of enforcing agreements. Responding to the pressures of anarchy, during peacetime countries will be inclined to deal with adversaries by arms racing and gaining allies, rather than by cooperating via arms control or other approaches for realizing common interests. Anarchy discourages cooperation because it requires states to worry about the relative gains of cooperation and the possibility that adversaries will cheat on agreements. In short, the standard structural-realist argument predicts that cooperation between adversaries, while not impossible, will be difficult to achieve and, as a result, will be rare and contribute relatively little to states' well-being.[1]

This characterization of structural realism is offered by both its proponents and its detractors. Kenneth Waltz argues that self-help systems "make the cooperation of parties difficult. . . . Rules, institutions, and patterns of cooperation . . . are all limited in extent and modified from what they might otherwise be." Summarizing the views of realists, Joseph Grieco says, "realism presents a fundamentally pessimistic analysis of the prospects for international coop-

Charles L. Glaser is Associate Professor and Acting Dean of the Irving B. Harris Graduate School of Public Policy Studies at the University of Chicago.

For helpful comments on earlier drafts, I would like to thank Matt Evangelista, Jim Fearon, Lloyd Gruber, Ted Hopf, Chaim Kaufmann, Barbara Koremenos, Andy Kydd, John Mearsheimer, Jonathan Mercer, Robert Powell, Duncan Snidal, Ivan Toft, Brad Thayer, Steve Walt, and Ken Yao, and participants in seminars at the University of Chicago's Program on International Politics, Economics and Security and at Stanford's Center for International Security and Arms Control.

1. Structural realists are sometimes referred to as neorealists. Kenneth N. Waltz, *Theory of International Politics* (New York: Random House, 1979) remains the most important statement of these arguments. Some authors want to reserve "neorealism" to refer to the theory as articulated by Waltz, while using structural realism to refer to a broader family of systemic theories; see Barry Buzan, Charles Jones and Richard Little, *The Logic of Anarchy: Neorealism to Structural Realism* (New York: Columbia University Press, 1993). In this essay, I use "structural realist" as an ideal type—an analyst who believes that only international or systemic-level factors influence international politics. I recognize, however, that virtually all structural realists actually believe that other levels of analysis have some influence.

International Security, Winter 1994/95 (Vol. 19, No. 3)
© 1995 by the President and Fellows of Harvard College and of the Massachusetts Institute of Technology.

eration." Critics essentially agree. Robert Keohane concludes that, "realism sometimes seems to imply, pessimistically, that order can be created *only* by hegemony. If the latter conclusion were correct . . . at some time in the foreseeable future, global nuclear war would ensue. . . . No serious thinker could, therefore, be satisfied with Realism." Steve Weber declares that structural realism claims that any cooperation that emerges under anarchy will "be tenuous, unstable, and limited to issues of peripheral importance."[2]

I argue that this pessimism is unwarranted. Contrary to the conventional wisdom, the strong general propensity for adversaries to compete is not an inevitable logical consequence of structural realism's basic assumptions. Structural realism properly understood predicts that, under a wide range of conditions, adversaries can best achieve their security goals through cooperative policies, not competitive ones, and should, therefore, choose cooperation when these conditions prevail.

This article focuses on states' military-policy options during peacetime. In this context, "cooperation" refers to coordinated policies designed to avoid arms races,[3] while competition refers to unilateral military buildups, which are likely to generate arms races, and to alliance formation.[4]

The implications of my reevaluation are not limited to peacetime policies, however. Adversaries find peacetime cooperation desirable because it enables

---

2. Kenneth N. Waltz, "Reflections on *Theory of International Politics*: A Response to My Critics," in Robert O. Keohane, ed., *Neorealism and Its Critics* (New York: Columbia University Press, 1986), p. 336; Joseph M. Grieco, *Cooperation Among Nations: Europe, America and Non-tariff Barriers to Trade* (Ithaca, N.Y.: Cornell University Press, 1990), p. 27; Robert O. Keohane, "Theory of World Politics: Structural Realism and Beyond," in Ada W. Finiter, ed., *Political Science: The State of the Discipline* (Washington, D.C.: American Political Science Association, 1983), p. 532, reprinted in Keohane, *Neorealism and its Critics*; and Steve Weber, "Realism, Detente, and Nuclear Weapons," *International Organization*, Vol. 44, No. 1 (Winter 1990), pp. 58–59. Weber claims further that realism "cannot comfortably encompass the more constraining provisions of SALT," the Strategic Arms Limitation Treaty.

3. In other contexts, cooperation can refer to decisions to make concessions during a crisis and to decisions to forgo launching a war. Cooperation—including both formal and informal reciprocated restraint—is not the only alternative to competitive policies. Uncoordinated but unthreatening, and therefore uncompetitive, policies can sometimes be a second key alternative. For example, if defensive forces have an advantage over offensive forces, then countries could choose defense, independent of others' choices.

4. I consider alliance formation to be a type of competition because, although the allies are cooperating with each other, they are competing with a common adversary. Since balancing in the form of alliance formation is probably the most prominent and widely accepted prediction of structural realism, the standard pessimism about cooperation presumably does not count alliances as cooperation. The key questions about cooperation therefore focus on cooperation between adversaries. However, because today's ally could be an adversary in the future, the line between allies and adversaries is not always sharp, and under certain conditions concern about relative gains could inhibit cooperation between allies.

them to moderate causes of war that already exist or to avoid competition that would intensify causes of war. Consequently, beyond being more optimistic about the prospects for peacetime cooperation, my alternative structural-realist analysis, which I label *contingent realism,* is also more optimistic about the likelihood of avoiding war than is the standard structural-realist analysis.

My argument draws on various strands of international relations theory, including arguments about the security dilemma, costly signaling, relative-gains constraints, arms control, and cooperation under anarchy. I develop a number of specific arguments that are required to apply these strands of theory to the security realm and to integrate them fully into a structural-realist argument. However, the overall argument is bigger than the sum of the individual strands: it offers a direct and thorough challenge to the standard structural-realist explanation of the prevalence of international competition.

Recent critics of structural realism have come to be viewed as advancing a competing theory, instead of correcting flaws within structural realism.[5] In part, this is because the critics have emphasized factors such as institutions and regimes that structural realists believe have little explanatory power, and have underplayed factors that structural realists believe are critical, such as the relative gains of cooperation. This article focuses more closely on the elements that structural realists identify as most important. Therefore, my argument should be understood as identifying basic corrections that follow deductively from structural realism's core assumptions, not as another theory being counter-posed against structural realism.

Contingent realism challenges neo-institutionalists, who see institutions as the key to cooperation, by explaining international cooperation without focusing on institutions. Moreover, to the extent that institutions facilitate cooperation, contingent realism explains why they are necessary and how they help.

The first section of this article summarizes the "standard" structural realist explanation for competition. The next section presents the three arguments that together constitute contingent realism. The first argument shows that the stan-

---

5. One challenge comes from cooperation theory, which employs game theory to study the implications of potential cheating. Robert Axelrod, *The Evolution of Cooperation* (New York: Basic Books, 1984), provides the foundation for much of this work. Key works include Robert O. Keohane, *After Hegemony: Cooperation and Discord in the World Political Economy* (Princeton, N.J.: Princeton University Press, 1984); and Kenneth A. Oye, ed., *Cooperation Under Anarchy* (Princeton, N.J.: Princeton University Press, 1986). Cooperation theory has been criticized for overlooking constraints imposed by concern over relative gains; see Grieco, *Cooperation Among Nations.* David A. Baldwin, ed., *Neorealism and Neoliberalism: The Contemporary Debate* (New York: Columbia University Press, 1993), includes many of the key articles in this debate. Robert Powell, "Anarchy in International Relations Theory: The Neorealist-Neoliberal Debate," *International Organization,* Vol. 48, No. 2 (Spring 1994), pp. 313–44, explores many of the key issues.

dard explanation is biased, because it emphasizes the benefits of competition while overlooking its risks, and it implies that "self-help" necessitates competition; in fact, cooperative policies are an important type of self-help. The second corrects problems with how the standard formulation deals with states' military capabilities, specifically their ability to perform military missions. In assessing their security, states should focus on their ability to perform military missions. However, the standard structural-realist argument is cast in terms of power.[6] Power influences mission capability, but is only the beginning of the story. Contingent realism corrects this mis-specification by integrating offense-defense variables into structural-realist theory. This integration shows that, as the security-dilemma literature argues, cooperation can be a country's best option, and identifies the conditions under which states should prefer arms control or unilateral defensive policies to arms racing.

The third argument shows that basic structural-realist assumptions leave open the possibility that a country can use its military policy to communicate information that should lead its adversaries to reassess its motives and intentions. Thus, contrary to the standard argument, countries should not focus solely on capabilities, but also on motives. Consequently, countries should sometimes exercise self-restraint and pursue cooperative military policies, because these policies can convince a rational opponent to revise favorably its view of the country's motives. I explore the conditions under which these considerations favor cooperation.

The third section of this article addresses the three major arguments that structural realists use to support their standard prediction of competition, and that could be used to counter the conclusions that flow from my reformulation. These potential counter-arguments are: 1) states try to maximize relative power, which creates a zero-sum situation that usually precludes cooperation; 2) states' concerns over relative gains make security cooperation especially difficult; and 3) states adopt competitive policies because the possibility of cheating makes cooperation too risky. I explain how each of these arguments is seriously flawed, holding only under certain conditions, and not under others.

---

6. To avoid confusion, it is important to distinguish the role that power plays in two major strands of realism. Classical realists hold that power is an end in itself; in contrast, structural realists hold that security is an end, and according to the standard argument, states measure their ability to achieve this end in terms of power. My discussion accepts the structural-realist assumption that security is the end, and explores problems that arise from focusing on power as the means to this end. Hans J. Morgenthau is often credited with presenting the fullest statement of classical realism; see his *Politics Among Nations*, 5th ed. (New York: Knopf, 1973). Robert O. Keohane, "Realism, Neorealism and the Study of World Politics," pp. 7–16, in Keohane, ed., *Neorealism and Its Critics*, compares classical and structural realism.

The final section briefly considers implications for theoretical and policy debates. Contingent realism emphasizes that offense-defense variables and the security dilemma are central to the logic of structural realism, not a separate body of theory. Integrating these variables yields a set of conditional structural-realist predictions about when states should compete and when they should cooperate. Because structural realism is a parsimonious theory of rational behavior, these predictions establish an important baseline against which to compare theories that are less parsimonious or that deal with sub-optimal behavior. The thrust of my argument is not that contingent realism necessarily explains states' behavior correctly, but rather that such a baseline is essential for assessing the explanatory power of structural realism relative to theories built on other assumptions and at other levels of analysis.

Contingent realism makes clear that the standard structural-realist claim about the strong tendency for states to pursue competitive military policies is at best incomplete. Because contingent realism makes conditional predictions about cooperation and competition, a structural-realist case against cooperation must demonstrate that the conditions necessary for cooperation have not occurred; structural-realists have not provided this type of evidence. Furthermore, contingent realism contradicts the conventional wisdom that while structural realism does a good job of explaining the Cold War, it is severely challenged by the end of the Cold War, which runs counter to the theory's supposed predictions of competitiveness. Contingent realism suggests that structural realism, correctly understood, can explain the end of the Cold War relatively easily, but has greater difficulty explaining the latter half of the Cold War. The need for additional theories is clearest when trying to explain this competitive period. In terms of the future, contingent realism provides more optimistic predictions than those now often associated with structural realism.

Review of the "Standard" Structural-realist Argument

Structural realism is built on a small number of basic assumptions: that states can be viewed as essentially rational unitary actors; that states give priority to insuring their security; and that states confront an international environment that is characterized most importantly by anarchy.[7] Structural realism is a

---

7. This formulation is consistent with Waltz, *Theory of International Politics*. For Waltz's view on rationality, see "Reflections on *Theory of International Politics*," pp. 330–331. Waltz does make other assumptions and basic arguments that significantly influence his conclusions, including claims that power is fungible. For discussion and criticism of his formulation see Buzan, Jones, and Little, *The Logic of Anarchy*. For useful discussions of the assumptions of realism, see Keohane, "Theory of

third-image theory: the constraints and opportunities created by the international system are used to explain states' behavior; and states view each other as "black boxes"—they focus on other states' observable behavior, not their type of government, the quality of their decision-making, or particular features of their leaders.[8]

Structural realism does not preclude the possibility that states have important motives in addition to security. States must worry that others have non-security ("greedy") motives that call for expansionist policies,[9] but structural realism does not assume the presence of greedy states in the system.[10] Central to the structural realist argument is the conclusion that security competition and war are possible even when there are no greedy states in the system, since states might seek to increase their security through expansion.

THE STANDARD ARGUMENT

Working from these basic assumptions,[11] structural realists argue that states live in a "self-help" world that results from international anarchy: without an

---

World Politics," pp. 163–169, and Robert G. Gilpin, "The Richness of the Tradition of Political Realism," pp. 304–305, both in Keohane, *Neorealism and Its Critics.* Another common assumption is that states are the major actors in the international system. I do not include this as an assumption, preferring to leave open to analysis the question of whether states would create or allow other actors that would replace them as the major actors.

8. On the third image, see Kenneth N. Waltz, *Man, the State and War* (New York: Columbia University Press, 1959), esp. chaps. 6 and 7. Other useful discussions of levels of analysis include J. David Singer, "The Level-of-Analysis Problem in International Relations," in James N. Rosenau, ed., *International Politics and Foreign Policy* (New York: The Free Press, 1969), pp. 20–29; and Robert Jervis, *Perception and Misperception in International Politics* (Princeton, N.J.: Princeton University Press, 1976), chap. 1.

9. Because expansion can be motivated by greed as well as insecurity, I do not use the terms "expansionist" and "aggressive" to define types of states. For similar reasons, I do not use the term "status quo" to define states that are motived only by insecurity; pure security seekers may be unwilling to accept the status quo. For more on these points, see Charles L. Glaser, "Political Consequences of Military Strategy: Expanding and Refining the Spiral and Deterrence Models," *World Politics,* Vol. 44, No. 4 (July 1992), pp. 497–538.

10. Although the standard structural-realist explanation says little about the probability and severity of greedy states in the system, these variables and states' beliefs about them would influence their choices between cooperation and competition; see Glaser, "Political Consequences of Military Strategy," and the discussion below. Therefore, a more complete theory would incorporate variations in greed and generate a family of predictions, while holding other variables constant. In this spirit, see Randall L. Schweller, "Bandwagoning for Profit: Bringing the Revisionist State Back In," *International Security,* Vol. 19, No. 1 (Summer 1994), pp. 72–107.

11. The following description of the standard argument does not include some important nuances and it blurs some differences between authors that I have lumped together as contributors to the standard structural-realist analysis. Nevertheless, I believe that it captures the basic thrust of the standard argument. For a good summary of the realist literature, see Arthur A. Stein, *Why Nations Cooperate: Circumstances and Choice in International Relations* (Ithaca, N.Y.: Cornell University Press, 1990), pp. 4–13.

international authority capable of protecting them, major powers must look out for themselves.[12] The standard interpretation equates self-help with states' pursuit of unilateral, competitive policies.[13] This inclination toward competition is reinforced by doubts about the adversary's motives and intentions. Intentions are unknowable, and even if known, could be different tomorrow. This uncertainty works against cooperation.[14] States must not overlook the possibility that potential adversaries will use their full capabilities against them, and they therefore must focus on adversaries' capabilities instead of their intentions. Thus, at a minimum, cooperation is difficult because states are sensitive to how it affects their current and future relative capabilities;[15] moreover, cooperation is often impossible because states find military advantages to be especially valuable and thus compete to acquire them.[16] Making matters still worse, falling behind in this competition can carry extremely high costs: it invites war and, in the worst case, a major power can lose its sovereignty.[17] Consequently, competition tends to be intense and cooperation is rare because the risks of being cheated are large.

In short, according to the standard structural-realist explanation, states prefer competitive policies for multiple, reinforcing reasons. Arms races occur because

---

12. On the nature and implications of self-help, see Waltz, *Theory of International Politics*, pp. 105–107, 111–112. The necessity of self-help also depends on the assumption that states do not believe that other states are highly altruistic—specifically, that they would be willing to risk their own security to guarantee others' security. If they were, then even under anarchy, states would not have to rely entirely on self-help; instead, they could count on others coming to their aid, even when the other states' security was not in jeopardy. However, altruism is not the key issue for structural realists; under anarchy, the more immediate concern is the extent of opposing states' current and future malign intentions; states cannot count on others being benign, let alone altruistic.
13. For example, Christopher Layne, "The Unipolar Illusion: Why New Great Powers Will Rise," *International Security*, Vol. 17, No. 4 (Spring 1993), p. 11, argues: "Because it is anarchic, the international political system is a self-help system in which states' foremost concern must be with survival. In an anarchic system, states must provide for their own security and they face many real or apparent threats. International politics is thus a competitive realm." In his critique of structural realism, Alexander Wendt, "Anarchy is What States Make of It: The Social Construction of Power Politics," *International Organization*, Vol. 46, No. 2 (Spring 1992), p. 392, argues: "The self-help corollary to anarchy does enormous work in neorealism, generating the inherently competitive dynamics of the security dilemma and collective action problem." See also ibid, p. 396. Waltz appears to agree that self-help leads to competition: "In self-help systems, the pressures of competition weigh more heavily than ideological preferences or internal political pressures." Waltz, "Reflections on *Theory of International Politics*," p. 329; see also the quotation previously cited in fn. 2.
14. Waltz, *Theory of International Politics*, p. 105.
15. Waltz, *Theory of International Politics*, p. 105; Grieco, *Cooperation Among Nations*, p. 45.
16. John J. Mearsheimer, "Back to the Future: Instability in Europe After the Cold War," *International Security*, Vol. 15, No. 1 (Summer 1990), p. 12.
17. For example, Mearsheimer, "Back to the Future," p. 12, argues "there is little room for trust among states because a state may be unable to recover if its trust is betrayed."

states must rely on their own means; because states must avoid reductions in their capabilities and often desire military advantages; and because, even if interested in avoiding a race, states must insure against falling behind if the adversary cheats on agreements. In its most succinct version, the standard argument sees the search for security that flows from anarchy as sufficient to explain competition: "realists argue that states are preoccupied with their security and power; *by consequence,* states are predisposed toward conflict and competition."[18] Cooperation between adversaries, although not impossible, will be rare and limited to areas of at best secondary importance.

This conclusion is implicit in Waltz's focus on arms competition and alliance formation. In broad terms, states can choose from three approaches for acquiring and maintaining the military capabilities required to meet their security needs: building arms, gaining allies, and reaching arms control agreements.[19] In principle, the approaches could be equally important. Waltz acknowledges that some cooperation (i.e., arms control) is possible,[20] but he then excludes cooperation with adversaries from the basic alternatives available to states in a self-help system:

States, or those who act for them, try in more or less sensible ways to use the means available in order to achieve the ends in view. Those means fall into two categories: internal efforts (moves to increase economic capability, to increase military strength, to develop clever strategies) and external efforts (moves to strengthen and enlarge one's own alliance or to weaken and shrink an opposing one).[21]

Contingent Realism

Although widely accepted as an accurate statement of structural realism, the standard structural-realist argument is deeply flawed. A more complete and

---

18. Grieco, *Cooperation Among Nations,* p. 4 (emphasis added).

19. "Arms control" is used here to refer to the full range of reciprocated restraint in the deployment, operation, and monitoring of forces; it is not restricted to formal agreements. On this broader definition see Thomas C. Schelling and Morton H. Halperin, *Strategy and Arms Control* (New York: Twentieth Century Fund, 1961), pp. 2–5; on the relative strengths of formal agreements and tacit bargaining, see George W. Downs, David M. Rocke, and Randolph M. Siverson, "Arms Control and Cooperation," in Oye, ed., *Cooperation Under Anarchy.*

20. Waltz, *Theory of International Politics,* pp. 115–116; also, Waltz, "A Response to My Critics," p. 336.

21. Waltz, *Theory of International Politics,* p. 118; see also Waltz, "The Origins of War in Neorealist Theory," in Robert I. Rotberg and Theodore K. Rabb, eds., *The Origin and Prevention of Major Wars* (Cambridge: Cambridge University Press, 1989), p. 43: "Their individual intentions aside, collectively their actions yield arms races and alliances."

balanced assessment, while starting from the same structural-realist assumptions, leads to quite different conclusions. Under a wide range of conditions, cooperation should be a country's preferred option; significantly, two or more countries could simultaneously reach this conclusion, thereby making security cooperation feasible. The following discussion also demonstrates that under other conditions structural realism does not identify a clear preference for competition versus cooperation.

My contingent-realist analysis develops three lines of argument. First, it eliminates the unwarranted bias toward competition that exists in the standard argument. Second, to capture more faithfully the logic that flows from structural realism's basic assumptions, contingent realism focuses on military capabilities—the ability to perform military missions—instead of on power.[22] This is accomplished by more fully integrating the security dilemma into structural realism. Third, contingent realism recognizes that the rational-actor assumptions that form the foundation of structural realism allow states to use military policy to communicate information about their motives. As a result, states seeking security should see benefits in cooperative policies that can communicate benign motives.

ELIMINATING THE "COMPETITION" BIAS

The standard argument focuses on the risks of cooperation; by underplaying and overlooking the risks of competition, it contains an unwarranted bias toward competition. The bias is the result of several mistakes. First, although the standard argument equates self-help with pursuit of competitive policies, in fact cooperative policies are an important type of self-help. For example, an adversary will engage in reciprocal restraint only if arms control promises to provide it with greater security than the competitive alternatives; this is possible only if the adversary believes that an arms race would be risky. Consequently, a country gets an adversary to cooperate by relying on its own resources—through self-help—since the country's ability to engage in an

---

22. To avoid confusion, I stress that the term "military capabilities" refers to the capability to perform military missions. Some authors use "military capabilities" to refer to military forces, that is, as a measure of the forces a country has deployed, not as a measure of the ability of forces to perform missions against an adversary's forces. As an example of the former use, Waltz explains that "capabilities are attributes of units [states]" and he includes "military strength" among the components of overall capability; Waltz, *Theory of International Politics*, pp. 98, 131. The distinction is very important because a state's ability to perform military missions is not determined by the size, type, and quality of its own military forces or resources, but by how these resources compare with and would fight against the adversary's forces.

arms race is a central condition for its adversary's belief that arms racing is risky, and thus for its willingness to cooperate. Thus, by itself, self-help tells us essentially nothing about whether states should prefer cooperation or competition.

Second, although the standard argument is correct in maintaining that the desire to avoid losses of capability and to gain military advantages can force states to compete, it is also true that this desire can lead states to cooperate. If military advantages are extremely valuable, then military disadvantages can be extremely dangerous. Therefore, when uncertain about the outcome of an arms race, which it would like to win, a risk-averse state could prefer an arms control agreement that accepted the current military status quo to gambling on prevailing in the arms race.[23] In addition, countries can prefer cooperation even when they are sure that they would not lose the arms race. For example, a country concerned about maintaining its military capabilities could prefer arms control when an arms race would result in advances in weapons technology that, when deployed by both countries, would have the unfortunate effect of leaving both countries more vulnerable to attack. And a country could prefer arms control when equal increases in the size of forces might decrease, not increase, its ability to defend itself.[24] The central message of modern arms control theory is that under certain conditions *both* countries could prefer these kinds of cooperation.[25]

Third, although it is correct in stating that uncertainty about the adversary's motives creates reasons for a state to compete, the standard argument fails to recognize that uncertainty about motives also creates powerful reasons for states to cooperate. Each faces uncertainty about the other's motives; such

---

23. Doubts about the outcome of the race could reflect uncertainties about which country is wealthier, better able to extract resources for military purposes, or better able to develop and exploit military technologies.
24. Moreover, the choice of arms racing over cooperation must compare arms racing not only to the military status quo but also to the possibility that reductions from the status quo might improve capabilities. Of course, the choice between arms racing, arms control and allies will also be influenced by domestic factors. For example, a country might prefer to avoid an arms race, which would not reduce its security, simply to avoid the economic costs of further arming. On domestic factors in the choice between arming and allies, see James D. Morrow, "Arms Versus Allies: Tradeoffs in the Search For Security," *International Organization*, Vol. 47, No. 2 (Spring 1993), pp. 207–233.
25. See Schelling and Halperin, *Strategy and Arms Control;* and Donald G. Brennan, ed., *Arms Control, Disarmament and National Security* (New York: George Braziller, 1961). Thomas C. Schelling, "A Framework for the Evaluation of Arms-Control Proposals," *Daedalus*, Vol. 104, No. 3 (Summer 1975), pp. 187–200, explores the implications of a country's preferences for an arms race, an unmatched unilateral buildup, or the military status quo.

uncertainty is dangerous because it can fuel insecurity, which structural realism identifies as the key source of international conflict. This generates two reasons for a state to cooperate. Even if cooperation leaves the adversary's uncertainty about a state's motives unchanged, cooperation is valuable if it reduces the adversary's insecurity by reducing the military threat it faces. Moreover, cooperation is valuable if it can reduce the adversary's uncertainty, convincing it that the first state is motivated more by insecurity than by greed; this would further reduce the probability of conflict caused by an opponent's insecurity. The benefits of competition, specifically gaining military advantages, must be weighed against these benefits of cooperation. This tradeoff lies at the core of the security dilemma, is a central component of structural realism, and cannot be generally resolved in favor of competition.

In sum, eliminating the bias in the standard structural-realist argument shows that states face a variety of countervailing pressures for cooperation as well as competition. Nothing in the basic structural-realist argument resolves these tradeoffs in general in favor of competition. The standard argument stresses only the risks of cooperation, but both cooperation and competition can be risky. Launching an arms buildup can make the adversary more insecure and, therefore, harder to deter. Pursuing military advantages forgos the possibility of avoiding an arms race in which the state could fall temporarily or permanently behind. When the risks of competition exceed the risks of cooperation, states should direct their self-help efforts toward achieving cooperation. Thus, contingent realism makes it clear that we need to replace essentially unconditional predictions of competition with conditional predictions of when states should cooperate and when they should compete.

SHIFTING THE FOCUS FROM POWER TO MILITARY CAPABILITIES: BRINGING IN CONSIDERATIONS OF OFFENSE AND DEFENSE
A security-seeking state that is comparing competition and cooperation must confront two fundamental questions. First, which will contribute more to its military capabilities for deterring attack, and for defending if deterrence fails? Second, appreciating the pressures created by anarchy and insecurity, the state should ask which approach is best for avoiding capabilities that threaten others' abilities to defend and deter, while not undermining its military capabilities? The tension that can exist between these two objectives lies at the core of the security dilemma.

WHY REFORMULATION IS NECESSARY. According to the standard structural-realist argument, states evaluate their ability to achieve security in terms of power.[26] Great powers are defined in terms of aggregate resources, including size of population, economic and industrial assets, and military assets. Power is defined in terms of the distribution of these resources among the states in the system. States seeking security endeavor to maintain their position in the system, and therefore they seek to maintain their relative resource rankings.[27]

This formulation is problematic because, as noted above, security-seeking states should assess their military requirements in terms of their ability to perform necessary military missions and to forgo the ability to perform certain other missions. Considerations of power do influence the answers to these questions, but they only begin to tell the story. For example, under certain conditions, two equally powerful states might have good prospects for defending against each other, while under other conditions their prospects for defending successfully could be relatively poor.

To shift from a structural theory based on power to one based on military capabilities and strategy, we need to include the dimensions of the security dilemma—the offense-defense balance and offense-defense distinguishability—as key variables. The offense-defense balance determines how much military-mission capability a country can get from its power; more specifically, for a country with a given amount of power, including the offense-defense balance in our analysis improves our ability to evaluate the country's prospects for defending itself. The offense-defense balance can be defined in terms of the investment in forces that support offensive missions that an opponent must make to offset a defender's investment in forces that support defensive missions. Defense enjoys a larger advantage when the required investment in offense is larger. The offense-defense balance is the ratio of the cost of the offensive forces to the cost of the defensive forces.[28]

---

26. We need to be clear on whether power is a "relational concept" defined in terms of the ability to influence another's actions, or a "property concept," something that can be defined and measured without reference to other countries. See David A. Baldwin, *Economic Statecraft* (Princeton, N.J.: Princeton University Press, 1985), esp. pp. 18–24. I am using "power" as a relational concept, which is consistent with Waltz, who defines power in terms of the *distribution* of capabilities (by which he means resources) in *Theory of International Politics*, pp. 98, 192. However, "power" is often used to refer to a state's resources, in which case assessments of influence need to be cast in terms of relative power.

27. Waltz, *Theory of International Politics*, pp. 131, 98, 192, and 126; Grieco, *Cooperation Among Nations*, pp. 10, 39–40. What I am referring to as resources, Waltz refers to as capabilities; see note 22 for why I avoid using "capabilities."

28. Robert Jervis, "Cooperation Under the Security Dilemma," *World Politics*, Vol. 30, No. 2 (January 1978), p. 188; on the variety of definitions of the offense-defense balance and potential problems that this creates see Jack S. Levy, "The Offense/Defense Balance of Military Technology: A Theoretical and Historical Analysis," *International Studies Quarterly*, Vol. 28, No. 2 (Spring 1990), pp. 222–230.

Therefore, the defender's power (which is a function of the ratio of its aggregate resources to the adversary's aggregate resources) multiplied by the offense-defense balance tells us much more about the defender's prospects for maintaining effective defensive capabilities than does considering power alone. Put slightly differently, the offense-defense balance provides information about the ratio of resources required by a country to maintain the military capabilities that are necessary for deterrence and defense. As the advantage of defense grows, the ratio of resources required by the defender decreases.

Including offense-defense distinguishability in our analysis enables us to consider whether states can choose to convert their power into different types of military capability, specifically, offensive or defensive-mission capability. When offense and defense are completely distinguishable, the forces that support offensive missions do not support defensive missions, and vice versa; when offense and defense are not at all distinguishable, the forces that support offensive missions can be used as effectively in defensive missions. Therefore, the extent to which military power can be disaggregated, making offense and defense distinguishable, is important for answering a key question—whether defenders can avoid having offensive-mission capabilities while maintaining defensive ones.

These offense-defense variables depend on a variety of factors, significantly including the nature of military technology and geography.[29] Integrating them into a structural-realist analysis enables us to shift from a *balance-of-power* theory to a *military-capabilities* theory, specifically a theory cast in terms of countries' abilities to perform military missions.[30] This transformation constitutes an important advance because security is much more closely correlated with mission capabilities than with power.

Some implications of variation in these two key dimensions of the security dilemma have been explored previously.[31] Moreover, some analysts have sug-

---

29. Other factors that may influence the overall offense-defense balance include the cumulativity of resources and strategic beliefs, in particular, states' beliefs about others' propensity to balance versus bandwagon. See, for example, Ted Hopf, "Polarity, the Offense-Defense Balance and War," *American Political Science Review,* Vol. 85, No. 2 (June 1991), pp. 475–494; and Jack Snyder, *Myths of Empire: Domestic Politics and International Ambition* (Ithaca, N.Y.: Cornell University Press, 1991).

30. I say "capabilities" here instead of "balance of capabilities" because states should care most about their capabilities for performing necessary missions, not about relative capabilities or a balance in capabilities. For example, a state that has high confidence in its ability to defend may not care about whether its potential adversary has even greater confidence in its ability to defend; security does not depend on a balance of capabilities. The key qualification arises when an "imbalance" in capabilities would leave one state more vulnerable to an arms race.

31. See John H. Herz, "Idealist Internationalism and the Security Dilemma," *World Politics,* Vol. 2, No. 2 (January 1950), pp. 157–180; George Quester, *Offense and Defense in the International System* (New York: John Wiley & Sons, 1977); Jervis, "Cooperation Under the Security Dilemma," pp. 167–

gested the need to combine security-dilemma considerations with overall power to generate predictions about state behavior. They have not, however, explored all of the implications for the predictions of structural realism, especially regarding security cooperation between adversaries.[32] Two basic points should be emphasized.

First, the basic argument of structural realism is not altered by using the dimensions of the security dilemma to shift from a focus on power to a focus on military capabilities. Indeed, to capture the central logic of the structural-realist argument requires that we assess how much and what types of military capability a state can produce with its power, since security-seekers should evaluate the international environment and their policy options in terms of military capabilities. Bringing in offense-defense variables is not optional, but necessary. Specifying the theory primarily in terms of power has distorted the insights that should flow deductively from structural realism's assumptions. Contingent realism eliminates this distortion.

Second, explicitly including the dimensions of the security dilemma as variables increases the ability of a structural theory to explain variations in states' choices between competitive and cooperative options for acquiring necessary military capabilities.[33] In contrast, Waltz's formulation focuses on a single variable—the degree of polarity—and explores its implications for the probability of war.[34] However, the preceding arguments suggest that states' choices

---

214; Stephen W. Van Evera, "Causes of War" (Ph.D. dissertation, University of California, Berkeley, 1984), esp. chap. 3; and Glaser, "Political Consequences of Military Strategy." Important criticisms of offense-defense arguments include Levy, "The Offense/Defense Balance of Military Technology: A Theoretical and Historical Analysis," pp. 137–168; and Jonathan Shimshoni, "Technology, Military Advantage and World War I," *International Security*, Vol. 15, No. 3 (Winter 1990/91), pp. 187–215.

32. However, Snyder makes an argument similar to the one I am presenting here in *Myths of Empire*, pp. 11–12 and 21–26, although he focuses on the question of expansion and suggests that defense usually has the overall advantage, largely because of states' propensity to balance. See also Sean Lynn-Jones, "The Implications of Security Dilemma Theory as a Theory of International Politics" (unpublished memo, September 1993). Others who have combined offense-defense considerations with structural-realist logic include Barry R. Posen, *The Sources of Military Doctrine* (Ithaca, N.Y.: Cornell University Press, 1984); Thomas J. Christensen and Jack Snyder, "Chain Gangs and Passed Bucks: Predicting Alliance Patterns in Multipolarity," *International Organization*, Vol. 44, No. 1 (Spring 1990), pp. 137–168; and Stephen M. Walt, *The Origins of Alliances* (Ithaca, N.Y.: Cornell University Press, 1987).

33. Other variables also matter in assessing capabilities: for example, the level of uncertainty about key variables, including the forces the adversary has deployed and the rate at which it could build additional forces, and the offense-defense balance. In addition, if states suffer evaluative biases, then this type of theory will still be inadequate for explaining behavior. Thus, for example, Christensen and Snyder, "Chain Gangs and Passed Bucks," include the quality of states' perceptions as an additional variable.

34. Waltz, *Theory of International Politics*, esp. chaps. 5 and 8.

between arms racing and arms control could vary substantially even when the degree of polarity does not vary, for example, within a bipolar system.

To appreciate the central role of variations in the severity of the security dilemma in structural-realist theory, consider the implications of anarchy if there were no security dilemma. States that were seeking only security could deploy adequate military capabilities without threatening other states. Moreover, uncertainty about motives would be reduced, if not eliminated, since security-seekers would not need offensive capabilities. Insecurity could be virtually eliminated.[35] Competition would arise only if one or more major powers were motivated by greed, rather than security.

IMPLICATIONS OF VARIATION IN THE DIMENSIONS OF THE SECURITY DILEMMA. Under what conditions should security-seeking states find cooperative policies to be desirable and feasible?[36] The types of policies that states can choose from depend on whether the forces required to support offensive strategies are distinguishable from those required to support defensive strategies. If they are distinguishable, then states can choose to build offense, defense, or both; they can also engage in arms control to limit offensive forces, defensive forces, or both. Given these choices, three approaches for gaining security are especially interesting: cooperation via arms control; unilateral defense, that is, deploying

---

35. Jervis makes this point in "Cooperation Under the Security Dilemma," p. 187, and provides qualifications. Waltz notes that, as a result of their situation, states face a security dilemma; he thereby gives it standing as part of a systemic explanation. See, for example, Waltz, *Theory of International Politics*, pp. 186–187; and Waltz, "The Origins of War in Neorealist Theory," pp. 41–42. However, he says little about the implications of variations in its severity. Waltz also argues that changes in military technology, including nuclear weapons, are a unit-level change. Waltz, "Reflections on *Theory of International Politics*," in Keohane, *Neorealism and Its Critics*, p. 327; and Waltz, "The Origins of War in Neorealist Theory," pp. 50–51. This seems problematic, however, since these changes influence the security dilemma, which is a systemic variable. This problem is noted by Joseph S. Nye, Jr., "Neorealism and Neoliberalism," *World Politics*, Vol. 40, No. 2 (January 1988), p. 243; and Daniel Deudney, "Dividing Realism: Structural Realism versus Security Materialism on Nuclear Security and Proliferation," *Security Studies*, Vol. 2, No. 3/4 (Spring/Summer 1993), pp. 13–14.

36. The following discussion assumes that states motivated primarily by security would prefer situations in which all countries lack effective offensive capabilities to situations in which all countries have effective offensive capabilities. However, pure security seekers might see some benefits in offensive capabilities under a variety of circumstances. For example, offense might contribute to deterrence by providing the capability to credibly threaten a punishing counteroffensive, might enhance the country's ability to defend its territory by providing the capability to regain lost territory, and might enable a declining state to insure its security by launching a preventive war. These benefits would have to be weighed against the dangers of increasing the adversary's insecurity. In addition, given the choice of both states having or both lacking offense, each state needs to consider the dangers posed by an increase in the adversary's offensive capability. On factors that influence this choice see Stephen Van Evera, "Offense, Defense, and Strategy"; Posen, *The Sources of Military Doctrine*, pp. 67–71; and Glaser, "Political Consequences of Military Strategy."

defensive forces independent of the strategy one's adversary chooses; and arms racing.[37] On the other hand, if offense and defense are indistinguishable, the basic choice facing states is whether to build larger forces, and risk generating an arms race, or to pursue arms control that reduces or caps the size of their forces.[38]

Arms control can be especially useful when the forces that support offensive missions can be distinguished from forces that support defensive missions.[39] If they can be distinguished, then agreements can restrict offensive capabilities by limiting specific types of forces; both countries will have better defensive capabilities and appear less threatening than if they had both deployed offensive forces.

Whether arms control is the preferred policy will vary with the offense-defense balance. When defense has a large advantage, arms control will be largely unnecessary. Countries can instead pursue unilateral defense, choosing to deploy defensive forces independent of whether their adversaries do. Even if one country decides to pursue offense, the competition should be mild due to the advantage of the defense. Two countries motivated primarily by security are both likely to choose unilateral defense, resulting in even less intense military competition.

In contrast, if offense has an advantage over defense, arms control has far more to contribute. Limiting offensive weapons while allowing defensive ones would establish a military status quo in which both countries are better able to defend themselves and in which first-strike incentives are smaller than if the countries invested primarily in offensive forces.[40] Arms control would likely be necessary to avoid this emphasis on offensive forces and on the arms race that could ensue, since both countries would find it difficult, technically or economically, to counter the adversary's offense with defense. Beyond improving the military status quo, arms control could help avoid some of the

---

37. Unilateral defense has much in common with cooperative policies in that it does not threaten the adversary's security, and usually will not generate threatening reactions from an adversary motivated primarily by security. However, pursuit of unilateral defense is not cooperation because the defender can productively pursue unilateral defense without coordinating with the adversary. Unilateral defensive policies therefore reflect a situation of harmony, not cooperation; see Keohane, *After Hegemony*, pp. 51–55.
38. To simplify the discussion, I do not address qualitative arms control that limits technological innovation.
39. Robert Jervis, "Security Regimes," *International Organization*, Vol. 36, No. 2 (Spring 1982), p. 362, comments on some of the following points.
40. On the dangers of offense see Stephen Van Evera, "The Cult of the Offensive and the Origins of the First World War," *International Security*, Vol. 9, No. 1 (Summer 1984), pp. 58–107.

"dynamic" risks that an arms race itself could generate. When defense does not have the advantage, falling temporarily behind in a race, which creates a "window" of disadvantage, becomes more dangerous.[41]

This case for arms control is not entirely clear-cut, however, because countries face an increasingly severe tradeoff as the advantage of offense increases. This is because cheating poses a greater danger: as the advantage of offense grows, a given amount of cheating would provide a larger advantage and, therefore, allowing the adversary to gain a headstart in a renewed arms race is more dangerous. This makes it more difficult to monitor an agreement satisfactorily, which makes it harder for arms control to increase the states' security.

Therefore, in addition to the clear benefits that arms control could provide with regard to the military status quo, states must compare the dynamic risks of arms control and arms racing. When offense and defense are distinguishable, countries can reduce the dangers of cheating, and therefore the requirements for monitoring, by allowing large defensive forces while banning offensive ones, creating a defensive barrier to cheating. However, there is no general resolution of the tradeoff between these dynamic considerations; it will depend on the specifics of monitoring capabilities and the rates at which countries can break out of agreements, as well as the effectiveness of a defensive barrier.[42] Nevertheless, because arms control can definitely improve the military status quo, states should be inclined to prefer arms control.

When the forces required for offensive and defensive missions are not distinguishable, arms control is less clearly useful. Agreements that limit the size of forces may leave offensive and defensive capabilities essentially unchanged, in which case they would have little effect on a country's ability to deter.[43] In contrast to the case in which offense and defense are distinguishable, arms control cannot promise to improve the military status quo. However, this observation applies equally to arms racing: competition that increases the size of the countries' forces may not increase their deterrent capabilities. Thus, when

---

41. On windows see Van Evera, "Causes of War," esp. chap. 2; and Charles L. Glaser, *Analyzing Strategic Nuclear Policy* (Princeton, N.J.: Princeton University Press, 1990), pp. 150–155.
42. A defensive barrier increases the time required to gain an offensive advantage, but does not necessarily reduce the benefits of cheating. However, if there are uncertainties about relative rearmament rates, then defensive barriers would increase uncertainty about whether breaking out of an agreement will provide military advantages, which could contribute to deterrence. See Thomas C. Schelling, *Arms and Influence* (New Haven, Conn.: Yale University Press, 1966), pp. 248–259; and Glaser, *Analyzing Strategic Nuclear Policy*, pp. 178–179.
43. This depends on whether the the offense-defense balance varies with the size of deployed forces. To see that it can, consider the deterrence requirements of nuclear forces, or force-to-space requirements of conventional forces designed to defeat breakthrough battles.

offense and defense are indistinguishable, there is no general conclusion about whether states should prefer arms control or arms racing. To analyze specific cases, states would have to perform net assessments of the variation in mission capability as a function of force size.[44]

Here again, the offense-defense balance matters. When defense has a large advantage, countries will find that arms control is largely unnecessary for avoiding competition. Because large unmatched increases in forces are required to gain significant military advantages, military competition should be mild and countries should enjoy high levels of security.[45] When offense has the advantage, arms control will be necessary for avoiding arms races, but will be harder to achieve and riskier than in the case in which offense and defense are distinguishable. Reaching agreement on the forces that will be permitted will be harder because, as noted above, limits are less likely to improve military capabilities and small differences in force size may be more important. Agreements will be riskier than in the case in which offense and defense are distinguishable because large defensive forces cannot be deployed as a hedge against cheating.

In sum, adding offense-defense variables does not shift the basic emphasis of structural theories, but instead eliminates distortions that result when the theory is cast primarily in terms of power. Considering not just power, but also how much and what types of military capability a state can produce with its power, is essential for understanding the pressures and opportunities that countries face when seeking security in an anarchic system. Given this formulation, a country's concern about its military capabilities should lead it to reject competitive policies under a range of conditions. In fact, contrary to the standard structural-realist analysis, arms racing is only clearly preferred to less competitive policies under rather narrow conditions: when offense has the advantage and is indistinguishable from defense, and when the risks of being cheated exceed the risks of arms racing.

INCORPORATING MOTIVES AND INTENTIONS: MILITARY POLICY AND SIGNALING

A state seeking security should be concerned about whether its adversary understands that its motivations are benign. Uncertainty about the state's motives, or even worse, the incorrect belief that the state is motivated by greed

---

44. However, even when larger forces are desirable, it is unclear that states should prefer truly competitive policies. One alternative is simply to coordinate increases in force size up to but not above a level at which both countries believe their deterrent capabilities would be enhanced.
45. See Malcolm W. Hoag, "On Stability in Deterrent Races," *World Politics*, Vol. 13, No. 4 (July 1961), pp. 505–527.

rather than security concerns, will increase the adversary's insecurity, which in turn will reduce the state's own security. Thus, structural realism suggests that states should be very interested in demonstrating that their motives are benign. The problem, according to the standard formulation, is that states acting within the constraints imposed by the international structure cannot communicate information about motives;[46] this type of information is seen as available only at the unit level.

Here again, however, the conventional wisdom is flawed. The rational actors posited by structural realism can under certain conditions communicate information about their motives by manipulating their military policies.[47]

Because greedy states have an incentive to misrepresent their motives, a pure security seeker can communicate information about its motives only by adopting a policy that is less costly for it than it would be for a greedy state.[48] A greedy state would like to mislead its adversaries into believing that it is interested only in security, since its adversaries would then be more likely to pursue policies that leave them vulnerable, enabling the greedy state to meet its expansionist objectives. However, when the policies that indicate that a state is not greedy are more costly for greedy states than for pure security seekers, greedy states are less likely to adopt them. Consequently, by adopting such a policy a state can communicate information about which type of state it is, that is, about its motives.

States can try to communicate their benign intentions via three types of military policies: arms control, unilateral defense, and unilateral restraint.[49] Agreeing to limit offensive capabilities, when offense has the advantage, can shift the adversary's assessment of the state's motives. Although a greedy state might accept this arms control agreement, because limits on its adversary's offense would increase its security, the agreement is costly for a greedy state because it reduces its prospects for expansion. Thus, although both states that are pure security-seekers and states that are motived by greed as well as

46. This view plays a central role in Wendt, "Anarchy is What States Make of It," pp. 391 and 392.
47. For formal treatments that focus on this possibility see George W. Downs and David M. Rocke, *Tacit Bargaining, Arms Races, and Arms Control* (Ann Arbor: University of Michigan Press, 1990), chap. 4; and Andrew Kydd, "The Security Dilemma, Game Theory, and WWI," paper presented at the 1993 annual meeting of the American Political Science Association. See also Robert Jervis, *The Logic of Images in International Relations* (Princeton, N.J.: Princeton University Press, 1970); and Jervis, "Cooperation Under the Security Dilemma."
48. On "costly signals," see James Dana Fearon, "Threats to Use Force: Costly Signals and Bargaining in International Crises" (Ph.D. dissertation, University of California, Berkeley, 1992).
49. See also Glaser, "Political Consequences of Military Strategy."

security might accept such an agreement, the costs of agreement are higher for the greedy state; moreover, the greedier the state was, the less likely it would be to accept the agreement. Consequently, although accepting the arms agreement should not entirely convince the adversary that it does not face a greedy state, it does nevertheless provide valuable information. By comparison, agreeing to limit offense when defense has the advantage provides less information, since an arms race is less likely to make expansion possible. Consequently, a greedy state would find such an agreement less costly, narrowing the cost-differential between greedy and non-greedy states, and thus limiting the information conveyed by such a policy.

Agreeing to limit the size of forces when offense and defense are indistinguishable can also communicate information about motives. Assuming that both countries have some chance of gaining an offensive military advantage in the race, the costs of accepting limits on force size will be greater for greedier states. The clearest signal will come from a state that has good prospects for winning the race, but nevertheless agrees to some form of parity.

Under certain conditions, a country may be able to communicate more effectively with unilateral defensive policies than with arms control. When offense has the advantage, a country that decides to meet its military requirements with defensive means will have to make larger investments in military forces than if it had chosen the offensive route. Compared to the arms control approach, this state will have indicated not only its willingness to forgo offensive capabilities, but also a willingness to invest greater resources to send this message.[50]

Finally, a country can try to communicate benign motives by employing unilateral restraint—that is, by reducing its military capability below the level it believes would otherwise be necessary for deterrence and defense.[51] This should send a clear message for two reasons: the state has reduced its offensive capability, which a greedy state would be less likely to do; and the state has incurred some risk, due to the shortfall in military capabilities, which the adversary could interpret as a further indication of the value the state places on improving relations. Of course, this security risk will make states reluctant to adopt an ambitious policy of unilateral restraint. Consequently, states are

---

50. Of course, if its adversary also shifts to a defensive policy, the cost of sustaining the defensive policy will be similar to the costs under an arms control agreement.
51. The uses of unilateral restraint are emphasized by Charles E. Osgood, *An Alternative to War or Surrender* (Urbana: University of Illinois, 1962). In *Tacit Bargaining, Arms Races and Arms Control*, pp. 41–51, Downs and Rocke assess Osgood's arguments.

likely to turn to unilateral restraint only when other options are precluded, e.g., when unilateral defense is impossible because offense and defense are indistinguishable, or when it is unaffordable, because offense has a large advantage over defense, or when they conclude that an especially dramatic gesture is necessary.

In short, the essentially rational actors posited by structural realism will under certain conditions be able to use cooperative or other unthreatening military policies to improve understanding of their motives. For states motivated primarily by security, such opportunities will be especially attractive when cooperative policies can also enhance their military capabilities. By comparison, when communication of benign motives requires a state to reduce necessary military capabilities, states face a much more difficult choice, especially since they must worry not only about deterring, but also about defending if deterrence fails.

The standard structural-realist argument overlooks the possibility of clarifying motives. Although uncertainty about the adversary's motives can sometimes call for competitive policies, the adversary's uncertainty about the state's motives can call for the opposite. A balanced assessment of alternative approaches must weigh these potentially countervailing pressures, as well as the possibility of acquiring improved military mission capabilities via cooperative means.

Flaws in the Standard Structural-realist Counter-arguments

Three major arguments are commonly used in support of the standard structural-realist argument, and could be used to counter the overall thrust of contingent realism. However, each argument suffers serious flaws or limitations; none weakens contingent realism.

"STATES TRY TO MAXIMIZE RELATIVE POWER, WHICH CREATES A ZERO-SUM
SITUATION THAT MAKES COOPERATION DIFFICULT"
Although the claim that states try to maximize relative power has been rejected by some prominent structural realists, most notably Waltz,[52] it has been presented forcefully by others. For example, John Mearsheimer argues that "states seek to survive under anarchy by maximizing their power relative to other

---

52. Waltz, "Theory of International Politics," p. 118, 126, and 127; and Waltz, "Reflections on *Theory of International Politics*," in Keohane, *Neorealism and its Critics*, p. 334. See also Robert Gilpin, *War and Change in International Politics* (Cambridge: Cambridge University Press, 1981), esp. pp. 86–88.

states, in order to maintain the means for self-defense."[53] If states try to maximize relative power, international relations will be highly competitive, since states will then "seek opportunities to weaken potential adversaries and improve their relative position."[54] Adversaries attempting to maximize their relative power face a zero-sum situation—increases in one state's relative power necessarily result in decreases in the other's relative power. Cooperative policies will be rare because they preempt the possibility of achieving advantages in relative power.

The key to assessing this claim is to recognize that, for structural realists, conclusions about maximizing power are conclusions about means, not ends. Structural realism assumes that, in an anarchic system, security is the end to which states will give priority. States may pursue other goals, but structural realism does not assume that they do. Consequently, showing that structural realism predicts that states try to maximize relative power requires demonstrating that doing so is the best way for states to gain security.

Three arguments suggest that pursuing increases in relative power is not always the best way to increase security. First, the claim in favor of maximizing relative power overlooks the security dilemma: a state that increased its relative power might nevertheless decrease its security because its increased relative power could make its adversary less secure, which could in turn increase the value its adversary places on expansion. War could become more likely, since any deterrent value of increased relative power might be outweighed by the increased benefits that a security-seeking adversary would see in expansion. Consequently, a country could reasonably conclude that accepting rough parity in military capabilities would provide greater security than maximizing its relative power. Notwithstanding the claim that states try to maximize power, structural realism leaves this question wide open.[55]

---

53. Mearsheimer, "Back to the Future," p. 12. See also Fareed Zakaria, "Realism and Domestic Politics: A Review Essay," *International Security*, Vol. 17, No. 1 (Summer 1992), pp. 193–194. In this argument, "power" is being used as a property concept, not a relational concept; see footnote 26. Although I prefer the relational use, in this section I use relative power to maintain consistency with the quotations.

54. Mearsheimer, "Back to the Future," p. 12.

55. Factors important in resolving this tradeoff include: 1) the extent of increases in relative power: military advantages that are so overwhelming that they clearly deny the adversary any chance of victory probably reduce the probability of war, whereas smaller military advantages that leave some doubt about the adversary's prospects for victory might increase the probability of war; 2) the offense-defense balance, as discussed above; 3) the adversary's motives: military advantages will be less valuable against states motivated primarily by insecurity and more valuable against states motivated primarily by greed; and 4) the quality of the adversary's evaluative capabilities, which influences the extent of insecurity that launching an arms buildup or arms race would generate.

Second, trying to maximize power could increase the probability of losing an arms race. Even a country that would prefer to win an arms race—that is, that would prefer superiority to parity—might choose cooperation over arms racing to avoid the risk of losing the race.

Third, by failing to distinguish between offensive and defensive potential, the claim that states try to maximize relative power disregards the fact that maximizing relative power may not maximize the military capabilities that a country needs for defense and deterrence. Consider the case in which, to maximize its power, a country must compete in the deployment of offensive capabilities, and its alternative is to accept parity in defensive capabilities. The offensive race could decrease the winner's security by reducing its ability to defend against attack and by increasing crisis instability. Thus, even setting aside dangers that could result from decreasing the adversary's security and losing a race, maximizing power could decrease one's own security.

In short, states motivated primarily by security should not as a general rule try to maximize their relative power. Proponents of the relative-power–maximization argument sometimes try to defend their claim by adding the qualification that states maximize relative power when they can. This qualification is actually quite significant, suggesting that the claim is about what states want, not about how they behave. If so, their claim is potentially quite misleading, since constraints on state behavior can create a large gap between what a state would like to achieve and what it actually tries to achieve. Moreover, the qualification is inadequate because it does not deal with the first and third arguments presented in this section. Therefore, analyses that start from the claim that states try to maximize relative power exaggerate the extent to which structural realism predicts that international politics will be highly competitive.

"STATES' CONCERN OVER RELATIVE GAINS MAKES SECURITY COOPERATION ESPECIALLY DIFFICULT"

Structural realists believe that states must be concerned not only about whether cooperation will provide them with gains, but also with how these gains will be distributed.[56] If cooperation enables a state's adversary to gain more, the adversary may be able to convert this advantage into a capability for effectively coercing the state or, in extreme cases, defeating it in war. As a result, states

---

56. Waltz, *Theory of International Politics*, pp. 105, 175; Grieco, *Cooperation Among Nations*; Grieco, "Anarchy and the Limits of Cooperation: A Realist Critique of the Newest Liberal Institutionalism," *International Organization*, Vol. 42, No. 3 (Summer 1988), pp. 485–507.

must be concerned about relative gains, that is, about which state gains more from cooperation. States may conclude that the danger of relative losses exceeds the benefit of absolute gains, making cooperation undesirable. Relative-gains problems are generally believed to be more severe in the security realm than in the economic realm, thereby making security cooperation especially difficult.[57]

The following arguments, however, show that under a wide range of conditions, states interested in security cooperation should not be constrained by a relative-gains problem.[58]

THE RELATIVE-GAINS PROBLEM IS NOT ABOUT RELATIVE MILITARY ASSETS. The key to understanding relative gains in the security realm is to frame the issue correctly. We first must distinguish the instruments of policy from the ends of policy, that is, the value the policy produces. In the security realm, military assets are instruments of policy, while security is the end. In the economic realm, tariffs and other barriers to trade are instruments of policy, while wealth is the end.[59] A policy provides a state with "gains" when it increases what the state values, not when it increases the instruments the state has available or employs.

Consider the tradeoff posed by the relative-gains problem. In describing states' concern for relative gains, Waltz argues that states "are compelled to ask not 'Will both of us gain?' but 'Who will gain more?'"[60] The first question focuses on absolute gains, the second on relative gains. The implication is that if only absolute gains mattered, then states would need to answer only the first question to determine whether cooperation was desirable. Desirability would

---

57. For example, Grieco, *Cooperation Among Nations,* p. 46, argues that, "a state's sensitivity to gaps in gains is also likely to be greater if a cooperative venture involves security matters than economic well-being"; see also ibid, p. 14. This view of the conventional wisdom is also described by Robert Powell, "Absolute and Relative Gains in International Relations Theory," *American Political Science Review,* Vol. 85, No. 4 (December 1991), p. 1303.

58. Moreover, they also suggest that concern about relative gains will be less constraining in security cooperation, specifically in arms control, than in economic cooperation.

59. For the sake of contrast, I am using "security realm" to refer to policies that influence the size and type of forces, and "economic realm" to refer to policies that influence the type and severity of trade barriers. I do not mean to imply that policies in the economic realm lack security implications and vice versa. Thus, these statements include important simplifications: they exaggerate the extent to which manipulation of instruments in one realm produces only one type of value. For example, policies in the economic realm can generate changes in relative wealth, which can in turn have security implications; moreover, cooperation in the security realm can have implications for future relative wealth. I address the implications below.

60. Waltz, p. 105. A state really only needs to ask "will I gain?" to determine whether cooperation is desirable; however, it may need to ask "will both of us gain?" to assess whether cooperation is feasible.

be determined by "gains," which must therefore refer to the value produced by cooperation.[61]

This formulation helps us correct a common mistake: analysts argue that states care a great deal about relative changes in military assets, and then conclude that countries are highly sensitive to relative gains.[62] However, although states do care about relative changes in military assets, this concern is not due to a relative-gains problem. A state evaluating the impact of cooperation on relative force size is comparing changes in instruments, not changes in the achievement of ends. This does not reflect a relative-gains problem, since states are concerned with relative gains when they compare relative changes in their achievement of things they value, not when they compare the instruments employed. The analogous but perhaps more obvious mistake in the economic realm would be to evaluate relative gains by comparing the extent to which trade barriers were loosened instead of comparing the economic benefits that this loosening would generate. This error is rarely made in economic analysis.

Consequently, although I agree with proponents of the flawed formulation that states care about relative military assets, I explain this concern in a different, more straightforward way. Correctly formulated, in the security realm the "absolute gains" from cooperation refer to an increase in security.[63] When cooperation would result in a relative loss in military assets, and when this loss reduces mission capability and security, the state will refuse to cooperate.[64]

---

61. We can reach the same conclusion by considering the evolution of the debate over absolute and relative gains. Grieco, "Anarchy and the Limits of Cooperation" argued that neoliberals focused on absolute gains in the repeated prisoner's dilemmas, while overlooking relative gains in establishing the preference orderings in their two-by-two games. Because preferences in these games are defined across outcomes produced by cooperation and defection, "absolute gains" must refer to the value produced by policies, not to increases in the means employed.

62. This formulation also helps us to clarify a closely related point of confusion: the first two arguments of this section—(1) that states maximize relative power and (2) that states are constrained by concern about relative gains—are sometimes thought to be the same argument. However, the first argument focuses on states' choices regarding policies that manipulate means—the instruments that can produce security—whereas the second argument focuses on states' concern about relative achievement of value.

63. Absolute gain could also refer to economic savings, if the arms control agreement enables the country to reduce investment in military forces. However, although saving money is one of the three classic objectives of arms control, security is usually the priority goal of cooperation. On the classic objectives see Schelling and Halperin, *Strategy and Arms Control*, p. 2. For a dissenting view on the role of saving money see Bernard Brodie, "On the Objectives of Arms Control," *International Security*, Vol. 1, No. 1 (Summer 1976), pp. 17–36.

64. Three points are worth noting briefly: (1) as discussed below, losses in relative military assets might not reduce the state's security if they increase the adversary's security; (2) a state's sensitivity to relative losses in military assets will depend on the offense-defense balance; (3) a state's military capability could increase, even if it suffers a relative loss in military assets, if the offense-defense balance varies with force size.

However, this refusal would reflect the failure of cooperation to increase secu-rity, that is, to provide absolute gains, not the state's concern over relative gains.[65]

In short, although the relative-gains problem is often apparently viewed in terms of concern over relative gains in military assets, this is the wrong way to formulate the issue. If there is a relative-gains problem in the security realm, it must lie elsewhere. The two possibilities, discussed below, are relative gains in security and relative gains in wealth resulting from security cooperation. However, exploration of these areas casts serious doubt on whether relative-gains concerns are severe in the security realm and suggests further that states will usually not be constrained by them.

RELATIVE SECURITY GAINS AND COMPARISONS OF SECURITY. Since the goal of cooperation is to increase security, relative-gains logic suggests that we explore whether concern over the distribution of security gains should inhibit coopera-tion. A country is concerned about relative gains in security if cooperation would increase its adversary's security more than its own, and if this relative loss in security would in turn reduce its own security. If we narrowly equate security with military capability, then this situation could arise if an arms control agreement increased both countries' denial capabilities, but not equally.

However, following security-dilemma logic, all else being equal, increases in the adversary's security often increase one's own security because a more secure adversary has smaller incentives for pursuing an expansionist foreign policy, and therefore will pose a smaller threat. This argument does not depend on whether the increase in the adversary's security exceeds or trails the increase in the defender's security, because the change in the adversary's motives reflects its absolute security, not a relative measure of its security compared to the defender's.

Objections and qualifications to this argument focus on two types of cases. First, when facing an adversary that is motivated by greed, as well as security, increasing the adversary's security could increase its willingness to pursue its expansionist objectives. This danger could result from cooperation that at-tempted to increase both countries' security by reducing both countries' offen-sive capabilities. The defender's denial capability would be enhanced, but its ability to deter via punishment would likely be reduced, since mutual reduc-

---

65. One possible counter to this argument is that mission capability, and therefore, security are themselves relative, not absolute measures. This is incorrect. Although a country's ability to perform military missions depends on how its forces compare to the adversary's, we measure mission capability in absolute terms. For example, an estimate of the probability that a country can defeat an invasion is an absolute measure.

tions in offense would reduce the defender's counteroffensive capability. An adversary that was especially impressed by the risks posed by punishment capabilities might conclude that the deterrent value of the defender's military capabilities had been reduced.[66]

Although important, the issue raised by this case is not about relative gains, but rather about whether cooperation that reduces both countries' offensive capabilities would provide the defender with absolute gains in security. If this cooperation reduces the defender's ability to deter, then the defender would not achieve an absolute gain in security, thus making cooperation undesirable. The problem is not that the adversary gains more security, but rather that the defender does not gain.

The second type of case comes closer to presenting the defender with a relative-gains problem. In these cases, the countries have conflicts of interest that lie beyond their primary security interests, that is, beyond their concern for protecting their homelands and possibly their major allies. Relative gains in security could influence countries' abilities to prevail in these secondary conflicts, if the advantaged country is willing to risk major war to prevail. A country's credibility in this competition in risk-taking will depend on the costs of major war. Therefore, cooperation that provides a country with relative gains in security by reducing the costs of major war could advantage that country in these secondary disputes. Nevertheless, the country that suffers a relative loss in security could still favor cooperation, since its primary security interests would be better protected.

In short, contrary to the problem identified by the logic of the relative-gains problem, if cooperation increases a country's security, then increases in the adversary's security are usually desirable, whether or not they exceed increases in the defender's security. In the security realm, instead of a relative-gains problem, we often have a mutual-gains benefit.

RELATIVE ECONOMIC SAVINGS AND ECONOMIC GROWTH. The second line of argument shifts the focus of the relative-gains argument from comparisons of security gains to comparisons of economic growth that are made possible by

---

66. On the value of counteroffensive capabilities for deterrence, see Samuel P. Huntington, "Conventional Deterrence and Conventional Retaliation in Europe," *International Security*, Vol. 8, No. 3 (Winter 1983/84), pp. 32–56; and Barry R. Posen, "Crisis Stability and Conventional Arms Control," *Daedalus*, Vol. 120, No. 1 (Winter 1991), pp. 217–232. The overall effect on the defender's prospects for deterrence would then depend on weighing countervailing factors: even a greedy adversary would be easier to deter, because increasing its security would reduce its interest in expansion; the defender, however, would be left with a less effective mix of deterrent capabilities.

security cooperation. This argument traces the danger in security cooperation through relative increases in the adversary's wealth, which the adversary can eventually convert into superior military forces. More specifically, when security cooperation saves the adversary greater resources than it saves the defender, the adversary will be able to redirect greater resources into future security competition, which will enable it eventually to pose a greater security threat than if cooperation had never occurred.

Although this argument appears to hinge on differences in savings, in fact it hinges on the relationship between reduced defense spending and economic growth. Assume that both countries reserve their savings for a future arms race. If the agreement breaks down, the country that saved more cannot compete more effectively than if an agreement had never been reached, since it has only the resources it would have invested earlier. The agreement defers the arms race, but does not advantage the country that saves more. Consequently, savings can have security implications only if they generate economic growth. In this case, the country that saves more can achieve relative gains in GNP. If the agreement then breaks down, the countries' abilities to engage in an arms race would have changed.

The problem with this line of argument is that studies have not established a strong relationship between defense spending and economic growth.[67] The basic concern is that defense spending crowds out private investment, which would otherwise contribute more to economic growth. However, there is no agreement on whether even U.S. defense spending during the Cold War slowed the growth of the American economy.[68] Moreover, if the country that would save less from an arms agreement were nevertheless worried about the long-term growth implications, it could adopt a variety of economic policies that would reduce the risks.[69]

---

67. Aaron L. Friedberg, "The Political Economy of American Strategy," *World Politics*, Vol. 41, No. 3 (April 1989), pp. 395–405; Charles A. Kupchan, "Empire, Military Power, and Economic Decline," *International Security*, Vol. 13, No. 4 (Summer 1989), pp. 40–47; and Steve Chan, "The Impact of Defense Spending on Economic Performance: A Survey of Evidence and Problems," *Orbis*, Vol. 29, No. 2 (Summer 1985), pp. 403–434.

68. For opposing views see Kenneth A. Oye, "Beyond Postwar Order and New World Order," in Kenneth A. Oye, Robert J. Lieber, and Donald Rothchild, *Eagle in a New World* (New York: HarperCollins, 1992), pp. 7–11; David Gold, *The Impact of Defense Spending on Investment, Productivity and Economic Growth* (Washington, D.C.: Defense Budget Project, 1990) and Friedberg, "The Political Economy of American Strategy," pp. 398–405.

69. These could include policies that would encourage savings and investment. See, for example, Friedberg, "The Political Economy of American Strategy," p. 400.

The feasibility of such policies depends on the size of the differential in saved defense spending: the smaller the relative loss in savings, the easier it is to compensate by revising domestic economic policy. Consequently, it is significant that an arms agreement can rarely promise to save a significant percentage of GNP. An agreement that saved the United States one percent of GNP per year would have to be quite dramatic.[70] An agreement that resulted in a difference in savings of this magnitude would have to be at least as dramatic and highly asymmetric in its effect on savings, which is unlikely.

In sum, although it is analytically sound to focus on the possibility that security cooperation could generate relative gains in economic growth, it appears that the dangers posed by this possibility should rarely, if ever, be a major barrier to security cooperation. This should be especially true for states that give priority to security, since they should be more willing to adjust domestic economic policies if necessary to gain the immediate security benefits of cooperation.

FACTORS THAT WOULD INFLUENCE THE SECURITY IMPLICATIONS OF RELATIVE ECONOMIC GAINS. In cases in which security cooperation would generate differential economic growth, three additional considerations influence whether the risks would outweigh the defender's direct gains in security, thereby making security cooperation undesirable. The first consideration applies only to security cooperation, while the latter two apply to economic cooperation as well. First, the beneficial effects of the adversary's increased security make its increased relative economic strength less threatening, since it would be less inclined to use this economic potential for security-driven expansion. Thus, the defender should find relative economic losses produced by security cooperation somewhat less threatening than comparable relative losses produced by economic cooperation.

Second, the magnitude of relative gains influences the potential security threat. Small relative gains, compared to GNP, would rarely pose a major threat. If cooperation breaks down, the disadvantaged country would be able to offset any increased military threat made possible by growth in the adversary's GNP by increasing the percentage of GNP that it spends on defense. Thus, when the adversary's relative economic gains are small, the defender risks a loss of prosperity, but not of security. If the agreement (while it holds) provides large security gains, risking this loss would usually be warranted.

---

70. For example, during much of the Cold War the United States spent approximately one percent of its GNP on nuclear forces; an agreement to ban nuclear weapons might therefore have saved approximately this much per year.

Third, the offense-defense balance influences the security implications of relative economic gains.[71] Relative economic gains matter less as the advantage of defense grows, because acquiring effective offensive capabilities requires the adversary to make increasingly disproportionate investments in military forces. Thus, when defense has a large advantage over offense, the possibility of relative gains should do little to inhibit economic or security cooperation.[72] Consequently, countries that possess large nuclear arsenals and that rely heavily on nuclear deterrence for their security should not be inhibited from security or economic cooperation by security-related relative-gains constraints, since nuclear weapons create a very large advantage for the defense.[73]

These arguments suggest that under most conditions countries should focus on the absolute security gains offered by security cooperation, since these gains would rarely be jeopardized by relative economic gains. Exceptions are most likely when gains in relative economic growth would be significant in terms of overall national wealth and when the offense-defense balance favors offense.

"STATES ARE COMPETITIVE BECAUSE THE POSSIBILITY OF CHEATING MAKES
COOPERATION TOO RISKY; INSTITUTIONS CANNOT SOLVE THE PROBLEM"
The third broad argument, that states will not engage in extensive security cooperation focuses on the danger posed by the adversary's ability to cheat on arms control agreements (whether formal or tacit). The possibility of cheating is important only for cases in which cooperation, assuming it holds, would increase the country's security, and therefore is desirable. Thus, the implications of cheating matter only after the preceding standard structural-realist arguments have been rejected.

The standard structural-realist argument notes that since under anarchy there is no authority that can enforce agreements, states will cheat when doing so serves their interests. The possibility of cheating means that a country's true choice may not be between successful arms control and arms racing, but

---

71. A second structural factor that can influence the implications of relative gains is the number of major states in the system. See Duncan Snidal, "Relative Gains and the Pattern of International Cooperation," *American Political Science Review*, Vol. 85, No. 3 (September 1991), pp. 701–726.

72. Powell, "Absolute and Relative Gains in International Relations Theory," pp. 1303–1320, reaches a similar conclusion, but has cast it in terms of the cost of fighting, not the offense-defense balance. See also Helen Milner, "International Theories of Cooperation Among Nations: Strengths and Weaknesses," *World Politics*, Vol. 44, No. 3 (April 1992), pp. 483–484. Waltz, *Theory of International Politics*, p. 195, suggests this logic but does not spell it out.

73. For similar points, see Kenneth N. Waltz, "The Emerging Structure of International Politics," *International Security*, Vol. 18, No. 2 (Fall 1993), p. 74. Layne, "The Unipolar Illusion," pp. 44–45, appears to disagree.

instead between risking being left behind when the adversary cheats and racing from the start to insure that the adversary fails to gain a lead. The standard structural-realist argument emphasizes the dangers of being cheated and suggests that this will usually prevent significant cooperation, especially security cooperation, since states are especially reluctant to risk shortfalls in military capability.[74]

We have already seen that contingent realism rejects cheating as a dominating influence. Correcting the bias in the standard argument requires, among other things, emphasizing the risks of arms racing, as well as the risks of arms control, and specifically of cheating; this correction creates a balance that is missing in the standard argument. In addition, exploring the implications of incorporating the security dilemma into structural realism showed that the risks of cheating, and therefore its implications for cooperation, vary with offense-defense considerations. Thus, contingent realism recognizes that the possibility of cheating matters, but proceeds to focus on the conditions under which major powers are likely to find that, when all factors are considered, cooperation remains desirable. The following subsection draws on two bodies of literature that help to elaborate the overall thrust of this analysis.

ARMS CONTROL THEORY. The literature on modern arms control theory recognizes the danger posed by the adversary's cheating.[75] But, as Schelling and Halperin argue, the risks of cheating must be weighed against the benefits the agreement would provide, assuming it holds. They argue that the danger of cheating depends on: the probability of detecting violations of a given size; the strategic implications of a given degree of cheating, which depends upon the level and type of forces allowed by the agreement; and the ability to respond to violations by joining the renewed arms race.[76]

To reduce the risks of cooperation, a formal arms control agreement could include provisions for monitoring that insure the ability to react before the advantage of cheating becomes too large, that is, to ensure that the benefits of

---

74. This view of the role of cheating in making security cooperation more difficult than economic cooperation is supported by important articles in cooperation theory; for example, Robert Jervis, "Security Regimes," in Stephen Krasner, ed., *International Regimes* (Ithaca, N.Y.: Cornell University Press, 1983); and Charles Lipson, "International Cooperation in Economic and Security Affairs," *World Politics*, Vol. 37, No. 1 (October 1984), pp. 1–23, esp. 12–18. Both articles do, however, point to conditions that increase the probability of security cooperation.

75. See Schelling and Halperin, *Strategy and Arms Control*, esp. 67–74, 91–106; see also Abram Chayes, "An Inquiry Into the Working of Arms Control Agreements," *Harvard Law Review*, Vol. 85, No. 5 (March 1972), pp. 905–969, esp. 945–961; and James A. Schear, "Verification, Compliance, and Arms Control: The Dynamics of the Domestic Debate," in Lynn Eden and Steven E. Miller, eds., *Nuclear Arguments* (Ithaca, N.Y.: Cornell University Press, 1989).

76. Schelling and Halperin, *Strategy and Arms Control*, pp. 67–74.

taking the first step in the arms race are not too large. If, however, the countries' independent national monitoring capabilities already provide information that makes the benefits of cheating small, deals to accept the military status quo may not require formal agreement, but can instead be accomplished by unilateral statements that a state plans to build only if the adversary builds. Schelling and Halperin conclude that "it cannot be assumed that an agreement that leaves some possibility of cheating is necessarily unacceptable or that cheating would necessarily result in strategically important gains."[77]

Although this line of argument was well established by the early 1960s, the standard structural-realist argument neither incorporates it nor seriously disputes it. The burden to confront these conclusions lies with the structural-realists, since none of the essential elements of arms control theory run counter to structural realism's basic assumptions. Some critics will fall back on self-help as an argument, but, as we have seen, cooperation is an important type of self-help, and this includes cooperation in monitoring agreements. Moreover, as argued below, the types of institutions that might be required to make arms control desirable are not precluded by structural realism.

COOPERATION THEORY. Support for contingent realism also comes from the literature that uses game theory to explore cooperation under anarchy.[78] Cooperation theory provides insights that parallel those offered by arms control and offense-defense theories, and emphasizes the importance of each countries' beliefs about its adversary's preferences. A simple model of the choice between an arms control agreement and an arms race assumes that if an agreement is reached and cheating is then detected, the arms race begins and is not halted again by another agreement.[79] Given this assumption, the country comparing the value of the arms agreement and the risks of being cheated faces four possible outcomes: the agreement prevails (CC); the adversary cheats, leaving the country one step behind in the ensuing arms race (CD); an equal arms race (DD); or, the country cheats, gaining a one step lead in the arms race (DC).[80]

---

77. Schelling and Halperin, *Strategy and Arms Control*, p. 69.
78. See citations in fn. 5; also Schelling, "A Framework for the Evaluation of Arms-Control Proposals."
79. More complex assumptions would allow for reestablishing an agreement at any point during the ensuing race. Although renegotiation would be possible, the simplified assumption seems to do an adequate job of capturing the options that states would consider in joining and breaking out of a major arms control agreement. Relaxing this simplifying assumption opens up the possibility in iterated-game models of tit-for-tat type strategies, which play a central role in the literature on cooperation under anarchy, but not in this discussion.
80. "C" stands for cooperation, which in this example means abiding by the agreement; "D" stands for defection, which in this example means cheating on the agreement. CC refers to the outcome in which both countries cooperate; DD refers to the outcome in which both countries defect; and DC and CD refer to outcomes in which one country cooperates and the other defects.

A country is concerned with the implications of cheating only if it prefers the arms agreement to the equal arms race, CC > DD.[81] If in addition, the country prefers the arms agreement to an arms race in which it gets a one-step lead (CC > DC), and if its adversary has the same preference ordering, then the countries face a "stag hunt."[82]

Unlike the prisoner's dilemma, in a stag hunt it can be individually rational for two countries to cooperate.[83] However, cooperation is not assured if the countries are unsure of each other's preference orderings. For example, a country with stag-hunt preferences believing that it faces a country with prisoner's-dilemma preferences should defect. A country that is unsure about its adversary's preferences, and therefore unsure about whether the adversary will abide by the arms agreement, should consider the magnitude of the differences between its payoffs.[84] This is when the magnitude of the danger posed by cheating comes into play.

To determine when the risks of cooperation are "too large," the defender compares an arms race in which it starts one step behind (CD) to both an arms race started on equal footing (DD) and to the arms agreement (CC). The country's willingness to risk cooperation grows as: (1) the difference between falling behind by a step and running an equal arms race (CD-DD) decreases; and (2) the difference between the arms control agreement and the equal arms race (CC-DD) increases. As discussed in the arms control and security dilemma literatures, the difference between CD and DD depends on the forces allowed by the agreement, the offense-defense balance, and the quality of monitoring and reaction capabilities. For example, improving the country's ability to monitor an agreement reduces the difference between the adversary getting a lead and starting the race on equal footing, that is, it reduces CD-DD, thereby making cooperation more desirable.

To translate this argument into the kind of model that is commonly used in cooperation theory, we can envision the arms control–arms race choice as a

---

81. Standard structural-realist arguments argue that this condition is not fulfilled. For example, the argument that cooperation theory is flawed because it fails to take into account countries' concerns about relative gains amounts to saying that for one country DD > CC.

82. This also includes the reasonable assumption that DC > DD > CD. For a discussion of how a stag hunt compares to other games where cooperation is necessary for states to achieve mutual gains, see Kenneth A. Oye, "Explaining Cooperation Under Anarchy: Hypotheses and Strategies," in Oye, *Cooperation Under Anarchy,* pp. 6–9.

83. For a discussion of when competition will nevertheless occur in a stag hunt, see Downs, Rocke, and Siverson, "Arms Races and Arms Control," pp. 133–137.

84. The country must also worry about whether its adversary correctly understands its own preferences, since misunderstanding could lead a country that would otherwise cooperate to defect.

series of decisions made over time; each decision constitutes a single play of a game, which is then repeated.[85] The simplifying assumption used above—that once cheating is detected the arms race begins and is not halted again by another agreement—translates into a model in which each country's strategy is to always defect after its adversary's first defection. The prospects for cooperation depend on the countries' preferences in the game. Cooperation should occur if the countries believe they are playing stag hunt. However, cooperation can also be possible if the countries believe they are playing prisoner's dilemma, since, given their strategy for dealing with defection, the overall game that results with iteration can be a stag hunt.[86] Thus, a way to get the stag hunt discussed in the previous paragraphs is from an iterated prisoner's dilemma played under certain conditions.

In sum, the arguments presented in the arms control literature and later in the cooperation theory literature make it clear that whether the dangers of cheating more than offset the potential benefits of arms control depends on a variety of specific factors, including the terms of the agreement and the countries' abilities to monitor it and to respond to breakout. Thus, according to contingent realism, although the possibility of cheating could make cooperation undesirable under certain conditions, under other conditions arms control would remain preferable to arms racing.

INSTITUTIONS. Contingent realism does not establish an important role for institutions. This clarification is necessary because influential cooperation theorists have emphasized the importance of institutions and regimes in making

---

85. However, the assumption of this type of model, that the payoffs do not change over time, can be problematic for certain arms agreements and races. For example, in an agreement that establishes low levels of forces, a given amount of cheating in the first play of the game could have dramatically different implications than cheating of the same magnitude once the renewed arms race has continued through many plays. In addition, because a war could stop the repetition of the game, a model that includes the possibility of war after each play of the game might capture more of what we care about. The probability of war after each move would depend on the countries' military capabilities at that stage of the race, thereby reflecting the cumulative nature of the arms race. Powell, "Absolute and Relative Gains in International Relations Theory" develops this type of model for cooperation on trade issues. This type of model would be unnecessary, however, if states' preferences for each outcome incorporate their assessment of the probability of war as an element of their security.

86. On this possibility and complications see David M. Kreps, *A Course in Microeconomic Theory* (Princeton, N.J.: Princeton University Press, 1990), pp. 503–515. Whether it is a stag hunt or a prisoners' dilemma depends on the cost of being cheated in a single play and on the country's discount rate. The intuition is as follows: assuming a prisoner's dilemma for each iteration of the game, although a country can do better than mutual cooperation by cheating on the first move, it does less well than mutual cooperation on each following move. If the first move is not valued much more than future moves (that is, if the discount rate is sufficiently low), then eventually the costs suffered in all following moves will outweigh the gains of taking advantage in the first move. In effect, the prospect of restarting and prosecuting the race is sufficient to deter initial cheating.

cooperation feasible.[87] In contrast, contingent realism leaves open the question of whether institutions will play a role in making cooperation possible.[88] Although the prospects for cooperation vary with the quality of information about cheating, whether states need to cooperate to make this information available varies greatly with the specific case. For example, the invention of satellites made available information that was critical for strategic arms agreements, but required little cooperation. Moreover, even when cooperation is required, *ad hoc* agreements, which would not by themselves count as institutions,[89] could provide the necessary information.

Further, the type of institutions in question—those that provide information and reduce transaction costs—do not pose a problem for structural realism. Nothing about the roles performed by this type of institution conflicts with structural realism's basic assumptions. States remain the key actors, and anarchy remains unchanged; from this perspective the role played by these institutions is modest. If institutions of this type would make cooperation desirable, then structural realism predicts that states would create them for essentially the same reason that under certain conditions they should pursue advances in technology or increases in force size: these policies would enhance their military capabilities. The more ambitious purposes of institutions—for example, changing states' motives from self-interest to altruism, instilling confidence in benign shifts in motives, or eliminating anarchy by granting tremendous control to an international authority—appear to violate structural realism's core assumptions or its basic insights. But the debate between neorealists and neoinstitutionalists is not primarily over these more ambitious institutions. Therefore, if there is really anything to disagree over, this debate needs to be refocused.

---

87. Key works include Keohane, *After Hegemony;* Robert Axelrod and Robert O. Keohane, "Achieving Cooperation under Anarchy: Strategies and Institutions," in Oye, *Cooperation Under Anarchy;* and Krasner, ed., *International Regimes.* The relationship between the literatures on regimes and institutions and that on structural realism is complex, because although their assumptions are not logically inconsistent, their connotations are different. See Stephen D. Krasner, "Global Communications and National Power: Life on the Pareto Frontier," *World Politics,* Vol. 43, No. 3 (April 1991), pp. 360–362, who explains that, "the connotation of a research program suggests which questions are most important, what kind of evidence should be gathered, and, often tacitly, which issues should be ignored."

88. Keohane seems to waver on this issue, sometimes arguing only that institutions help make cooperation possible, while elsewhere suggesting the much stronger position that cooperation is possible only when institutions are present. For example, *After Hegemony,* p. 245: "Institutions are necessary, even on these restrictive premises, in order to achieve *state* purposes"; see also pp. 13, 78, and 245–247.

89. On the distinction between *ad hoc* agreements and institutions see Keohane, *After Hegemony,* pp. 51–54.

Contingent realism helps us to understand the confusion. The standard structural-realist argument predicted less cooperation than structural realism should have, leaving a gap that was filled by institutionalist arguments, which purported to diverge from structural realism.[90] In effect, contingent realism reclaims much of the territory that the standard argument gave to neoinstitutionalists.

However, more is at issue than deciding which arguments belong to which theories, because contingent realism identifies the possibility of extensive cooperation without focusing on institutions. This is not because structural realism finds that institutions do not matter. Rather, contingent realism sees institutions as the product of the same factors—states' interests and the constraints imposed by the system—that influence whether states should cooperate. Consequently, it sees institutions not as having much explanatory power of their own, but instead as part of what is being explained. Structural realism can, therefore, provide a partial foundation for a theory of international institutions.

Implications for Structural-realist Arguments

Contingent realism has a number of implications for the study and application of structural theories. First, because contingent realism predicts cooperation under certain conditions and competition under others, a structural-realist case against cooperation must demonstrate that the conditions necessary for cooperation have not occurred or will not occur in the future. This empirical assessment should be a key component of the argument explaining the prevalence of international competition. However, the standard structural-realist case about the competitive nature of international politics has not been built on this type of evidence.[91] These arguments are therefore incomplete; whether their conclusions are nevertheless correct remains an open question.

---

90. For example, Robert Keohane, "Institutionalist Theory and the Realist Challenge After the Cold War," in Baldwin, *Neorealism and Neoinstitutionalism*, p. 277, states that "institutionalism accepts the assumptions of realism about state motivation and lack of common enforcement power in world politics, but argues that *where common interests exist,* realism is too pessimistic about the prospects for cooperation and the role of institutions."

91. Nevertheless, the debate over the competitive policies that preceded World War I can be read from this perspective with Scott D. Sagan, "1914 Revisited: Allies, Offense, and Instability," *International Security*, Vol. 11, No. 2 (Fall 1986), pp. 151–176, arguing the greater explanatory power of structural explanations, and Van Evera, "The Cult of the Offensive and the Origins of the First World War," and Jack Snyder, *The Ideology of the Offensive: Military Decision Making and the Disasters of 1914* (Ithaca, N.Y.: Cornell University Press, 1984), emphasizing the shortcomings.

Second, development of an improved structural-realist baseline improves our ability to explore the value of alternative explanations for competitive and cooperative policies.[92] For example, since contingent realism predicts cooperation in certain cases, alternative and complementary explanations for cooperation—for example, institutions and regimes—could become less compelling. On the other hand, in cases where contingent realism predicts extensive cooperation but little occurs, other theories that explain competition become more important. A variety of important possibilities have received extensive attention—for example, that greedy motives, in addition to insecurity, make cooperation less likely if not impossible, and that a variety of individual and state-level misperceptions could lead countries to pursue undesirable competition.[93] Our ability to compare the explanatory strength of these theories depends on having established a structural-realist baseline that explains cooperation, as well as competition, and the conditions under which each is predicted.

Third, because contingent realism identifies countervailing pressures, it will, at least sometimes, not clearly prescribe either competitive or cooperative policies. In these cases, other levels of analysis will necessarily play a more important role in explaining state behavior. Structural pressures will bound the possibilities, while leaving states with substantial choice between more cooperative and more competitive approaches. Although the levels-of-analysis debate is often viewed as a competition between different levels of explanation, this argument suggests that they are often necessarily complementary. A related point focuses on implications for policy analysis: when structural arguments do not provide clear guidance, the choice between cooperative and competitive policies could hinge on the anticipated effects of various policy options on the opponent's domestic politics.[94] .

Fourth, contrary to what appears to be the conventional wisdom, structural realism, properly understood, has more trouble explaining the competitive military policies the superpowers pursued during the latter half of the Cold War than it does explaining the less competitive policies that have followed it.

---

92. Noting the importance of a "rationalist baseline," although focusing on different issues, is Fearon, "Threats to Use Force," chap. 2.
93. On individual misperceptions see Jervis, *Perception and Misperception in International Politics;* on national-level explanations see Snyder, *Myths of Empire,* and Van Evera, "Causes of War."
94. On the interaction between international policy and domestic politics see Peter Gourevitch, "The Second Image Reversed: The International Sources of Domestic Politics," *International Organization,* Vol. 32, No. 4 (Autumn 1978); Jack Snyder, "International Leverage on Soviet Domestic Change," *World Politics,* Vol. 42, No. 1 (October 1989), pp. 1–30; and Glaser, "Political Consequences of Military Strategy," pp. 519–525.

Because structural realism is commonly understood to predict highly competitive international relations, the end of the Cold War was interpreted as a severe defeat for structural-realist theories and as a boost for unit-level, country-specific theories. For the same reason, some analysts argued that even the limited cooperation that did occur during the Cold War could not easily be explained by structural realism.[95] Others argued that the limited contribution of arms control to slowing the superpowers' military buildups and reducing the probability of war provides support for the standard structural-realist claim that cooperation can play only a marginal role in major powers' security policies.[96]

However, contingent realism suggests that it is the competition that occurred during the latter half of the Cold War that poses the more serious challenge to structural realism properly understood. The security dilemma facing the United States and Soviet Union was greatly reduced, if not entirely eliminated, by the superpowers' acquisition of assured destruction capabilities, which appeared virtually certain to occur by the mid-1960s at the latest: the superpowers' deployment of large survivable nuclear arsenals established clear defense-dominance, and the technology of nuclear weapon delivery systems and various types of offensive counterforce provided the opportunity to distinguish offense and defense.[97] At the same time, bipolarity reduced the complexity of the arms control agreements that were required to slow competition. Under these conditions, instead of a marginal role, contingent realism predicts a major role for arms control or other non-competitive policies. The nuclear arms race should have ground to a halt and the full spectrum of the most threatening nuclear forces should have been limited either by arms control agreements or unilaterally. Thus, rather than providing support, the continuing military competition cuts against structural realism and must be explained by other theories.

In addition, the U.S. need to protect Western Europe should have been seriously questioned, if not terminated, since the United States would have been able to protect its homeland against a conventional attack by a European

---

95. For example, Weber, "Realism, Detente and Nuclear Weapons."

96. See, for example, John J. Mearsheimer, "Correspondence: Back to the Future, Part II: International Relations Theory and Post–Cold War Europe" *International Security,* Vol. 15, No. 2 (Fall 1990), p. 197, footnote 6; in disagreeing with Mearsheimer on this point I do not intend to endorse the position he is arguing against—that institutions necessarily play a major role in security cooperation.

97. This conclusion depends on judgments about U.S. requirements for counterforce to extend deterrence and on implications for the security dilemma facing the United States. See Glaser, *Analyzing Strategic Nuclear Policy,* pp. 94–99, 207–256.

hegemon.[98] Likewise, the Soviet need to control Eastern Europe should have been greatly reduced or eliminated, since the Soviet Union would have been able to deter a Western invasion without using Eastern Europe as a security buffer. Thus, it is the ending of the Cold War rather than the latter half of the Cold War that is in many ways easier for structural realism to explain.[99]

A fifth implication of contingent realism is that, contrary to the standard interpretation, structural-realist analysis offers generally optimistic predictions about the future of conflict between Europe's major powers. For example, because states pursue security, not advantages in relative power, structural realism does not predict that the West will try to take advantage of current Russian weakness. This is fortunate because military competition and a lack of economic cooperation would risk an increase in future threats to Western security: Russia already has large nuclear forces and is likely eventually to regain economic strength and with it the wherewithal to maintain large modern conventional forces. Competitive Western policies designed to keep Russia down are likely to be counterproductive, leaving Russia with enormous military capability, while signaling that the West is a threat to Russian economic and political well-being. By contrast, the cooperative policies the West is now pursuing—providing economic support, continuing with arms control instead of launching an arms race, and coordinating on foreign policy—hold better prospects for advancing its long-term security interests.

In addition, contingent realism finds that security-driven concern over relative economic gains should not damage trading relations among Western Europe's major powers, and between the United States and these countries, and therefore should not be a source of political tension. The large defensive advantages provided by nuclear weapons should dwarf any security risk that might otherwise result from advantages in relative economic growth. This is especially true since Germany is the focus of fears about disproportionate economic growth, but the other major Western powers have nuclear weapons.

Furthermore, this analysis suggests that the dangers of a shift to multipolarity in Europe have been exaggerated because offense-defense considerations have not been adequately integrated with polarity arguments. Many of the dangers that can be generated by multipolarity do not arise when defense has

---

98. Robert J. Art, "A Defensible Defense: America's Grand Strategy After the Cold War," *International Security*, Vol. 15, No. 4 (Spring 1991), pp. 11–23; Charles L. Glaser and George W. Downs, "Defense Policy: U.S. Role in Europe and Nuclear Strategy," in Oye, Lieber, and Rothchild, *Eagle in a New World*, pp. 72–78.

99. For elements of such an argument, see Daniel Deudney and G. John Ikenberry, "The International Sources of Soviet Change," *International Security*, Vol. 16, No. 3 (Winter 1991/92), pp. 74–118.

a large advantage:[100] uncertainties about whether allies will meet their commitments matter less because countries can maintain adequate deterrent capabilities on their own; increases in the miscalculation of capabilities will be smaller because capabilities are less sensitive to differences in the size and quality of forces; and the ability of major powers to gain military superiority by ganging up against other major powers is greatly reduced if not eliminated.[101] Because nuclear weapons provide very large advantages for the defense, a multipolar Europe can largely avoid these problems.

Finally, this analysis also indicates a likely source of tension. Current nuclear powers will face conflicting pressures if other major or intermediate powers—most obviously, Germany and Ukraine—decide they need nuclear weapons. On the one hand, structural arguments hold that the nuclear powers should welcome the security that nuclear weapons can provide to other major powers. On the other hand, the acquisition of nuclear capabilities will reduce the ability of current nuclear powers to deter conventional attacks, or at least their confidence in their abilities,[102] and might increase the damage they would suffer if war occurs. At least initially, therefore, proliferation is likely to be an unwelcome change and to strain relations in Europe. Fortunately, there is a readily available solution for avoiding these strains in the case of Germany. Preserving NATO, and thereby U.S. security guarantees to Germany, should essentially eliminate Germany's need for nuclear weapons.[103] Unfortunately, there is no comparable solution for Ukraine's security requirements.[104]

In closing, contingent realism paints a picture that diverges dramatically from that offered by the standard structural-realist argument. Instead of a strong propensity toward security competition, we find that states' choices

---

100. Even without including the offense-defense balance, the overall deductive case against multipolarity is mixed; see Stephen Van Evera, "Primed for Peace: Europe After the Cold War," *International Security*, Vol. 15, No. 3 (Winter 1990/91), pp. 33–40. For a different challenge to the explanatory value of polarity arguments see Hopf, "Polarity, the Offense-Defense Balance and War."

101. Mearsheimer, "Back to the Future," notes these points but does not fully integrate them into his predictions about the shift to multipolarity; Waltz, "The Emerging Structure of International Politics," p. 74, agrees that nuclear weapons transform the implications of multipolarity.

102. The argument here follows the logic of the stability-instability paradox. There is, however, a sound argument that nuclear powers should not be very worried about their ability to deter; see Robert Jervis, *The Meaning of the Nuclear Revolution* (Ithaca, N.Y.: Cornell University Press, 1989), pp. 19–22.

103. I present the case for NATO in Glaser, "Why NATO is Still Best: Future Security Arrangements for Europe," *International Security*, Vol. 18, No. 1 (Summer 1993), pp. 5–50.

104. For competing views on Ukrainian proliferation see John J. Mearsheimer, "The Case for a Ukrainian Nuclear Deterrent," and Steven E. Miller, "The Case Against a Ukrainian Nuclear Deterrent," both in *Foreign Affairs*, Vol. 72, No. 3 (Summer 1993), pp. 50–66 and 67–80.

between cooperation and competition are highly conditional, with no general preference for competition. This conclusion flows from the same assumptions that are employed in the standard structural-realist analysis. However, by eliminating the bias in that analysis, integrating offense-defense considerations to determine how much and what types of military capability countries can generate from their power, and explaining how military policies can signal valuable information about motives, contingent realism corrects a variety of shortcomings. It provides a set of conditional structural-realist predictions that improve our ability to explore past cooperation and competition, are necessary for assessing competing explanations, and provide better guidance for designing future policies.

Part IV:
Real Flaws? Criticisms of Realism

Historical Reality vs. Neo-realist Theory

Paul Schroeder

Realism has been for some time the reigning tradition in international theory and remains a major current in it.[1] The neo-realism or structural realism developed in Kenneth N. Waltz's *Theory of International Politics* is generally considered a major advance on the classical version of Hans Morgenthau and others. The central argument is that the broad outcomes of international politics derive more from the structural constraints of the states system than from unit behavior. The theory proceeds in a series of logical inferences from the fundamental postulate of a states system in which all units are autonomous, so that the system is structured by anarchy rather than hierarchy; to the primacy of

The author is a member of the Departments of History and Political Science at the University of Illinois, Urbana.

Much of the research and writing of this article was done while the author was a Jennings Randolph Peace Fellow at the United States Institute of Peace; its support is here gratefully acknowledged. Helpful criticism and suggestions have been given by Robert Jervis, Jack Snyder, Robert O. Keohane, Patrick Morgan, Edward Kolodziej, Bruce Russett, Joseph Kruzel, Jennifer Mitzen, Michael Lund, Joseph Klaits, and the members of seminars at the U.S. Institute of Peace, Columbia University's Institute for War and Peace Studies, and the University of Chicago's Program on International Politics, Economics, and Security. They are likewise gratefully acknowledged.

1. The central work is Kenneth N. Waltz, *Theory of International Politics* (Reading, Mass.: Addison-Wesley, 1979). Other expositions by Waltz of his position are his *Man, the State, and War: a Theoretical Analysis* (New York: Columbia University Press, 1959); "The Origins of War in Neo-realist Theory," in Robert I. Rotberg and Theodore K. Rabb, eds., *The Origin and Prevention of Major Wars* (Cambridge: Cambridge University Press, 1989), pp. 39–52; and "The Stability of a Bipolar World," *Daedalus*, Vol. 93, No. 3 (1964), pp. 881–909. Robert J. Art and Kenneth N. Waltz, eds., *The Use of Force: Military Power and International Politics*, 4th ed. (Lanham, Md.: University Press of America, 1993) contains many articles exemplifying neo-realist arguments and assumptions, including three by Waltz. Other versions and applications of realist theory may be found in Stephen M. Walt, *The Origins of Alliances* (Ithaca, N.Y.: Cornell University Press, 1987); Barry R. Posen, *The Sources of Military Doctrine: France, Britain, and Germany Between the World Wars* (Ithaca, N.Y.: Cornell University Press, 1984); Robert Gilpin, *War and Change in World Politics* (Cambridge: Cambridge University Press, 1981); and John Mearsheimer, *Conventional Deterrence* (Ithaca, N.Y: Cornell University Press, 1983). For a good introduction to realism and its chief current rival, idealism, see Joseph S. Nye, Jr., *Understanding International Conflicts: An Introduction to Theory and History* (London: HarperCollins, 1993). The classic work of the older realism, emphasizing the state's natural drive for power rather than structural constraints as the chief source of power politics and conflict, is Hans Morgenthau, *Politics Among Nations: The Struggle for Power and Peace* (New York: Knopf, 1948).

International Security, Vol. 19, No. 1 (Summer 1994), pp. 108–148
© 1994 by the President and Fellows of Harvard College and the Massachusetts Institute of Technology.

survival, security, and independence for each unit wishing to remain part of the system; to the mandate of self-help this need imposes upon each unit; and to a resultant competition between units which produces a recurrent pattern of various balances of power. (See Figure 1.)

Much current debate over neo-realism centers on what implications the end of the Cold War might have for realist theory, in terms of its ability both to explain this particular outcome and to prescribe future policy.[2] This essay

Figure 1. Neo-realism.

States system

↓

Structural anarchy

↓

Primacy of security

↓

Self-help

↓

Balance of power

---

2. For current neo-realist arguments, see John Mearsheimer, "Back to the Future: Instability in Europe After the Cold War," *International Security*, Vol. 15, No. 1 (Summer 1990), pp. 5–55; Christopher Layne, "The Unipolar Illusion: Why New Great Powers Will Rise," *International Security*, Vol. 17, No. 4 (Spring 1993), pp. 5–51; and Kenneth N. Waltz, "The Emerging Structure of International Politics," *International Security*, Vol. 18, No. 2 (Fall 1993), pp. 44–79. Layne's argument is analyzed more closely below. For divergent views, see Robert Jervis, "International Primacy: Is the Game Worth the Candle?" *International Security*, Vol. 17, No. 4 (Spring 1993), pp. 52–67; Jervis, "A Usable Past for the Future," in Michael J. Hogan, ed., *The End of the Cold War: Its Meaning and Implications* (Cambridge: Cambridge University Press, 1992), pp. 257–268; and John Mueller, "Quiet Cataclysm: Some Afterthoughts on World War III," in Hogan, *The End of the Cold War*, pp. 39–52. See also Kenneth A. Oye, Robert J. Lieber, and Donald Rothchild, *Eagle in a New World: American Grand Strategy in the Post-Cold War Era* (London: HarperCollins, 1992); Mark Bowker and Robin Brown, eds., *From Cold War to Collapse: Theory and World Politics in the 1980s* (Cambridge: Cambridge University Press, 1993); Geir Lundestad and Odd Arne Westad, eds., *Beyond the Cold War: Future Dimensions in International Relations* (Oxford: Oxford University Press, 1993); and Stanley Hoffmann, Robert O. Keohane, and Joseph S. Nye, Jr., eds., *After the Cold War: International Institutions and State Strategies in Europe, 1989–91* (Cambridge, Mass.: Harvard University Press, 1993).

will not, however, discuss how neo-realist theory fits recent and current history. Instead it takes up a question seldom if ever discussed, yet clearly important for international historians and arguably also for international relations theorists, namely, whether neo-realist theory is adequate and useful as an explanatory framework for the history of international politics in general, over the whole Westphalian era from 1648 to 1945, the period in which the validity of a realist paradigm of some sort is widely accepted even by non-realists.[3]

This question could have some implications for the debate over neo-realism and the end of the Cold War. For example, a finding that the neo-realist structural analysis of international politics did succeed in explaining the general operation and dynamics of the modern European states system over this long span of time might suggest that, with modifications to accommodate current changes, it should remain valid today; an opposite verdict would bolster the call for more radical revision or abandonment. Investigating the long-term fit between neo-realist theory and international history might also shed some indirect light on other current questions and issues in international relations theory, such as the obsolescence or continued utility of nuclear weapons;[4] the problems and uses of deterrence;[5] the comparative incidence of balancing versus bandwagoning in international politics;[6] hegemony in theory and practice;[7] the development of an international society under conditions of anarchy;[8] the necessity and possibility of developing rules and

---

3. It is striking, for example, that a strong opponent of realism, Bruce Russett, seems to accept the validity of the realist paradigm for this period in writing: "It may be possible in part to supersede the 'realist' principles (anarchy, the security dilemma of states) that have dominated practice to the exclusion of 'liberal' or 'idealist' ones since at least the seventeenth century." Russett, *Grasping the Democratic Peace* (Princeton, N.J.: Princeton University Press, 1993), p. 24.
4. Robert Jervis, *The Meaning of the Nuclear Revolution* (Ithaca, N.Y.: Cornell University Press, 1989); John Mueller, *Retreat from Doomsday* (New York: Basic Books, 1989).
5. Paul Stern, et al., eds., *Perspectives on Deterrence* (New York: Oxford University Press, 1989); Paul K. Huth, *Extended Deterrence and the Prevention of War* (New Haven: Yale University Press, 1988); Richard N. Lebow and Janice Gross Stein, "Deterrence: The Dependent Variable," *World Politics*, Vol. 47, No. 3 (April 1990), pp. 336–369 ; Paul Huth and Bruce Russett, "Testing Deterrence Theory: Rigor Makes a Difference," *World Politics*, Vol. 47, No. 4 (July 1990), pp. 466–501.
6. Walt, *Origins of Alliances.*
7. Robert Gilpin, *The Political Economy of International Relations* (Princeton, N.J.: Princeton University Press, 1987); Kenneth A. Oye, ed., *Cooperation under Anarchy* (Princeton, N.J.: Princeton University Press, 1986); Robert O. Keohane, *After Hegemony: Cooperation and Discord in the World Political Economy* (Princeton, N.J.: Princeton University Press, 1984).
8. Hedley Bull, *The Anarchical Society* (New York: Columbia University Press, 1977); Martin Wight, *Systems of States* (Leicester: Leicester University Press, 1977); Evan Luard, *International Society* (London: MacMillan, 1990).

norms for greater international order and peace;[9] the possible transformation of international politics through the effects of dependence and interdependence and the emergence of new transnational actors and institutions;[10] and the historical conditions and negotiating postures and techniques best suited for peaceful resolution of conflicts.[11] Therefore the question is not irrelevant to theory; theorists of different schools might wish to see such an investigation done for their purposes and tailored to their interests and needs. But I wish to make clear that it is being done for the interests and needs of the historian. The primary aim is *not* to test neo-realist theory with historical evidence in order to help political scientists determine what is sound or unsound about it.

This investigation necessarily examines certain theses or generalizations advanced by neo-realists in some historical detail, in particular the following: (1) States generally tend to balance against power or threat; (2) States are not functionally differentiated in international politics; (3) Potential hegemons are countered and defeated by the balancing efforts of other states; and (4) Unipolar periods motivate other states to rise to great power status, as part of the general tendency to balance and to emulate successful military and organizational development.[12] The central purpose of this essay, however, is not to amass historical evidence pro and con on these particular points or on other tenets and implications of neo-realist theory.[13] It has a different

---

9. Friedrich Kratochwil, *Rules, Norms, and Decisions* (Cambridge: Cambridge University Press, 1989); Samuel S. Kim, *The Quest for a Just World Order* (Boulder, Colo.: Westview, 1984); Lynn H. Miller, *Global Order*, 2d ed. (Boulder, Colo.: Westview, 1990); Dorothy V. Jones, *Code of Peace* (Chicago: University of Chicago Press, 1991); Charles R. Beitz, *Political Theory and International Relations* (Princeton, N.J.: Princeton University Press, 1979); Emanuel Adler and Beverly Crawford, eds., *Progress in Postwar International Relations* (New York: Columbia University Press, 1991); Christ Brown, *International Relations Theory: New Normative Approaches* (New York: Columbia University Press, 1992).

10. James N. Rosenau and Ernst-Otto Czempiel, eds., *Governance without Government: Order and Change in World Politics* (Cambridge: Cambridge University Press, 1992); Charles F. Doran, *Systems in Crisis: New Imperatives of High Politics at Century's End* (Cambridge: Cambridge University Press, 1991).

11. Stephen R. Rock, *Why Peace Breaks Out: Great Power Rapprochement in Historical Perspective* (Chapel Hill: University of North Carolina Press, 1989); Alexander George, *Forceful Persuasion: Coercive Diplomacy as an Alternative to War* (Washington, D.C.: United States Institute of Peace Press, 1991); I. William Zartman and Maureen R. Berman, *The Practical Negotiator* (New Haven: Yale University Press, 1982).

12. I owe the formulation of these four generalizations to Sean Lynn-Jones.

13. This may help explain why I have not followed some of the suggestions offered by friends and critics, even though I appreciate them. Such an attempt would not only vastly overstep the bounds of a journal article, but also bog down in debates over differing definitions of terms, divergent interpretations of historical data, the proper methods of "operationalizing" historical

purpose and poses a different broad question, namely, whether neo-realist theory works for international history, provides a sound model or paradigm for understanding the general nature of international politics, and therefore for explaining its history in terms of its broad outcomes and general patterns.

Neo-realists advance this claim for the theory, and many historians accept it, making the question pertinent for both sides. This setting and purpose also shape the form of my argument. It concentrates initially upon Waltz's ideas, not because he is the only important realist or his version of realism the only possible one, but because he most clearly and explicitly grounds the claim of realist theory to account for the broad outcomes of international history. It then focuses on Christopher Layne's recent use of neo-realist theory to explain and to predict international history, because Layne's article represents a typical instance of the results of applying the neo-realist paradigm to international history in the era where it is supposed to work best.

I do not, finally, claim a monopoly for historians in judging how theorists, especially neo-realists, use history. The fit between theory and international history is one for both theorists and historians to discuss. I come to it as a historian, but recognize the right and duty of theorists to weigh in from their side, evaluating the way historians use theory and historical evidence.[14]

This article, therefore, is not just another attempt to revise and improve neo-realist theory,[15] or to use history to improve international relations theory in general. While theorists and policy scientists aspiring to lengthen the shadow of the future may use this article in that pursuit, my aim is to sharpen and deepen the shadow of the past.

The Neo-realist Historical World

Two things are interesting about the role of history in neo-realist theory, especially Waltz's work, and in the discussion and criticism of it represented

---

evidence to make it yield reliable results for political science, and the extent to which neo-realist categories can or cannot accommodate the evidence adduced.

14. For a detailed attempt to demonstrate how the realist paradigm does not explain a long and crucial period, see Paul W. Schroeder, *The Transformation of European Politics, 1763–1848* (Oxford: Clarendon Press, 1994). No short journal article can really prove the kind of case I intend to lay out except in a *prima facie* way.

15. Barry Buzan, *People, States, and Fear: The National Security Problem in International Relations* (Chapel Hill: University of North Carolina Press, 1983); Barry Buzan, Charles Jones, and Richard Little, *The Logic of Anarchy: Neorealism to Structural Realism* (New York: Columbia University Press, 1993).

in *Neo-Realism and Its Critics*.[16] Some critics, especially Robert O. Keohane, Richard K. Ashley, and John G. Ruggie, contend that neo-realism is too static a theory and fails to allow or account for change and development in the international system. This charge of failing to account for historic change, also raised in other works,[17] apparently does not especially worry Waltz, judging by his reply to his critics in the Keohane volume (pp. 322–345). His answer to the various criticisms of failure to account for historical change is that, to the extent that they are true, they do not affect the core of the theory. The historical question of how the current states system with its structural anarchy came to develop is of no particular importance for theoretical purposes. Structure does not account for everything, nor does theory explain or predict everything. The changes in international politics cited by critics occur at the unit level; only if hierarchy replaced anarchy would its structure be changed. Enriching the theory as critics propose, Waltz argues, would only marginally improve its descriptive accuracy while reducing its theoretical rigor and predictive power.

Thus neo-realism seems resistant to refutation on the charge that it is unhistorical, at least at the theoretical level. At the same time, critics and proponents of rival theories or approaches do not, to my knowledge, challenge the historical generalizations Waltz makes, at least in connection with the main era to which they apply, the international states system since 1648.[18] In fact, Waltz's assumptions about the historic character of international politics seem common to realism as a whole, and to be shared even by critics and members of other schools as well.

Two main assertions concerning international politics over history are made by Waltz in various forms and contexts throughout his work, especially in his *Theory of International Politics:* first, he asserts that the conduct of states in international politics has always been basically the same: all states are

---

16. Robert O. Keohane, ed., *Neo-Realism and Its Critics* (New York: Columbia University Press, 1986). For another critique of neo-realism, see Keohane, *International Institutions and State Power* (Boulder, Colo.: Westview, 1989), pp. 35–73.
17. E.g., Doran, *Systems in Crisis*, pp. 2–3, 258; Buzan, Jones, and Little, *Logic of Anarchy, passim.* See also the discussion in William C. Olson and A.J.R. Groom, *International Relations Then and Now: Origins and Trends in Interpretation* (London: HarperCollins, 1991), pp. 262–284.
18. This may not be true of Buzan, Jones, and Little, *Logic of Anarchy,* one of whose chief aims in moving (in their terms) from neo-realism to structural realism is to make the theory more open to history. Their arguments, however, often seem abstract and obscure, and while they refer to Chinese, Greek, Roman, Hellenistic, and medieval history, they never deal with the European international system from 1648 on.

guided by structural constraints and imperatives of anarchy, self-help, and balance of power, and must be if they hope to survive and prosper.[19]

Second, states are not functionally differentiated within the structure of international politics. Their common, primary function, structurally determined, is to survive and remain independent through self-help. What differentiates states is instead their position within the system, i.e., their power relative to others. Domestic society, structured by hierarchy and heteronomy, enforces upon its units the mandate of specialization in order to survive. International society, structured by autonomy and anarchy, imposes on its units the mandate not to specialize but to concentrate their resources first and foremost on security. Only after that requirement is at least minimally met dare they pursue their particular aims. States ignoring this rule suffer serious consequences.[20]

Both historical generalizations are asserted as self-evident, something everyone knows, rather than based on much evidence or on inductive as opposed to deductive argument. In *Theory of International Politics*, Waltz uses historical evidence, drawn mainly from the recent past, primarily for purposes of instantiation and to back up certain other particular theses, e.g., that a bipolar balance is superior to a multipolar one, or that force has not declined in utility in the recent past. His most extended historical discussion of how structure shapes outcomes in international politics draws on material from domestic rather than international politics, arguing that the different British and American political systems have historically produced different kinds of leaders. Other broad historical assertions accompany and support his two main ones, for example, the contentions that "states prefer to join the weaker of two coalitions" and that "secondary states, if they are free to

---

19. "The daily presence of force and recurrent reliance on it mark the affairs of nations. Since Thucydides in Greece and Kautilya in India, the use of force and the possibility of controlling it have been the preoccupations of international-political studies." Waltz, *Theory of International Politics*, p. 186. "Balance-of-power politics in much the form that we know it has been practiced over the millennia by many different types of political units, from ancient China and India, to the Greek and Italian city states, and unto our own day." Waltz, "A Response to My Critics," in Keohane, ed., *Neo-Realism*, p. 341. "Over the centuries states have changed in many ways, but the quality of international life has remained much the same." Waltz, *Theory of International Politics*, p. 110. More such statements could be cited.
20. Waltz, *Theory of International Politics*, pp. 97–99, 107, 126, and *passim*. It is worth noting that these generalizations are not solely Waltz's but are widely shared by neo-realists, and constitutive of the theory. For example, another eminent realist, Robert Gilpin, shares them in both *War and Change* and *Political Economy*, and these general premises form the specific bases of the arguments of Mearsheimer, "Back to the Future"; and Layne "The Unipolar Illusion," as discussed below.

choose, flock to the weaker side; for it is the stronger side that threatens them," likewise without adducing historical evidence or argument.[21]

Yet both of Waltz's central assertions concerning the conduct of international politics throughout history are vital to neo-realist theory, for according to Waltz, the broad outcomes of international politics over the ages and its sameness and repetitive character can be explained only by the structure of international politics as he presents it. The theory also purports to predict and explain the persistent strong tendency toward balance in the system,[22] and to account for the absence of functional differentiation among units and their differentiation solely by their position (i.e., relative power and capability) within it. Waltz also argues elsewhere that the placement of countries within the system by their relative power is the main determinant of their behavior within it, and this time cites historical examples as proof.[23]

A Historian's View of the Neo-realist Historical World

Some facts in the history of international politics seem to hold broadly for the modern European states system through much of its existence and thus give the Waltzian picture a *prima facie* plausibility. It is generally true, though not at all uniformly so, that states in the modern era, regardless of their ideology, domestic structure, individual aims, etc., have claimed exclusive sovereignty over their territory and the sole right to the legitimate use of force within it, have set a high value on their independence and security, have upheld their right to use force in self-defense, have tried to provide means for their defense, and have conducted foreign policy with an eye to maintaining their security and independence. This is obvious and familiar. Nevertheless, the more one examines Waltz's historical generalizations about the conduct of international politics throughout history with the aid of the historian's knowledge of the actual course of history, the more doubtful—in fact, strange—these generalizations become.

---

21. Waltz, *Theory of International Politics*, pp. 126–127.
22. Ibid., pp. 124, 128.
23. In Waltz, "America as a Model for World? A Foreign Policy Perspective," *PS: Political Science and Politics* (December 1991), pp. 667–70, Waltz contends that because the United States and the Soviet Union were similarly placed since 1945 by their power, their behavior was also similar, and he explains the "arbitrary and arrogant behavior" of such past rulers as Charles V, Louis XIV, Napoleon, and Kaiser Wilhelm II chiefly by their "surplus of power" (p. 669).

SELF-HELP: THEORY CONFRONTS PRACTICE

Do all states, or virtually all, or all that really count, actually resort to self-help in the face of threats to their security and independence? Though Waltz does not clearly define self-help or describe its practice, one may reasonably infer, given the link frequently drawn between self-help and the balance of power, and given Waltz's insistence on the primacy of power and the structural role of the potential and actual use of force in international politics, that self-help means, at least generally and primarily, the potential or actual use of a state's own power along with that of other units for the purposes of compellence, deterrence, and other modes of controlling the actions of one's opponents. By Waltz's rules for testing theories, neo-realist theory should correctly predict or confirm this kind of conduct in international politics throughout history, and Waltz clearly believes it does so. So, as discussed below, does Christopher Layne, and so do (and to some extent must) other realists.

I do not. I cannot construct a history of the European states system from 1648 to 1945 based on the generalization that most unit actors within that system responded to crucial threats to their security and independence by resorting to self-help, as defined above. In the majority of instances this just did not happen. In each major period in these three centuries, most unit actors tried if they possibly could to protect their vital interests in other ways. (This includes great powers as well as smaller ones, undermining the neo-realist argument that weaker states are more inclined to bandwagon than stronger ones, as discussed below.) The reasons are clear. For one thing, most states, most of the time, could not afford a strategy of self-help of this kind. They were like landowners with valuable property which they knew they could not possibly insure, first because insurance premiums were ruinously expensive, second because against the most devastating dangers no insurance policy was available at any price, and third because the very attempt on their part to take out an insurance policy would encourage robbers to attack them.[24] Hence the insurance policies they took out and maintained

---

24. A classic example of this can be seen in the origins of the War of the Austrian Succession in 1740. The Habsburg monarch and German Emperor Charles VI had devoted years of costly diplomacy to trying to insure the rights of his daughter Maria Theresa to inherit his Austrian lands against any challenge to the succession on his death, by getting all interested powers including Prussia formally to endorse the so-called Pragmatic Sanction of her title. Frederick II of Prussia, seeing Charles rely on this insurance policy, and knowing that others were likely also to disregard their obligations under it, immediately seized Austrian Silesia when he and Maria Theresa acceded to their thrones in 1740, and France and Bavaria quickly joined in the

in the form of armed forces, alliances, and diplomacy were mostly intended to protect against minor risks and to deter casual attacks or vandalism, with the full knowledge that if something more serious threatened, another recourse would be necessary.

Other strategies were available and often tried. One commonly employed was *hiding* from threats. This could take various forms: simply ignoring the threat or declaring neutrality in a general crisis, possibly approaching other states on one or both sides of a quarrel to get them to guarantee one's safety; trying to withdraw into isolation; assuming a purely defensive position in the hope that the storm would blow over; or, usually as a later or last resort, seeking protection from some other power or powers in exchange for diplomatic services, friendship, or non-military support, without joining that power or powers as an ally or committing itself to any use of force on its part.[25] A strategy less common, but far from unusual or unknown, was *transcending*, i.e., attempting to surmount international anarchy and go beyond the normal limits of conflictual politics: to solve the problem, end the threat, and prevent its recurrence through some institutional arrangement involving an international consensus or formal agreement on norms, rules, and procedures for these purposes. Efforts of this kind were made in every era of these centuries. Another strategy was *bandwagoning*, i.e., joining the stronger side for the sake of protection and payoffs, even if this meant insecurity *vis-à-vis* the protecting power and a certain sacrifice of independence. Against the views of some, such as Waltz and Stephen M. Walt,[26] I see bandwagoning as historically more common than balancing, particularly by smaller powers. Finally comes the strategy which, according to Waltz and others, is dominant and structural in international politics: *self-help* in the form of balancing against an actual or potential hegemon. Once again, con-

---

attack on Austria. For the historical details, see on the French and European side especially Paul Vaucher, *Robert Walpole et la politique de Fleury (1731–1742)* (Paris: Plon-Nourrit, 1924); on the Austrian, Max Braubach, *Versailles und Wien von Ludwig XIV bis Kaunitz* (Bonn: L. Röhrschild, 1952).

25. What I here call "hiding" may be related to "buckpassing"; see Thomas J. Christensen and Jack Snyder, "Chain Gangs and Passed Bucks: Predicting Alliance Patterns in Multipolarity," *International Organization*, Vol. 44, No. 2 (Spring 1990), pp. 137–168. Hiding, however, would seem to be broader in scope, often involving not just an effort to pass the costs of international politics to someone else, or to avoid any active participation in it, but a search for some method of handling the threat apart from being drawn into the power-political fray, often by a very active foreign policy. "Hiding" may therefore be somewhat misleading as a blanket term for all these forms of conduct, but I can think of no more satisfactory one.

26. Walt, *Origins of Alliances*.

trary to the view of many scholars including historians, I see this as having been relatively rare, and often a fallback policy or last resort.[27]

A concrete example illustrating these different strategies in practice is the crisis in Germany (the Holy Roman Empire or Reich) caused by the Austrian Emperor Joseph II's attempt in 1785 to carry through the exchange of the Austrian Netherlands (Belgium) for Bavaria.[28] Almost all German states and principalities saw this move as a threat to the German "balance"—by which they meant not simply the balance of power between the German great powers, Austria and Prussia, and their respective clients, but even more importantly for some states, the balance provided by the Reich constitution between the sovereign powers of Germany's various states and the limits to individual state power and guarantees of corporate "liberties" (i.e., privileges) within those states. The reason the proposed move would threaten the independence and security of the Reich and its members was not just that it would strengthen Austria, but also and mainly that it would damage the Reich as a legal order guaranteeing the liberties of all its members (another indication of the ways in which a purely power-political view of international politics is too crude to capture vital elements of the process).[29] Many units hid from the threat, i.e., simply ignored the issue or remained neutral, even though they knew the outcome might affect them critically. Some balanced against it. Prussia and Hanover, old rivals, joined to exploit an idea already current, that of forming a Protestant League of Princes to check the Catholic Emperor and his ecclesiastical princely clients.[30] Some began by hiding out,

---

27. This list of the ways states have reacted to international crises and threats or tried to use them is not proposed as exhaustive. It was common, for example, to try to exploit threats, i.e., use them to gain some particular advantage for one's own state, often at the expense of another state than the one posing the threat. This strategy, however, seems impossible to characterize as a particular response to threats, since it always or almost always plays into attempts to balance or bandwagon, and frequently is involved in attempts to hide and transcend as well. Thus it would seem characteristic of competitive power politics in general, and not a particular mode of response to threats within it.

28. Good discussions are in K.O. von Aretin, *Heiliges Römisches Reich 1776–1806*, 2 vols. (Wiesbaden: F. Steiner, 1967); and Max Braubach, *Maria Theresias jüngster Sohn Max Franz, letzter Kurfürst von Köln* (Vienna: Herold, 1961).

29. Aretin, *Heiliges Römisches Reich*, repeatedly stresses this theme, but it is also generally recognized by students of the constitutional history of the Empire. See for example John C. Gagliardo, *Reich and Nation: The Holy Roman Empire as Idea and Reality, 1763–1806* (Bloomington: Indiana University Press, 1980); Jean-François Noël, *Le Saint Empire* (Paris: Presses Universitaires de France, 1976). This tension between balance of power and balance of rights, *Machtordnung* and *Rechtsordnung*, prominent especially in the old regime but important in all eras, tends to be blurred or erased by the neo-realist approach.

30. T.C.W. Blanning, "George III and the Fürstenbund," *Historical Journal*, Vol. 20, No. 2 (June 1977), pp. 311–344.

then saw that Emperor Joseph would lose his nerve, and bandwagoned to the winning Prussian side. But some also tried to transcend; that is, certain lesser princes attempted to form a union of smaller states not to stop Prussia or Austria by force (which they knew was beyond their resources) or to balance with either great power or against both, but to rise above the quarrel, reviving and reforming the institutions and constitution of the Empire so as to provide guarantees for everyone's territorial rights, and a machinery for the arbitration of future disputes.[31]

This kind of scenario, in which different states perceiving the same threat or similar ones adopted differing strategies to meet them, is seen in almost every major crisis throughout the centuries in question. For this reason alone, neo-realist theory cannot accommodate the history of international politics as I know it; too many facts and insights vital for explaining broad developments and results do not pass through its prism.

To be sure, this assertion has been supported here only by example rather than proof; even after a thorough historical elaboration it would still remain controversial, given the debates over historical interpretation and the notorious difficulties of deciding which motives and strategies guided historical actors. Yet the problem of divergent strategies here indicated is not unknown to theorists. Stephen Walt proposes to meet it with an argument that states balance against threats rather than simply against power. This does not, however, really help answer the question of which of the four strategies—hiding, transcending, bandwagoning, or self-help—or which combination of them, prevailed in each instance. Walt's thesis, designed to help neo-realist theory explain why states so often join overwhelmingly powerful coalitions, actually makes it virtually impossible to distinguish between "balancing" and "bandwagoning" or to determine the real motives of actors, since any bandwagoning state is likely to claim that it is actually "balancing" against a threatening enemy. The argument thus begs the very question it is supposed to answer, namely, whether weaker states tend to balance or to bandwagon in the face of threats from more powerful states.[32] Besides, states seldom

---

31. For evidence that this kind of transcending was not an uncommon occurrence, but a frequent feature of Imperial politics, see K.O. von Aretin, ed., *Der Kurfürst von Mainz und die Kreisassoziationen 1648–1746* (Wiesbaden: F. Steiner, 1975).
32. An example: when Japan and China declared war on Germany during the First World War, they were plainly bandwagoning—Japan in order to seize German possessions in Asia, China to escape isolation and gain British and French protection against Japan and Imperial Russia. Yet both Japan and China claimed to be balancing against German imperialism. Or in 1939–40, when various states in southeastern Europe (Hungary, Rumania, Bulgaria, and momentarily

choose a strategy unconditionally or without mixed motives, and in particular they consider what strategy will yield the greatest side payments (territorial gains, future alliances, political concessions, prestige, etc.).[33]

Even if no ironclad case can be made from history, I can back the assertion that neorealism is incorrect in its claims for the repetitiveness of strategy and the prevalence of balancing in international politics, with brief examples of how the various competing strategies were used in the face of threat in four major periods of war: the French revolutionary and Napoleonic wars (1792–1815), the Crimean War (1853–56), the First World War (1914–18), and the Second World War (1939–45). These make a *prima facie* case against Waltz's generalizations.

FRENCH REVOLUTIONARY AND NAPOLEONIC WARS. The French revolutionary and Napoleonic wars are often considered a classic case of balancing, with allied coalitions repeatedly being formed to defeat France's bid for hegemony and restore the balance of power. However, this view will not stand examination. The First Coalition (1792–97) was formed against France at a time when, though it provoked the coalition into being and started the war by its aggressive behavior and ideology, France was militarily extremely weak and vulnerable and had lost all its allies and political influence in Europe. Austria and Prussia (or at least most of their leaders) expected to win the war easily; the smaller states, if they could not hide from the conflict, gravitated toward the apparently overwhelmingly superior allied coalition, which included Spain, Piedmont, Tuscany, Naples, and various German states, soon joined in early 1793 by Great Britain. Once France's real revolutionary power became apparent from late 1793 on, states began hiding by leaving the coalition (Prussia, Tuscany, and some German states) or bandwagoning by joining France, as Spain did.[34] The same thing happened to the Second Coalition (1798–1801): states hid or bandwagoned to the allied side so long as it was winning, to mid-1799, and then bandwagoned to France's side from late 1799

Yugoslavia) allied with Germany, they were plainly bandwagoning—but also, perhaps genuinely, balancing against the threat from the USSR.

33. A good example is the conduct of Piedmont-Savoy under King Victor Amadeus II before and during the War of the Spanish Succession (1702–14). He always bandwagoned with the stronger side, shifting alliances to do so; he always exacted the highest possible price for doing so; and he always claimed (and conceivably to some extent believed) that he was balancing against the greatest threat to his state and Europe. For his policy, see Geoffrey Symcox, *Victor Amadeus II* (Berkeley: University of California Press, 1983), chaps. 8, 10, and 12.

34. I draw here on the account in my *Transformation of European Politics*, chap. 3; but see also T.C.W. Blanning, *The Origins of the French Revolutionary Wars* (London: Longman's, 1986).

on. Even Russia, a main founder of the Second Coalition, did so.[35] In every succeeding war from late 1799 to mid-1813, despite the fact that France under Napoleon had become by far both the most powerful Continental state and the most ambitious and insatiable one, the French-led coalition was always larger and stronger than its counterpart; more states always bandwagoned than balanced. In several instances Napoleon was able to organize most of Europe for war against a single isolated foe (Britain in 1803 and 1807, Prussia in 1806, Spain in 1808, Austria in 1809, Russia in 1812). In short, the main response to Napoleonic hegemony and imperialism by European states, large and small alike, was not balancing but either hiding or bandwagoning. (There were also attempts to transcend, mainly in the form of trying to transform French conquest and domination into a new federal order for Germany and Europe, but these proved futile in the face of Napoleon's militarism.) Besides the smaller, weaker states who bandwagoned as Napoleon's satellites, many of them willingly and profitably, every major power in Europe except Great Britain—Prussia, Austria, Russia, Spain—bandwagoned as France's active ally for a considerable period. Wars continued to break out mainly not because European states tried to balance against France as a hegemonic power, but because Napoleon's ambition and lawless conduct frustrated their repeated efforts to hide or bandwagon. This happened to Prussia from 1795 to 1806 and from 1807 to 1810, Spain from 1795 to 1808, Austria in 1806–08 and 1809–13, and Russia in 1807–12.[36] Even after Napoleon's disastrous defeat in Russia in 1812, the Continental coalition that Russia and Prussia formed in early 1813 to "balance" against France was smaller than the coalition Napoleon re-formed from his allies and satellites, and was initially defeated by it. Only after the failure of Austria's attempt to transcend the crisis, by mediating a negotiated peace in the summer of 1813, did Austria join the coalition (for purposes of controlling and ending rather than winning the war), and only after the decisive defeat of Napoleon's army at Leipzig in October 1813 did his coalition break up, with smaller states bandwagoning to the winning allied side.[37]

THE CRIMEAN WAR. The Crimean War, originally seen by most Britons and still viewed by some historians as a case of "balancing" against Russian

---

35. Paul W. Schroeder, "The Collapse of the Second Coalition," *Journal of Modern History*, Vol. 59, No. 2 (June 1987), pp. 244–290.
36. For a brief survey of the evidence, see Paul W. Schroeder, "Napoleon's Foreign Policy: A Criminal Enterprise," *Journal of Military History*, Vol. 54, No. 2 (April 1990), pp. 147–162.
37. Again, this is shown in detail in my *Transformation of European Politics*, chaps. 5–8, 10–12.

domination of Europe, actually began with a clearly superior allied coalition (Britain, France, and the Ottoman Empire) facing a Russia diplomatically isolated, politically and militarily threatened, aware of its peril, and looking for an honorable retreat. No neutral state in Europe therefore considered Russia a military threat at that time. Even Austria, which had a general fear of Russian domination of the Balkans, recognized that this danger was for the moment allayed, and tried hard to prevent the war. Most German states, including Prussia, considered the Anglo-French coalition a greater military and political threat to their security and interests. Yet Sardinia-Piedmont joined the dominant coalition militarily, Austria did so politically, and even Prussia and the German Confederation, although sympathetic to Russia and wanting only to hide from the conflict, were dragged into helping force Russia to admit defeat and accept an imposed settlement. In short, some states, great and small, bandwagoned; others tried to hide and then bandwagoned; still others, like Sweden, Denmark, and the Low Countries, remained in hiding; none balanced against Anglo-French domination. Once again, moreover, there was a major effort to transcend: Austria's attempt to stop the war short of victory by a negotiated settlement intended to produce a new concert and a permanent solution to the Eastern question.[38]

THE FIRST WORLD WAR. The distinction between balancing and bandwagoning becomes especially difficult to draw in the First World War. It is possible, though far from clear, that initially both sides were balancing against the other's threat rather than bidding for hegemony. However, the distinction between aiming for balance or hegemony, always problematic, becomes virtually meaningless here, since, once engaged in war, both sides could envision security only through clear military supremacy, and both fought for imperialist goals designed to insure it.[39] Moreover, other states plainly preferred either to hide (Spain, Holland, Denmark, Sweden, Switzerland) or to bandwagon with the victor so as to defeat their particular enemies and make gains at their expense (Turkey, Bulgaria, Italy, Rumania, Greece, Japan, and China). As things turned out, only two powers joined the smaller and pu-

---

38. See Paul W. Schroeder, *Austria, Great Britain and the Crimean War* (Ithaca, N.Y.: Cornell University Press, 1972); Winfried Baumgart, *Der Frieden von Paris 1856* (Wiesbaden: F. Steiner, 1972); Ann Pottinger Saab, *Origins of the Crimean Alliance* (Charlottesville: University of Virginia Press, 1977); and Norman Rich, *Why the Crimean War?* (Hanover, N.H.: University Press of New England, 1985).
39. A brilliant recent study proving this with massive evidence, especially for the Allied side, is G.-H. Soutou, *L'Or et le Sang: les buts de guerre économiques de la Premiere Guerre mondiale* (Paris: Fayard, 1989).

tatively weaker Central Powers (Bulgaria and Turkey, both under a degree of duress); more joined the larger allied one (Italy, Rumania, Greece, Japan, China, the United States, and all the British Dominions). Certain of these, especially Italy and Rumania, explicitly tried to bandwagon with the victorious side at the right moment to share the spoils. Moreover, one cannot overlook attempts by neutrals (the Papal State, Sweden, Switzerland, the United States) and even certain belligerents (Austria-Hungary and the Russian Provisional Government in 1917) to transcend the conflict by promoting a negotiated peace.[40]

WORLD WAR TWO. The pattern is a bit clearer in World War Two in Europe. Even before the war, Germany's growing power and political success promoted extensive hiding and bandwagoning in Western and Eastern Europe. Belgium dropped its ties to France in 1936 and reverted to neutrality; Holland, Denmark, and Norway not only remained ostentatiously neutral but declined even to arm for self-defense before they were overrun. Chamberlain's appeasement policy was certainly not balancing, but an attempt at a British partnership with Germany for peace; Daladier's abandonment of Czechoslovakia can be seen as France's attempt to avoid war by hiding. The Little Entente of Czechoslovakia, Rumania, and Yugoslavia, a potential instrument for balancing against Germany, fell apart even before Munich; the French-Czech-Russian alliance collapsed at Munich; and Poland and Hungary joined with Germany in despoiling Czechoslovakia. Italy, despite Mussolini's and Ciano's fears of Germany, moved decisively to Hitler's side in May 1939, and the Soviet Union followed in August. The Poles, although standing firm against German demands and accepting a British guarantee, steadfastly refused to join a balancing alliance with Russia against Germany and essentially pinned their hopes of salvation on hiding in independent neutrality. After France's defeat, the Vichy regime tried to bandwagon with Hitler's Germany. Hungary, Bulgaria, and Rumania joined his camp, while Yugoslavia's apparent reversal of its decision to do so in March 1941 was actually a purely domestic political coup. Even neutrals (Sweden, Turkey, Switzerland, Spain) leaned toward Germany so long as the tide of war was going Hitler's way. Once the tide of battle turned in 1941–42, however, states began bandwagoning with Hitler's enemies, many joining the "United Nations." Even Franco's Spain and Perón's Argentina finally leaned toward the Allies (al-

---

40. The literature here is too massive to summarize; a good recent overview is David Stevenson, *The First World War and International Politics* (Oxford: Clarendon, 1988).

though Spain felt a threat from Britain and Argentina from the United States), while Fascist Italy did an eighteenth-century *volte-face* and joined them as a co-belligerent.

Even if one allows considerable room for differences of interpretation of these well-known developments, neo-realist generalizations about the repetitiveness of strategy and the prevalence of balancing in international politics do not withstand historical scrutiny.

The neo-realist answer is likely to be that regardless of all the supposed variations in unit behavior, neo-realism still explains and predicts the broad patterns of behavior and overall outcomes of international history. Hiding, transcending, and bandwagoning are all just different forms and strategies of self-help; and in the last analysis, bids for hegemony are defeated, and new balances of power do emerge. The historian's preliminary reply would be, first, to ask what serious content remains to the concept of self-help if it includes strategies so diverse and even contradictory as these. Indeed, what becomes of the structural constraints of anarchy if they are elastic enough to allow some of the behaviors involved in transcending? Second, it is far from obvious (as discussed below) that in the long run bids for hegemony always fail and new balances emerge. Finally, if these central generalizations of neo-realist theory do not hold, what use is it to the historian? What does it really explain and predict?

THE FACT OF FUNCTIONAL DIFFERENTIATION

Waltz's second generalization is that states are differentiated in the international system not by their functions but only by their power position within it. In fact, however, during every period of the Westphalian era, states of various sizes defined their place and role within the system, and were accorded status and recognition by other states, not simply according to their positions of power, even relative to other adjacent units, but also, and often mainly, on the basis of their specific functions within the system. My claim is not that the functional differentiation here alluded to, within the international system, is equivalent to what Waltz or other neo-realists mean by functional differentiation within hierarchical systems, e.g., between various offices within a domestic government, or between firms in a domestic economy. Obviously the two are not the same, in either kind or degree. Nor is this merely a general complaint that more functional differentiation of some sort has been involved in the history of international politics than neo-realism recognizes.[41] Even if true, that might be unimportant as an objection to the theory.

The issue involved is again the central one of this essay: does neo-realism adequately explain the broad outcomes and general pattern of international history? The question of functional differentiation is raised here to address this point, first, by showing that Waltz's argument—that "the domestic imperative is 'specialize!'" and "the international imperative is 'take care of yourself!'" so that "what each state does for itself is much like what all of the others are doing"[42]—is unsound even as a broad historical generalization; and second and still more important, by arguing that major outcomes and overall patterns in international history cannot be explained adequately unless one recognizes and allows for a great amount of functional differentiation of a particular kind.

To be specific: throughout the Westphalian era states both great and small, aware of their vulnerability and threats, sought survival in the international arena not only by means of strategies other than balancing (by bandwagoning, hiding, and transcending) but also, precisely, by specializing. They claimed, that is, an ability to perform certain important international functions or fill particular vital roles within the system that no other unit could do or do as well, and expected other powers to recognize these functions, to give them support or assistance, and even to accept their leadership on these functional grounds. These claims, far from being regularly dismissed as propaganda or window-dressing, were often discussed and debated. Questions of how functions and roles were assigned to individual actors within the international system, whether these roles were necessary and justified, and how well the actors were fulfilling them, became major issues in international politics (and still are), and formed the basis for many decisions and actions. Most important, they affected broad outcomes. The survival of states could depend on them: states that successfully specialized within the international system could continue to exist and prosper long after they were unable or unwilling to defend themselves, while states that failed to specialize or whose specialty lost its international relevance might be destroyed. In other words, the international imperative was not just "Take care of yourself!" but also, in a real sense, "Specialize!"; failure to specialize in the international system could equally well be punished. Furthermore,

---

41. See Buzan, Jones, and Little, *Logic of Anarchy*, pp. 131, 146, and 238–239.
42. Waltz, *Theory of International Politics*, pp. 106–107.

the durability, stability, and peaceful or bellicose character of the system of international politics in different eras could and did depend to a major degree upon whether this kind of functional differentiation between states was allowed and promoted, or was discouraged and destroyed.

To prove these assertions in detail would spring the bounds of this article, but a list of examples drawn from the first half of the nineteenth century (1815–48) will illustrate the functional differentiation posited here:

Britain, for example, claimed during this period and others to be the special holder of the European balance, protecting small states, promoting constitutional liberty, encouraging commerce, and preserving peace.

Russia claimed to be the guardian of the monarchical order in Europe, defender of all states against revolution, and protector especially of smaller states against threats or domination by other great powers.

The United Netherlands after 1815 claimed special treatment, and after 1830 Belgium claimed guaranteed neutrality, because the Low Countries served Britain and others as a barrier against French expansion, and served Austria, Prussia, and the lesser German states as a vital economic and political link connecting Britain to the Continent and Central Europe, curbing its drift toward isolation and preoccupation with its empire.

Switzerland had special functions as a neutral state under joint European guarantee, which were both strategic—to keep the passes between Germany and Italy out of any one great power's control—and broadly political—to make France, Austria, and Germany jointly responsible for a crucial area.

Denmark and Sweden undertook roles as neutrals guarding the entrance to the Baltic, thus serving everyone's commercial interests and preventing the constant struggles over the region from 1558 to 1815 from flaring up again.

The Papal State functioned as the political base for the Pope's independent reign as head of the Catholic church, which was considered vital by many states, including Protestant ones, to prevent international struggles over control of the church and religion.

The Ottoman Empire played roles both strategic—keeping the Turkish Straits and other vital areas out of great-power hands—and political—buffering against possible Austro-Russian clashes over influence in the Balkans, or Anglo-Russian conflict over the routes to India.

The smaller German powers played roles as independent states in forestalling struggles between Austria or Prussia for control of Germany, or attempts by France or Russia to dominate it from the flanks; as well as buffers and decompression zones between the absolutist East and the liberal-constitutionalist West.

Many special international functions were assigned to the German Confederation from 1815 on: regulating and controlling conflicts between individual German states, between estates and princes within individual states, between the Confederation and the individual states, between Protestants and Catholics, and between the great powers Austria and Prussia, former bitter rivals for supremacy in Germany and now required to work together to manage the Confederation.

Any historian knowledgeable in this area could extend this list. It is hard to conceive an international history of this period or any other which did not explicitly or implicitly deal with the different roles and functions filled by various units within the international system, and their effects. It is no answer to say that many of these special international functions were related to questions of security, and therefore can be considered as aspects of the states' relative power position within the structure. Of course they were often (but not always) *related* to questions of power and security. That is almost axiomatic in an international system. But this does not mean that these roles can be *reduced* to security factors and considered solely for their effects on security and the balance of power. Moreover, one can easily show in many instances that these functions and roles modified the behavior of states, including great powers, and significantly changed their purposes and methods in using power. For example, one reason Russia's conduct toward the Ottoman Empire in this period differed so strikingly from that in the previous half-century was the Russian Tsars' new self-conception as guardians of the European order and peace.[43] Britain's continental policy was powerfully influenced by its self-imposed role of advancing liberalism and constitutionalism.[44] Finally, to reduce or subordinate functional differentiation as here described to purposes of security and balance of power would be stand its meaning, purposes, and effects in international history on their heads. The basic point of making these functional claims and of differentiating roles in all eras, but above all in 1815–48, is that states and their leaders, seeing that certain problems if left unmanaged would lead to dangerous

---

43. See, for example, Barbara Jelavich, *Russia's Balkan Entanglements 1806–1914* (New York: Cambridge University Press, 1991).
44. Anselm Doering-Manteuffel, *Vom Wiener Kongress zur Pariser Konferenz. England, die deutsche Frage und das Mächtesystem 1815–1856* (Göttingen: Vandenhoeck & Ruprecht, 1991).

security issues and balance of power confrontations, used the device of functional differentiation to remove problem areas and states from power politics and balance of power competition by recognizing and sanctioning particular roles and functions for particular states. Every example of functional differentiation in the Vienna system noted above illustrates this rule. They were all, in other words, instances not of balancing but of transcending, often in a collective, consensual way.[45]

The ideal example to show that the role of a state within the international system cannot be reduced to its power position, but must include its wider systemic functions, is the Habsburg Monarchy. Since its emergence as a great power in the late seventeenth century, the Monarchy had vital security interests to protect and strategic roles to play. In the Vienna system from 1815 on it was supposed to control Italy, help check Russia and France, help preserve the Ottoman Empire, and share in the organization and leadership of the German Confederation with Prussia, all in the interests of a peaceful, independent, defensively-oriented central Europe. But besides these security-related functions, which, if one were determined to do so, could all somehow be subsumed under the protean category of "balance of power," Austria also had other roles and functions, widely recognized (though not in formal treaties) and at least as indispensable for European peace and stability as its strategic-security ones, especially as the century wore on. It was fated by its own history, geography, and ethnic composition to be an arena where the two largest ethnic groups in Europe, Germans and Slavs, met and interpenetrated, along with other peoples neither German nor Slav. Within the Monarchy, as elsewhere in Eastern Europe, different cultures, religions, and nationalities crossed, clashed, and mingled with each other, making Austria, like it or not, the main seed-bed and nursery for one of the most important developments in nineteenth-century international history: the awakening of the peoples of east-central Europe to a consciousness of their nationality and a desire for political autonomy, if not independence. Only Austria conceivably had a chance to manage that process within and without its own borders in the interest of international stability; only if Austria continued to exist as

---

45. Though this principle applies especially to 1815–48, it was never absent from other periods. For example, the long sixteenth-seventeeth century contest between Habsburg Spain and France, often seen as a straightforward struggle for hegemony, has been shown also to have been a struggle over which power was better fitted and entitled to fill the vital European functions of leading Christendom and guaranteeing peace. See, *inter alia*, Eberhard Straub, *Pax et Imperium: Spaniens Kampf um seine Friedensordnung in Europa zwischen 1617 und 1635* (Paderborn: Schöningh, 1980).

an independent state, moreover, could Europe seriously hope to avoid an eventual struggle between Teuton and Slav for control of this area, and with it the mastery of Europe. It is therefore critical to an understanding of the nineteenth-century international system and of its two most important power-political problems—the emergence of nationalities and national states, and the potential struggle between Teuton and Slav for mastery in east-central Europe—to see that the system's functioning in a real sense depended upon Austria-Hungary's filling certain special, vital functions and roles, whether it wanted to or not. The character of international politics generally, and the survival of the system, would depend very heavily on both whether Austria proved able and willing to carry out these tasks, and whether the prevailing systemic rules and principles of international conduct in various periods allowed and encouraged this functional differentiation, or instead discouraged, punished, and ultimately destroyed it. Much of nineteenth-century European international history—indeed, the heart of it—must be seen in these terms. Otherwise one cannot really understand or explain either the remarkable peacefulness of the system in 1815–48 (the real "Long Peace" of international history, in most respects far superior to the much-celebrated "Long Peace" since 1945), the wars and strains of the mid-century, or the final degeneration and collapse by 1914.[46] A theory that holds that states are differentiated within the system solely by their relative power position cannot possibly deal successfully with this history or its outcome, any more than Newtonian physics can work for quantum mechanics. This neo-realist assumption, like its view of the unchanging, repetitive nature of balance-of-power politics and outcomes throughout the ages, may make its theory of international politics simple, parsimonious, and elegant; they also make it, for the historian at least, unhistorical, unusable, and wrong.

The Neo-realist Theory of History Applied

The probable response from neo-realists will be to repeat, perhaps with weary exasperation, that predictive power rather than descriptive accuracy is the

---

46. For an elaboration of this thesis, see Paul W. Schroeder, "World War I as Galloping Gertie: A Reply to Joachim Remak," *Journal of Modern History*, Vol. 44, No. 3 (September 1972), pp. 319–344; for Austrian foreign policy, see above all F.R. Bridge, *The Habsburg Monarchy among the Great Powers, 1815–1918* (New York: Berg, 1991). For another instance of the major effects of eliminating small states and their special functions in the system, see Paul W. Schroeder, "The Lost Intermediaries: The Impact of 1870 on the European System," *International History Review*, Vol. 6, No. 1 (February 1984), pp. 1–27.

goal of theory. All these alleged attempts of states to hide, "transcend," or differentiate themselves functionally reflect unit-level differences in behavior, but do not change the essential structure in which the great powers, their power positions, and the balance of power remain decisive. The historian is free to describe the events of international politics as the detailed evidence seems to require; neo-realist theory points to its systemic structure and essential dynamics to explain and predict the broad outcomes and patterns of the story.

I have tried to show by historical argument and examples that it is precisely the broad outcomes and general patterns of international history which neo-realist theory does not explain, or even recognize. Pursuing this point further on a theoretical level could lead to a sterile debate over just how broad and general outcomes or patterns have to be in order to be captured by neo-realist theory. Instead, therefore, let us examine a particular instance in which neo-realist theory is used specifically and in fairly detailed fashion by a neo-realist to explain and predict historical outcomes and patterns which neo-realist theory itself considers vital and claims to explain by its system dynamics, and see whether this application of neo-realism can withstand historical scrutiny.

Christopher Layne's article "The Unipolar Illusion" is ideally suited to this experiment. True, his ultimate purpose in the article is to base certain predictions of the future course of international politics and prescriptions for current policy on the broad patterns and outcomes he finds and explains in history through neo-realist theory. These predictions and prescriptions, however, as well as other related ones, do not concern us here.[47] The question is solely what happens when neo-realist theory is used to explain and predict its version of the important broad outcomes and patterns in international history.

Having founded his case explicitly on standard neo-realist premises concerning the prevalence, rationale, and pervasive effects of balancing in international politics,[48] Layne sets out to demonstrate the correctness and impor-

---

47. Layne, "The Unipolar Illusion." See also, e.g., Mearsheimer, "Back to the Future"; Mearsheimer, "The Case for a Ukrainian Nuclear Deterrent," *Foreign Affairs*, Vol. 72, No. 3 (Summer 1993), pp. 50–66; Kenneth N. Waltz, "The Emerging Structure of International Politics," *International Security*, Vol. 18, No. 2 (Summer 1993), pp. 44–79.

48. Some characteristic assertions are that "states balance against hegemons," even would-be benevolent ones like the United States; that "in international politics, overwhelming power repels and leads other states to balance against it"; that balancing is done "to correct a skewed distribution of relative power in the international system"; and that it "has especially strong

tance of a particular prediction of structural realism, namely, that whenever a dominant or hegemonic power emerges at particular times, producing a "unipolar system," tight systemic constraints lead weaker states to balance against that power and "eligible" states to become great powers in response. The historical part of the article is devoted to showing how the emergence of new great powers in two eras, 1660–1713 and 1860–1910, represented "a response to unipolarity" and "an eligible state's adjustment to the international system's structural constraints" (pp. 16 and 20), and thus confirm neo-realist predictions. The system dynamics of neo-realist theory, he insists, directly produce broad historical effects:

The rise of England and Habsburg Austria—that is, the international system's transformation from unipolarity to multipolarity—is directly traceable to anarchy and its consequences: the sameness effect and balancing. Because French dominance threatened their security and autonomy, England and Austria responded by: (1) organizing the Grand Alliances that, in the Nine Years' War and the War of the Spanish Succession, sought to contain France and counter its power; and (2) reorganizing themselves administratively, militarily, and economically to acquire great power capabilities comparable to France's (p. 18).

He further claims that in 1860–1910 Germany in a similar fashion, and the United States and Japan in a slightly different but equally "structurally determined" way (p. 23) became great powers in imitation of and response to Britain's hegemony (pp. 20–31). He concludes, therefore, that: "The historical evidence from 1660–1714 and 1860–1914 strongly supports the hypothesis derived from neo-realist theory: unipolar moments cause geopolitical backlashes that lead to multipolarity" (p. 32).

Both the thesis, widely held by neo-realists, and the claim that the historical record confirms it are admirably clear. Since the periods covered are extensive, the historical problems complex, and the literature massive, my attempt to test these claims here must be highly compressed and oversimplified. Yet enough can be offered to justify a conclusion.

Historians might raise serious objections to characterizing France's situation in 1660 as a "unipolar moment" in a sense comparable to that of the United States today, as Layne does. The reasons are numerous: France's

---

explanatory power in accounting for the facts that unipolarity tends to be short-lived and that would-be hegemons *invariably* fail to achieve lasting dominance." Layne, "The Unipolar Illusion," pp. 7–12.

reach was limited to western and northwestern Europe; it was unable to control the struggles in northern Europe, the Baltic, and southeastern Europe; France's naval, commercial, and colonial position, while important, was never dominant; some of its frontiers were not secure, especially in the north and east; even its wealth was great only in comparison to the extreme poverty of most states and princes.[49] Neither France nor any other seventeenth-century state could achieve any stable alliances or spheres of influence.[50] Basically, therefore, France was dominant only where it could bring its superior army to bear, and that was not very far, or in many places at once, a fact crucial in the outcome.[51]

Yet if Layne's "unipolar moment" thesis is debatable, historians would nonetheless agree that France was the most powerful state in Europe in 1660, that it may have had a chance for peaceful hegemony in the West (at least two of Louis's foreign ministers urged him to seek this instead of conquests), and that Louis XIV clearly lost this chance and temporarily exhausted France in a series of wars from 1667 to 1714. This outcome, Layne claims, is predicted by neo-realist theory, and resulted from systemic constraints that led weaker powers, especially England and Austria, under the threat of French hegemony and the imperatives of balance of power politics, to respond by imitating or adapting French institutions, developing their own power, and

---

49. France in 1660 had just emerged from a century of religious, civil, and international wars which it had often barely survived, and was not so much powerful in its own right as by virtue of the weakness, decline, and undeveloped state of almost all the other powers, at a time when the European international system was still being formed and hardly represented a single system at all. Much modern modern scholarship emphasizes the limits of the actual power and reach of most early modern states, their narrow military and fiscal resources, and their vulnerability to internal revolt and external attack and subversion. Some major works are Richard Bonney, *Political Change in France under Richelieu and Mazarin* (New York: Oxford University Press, 1977); Brian M. Downing, *The Military Revolution and Political Change* (Princeton, N.J.: Princeton University Press, 1991); Pierre Goubert, *Mazarin* (Paris: Fayard, 1990); David Parker, *The Making of French Absolutism* (London: Edward Arnold, 1983); Perez Zagorin, *Rebels and Rulers, 1500–1660*, 2 vols. (Cambridge: Cambridge University Press, 1982); Fritz Redlich, *The German Military Enterpriser and His Work Force*, 2 vols. (Wiesbaden: F. Steiner, 1964); André Corvisier, *Armies and Societies in Europe, 1494–1789* (Bloomington: Indiana University Press, 1979); Corvisier, *La France de Louis XIV, 1643–1715* (Paris: SEDES, 1979); and G.N. Clark, *War and Society in the Seventeenth Century* (Cambridge: Cambridge University Press, 1958).
50. For good discussions of the possibilities and limits of foreign policy in that age, see Heinz Duchhardt, ed., *Rahmenbedingungen und Handlungsspielräume europäischer Aussenpolitik im Zeitalter Ludwigs XIV* (Berlin: Duncker and Humblot, 1991); Johannes Kunisch, ed., *Expansion und Gleichgewicht* (Berlin: Duncker and Humblot, 1986).
51. For example, in the various wars of Louis XIV France could not conquer the flooded Dutch heartland, nor hold onto the German Rhineland while campaigning in the Netherlands, nor defend its own frontiers while providing enough help to its Spanish and German allies, nor sustain its ally Sweden against Brandenburg.

balancing against France to create a new multipolar balance of power. Does this broad interpretation fit the facts of history?

THE RESPONSE TO FRENCH HEGEMONY, 1660–1713

The only enemy of France and "balancer" against it in 1660 was Habsburg Spain, which had been finally defeated and exhausted by France in a long series of wars ending in the Peace of the Pyrenees in 1659. Louis XIV's first target, for reasons of military glory, prestige and status, and security, was the Spanish Netherlands (Belgium). The King's program of expansion in the Low Countries directly endangered the Dutch Republic (curiously omitted from Layne's account, although it is central to the whole story) and would ultimately threaten England. Neo-realist theory therefore would predict that England and the Dutch would join with Spain to contain France, especially when Louis attacked the Spanish Netherlands in the War of Devolution in 1667–68. Nothing of the sort occurred. Instead, Charles II of England, having earlier tried unsuccessfully for a marriage and subsidy alliance with Spain for dynastic reasons, allied with France and launched a war against the Dutch Republic in 1664 in order to destroy Dutch commerce. The Dutch, led by the Amsterdam-centered republican (i.e., anti-Orangist Stadholder) party and its leader Johan De Witt, while fighting the English, negotiated with their old allies, the French, for a deal in which each would take part of the Spanish Netherlands while preserving a portion as a joint buffer state. This Dutch effort at security by bandwagoning with France failed, at the same time the English naval war against the Dutch turned sour, leading Britain and the Netherlands to end their war in 1667 and negotiate a Triple Alliance with Sweden, ostensibly to defend Spain from France. This apparent balancing against France, however, was deceptive; both powers never intended to defend Spain but rather to make Spain subsidize Sweden (which it finally did), while they used their alliance to induce France to make a mutually profitable deal with them at Spain's expense. Hence in this first decade of Louis's rule everybody except Spain, which as victim and loser had no choice, bandwagoned with France and increased the French hegemonic threat.[52]

---

52. For general surveys, see Derek McKay and H.M. Scott, *The Rise of the Great Powers 1648–1815* (London: Longman, 1982); and Gaston Zeller, *Les Temps Modernes*, 2 vols. (Paris: Hachette, 1953–55); for France, Louis André, *Louis XIV et l'Europe* (Paris: Michel, 1950); for England, Keith G. Feiling, *British Foreign Policy 1660–1672* (London: F. Cass, 1968 [original ed., 1930]), and G.M.D. Howat, *Stuart and Cromwellian Foreign Policy* (New York: St. Martin's, 1974); for the Dutch Republic, Herbert H. Rowen, *Johan de Witt: Statesman of the "True Freedom"* (Cambridge:

This pattern continued. In 1670, with Louis bent on further expansion into the Netherlands, Charles II of England signed the secret Treaty of Dover committing England to a joint war with the French against the Dutch; England joined the French in the attack on the Dutch in 1672. The Dutch Republic under De Witt, having tried unsuccessfully to appease France by proposing an alliance and a favorable deal on the Spanish Netherlands, faced virtual collapse in mid-1672 under the sudden French onslaught, and offered France peace on very favorable terms (more appeasement). Louis's foreign minister urged him to accept, but the king, following his own instincts and his war minister's advice, chose military conquest over a glorious hegemonic peace. The Dutch, left no choice but to fight on, resorted to desperate measures, cutting the dikes to stop the French army, and assassinating De Witt and restoring the Stadholderate under William of Orange. This resistance, combined with other factors (Louis's indecision in prosecuting and concluding the war he had started, French threats to Germany which brought in the German Empire, Dutch victories at sea, and English war-weariness[53]) made the war drag on to a decisive but not total French victory and peace at Nijmegen in 1679.[54] If Louis's gains, as a result, fell short of his aims, this was neither the result of a balancing policy by weaker powers, nor an encouragement to them to balance in the future. Stephen B. Baxter, William's biographer, argues just the opposite: that in effect the war had discredited balancing and promoted bandwagoning and hiding by proving that "an alliance could not fight on equal terms with a single great power." In con-

Cambridge University Press, 1986); for Spain, R.A. Stradling, *Europe and the Decline of Spain: A Study of the Spanish System 1580–1720* (London: Allen and Unwin, 1981). For an introduction to the literature for the whole early modern period, see two indispensable works by Heinz Duchhardt, *Gleichgewicht der Kräfte, Convenance, europäisches Konzert: Friedenskongresse und Friedensschlüsse vom Zeitalter Ludwigs XIV bis zum Wiener Kongress* (Darmstadt: Wissenschaftliche Buchgesellschaft, 1976); and *Altes Reich und europäische Staatenwelt 1648–1806* (Munich: R. Oldenbourg, 1988).

53. The English Parliament and political elite opposed the war and the French alliance, it is worth noting, not for balance of power reasons, but for the more powerful and typical seventeenth century reasons of religion, taxes, and commerce. Not only was the war costing money and hurting English trade, but the French alliance and Louis's subsidies to Charles, they rightly suspected, were intended to return England to the Catholic church.

54. In addition to the sources in note 50, see Herbert H. Rowen, *The Ambassador Prepares for War: The Dutch Embassy of Arnauld de Pomponne, 1669–1672* (The Hague: M. Nijhoff, 1957); Paul G. Sonnino, *Louis XIV and the Origins of the Dutch War* (New York: Cambridge University Press, 1988); Carl J. Ekberg, *The Failure of Louis XIV's Dutch War* (Chapel Hill, N.C.: University of North Carolina Press, 1979); P. Höynek, *Frankreich und seine Gegner auf dem Nymwegener Friedenskongress* (Bonn: Röhrscheid, 1960); and K.H.D. Haley, *An English Diplomat in the Low Countries: Sir William Temple and John De Witt, 1665–1672* (New York: Clarendon Press, 1986).

sequence, he writes, "In the years after the conclusion of the treaties of Nijmegen, alliances, or 'social war' as it was called at the time, were at a steep discount. Social war had failed. Almost every individual state in Europe would find it advantageous to make its own terms with the enemy and to hope for the best."

What prevented hiding and bandwagoning, or appeasement, from working, as Baxter points out, was that in the long run two particular groups "could never hope to make a private arrangement with Louis XIV": first, Habsburg Spain and Austria, directly attacked or threatened by French expansion in the Netherlands, Spain, Italy, and the Empire; and second, the sea powers England and the Dutch Republic, also threatened on land, at sea, and commercially. Nonetheless, leaders in these countries, including William of Orange, the main spokesman for a balance of power, still tried for deals with Louis.[55] States, in other words, did not balance against France as a response to French hegemony in accordance with the constraints of structural anarchy. Rather, they tried to hide or bandwagon, and failed because France would not let their efforts succeed; they resisted because France kept on attacking them.[56]

But perhaps this changed from 1688 to 1714, when, according to Layne, England and Austria organized alliances "to contain France and counter its power," and "the English King William III" set out to maintain "England's security by establishing a balance of power to preserve 'the peace, liberties, and well-being of Europe'" (p. 18).

The first observation is that the "English King William III" was not English but Dutch, had been Dutch Stadholder since 1672, and became English King in 1689 only by exploiting (indeed, promoting) a revolution in Britain which originated not in foreign policy or the European balance of power, but in religion and domestic politics. Had not William III become king of England through a successful invasion and conquest of England with his Dutch

---

55. Stephen M. Baxter, *William III and the Defense of European Liberty 1650–1702* (New York: Harcourt, Brace, and World, 1966), p. 160.

56. Louis's reasons for doing this (or, for that matter, the motives of leaders of other eras for making supposed bids for hegemony) do not concern us here. I would insist only that these reasons, like the nature of the bids themselves, are contingent historical variables, very different in different times and circumstances, and must be explained from historical evidence, not by an overarching theory. If neo-realists wish to claim credit for predicting and explaining the phenomenon described here, namely, that states faced with mortal threats, having failed to avert them by any other means, generally choose to resist if they possibly can rather than simply submit, I have no objection.

army,[57] England would never have balanced against France. The legitimate Stuart King James II whom William overthrew depended upon Louis to support and subsidize him in his religious-political struggle with Parliament and the Church of England.[58] William III's reasons for taking England into the Nine Years' War on the continent (1688–97), moreover, were strictly Dutch; saving "the European balance of power" was a way of saving the Dutch state and its way of life, including its religion. In England this European aspect of the war, in particular the alliance with the Dutch who were still England's main trade rivals, was unpopular. What made the Nine Years' War necessary and popular in England was its connection with the Glorious Revolution (i.e., the victory of Parliament, the aristocracy, and the Anglican church over James) and William's conquest of Ireland. In this war (which historian Mark A. Thomson calls "The War of the English Succession"[59]) and the next as well, the primary British motive would be domestic, not international—to defend the Glorious Revolution and its subsequent ecclesiastical, political, and property establishments in England, Ireland, and Scotland (joined to England in 1707) against James and his supporter Louis.

Layne's interpretation of Austria's emergence as a great power in the late seventeenth and early eighteenth centuries as a response to France's hegemonic threat fits the facts no better. First, Austria's expansion was not "also" (as Layne has it) but primarily, and overwhelmingly, directed to the southeast against the Ottoman Empire, and it was a largely unexpected, contingent development following almost two centuries of defense against the Ottoman threat. This southeastern expansion, moreover, tended to turn Austria away from its long-standing contest with France, which was partly a continuation

---

57. At the last minute, he secured an invitation to come from English leaders who were hostile to James II's plans for full toleration of Catholicism and fearful that the Stuart dynasty would be perpetuated, but he had decided on and planned the invasion before the invitation, and Dutch, Danish, and Huguenot troops, not English, finally defeated James's forces at the Battle of the Boyne in 1690. See Jonathan Israel, "The Dutch Role in the Glorious Revolution," in Jonathan Israel, ed., *The Anglo-Dutch Moment: Essays on the Glorious Revolution and its World Impact* (Cambridge: Cambridge University Press, 1991), pp. 105–162; John Carswell, *The Descent Upon England* (London: Barrie and Rockliff, 1969).
58. Clyde L. Grose, "Louis XIV's Financial Relations with Charles II and the English Parliament," *Journal of Modern History*, Vol. 1, No. 22 (June 1929), pp. 177–204.
59. For more on these developments and facts, most of them well known, see: Baxter, *William III*; Stephen M. Baxter, ed., *England's Rise to Greatness 1660–1763* (Berkeley: University of California Press, 1983); Ragnhild M. Hatton, *Studies in Diplomatic History* (Harlow, U.K.: Longman, 1970); Ragnhild M. Hatton and J.S. Bromley, eds., *William III and Louis XIV: Essays by and for the Late Mark A. Thomson* (Liverpool: University of Liverpool Press, 1968); and W.A. Speck, *Reluctant Revolutionaries: Englishmen and the Revolution of 1688* (New York: Oxford University Press, 1988).

of the traditional Habsburg-Valois and Habsburg-Bourbon rivalries, mainly a result of the French threat to Austria's southwest German lands and its historic role as leader and protector of the Holy Roman Empire. Austria's Emperor Leopold I (1658–1705), though certainly anti-French, was, like most Habsburg monarchs, reluctant to fight France for the sake of other German princes or the German Empire, much less for the sake of the European balance of power. He had not tried to break up the French-led League of the Rhine, formed by Cardinal Mazarin in 1658, which constituted a kind of French protectorate in west and southwest Germany; in 1668 he had concluded a secret alliance with Louis to divide Spain's possessions in Europe upon the expected death of King Carlos II without issue (a clear instance of bandwagoning). Leopold's main aim, like that of his great commander Prince Eugene of Savoy, was to expand his hereditary domain into a solid central and southeastern European great power which would be essentially independent of the Reich and its burdens; this policy was no help to the threatened German princes or the balance of power on the Rhine.

What pulled Austria first into the League of Augsburg in 1686 (a league designed to deter France rather than drive it back), and then into the Nine Years' War, was once more unrelenting French aggression: a program of territorial expansion at German expense in the Rhineland (the "réunions"); Louis's alliance with the Turks and aid to them against Austria; his revocation of the Edict of Nantes and expulsion of the Huguenots, arousing fear and anger among the Protestant estates in the German Empire; and finally, when war broke out, French scorched-earth warfare in the Rhineland. These gave the Habsburgs no choice but to fight if they wished to save their traditional position in Germany and their elective German Emperorship.[60] It makes more sense to say that Louis was balancing against Austria and its gains in the East than the other way around.[61]

True, the Nine Years' War ended more or less in a draw and the Treaty of Rijswijk seemed to establish a rough equivalence of power in western Europe, an outcome which, though really contingent and unintended, might be as-

---

60. Louis in fact aspired to take the emperorship away from the Habsburgs, and had considered campaigning for the election in 1658.
61. In addition to the sources in fn. 50, see Charles W. Ingrao, *In Quest and Crisis: Emperor Joseph I and the Hapsburg Monarchy* (West Lafayette, Ind.: Purdue University Press, 1979); Oswald Redlich, *Das Werden einer Grossmacht, Österreich von 1700 bis 1740*, 2d ed. (Brünn: R.M. Rohrer, 1942); Max Braubach, *Prinz Eugen von Savoyen*, 5 vols. (Munich: R. Oldenbourg, 1963–65); Derek McKay, *Prince Eugene of Savoy* (London: Thames and Hudson, 1977); Andrew Lossky, *Louis XIV, William III, and the Baltic Crisis of 1683* (Berkeley: University of California Press, 1954).

cribed by realists to balancing. But neo-realist theory would then predict that following this peace England, Austria, and the Dutch Republic, especially under William III's leadership, would carefully maintain their alliance and the hard-won balance against France, still easily the strongest land power. This, however, did not happen. Instead, William promptly made a deal with Louis XIV to divide the Spanish inheritance after the death of Carlos II, then imminent—a deal which advanced British commercial and imperial interests and protected Dutch ones, but shut Austria out of the negotiations and would have greatly enhanced French power on the Continent. When Leopold, naturally, rejected the agreement and, more important, so did the Spaniards whose possessions were to be divided, this agreement between two dominant powers at the expense of weaker ones broke down, and war ensued between France and Austria over the Spanish inheritance. Neo-realist theory would predict that the British and Dutch would promptly rally to Austria's side to prevent France from establishing its hegemony by defeating the Austrians, who were weaker, poorer, and distracted by the Ottoman threat and their troubles in recently conquered Hungary. Instead the British government, including William III, showed every intention of staying out of the fight, entering the war along with the Dutch only after Louis seemed deliberately to provoke them into it. Not only did he accept the whole Spanish inheritance for his grandson Philip as Philip V of Spain, but he supported Philip's rights to succeed to the French throne as well, and above all he endorsed the claim of James III to the throne of England, making the War of the Spanish Succession one of the English succession as well. The question of why Louis forced England into the war remains open, though it has many plausible answers.[62] One theory of the war's origins that is not plausible or even tenable, however, is the one expounded by Layne and predicted by neo-realist theory: that it was an Anglo-Austrian response to French hegemony for preserving the European balance of power.[63]

---

62. Louis's most important motives (although many entered in), were probably pride, honor, and monarchical principle. He genuinely believed in his right to preeminence in Europe, and still more in his and his grandson Philip's proprietary rights to the French and Spanish thrones, and felt he would compromise his own legitimacy by yielding on them. See Herbert H. Rowen, *The King's State: Proprietary Dynasticism in Early Modern France* (New Brunswick, N.J.: Rutgers University Press, 1980). At the same time, he had important security concerns and territorial and dynastic ambitions, and probably considered that it would prove impossible to limit the war anyway. In other words, the general chaos and unpredictability of seventeenth century international politics promoted a policy of *va banque*.

63. The old standard work on the origins of the war is Arsène Legrelle, *La diplomatie française et la Succession d'Espagne*, 4 vols. (Ghent: F. Dulle and L. Plus, 1888–92). See also, in addition to

The conduct and diplomacy of the war confirm neo-realist predictions no better. It is true that Britain committed itself more fully to this war on the Continent than to any other between the Hundred Years' War and the First World War. But again, contingent developments rather than concern for the balance of power caused this, including the political and military leadership of the Duke of Marlborough, the support given him for religious and personal reasons by Queen Anne and for political ones by his Whig colleagues, and the remarkable military success of his collaboration with Prince Eugene. Despite British victories, the unpopularity of continental war and continental allies grew in England as the war went on and its costs and losses mounted. Balance of power, although a good slogan, was always less important in war aims than the domestic factional struggle for power, religious-dynastic concerns, and imperial, colonial, and commercial gains, acquired at the expense more of the Spaniards and the Dutch than of France. When France, defeated and nearing exhaustion, sought peace in 1708 and after, the Whigs insisted on total victory instead, demanding that Louis not only accept great sacrifices himself (to which he consented) but also help overthrow his grandson Philip V in Spain in favor of the Austrian claimant Archduke Charles. This extreme program, designed partly to help the Whigs stay in power at home against the Tories, but mainly to enable the British and the Dutch to extort commercial concessions in the Spanish Empire from Charles, was maintained by the Whigs even in 1711 when the Archduke became Emperor Charles VI, though this would mean a union of the thrones of Austria and Spain that would menace the European balance almost as much as a union of the French and Spanish crowns would. The Tories, on the other hand, came to power in Britain by exploiting the widespread British eagerness to end the war, and in order to do so deliberately betrayed their Dutch and Austrian allies in negotiations and on the battlefield. Their defection enabled France to recover and defeat its other enemies, so that the Peace of Utrecht-Rastadt left France intact and Philip V ruling in Spain. In other words, the British allowed France to consolidate its supremacy in Western Europe and to end the long-standing

---

works mentioned above, C.V. Picavet, *La diplomatie française au temps de Louis XIV, 1661–1715* (Paris: F. Alcan, 1930); W.J. Roosen, *The Age of Louis XIV: The Rise of Modern Diplomacy* (Cambridge, Mass.: Schenkman, 1976); John C. Rule, ed., *Louis XIV and the Craft of Kingship* (Columbus: Ohio State University Press, 1970); John B. Wolf, *Toward a European Balance of Power, 1620–1715* (Chicago: Rand McNally, 1970); John B. Wolf, *Louis XIV* (New York: Norton, 1968); Alfred Coville and H.W.V. Temperley, eds., *Studies in Anglo-French History during the Eighteenth, Nineteenth, and Twentieth Centuries* (Cambridge: Cambridge University Press, 1935); and François Bluche, *Louis XIV* (Paris: Fayard, 1986).

threat from Spain, for the sake of English naval and overseas supremacy and colonial gains. The Dutch, once William III died in 1702, concentrated primarily on escaping from further war and the destruction of their commercial prosperity, seeking security by getting England to guarantee them a barrier system in the southern Netherlands to be paid for and defended, against its will, by Austria. This policy, carried through by Anglo-Dutch pressure on Austria, enabled the Dutch to hide and to pass the buck at the same time. Austria, despite some gains in the settlement, soon lost the precarious power and security it had gained.[64]

The obvious neo-realist reply would be that regardless of the particular motivations and policies of individual statesmen and units, the broad outcome was what neo-realist theory predicts: France's hegemony was overthrown, and new great powers and a balance of power emerged. To this there are some immediate responses, as well as a further one which is introduced below. First, neo-realist theory, and Layne's argument, do not represent these broad outcomes as the generic results of a general free-for-all scramble in international politics, but as the specific results of systemic constraints derived from structural anarchy leading states to particular kinds of international conduct, especially balancing. The facts refute this view. A theory, to be valid, needs not merely to predict a general outcome, but to explain its development and etiology, which neo-realist theory here proposes to do and fails. Second, this description of the overall outcome from 1660 to 1721 (hegemony overthrown and new great powers and a new balance emerging), examined historically, proves equally unsatisfactory. It ignores some important results of the struggle in Western Europe, and all of them in the rest of Europe and much of the rest of the world. There was another great contest in Europe from 1660 to 1721, never mentioned by Layne: a series of wars involving Russia, Sweden, Denmark, Prussia, Poland, Hanover, other smaller German states, and the Empire, over territorial and commercial domination of the Baltic regions. Its climax came in the Great Northern War of 1700–21, which involved bids for hegemony even clearer than

---

64. In addition to works cited earlier, see Edward Gregg, *The Protestant Succession in International Politics 1710–1716* (New York: Garland, 1986); Gregg, *Queen Anne* (London: Routledge Kegan Paul, 1980); Ragnhild M. Hatton, *George I, Elector and King* (Cambridge, Mass.: Harvard University Press, 1978); Douglas Coombs, *The Conduct of the Dutch: British Opinion and the Dutch Alliance during the War of the Spanish Succession* (The Hague: M. Nijhoff, 1958); Roderick Geikie, *The Dutch Barrier, 1705–1719* (Cambridge: Cambridge University Press, 1930; and A.C. Carter, *Neutrality and Commitment: The Evolution of Dutch Foreign Policy, 1667–1795* (London: E. Arnold, 1975).

Louis XIV's and struggles for survival even more dramatic than Holland's.[65] The outcome of these wars was not a new multipolar balance of power in northern Europe, but the emergence of a new hegemony, that of Russia—a hegemony, moreover, which defied neo-realist predictions by enduring and expanding to embrace much of eastern, central, and southeastern Europe, despite challenges, for about 150 years into the latter nineteenth century.[66] This Great Northern War further defies neo-realist predictions about balancing and bandwagoning by smaller powers. After the army of Charles XII of Sweden was destroyed by Tsar Peter the Great's forces at Poltava in 1709, all the smaller states involved in the contest saw Russia as a new hegemonic threat and feared it. Nonetheless, they bandwagoned with it against Sweden, partly out of this fear of Russia, mainly to gain their share of the Swedish empire or prevent other rivals from getting more than they.

While ignoring what happened in northern and eastern Europe, the neo-realist analysis also distorts results in the West, where in fact another hegemony emerged to replace France's, that of Britain. Britain's world-wide maritime, colonial, and commercial hegemony was founded in 1688–1715, both by the defeat of France and by the exhaustion of the Dutch and weakening of Spain, and it endured into the twentieth century.[67] Moreover this outcome—British colonial, maritime, and commercial paramountcy—can much better be defended as the real British motivation and goal, rather than the concern for the "balance of power" and "liberties of Europe" which Layne

---

65. Some English, German, and French works on the Northern Question are: for its origins, Walter Kirchner, *The Rise of the Baltic Question* (Newark: University of Delaware Press, 1954); for a convenient survey, Jill Lisk, *The Struggle for Supremacy in the Baltic 1660–1725* (London: University of London Press, 1967); on Sweden, Ragnhild M. Hatton, *Charles XII of Sweden* (London: Weidenfeld and Nicolson, 1968); Michael Roberts, *The Swedish Imperial Experience, 1560–1718* (New York: Cambridge University Press, 1979); Michael Roberts, *From Oxenstierna to Charles XII: Four Studies in Swedish History* (Cambridge: Cambridge University Press, 1991); and Claude Nordmann, *Grandeur et liberté de la Suède (1660–1792)* (Paris: Béatrice-Nauwelaerts, 1971). For Russia, see M.S. Anderson, *Peter the Great* (London: Thames and Hudson, 1978); Klaus Zernack, *Studien zu den schwedisch-russischen Beziehungen in der 2. Hälfte des 17. Jahrhunderts* (Giessen: W. Schmitz, 1958); and Walther Mediger, *Mecklenburg, Russland und England-Hannover 1706–1721*, 2 vols. (Hildesheim: Lax, 1967). For the Anglo-Hanoverian involvement, see also Hatton, *George I*; and John J. Murray, *George I, the Baltic and the Whig Split of 1717* (London: Routledge Kegan Paul, 1969).

66. For Russia's use of its hegemonic position and its further rise in power, see especially Walther Mediger, *Moskaus Weg nach Europa. Der Aufstieg Russlands zum europäischen Machtstaat im Zeitalter Friedrichs des Grossen* (Braunschweig: G. Westermann, 1952).

67. The title of Vol. 6 of the *New Cambridge Modern History* thus aptly describes the real results of this era for the international system: J.S. Bromley, ed., *The Rise of Great Britain and Russia, 1688–1715/25* (Cambridge: Cambridge University Press, 1970).

cites and about which British leaders talked. The Peace of Utrecht was deliberately designed to gain Britain vital advantages overseas while freeing it
from continental commitments and forcing others (especially Austria) to bear
the burden of containing France in Europe. British policy after 1714 fits the
same pattern: alliance with France to force the terms of Utrecht on a resentful
Austria and a rebellious Spain; friction with the Dutch who were still allies
but now a burden; pleasure at the emergence of Prussia and Russia as
possible substitutes for Austria in checking France; and serious quarrels with
Austria which nearly led to war because Austria resisted the burden of
defending Holland, resented the terms of Utrecht and, worst of all, tried to
become a commercial rival to Britain.[68] For the English the phrase "balance
of power," when it was not a substitute for thought, regularly meant nothing
more than any arrangement whereby France or any other power that might
threaten or compete with Britain would be checked by the exertions of others
at their own expense, allowing Britain to concentrate on trade and empire.
The real British definition of a "balance of power" thus becomes a system
enabling Britain to enjoy hegemony and pass its costs to others.[69] This is no
criticism of British policy: Britain was simply more successful than most in
achieving what everyone sought under the rubric of "balance of power,"
some kind of free security, advantage, or domination for themselves. It does,
however, have major implications for neo-realism or any theory which regards the balance of power as either a prime motive or a predictable outcome
of international politics.

Hence a summary of the broad outcome of international competition in
1660–1720 would read as follows: a French bid for Western European hegemony, serious but local and never all-out, was defeated for a time. A serious
and all-out but unrealistic Swedish bid for North European hegemony was
crushed, never to be seriously revived.[70] One new but very marginal and
insecure great power (Austria) emerged.[71] One former great power, Spain,

---

68. See especially Jeremy Black, *British Foreign Policy in the Age of Walpole* (Edinburgh: John
Donald, 1983); Derek McKay, *Allies of Convenience: Diplomatic Relations between Great Britain and
Austria, 1714–1719* (New York: Garland, 1986).
69. For an explicit recognition of this fact, and an excellent account of how the concept worked
after 1763, see H.M. Scott, *British Foreign Policy in the Age of the American Revolution* (Oxford:
Clarendon Press, 1990).
70. On Swedish policy after Charles XII's death, see Michael Roberts, *The Age of Liberty: Sweden,
1719–1772* (Cambridge: Cambridge University Press, 1986).
71. Charles Ingrao, *In Quest and Crisis*, makes the relative insecurity and weakness of Austria
the key to its rise as a great power, in a comment equally acute as an analysis of Austria's
position and, unwittingly, as a refutation of Layne's: "After examining the path of the Habsburg

was reduced still further. One state, the Dutch Republic, which enjoyed great power status at the beginning of the period, was exhausted and driven from the great power game. Numerous lesser powers either rose (e.g., Prussia and Savoy-Piedmont) or fell (e.g., Denmark and Poland). Above all, two great powers achieved positions of important, durable, profitable, and dangerous hegemony, and were set on the road to world power. This is not the sort of result neo-realist theory either predicts or explains.[72]

As for Layne's argument that Britain and Austria deliberately acted to increase their power in response to French hegemony by transforming their state machinery, economies, military establishments, and other instruments of power, in some instances in imitation of French models, two comments are in order. First, it is not persuasive to attempt to explain broad, deeply rooted, organic trends and developments in early modern Europe—such as the formation and expansion of bureaucratic-absolutist states, the centralization of governmental authority, and the development of standing armies or navies and the taxes and administrative machinery to support them, or the growth of the British mercantile economy and banking system—as results of, or responses to, specific threats or needs in international politics. Of course these developments in various states (not just Britain and Austria) were in many ways responses to problems and opportunities they faced both at home and in the world around them. Of course war, domestic and international insecurity, and international competition had a good deal to do with them. But to make the dynamics of the international system, or a particular crisis in it, in some sense the prime mover or a direct cause of these processes is an extreme form of the old, discredited principle of the primacy of foreign policy which not even its nineteenth-century exponents such as Leopold von Ranke would have defended.

Monarchy's internal development and foreign policy during the last quarter of the seventeenth and first half of the eighteenth century, one is tempted to conclude that its fundamental strength and reason for success lay in its very weakness as a military power. While not posing a threat to the balance of power or even to its own neighbors, the Habsburg Monarchy was between 1681 and 1720 the principal beneficiary of a series of coalitions aimed against France and Turkey. With the ultimate defeat of these two powers, however, it ceased to benefit from the dynamics of balance of power war and diplomacy and entered upon a period of diplomatic insecurity and isolation." Ibid., p. 1.

72. This answers, incidentally, the possible argument that even if balancing is not a conscious policy induced by the dynamics of anarchy and the requirements of self-help, at least a kind of Smithian "invisible hand" mechanism produced balance out of the egoistic international power struggle. The reply is clear: the outcome was not balanced. Any balance reached in western and central Europe served to promote hegemony in other wider spheres, making possible the emergence of Britain, Russia, and later the United States as world powers.

Second, the argument is not factually sound. Britain, as already noted, built itself up commercially more against the Dutch than against France.[73] Amsterdam, not Paris, was the great competitor to be overtaken in trade and finance.[74] As for Austria, it carried out little internal reform and transformation at this time, and when later in the eighteenth century it did, it was responding to a challenge from Prussia, not France.[75]

BRITISH HEGEMONY AND THE RISE OF NEW POWERS, 1860–1910

Layne's second instance of a "unipolar moment," Britain in 1860, offers less of a case to answer. First, Britain at that time did not enjoy anything comparable to the current dominant position of the United States in the international system. For four decades after 1815, Britain enjoyed a certain kind of leadership in Europe, along with its wider maritime, commercial, and colonial lead.[76] During that period of half-hegemony, however, no European power tried seriously to balance against Britain, not even its supposed rivals France and Russia; all bandwagoned, seeking Britain's alliance and partnership, again a problem for neo-realist theory. And in any case, by 1860 things had changed. It is hard to find two decades in British history from 1688 to 1945 in which it exerted less influence in Europe or control over the international system than 1855 to 1875.[77] All the major developments of these decades in European politics, and some in world politics, were ones which Britain either failed to control or simply observed without important participation: the Peace of Paris after the Crimean War; the liberation and beginnings of national unification of the Danubian Principalities (Rumania); the unification of Italy; the building of the Suez Canal by Egypt under French guidance; Russia's completion of its conquest of the Caucasus and steady penetration into Central Asia and toward India's Northwest Frontier; huge Russian gains in China; French annexation of Nice and Savoy, ruining the Anglo-French alliance and producing a semi-serious war and invasion scare;

---

73. See, for example, Charles H. Wilson, *Profit and Power: A Study of England and the Dutch Wars* (London: Longmans Green, 1957).
74. For the story, especially from the Dutch side, see Jonathan H. Israel, *Dutch Primacy in World Trade, 1585–1740* (Oxford: Clarendon Press, 1989).
75. See especially Ingrao, *In Quest and Crisis.*
76. For example by Robert Gilpin, *Political Economy of International Relations,* and in a different way by Schroeder, "Did the Vienna Settlement Rest on a Balance of Power?" *American Historical Review,* Vol. 97, No. 3 (June 1992), pp. 683–706, 733–735.
77. The only competitor would be 1763–83, and that could be seen as a trough following the unsustainable peak of victory in the Seven Years' War. See Scott, *British Foreign Policy.*

Austro-Prussian conquest of Britain's client Denmark, despite British diplomatic intervention; serious troubles with the United States over the American
Civil War; an Austro-Prussian war destroying the German Confederation,
ousting Austria from Germany, redrawing the map of Central Europe, and
drastically changing the balance of power; a Franco-German war in 1870
which Britain tried half-heartedly to prevent, and which further revolution-
ized the European system; Russia's repudiation of the Black Sea clause of
the Peace of Paris; and the isolation of France in Europe and the renewal of
Austro-German-Russian ties in the Three Emperors' League after 1871. Only
in 1875 was Britain aroused from its international torpor by a new Franco-
German war scare, the fiscal collapse of Egypt raising the question of control
of the Suez Canal, and a new crisis and danger of Russian expansion in the
Balkans.[78] No historian recognizes this period as a British "unipolar moment";
the question is how to explain Britain's isolation and apathy in international
politics.[79]

   None of this, of course, represented serious defeats or losses for Britain or
undermined its world position (though many British were remarkably insou-
ciant about the long-range effects of Bismarck's revolutionizing of the European system). Britain's power, prosperity, and security rested on its insular
position, naval supremacy, industrial and commercial preeminence, fiscal
strength, and an unchallenged and inexpensive paramountcy in many areas
of the world, all largely shielded from the ups-and-downs of European
international politics. It would last so long as these foundations remained
sound (which, to be sure, they did not for very long after 1870). Still, Britain
cannot be termed a unipolar hegemon in 1860.

   Nor can one speak of Germany, the United States, and Japan as becoming
great powers in response to British hegemony, in accordance with the con-

78. For general information on the Crimean War see the works listed in fn. 38; on Italy, Derek
Beales, *England and Italy, 1859–1860* (London: Nelson, 1961); and Denis Mack Smith, *Victor
Emmanuel, Cavour, and the Risorgimento* (London: Oxford University Press, 1971); on Russia, W.E.
Mosse, *The Rise and Fall of the Crimean System, 1855–1871* (New York: Macmillan, 1963); on
Rumania, T.W. Riker, *The Making of Roumania* (London: Oxford University Press, 1931); on
Britain and the German question, W.E. Mosse, *The European Powers and the German Question
1848–1871* (Cambridge: Cambridge University Press, 1958); and Richard Millman, *British Foreign
Policy and the Coming of the Franco-Prussian War* (Oxford: Oxford University Press, 1965; on Anglo-
American relations, Kenneth Bourne, *Britain and the Balance of Power in North America, 1815–1908*
(Berkeley: University of California Press, 1967); on the competition with Russia in Asia, David
Gillard, *The Struggle for Asia, 1828–1914* (London: Methuen, 1977).
79. For an interesting interpretation, see Klaus Hildebrand, "Die britische Europapolitik
zwischen imperialem Mandat und innerer Reform 1856–1876," *Rheinisch-Westfälische Akademie
der Wissenschaften: Vorträge* G322 (Opladen: Westdeutscher Verlag, 1993), pp. 7–27.

straints of the balance of power system. To concentrate on Germany, Layne's prime example: it did after 1870 become a true great power. But it did so militarily and politically by defeating first Austria and then France, annexing or subordinating all the lesser German states in the process and half persuading, half threatening Russia into accepting the outcome. Thus the only major power against which Germany did not in some measure direct its expansion was Britain. Bismarck expected, with good reason, the British more than any other people to accept the new Germany and grow to appreciate it. It would be a peaceful, satiated, progressive, Protestant power, a useful commercial partner, and a good guarantor of peace in Europe against a restless France and a dangerous Russia—everything the British wanted. And for a long time Bismarck seemed to be basically right. The main pattern of Anglo-German relations until well after his fall in 1890 was cooperation more than rivalry. The "New Course" of Bismarck's successor General von Caprivi was avowedly pro-English, and much of Germany's later policy can best be explained as an ill-advised attempt to pressure the British into friendship. Even the obvious and serious challenge to Britain after 1900 of Admiral Tirpitz's battle fleet was intended by most German leaders (although not by Tirpitz) only to help keep Britain neutral in any clash between Germany and its real opponents, France and Russia.

Hence one cannot interpret Germany's political and military strategy in 1860–1910 as an attempt to balance against Britain. Many Germans, tragically, by 1914 expected a great struggle between Teuton and Slav for the mastery of Europe, and some still believed in a contest between the Teutonic and Latin peoples, but very few indeed considered England the enemy. The hatred of England boiling up in Germany in World War One reflected in good part the feeling that their brothers had betrayed them and had fallen upon them.[80]

As for the economic growth that made Germany a great power, this represented simply an acceleration after 1870 of an autonomous, profoundly organic process of industrialization, modernization, national and social integration, and economic expansion begun decades earlier with Prussia's economic reforms and the formation of the German *Zollverein* in 1833.[81] Once

---

80. The standard work on Anglo-German rivalry is Paul M. Kennedy, *The Rise of Anglo-German Antagonism 1860–1914* (London: G. Allen and Unwin, 1980). A good survey of this and other aspects of nineteenth-century politics is Norman Rich, *Great Power Diplomacy 1814–1914* (New York: McGraw-Hill, 1992).
81. For evidence, see Helmut Böhme, *Deutschlands Weg zur Grossmacht*, 2d ed. (Cologne: Kie-

again, one cannot argue that this societal transformation, widespread if not universal in Europe, was the result of the constraints of the international system or a response to British hegemony. Naturally the Germans measured their economic progress against that of Britain, as commercial and industrial competitors always do. Naturally each sought to adapt and learn from the other, the Germans in this instance more successfully. Naturally both powers competed—and cooperated—economically and commercially, as industrial states always do. But to see in this emulation and competition a kind of force prompting Germany's growth in power, produced by the dictates of international politics, is surely a strangely mystical form of "realism."

To Layne's similar argument that the United States and Japan emerged as great powers in response to British hegemony and the imperatives of balance of power politics, one need remark only that the United States had no foe or threat against which to balance, that Japan's primary enemy was Russia, and that by the time both the United States and Japan emerged as great powers early in the twentieth century, the United States had become something of a partner to Britain and Japan was Britain's formal ally.

Conclusions

The purpose of examining Layne's argument is not to contend that neo-realist theory falls simply because Layne's application of it cannot stand. The point is to show how a normal, standard understanding of neo-realist theory, applied precisely to the historical era where it should fit best, gets the motives, the process, the patterns, and the broad outcomes of international history wrong, and predicts things of major theoretical and historical importance which on closer examination turn out not to be so. It indicates the central problem of neo-realism with international history: that it prescribes and predicts a determinate order for history without having adequately checked this against the historical evidence. What led Layne astray was not any insufficiency in his historical research so much as his theoretical presuppositions. Armed with neo-realist theory, he knew what was essentially to be found in the historical record at the outset, and this helped him find it.

---

penheuer and Witsch, 1972); Hans-Ulrich Wehler, *Deutsche Gesellschaftsgeschichte (1700–1849)*, 2 vols. (Munich: R. Oldenbourg, 1987). On the *Zollverein*, see especially Hans-Werner Hahn, *Geschichte des Deutschen Zollvereins* (Göttingen: Vandenhoeck and Ruprecht, 1984).

Thus the main fault lies with neo-realist theory. Its insistence on the sameness effect and on the unchanging, structurally determined nature of international politics make it unhistorical, perhaps anti-historical.[82] This has special deleterious effects on its handling of international history. Neo-realist theory not only prevents scholars from seeing and explaining the various strategies alternative to balancing, or the different functions and roles of various actors within the system, but even blocks a genuine historical understanding of balancing conduct and the balance of power itself as a historical variable, changing over time, conditioned by historical circumstances, and freighted with ideological assumptions.[83] Other harmful effects may spread beyond international history to history in general. Rather than illuminating it, the kind of approach involved in neo-realist theory renders it incomprehensible. It obstructs new insights and hypotheses, leads scholars to overlook or explain away large bodies of inconvenient facts, flattens out vital historical distinctions. It may even encourage an attitude toward history not uncommon among scholars of many kinds: an unconscious disdain for it, a disregard of its complexity and subtleties and the problems of doing it well or using it wisely; an unexamined assumption that its lessons and insights lie on the surface for anyone to pick up, so that one can go at history like a looter at an archeological site, indifferent to context and deeper meaning, concerned only with taking what can be immediately used or sold.[84]

Whether neo-realist theory can be revised to apply usefully to all of international history, and not simply the element of power-political competition which has always bulked large in it and still does, is a question best left to others, or at least to another time and place. This essay will close with advising international historians not to adopt the neo-realist paradigm, and theorists not to assume that the facts of international history support one.

---

82. Waltz argues in *Theory of International Politics*, p. 117, that the principles of Realpolitik noted by Thucydides and expounded by Machiavelli have always governed international politics for structural reasons; this view is widely shared. Yet while some basic ideas and practices associated with Realpolitik are old, Realpolitik as it emerged in the middle of the nineteenth century was very much a historical construct. Both the term itself (coined by a German political theorist, Ludwig August von Rochau) and its principles represented a particular ideology which had to fight for acceptance against rival outlooks in Germany, winning decisively only when Prussia defeated Austria in 1866. Karl-Georg Faber, "Realpolitik als Ideologie," *Historische Zeitschrift*, Vol. 203, No. 1 (August 1966), pp. 1–45.

83. For a discussion of the actual divergent meanings of "balance" as used by nineteenth-century statesmen, see Schroeder, "The Nineteenth Century System: Balance of Power or Political Equilibrium?" *Review of International Studies*, Vol. 15, No. 2 (1989), pp. 135–153.

84. This is not directed solely or mainly at realists or political scientists; the most striking examples of this attitude I have encountered in recent years are Francis Fukuyama's *The End of History and the Last Man* (New York: Free Press, 1992); and Henry Kissinger, *Diplomacy* (New York: Simon and Schuster, 1994).

Realism and Domestic Politics

Fareed Zakaria

A Review Essay

Jack Snyder, *Myths of Empire: Domestic Politics and International Ambition.* Ithaca N.Y.: Cornell University Press, 1991.

In the literature of international relations, it is fast becoming commonplace to assert the importance of domestic politics and call for more research on the subject.[1] After over a decade of vigorous debates about realism, structural realism, neoliberal institutionalism, and hegemonic stability theory, political scientists are shifting their attention to the internal sources of foreign policy.[2] Some even contend that realism's dictum about the "primacy of foreign policy" is wrong, and that the domestic politics of states are the key to understanding world events. *Innenpolitik* is in.

Diplomatic history has been under fire for over two decades for its focus on elite decision-making,[3] and with the rise of the "new history," younger

Fareed Zakaria is a Ph.D. candidate in the Department of Government, and a fellow at the Olin Institute for Strategic Studies, at Harvard University. He is writing a dissertation entitled, "The Rise of a Great Power: National Strength, State Structure, and American Foreign Policy, 1865–1917."

I would like to thank Thomas Christensen, Stanley Hoffmann, Robert Keohane, Jonathan Mercer, Joseph Nye, the anonymous reviewers for *International Security*, and especially, Gideon Rose, and Andrew Moravcsik for their comments on earlier drafts of this essay.

1. See for example, Joseph S. Nye, Jr., and Sean M. Lynn-Jones, "International Security Studies," *International Security*, Vol. 12, No. 4 (Spring 1988), pp. 25–27; Robert O. Keohane, *International Institutions and State Power* (Boulder, Colo.: Westview, 1991), pp. 173–174; Benjamin Cohen,"The Political Economy of International Trade," *International Organization*, Vol. 44, No. 2 (Spring 1990), pp. 268–270; and especially Jack S. Levy, "Domestic Politics and War," in Robert I. Rotberg and Theodore K. Rabb, eds., *The Origin and Prevention of Major Wars* (Cambridge: Cambridge University Press, 1989), pp. 79–101.
2. While the international relations literature of the last decade was dominated by debates about the international system, exceptions exist, the most prominent of which include Peter J. Katzenstein, ed., *Between Power and Plenty: The Foreign Economic Policies of the Advanced Industrial States* (Madison: University of Wisconsin Press, 1978); Michael Doyle, "Kant, Liberal Legacies, and Foreign Affairs: Parts I and II," *Philosophy and Public Affairs*, Vol. 12, No. 3 and 4 (Summer, Fall 1983), pp. 205–235, 323–353; and Robert Putnam, "Diplomacy and Domestic Politics: The Logic of Two-Level Games," *International Organization*, Vol. 42, No. 3 (Summer 1988), pp. 427–460. For a review of recent work, see Levy, "Domestic Politics and War."
3. See, for example, three modern classics in the field: William Langer, *European Alliances and*

International Security, Summer 1992 (Vol. 17, No. 1)
© 1992 by the President and Fellows of Harvard College and of the Massachusetts Institute of Technology.

historians have increasingly written about the underlying social, economic, and ideological influences on high politics.[4] They have not, however, placed their particular explanations within the context of international relations theory. Most theorists of international politics, on the other hand, have focused on the nature of the international system and ignored what goes on behind state doors, treating it as the province of comparative politics, a different sub-field of political science.[5]

Jack Snyder tries to bridge this gap between domestic and international affairs in his ambitious new book, *Myths of Empire*,[6] constructing a domestic politics model that he claims stays within the realist tradition. The book raises important issues with great sophistication and displays a mastery of both comparative politics and international relations. Ultimately, however, it highlights the difficulties of constructing a theory in which domestic politics determines international events. In this essay I will argue that Snyder, while purporting to combine domestic and international levels of analysis, can do so only because he adopts an erroneous—though increasingly common—interpretation of realism that minimizes the powerful effects of the international system on state behavior. In the end we are left not with a novel combination of systemic and domestic determinants, but with a restatement of the traditional *Innenpolitik* case. Future research should build on the many insights of *Myths of Empire*, but must attempt to construct domestic explanations that take full account of systemic pressures. This will require that

---

Alignments, 1870–1890, 2nd ed. (New York: Knopf, 1950); Ronald Robinson and John Gallagher, *Africa and the Victorians* (London: Macmillan, 1961); and A.J.P. Taylor, *The Origins of the Second World War* (London: Hamilton, 1961).

4. An important critique of traditional diplomatic history is Arno J. Mayer, "Internal Causes and Purposes of War in Europe, 1870–1956: A Research Assignment," *Journal of Modern History*, Vol. 41 (September 1969), pp. 291–303. For an overview that details the best "new" diplomatic history, see Charles Maier, "Marking Time: The Historiography of International Relations," in Michael Kammen, ed., *The Past Before Us: Contemporary Historical Writing in the United States* (Ithaca, N.Y.: Cornell University Press, 1980), pp. 366–387; and for reactions from other diplomatic historians, see "Responses to Charles Maier's 'Marking Time'," *Diplomatic History*, Vol. 5, No. 4 (Fall 1981), pp. 353–373. Also see Gordon Craig, "Political History," *Daedalus*, Vol. 100, No. 2 (Spring 1971), pp. 323–339; and Ernest May, "The Decline of Diplomatic History," in George Billias and Gerald Grob, eds., *American History: Retrospect and Prospect* (New York: Free Press, 1971), pp. 399–430.

5. See Stanley Hoffmann, "An American Social Science: International Relations," *Daedalus*, Vol. 106, No. 1 (Summer 1977), pp. 41–60.

6. Jack Snyder, *Myths of Empire: Domestic Politics and International Ambition* (Ithaca, N.Y.: Cornell University Press, 1991). Subsequent references to *Myths of Empire* appear in parentheses in the text.

scholars develop a tolerance for more limited—but also more accurate—generalizations.

Aussenpolitik and Innenpolitik

The concept of the *Primat der Aussenpolitik*—"the primacy of foreign policy"—has two distinct, though related, meanings in realist thought. The first, from which the phrase comes, is tangential to this discussion. It is the claim that international relations strongly affects a state's domestic arrangements: "throughout the ages pressure from without has been a determining influence on internal structure."[7] In fact, Leopold von Ranke, with whose writings the phrase *Primat der Aussenpolitik* is most strongly associated, used it in this sense only, urging the Prussian state to organize itself internally so that it would succeed externally.[8] More recently Charles Tilly and Peter Gourevitch have elaborated on this concept, which Gourevitch calls "the second image reversed."[9]

The second meaning of the "primacy of foreign policy," which is more relevant here, is that states conduct their foreign policy for "strategic" reasons, as a consequence of international pulls and pushes, and not to further domestic ends. Realists have long thought of inter-state relations as a realm apart from domestic politics.[10] Indeed realism as a school of thought developed in conjunction with the growth of strong states, distinct from the societies that they ruled, interacting with one another. From the sixteenth-century Italians, who spoke of an external force of nature that controlled

7. Otto Hintze, "Military Organization and the Organization of the State," in Felix Gilbert, ed., *The Historical Essays of Otto Hintze* (New York: Oxford University Press, 1975), p. 183.
8. See Ranke, "A Dialogue on Politics," reprinted in Thedore H. von Laue, *Leopold Ranke: The Formative Years* (Princeton, N.J.: Princeton University Press, 1950), pp. 152–180, esp. pp. 167–168; also see pp. 98–99.
9. Charles Tilly, "Reflections on the History of European State-making," in Charles Tilly, ed., *The Formation of National States in Western Europe* (Princeton, N.J.: Princeton University Press, 1975); and Peter Gourevitch, "The Second Image Reversed: The International Sources of Domestic Politics," *International Organization*, Vol. 32, No. 4 (Autumn 1978), pp. 881–911, which contains a literature review. Important work since then includes Peter J. Katzenstein, *Small States in World Markets: Industrial Policy in Europe* (Ithaca, N.Y.: Cornell University Press, 1985); and Brian M. Downing, *The Military Revolution and Political Change* (Princeton: Princeton University Press, 1992).
10. This aspect is emphasized by "systemic" theories; see, for example, Kenneth N. Waltz, *Theory of International Politics* (New York, Random House, 1979), pp. 80–101; and Stanley Hoffmann, *The State of War* (New York: Praeger, 1965), p. 26.

state behavior, to Kenneth Waltz's balance-of-power theory, realists have argued that systemic pressures determine states' foreign policy behavior.[11] Realists do not deny that domestic politics influences foreign policy, but they contend that "the pressures of [international] competition weigh more heavily than ideological preferences or internal political pressures."[12]

Critics of realism have typically reversed this logic, asserting that pressure from *within* determines external politics. Periodically, thinkers from Plato on have espoused this view, and it has become part of a coherent critique of realism over the last two centuries. One of the intellectual legacies of the Enlightenment was a challenge to the assumption, fundamental to realism, that history is cyclical, thus offering hope for a future without perpetual conflict. Since then both Marxists and liberals have argued that all states are *not* alike, that the causes of international conflict often lie within states, and that peace will be obtained, not when the distribution of external power is stable, but rather when the distribution of internal power is just.[13]

These philosophical critiques led to the growth of what can be termed the *Innenpolitik* school, an ongoing tradition of scholarship that, dismissing the strategic rationales of statesmen, locates the roots of foreign policy in the social and economic structure of states. Such theories came into prominence in the early twentieth century as intellectuals attempted to explain two particular phenomena: British imperialism and German *Weltpolitik*. John Hobson's now famous explanation of Britain's scramble for Africa began a long and contentious debate about the sources of imperialism.[14] Discussion about the domestic roots of German foreign policy began during the First World War itself with Thorstein Veblen's study of German industrialization and, in 1919, with Joseph Schumpeter's more general critique of atavistic expansionism.[15] The interwar German historian Eckart Kehr made more specific claims,

---

11. On the origins of realism and "interest theorists," see Friedrich Meinecke, *Machiavellism*, trans. Douglas Scott (New Haven, Conn.: Yale University Press, 1957); Felix Gilbert, *To the Farewell Address* (Princeton, N.J.: Princeton University Press, 1961), pp. 85–95; and Friedrich Kratochwil, "On the Notion of 'Interest' in International Relations," *International Organization*, Vol. 36, No. 1 (Winter 1982), pp. 1–24.
12. Waltz, "A Response to My Critics," in Robert O. Keohane, ed., *Neorealism and its Critics* (New York: Columbia University Press, 1986), p. 329.
13. The best discussion of this school of thought remains Kenneth Waltz, *Man, the State, and War* (New York: Columbia University Press, 1954), pp. 80–159.
14. J.A. Hobson, *Imperialism: A Study* (London: Allen and Unwin, 1902, repr. 1938). Lenin popularized Hobson's thesis, although the two disagreed on the solution to imperialism; see V.I. Lenin, *Imperialism: the Highest Stage of Capitalism* (New York: International Publishers, 1916, repr. 1939).
15. Thorstein Veblen, *Imperial Germany and the Industrial Revolution* (New York: Viking, 1915,

based on archival research, that the domestic concerns of elites drove German foreign policy.[16] Kehr has been called the father of modern revisionism because his work has had an important influence on subsequent revisionists in both Germany and America, including Charles Beard, William Appleman Williams, Fritz Fischer, and Hans Ulrich Wehler.[17]

Myths of Empire

Jack Snyder's work follows explicitly in the *Innenpolitik* tradition. Joining together the German and English schools of revisionism, he asks the broader question: why do great powers "overexpand" so often? (p. 1) By overexpansion he means expansion that provokes an overwhelming balancing coalition or where the costs exceed benefits (pp. 6–7). He thus combines Kehr's concern about Germany's self-encircling policies with Hobson's concern about Britain's costly imperialism. Snyder's answer is also a composite, mixing and matching individual revisionist arguments to create a complex domestic politics model to explain the overexpansion of the great powers over the last two hundred years (pp. 61–62). He applies his model to five great powers during what he deems their periods of overexpansion: Germany (1866–1945); Japan (1868–1945); Britain (1830–1890); the Soviet Union (1945–1989); and the United States (1945–1989). He considers, but discards as inadequate, realist and cognitive explanations for these states' behavior.

Snyder's argument has three steps:

repr. 1954); and Joseph Schumpeter, "The Sociology of Imperialism," in *Imperialism and Social Classes*, trans. Heinz Norden (New York: Augustus M. Kelley, 1951), pp. 3–83. Schumpeter's essay was first published in 1919 in *Archiv für Sozialwissenschaft un Socialpolitik*, Vol. 46 (1919), pp. 1–39, 274–310.

16. Eckart Kehr, *Battleship Building and Party Politics in Germany, 1894–1901: A Cross Section of the Political, Social, and Ideological Preconditions of German Imperialism*, trans. Pauline R. Anderson and Eugene N. Anderson (Chicago: University of Chicago Press, 1930, repr. 1973). Kehr's essays were collected and published in Germany by Hans Ulrich Wehler in 1965 under the title *Der Primat der Innenpolitik*. The American edition is Eckart Kehr, *Economic Interest, Militarism, and Foreign Policy: Essays on German History*, trans. Grete Heinz (Berkeley: University of California Press, 1977).

17. Beard publicized Kehr's writings in America, and Wehler collected and edited his essays; see Gordon Craig's introduction in Kehr, *Economic Interests*, pp. vii–xxi. Also see Maier, "Marking Time," p. 365; and Arthur Lloyd Skope, "The Primacy of Domestic Politics: Eckart Kehr and the Intellectual Development of Charles Beard," *History and Theory*, Vol. 13 (1974), pp. 119–131. Also see Fritz Fischer, *War of Illusions: German Policies from 1911 to 1914*, trans. Marian Jackson (New York: Chatto and Windus, 1975); Fischer's work also spawned a controversial debate about Germany's responsibility for World War I.

(1) *Why overexpansion?* A state overexpands because expansion always benefits a few people greatly and costs many people only a little. Parochial interest groups—such as the military, foreign offices, and big business—may or may not want imperialism per se, but they benefit from imperial, militarist, or autarkic policies. These groups hijack the organs of government for their selfish goals. The taxpayers who foot the bill lack the organization and access to the state that would allow them to lobby successfully for their interests (pp. 31–33).

(2) *How?* In order to gain broad support for their narrow policies, proexpansionists create strategic rationalizations for their policies and hoodwink the public with these "myths of empire," which include a belief in the riches to be gained through conquest, falling dominoes, the advantage of offensive strategies, and the efficacy of threats. Over time some elites begin to believe the myths that they themselves created, which makes retrenchment highly unlikely (pp. 2–6, 35–39).

(3) *Why acute overexpansion?* Expansion is often so extreme, beyond what any one group wants, because of a process of logrolling between various factions, each of whom is willing to back the others' imperial projects if its own ambitions are supported in turn. This synergy usually creates "multiple expansion," though if the bargaining process also involves key anti-imperial interests it may result in an awkward combination of aggressive behavior in some areas and conciliation in others, which Snyder terms "offensive detente." It follows that overexpansion will be most acute in countries with many concentrated interest groups, a phenomenon that Snyder calls "cartelization" (pp. 39–49).

Snyder distinguishes unitary, democratic, and cartelized systems and explains that overexpansion is "moderate" in the first two (pp. 43–54). Unitary systems are ruled by a single leader or an oligarchy whose members share common interests. Dominant and self-confident oligarchies—Snyder's examples are the British Whig aristocracy, the American East-coast establishment, and the post-Stalin Soviet Politburo—have a proprietary interest in the long-term health of the society, and are unlikely to engage in ruinous expansion. Dictators, Snyder concedes, are unpredictable. They may be gross overexpanders, since nothing in the domestic system checks them, but they have the power to overrule imperial cartels and may hence behave sensibly. Democracies are only moderate expanders because they empower the many who pay for expansion and allow them to check concentrated interests through elections and accountability. Though overexpansion is least common in unitary and democratic states, all domestic systems have periods of cartelization, and therefore of overexpansion. An uneasy coalition of elites anywhere may lead to logrolling, myth-making, and overexpansion.

To explain why some states develop cartelized systems, Snyder examines the timing and pattern of industrialization in the countries under study. In Britain and the northern United States, "early" industrialization ensured that social and political changes moved in step with economic transformation, and these societies modernized in an evolutionary manner. Wilhelmine Germany, however, experienced "late" industrialization. Because Germany was, in a sense, "catching up" with Britain, German industrialization was rapid, centralized, and state-assisted. This created large business interests and left pre-industrial feudal and military elites unassimilated into the nation's economic transformation. The Japanese pattern of development was similar to the German one. Russia's variant, "late late industrialization," created a new pattern of development, vesting power in a modernizing elite with broad interests (the Communist party). This made it a unitary system in Snyder's terms. Snyder summarizes his causal chain succinctly: "Late industrialization produces a cartelized political structure, which magnifies the effectiveness of concentrated interests in expansion, favors the development of expansionist strategic myths, and promotes self-encirclement and imperial overexpansion" (p. 58).

The first step of Snyder's model (why overexpansion?) derives from the work of Hobson, Schumpeter, and Stephen Van Evera, all three of whom emphasize the selfish imperial motivations of powerful groups within states (pp. 14–15, notes 44 and 45). The second (how?) applies Van Evera's ideas about "national mythmaking," and strategic "non-evaluation" to the cases under study (pp. 2–3, notes 2–3). The third step (why acute overexpansion?) turns Eckart Kehr's model of elite logrolling in Wilhelmine Germany into a general model (p. 18, note 51). Snyder's discussion of industrialization and its effects on elite politics draws heavily on the work of Veblen, Schumpeter, and especially Alexander Gerschenkron and Barrington Moore (p. 18, note 51; pp. 55–60, note 95).

Evaluating Myths of Empire

Myths of Empire is a work of scholarly synthesis rather than one of original historical research, and should be judged as such. Specifically it should be evaluated on two grounds. First, is Snyder's domestic politics model—his

independent variable—a powerful and generalizable explanation of overexpansionist foreign policies? Second, how much of his dependent variable—
overexpansion—is explained by domestic factors as opposed to systemic
ones? I will discuss the first question only briefly, because the various theories
that Snyder draws on to make up the logical chain of his model have been
subjected to substantial scrutiny by historians and scholars of comparative
politics.[18] More important, the value of this model for the literature of international relations depends on how well it integrates domestic and systemic
levels of analysis, and thus turns on the second question.

As a theoretical synthesis, *Myths of Empire* is a *tour de force*. Snyder brings
together previously compartmentalized scholarly discussions about imperial
overextension and about provocative foreign policies, arguing persuasively
that both should be considered part of a state's grand strategy. He creates a
complex argument that focuses on crucial domestic factors like industrialization and domestic coalitions, and then connects them to foreign policy.
His own theoretical contribution, the discussion of cartelized, unitary, and
democratic systems, is ingenious and provocative, leading to some counterintuitive hypotheses, for example, that dictators and clubby oligarchies may
be good for a state's foreign policy.

Does the book, however, advance the debate over *Aussenpolitik* versus
Innenpolitik, moving us beyond simple assertions of the primacy of one or
the other? Does it integrate international and domestic sources of international relations into a coherent model of state behavior? Is it, as Snyder
claims, compatible with a realist systemic theory? (pp. 11–12). Unfortunately
not. The central flaw in *Myths of Empire* is that it accords little weight to
systemic causes. This would be less troublesome but for the fact that the
phenomenon Snyder wishes to explain is a systemic outcome. Snyder defines
his dependent variable not as attempted expansion, which can be measured
by looking at a state's policies, but rather as overexpansion—which he defines

---

18. Many of Snyder's domestic variables and relationships—though not all—are derived from
the *Innenpolitik*–neo-Marxist school that I have outlined above, critiques of which are well known.
See for example, Craig, "Political History"; James J. Sheehan, "The Primacy of Domestic Politics:
Eckart Kehr's Essays on Modern German History," *Central European History*, Vol. 1, No. 2 (June
1968); Charles Maier, "Foreword to the Cornell University Press Edition," in Alexander Ger-
schenkron, *Bread and Democracy in Germany* (Ithaca, N.Y.: Cornell University Press, 1989); David
Blackbourn, *Class, Religion, and Local Politics in Wilhelmine Germany* (New Haven, Conn.: Yale
University Press, 1980); D.C.M. Platt, *Finanace, Trade, and Politics in British Foriegn Policy, 1815–
1914* (Oxford: Oxford University Press, 1968); D.K. Fieldhouse, *Economics and Empire* (Ithaca,
N.Y.: Cornell University Press, 1973); and Benjamin J. Cohen, *The Question of Imperialism* (New
York: Basic Books, 1973).

as *unsuccessful expansion*—which must be measured by looking at the success of a state's policies in the international arena. The *attempt* at expansion may be chiefly linked to a state's domestic politics, but the *success* of its expansionist policies is surely related to the international environment in which it was tried. By failing to separate systemic and domestic factors, Snyder's treatment of his cases remains incomplete.

Consider, for example, Snyder's discussion of the Soviet Union and the United States (pp. 212–254). Finding equally "moderate" patterns of cartelization in both domestic polities, he labels both countries equally "moderate" overexpanders (pp. 63–64, 212). By his own criteria, however, the Soviet Union was clearly an "extreme" overexpander, closer to Wilhelmine Germany and pre–World War II Japan than to the United States. Snyder measures overexpansion by its success, specifically by whether a state's policies provoke an overwhelming coalition and whether its costs exceed benefits. On this score the Soviet Union can hardly be placed in the same category as the United States. The Soviet Union's postwar expansionism provoked a balancing coalition of states that comprised between 60 and 80 percent of world gross national product (GNP).[19] In forty years its behavior resulted in collapse, bankruptcy, and dismemberment, reducing Russia, for the first time in two hundred years, to a second-rank power.

U.S. expansion, by contrast, never resulted in the formation of a countering coalition that even approached its own industrial power, let alone the combined power of its allies. It remains today, as it was in 1945, the strongest nation in the world, and even if the "declinists" are entirely right, it will move only to second or third place over the next twenty-five years.[20] Were Snyder explaining the two state's *attempts* to spread their influence and interests abroad, measured by the number of interventions initiated or missiles built, the Soviets and the Americans come out roughly similar.[21] But if the yardstick is success, their behavior falls into very different categories. This is not simply a miscoding of one case, but rather points to Snyder's general error. Why do two equally cartelized states have different levels of overexpansion? It is because of the international context in which their actions

---

19. Stephen M. Walt, *The Origins of Alliances* (Ithaca, N.Y.: Cornell University Press, 1987), pp. 289–291.
20. Paul Kennedy, *The Rise and Fall of the Great Powers: Economic Change and Military Conflict from 1500–2000 (New York: Random House, 1987), pp. 515–534.
21. Kenneth Waltz does this in "America as a Model for the World," *PS: Political Science and Politics*, Vol. 24, No. 4 (December 1991), p. 668.

occurred. The failure of Soviet expansion—its extreme overexpansion—and the success of American expansion—its moderate, even low, overexpansion—had little to do with their levels of cartelization, but rather more to do with a key systemic variable: relative power. Soviet expansionism's failure and American expansionism's success were caused by the same set of factors: the West's vastly greater relative economic power, the technological gap between the two blocs, and the productivity of capitalism versus communism. Gerschenkron points out that France, Italy, and Austria-Hungary also experienced the "German" pattern of late industrialization.[22] Yet Germany alone was overexpansionist, in part because it faced unusual systemic pressures and opportunities.

Snyder's five cases provide an opportunity to demonstrate how a spare systemic explanation can better explain systemic outcomes than a complex domestic politics model does. For simplicity's sake I will use two key variables only: the relative power of the expansionist state, and the polarity of the international system in which the expansion was attempted (unipolar, bipolar, or multi-polar).[23] Consider two more of Snyder's cases: he terms Britain a "moderate" overexpander and Japan an "extreme" one (p. 63). Yet during the nineteenth century, Britain asserted political control over one-quarter of the world's population and built the largest imperial bureaucracy and navy in history. In 1914 it ruled over a world empire twice as large as the Roman empire at its peak.[24] Japan, by contrast, made a bid for regional supremacy in what was then a peripheral area of the world. Because he measures their respective expansionism by the results that followed, however, Snyder comes to the conclusion that Japan was the greater overexpander. Britain's policies, however, met with greater success than Japan's not because it was a less cartelized state, but rather because it was more powerful state.

In the mid- and late nineteenth century Britain's relative power was greater than any European state's since Rome. If we use GNP as a crude but simple measure of a state's relative power, we find that during this period Britain comprised over 20 percent of world GNP and, more important, close to 50

22. Gerschenkron, *Economic Backwardness*, p. 16.
23. Introducing additional factors such as technology, the offense-defense balance, and geography would help explain each case even better.
24. See D.K. Fieldhouse, *The Colonial Empires* (New York: Macmillan, 1965); Fieldhouse, *Economics and Empire*; William Langer, *Diplomacy of Imperialism, 1890–1902* (New York: Knopf, 1935); and Michael W. Doyle, *Empires* (Ithaca, N.Y.: Cornell University Press, 1986), pp. 104–122, 141–307.

percent of Europe's GNP.[25] Such a raw measure underestimates British power, if anything. With Napoleonic France defeated, Britain was the superpower of the nineteenth century: it was the financial center of the world, the balancer of Europe and the unrivaled hegemon outside it (in what Michael Doyle called a "unipolar world-peripheral system"). Britain could not have been met with an "overwhelming" balancing coalition. Furthermore, the absence of strong nationalism in its colonies kept imperial costs down until well into the twentieth century. In Paul Kennedy's words, "[Britain's] successful imperialism and world influence on the cheap was due, of course, to the fact that outside Europe Britain largely operated in a power-political vacuum."[26] Japan, on the other hand, entered the great power system during a period of intense and competitive multipolarity. From the Meiji restoration to the Second World War it never rose above a 4 percent share of world GNP (in 1938). Hence it is hardly surprising that its expansion met with quick resistance.

Overexpansion, in other words, is easily and simply correlated with relative power and the degree of competitiveness in the international system. The two states that Snyder places at the extreme end of his spectrum of overexpansion, Germany and Japan, accounted for a small percentage of world GNP—between 4 percent and 14 percent—and both rose to great-power status in a multipolar world, i.e., a world in which the possibilities for a countervailing coalition were great. Britain and the United States, in contrast, rose to great power status in unipolar and bipolar systems respectively. If Britain's share of world and European GNP made formation of an "overwhelming" coalition against it *virtually* impossible, in the case of the United States, it was power made it *literally* impossible. With 50 percent of world GNP in 1945, the United States could not provoke a balancing coalition greater than its own strength, no matter what kind of expansionism it engaged in. The Soviet Union, with under 15 percent of world GNP, fits in along with Germany and Japan as a weak and therefore unsuccessful great power, though since it expanded in a less competitive, bipolar system—and one with nuclear deterrence—the result was less catastrophic for it than for those two states.

---

25. All of the following figures are taken from Paul Kennedy, *The Rise and Fall of the Great Powers*, pp. 149, 330, 436.
26. Paul Kennedy, *The Realities Behind Diplomacy: Background Influences on British External Policy, 1865–1980* (London: Fontana, 1981), 33. The phrase "unipolar world-peripheral system" is from Doyle, *Empires*, p. 236.

One might rephrase Snyder's question to be: Why do states foolishly attempt expansion when they know it will fail? The question points to a flawed understanding of both realism and systemic pressures, which I discuss in greater detail in the next section. But briefly, there are two responses to this question. First, states can rarely "know" beforehand what specific international outcomes will follow from their individual actions. Outcomes in the international system result from the myriad interactions of myriad actors, further complicated by system-wide forces like polarity and technological change. Uncertainty, misperceptions, and unintended consequences characterize anarchic systems.[27] In fact if specific systemic outcomes could be predicted from any one state's actions, then the rationale of conceiving of the system as a separate analytic concept would disappear. The international system is central to international relations theory precisely because its characteristics intervene powerfully between state actions and international outcomes.

Second, states do not choose in what era they will rise to great wealth and power. Traditionally, realists have argued that a state's intentions are shaped by its capabilities; in Hans Morgenthau's terms a nation's "interests" are shaped by its "power."[28] Differential rates of national growth mean that some states grow rich, others poor. As a state's relative power increases, it attempts to expand its interests and influence abroad. Part of this process is almost involuntary; a growing state acquires more and more economic and political interests in the outside world, often bumping up against the interests of other states. When a state climbs to the highest rungs of the international ladder it will, in Robert Gilpin's words, "try to expand its economic, political, and territorial control; it will try to change the international system in accordance with its own interests."[29] Sometimes this rise to great power status succeeds and sometimes it fails; realists argue that these systemic outcomes might depend on the international environment. The external structure does not always determine outcomes, but if structural causes are not separated from domestic ones, we cannot know when it does.

27. As Geoffrey Blainey puts it, "War is usually the outcome of a diplomatic crisis which cannot be solved because both sides have conflicting estimates of their bargaining power." See Geoffrey Blainey, *The Causes of War*, 3rd ed. (New York: Free Press, 1988), p. 114.
28. Hans Morgenthau, *Politics Among Nations*, 5th ed. (New York: Knopf, 1973), p. 5.
29. Robert Gilpin, *War and Change in World Politics* (Cambridge: Cambridge University Press, 1984), pp. 94–95.

The problem of defining and measuring state strategies by their success reappears in Snyder's discussion of states that are "bad learners." Snyder assumes that failed expansion must be the result, in part, of bad learning; why, after all, would states take actions that result in their own ruin? Conversely, successful expansion must be the result of good learning. As with expansion, however, Snyder should have defined and measured learning separate from the outcomes that followed it. For example, Snyder labels the United States a "good learner" (when in Vietnam) and the Soviet Union a bad one (when in Afghanistan). But if one examines the actual process of learning, the United States comes across as a terrible learner. It took six years for Washington to decide to withdraw from Vietnam, and another six years to actually pull out.[30] Snyder calls this good learning because it did not result in the catastrophe that Soviet overextension in Afghanistan did. But American expansion was less costly than the Soviet experience in Afghanistan only because the United States was a stronger power.

The outcomes of national policies— such as overexpansion or war—cannot be simply explained by placing states in two categories, one good and the other bad. There may well be types of states that are more greedy and rapacious than others. But to directly infer such attributes from international outcomes is to make what psychologists call the "fundamental attribution error" and physical scientists call "reductionism."[31] The situation in which states are placed contributes to these outcomes, and an analysis of these environmental effects must take the environment into account. Often it remains unclear—especially to the leaders of a state—whether its policies will trigger a balancing coalition or whether their expansion is in fact *part* of a balancing process. Was Britain's climb to world empire an example of expansion that led to Wilhelmine Germany's balancing response?[32] England itself

30. Leslie Gelb and Richard Betts, *The Irony of Vietnam: The System Worked* (Washington, D.C.: Brookings, 1979), makes a powerful case that domestic structures and politics delayed learning about Vietnam.
31. See, for example, Jonathan L. Freedman, David O. Sears, and J. Merrill Carlsmith, *Social Psychology*, 4th ed. (Englewood Cliffs, N.J.: Prentice-Hall, 1981), pp. 153–155; Lee Ross, "The Intuitive Psychologist: Distortions in the Attribution Process," in Leonard Berkowitz, ed., *Advances in Experimental Social Psychology* (New York: Academic Press, 1977), pp. 184–186. For a powerful critique of reductionist explanations that move from systemic outcomes to national attributes, see Waltz, *Theory of International Politics*, pp. 18–37.
32. Recall Churchill's famous counsel to the British cabinet during the Anglo-German arms race: "We have got all we want in territory, and our claim to be left in unmolested enjoyment of vast and splendid possessions, mainly acquired by violence, largely maintained by force, often seems less reasonable to others than to us." Quoted in Kennedy, *Realities Behind Diplomacy*, pp. 69–70.

was balancing against Napoleonic France and then the Holy Alliance. The tragedy of international relations, as theorists from Thucydides to Rousseau to Waltz have understood, is that it does not take bad states to produce bad outcomes.

That systemic pressures on state behavior are greater than Snyder acknowledges does not mean that domestic politics was irrelevant to foreign policy choices in the five case studies he looks at. Snyder's theory persuasively demonstrates how pro-imperial interests can fool the public, and how logrolling over foreign policy can result in multiple imperial projects. The theory rings truest for pre–World War II Japan and Wilhelmine Germany, but those countries' expansionism is overdetermined; there are powerful international, domestic, bureaucratic, ideological, and personality-based explanations for their aggressive behavior. Germany and Japan *were* militarized states with powerful pro-expansionist elements. But these domestic traits ensured only that the states would be expanders, not that they would be *unsuccessful* expanders. Louis XIV's France and Elizabethan England were also militarized and expansionist states; their expansion happened to work.[33] Some expansion may well be doomed from the start by the folly of statesmen or the domestic political process in which they operate, but some unsuccessful expansion is caused by the anarchy of international life. Because Snyder does not weigh the systemic causes of overexpansion, he cannot separate these two factors and determine when internal factors caused external failure and when environmental factors conjoined to undo a rising power's bid for influence.

Defensive Realism

Snyder argues that he has, in fact, taken systemic factors into account in his model. His interpretation of realism, which he calls "defensive realism," assumes that the international system provides incentives only for moderate, reasonable behavior. Immoderate, unreasonable behavior contradicts "true" systemic incentives and must be caused at some other level of analysis (pp. 10–13, 108). Thus he asks why states overexpand, and when he finds unsuccessful expansion, he assumes that by definition this behavior could not explained by systemic causes because it results in a sub-optimal outcome

---

33. See Kennedy, *The Rise and Fall of the Great Powers*, pp. 73–139.

(p. 117). Systemic factors then drop out of his analysis and he moves to a domestic explanation. *Myths of Empire* highlights an increasingly common, but erroneous, starting point that has been adopted by many scholars, often referred to as neo-realists (many of them are, in fact, students of Kenneth Waltz). The rest of this essay will argue, however, that these scholars have misinterpreted realism substantially. While they have different approaches and concerns, they do adopt certain key assumptions that drive their work, and hence they can be thought of as a school. Since this school is currently at the center of the field of international security studies, an analysis and critique of its assumptions should prove useful—particularly in this journal which has been the forum for much of its work.

Snyder begins his analysis with assumptions about how the international system affects a state's foreign policy. He argues that his domestic politics model accounts for state behavior that contradicts these systemic incentives, and thus is compatible with defensive realism (pp. 10–13). Defensive realism's base assumption is that a rational state expands only to achieve security. Snyder and other defensive realists argue that the *systemic cause* for state expansion is its attempt to "cause" or "buy" security and that state behavior is best explained as a response to external threats. When the defense has the advantage (technologically and geographically), states are more likely to feel secure and hence to behave calmly. When the offense has the advantage, states will feel threatened and become aggressive. Expansion thus results from insecurity.[34] Notice that this assumption is strikingly different from the traditional realist one, that states expand as a consequence of increasing power resources.

---

34. The important works espousing these views include: Stephen Van Evera, "Causes of War" (Ph.D. dissertation, University of California, Berkeley, 1984); Van Evera, "The Cult of the Offensive and the Origins of the First World War," *International Security* Vol. 9, No. 1 (Summer 1984), pp. 58–108; Van Evera, "Why Cooperation Failed in 1914," *World Politics*, Vol. 38, No. 1 (October 1985), pp. 80–118; Barry R. Posen, *The Sources of Military Doctrine: France, Britain, and Germany Between the World Wars* (Ithaca, N.Y.: Cornell University Press, 1984); Barry R. Posen and Stephen Van Evera, "Reagan Administration Defense Policy: Departure from Containment," in Kenneth A. Oye, Robert J. Lieber, Donald Rothchild, eds., *Eagle Resurgent? The Reagan Era in American Foreign Policy* (Boston: Little Brown, 1987); Stephen M. Walt, *The Origins of Alliances;* Walt, "The Case for Finite Containment," *International Security*, Vol. 14, No. 1 (Summer 1989), pp. 5–50; Jack Levy, "Declining Power and the Preventive Motive for War," *World Politics*, Vol. 40, No. 1 (October 1987), pp. 82–107; Jack Snyder, *The Ideology of the Offensive: Military Decision Making and the Disasters of 1914* (Ithaca, N.Y.: Cornell University Press, 1984); and Ted Hopf, "Polarity, the Offense-Defense Balance, and War," *American Political Science Review*, Vol. 85, No. 2 (June 1991), pp. 476–493. Much of the inspiration for this school's assumptions comes from Robert Jervis, "Cooperation Under the Security Dilemma," *World Politics*, Vol. 30, No. 3 (January 1978), pp. 167–214.

Defensive realists make a second assumption: that the workings of the international system demonstrate that a state's security requires limited external interests, small armies, and carefully restrained foreign policies. States expand for security, and neo-realism shows that "security [is] plentiful,"[35] aggression is quickly counter-balanced, and technology and geography usually favor defenders. Anything beyond a moderate, incremental foreign policy is unnecessary and counterproductive.[36] In practice, of course, states often try to expand beyond these objective security requirements, but defensive realism refuses to attribute any of this expansion to systemic incentives. The international system pressures states towards moderate behavior only; anything else must be explained at some other level of analysis because it cannot be a rational response to the international environment. Thus defensive realism's systemic explanation of state behavior actually explains very little foreign policy behavior. From this perspective most great powers in modern history are exceptions to be accounted for; indeed much of the scholarship of defensive realism strives to explain behavior that, as Snyder admits, is "common" and "widespread" (pp. 1, 2–10). Not only is most great power behavior inexplicable, it is also pathological. The diagnoses offered by defensive realists invariably revolve around domestic deformities within the body politic of states that cause them to expand—for example, militaristic general staffs, strategic mythmakers, and imperialistic cartels.[37]

The assumption that the system provides incentives for cautious behavior explains little great power behavior in history. Thus it proves to be unhelpful, and defensive realists must construct theories of domestic politics that try to explain the anomalies that their "first-cut" assumption has generated.[38] These auxiliary theories, like Snyder's, must find similarities at the domestic level across a wide spectrum of domestic regimes. Neorealism is often loosely characterized as "leaving domestic politics out," but in fact defensive realism

---

35. Walt, *Origins of Allianices*, p. 49.
36. See, for example, Posen, *Sources of Military Doctrine*, pp. 68–69; Stephen Walt, "The Search for a Science of Strategy: A Review Essay on *Makers of Modern Strategy*," *International Security*, Vol. 12, No.1 (Summer 1987), pp. 140–166; and Snyder, *Myths of Empire*, pp. 1–31.
37. Van Evera, "Cult of the Offensive"; Snyder, *Ideology of the Offensive*; Snyder, *Myths of Empire*. Key revisionist histories that support these interpretations include: Kehr, *Battleship Building*; Kehr, *Economic Interests*; Hans Ulrich Wehler, *The German Empire, 1871–1918* (Leamington Spa/ Dover, N.H.: Berg Press, 1985); Arno J. Mayer, *The Persistence of the Old Regime: Europe to the Great War* (New York: Pantheon, 1981).
38. "[Imre] Lakatos' discussion of scientific research programs leads us to expect that when confronted with anomalies, theorists will create auxiliary theories." Robert Keohane, "Theory of World Politics," in Keohane, *Neorealism*, p. 185.

has the opposite tendency; it uses domestic politics to do all the work in its theory. Defensive realism begins with a minimalist systemic assumption that explains very little state behavior, generating anomalies instead. It then uses auxiliary domestic politics theories to explain away these inconvenient cases—which comprise much of modern diplomatic history. Imre Lakatos terms such projects theoretically "degenerative."[39]

Defensive realists assume that the international system provides incentives for moderate behavior because they misconstrue the manner in which the system affects states. Defensive realism is premised on the notion that the system teaches states to seek only minimal security because aggression always faces balancing, the costs of expansion quickly exceed the benefits, and defenders usually have the advantage.[40] But systemic imperatives do not operate in this manner. Waltz suggests that the international system affects states in two ways: "socialization," and "competition and selection." Socialization causes all states to become more alike; competition and selection generates an order because some states do better than others.[41] This does not mean, however, that the system teaches states wisdom.

To develop an analogy that Waltz and others have used, the international system affects states in much the same way that the market affects firms. Economists assume that a self-help environment forces firms to attempt "profit-maximization." In reality, some firms choose risky, short-term, high-profit strategies and others pursue more cautious, longer-term strategies that generate smaller immediate gains. Rather than assume that all firms strive for "reasonable" profits, microeconomics starts with the theoretical assumption that firms attempt to maximize profit.[42] Periodically, technological shifts, recessions, bankruptcies, and market failures cause many firms of both types to lose money; some even go bankrupt. Yet few economists would argue that these market outcomes can be predicted from the behavior of individual pathological firms. Rational strategies by firms can lead to sub-optimal out-

---

39. Imre Lakatos, "Falsification and the Methodology of Scientific Research Programmes," in Imre Lakatos and Alan Musgrave, eds., *Criticism and the Growth of Knowledge* (Cambridge: Cambridge University Press, 1970), pp. 117–118.
40. See especially Posen, *Sources of Military Doctrine*, pp. 67–69; and Walt, "The Search for a Science of Strategy."
41. Waltz, *Theory of International Politics*, pp. 74–77; and Waltz, "A Response to My Critics," in Keohane, *Neorealism*, pp. 330–332.
42. Despite all the additional constraints placed on the concept of profit-maximization, economists believe it is "certainly the place to start." Stanley Fischer and Rudiger Dornbusch, *Economics* (New York: McGraw-Hill, 1983), pp. 139–141.

comes. The nineteenth-century company that made stage-coaches may have been the best-run company in the world; it went bankrupt for systemic reasons. To assume rationality is not to assume foresight.

The international system affects states similarly; therefore even though states behave in various manners—some are cautious appeasers, while others are bold risk-takers—we must start with the *theoretical assumption* that the existence of an anarchic environment causes states to attempt self-help continuously. States are driven by the system's competitive imperative, which produces what could be termed "influence-maximizing" behavior.[43] The results are not always salutary either in economics or international relations, due to "the tyranny of small decisions":

It is an inherent characteristic of a consumer-sovereign, market economy that big changes occur as an accretion of moderate-sized steps, each of them the consequence of "small" purchase decisions—small in their individual size, time perspective, and in relation to their total, combined ultimate effect. Because change takes place in this fashion, it sometimes produces results that conflict with the very values the market economy is supposed to serve.[44]

In the same way, rational short-term behavior on the part of individual states can lead to sub-optimal outcomes in the international arena. Charles Maier has explained, for example, that the length and terror of World War I, not desired by *any* of the states involved, was the result of individual decisions

43. I use the term "influence-maximizing" rather than "power-maximizing" to avoid the pitfalls of the vague concept of power. Realists in the past have used power-maximization to suggest alternately that states expand *for* increased resources or *as a consequence* of increased resources. I adopt the second meaning. The stronger a state gets, the more influence it wants. Waltz's own writings are confused and contradictory on this issue. He attempts—for almost aesthetic reasons—to distance himself from the classical realists' concept of power (influence) maximizing, but at the same time he makes clear that the opposite—influence-minimization—is implausible, because states can never have limited conceptions of their security. See Waltz, *Man, the State, and War*, pp. 37–38, 227. He also frequently cites the example of firms attempting profit-maximization as a parallel to state behavior and insists that units in any self-help environment will display "maximizing" behavior. Waltz chooses, however, not to regard influence-maximizing behavior as the equivalent of profit-maximizing behavior, using instead the concept that states constantly attempt self-help or seek survival. The difference between this assumption and influence-maximization is semantic. The urge to "constantly seek survival" will produce the same behavior as influence-maximizing, because anarchy and differential growth-rates ensure that "survival" is never achieved and the state is never allowed to relax its efforts. See Waltz, *Theory of International Politics*, pp. 74–76, 117–119, 136–137.
44. Alfred E. Kahn, "The Tyranny of Small Decisions," *Kyklos*, Vol. 19, No. 1 (1966), repr. in Bruce Russett, ed., *Economic Theories of International Relations* (Chicago: Markham, 1968), p. 537. On relating "market-failure" to international relations, see Robert O. Keohane, *After Hegemony: Cooperation and Discord in the World Political Economy* (Princeton: Princeton University Press, 1984), pp. 82–83.

that were rational *"given what was known to the decision-makers at the time,* and yet each [led] to horrendous consequences."[45] Defensive realists have confused the system's effects on states with the lessons that *they* believe states should learn from that system's operation. In fact, such "lessons" unfold over long time spans and are highly subjective. (Did the outbreak of World War I teach nations that they balanced too much, or too little?) Outside of the general influence-maximizing imperative that the system forces on states, longer-term lessons have always been the subject of heated debates. The key points of all of the writings on the lessons of international history are that nations rarely learn any one lesson from specific events in the past, what each nation learns is never the same as the other, and each applies these lessons in a different manner.[46] Moreover if states were socialized uniformly by the lesson that balancing occurs, a massive collective action problem would inevitably result, since for any given state the incentive to "free-ride" would be enormous. Thus, the logic of defensive realists' understanding of systemic incentives would make balancing behavior less common than they claim it is.[47] This flawed understanding of socialization makes Barry Posen refer to his theory as "historical" realism versus the older and cruder ahistorical realism.[48] For Waltz, however, realism is *explicitly* ahistorical. It rests on the assumption that "through all the changes of boundaries, of social, economic, and political form, of economic and military activity, the substance and style of international politics remains strikingly constant."[49]

One may agree with defensive realists that states should learn certain lessons from the international system, but good theory explains how the

45. Charles S. Maier, "Wargames: 1914–1919," in Rotberg and Rabb, *The Origin and Prevention of Major Wars*, pp. 249–281. The quotation is from another essay in the same volume in which Bruce Bueno de Mesquita summarizes Maier's argument; ibid., p. 56.

46. Ernest May, *"Lessons" of the Past* (New York: Oxford University Press, 1973); Ernest May and Richard Neustadt, *Thinking in Time* (Cambridge: Harvard University Press, 1987); Yuen Foong Khong, *Analogies at War* (Princeton, N.J.: Princeton University Press, 1992); Michael Howard, *The Lessons of History* (New Haven, Conn.: Yale University Press, 1991), pp. 6–49, 177–201.

47. For a discussion of this issue in an empirical context, see Fareed Zakaria, "The Reagan Strategy of Containment," *Political Science Quarterly*, Vol. 105, No. 3 (Fall 1990), pp. 391–392. A version of the collective action problem is nicely dealt with in Thomas J. Christensen and Jack Snyder, "Chain Gangs and Passed Bucks," *International Organization*, Vol. 44, No. 3 (Summer 1990), pp. 137–168.

48. Posen, *Sources of Military Doctrine*, pp. 68–69.

49. Waltz, "A Response to My Critics," p. 329. Virtually the same sentence can be found in Waltz, *Theory of International Politics*, p. 110.

world *does* work, not how it *should* work. By smuggling in normative assumptions about state behavior, defensive realism ends up regarding much
foreign policy as abnormal and then explaining it by attributing abnormality
to guilty parties. Ironically, one detects in this school of thought many of the
idealistic assumptions that realists have traditionally scorned: the assumption
that states can be easily satisfied; the conviction that nations can learn the
"true" lessons of the past; and the belief that expansionism and international
conflict, far from normal, are the result of domestic disorders within states.
One wonders if defensive realists believe that if the diseases were cured—
the military bureaucracies, mythmakers, and cartels abolished—states would
pursue enlightened self-interests that would never trigger balancing coalitions, and the result would thus be a perpetual peace.[50]

Conclusions and Future Research

Jack Snyder's *Myths of Empire* is an ambitious attempt to enlarge the discourse
of international relations by studying domestic politics. He demonstrates
how comparative-politics theories can be used and expanded to shed light
on foreign policy. Future work in international relations should build on the
three great strengths of *Myths of Empire*: first, its insistence that imperialism
in the periphery and foreign policy at the core should be studied together
because they emanate from the same metropol; second, its impressive synthesis of comparative politics theories, in particular its emphasis on logrolling;
and third, its demonstration that strategic rationales are often cynically put
forward by statesmen to garner popular support for their policies.

But future work should also avoid Snyder's pitfalls. He is unable to provide
a model of domestic politics that is compatible with system-level influences
chiefly because his theoretical ambitions undermine his analysis. Snyder
attempts to build a domestic explanation with the same power and sweep
as systemic ones. (This may explain why he, and other *Innenpolitikers*, are
drawn to neo-Marxist explanations. Only Marxist explanations can match
realism's generalizability.) He fails for two reasons. First, he tries to explain
an international outcome, the success of expansion, which cannot be explained without recourse to system-level factors. Second, even if he were
explaining state policies, he should have begun by separating the systemic

---

50. I have benefited from conversations with Andrew Moravcsik on this point.

causes of state behavior from the domestic ones. A good theory of foreign policy should first ask what effect the international system has on national behavior, because the most powerful *generalizable* characteristic of a state in international relations is its relative position in the international system. A first-cut theory of foreign policy should begin by looking at the effect of this relative standing on a state's preferences. Theories of foreign policy that place chief emphasis on internal—national, bureaucratic, or individual— causes often make hidden assumptions about the way the international environment shapes a state's range of choices. Such theories typically consider only those cases where the behavior they are examining exists, biasing their conclusions. Snyder's case selection is an example. He only considers great powers "at the height of their expansionism," thus selecting only those cases where the behavior he expects occurs (p. 2). Had he chosen other powers with similar patterns of industrialization or cartelization but without a pattern of overexpansion,[51] he would have recognized that systemic factors were present in the cases of overexpansion and absent in other cartelized systems.[52]

A good explanation of foreign policy should not ignore domestic politics or national culture or individual decision-makers. But it must separate the effects of the various levels of international politics. In order to achieve balance between the parsimony of a spare theory and greater descriptive accuracy, a first-cut theory can be layered successively with additional causes from different levels of analysis focusing on domestic regime types, bureaucracies, and statesmen. As Robert Keohane writes:

The larger the domain of a theory, the less accuracy we expect . . . The domain of theory is narrowed to achieve greater precision. Thus the debate between advocates of parsimony and proponents of contextual subtlety resolves itself into a question of *stages*, rather than either-or choices. We should seek parsimony first, then add on complexity while monitoring the adverse

---

51. Gerschenkron's complete list of countries that experienced late industrialization includes Germany, Austria, Italy, Switzerland, France, Belgium, and large parts of the Austro-Hungarian empire. See Gerschenkron, *Economic Backwardness*, p. 16.
52. Snyder avoids an interesting and hard case for his analysis that would possibly falsify his thesis. The U.S. period of industrialization in 1865–1929, with a mixed pattern of industrialization, early in the north and late in the south, produced an uneasy coalition of elites who logrolled on many policy issues. It was also a period of foreign "under-expansion" compared with any other great power. Yet Snyder chooses to consider post–World War II American foreign policy, clearly selecting "on the dependent variable." Schumpeter's discussion of atavistic imperialism has the same case-selection bias.

effects this has on the predictive power of our theory: its ability to make significant inferences on the basis of limited information.[53]

Over the last decade, scholars of international relations have either ignored the international system or never moved beyond it. Instead, a good account of a nation's foreign policy should include systemic, domestic, and other influences, specifying what aspects of the policy can be explained by what factors. Paul Kennedy's essay on the Kaiser's role in German *Weltpolitik* is a rare example of this kind of comprehensive analysis.[54]

Domestic politics has a crucial influence on foreign policy. It is a mistake, however, to place it in competition with international factors when constructing general explanations of state behavior, not least because it will lose the contest. Domestic factors often seem more important than international ones in any particular case, like Hitler's Germany, but *in general*, across time and space, states' positions in the anarchic international system prove to provide the simplest, shortest guide to international relations. This is hardly a cause for disappointment. The parsimony of a systemic theory is useful for some purposes, but more accurate theories are far more useful for many other purposes.[55] Domestic politics explanations can be most useful in explaining events, trends, and policies that are too specific to be addressed by a grand theory of international politics. That comprises most of international life.

---

53. Keohane, "Theory of World Politics," pp. 187–188.
54. Kennedy distinguishes what parts of Wilhelmine foreign policy can be explained by systemic factors, what parts by domestic structures and finally, what parts by Kaiser Wilhelm's personal idiosyncrasies. See Paul Kennedy, "The Kaiser and German *Weltpolitik*: Reflections on Wilhelm II's Place in the Making of German Foreign Policy," in John C.G. Rohl and Nicholas Sombart, eds., *Kaiser Wilhelm II: New Interpretations* (New York: Cambridge University Press, 1982), pp. 143–167. Among historians, Kennedy has thought most seriously about levels of analysis (though he would never use the term). See especially Paul Kennedy, "A.J.P. Taylor and 'Profound Forces' in History," in Chris Wrigley, ed., *Warfare, Diplomacy, and Politics: Essays in Honor of A.J.P. Taylor* (London: Hamish Hamilton, 1986), pp. 14–29.
55. Robert Keohane starts his analysis of the sources of cooperation with a structural realist theory of international politics and then layers onto it additional variables that provide more determinate predictions. See Keohane, *After Hegemony*, pp. 5–31. Other works that blend levels of analysis include Doyle, *Empires*; and Katzenstein, *Between Power and Plenty*. For a recent analysis that starts with systemic factors and then layers on domestic ones to yield clearer predictions, see Randall L. Schweller, "Domestic Structure and Preventive War," *World Politics*, Vol. 44, No. 2 (January 1992), pp. 235–270.

Institutions and Cooperation

Lisa L. Martin

Sanctions During the Falkland Islands Conflict

$\mathbf{A}$t the beginning of April 1982, a long-running dispute between Great Britain and Argentina about sovereignty over the Falkland Islands (called the Malvinas in Latin America) broke into open conflict when Argentine forces invaded the islands. During the next two months, at Britain's urging, many states imposed economic sanctions against Argentina. Sanctions both preceded and accompanied British military action. In this article I examine Britain's success in gaining the cooperation of other states, particularly the members of the European Economic Community (EEC). The high level of cooperation cannot be explained on the basis of narrowly-defined national self-interest, because only Britain had a strong interest in reacting to Argentina's moves, while other states had good reasons to prefer to avoid imposing sanctions.[1] Resistance to imposing sanctions increased as the crisis escalated and derived primarily from political concerns about supporting Britain in war and, to a lesser extent, from the economic costs of sanctions. I argue that British manipulation of the EEC's institutional incentives overcame members' resistance.

A number of international relations theorists have presented arguments about the role that international institutions might play in facilitating cooperation among states. By means such as providing information about the actions of other states, setting standards by which to evaluate others' behav-

Lisa L. Martin is a National Fellow at the Hoover Institution on War, Revolution and Peace, Stanford University, and Assistant Professor of Political Science at the University of California, San Diego. She is the author of Coercive Cooperation: Explaining Multilateral Economic Sanctions *(Princeton University Press, forthcoming 1992).*

My thanks to James Alt, Robert Keohane, Gary King, Stephen Krasner, Peter Yu, and three anonymous readers for their comments and suggestions. This research was assisted by an award from the Social Science Research Council's Program in Foreign Policy Studies.

1. The level of cooperation achieved in this case is well above the average for post-1945 cases of economic sanctions. One comprehensive study gives the Falklands case a cooperation score in the top 25 percent of all sanctions episodes since 1945. See Gary Clyde Hufbauer, Jeffrey J. Schott, and Kimberly Ann Elliott, *Economic Sanctions Reconsidered: Supplemental Case Histories*, 2d ed. (Washington, D.C.: Institute for International Economics, 1990), p. 544.

International Security, Spring 1992 (Vol. 16, No. 4)
© 1992 by the President and Fellows of Harvard College and of the Massachusetts Institute of Technology.

ior, or establishing penalties for non-compliance, such institutions may allow states to overcome collective action problems.[2] Studies have also shown how, in domestic contexts, institutions can provide for cooperation among self-interested individuals by allowing them to make credible commitments and by assigning property rights.[3] Yet, on the international level, scholars working in the realist tradition maintain a well-founded skepticism about the empirical impact of institutional factors on state behavior. This skepticism is grounded in a lack of studies that show precisely how and when institutions have constrained state decision-making.[4] This study addresses the question of institutional constraint by providing micro-level evidence that decisions made by the EEC directly influenced the foreign policy decisions of its members, even when governments faced political and economic incentives to defect from the sanctions effort. While a single case cannot conclusively prove a particular hypothesis correct, process-tracing such as this is a necessary complement to aggregate-level results showing correlations between institutions and cooperation.[5]

This article begins with a brief chronology of the Falklands War and economic sanctions imposed during this episode. While Britain took the lead in imposing sanctions, gaining the cooperation of other states and the approval of international institutions were also matters of high priority for the British government. After this overview, I discuss in more depth the involvement of the EEC and the decisions that led to the Community's imposition of

2. A collective action problem results when states can only achieve their goals through joint action, while each has incentives to defect from joint efforts. See Robert O. Keohane, *After Hegemony: Cooperation and Discord in the World Political Economy* (Princeton: Princeton University Press, 1984); Keohane, "International Institutions: Two Approaches," *International Studies Quarterly*, Vol. 32, No. 4 (December 1988), pp. 379–396; Kenneth A. Oye, "Explaining Cooperation under Anarchy: Hypotheses and Strategies," in Oye, ed., *Cooperation under Anarchy* (Princeton: Princeton University Press, 1986), pp. 1–24.
3. See Douglass C. North and Barry R. Weingast, "Constitutions and Commitment: The Evolution of Institutions Governing Public Choice in Seventeenth-Century England," *Journal of Economic History*, Vol. 49, No. 4 (December 1989), pp. 803–832; Paul R. Milgrom, Douglass C. North, and Barry R. Weingast, "The Role of Institutions in the Revival of Trade: The Law Merchant, Private Judges, and the Champagne Fairs," Hoover Institution Working Papers in Political Science P-90-1 (Stanford, Calif.: Stanford University, January 1990); Douglass C. North, *Structure and Change in Economic History* (New York: W.W. Norton, 1981).
4. Oran R. Young, *International Cooperation: Building Regimes for Natural Resources and the Environment* (Ithaca: Cornell University Press, 1989), p. 206; Susan Strange, "*Cave! Hic Dragones*: A Critique of Regime Analysis," in Stephen D. Krasner, ed., *International Regimes* (Ithaca: Cornell University Press, 1983), p. 354.
5. For aggregate results of cooperation on economic sanctions, see Lisa L. Martin, *Coercive Cooperation: Explaining Multilateral Economic Sanctions* (Princeton: Princeton University Press, forthcoming 1992).

sanctions. The pattern of decision-making shows that individual states formulated their sanctions policies contingent on the organization's decisions. The course of EEC sanctions can be divided into three distinct phases. In the first, states saw sanctions as an alternative to military action, and were involved in an assurance game where most were willing to cooperate contingent on multilateral action.[6] In the second, after the outbreak of military conflict in the South Atlantic, EEC members became much more reluctant to continue imposing sanctions. The third phase involves intensive negotiations over the renewal of sanctions in mid-May, as fighting continued. Intra-EEC politics show that linkage across issues was vital to Britain's ability to gain the cooperation of other states, particularly in the latter two phases. I argue that a link between ongoing budget discussions and the Falklands issue became central to the renewal of sanctions in mid-May.

The final section relates this history to the theoretical debate on the role of international institutions in cooperation problems. The Falklands case illuminates the reasons for international cooperation on economic sanctions and the role of institutions, if any, in facilitating such cooperation. This study shows that common interests alone did not explain cooperation. Instead, cooperation resulted from the intense interest of one state, which relied on bargains across issues to consolidate a coalition. An institution played a key role in this process, reducing transaction costs and making the cross-issue linkages credible. Neither neoliberals nor realists have fully anticipated the specific impact of institutions found here. The EEC did not solve a symmetrical collective action problem, as in neoliberal theories, but neither was it irrelevant or epiphenomenal, as most realist theorizing would describe it.

This sanctions problem is not an easy test for the proposition that institutions have an impact on state decisions. The Falklands case represents a situation with clear conflicts of interest among states that made the emergence of cooperation problematic. While from an institutional perspective the EEC is an unusually strong international organization, at the time of the Falklands crisis in 1982, European Political Cooperation (EPC), the forum in

---

6. In a Prisoners' Dilemma or assurance game, state interests are symmetric in that each places desired outcomes in the same order. In a Prisoners' Dilemma, states rank outcomes as follows, with the most-preferred first: unilateral defection (DC), mutual cooperation (CC), mutual defection (DD), unilateral cooperation (CD). In an assurance game, the first two payoffs are reversed, so that the ranking is CC>DC>DD>CD, and mutual cooperation is an equilibrium outcome. In an asymmetrical game, states' preference orderings differ from one another. For example, Britain might have assurance preferences while its partner has a Prisoners' Dilemma preference ordering.

which members sought to coordinate their foreign policies, was weak. In addition, this case is interesting from a substantive perspective. With the demise of the Cold War, economic sanctions are an ever more important tool of statecraft. The Falklands example exhibits striking analogies, on a smaller scale, to sanctions against Iraq in 1990–91, and therefore suggests lessons about the possibilities and problems surrounding the use of this instrument of statecraft. In both cases one state took the lead in organizing sanctions, turned to a formal international organization for this purpose, and relied on tactical linkages to convince recalcitrant states to join in the sanctions effort. These similarities suggest that the Falklands case was not unique. Tracing the process of state decision-making in 1982, therefore, offers an opportunity to gain both theoretical insight and practical understanding of multilateral economic sanctions.

The Falklands Crisis, 1982

Argentina and Britain have contested sovereignty over the Falkland Islands for the last two centuries. The Falklands are located in the South Atlantic, 480 miles northwest of Cape Horn. Their discovery is variously claimed by representatives of Spain and England at different dates in the sixteenth century. Spain forced out a small British colony on the islands in the 1770s; the Spanish settlers then withdrew in 1811 due to the high costs of maintaining a colony in such cold, barren surroundings. In 1820 Argentina declared sovereignty over the Falklands, sending settlers to stake its claim. In 1831, the United States briefly became involved in this drama, deporting the Argentine settlers and declaring the islands free of any government. Argentines, however, returned to establish a penal colony. In 1833, British warships landed on the islands to reclaim them. The Argentine settlers left peacefully, but under protest. Britain has exercised sovereignty over the islands since then, although Argentina has continued to argue that the Falklands were illegally taken by force.[7]

In 1965, Argentina took the Falklands case to the United Nations, which sporadically sponsored negotiations between the two claimants. These ne-

---

7. For histories of the Falkland Islands, see Julius Goebel, *The Struggle for the Falkland Islands: A Study in Legal and Diplomatic History*, 2d ed. (New Haven: Yale University Press, 1982); Ian J. Strange, *The Falkland Islands*, 3d ed. (Newton Abbott, London: David and Charles, 1983); Friedrich Kratochwil, Paul Rohrlich, and Harpreet Mahajan, *Peace and Disputed Sovereignty: Reflections on Conflict Over Territory* (Lanham, Md.: University Press of America, 1985).

gotiations made little progress, as neither side was willing to concede on the central issue of eventual sovereignty. In March 1982, negotiations broke down once again, with Argentine representatives warning that they would have to take stronger measures to advance their cause.[8] Apparently, this warning was not taken seriously in London, and there is no evidence that the Argentine government planned to invade in early March although invasion scenarios may have been considered by some in the military.

As of 1982, the Falklands were inhabited by about 1800 "kelpers" of British origin. The Falklanders are fiercely loyal to Britain, and just as fiercely disdainful of the Argentines. Most refuse to learn Spanish and maintain a willful ignorance of anything about Argentina.[9] The Falklanders want their island to remain a British dependency, and the British argument for sovereignty rests on the islanders' right of self-determination. Yet, because Argentina refuses to maintain regular communications and other services with the islands, the British government has found the cost of maintaining the Falklanders quite high.[10] The "Falklands lobby" in Parliament is disproportionately powerful and has frustrated occasional attempts by the Foreign and Commonwealth Office to give serious consideration to mechanisms that eventually would transfer sovereignty to Argentina.[11] The influence of the "Falklands pressure group" is perplexing. One analyst traces it to a parliamentary scandal and collapse of Anglo-Argentine negotiations in 1968.[12]

The 1982 Falklands crisis began somewhat haphazardly when on March 19 an Argentine scrap metal merchant landed on South Georgia, another British dependency about 600 miles east of the Falklands, and raised the Argentine flag. The captain apparently had the implicit backing of the Argentine navy, which expected little or no British response. Instead, Prime

---

8. Alexander M. Haig, Jr., *Caveat: Realism, Reagan, and Foreign Policy* (New York: Macmillan, 1984), p. 263.
9. See Strange, *The Falkland Islands*, pp. 247–254.
10. These costs kept the British from maintaining forces there before 1982 that were capable of defending the islands. After June 1982, the population of the island tripled as the number of military personnel stationed there far exceeded the original 1800 inhabitants. All in all, Britain's 1982 victory was an expensive one.
11. For a discussion of the positions of various parts of the British government on the Falklands, see "British Foreign Office," *The Economist*, November 27, 1982, pp. 19–26. For a history of the negotiations, see Max Hastings and Simon Jenkins, *The Battle for the Falklands* (New York: W.W. Norton, 1983), pp. 15–44.
12. Virginia Gamba, *The Falklands/Malvinas War: A Model for North-South Crisis Prevention* (Boston: Allen and Unwin, 1987), pp. 90–95. See also G.M. Dillon, *The Falklands, Politics and War* (London: Macmillan, 1989), pp. 55–89.

Minister Thatcher sent the ice patrol ship *HMS Endurance* from the Falklands to South Georgia.[13] The Argentine government, headed by President Leopoldo Galtieri and under intense domestic pressure due to rapidly deteriorating economic and political conditions, felt it had to respond and did so by landing Argentine commandos on South Georgia on March 25. The junta also decided to plan an invasion of the Falklands, apparently believing that the South Georgia incident provided an opportunity and that the invasion would direct domestic attention away from new austerity measures.[14]

By March 30, British Foreign Secretary Lord Carrington warned Parliament that Argentina had created a "potentially dangerous" situation in the South Atlantic. At Britain's request, the United Nations Security Council took up the Falklands issue on April 1; the President of the Council called on both sides to exercise restraint and avoid the use of force.[15] Carrington's warnings were confirmed when Argentina invaded the Falklands, South Georgia, and South Sandwich islands that night. About 300 marines landed in Port Stanley, the capital of the Falklands. The British forces defending the islands killed four Argentines and wounded two before surrendering; the Argentine forces were under orders not to harm the British forces, and did not return fire.

Sir Anthony Parsons, the British Permanent Representative to the UN, immediately called an emergency session of the Security Council on the morning of April 2. He demanded a vote within 24 hours on a resolution drawn up by Britain, demanding an immediate cease-fire and Argentine withdrawal. On April 3, the Security Council approved the British document, Resolution 502, by a vote of ten in favor (including the United States), only one against (Panama), and four abstaining (including the Soviet Union, which declined to use its veto power to kill the resolution).[16] Later, UN diplomats called the rapid passage of Resolution 502 "miraculous."[17] Delighted by this unexpected level of international support, Britain based its future actions on Resolution 502, refusing to ask for further Security Council or General As-

---

13. The British government had recently decided to decommission the *Endurance*, one of many moves that convinced the Argentine junta that the British were not seriously committed to defending the Falklands.

14. Hastings and Jenkins, *The Battle for the Falklands*, pp. 54–60.

15. "Falkland Islands (Islas Malvinas)," *UN Chronicle*, Vol. 19, No. 5 (May 1982), p. 3.

16. See Anthony Parsons, "The Falklands Crisis in the United Nations, 31 March–14 June 1982," *International Affairs*, Vol. 59, No. 2 (Spring 1983), pp. 169–172; "Council Calls for Withdrawal of Argentine Forces from Falklands," *UN Chronicle*, Vol. 19, No. 5 (May 1982), pp. 5–10.

17. David Tonge, "Britain Wary of Pushing UN for Support," *Financial Times*, April 28, 1982, p. 4.

sembly action. Since the Security Council would have to approve further UN actions, such as sending peacekeeping forces, any permanent member of the Security Council could veto the use of force. British officials believed that attempts to enforce 502 by approving UN activities intended to force Argentina to withdraw would meet with a Soviet veto. Thus, the UN's role in the unfolding conflict became more limited after April 3.

On April 3, the British government also broke diplomatic relations with Argentina and imposed economic sanctions. These sanctions, which were clarified over the next few days, included a freeze on Argentine assets in British banks (valued at about $1.5 billion), embargo of arms sales to Argentina, suspension of export credit insurance, and a ban on Argentine imports. However, the ban excluded goods already in transit, as well as Argentine assets in overseas branches of British banks. The freeze on assets was potentially the most damaging of these economic measures, as the already acute financial situation in Argentina meant that the government would need to borrow more than $7 billion on the international market in the remaining months of 1982. The leading role of the City of London in syndicated loans meant that international finance for Argentina might dry up.[18] Thatcher told the House of Commons, recalled on a Saturday for the first time in more than thirty years, that she saw the freeze of assets as "an appropriate precautionary and, I hope, temporary measure."[19]

London banks worried that the financial measures could harm their reputation as reliable sources of funds, and pressed the Bank of England for an "enlightened interpretation" of the sanctions regulations that would minimize damage to their long-term interests.[20] When the Bank of England came out with its clarified guidelines on April 13, they covered a wide range of transactions; British banks were not allowed to make any new loans to Argentina or to disburse funds from existing lines of credit. However, these restrictions did not apply to overseas branches of British banks, and so were acceptable to London financial interests.[21] Despite the exception for overseas branches, bankers expected the measures to deal a "sharp blow" to Argen-

---

18. Paul Cheeseright and John Wyles, "UK Bans All Argentine Imports," *Financial Times*, April 7, 1982, p. 1.
19. Great Britain, House of Commons, *The Falklands Campaign: A Digest of Debates in the House of Commons, 2 April to June 1982* (London: Her Majesty's Stationery Office, 1982) p. 4.
20. William Hall, "Bankers Fear Freeze has Harmed City's Reputation," *Financial Times*, April 10, 1982, p. 2.
21. William Hall and Alan Friedman, "Bank Guidance on Argentine Assets," *Financial Times*, April 14, 1982, p. 1.

tina's ability to borrow. Argentina responded to these measures by freezing British assets in Argentina, banning British imports (worth about $411 million annually),[22] and suspending payments to British banks. However, both British and Argentine financial interests leaned strongly against declaring Argentina formally in default on its British loans. One such declaration could trigger a spiderweb of cross-default clauses, with drastic effects on the international financial system. Thus, Argentina claimed that it was continuing to make payments on British debt to an escrow account set up in New York, and London banks were spared the necessity of finding Argentina in default.

Coincident with its own imposition of sanctions, the British government asked other states to take economic measures against Argentina. As detailed below, Britain formally asked the EEC to impose economic sanctions. British officials described intensive discussions with EEC states as the centerpiece of diplomatic efforts to isolate Argentina.[23] British diplomatic efforts focused on West Germany, Argentina's largest trade partner in the Community and a significant source of military goods.[24] Prime Minister Thatcher also communicated personally with the leaders of Commonwealth states, Western European nations, Japan, and the United States, asking for expressions of support. Many nations including France, West Germany, Belgium, Austria, the Netherlands, and Switzerland responded immediately by embargoing arms sales to Argentina. Australia, New Zealand, and Canada withdrew their ambassadors from Buenos Aires, and New Zealand banned all trade with Argentina.[25] The United States and Japan took no immediate actions.

The U.S. government found itself in the difficult position of being asked to choose between two allies. Faced with this dilemma, the government decided the best course was to remain neutral for the time being and to try to prevent the conflict from escalating to open warfare. Thus, Washington refused to impose sanctions and sent Secretary of State Alexander Haig to

---

22. Gary Clyde Hufbauer and Jeffrey J. Schott, *Economic Sanctions Reconsidered: History and Current Policy* (Washington, D.C.: Institute for International Economics, 1985), p. 717.
23. Cheeseright and Wyles, "UK Bans All Argentine Imports," p. 1.
24. EEC sanctions were lifted in June 1982. West Germany went ahead with delivery of four frigates to Argentina in September in spite of British objections. See Foreign Staff, "Bonn Lifts Argentine Arms Ban," *Financial Times*, September 27, 1982, p. 3.
25. Janis A. Kreslins, "Chronology: The Falklands War," *Foreign Affairs*, Vol. 60, No. 3 (America and the World 1982), p. 740; Foreign Staff, "Australia and Canada Recall Envoys," *Financial Times*, April 7, p. 4; House of Commons, *The Falklands Campaign*, p. 75.

attempt to negotiate a settlement to the dispute. However, evidence that has come out since 1982 shows that, at least in the lower levels of government and within the military, the United States was never neutral. The Defense Department, in particular, provided important assistance to the British task force from the beginning.[26] The president took no action to inhibit this support, although he might have if the support had become public while Haig's mission was unfolding.

For most of the month of April, the course of the crisis was dominated by Haig's shuttle diplomacy and the movement of the British task force toward the Falklands. The approach of a task force of more than 100 ships and 28,000 men placed a *de facto* time limit on negotiations, although the Argentines and many others remained unconvinced that the British were actually willing to risk lives over a few barren rocks 8000 miles from Britain. However, domestic political pressures and Thatcher's own preferences reduced the probability that Britain could back down from its stand on the Falklanders' right of self-determination at this time. At home, the conflict led to a burst of support for Thatcher's Conservative party, which otherwise was in electoral trouble.[27] In the House of Commons, support for a strong response to the actions of the "tinpot fascist junta" was almost universal.[28] Any outcome that looked like a British surrender would almost certainly have led to demands that Thatcher resign.

On April 8, Britain announced a 200-mile blockade around the Falklands effective April 12 and threatened to sink any Argentine vessel within this area. Haig continued his negotiations, but Argentina repeatedly rejected any deal that did not guarantee eventual Argentine sovereignty over the islands. The Organization of American States (OAS) formally began to discuss the conflict on April 21, where the majority of votes were, predictably, in Argentina's favor. However, the OAS never called for sanctions against Britain.

Until April 25 the Falklands dispute remained a matter of diplomacy rather than military confrontation, but on that date, the task force reached South Georgia and recaptured it in a two-hour battle. Britain would have sufficient

---

26. "America's Falklands War," *The Economist*, March 3, 1984, p. 29; Haig, *Caveat*, p. 266.
27. Robert Worcester and Simon Jenkins, "Britain Rallies 'Round the Prime Minister," *Public Opinion*, Vol. 5 (June/July 1982), pp. 53–55; Helmut Norpoth, "Guns and Butter and Government Popularity in Britain," *American Political Science Review*, Vol. 81, No. 3 (September 1987), pp. 949–959.
28. See House of Commons, *The Falklands Campaign*, p. 1.

forces in the area by April 30 to enforce the 200-mile blockade, and warned that it would do so. However, even this threat was insufficient to convince the Argentines to back down. At this time, many observers had doubts about Britain's ability to win a military confrontation. Argentina had a logistical advantage, with British forces having to operate 8000 miles from home. Argentine military forces were equipped with advanced, modern armaments, some of them purchased from Britain. In addition, the Argentine forces had the advantage of defending, rather than trying to invade, the islands.

When it became obvious on April 30 that neither Argentina nor Britain would back down, the United States announced its unqualified support for Britain. The U.S. government imposed some limited sanctions against Argentina, including an arms embargo, and offered overt support to the British task force. The next day, fighting began in the Falklands with British bombers attacking airfields on the islands. On the night of May 2–3, a British submarine sank the Argentine cruiser *General Belgrano*, which was outside the declared exclusion zone. More than 300 Argentine sailors were killed in this attack. This action shocked most of the world, as it realized the potential for widespread casualties in the Falklands. The sinking had a negative impact on sympathy for the British in Europe, where many felt that Britain had acted too aggressively. Ireland called for an end to EEC sanctions.[29] On May 4, Argentina sank *HMS Sheffield*, killing 30 and claiming retaliation for the *Belgrano*.

After the failure of Haig's negotiating efforts, UN Secretary General Javier Perez de Cuellar attempted to find a solution to the conflict. However, despite personal appeals to Prime Minister Thatcher and President Galtieri, his efforts were fruitless. Peru, which had sided with Argentina from the beginning of the conflict, also attempted to play the role of mediator without success. Fighting continued, with Britain gaining a foothold on the islands on May 21. British forces continued to gain ground and Argentina finally surrendered at Port Stanley on June 14. Over the next week, arrangements were made for the exchange of prisoners; the British governor of the Falklands returned on June 26. The defeat contributed to the fall of the Argentine military junta within a matter of months.[30]

---

29. Olivia O'Leary, "All-Out War Feared as Belgrano Sinks with Many Missing," *Irish Times*, May 4, 1982, p. 1.
30. See Alejandro Dabat and Luis Lorenzano, *Argentina: The Malvinas and the End of Military Rule* (London: Verso, 1984).

The Falklands and the European Economic Community

After its initial success in the UN, British efforts to gain international support centered on the EEC. In this section, I examine the series of EEC decisions on economic sanctions. I argue that Britain had to persuade other EEC members, who would not, especially after the start of hostilities, have imposed sanctions without sustained British efforts. As discussed below, governments faced varying degrees of domestic opposition to sanctions and would derive few direct benefits from them. As long as Britain was taking a strong stand against the dangerous precedent set by Argentina's actions, they would have preferred to free-ride on British actions. Examination of political and economic interests, and of statements made at the time, reveal that only Britain was willing to impose unilateral sanctions. In such a situation of asymmetrical interests, cross-issue linkages would provide one of the few levers for gaining the cooperation of recalcitrant states.[31] In this case, the linkage was provided by an ongoing dispute over the EEC budget and the Common Agricultural Policy (CAP); British concessions on the budget issue were linked to renewal of EEC sanctions in mid-May. Examination of EEC involvement provides persuasive evidence of the importance of international organizations in facilitating cooperation. Many of the smaller member states did not impose sanctions until the EEC formally called for them, as the larger problems of Community solidarity and political cooperation became intertwined with the somewhat obscure issue of sovereignty in the Falklands.

For analytical clarity, I divide EEC sanctions into three phases. During the first, most member states had an interest in supporting Britain with multilateral sanctions, seeing them as an alternative to politically costly military conflict. In this phase, the EEC as an organization provided member states with assurance that they would not be acting unilaterally, but it was not necessarily central to their sanctions decisions. The second phase began as military action broke out, and presented Britain with a more difficult cooperation problem. Now, some members preferred to defect rather than to continue with multilateral sanctions, and only maintained them because the EEC as a whole would not agree to withdraw them. Finally, the third phase of sanctions involved crucial negotiations over their renewal in mid-May. At

---

31. Cross-issue linkages result when a government makes its actions on a particular issue, such as sanctions, contingent on others' actions on independent issues, such as economic policy.

this time, most EEC members preferred no sanctions to continued cooperation unless they received a side-payment from Britain, which took the form
of concessions on a budget rebate.

INITIAL EEC SANCTIONS: AN ASSURANCE GAME

In this section, I argue that most EEC members were willing to support
Britain with sanctions prior to military engagement, as long as they were
assured that the rest of the Community would act in the same manner.
Because European states believed that a broad ban on Argentine imports
would provide sufficient leverage to force the junta to back down, they saw
multilateral sanctions as an effective alternative to military conflict. In addition, because EEC members did not expect sanctions to last longer than a
few weeks, governments anticipated low costs. Although some members
were more reluctant than others to impose sanctions due either to high direct
costs or unwillingness to support Britain, all eventually acquiesced in the
Commission's initial decision to take action. Thus, this phase presents a
somewhat weak case for institutional impacts on state decisions.

One of the most striking features of EEC involvement in the Falklands is
the speed with which the normally slow-moving Community acted. As one
EEC official said, "We have done in a day what it usually takes a year to
do."[32] British diplomacy deserves any credit for this rapid response, as gaining the cooperation of others in imposing sanctions received sustained attention at the highest levels of government. The prime minister, foreign secretary, and various ambassadors immediately called on other nations to support
the British cause, framing the issue as one of responding to unlawful international aggression. On Monday, April 5, just four days after the invasion,
the Secretary of State for Trade informed Parliament that "any helpful economic response in this dispute can best proceed if we are supported fully by
our nearest allies in the European Community."[33] The British government
quickly realized that its economic pressure on Argentina would be minimal
unless other states also cut imports, export credits, and arms exports. Since
the EEC accounted for approximately 20 percent of Argentina's exports, a
Community-wide ban on imports could, politicians believed, put intense
economic pressure on Buenos Aires.[34]

---

32. "Waging Economic Warfare," *Time*, April 26, 1982, p. 31.
33. House of Commons, *The Falklands Campaign*, p. 23.
34. Eberhard Rein, "The Community and the Falklands: A Stand Against Aggression," *Europe
82*, No. 5/6 (May/June 1982), p. 15.

West Germany was Argentina's largest trading partner in the European Community in 1982, with Argentine exports to West Germany worth almost $565 million and West German exports to Argentina worth $1 billion. Thus, British efforts first centered on the West German government. Foreign Minister Hans-Dietrich Genscher had extensive discussions with Lord Carrington on April 1 and 2. On April 5, British ambassador Sir Jock Taylor met with Foreign Ministry State Secretary Bernd von Staden. At this time, German representatives felt that it was too early to discuss economic sanctions. However, they reached an informal agreement to stop the shipment of West German–built frigates if the conflict escalated. One West German diplomat said, "We would do our utmost to comply with Britain's wishes." Belgian Foreign Minister Leo Tindemans, then serving as the president of the EEC Council of Ministers and a proponent of EPC, also became the target of British lobbying efforts. His initial response was generally supportive.

Although the EEC quickly condemned Argentina's use of force and called for its withdrawal from the islands, the question of imposing economic sanctions that could be costly for the Community if they stayed in place for any significant time remained undecided. EEC trade with Argentina in 1980 totaled about $4 billion, with a $460 million trade surplus.[35] Banning Argentine imports would not cost much to the Community as a whole, since most Argentine imports such as meat and other agricultural products were already over-produced by member states. However, Italy and Ireland could suffer from termination of leather imports for their shoe industries. In addition, the EEC fully expected that Argentina would retaliate by banning Community imports, as it had when Britain announced sanctions on Argentine imports.[36] Thus, the cost of sanctions lay not only in lost imports, but the near-certainty of losing the Argentine market as well. In fact, on April 9 Argentina formally protested EEC discussions of sanctions and threatened to (and later did) adopt "pertinent measures responding to those liable to affect its foreign trade and international economic relations."[37]

By April 6, initial soundings from Community members were encouraging enough for Britain to call formally for EEC sanctions against Argentina. Britain asked only for measures that did not exceed steps it had taken

35. Reuters North European Service, April 5, 1982.
36. Cawl Cosgrove Twitchett, "The Falklands: Community Diplomacy at Work," *Europe 82*, No. 7 (July 1982), p. 11; John Cooney, "Ireland Agrees to EEC Embargo," *Irish Times*, April 12, 1982, p. 6.
37. Reuters North European Service, April 9, 1982.

unilaterally. It requested an embargo on arms sales, to which the Netherlands and West Germany, followed by Belgium and France, had already agreed. Since Argentina relied heavily on French and West German arms, these moves were significant. The French were highly supportive of the British position, probably because Argentine success in the Falklands would set an unwelcome precedent for various disputed French colonial possessions. Most importantly, Britain asked for a ban on some Argentine imports (including beef, steel, textiles, and leather goods), an end to preferential treatment of other Argentine imports, and termination of export credits.

Over the next few days, EEC ambassadors consulted with their governments on the issue of sanctions. While West Germany and France seemed willing to go along with the British request, some of the other EEC members were more reluctant. Ireland, in particular, questioned the wisdom of sanctions. Prime Minister Charles Haughey was reported to be cool to the British request and to believe that sanctions would be "counter-productive."[38] During four hours of talks on April 8, the political directors from EEC foreign ministries decided to defer a decision on sanctions, awaiting further instructions from their governments.[39] They did, however, agree to terminate all supplies of arms and military equipment. In spite of general support for Britain, as of April 9 reports from EEC sources suggested that Community action would fall short of an import ban.[40] Denmark stated that it would not accept any sanctions that were not administered on the national, as opposed to supra-national, level. Italy, in addition to benefiting from leather imports, had a large emigrant population in Argentina and so was reluctant to break off relations. In addition, West Germany was reportedly worried about proposed limitations on export credits.[41]

On Saturday, April 10, EEC members overcame their reservations and imposed a total ban on Argentine imports, along with an embargo on arms exports.[42] Press reports called these the "toughest sanctions ever imposed" by the Community, comparing them to the "almost laughable" sanctions

---

38. Denis Coghlan, "Haughey Cool on Sanction Plan," *Irish Times*, April 7, 1982, p. 1.
39. Renagh Holohan, "No Final Stance Yet on Sanctions," *Irish Times*, April 8, 1982, p. 8.
40. Reuters North European Service, April 9, 1982, AM cycle.
41. Giles Merritt, "Britain Secures Arms Embargo from All Countries in EEC," *Financial Times*, April 10, 1982, p. 2.
42. "Statement of the Ten on the Falklands (Brussels, 10 April 1982)," reprinted in *European Political Co-operation (EPC)*, 5th ed. (Federal Republic of Germany: Clausen and Bosse, 1988), pp. 150–151.

imposed against the Soviet Union and Poland in the previous two years.[43] The date on which sanctions would come into effect and their duration remained unclear.

Thatcher, speaking to Parliament, noted the government's "heartening degree of success" in convincing the EEC to take action, calling it a "very important step, unprecedented in its scope and the rapidity of the decision." The Prime Minister also noted that economic self-interest could not explain the EEC action. "The decision cannot have been easy for our partners, given the commercial interests at stake."[44] Other governments agreed with this assessment. A spokesman for the Belgian president of the EEC corroborated Thatcher's point, noting that a great deal of persuasion had been required to convince both Ireland and Italy to join in the sanctions effort.[45] A West German official, speaking of negotiations on the import ban, said, "Here was a case where we were doing something for the Community with no national profit to be gained, in fact quite the opposite."[46]

Given the economic and political interests at stake, most European states were willing to participate in multilateral sanctions as an alternative to war, but were not willing to bear the costs of unilateral sanctions, which they saw as ineffective. The interests leading to support for multilateral sanctions included concern over Argentina's aggressive move against a member's territory and recognition of similarly vulnerable areas, such as West Berlin.[47] With the possible exception of Ireland and Italy, members found themselves in an assurance game where multilateral cooperation was desirable. For these states, the EEC played a useful but perhaps not vital role. Involvement of this formal multilateral organization meant that states agreed on the precise obligations of each in the sanctions effort, setting standards about what constituted cooperation and defection. Through the provision of information and setting of standards, the EEC allowed these members to overcome doubts about the utility of their own sanctions, and thus facilitated cooperation. For the members with a weaker interest in sanctions, due to higher economic

---

43. R.W. Apple, Jr., "Europeans Ending Argentine Imports," *New York Times*, April 11, 1982, p. 1; Gary Yerkey, "W. Europe Stands with Britain," *Christian Science Monitor*, April 12, 1982, p. 12.
44. House of Commons, *The Falklands Campaign*, pp. 74–75.
45. Cooney, "Ireland Agrees to EEC Embargo, " p. 6.
46. John Wyles, "Community May Owe Debt to Argentina," *Financial Times*, April 27, 1982, p. 2.
47. Lawrence Freedman and Virginia Gamba-Stonehouse, *Signals of War: The Falklands Conflict of 1982* (London: Faber and Faber, 1990), p. 152.

and domestic political costs and no immediate geopolitical benefits, the EEC was more important. For Italy and Ireland, the diffuse benefits provided by the Community created an interest in "solidarity," prompting them to co-operate. Later, however, when the realized costs of sanctions grew, "solidarity" would no longer be a sufficient payoff.

EEC members viewed sanctions not as an adjunct to military activity, but as an alternative. British Foreign Minister Francis Pym (who replaced Lord Carrington when the crisis began) claimed that the sanctions caught Argentina by surprise, and were "a body blow to its already rather shaky economy."[48] Officials recognized that EEC ministers were willing to impose sanctions quickly because they hoped that this action might prevent escalation of the conflict into a military confrontation. The "European plan" was to use economic and diplomatic pressure to force Argentina to compromise.[49] In the House of Commons, one member noted that "We are fortunate in having the EEC's backing, but I suspect that it wants not only to provide us with support but to act as a restraining force on any over-adventurousness on our part."[50] As events were to prove, this member's assessment was correct. EEC members hoped that joint sanctions could have a significant impact on Argentina because it was highly dependent on the international economy.

However, as in the Argentines' assessment of British motives, the Europeans underestimated the importance of domestic political pressures on the junta. Like Thatcher, Galtieri could not afford to back down once he had taken his stand in the Falklands.[51] Argentina hoped to counter sanctions with assistance from Latin American countries and the Soviet Union. It also surmised correctly that international financial markets could not afford to force the country into default. Thus, even the impressive level of cooperation exhibited by the EEC and other countries was not sufficient to prevent the Argentines from fighting over the Falklands.

The EEC did not immediately implement its April 10 decision to ban imports. Representatives struggled with a number of legal and technical difficulties. Reports suggested that the import ban would probably be limited

---

48. House of Commons, *The Falklands Campaign*, pp. 102–103.
49. Yerkey, "W. Europe Stands," p. 12.
50. House of Commons, *The Falklands Campaign*, p. 85.
51. This could be considered a problem of non-overlapping win sets, meaning that there existed no agreement that would be approved by the relevant constituencies in both countries. See Robert D. Putnam, "Diplomacy and Domestic Politics: The Logic of Two-Level Games," *International Organization*, Vol. 42, No. 3 (Summer 1988), pp. 427–460.

to two weeks.[52] By April 14 officials had sorted out these difficulties. Sanctions went into effect on April 17 and were initially approved for a period of four weeks. After four weeks, the Community would lift the sanctions if progress toward a diplomatic solution were evident. Approval of the one-month import ban was considered a victory for the British, since the European Commission had proposed a two-week limit.[53] The economic interests of member states received one crucial concession in the final negotiations, in that contracts concluded prior to April 16 were exempted from the import ban.[54] Given the time it takes for goods to travel from Argentina to Europe and expectations that the conflict would be settled within a few weeks, this provision meant that the ban would have only a minor economic impact if the dispute were settled quickly. In spite of this concession, Italy continued to express reservations about the proposed sanctions and refused to approve the official documents until the last minute, on Friday, April 16.

Ireland and Belgium also showed a notable reluctance to impose sanctions. Other EEC members expressed more whole-hearted support for Britain. In France, President Mitterrand and the rest of the government fully supported the British effort, although the French press continued to portray the conflict as a farce. One analysis suggested that the French "government's reason for rallying early to the British cause has been to provide a precedent for joint EEC action in the event of a threat to France's overseas territorial possessions."[55] In West Germany, public, government, and press support appeared strong. Analogies were drawn to the situation in Berlin. Economics Minister Otto Lambsdorff sounded one discordant note, declaring that EEC sanctions against Argentina did not change his belief that economic sanctions were not very useful as a political lever.[56] He hoped that the dispute would be settled quickly so that the Community could lift its sanctions.

Thus, there was a range of opinion in Europe about the utility of supporting Britain with sanctions. Despite their misgivings, European states were willing to take economic measures as an alternative to military conflict, and because they did not expect that sanctions would cost them much, as long as they worked. British requests had been designed to keep costs relatively low, e.g.,

---

52. Giles Merritt, "EEC Ban Likely to be Delayed," *Financial Times*, April 14, 1982, p. 1.
53. John Cooney, "EEC Ban on Trade Begins," *Irish Times*, April 15, 1982, p. 4.
54. Council Regulation (EEC) No. 877/82, *Official Journal of the European Communities*, Vol. 25, No. L 102 (April 16, 1982).
55. David Housego, "French Treat Conflict as a Farce," *Financial Times*, April 16, 1982, p. 4.
56. Reuters North European Service, April 22, 1982.

avoiding a Community-wide freeze on Argentine assets that West German representatives had opposed.[57] States' willingness to cooperate had one strong condition: that other EEC members also impose sanctions. Measures taken by just a few countries would have little impact on Argentina, so governments were willing to participate only in a multilateral effort. The EEC machinery provided assurance that all states were taking the same measures. Members' reputations were now tied to national enforcement of particular measures. However, given the expectation that sanctions would quickly work, a determinative role for the EEC cannot be claimed at this stage, except perhaps in the case of the most reluctant members.

SANCTIONS AFTER THE *GENERAL BELGRANO* SINKING: INSTITUTIONAL COERCION

EEC solidarity began to waver as soon as the first shot was fired in the Falklands War. Members had hoped that economic pressure would be sufficient to prevent Argentina from going to war with Britain. Some, especially Ireland, were strongly opposed to imposing sanctions that could be seen as an adjunct to military activity. In addition, the economic costs of sanctions would now increase, as it became obvious that the conflict would not be resolved overnight. As early as April 20, Tindemans refused to agree that EEC support for Britain would continue if force were used.[58] Newspapers reported that if Britain began firing, EEC public and governmental backing for Thatcher would likely evaporate.[59] During this second phase of sanctions, preferences became more asymmetric, with Britain desiring continued strong support while other states grew less willing to keep sanctions in place. Britain continued to have a dominant strategy of imposing sanctions, while other EEC members now derived fewer immediate benefits from multilateral sanctions than from defecting from the joint effort, due to domestic resistance to military action and increased economic costs. The game during this phase became one in which Britain had to exert significant pressure on some members to gain their continued cooperation, as the payoff for multilateral sanctions decreased. The EEC framework provided this leverage.

After the British recapture of South Georgia on April 25, EEC foreign ministers met in Luxembourg to discuss the status of sanctions. Although

57. John Cooney, "EEC Nations Fail to Agree on Sanctions," *Irish Times*, April 9/10, 1982, p. 1.
58. Reuters North European Service, April 20, 1982.
59. David K. Willis, "Each Day the Fleet Sails, Thatcher's Options Narrow," *Christian Science Monitor*, April 22, 1982, p. 9.

some reports suggested that officials urged Thatcher to continue negotiating with Galtieri and warned that they would have to re-evaluate their support for sanctions if force were used, the public stance of solid EEC support remained firm.[60] Tindemans announced continued backing of Britain. On the other hand, Irish diplomats argued that with the start of military action the EEC was involved in "a whole new ballgame."[61]

West Germany, on the whole, remained committed to sanctions. Foreign Minister Genscher argued that solidarity was in NATO's interest as well as the EEC's; since all but Ireland were members of NATO, this cross-institution tie could have persuaded some representatives. Genscher argued that the value of EEC backing would be diluted if internal differences were made public; thus, Tindemans' public statements downplayed any dissent. At the Luxembourg meeting, Britain did not request any further sanctions and there was apparently no formal discussion of what actions the EEC might take if fighting became serious.[62] Tindemans did, however, link continued support to negotiations between Britain and Argentina, particularly Haig's ongoing shuttle diplomacy. Other officials, including Italian Foreign Minister Emilio Colombo, voiced similar concerns. One official said, "The aim of Common Market sanctions was to put diplomatic pressure on Argentina, and the whole ball game will be completely different if the British attack the Falklands."[63] Newspapers in Europe echoed this reluctance to see military force used.[64]

In spite of these warnings, on May 2 British forces sank the Argentine cruiser *General Belgrano* outside of the declared 200-mile exclusion zone around the Falklands. Tindemans immediately reiterated EEC support for Britain and for a negotiated settlement to the dispute, saying that no government formally had changed its stance on sanctions.[65] However, in Ireland, Denmark, and West Germany officials quickly began to question sanctions. The Irish Minister for Defense, Patrick Power, said on May 3 that Britain was now the aggressor in the Falklands, and compared the British to a hit-and-

60. R.W. Apple, Jr., "Britain Imposing Blockade on All Shipping and Flights Near Falklands Tomorrow," *New York Times*, April 29, 1982, p. A1.
61. Dennis Kennedy, "Envoy Sent to Put Argentine Case to Irish Government," *Irish Times*, April 27, 1982, p. 6.
62. John Cooney, "Pym Describes EEC Support as 'Very Robust'," *Irish Times*, April 28, 1982, p. 8.
63. Reuters, April 28, 1982, AM cycle.
64. Twitchett, "The Falklands," p. 11.
65. Reuters North European Service, May 3, 1982.

run driver. Reports in Irish newspapers suggested that renewal of sanctions when they expired on May 17 was now "extremely unlikely."[66] In addition to the sinking of the *Belgrano*, air attacks on Port Stanley, which had begun on April 30, and U.S. support for Britain were cited as factors that had changed the situation considerably. Leaders of most European countries, including France and Germany, called for an immediate ceasefire.[67]

When the news of the *Belgrano* sinking reached Dublin, Irish cabinet ministers were relieved about a decision they had made earlier in the day, to ask the EEC to agree to a lifting of sanctions and to call for an emergency UN Security Council meeting in light of the likelihood of military conflict. There was now little ambiguity about the Irish position. The new policy, calling Britain an aggressor and calling for an end to sanctions, was formally adopted in a cabinet meeting on Tuesday, May 4. The government stated that it was, "appalled by the outbreak of what amounts to open war . . . and at reports that hundreds of lives have already been lost. They see the present situation as a serious threat to world peace. . . . The Irish Government regard the application of economic sanctions as no longer appropriate and will, therefore, be seeking the withdrawal of these sanctions by the Community."[68]

Haughey declared, however, that Ireland would not lift sanctions unilaterally. A Dublin paper explained the reasoning: "There is no compulsion on Ireland or any other country to fall into an EEC line, but the desirability of such solidarity itself becomes a factor in deciding policy."[69] Afraid of threatening other Community benefits, particularly farm subsidies and access to the British market at favorable tariff rates, the government was worried about unilateral withdrawal from sanctions to which they had previously committed themselves.

Prime Minister Haughey explained that Irish neutrality was the major obstacle to continuing sanctions, now that they were a complement to British military action. Neutrality meant that Irish options were "more limited" than those of other EEC members. Haughey stated that, "we were never very enthusiastic about the imposition of sanctions but the argument was persuasive that they could be instrumental in applying pressure to achieve the implementation of Resolution 502 and so lead to a diplomatic solution."[70]

---

66. "EEC Unlikely to Renew Imports Ban," *Irish Times*, May 4, 1982, p. 6.
67. William Borders, "Falklands Casualties Bring Dismay in Europe," *New York Times*, May 5, 1982, p. A1.
68. Dick Walsh, "Government Wants Sanctions Lifted," *Irish Times*, May 5, 1982, p. 1.
69. Dennis Kennedy, "EEC Solidarity a Factor in Determining Ireland's Stance," *Irish Times*, May 3, 1982, p. 8.
70. Dick Walsh, "Haughey Explains Sanctions Change," *Irish Times*, May 7, 1982, p. 1.

He explained the timing of his decision to oppose sanctions by saying that prior to the attack on the *Belgrano,* the British task force appeared to be on a mission of blockade rather than invasion. Now, he reiterated that he wanted to maintain EEC solidarity, but would try to convince others to lift sanctions. He continued to be "very averse" to unilateral action.[71]

West Germany and Italy reportedly continued to favor an arms embargo, but questioned the further utility of trade sanctions. If its purpose was to prevent fighting, now that the shooting had started there seemed little reason to continue the ban on imports. West Germany also expressed fears that escalation of violence in the Falklands would provide an opportunity for the Soviet Union to increase its influence in Latin America.[72] West Germany in particular was disappointed and surprised by the failure of U.S. efforts at mediation. Officials noted that U.S. negotiations had been an important factor in convincing the EEC to impose sanctions. However, the failure of negotiations made sanctions look like a "blank check" for British military action, which was not what the Community had intended.

West Germans said that a "grave question mark" hung over the future of EEC sanctions, and noted that their initial support had been given only with "serious misgivings," considering significant West German economic interests in Argentina and the fact that sanctions were unlikely to work.[73] West German businessmen began to worry more about the economic impact of sanctions, especially since Argentina began to threaten that extension of the sanctions past May 17 could result in long-term damage to relations.[74] While the credibility of this threat remains open to question, the prospect of losing a market worth over half a billion dollars annually due to a colonial dispute between Britain and Argentina was unsettling. A debate in the European Parliament showed the extent to which public opinion for sanctions had waned. On April 22, the Parliament had voted 203 to 28 in support of sanctions; on May 12, a vote on the same question passed by only 137 to 79.[75]

By May 4, support for continued sanctions seemed to be in serious trouble. Prime Minister Haughey publicly called for the EEC to lift its sanctions immediately, but said that if the EEC would not agree to lifting sanctions,

71. Ella Shanahan, "Dead on, Baby, Lenihan Tells Cashman," *Irish Times,* May 7, 1982, p. 9.
72. Reuters North European Service, May 4, 1982.
73. Jonathan Carr, "Bonn Fears Worsening Crisis," *Financial Times,* May 6, 1982, p. 4.
74. Foreign Staff, "Sympathy in Western Europe Wears Thin," *Financial Times,* May 5, 1982, p. 1.
75. Freedman and Gamba-Stonehouse, *Signals of War,* p. 347.

Ireland would not do so unilaterally. Given the outrage in Ireland over the *Belgrano* sinking and general antipathy toward the British, in which support for Britain was "almost an affront to a national tradition," this condition was a strong statement of the power of institutional decisions on national policies.[76] The rest of the EEC, however, was unprepared for the Irish request and unlikely to agree quickly. This cautious attitude was reinforced on May 4, when Argentina sank *HMS Sheffield*, making the military conflict appear less one-sided.

The escalation of the Falklands conflict to the military level had profound implications for state preferences. Some, like West Germany, found themselves questioning the level of support they had given Britain. Others, particularly Ireland, now faced severe domestic pressure to pull out of the sanctions. However, the EEC decided to put off a decision until the original sanctions expired, on May 16. In this situation, Ireland anticipated that its EEC benefits, such as farm subsidies and access to EEC markets, would be threatened by a unilateral withdrawal from the Community's policy. Thus, institutional considerations forced Dublin to stick with the sanctions in spite of domestic demands to pull out. Only the pressure of institutional commitments can explain continued Irish cooperation. Although the conflict between institutional and domestic pressures became most public in Ireland, other members faced a similar conflict, to varying degrees. The EEC's decision to maintain the original agreement helped push governments to continue sanctions.

RENEWING SANCTIONS: CROSS-ISSUE LINKAGES

In the third and final phase of sanctions, most EEC members were reconsidering their costs and benefits, while Britain continued to look for cooperation. It was becoming obvious that the conflict was likely to drag on, leading to much higher costs of imposing sanctions than states had originally anticipated. In addition, many Europeans felt that since sanctions had failed to avert hostilities, the economic measures should now be dropped. In light of higher costs, members demanded a side-payment from Britain in the form of a concession on a persistent budget problem. The organization fostered continued cooperation, in the face of now highly asymmetrical interests, by allowing its members to link these two issues. The nature of strategic inter-

---

76. Ibid.

action and coercive bargaining that led to the continuation of sanctions conforms more closely to realist than to neoliberal expectations, as explained below, but the institutional dimension remained essential to the cooperative outcome.

Over the weekend of May 8–9, European foreign ministers met in Belgium, in what was described as "an extremely acrimonious" meeting, to discuss renewal of sanctions, which were due to expire on May 17.[77] Other issues were on the agenda as well, including the British budget contribution. British sources began to suggest that refusal to renew sanctions, or linkage of sanctions to other issues, might lead Britain to pull out of the EEC. They also emphasized that British ships were being lost, and that the government was now cooperating in UN efforts at negotiation, under the secretary general. These efforts would, diplomats hoped, convince their EEC partners that Britain was genuinely interested in a negotiated solution to the conflict and so increase the chances of renewing sanctions.[78]

Throughout the crisis, some members had quietly suggested that Britain should be willing to make concessions in a long-running intra-Community budget dispute in exchange for EEC solidarity on the Falklands issue. Britain had been demanding a reduced contribution to the EEC budget, arguing that it was one of the poorest countries in the Community and that therefore its budget assessment was out of line. In an attempt to force other members to concede on the budget issue, Britain had been holding up an increase in farm price supports under the Common Agricultural Policy (CAP).

Suggestions of linkage first arose in Ireland and Belgium. As early as April 12, the *Irish Times* had suggested that, "in return for this show of solidarity Britain may now be expected by her partners to take a more conciliatory approach to the review of farm prices, already a week overdue."[79] On April 16, the *Financial Times* noted the sentiment in favor of linkage in Belgium. "Belgium, at any rate, has not forgotten that the intra-EEC disputes of budget payments and farm prices that tend to separate Britain from the rest of the EEC had to be hurriedly shelved on the outbreak of the crisis."[80] A Belgian farmers' weekly newspaper carried a headline suggesting that European farmers were being held hostage to 1,800 Britons in the Falklands. The

---

77. Geoffrey Edwards, "Europe and the Falkland Islands Crisis, 1982," *Journal of Common Market Studies*, Vol. 22, No. 4 (June 1984), p. 307.
78. John Wyles, "Bid to Renew Sanctions," *Financial Times*, May 8, 1982, p. 2.
79. Cooney, "Ireland Agrees to EEC Embargo," p. 6.
80. Housego, "French Treat Conflict as a Farce," p. 4.

Financial Times reported that questions of linkage were "floating eerily on the diplomatic breeze," and that Foreign Minister Pym was working hard to keep the Falklands issue separate from all others.[81] In West Germany, hints of linkage emerged as expressions of hope that the quick EEC response would improve the Community's image in Britain.

Irish sources, in the early phases of sanctions, were the most open about potential linkage. One newspaper reported in late April that, "to maintain EEC solidarity with Britain in the Falklands crisis, the Irish Government would like to see Britain show solidarity inside the EEC by approving this week the 1982–83 farm price increases."[82] A few days later, the Irish Minister for Foreign Affairs claimed that there had been no direct tradeoff between EEC sanctions and the farm price deal, but noted that he did not expect continued British obstruction of price increases. He went on to say that "there had been an expectation that Britain would soften its line on the farm price issue following the EEC's solidarity over the Falklands."[83] Other reports claimed that Pym had been given an ultimatum on this issue. By early May, West German Farm Minister Josef Ertl joined Irish, Belgian, and French suggestions that Britain would now have to make concessions on the budget/ farm price dilemma in order to gain continued support for sanctions.[84]

Irish and French sources, on the weekend of May 8–9, continued to suggest that Britain would have to concede on the budget issue in order to gain their cooperation on sanctions.[85] While EEC officials still avoided making explicit any link between the two issues, they did suggest that Britain could not expect continued backing in the Falklands if it continued to antagonize its partners on other issues. A West German official went so far as to say that "solidarity is not a one-way street."[86] Thus, Britain had an opportunity to link the two issues, thereby transforming two games of deadlock into a single game where both sides—Britain and the rest of Europe—could benefit.

However, Francis Pym adamantly rejected any such linkage at the weekend meeting. Britain opposed all suggested deals on the budget, precipitating a crisis in the organization. The Community also failed to come to a decision on the sanctions issue. Although Ireland agreed to continue its sanctions

81. Wyles, "Community May Owe Debt to Argentina," p. 2.
82. John Cooney, "EEC Support for Britain to Continue," *Irish Times*, April 27, 1982, p. 7.
83. John Cooney, "EEC Agrees to Extend Embargo," *Irish Times*, April 30, 1982, p. 1.
84. Foreign Staff, "Sympathy in Western Europe Wears Thin."
85. Anne Sington, "French Mood is Uneasy," *Irish Times*, May 8, 1982, p. 8.
86. Reuters North European Service, May 8, 1982.

until May 17, the ministers did not agree to British requests to extend them past this date.[87] Leo Tindemans reported continued EEC solidarity with Britain, and said that a decision on the renewal of sanctions would be made the next Sunday, May 16—just one day before sanctions were due to expire. The *Financial Times* noted the implicit link between the budget and sanctions: "In taking the final decision [on sanctions], governments such as Ireland, Italy and Denmark may well be influenced by the fact that the UK has refused to soften its 'no farm price increase without a budget deal' stand, while still expecting supporting action over the Falklands."[88]

Over the next week, individual countries clarified their positions on the renewal of sanctions. Italy began to emerge as a major problem for Britain, as the Italian Socialist Party, a member of Italy's governing coalition, came out strongly against any renewal while military action continued. Bettino Craxi, leader of the Socialist Party, said that he could see no reason to approve extension of the sanctions. Europeans saw this as a major embarrassment for Italian Prime Minister Giovanni Spadolini, who was known for his pro-European attitudes and thus had supported EEC solidarity.[89] The British press, however, guessed that Spadolini would win this domestic debate, and that Italy would be unwilling to drop sanctions if West Germany and France called for their renewal.[90] In other words, some analysts expected that institutional incentives would overcome domestic opposition to sanctions in Italy, as they had in the Irish case. Although the West German public expressed opposition to continued sanctions if this might draw West Germany more deeply into the conflict, the government was expected to continue supporting sanctions unless Britain took the rash step of attacking the Argentine mainland.

Ireland continued to oppose renewal of sanctions, arguing that its position of neutrality made support for sanctions especially difficult if fighting continued. In addition, Ireland had much to gain from the proposed farm price increases Thatcher was blocking. Anti-Anglo sentiment was running particularly high in Ireland for this reason, and also due to a mishap in which a British submarine caught the nets of an Irish trawler, sinking it. In spite of

---

87. Leonard Doyle, "Britain Rejects EEC Cash," *Irish Times*, May 10, 1982, pp. 1 and 6.
88. John Wyles, "EEC States Withhold Renewal of Sanctions," *Financial Times*, May 10, 1982, p. 1.
89. Alessandro Silj, "Pym Claims EEC Support as Criticism Begins to Grow," *Irish Times*, May 11, 1982, p. 4.
90. Wyles, "EEC States Withhold Renewal," p. 1.

these factors working against Irish approval of new sanctions, the government delayed a formal decision until the last minute, hoping to avoid isolation within the EEC.[91] As in Italy, systemic pressures against isolation were competing with domestic pressures to pull out of sanctions. On Thursday, May 14, the Irish government was reportedly ready to veto EEC sanctions.[92] Formally, Ireland could invoke the Luxembourg Compromise, which allowed EEC members to veto actions that affected their "vital national interests." By vetoing sanctions, Irish officials thought they might avoid some of the stigma attached to refusing to go along with an institutional decision approved by majority vote.

During this week, the French position, which had been strongly pro-British, underwent a revision. French officials seem to have realized that they could use the sanctions issue to get concessions from Britain on the budget and farm prices, problems that had been plaguing the Community for years. Foreign Minister Claude Cheysson went to London for talks with British officials on May 14. He met with Francis Pym for ninety minutes, and later in an extended interview with the British Broadcasting Corporation made explicit the linkage between the budget and sanctions. He accused Britain of not appreciating EEC solidarity and of being interested only in financial gains, and said that the impressive solidarity shown in the Falklands crisis had much to do with other issues of Britain's presence in the Community.[93]

The foreign ministers' meeting took place as scheduled in Brussels on Saturday. However, the ministers failed to reach any agreement then, and so moved to Luxembourg where a NATO meeting was due to begin on Monday. By the night of Sunday, May 16, they had not yet struck a deal on either sanctions or the British budget contribution. The ministers used an ambiguity in the drafting of the sanctions order to determine that sanctions would not expire until midnight, May 17, thus giving themselves one more day in which to reach agreement.[94] The most vociferous opposition to sanctions came, unexpectedly, from Italy rather than Ireland. The Italian foreign

---

91. Dick Walsh, "Government May Stall on Sanctions," *Irish Times*, May 13, 1982, p. 1.
92. Denis Kennedy, "Government Seems Ready to Veto Sanctions," *Irish Times*, May 14, 1982, p. 1.
93. David Tonge and David Housego, "Cheysson Sets Harsh Opening Tone," *Financial Times*, May 15, 1982, p. 2.
94. Steven Rattner, "Common Market Delays Vote to Retain Argentine Boycott," *New York Times*, May 17, 1982, p. A1.

minister argued that he could not approve continued sanctions due to domestic opposition, despite a personal visit from Secretary of State Haig urging him to support a renewal. Meanwhile, the Irish representative said nothing during the debates.

On the budget issue, the ministers renewed an earlier offer to reduce Britain's contribution by $810 million, and Pym again rejected it. While British officials continued to insist that the budget and sanctions were separate issues, representatives of the other nine EEC members continued to hold out for British budget concessions before they would renew sanctions. On Monday, a series of bilateral meetings took place throughout the day. Representatives could not agree on the budget, farm prices, or sanctions. Finally, the ministers, led by the French and German representatives, decided to renew sanctions for just seven days, rather than the minimum of four weeks that Britain had requested.

Irish aversion to isolation continued during this series of negotiations, and the Irish government delayed making its own decision, hoping the EEC as a whole would refuse to extend sanctions. However, when Britain refused to accept the budget rebate offers, Ireland would not go along with a continued trade embargo. It was saved from the embarrassment of complete isolation by the fact that the Italian representative was forced to argue and to vote against a renewal. Italy and Ireland invoked the Luxembourg Compromise to allow their abstention.[95] Both countries agreed to continue the arms embargo against Argentina, while the Irish government informally agreed to avoid circumventing the EEC import ban by transshipment of Argentine goods.[96]

The Italian Prime Minister found his government's decision difficult, but his coalition partners had vowed to bring down the government if he went ahead with sanctions, even for seven days.[97] Bettino Craxi stated that he believed sanctions "were a mistake from the beginning," and supported the government's decision not to go along with the rest of the EEC.[98] Foreign Minister Colombo, however, revealed the division between the Socialist and

---

95. Peter Calvert, *The Falklands Crisis: The Rights and Wrongs* (New York: St. Martin's Press, 1982), p. 125.
96. Pieter Jan Kuyper, "Community Sanctions against Argentina: Lawfulness under Community and International Law," in David O'Keeffe and Henry G. Schermers, eds., *Essays in European Law and Integration* (Deventer, The Netherlands: Kluwer B.V., 1982), p. 149; Leonard Doyle, "Ireland and Italy Demur as EEC Renews Sanctions," *Irish Times*, May 18, 1982, p. 1.
97. James Buxton, "Britain Asks Rome to Explain," *Financial Times*, May 19, 1982, p. 4.
98. Reuters North European Service, May 18, 1982.

Republican parties by stating that Italy still considered Argentina the aggressor and by stressing that the arms embargo remained in force.[99] Thus, Britain partially lost the cooperation of two states, while achieving a temporary commitment to continued cooperation from the other EEC members.

On Tuesday, May 18, a crisis arose over the question of farm price supports. Britain continued to refuse to allow increases to go through. Traditionally, the EEC had allowed member states to exercise veto power over such decisions on the grounds of "vital national interest." However, on May 18 the Council of Agriculture ministers decided to go ahead with the price increases against Britain's wishes, precipitating a constitutional crisis.[100] This decision also created a political crisis for Thatcher, as calls arose for Britain to change its status in the EEC or withdraw completely from the organization.[101] Although she protested the Community's action loudly, calling it a dangerous move toward majority rule, she took no concrete actions to retaliate. Considering that sanctions were due to be renewed again in just six days, she could not afford to continue to press on the budget issue. Reports suggested that the farm price decision had been politicized by the Falklands issue.[102]

On May 21, British forces landed on the Falkland Islands. EEC members largely refrained from commenting, particularly on the impact of this move on the renewal of sanctions. Tindemans said that the Community would look for ways to continue pressuring Argentina, but did not mention sanctions.[103] Diplomats in Brussels suggested that sanctions might not be renewed, although France and West Germany continued to favor them.

A foreign ministers' meeting on Monday, May 25, lasted until 3:00 in the morning, but the ministers finally reached a deal. Britain accepted a budget rebate of $875 million, very close to what had been offered a week earlier, while EEC members other than Ireland and Italy agreed to an indefinite renewal of sanctions.[104] As mentioned above, West Germany was the EEC country that had the greatest trade with Argentina. Thus, as Bonn did not

---

99. John Vinocur, "Market Countries Postpone a Stand," *New York Times*, May 22, 1982, p. 7.
100. H. Peter Dreyer, "EC Institutions: Agreeing to Disagree," *Europe*, No. 232 (July/August 1982), p. 29; Panayitois Ifestos, *European Political Cooperation: Towards a Framework of Supranational Diplomacy?* (Brookfield, Vt.: Gower, 1987), p. 316; John Cooney, "Farm Prices Vote Puts EEC in Crisis," *Irish Times*, May 19, 1982, p. 1.
101. Reuters, May 20, 1982, AM cycle.
102. "Falklands Fallout in Europe," *Christian Science Monitor*, May 20, 1982, p. 24.
103. Vinocur, "Market Countries Postpone a Stand," p. 7.
104. Steven Rattner, "8 Market Nations Again Extend Ban Against Argentina," *New York Times*, May 25, 1982, p. A1.

withdraw, the willingness of at least this government to sanction Argentina is more precisely explained by political than economic factors. As of Monday morning, the British delegation was still looking for a rebate of $1.1 billion, but negotiations during the day forced Pym "to compromise to an extent unacceptable two months ago," and accept $810 million.[105] The members also agreed during these negotiations to an offer from French Foreign Minister Cheysson for an indefinite extension of sanctions.[106] Ireland and Italy remained "neutral" on the sanctions decision and agreed not to circumvent the embargo. By conceding on the budget and CAP issues, Britain achieved a firm commitment to continued sanctions from the other EEC members.

EEC observers declared the settlement of the farm price, budget, and sanctions issues a victory for the institution. The *EC Bulletin* said that a crisis had been overcome, but denied that linkage among the issues had contributed to the settlement.[107] Given the series of events, however, this assertion is implausible. Analysts described the decisions on the Falklands as a success for EPC, the gradual movement toward coordination of foreign policies among EEC members.[108] Even taking the partial withdrawal of Italy and Ireland into account, the level of cooperation achieved is impressive.

In this final phase, states used the renewal of sanctions to gain British concessions on a long-standing institutional dilemma. Thatcher, although furious at the Community's override of the farm price veto, could not pull back from the institution because she needed the others' support on sanctions. Linkage between these issues created and sustained by the Community's organizational framework accounts for the high level of cooperation expressed by the indefinite renewal of economic measures against Argentina. Because the Falklands case was a game in which Britain had to engage in "high-level arm twisting" to gain the cooperation of others, cross-issue linkage created conditions for cooperation.[109] British budget concessions allowed the Community to agree to an indefinite extension of sanctions on May 25. As one group studying the Falklands crisis concluded, "The fact that the EEC cooperated with Britain at all was a result of intra-community politics. The

---

105. John Wyles, "Britain and EEC Partners Declare a Truce," *Financial Times*, May 26, 1982, p. 2.
106. John Cooney, "EEC Respite as Britain Accepts £578m," *Irish Times*, May 26, 1982, p. 9.
107. "A Crisis Overcome," *Bulletin of the European Communities*, Vol. 15, No. 5 (1982), pp. 7–9.
108. Economist Intelligence Unit, *European Trends*, No. 71 (May 1982), pp. 1–2.
109. Heritage Foundation Reports, International Briefing No. 10, June 21, 1982; Ifestos, *European Political Cooperation*, p. 317; F.S. Northedge, "Britain and the EEC: Past and Present," in Roy Jenkins, ed., *Britain and the EEC* (London: Macmillan, 1983), p. 34.

effective quid pro quo was the abandonment of the Luxembourg Compromise which had allowed Britain to veto EEC farm pricing policies."[110] Given the need to provide side-payments, the EEC structure lowered transaction costs by allowing Britain to strike a single multilateral deal rather than a complex set of *ad hoc* bilateral bargains, and made such linkages credible. In this instance, the creation and cementing of intergovernmental bargains was greatly facilitated by an institutional framework.

Issue Linkage, Institutions, and Paradigms

The foregoing history provides an empirical perspective on the realist-neoliberal debate in international relations theory. This section discusses the nature of this debate, focusing on the impact of international institutions and regimes. It then identifies the role of institutions in facilitating cross-issue linkage. While realists correctly highlight tactical linkages in interstate bargaining, the neoliberal perspective adds valuable insight into how such linkages can be created and maintained. Because institutions help states establish credible linkages, the neoliberal approach generates greater understanding of the processes leading to cooperation in this case.

The essential distinction between the neoliberal and realist approaches lies in their understanding of the nature of state interests. Neoliberals see a world of mixed-motive strategic interactions, where conflict coexists with significant room for mutual gains.[111] From these assumptions about the character of strategic interaction among states, derived from understandings about the impact of anarchy, neoliberals deduce an important role for international institutions in facilitating cooperative behavior. They find that institutions allow states to overcome conflicts of interest to achieve mutual gains.

Realists, on the other hand, argue that concerns with relative gains and with the existence of power differentials result in patterns of state interests characterized by purely conflictual situations, leaving no scope for mutual gains.[112] The resulting perspective on the role of institutions is ambiguous.

---

110. Latin American Bureau, *Falklands/Malvinas: Whose Crisis?* (London: Latin American Bureau, 1982), p. 112.
111. Keohane, *After Hegemony*, pp. 66–69; Robert Axelrod, *The Evolution of Cooperation* (New York: Basic Books, 1984).
112. Joseph M. Grieco, "Anarchy and the Limits of Cooperation: A Realist Critique of the Newest Liberal Institutionalism," *International Organization*, Vol. 42, No. 3 (Summer 1988), pp. 495–503.

On the one hand, Kenneth Waltz argues that the competitive nature of state interests marginalizes the impact of institutions.[113] Joseph Grieco, along the same lines, finds that anarchy forces states to behave as "defensive positionalists" rather than "rational egoists," imposing stringent restraints on international cooperation.[114] However, Grieco is not totally pessimistic about the role of institutions. He concludes that institutions do matter because they can perform a broad range of functions, such as narrowing gaps in payoffs and providing side-payments.[115] Earlier realists show a similar ambivalence about the role of international organization and law, with both Hans Morgenthau and E.H. Carr devoting considerable attention to these subjects.[116]

The realist paradigm is useful in directing our attention to the arm-twisting and tactical issue linkage that led to cooperation in the final phase of sanctions. As the Falklands crisis developed, the preferences of European states changed from a classic neoliberal formulation—an assurance game—to a more asymmetrical, coercive pattern. As the nature of the conflict became clearer and the relevance of military conflict increased, the scope of common interests between Britain and other members of the European Community narrowed considerably. Opposition resulted from the higher cost of long-term sanctions and from domestic political resistance to siding actively with Britain in a war with colonial overtones. In response to this change in state preferences, the processes that led to cooperation changed. However, contrary to expectations from a narrow realist perspective, the institutional structure of the EEC continued to provide a central mechanism for cooperation. The functioning of the institution varied in response to changes in the nature of the cooperation problem facing states, but at no point did the institution become irrelevant to, or merely the result of, the bargaining process. Britain finally achieved cooperation through a tactical issue linkage.[117] Thus, as

---

113. Kenneth N. Waltz, *Theory of International Politics* (New York: Random House, 1979), pp. 115–116.
114. Joseph M. Grieco, *Cooperation among Nations: Europe, America, and Non-Tariff Barriers to Trade* (Ithaca: Cornell University Press, 1990), p. 10.
115. Ibid., pp. 233–234.
116. Hans J. Morgenthau, *Politics among Nations*, 2d ed. (New York: Alfred A. Knopf, 1954), pp. 249–308; Edward Hallett Carr, *The Twenty Years' Crisis, 1919–1939*, 2d ed. (New York: Harper and Row, 1946), pp. 170–207.
117. On tactical issue linkage, see Ernst B. Haas, "Why Collaborate? Issue-Linkage and International Regimes," *World Politics*, Vol. 32, No. 3 (April 1980), pp. 357–405. For other discussions of issue linkage, see Haas, *When Knowledge is Power: Three Models of Change in International Organizations* (Berkeley: University of California Press, 1990), pp. 76–80; Kenneth A. Oye, "The Domain of Choice: International Constraints and Carter Administration Foreign Policy," in Oye,

realists would expect, when the degree of common interest declined, *quid pro quo* bargaining and tactical linkages assumed center stage.

However, the realist argument underestimates the importance of institutions in structuring such bargaining processes. In any case of tactical linkage, states face the problem of making commitments credible and durable.[118] Realists trace the credibility of linkages to underlying power capabilities of states. This emphasis on state resources as the primary determinant of outcomes cannot explain British success in this case, since the distribution of underlying capabilities among European states in 1982 shows no obvious disparity in favor of Britain. Instead, Britain drew on its "organizationally dependent" capability to link issues to gain the cooperation of other EEC members.[119] If the asymmetry of preferences between Britain and the rest of the Community had derived from overall power considerations, Thatcher's government could have drawn on its greater resources to exert leverage in favor of multilateral sanctions. However, in this case asymmetric preferences arose for more context-specific reasons, particularly British commitments to the Falklanders. Britain therefore relied on levers provided within the EEC to exert pressure. Britain's "power" in this case was created by its position within the organization.

Discussions of tactical issue linkage suggest how formal organizations can increase the utility of linkage as a bargaining tactic. Robert Keohane argues that problems of transaction costs can prohibit the use of side-payments in the absence of a regime.[120] In this case, without the Community as a forum for negotiation, Britain would have had to construct separate bilateral agreements with each EEC member in order to gain its cooperation. This would

Donald Rothchild, and Robert J. Lieber, eds., *Eagle Entangled: U.S. Foreign Policy in a Complex World* (New York, Longman, 1979), pp. 13–19; Arthur A. Stein, "The Politics of Linkage," *World Politics*, Vol. 33, No. 1 (October 1980), pp. 62–81; Robert D. Tollison and Thomas D. Willett, "An Economic Theory of Mutually Advantageous Issue Linkage in International Negotiations," *International Organization*, Vol. 33, No. 4 (Autumn 1979); James K. Sebenius, "Negotiation Arithmetic: Adding and Subtracting Issues and Parties," *International Organization*, Vol. 37, No. 2 (Spring 1983), pp. 281–316.
118. For discussions of credibility, see Thomas C. Schelling, *The Strategy of Conflict* (New York: Oxford University Press, 1960), pp. 31–32, 50–51; Oye, "The Domain of Choice," pp. 14–15; Haas, "Why Collaborate?" p. 372.
119. Robert O. Keohane and Joseph S. Nye, Jr., *Power and Interdependence* (Boston: Little, Brown, 1977), p. 55.
120. Keohane, "The Demand for International Regimes," in Krasner, ed., *International Regimes*, p. 156.

have involved much higher transaction costs, at a minimum delaying the imposition of sanctions for a significant length of time. Without the EEC framework, Britain would have had to "create" issues for linkage; the Community's agenda provided a natural source of such issues.

The institutional role in facilitating linkages goes beyond the provision of a negotiating arena. As Kenneth Oye has noted, "tradeoffs created by tactical linkages are inherently unstable."[121] The problem of credibility is an important source of instability. To create an effective linkage, Britain had to be credible in its threats of punishment or its promises of side-payments in exchange for cooperation on economic sanctions. In the absence of an institutional context in which Britain made a clear commitment to taking a specific action in exchange for specific actions from other members, establishing credibility would have been more problematic. This fits Keohane's observation that institutions "raise the costs of deception and irresponsibility," allowing states to make more credible commitments.[122]

Sociological research has noted the connection between organizations and credibility. Samuel Bacharach and Edward Lawler, for example, argue that "the greater the formalization of an organization, the greater the credibility (the likelihood of enforcement) of threats."[123] They reason that formalization allows codification of rules, so that uncertainty about what constitutes performance or non-performance is reduced. The application of this insight to the Falklands case is straightforward: without institutional constraints, interpretations of what constituted "economic sanctions" against Argentina would be subject to greater disagreement, as would decisions about what constituted British payment of promised inducements. As neoliberals would expect, the ability to set standards for performance and non-performance enhances credibility.

These insights from sociologists are consistent with lessons drawn from political scientists' study of international regimes. Stephen Krasner notes that regimes can have feedback effects on the ability of members to influence

121. Oye, "The Domain of Choice," p. 18.
122. Keohane, *After Hegemony*, p. 97.
123. Samuel B. Bacharach and Edward J. Lawler, *Power and Politics in Organizations* (San Francisco: Jossey-Bass, 1980), p. 197. See also Bacharach and Lawler, "Political Action and Alignments in Organizations," in Bacharach, ed., *Research in the Sociology of Organizations*, Vol. 2 (Greenwich, Conn.: JAI Press, 1983), pp. 83–107; William A. Gamson, *Power and Discontent* (Homewood, Ill.: Dorsey, 1968); Jeffrey Pfeffer, *Power in Organizations* (Marshfield, Mass.: Pitman, 1981).

others' behavior.[124] As this modified realist approach suggests, Britain could draw on an existing institution to increase its influence. By creating the opportunity to link issues and bolstering beliefs in British willingness to carry through with side-payments, the EEC altered behavioral outcomes in this case. Thomas Schelling has noted the requirement of "an occasion, an object, and a means of communication" in establishing credibility; the EEC provided these.[125]

This study of a specific case of international cooperation thus offers a critique of elements of both the neoliberal and realist approaches and develops the argument that the role of institutions in facilitating cooperation changes in the face of changing state preferences. After military conflict began, state preferences became highly asymmetric and cooperation resulted from explicit, *quid pro quo* bargaining and arm-twisting. Neoliberalism typically discounts the role of such coercive measures in sustaining cooperation, focusing instead on the existence of common interests, although there is no inherent contradiction between neoliberalism and coercive bargaining.[126] The realist argument, however, is also inadequate for understanding this pattern of cooperation in that it underestimates the ability of international institutions to transform conflict. Creating durable cross-issue linkages required establishing credibility, and the EEC as an institution facilitated this process. Thus, even in the face of coercive bargaining, institutions can have a direct impact on outcomes.

Conclusion

This article has two purposes: to demonstrate through process-tracing that institutions have an impact on state decision-making, and to explore the nature of that influence. Sanctions imposed during the Falklands crisis provide evidence that international institutions play a role in facilitating cooperation among states, even when state interests are asymmetric. In this case, the institutional framework of the European Community created linkages

---

124. Krasner, "Regimes and the Limits of Realism: Regimes as Autonomous Variables," in Krasner, ed., *International Regimes*, p. 364. For a discussion of this dynamic in North-South relations, see Krasner, *Structural Conflict: The Third World Against Global Liberalism* (Berkeley: University of California Press, 1985).
125. Schelling, *The Strategy of Conflict*, p. 51.
126. See Keohane, *After Hegemony*, p. 107.

across issues that allowed Britain to gain the cooperation of other members. The EEC quickly called for sanctions against Argentina, despite reluctance from some of its members. This decision had a direct impact on the foreign policies of member states, as they followed the Commission's decision and banned imports from Argentina.

Originally, EEC members did not expect sanctions to prove very costly, anticipating that they would contribute to a quick end to the crisis. Thus, even those states with only lukewarm support for Britain went along with the others in the early phase of sanctions. Here, the EEC helped states cooperate in an assurance game, since only Britain was interested in imposing unilateral sanctions. However, the contribution of the institution was relatively small at this stage.

Some governments' preferences changed dramatically, however, when military conflict broke out at the end of April, and the problems of cooperation became more demanding. Ireland, in particular, now came under intense domestic pressure to repudiate the Community import ban. The asymmetry of interests between Britain and the rest of the Community grew. However, when Irish representatives failed to convince other members to lift the sanctions, the Irish government decided that the benefits of EEC participation outweighed the costs of sanctions. Thus, Dublin continued to impose sanctions through their original term. Institutional considerations were essential to this decision.

Tactical linkages between sanctions and other Community issues became central to the renewal of trade measures in mid-May, during the third phase of the conflict. Britain, which had been willing to obstruct all EEC business in order to gain a large budget rebate, finally backed down on this demand in exchange for an indefinite renewal of sanctions against Argentina. In this instance, the institutional effect consisted of the creation of cross-issue linkages that transformed separate games without cooperative equilibria into a single game in which both sides benefited from cooperation. This result suggests that the impact of institutions is not confined to providing solutions to collective action problems as specified by neoliberals, but can also lead to creative solutions for independent issues, by linking them in a credible manner.

This case study suggests two paths for future research on institutions and cooperation. First, students of international politics should give more attention to the role that institutions can play when state interests are asymmetric, rather than fitting a model of symmetrical preferences such as a Prisoners' Dilemma or assurance game. Secondly, it suggests that institutions can create specific cross-issue linkages that would be much harder to forge on an *ad hoc* basis. Policymakers considering the use of multilateral sanctions should therefore recognize the instrumental value of working within an institutional framework, as should students of international politics and foreign policy. Such a framework solidifies otherwise tenuous tactical issue-linkages.

International Security
Center for Science and International Affairs
John F. Kennedy School of Government
Harvard University

The articles in this reader were previously published in **International Security**, a quarterly journal sponsored and edited by the Center for Science and International Affairs at the John F. Kennedy School of Government at Harvard University, and published by MIT Press Journals. To receive subscription information about the journal or find out more about other readers in our series, please contact MIT Press Journals at 55 Hayward Street, Cambridge, MA, 02142.